D0085959

Sport Psychology

Sport Psychology

Performance Enhancement, Performance Inhibition, Individuals, and Teams

Nicholas T. Gallucci

Psychology Press
Taylor & Francis Group

NEW YORK AND HOVE

Published 2008
by Psychology Press
270 Madison Avenue
New York, NY 10016
www.psypress.com

Published in Great Britain
by Psychology Press
27 Church Road
Hove, East Sussex BN3 2FA

Copyright © 2008 Nicholas T. Gallucci

Psychology Press is an imprint of the Taylor & Francis Group, an informa business

Typeset by RefineCatch Limited, Bungay, Suffolk, UK
Printed and bound in the USA by Sheridan Books, Inc. on acid-free paper
Paperback cover design by Design deluxe; cover image by Peggy Stewart

All rights reserved. No part of this book may be reprinted or reproduced or utilized in any
form or by any electronic, mechanical, or other means, now known or hereafter invented,
including photocopying and recording, or in any information storage or retrieval system,
without permission in writing from the publishers.

10 9 8 7 6 5 4 3 2 1

Library of Congress Cataloging in Publication Data
A catalog record for this book is available from the Library of Congress.

ISBN: 978-1-84169-485-6 (hbk)
ISBN: 978-1-84169-486-3 (pbk)

Contents

About the Author

Nicholas T. GALLUCCI is a professor and the chair of the Psychology Department at Western Connecticut State University. He received MA and PhD degrees in psychology at the University of Louisville, and a BA in psychology at Vanderbilt University. His research concerns personality and sport performance, and exercise and weight loss. He enjoys running, played intercollegiate soccer at Vanderbilt, and is a member of the St. Xavier High School Athletic Hall of Fame.

Preface

Sport Psychology: Performance Enhancement, Performance Inhibition, Individuals, and Teams is a textbook for university courses. It is intended for students and sportspersons interested in learning about psychology and sport and in applying this learning to realize their full potential. It provides a synthesis of most of the major topics in sport psychology, and, true to its title, emphasizes topics related to optimal performance. Consistently realizing optimal performance involves the practice of strategies for *enhancing performance* such as self-talk, enhancing concentration, mental imagery, relaxation training, goal setting, and promoting self-efficacy and sport self-confidence. Optimal performance is also more likely when the factors causing *performance inhibition* are limited. This book presents a thoroughgoing coverage of the causes of choking under pressure, self-handicapping, procrastination, perfectionism, helplessness, substance abuse, and disruptive personality factors. With this emphasis and the space limitations of a textbook, some topics, such as exercise psychology, are not included.

With both the factors that enhance and inhibit performance, the chapters were organized on the basis of the degree to which the skills are to be practiced at times proximal or distal to the performance. Skills are proximal when their practice occurs immediately prior to and during performances, whereas those that are rehearsed at times farther removed from performances and competitions are distal. Strategies for enhancing performance that are practiced immediately prior to and during performances are presented in Chapters 3, 4, and 5, and psychological strengths and competencies that have a more distal influence on performance are related in Chapters 6 through 9. Similarly, psychological liabilities that inhibit performance as a result of their occurrence during performances are detailed in Chapter 10, and more distal inhibiting factors are explained in Chapters 11 through 17. This organization of topics and chapters was influenced by practices that are common in areas of applied psychology.

That is, the most expeditious way to solve problems and enhance performance is to first teach the skills necessary for success. If difficulties cannot be resolved after the acquisition of necessary skills, then inhibiting factors are analyzed. Additionally, the distal causes of success and failure are often less apparent, are altered more slowly and with greater effort, and readers may find it unnecessary to alter the distal and more entrenched sources of success and failure if their performance improves adequately after making changes to the proximal factors. To some degree this information is universally applicable.

In addition, research with diverse populations is reviewed. The topics of gender and sport, ethnicity and sport, and youth and sport are addressed in Chapters 18 through 20. The influence of leadership and coaching styles is considered in Chapter 21, and team cohesiveness is evaluated in Chapter 22.

An introduction and history of sport psychology is provided in Chapter 1. Human motivation is the subject of Chapter 2; theories outlined here are important for understanding motivation for sport, academic and vocational achievement, and the pursuit of personal interests.

The material in each chapter is introduced with a vignette, and photographs, figures, and illustrations are included in the chapters for the purpose of clarifying the material in the text. The illustrations are generally derived from the popular press, primarily concern well-known sport figures, and present dramatic and sometimes humorous examples of concepts in the text. Several illustrations are drawn from outside of the world of sport and these represent especially clear examples of concepts. For example, throughout 27 years in prison, Nelson Mandela never lost confidence that he would reach his goal of transforming South Africa. **Boldface type** is used to identify key terms and names for study.

PART I
INTRODUCTION

Introduction to Sport Psychology

> I fell in love with football as I was later to fall in love . . .: suddenly, inexplicably, uncritically, giving no thought to the pain or disruption it would bring with it. (Hornby, 1994, p. 1)

And so it goes with sport. This sentiment expressed by an Englishman about the sport Americans call soccer has undoubtedly been experienced by millions of men and women throughout the world. Regardless of the specific sport, gender, ethnicity, or nationality, interest and passion in sport endures. For example, recent estimates are that 23 million youth in the USA between the ages of five and 16 participate in sports after school and another 6.5 million play sports that are sponsored by their schools (Participation Survey, 1999–2000).

Likewise, interest in psychology is widespread and enduring. In the year 2000, 74,060 Americans received bachelor's degrees with psychology

Getting started (photo © Natthawat Wongrat).

majors (US Department of Education, 2002). Sport psychology brings together these widespread interests.

What is Sport Psychology?

Sport psychology is defined as the application of the knowledge and scientific methods of psychology to the study of people in sport and exercise settings. This knowledge is also applied to enhance sport performance and enjoyment, and the health and fitness of sportspersons (Gill, 2000). The scope of sport psychology includes understanding how psychological factors affect performance and how involvement in sport and exercise activities relates to psychological development, adjustment, and wellbeing (Williams & Straub, 2006). It is not surprising that college students have a keen interest in sport psychology, as college students have consistently demonstrated the greatest interest in topics in psychology that have direct applications in their daily lives (Ruch, 1937; Zanich & Grover, 1989).

History of Sport Psychology

By the start of the 20th century, theories about the benefits of sport were well established. Theories to explain human motivation for involvement in sport and play were also developed. For example, play and sport were seen as inherently pleasurable, or as outlets for surplus energy (Hermann, 1921). At the psychological laboratory of Yale University, Edward W. Scripture developed a theory that was widely recognized. According to Scripture (1900), involvement in sport built character, or fostered the development of favorable qualities of personality. He studied the effects of athletics, calisthenics, and manual training on the development of self-control among young felons in the Elmira Reformatory. Scripture argued that character strengths developed by motor activity could be transferred to areas of everyday living.

Scripture was not alone in concluding that sport and play was a method by which people developed skills and qualities that would prepare them for life. Sport was said to develop qualities of alertness and sound judgment, and the capacity to react to changing environments. In scientific and popular literature, parallels were drawn between strong bodies and strong minds and between sportspersonship and fair play and ethical conduct in other areas of life functioning (Davis, Huss, & Becker, 1995).

Research and Training in the United States

Norman Triplett (1898) is credited with conducting the initial research in sport psychology at the University of Indiana. Triplett discerned that bicycle racing performances were faster when cyclists competed in the presence of other cyclists who functioned as pacemakers or as competitors. Performances were slowest when cyclists rode alone. Triplett reasoned that the presence of pacemakers or competitors was "dynamogenic" or served as a stimulus to release energy that was latent when cyclists rode alone. Visual and auditory cues from the other cyclists were also seen to inspire additional effort from cyclists. Triplett replicated these findings with children who were

Sport and character strengths (photo courtesy of Western Connecticut State University).

timed winding fishing reels, either alone or with another child. These results were later described as the **social facilitation** effect (Zajonc, 1965). This research was conducted while Triplett was in graduate school. He did not continue it, as his professional career was spent in teaching and administration.

The first American psychologist to devote a significant portion of his career to research, teaching, and service in sport psychology was **Coleman Roberts Griffith** (Gould & Pick, 1995). Griffith and his students had a major impact on the field between the years of 1920 and 1940, as his was the first program for systematic research and training in sport psychology. He has been called the father of American sport psychology, and was the director of the Research in Athletics Laboratory at the University of Illinois. This lab was founded in 1925, five years after the first sport psychology laboratory in the world was established at the Institute of Physical Education by Carl Diem in Berlin, Germany. In addition to his research in his laboratory, Griffith functioned as an educator and consultant, and his career therefore presaged the roles of future generations of sport psychologists. His books *Psychology of Coaching* and *Psychology of Athletics* were published in 1926 and 1928, and are considered classics. He also consulted with the Chicago Cubs professional baseball team and corresponded with the renowned Notre Dame football coach Knute Rockne.

Griffith developed a view of the scope of sport psychology. First, he recommended that sport psychologists study the techniques and principles practiced by the best coaches of their day. Sport psychologists were then to abstract and summarize these principles and communicate them to young and inexperienced coaches. In this way, sport psychologists could help in the development of more effective coaches.

Second, Griffith studied psychomotor learning and the relationship between personality factors and physical performance, and called for the integration of this information into sport psychology research. This practice has continued to the present day, and its extension is emphasized in this book. Third, Griffith recommended scientific, psychological research specific to sport psychology (Weiss & Gill, 2005). This research was to have practical applications in supporting improved athletic performance. Among the topics of research in his laboratory were the learning of athletic and motor skills and the influence of personality traits on athletic performance. Personality traits are ways of responding and behaving that are consistent over time and across situations.

Griffith introduced the concepts of automated responses and the development of optimal states of arousal for competitions. Automated responses occur without conscious or deliberate thought and are characteristic of sophisticated and elite motor responses and athletic performance (see Chapter 5). With the identification of optimal states of arousal, it was recognized that athletic performance could be inhibited if physiological activation was too low or too high. Arousal refers to the activation of the sympathetic branch of the autonomic nervous system. This activation is measured on the bases of heart rate, rate of breathing, systolic blood pressure, diastolic blood pressure, and galvanic skin response. Higher readings on these measures were considered indicative of players being ready for, or "up" for, games. Successful performance was seen to be associated with the majority of the team being prepared for competition. Current literature concerning the relationship between arousal and intensity will be reviewed in Chapter 3. Griffith was also interested in the psychological growth that could be fostered by sport and physical training.

Coleman Roberts Griffith (photo courtesy of the University of Illinois at Urbana-Champaign Archives; record series 39/2/20).

Rapid growth in sport psychology occurred between 1950 and 1980 (Landers, 1995; Wiggins, 1984). Topics in sport psychology were identified during this period that remain as active areas of scientific inquiry. These areas include: optimal states of arousal and performance, mental imagery and performance, modeling of adaptive motor and psychological responses, performance anxiety, and achievement motivation. Between 1950 and 1965 there was an emphasis on personality factors associated with involvement in athletics. This literature was not especially conclusive, probably due largely to the methodological limitations such as reliably measuring the personality factors. More recent and promising research is reviewed in Chapter 14.

In the 1970s, the **interactionism paradigm**, or the interaction between individuals and their environments, was emphasized in sport psychology research (Williams & Straub, 2006). Also in the 1970s, a movement began to move research away from laboratories in universities and toward sport venues. **Rainer Martens' 1979 article "About Smocks and Jocks"** was credited with stimulating research in sport settings, which was considered more ecologically valid or directly applicable to real-life issues in sport. Applied research occurred on a limited basis before the 1970s. For example, as early as 1952, psychologists studied the relationship between arousal and performance with professional American football teams (Freudenberger & Bergandi, 1994).

In the 1980s, and thereafter, the breadth of research in sport psychology increased. Topics such as the cognitive factors associated with optimal performance, overtraining and burnout, the effects of athletic injuries, goal orientations, and exercise adherence were examined.

In the late 1960s and early 1970s sport psychology regained the momentum on American campuses that it experienced prior to 1932 in Coleman Griffith's laboratory. During this era, textbooks and scientific journals specific to sport psychology were published, and college courses and graduate training in sport psychology were founded. Sport psychology classes were also offered in university departments of physical education, exercise, sport science, and kinesiology, and to a lesser extent in departments of psychology. Most of the graduate training in sport psychology has been provided in university departments of physical education, exercise, sport science, and kinesiology (Singer, 1989).

Recommendations for the enhancement of graduate training include increasing the numbers of faculty in clearly defined sport psychology departments and providing supervised practicum experiences for graduate students. Practicum experiences involve the applied practice of sport psychology, such as consulting with teams and athletes, under the supervision of faculty. The development of comprehensive practicum training has lagged behind the establishment of strictly academic coursework (Silva, Conroy, & Zizzi, 1999), but is improving, as doctoral students in sport psychology averaged 446 hours of supervised experience between 1994 and 1999 (Williams & Scherzer, 2003).

Research and Training in the Rest of the World

The development of sport psychology in Britain has been somewhat parallel to that in the USA. The study of motor learning and the development of skill in sport was advanced at Cambridge University in the 1940s and 1950s (Biddle, 1989). The tradition of research concerning personality factors and athletics was pursued both in the USA and Britain. The eminent British psychologist Hans Eysenck was a pioneer in the scientific study of personality, and he extended his research to the evaluation of the personality of sportspersons (Eysenck, Nias, & Cox, 1982). A substantial portion of Chapter 14 will be devoted to reviewing Dr. Eysenck's theory of personality and its application in sporting contexts. Professional organizations were developed, and in 1985 the British Association of Sports Sciences was formed, which was an amalgamation of the Biomechanics Study Group, British Society for Sport Psychology, and Society of Sports Sciences. The British Psychological Society formed the Division of Sport and Exercise Psychology in 2004. Also consistent with practices in the USA, academic programs in sport psychology have been developed and British sport psychologists have increasingly consulted with athletes. Since the 1980s, research in applied or sport settings has been more frequent, and the findings of this research will be presented in later chapters.

Similarly, sport and exercise psychology services have been available for many years in France, Germany, Australia, Canada, Italy, Sweden, Japan, the People's Republic of China, and the former Soviet Union (Pargman, 1998). For example, in 1925, Piotr Antonovich Roudik established the first sport psychology laboratory in the Psychology Department of the State Central Institute of Physical Culture in Moscow (Ryba, Stambulova, & Wrisberg, 2005), and soon thereafter, A. Z. Puni established a sport psychology laboratory at the Institute of Physical Culture in Leningrad (Roberts & Treasure, 1999). In 1946, Puni launched a department of sport psychology at the Institute. Beginning in the 1950s, and continuing for approximately three decades, a rivalry ensued between Drs. Puni and Roudik for the acknowledged leadership of sport psychology in the Soviet Union, and during this time period sport psychology was seen as an important ingredient in the success of Soviet Olympic athletes (Ryba et al., 2005).

The focus of Soviet/Russian sport psychology was on applied sport psychology and especially on interventions to optimize the performance of elite athletes (Stambulova, Wrisberg, & Ryba, 2006). Prior to 1963, applied sport psychology in the Soviet Union included consulting with athletes about preperformance preparation for competition, simulation training, mental rehearsals (see Chapters 4 and 5), goal setting (see Chapter 7), and the development of sport self-confidence (see Chapter 9; Ryba et al., 2005). Among Puni's contributions was a comprehensive model for optimal sport performance that included long- (e.g. goal setting) and short-term (e.g. practicing mental skills to realize optimal concentration) phases.

A great number of resources were devoted to performance enhancement with elite athletes in the former Soviet Union and East Germany. In these countries, elite athletes were exposed to as many as 30 hours of training in techniques to enhance performance such as autogenic training, visualization, and self-hypnosis (Williams & Straub, 2006). Professional journals devoted to exercise and sport psychology are available in most of these countries.

Sport psychology also developed as a more applied discipline in Canada than in the USA in the 1960s and 1970s. Unlike their American counterparts, Canadian sport psychology consultants were supported by their national sport governing organizations such as the Coaching Association of Canada. As a result, the utilization of psychological services was more widespread among coaches and athletes in Canada. As was the case in the Soviet Union, there was also a greater emphasis on interventions to enhance and maximize athletic performance (Stambulova et al., 2006).

Professional Activities of Sport Psychologists

Sport psychologists based in universities are actively involved in scientific research and therefore in the development of the basic facts and findings of the science of sport psychology. University-based sport psychologists also teach courses in sport and exercise psychology, and academia remains the primary area of employment for sport psychologists (Williams & Scherzer, 2003).

A group of sport psychologists consult with professional, university, and Olympic teams and athletes, and this **consultation** emphasizes the realization of optimal performance. Some of these consultants function as a "mental coach" in teaching athletes techniques to enhance performance and minimize inhibition. This consulting may involve techniques for decreasing anxiety during competition, as well as enhancing confidence and motivation (Singer, 1989). These consultants may be identified as **educational sport psychologists** and often have graduate training in sport and exercise science, physical education, and kinesiology as well as sport psychology (McCullagh & Noble, 2002). Other consultants are licensed clinical or counseling psychologists with specialized training in sport and exercise psychology. **Clinical psychologists** are licensed to diagnose and treat mental disorders and behavioral or adjustment problems. Examples of mental disorders that might be present among athletes are substance abuse, depression, and eating disorders. The practices of clinical and counseling psychologists have converged in recent years, as both have been increasingly involved in the delivery of psychotherapy. Psychotherapy is a verbal intervention by which the psychologist assists the client or patient in overcoming mental disorders or problems in living. Traditionally, counseling psychologists have been trained to identify impediments to psychological growth rather than discrete mental disorders.

Evolution of Consultation

From the 1960s to the present, the range of professional psychological services provided to athletes progressed. A sport psychologist was assigned to work with the US Olympic team for the first time in 1976, and in 1978 the Olympic Committee (USOC) recruited advisors in four branches of sport science: biomechanics, exercise physiology, nutrition, and sport psychology. The USOC established a Sport Psychology Committee and a registry of qualified sport psychologists who specialized in research, education, or clinical sport psychology by 1983 (USOC, 1983). In 1984 and thereafter, sport psychology services were routinely provided to US summer and winter Olympians. There were 11 psychological consultants for US athletes at the 1984 summer and winter Olympics, with academic backgrounds in physical education and motor learning, clinical psychology, and counseling psychology (Suinn, 1985). The psychological services most frequently provided by these consultants were training in concentration, relaxation, and the use of mental imagery and mental practice.

It is not uncommon for innovations derived from psychological practice to precede the validation of these innovations via experimental study. For example, in 1971 Richard M. Suinn developed an intervention for athletes that combined mental imagery and relaxation. Dr. Suinn's **visuo-motor behavioral rehearsal** will be discussed in Chapter 5. It has been highly influential and has subsequently received solid empirical support (Seabourne, Weinberg, Jackson, & Suinn, 1985). In 1997 it was described as perhaps the most studied mental practice procedure in the literature of sport psychology (Onestak, 1997). Robert Nideffer's influential description and assessment of attentional styles was developed in 1976 and will also be discussed in Chapter 4 and in other chapters.

Bruce Ogilvie has been called the father of North American applied sport psychology because of his leadership in providing psychological services to elite and professional athletes (Weinberg & Gould, 2003). His book *Problem Athletes and How to Handle Them* (1966; coauthored with Thomas Tutko) and questionnaire, the Athletic Motivational Inventory, were influential and controversial. Dr. Ogilvie and other pioneering consultants surveyed colleagues in 1979 regarding the training necessary for clinical psychologists to function effectively in consultation with athletes (Ogilvie, Haase, Jokl, Kranidiotis, Mahoney, & Nideffer, 1979). These clinicians placed the highest priority on knowledge about psychopathology, and they also made frequent use of relaxation training to reduce physiological anxiety. The clinicians stated that their experience as athletes competing at a high level was their most important experience or training to be an effective sport psychologist. They also valued the experience they gained in consultation with elite athletes.

These psychologists were probably self-trained or learned "on the job" to apply clinical services to athletes. Today, on the job training is not sufficient for certification as a sport psychologist. For example, the Division of Exercise and Sport Psychology of the **American Psychological Association** (APA) explicitly states that sport psychologists are not self-taught and also that experience as an athlete and training as a clinical psychologist do not provide the necessary education and training. Formal graduate coursework, supervised practice, and testing are necessary to insure that sport psychologists meet objective standards of competence and expertise. The **Association for the Advancement of Applied Sport Psychology** (AASP) developed criteria for certification for sport psychologists in 1991 that also require supervised experience, graduate coursework in psychology and counseling, as well as knowledge of the biomechanical and/or physiological bases of sport (Zizzi, Zaichkowsky, & Perna, 2002). The USOC requires this certification for consultants to work with Olympic programs. The clinicians in the 1979 survey (Ogilvie et al.) recognized an ethical concern that has been codified as an ethical standard of sport psychologists, in that they considered confidentiality within the consulting relationship to be a high priority. The concern with confidentiality persisted into the 1990s with sport psychologists (Petitpas, Brewer, Rivera, & Van Raalte, 1994).

Ethics and Sport Psychology

The ethical code of the AASP (1994) was modeled after that of the APA. The current ethical code of the APA (2002) is an admixture of five general principles and specific rules that follow the general principles and relate to specific situations in the field of psychology. The general principles (beneficence and nonmaleficence; fidelity and responsibility; integrity; justice; respect for people's rights and dignity) are considered universal or applicable to all human beings and to involve no contradictions (Whelan, Meyers, & Elkins, 2002). The specific rules are derived to some degree from the actual practice of psychology and are intended to enhance the wellbeing of the greatest majority of people. An example of a specific ethical obligation for professional psychologists is to maintain the confidentiality of information they obtain from clients (with certain exceptions) in professional counseling relationships.

Athletes' Views of Consulting Sport Psychologists

Given the abovementioned history of consultation with US Olympic athletes since 1976, it is not surprising that in more recent times elite athletes routinely consult with psychologists (Gould, 1999). However, perhaps due to less experience with sport psychologists (Maniar, Curry, Sommers-Flanagan, & Walsh, 2001), collegiate athletes in the USA and Britain are not entirely comfortable with the prospect of psychological consultations (Linder, Brewer, Van Raalte, & De Lange, 1991;Van Raalte, Brewer, Brewer, & Linder, 1992; Van Raalte, Brewer, Linder, & DeLange, 1990; Van Raalte, Brewer, Matheson, & Brewer, 1996). Sport psychologists are viewed as similar to mental health professionals such as clinical psychologists, counselors, and psychiatrists. However, they are often seen as less knowledgeable about mental health issues and more conversant with sport and physical topics than mental health professionals. Coaches generally view the consultations of sport psychologists positively and recognize a need for their services (Pargman, 1998).

Athletes have underutilized mental health services and have been reluctant to take advantage of the services of sport psychologists. They are more likely to seek emotional help and support from family and professionals identified primarily as sport professionals, such as coaches (Maniar et al., 2001). It appears that athletes are uncomfortable with the title of psychologist due to its association with mental disorders and problems (Ravizza, 1988). African American and male Division I intercollegiate athletes were particularly uncomfortable with the prospect of accessing

> ## Changing Attitudes toward Mental Health Professionals?
>
> Major League Baseball all-star and Most Valuable Player Alex Rodriguez has seen therapists for years to deal with personal issues such as being abandoned by his father at age nine. On the television show *Extra*, he commented, "I don't know where I'd be [without therapy]." "I think it's a different life that I've discovered and I thank Cynthia [his wife] for that because therapy is an incredible thing and you might get to know someone you didn't even know was in there," he said. "Why let the train wreck come before you fix it?" Cynthia Rodriguez explained, "it's because of therapeutic intervention that he's been able to discover and flourish as a person" (Amore, 2006). On June 8, 2005, Rodriguez became the youngest major league baseball player, at age 29, to hit 400 home runs. At age 32, on August 14, 2007, he became the youngest to hit 500 home runs.

help from sport psychologists, as they feared being stigmatized (Maniar et al., 2001; Martin, Wrisberg, Beitel, & Lounsbury, 1997).

Female athletes appear to be more willing to accesses consultation from sport psychologists, and acknowledge their need for help. Perhaps males are more likely to be socialized to be stoic, or to accept pain and the risk of injury without asking for help or complaining (S. B. Martin et al., 1997, 2001b). Female athletes are less likely to believe that others will label them as having psychological problems due to their consultation with a sport psychologist. These women and girls are also less likely to express a preference for working with a consultant of their same culture, ethnicity, or race (Martin, 2005). High school athletes are also more likely than Division I collegiate athletes to associate consultation with a sport psychologist with the stigma of having psychological problems (Martin, 2005).

Professional Associations and Journals

An important stimulus to the growth of sport psychology was the formation of academic societies and scholarly journals that fostered research and communication (Roberts & Treasure, 1999). The first journal to be devoted entirely to sport psychology was founded in 1970 and called the *International Journal of Sport Psychology*. It is the official journal of the **International Society of Sport Psychology** (ISSP), and the first president of ISSP and editor of the *International Journal of Sport Psychology* was the Italian psychiatrist Ferruccio Antonelli. The *Journal of Sport Psychology*, later called the *Journal of Sport and Exercise Psychology*, publishes basic and applied research and was established in 1979 (Weinberg & Gould, 2003).

Other important journals in this field are *The Sport Psychologist*, established in 1986; the *Journal of Applied Sport Psychology*, founded in 1989 and the official journal of the Association for the Advancement of Applied Sport Psychology (AASP); and the *International Journal of Sport and Exercise Psychology*, launched in 2005. The relative youth and rapid development of sport psychology is reflected in this timeline for the development of journals.

Associations for the study of sport psychology were established in the mid-1960s. In 1965, the International Society of Sport Psychology (ISSP) held the First International Congress of Sport Psychology in Rome, and in 1967 the first meeting of the North American Society for the Psychology of Sport and Physical Activity (NASPSPA) was held in Las Vegas (Landers, 1995; Wiggins, 1984). The Canadian Society for Psycho-motor Learning and Sport Psychology (CSPLSP) was established in 1969. It was initially under the auspices of the Canadian Association for Health, Physical Education and Recreation, but became independent in 1977 (Williams & Straub, 2006). The AASP was launched in 1985. In 1987, the Division of Sport and Exercise Psychology was established as the 47th division of the APA.

Accreditation

Accreditation provides an objective index of the quality of training for educational programs and individuals. AASP established standards for the accreditation of individual sport psychologists (Silva, 1989). Accreditation for graduate training programs in sport psychology has been recommended but is more controversial (Silva, 1989).

The precedent for accreditation was established by the APA for clinical psychology shortly after World War II (Report, 1947) – the APA is the oldest and largest professional organization of psychologists in the USA. This model is referred to both as the scientist-practitioner model, reflecting its emphasis on training in academic and applied psychology, and as the Boulder model, in that it was established in a meeting in Boulder, Colorado (Raimy, 1950). Accreditation indicates that the academic courses, faculty, and facilities of academic institutions are sufficient to train competent professional psychologists.

Accreditation of graduate programs in sport psychology has been seen as slow to develop (Silva et al., 1999). Perhaps it has not been universally embraced due to concerns about the cost of the accreditation process, fears that programs that fail to meet accreditation standards will be eliminated, and beliefs that academic freedom will be imperiled if curriculums are imposed by outside organizations such as AASP.

Websites of Interest

With the development of the Internet, websites provide useful sources of information about sport psychology.

Sport and Exercise Psychology in North America

American Alliance for Health, Physical Education, Recreation and Dance	www.aahperd.org
Association for the Advancement of Applied Sport Psychology	www.aaasponline.org
Canadian Society for Psychomotor Learning	www.scapps.org
Division 47 of the American Psychological Association	www.psyc.unt.edu/apadiv47
North American Society for the Psychology of Sport and Physical Activity	www.naspspa.org

Information about Sport

American College of Sports Medicine	www.acsm.org
Coaching Association of Canada	www.coach.ca
National Collegiate Athletic Association	www.ncaa.org
United States Olympic Committee	www.olympic-usa.org

Sport and Exercise Internationally

Asian South Pacific Association of Sport Psychology	www.humankinetics.com/ associations/aspasp/index.cfm
British Association for Sport and Exercise Sciences	www.bases.org.uk
Board of Sport Psychologists of the Australian Psychological Society	www.psychsociety.com.au/ units/colleges/sport
Canadian Society for Psychomotor Learning and Sport	www.scapps.org
European Federation of Sport Psychology	www.fepsac.org
International Olympic Committee	www.olympic.org
International Society for Sport Psychology	www.issponline.org

These issues appear to be less concerning to graduate students in sport psychology, as they are largely in favor of accreditation (Students' Vote, 1997).

Sport Psychology and the Scientific Method

As mentioned above, a substantial body of scientific research is summarized in each chapter of this textbook. Although there is some explanation of how this information was obtained, the content rather than the methods of this scientific research will be emphasized in the ensuing chapters. Before we continue with the presentation of this content, a brief discussion of the methods by which the information was obtained is warranted. Due to space limitations, these topics are only introduced in this text, and readers are encouraged to explore the issues more thoroughly by referencing the suggested readings at the end of this chapter.

Most of the research in this textbook was informed by the scientific method, which consists of developing hypotheses, often informed by prior research, and testing their correctness or accuracy with sophisticated experimental and statistical methodology. The minimal elements necessary for scientific research in sport psychology are therefore testable hypotheses, valid experimental designs, and statistical procedures that mathematically evaluate hypotheses. The question "How many angels can stand on the head of a pin?" may be of metaphysical interest to some but it does not represent a scientifically testable hypothesis. Tangible information cannot be obtained to test this question about angels. A question such as "Does pressure disrupt athletic performance?" is both testable and relevant to sport psychology.

Hypotheses are tested in **experiments** or **quasi-experiments**. True experiments have experimental and control groups, and participants or subjects are randomly assigned to both groups. Experimental groups are exposed to an intervention whereas control groups are given no intervention or an intervention that would be expected to have no effect on the behavior of interest. With random assignment it is assumed that the experimental and control groups are equivalent before the intervention.

Returning to the question about the effects of pressure on performance, a sport psychologist might conduct a true experiment in which sport performance is measured by the accuracy of putting a golf ball. Specifically, accuracy could be measured by the distance between the outcome of each putt and the target or pin. Pressure might be operationalized or represented in this experiment by filming students putting in the experimental condition, and informing them that golf coaches and other students would review the film. Undergraduate students without prior experience at golf might be randomly assigned to the experimental group that received instructions that their putting would be filmed and reviewed, or to a control group that was given no instructions or instructions that were not intended to produce pressure, such as to try their best.

Differences in putting accuracy between the experimental and control groups would then be compared with statistical tests such as a *t-test* – a test of differences between the means of the two groups (Lindman, 1974).

If between-groups differences are sufficiently large, then the *null hypothesis* – that the experimental and control groups are indistinguishable and that pressure has no effect on performance – would be rejected with some degree of statistical certainty. Experimental convention dictates that a .05 level of statistical significance or certainty is necessary to reject the null hypothesis, and at this level, the experimenter knows that differences as large as those recorded would occur by chance only five times in 100.

Returning to the putting study, the experimenter might find that the average distances between putts and pins was 10 inches for the experimental or pressured group and four inches for the control group. The t-test would likely demonstrate that this difference is significant, perhaps at least at the .05 level. The experimenter might then reject the null hypothesis with the certainty that a difference between groups this large would occur by chance only five times in 100 times. Following this procedure, the experimenter is also likely to conclude that the experiment has **internal validity** or that the intervention designed to induce pressure was responsible for the reduced putting accuracy of the pressured group.

The experimenter might pause before announcing that this study has external validity. **External validity** refers to the populations to which the results of a study can be generalized. This study was an analog study, i.e. a study in which realistic conditions were recreated in a laboratory environment. In that it was analogous but not identical to the study of pressure in actual sporting events, it is far from certain that the results of this hypothetical study can be generalized to all groups of golfers. For example, elite golfers may have developed skills for blunting the effects of pressure, or perhaps those susceptible to pressure quit so that only golfers relatively unsusceptible to pressure advance to elite ranks.

Perhaps a study in a golf tournament with skilled golfers would provide more convincing evidence about the effects of pressure on performance. However, it is highly unlikely that participants in a golf tournament could be subjected to experimental conditions intended to increase pressure. Instead, performance in naturally occurring situations that produce pressure might be compared to performance where pressure is less obvious. For example, a gallery might be present on certain holes and not on others, and scores for holes with and without galleries might be compared. This study would probably have **ecological validity** in that it was conducted in naturalistic conditions, and external validity in that it was conducted in the actual setting and with the population of interest. However, this study would lack the experimental control and random assignment necessary for true experiments, and therefore it would be a quasi-experiment (Cook & Campbell, 1979). Quasi-experiments are more open to challenges about causation or whether the experimental procedures resulted in the differences in measured variables (in this case scores on holes). The benefits of external and ecological validity are balanced with potential challenges to internal validity when one evaluates quasi-experiments.

Concerns about internal and external validity notwithstanding, true experiments and quasi-experiments allow for inferences about causation. Some of the studies in this book utilized procedures, such as correlation and qualitative analyses, that were descriptive but did not allow for causal inferences. **Correlational studies** demonstrate associations between variables. **Qualitative analyses** (e.g. Gould, Tuffey, Udry, & Loehr, 1996b; Lincoln & Guba, 1985; Patton, 1990) rely on semistructured interviews that are tape-recorded and transcribed verbatim. Independent investigators identify specific themes of the interviews, and the specific themes are subsequently organized into increasingly general themes. Qualitative analyses permit the discovery of information from the perspective of sportspersons. Another form of qualitative research, **ethnography**, has recently been advanced as a method of gaining insight into the behaviors and mental states of athletes. With ethnography, researchers become embedded in a particular sport and team, and collect data in the forms of participant-observations, interviews, photography, and questionnaires (Krane & Baird, 2005).

Information from true experiments, quasi-experiments, correlational studies, and qualitative analyses is integrated throughout this textbook. With this research the horizons of sport psychology are continually expanded.

Summary and Conclusions

Sport psychology is a rapidly maturing area of research, teaching, and practice. The maturity of sport psychology is evidenced by the number of professional journals and organizations devoted to advancing and communicating the science and practice of sport psychology. The importance of applied sport psychology is perhaps best demonstrated by the observation that sport psychologists have consulted with US Olympians since 1976.

As is true in other areas of applied psychology, such as clinical psychology, there have been periods of tension between practitioners and academics. Subsequent to the publication of Rainer Martens' 1979 article "About Smocks and Jocks," research in the actual venues of sport has been emphasized. Studies in such sport settings provide opportunities for research that is both ecologically and externally valid. This research diminishes the distance between academic and applied practice.

The effectiveness of psychologists in consulting, educational, and research settings is to some degree determined by the quality of their working alliances with students, supervisees, and clients. The effectiveness of working alliances merits monitoring on an ongoing basis. This monitoring may involve estimates of the degree of trust in the working alliance.

Key Terms and Names

Norman Triplett

Facilitation effect

Audience effects

Coleman Roberts Griffith

Rainer Martens' 1979 article "About Smocks and Jocks"

Consultation

Educational sport psychologists

Clinical psychologists

Visuo-Motor Behavioral Rehearsal

Bruce Ogilvie

International Society of Sport Psychology

Association for the Advancement of Applied Sport Psychology

American Psychological Association

Accreditation

Experiments

Quasi-experiments

Internal validity

External validity

Ecological validity

Correlational studies

Qualitative analyses

Suggested Readings

Heiman, G. W. (2003). *Applied statistics for the behavioral sciences* (5th ed.). Boston: Houghton-Mifflin.

Krane, V., & Baird, S. M. (2005). Using ethnography in applied sport psychology. *Journal of Applied Sport Psychology, 17,* 87–107.

Nideffer, R. (1992). *Psyched to win.* Champaign, IL: Human Kinetics Press.

Ryba, T. V., Stambulova, N. B., & Wrisberg, C. A. (2005). The Russian origins of sport psychology: A translation of an early work of A. C. Puni. *Journal of Applied Sport Psychology, 17,* 157–169.

Shadish, W. R., Cook, T. D., & Campbell, D. T. (2002). *Experimental and quasi-experimental designs for generalized causal inference.* Boston: Houghton-Mifflin.

Stambulova, N. B., Wrisberg, C. A., & Ryba, T. V. (2006). A tale of two traditions in applied sport psychology: The heyday of Soviet sport and wake-up calls for North America. *Journal of Applied Sport Psychology, 18,* 173–184.

Williams, J. M., & Straub, W. F. (2006). Sport psychology: Past, present, future. In J. M. Williams (Ed.), *Applied sport psychology: Personal growth to peak performance* (5th ed., pp. 1–14). Mountain View, CA: Mayfield.

Motivation for Sport and Achievement

2

Standing tightly packed with 9,000 other runners in Hopkinton, MA at the start of the Boston Marathon, Greta noticed some liquid splashing on her leg. Scowling, she realized the guy next to her was relieving himself in a paper cup. With his weak apology and the realization that at least her shoes and socks were not wet, she decided to save her energy for the next 26.2 miles. Besides, she was frustrated with the heat and sunshine. As was usually the case, it was much too hot on Patriot's Day in April to run a marathon.

Greta glanced at her wristband on which she recorded her target split times. She was particularly concerned with the 20 and 30 kilometer splits, knowing that if she was not at 20 kilometers after one hour and twenty minutes (1:20) and 30 kilometers after two hours, she would have no chance of reaching her goal to complete the marathon under 2:50. She reminded herself of the downhill bias over the first 30 kilometers and how exhausted her quadriceps felt last year when she exceeded these split times. Then noticing the heat again, she considered how ironic it was that she dreaded facing the cold every Saturday morning throughout the winter as she began her long runs of 30 kilometers.

Through Framingham and at the 20 kilometer split, Greta was right on schedule. In Newton, the downhill course bias ended, and at the 30-kilometer mark she was still making her split times. Then came Boston College, the final 10 kilometers and the race for the finish line began. On Boylston Street and with three miles to go, her legs felt like they weighed a ton, and she concentrated on keeping her form and making her splits. It became more difficult, however, to ignore nausea, and she knew that lactic acid from fatigued leg muscles was spilling into her bloodstream. Greta reminded herself, "This ain't supposed to be fun." Pushing herself down Boylston Street and toward the finish line, her nausea spilled over; yet she held her form.

Returning to work the next day, Greta tried to walk normally and not reveal the soreness in her quadriceps. What bothered her more, however, was her time of 2:53. In the afternoon she snuck a peek at the race results in the newspaper, and it was difficult not to feel proud that her time was the third fastest for women in her state. She mused "Next year if I train properly on hills and if the weather cooperates . . ."

Why do people strive to do their best? Why do people attempt to reach their full potential? These questions have intrigued humankind since at least the time of the ancient Greeks. Aristotle divided human activity into two categories: labor and leisure. The former was the kind of work that created wealth and earned material goods. Leisure activities, on the other hand, were responsible for the creation of goods of the spirit and of civilization (Murphy, 1993). Labor and business were considered necessary but not ennobling for human life. Work did little for the self-esteem of ancient Greeks. By contrast, leisure allowed people to grow morally, intellectually, and spiritually, and made life worth living. In Greek society, slaves were the laborers, while aristocrats and most educated citizens spent their time engaged in leisure and recreation and activities related to the arts, sciences, business, and military enterprises.

Judaism and Christianity redefined the value of work. In these religions, men and women could emulate God, who worked six days to create the world. A full day's work came to have the highest ethical value while play and leisure were seen to lead to sin. Work came to be seen as a virtue in itself. In 1904, the German sociologist **Max Weber** described the **Protestant work ethic** as a continual striving for perfection or at least self-improvement and to do one's best in every respect. Weber argued that the Protestant work ethic was catalyzed by John Calvin's theology of predestination. Pre-destination refers to the concept that heavenly salvation was pre-determined by God and not to be won by the accumulation of good works and especially the purchase of indulgences. However, the concept that salvation was pre-destined did little to allay fears about damnation. By striving for

Why do people strive to do their best? (Photo © Alan Heartfield.)

perfection or to imitate a Biblical figure a believer could discover whether he or she was one of the elect or predestined.

Approximately 100 years have passed since Weber's studies of work and achievement motivation. It may be disheartening to learn that after this interval a unitary and perhaps straightforward explanation of achievement motivation does not exist. In the pages that follow, nine theories of human motivation are presented (psychoanalytic, neo-analytic, humanistic, achievement motivation, social-cognitive, goals, attribution, motivational orientation, and flow). There are at least 32 distinguishable theories of motivation (Roberts, 2001), but these nine theories have influenced research and practice over decades. The underpinnings of these theories will be emphasized in this chapter and their application in sport settings will be described in detail in ensuing chapters.

Psychoanalytic Viewpoints

Modern psychology has considered an absence of ambition as evidence of inhibition or psychopathology (American Psychiatric Association, 2000; Galatzer-Levy & Cohler, 1993). However, **Sigmund Freud**, a Viennese physician and the developer of **psychoanalysis**, and considered one of the 100 most influential intellects of the 20th century (Gay, 1999), argued that work was not a response to some innate internal drive but rather a response to external pressures and opportunities to make a living. Freud thought that society's proper role was to provide external pressure or coercion for work. Otherwise, he reasoned that the majority of humans would not put forth the effort necessary to create new wealth and care for themselves. He regarded the masses as "lazy and unintelligent" and not "spontaneously fond of work" (Freud, 1927, p. 7). Freud argued that each human being was innately endowed with an **id**, or a psychological repository of libidinal or sexual and aggressive impulses. The **pleasure principle** – the motive to seek immediate pleasures and to eschew delays of gratification in the pursuit of long-term goals – governs the id. The pleasure principle is concordant with the **hedonic principle** – the assumption that human motivation is determined by efforts to maximize pleasure and minimize pain. The hedonic principle dominated the understanding of human motivation from the time of the ancient Greeks to the 20th century. It is the basic motivation assumption in psychological theories as diverse as psychobiology, behavioral psychology, decision making, and social psychology (Higgins, 1997).

The psychological structure that allows for adaptive responses to societal pressure for work is the **ego**. An important standard for psychological health is the ego's uninhibited capacity to respond adaptively to external pressures and opportunities to make a living (normality was also related to the ego's uninhibited capacity to respond freely to the id's demands for enjoyment). Freud considered work to be a means by which people anchored themselves to reality as they established roles in the fabric of their societies. Perhaps due to the opportunities provided by their environments and their talents, some people were considered to find additional sources of gratification in their work. These people sublimated or redirected narcissistic, aggressive, or libidinal urges from their ids into work productions.

Through processes of identification with parents and other important figures, children develop models for working, for persistence in solving difficult problems, and ultimately ego strength. The **superego** – the psychological structure that contains the values and mores – also plays a role in directing ambition. The superego also contains the **ego ideal**, or the standards by which individuals judge their behavior. Together, the superego and the ego ideal determine the levels of goals and the methods for obtaining the goals to which people aspire.

Freud's personal focus on work was notable. He had prodigious energy for work; he feared the regressive pull of full contentment and hence thrived on irritation (Mahoney, 1997). For optimal achievement, Freud needed disgruntlement in the form of physical fatigue or psychic misery. In the last years of the 19th century, he was at his most creative and at the same time was suffering most from his neurosis. He wrote of these phenomena:

> I returned to a sense of too much well-being and have since then been very lazy because the modicum of misery essential for intensive work will not come back. (Masson, 1985, letter of April 16, 1896, pp. 180–1)

> My style has unfortunately been bad because I feel too well physically; I have to feel somewhat miserable to write well. (Masson, 1985, letter of September 6, 1899, p. 370)

The effects of work in diminishing discontentment notwithstanding, Freud also wrote that he found joy in work: "Creative imagination and work go together with me; I take no delight in anything else" (Mend & Federn, 1963, letter of March 6, 1910, p. 35).

Ultimately, Freud came to define mental health as the capacity to work and to love. Freud's emphasis on the importance of work, especially efficient work, achievement, and performance as a standard of mental health has been accepted as axiomatic or essentially unequivocal. Indeed, the modern classification of mental disorders, the *Diagnostic and Statistical Manual of Mental Disorders, Fourth Edition, Text Revision* (DSM-IV-R; American Psychiatric Association, 2000) identifies mental disorders as causing dysfunction vocationally, interpersonally, or intrapsychically.

Neo-analytic Viewpoints

Psychoanalytic theorizing about the drive to reach one's full potential did not end with Freud. The neo-psychoanalytic perspective of self psychology considered the movement of children from activities that are merely playful to activities that are more purposeful to be motivated by wishes to obtain approval from important adults such as parents. Satisfaction in achieving self-set goals was considered to be integrated into the child's self-concept, and self-esteem was then partially determined by achievement (Wolf, 1997).

A member of Freud's inner circle, **Alfred Adler**, left to found the Society for Individual Psychology. One of the essential tenets of his theory of human motivation was that striving for success or superiority was the driving force behind human activity. Adler maintained that this drive was universal, as infants and children recognize their lack of stature and vulnerability, experience inferiority, and compensate with goals for superiority or success (Adler, 1964). Social recognition as a superior athlete was seen as an important motive for athletic participation among elite track and field athletes (Mallett & Hanrahan, 2004). Those with exaggerated feelings of inferiority strive for superiority regardless of the effects of their behavior on others. Psychologically secure people strive toward goals that are also consistent with the interests of their society.

Subsequent research inspired by Adler's work focused less on feelings of inferiority than on maintaining control over the factors that could influence the lives of others (Veroff, 1992). The **power motive** was understood to represent a fear of being in a weak position in relation to others and therefore unable to control one's fate. More recent and perhaps complementary empirical research concerning the power motive has not emphasized the fear of weakness but has conceptualized the power motive as the desire to influence others; to have authority, dominance, and leadership (Winter, 1992). The kind of power that was most important to people high in this latter power motive was direct and legitimate interpersonal power. These people are likely to make efforts to gain the attention of other people by making themselves more visible, and by building alliances with others. This power motivation is independent of motives for achievement, affiliation, and intimacy.

Humanistic Psychology

The most widely recognized theory of motivation, which is perhaps most at odds with Freud's notion that humans are inherently or instinctually lazy, may be that of the American humanistic psychologist, **Abraham Maslow** (1973). Maslow argued that humans were instinctually motivated toward growth and **self-actualization**, or the realization of their full human potential. He maintained that growth is rewarding in itself, and that the appetite for growth is whetted by growth rather than diminished by the realization of growth.

Self-actualization has at times been seen to be more compatible with community involvement – such as building better societies, nurturing the next generation, and helping others in need – than with individual pre-occupations such as financial success and occupational status (Kasser & Ryan, 1993, 1996). Financial success and occupational status have been associated with external motivations or extrinsic goals as the individual strives to meet standards that are determined and perhaps imposed by others. Those working to make a better world have been seen as motivated by internal motives, as they sought to reach standards that were of their own making.

However, the question of whether one's ambitions are selfish versus altruistic matters less than the motives for pursuing those ambitions (Carver & Baird, 1998). People may pursue altruistic goals, such as building a better world, because they are freely pursuing their own interests and values, or because of external pressure such as the desire to please others, or by external pressure that is internalized such as efforts to avoid or diminish guilt. Self-actualization is associated with goals that are self-selected or intrinsically rewarding regardless of whether one aspires to build a better world or simply better one's position in the world.

Intrinsic motivation involves the pursuit of activities because they are inherently rewarding, and people make their own decisions to pursue these goals. Conversely, if ambitions and goals are imposed externally, self-actualization is unlikely regardless of whether ambitions relate to financial success or community involvement.

With the mastery of skills and the development of competence come feelings of satisfaction and joy (Dweck, 1986). The development of competence and intrinsic motivation is somewhat domain specific, and people experience varying degrees of cognitive, social, and physical competence. Competence in the cognitive, social, and physical spheres is more commonly experienced in academic performance, in relationships, and in sport and exercise, respectively. The issue of intrinsic versus extrinsic motivation will be discussed in greater detail later in this chapter.

Achievement Motivation

The American psychologist **John Atkinson**'s theories and research on achievement motivation (1957, 1964) were developed in the early 1950s, and continue to influence the direction of current research. He recognized and demonstrated scientifically that people differed in terms of levels of **achievement motivation** or need for accomplishments, and that achievement motivation was a trait or a stable characteristic. However, even those with high levels of achievement motivation would not be expected to put forth maximum effort on all evaluations. Instead, tendencies to put forth optimal efforts and achieve success were determined by achievement motivation, the likelihood of being successful at a task, and the importance of the task. Interestingly, those with high levels of achievement motivation were not drawn to tasks that were so difficult that the chances of success were slim. They preferred tasks of moderate difficulty, or perhaps fair tests of their ability. These fair tests provide clear evidence of effort and ability. People with lower achievement motivation prefer easy or unreasonably difficult evaluations.

Atkinson also recognized a **motive to avoid failure** or **fear of failure**. Just as with achievement motivation, there are individual differences in the motive to avoid failure, and it is most strongly aroused by tasks of intermediate difficulty. Ultimately, when faced with a situation in which performance is evaluated, an achievement-oriented tendency is activated that is the result of the additive combination of the motive for achievement and the motive to avoid failure. If the motive to avoid failure exceeds achievement motivation, evaluations will be avoided. The motive to avoid failure is most influential for tasks of moderate difficulty or fair tests of ability and effort, and those with high levels of this motive most vigorously avoid these tasks. People dominated by the tendency to avoid failure spend more of their time working on easier jobs and tasks. Of course even those with extremely high levels of the motive to avoid failure cannot avoid all forms of evaluation.

With high levels of fear of failure, evaluations are seen as threats. For example, college students with high levels of fear of failure engaged in negative self-talk in which they blamed themselves for poor performances during recreational tennis (Conroy & Metzler, 2004). Ironically, this form of blame was what they most dreaded, and therefore this form of self-reproach appeared somewhat involuntary and automatic.

Even eminent performers experience fear of failure. Aspects of the fear of failure among elite female and male athletes and performance artists have been identified (Conroy, Poczwardowski, & Henschen, 2001, p. 318):

1 experiencing personal diminishment
2 demonstrating that I have low ability
3 demonstrating that I lack control
4 experiencing tangible losses
5 wasting my effort
6 making my future uncertain
7 losing a special opportunity
8 causing others to lose interest in me
9 disappointing or upsetting important others
10 experiencing an embarrassing self-presentational failure.

Achievement Motivation and Gender

Matina Horner (1973), another American psychologist, pioneered the examination of gender differences in achievement motivation in the context of Atkinson's expectancy value theory. She maintained that there was a psychological barrier that interfered with the achievement of women, and referred to this as the **motive to avoid success**. The motive to avoid success refers to the belief that negative consequences will accompany success. Horner reasoned that traditional conceptions of femininity involved the suppression of aggressive and competitive impulses. Therefore success and competition would engender anxiety in women, as they would fear social disapproval and a "loss of femininity" (Horner, 1973, p. 223). The motive to avoid success was understood to be more influential when women competed with men and engaged in tasks considered masculine, such as mathematics.

In the 34 years since the publication of Dr. Horner's research, her work has come under a considerable amount of criticism because independent researchers did not replicate her findings. For example, a study of medical students published in 1988 (Piedmont) demonstrated that fear of success imagery and achievement motivation did not differ for female and male medical students and for other groups of males and females. Differences between individual women and men were also highlighted. For example, high school women with a history of high achievement performed better than comparable males on very difficult memory tests (Costanzo, Woody, & Slater, 1992).

However, women as a whole may be more uncomfortable demonstrating high levels of competence in the presence of men and women who have much less competence (Piedmont, 1988). Perhaps women are more sensitive than men to the emotional reactions of others and imagine that less capable peers will be discomforted by their demonstration of prowess.

Both female and male elite athletes and performers acknowledged aspects of fear of success (Conroy et al., 2001, p. 318):

1 not learning and improving
2 facing an overly rigid future
3 accomplishing all my goals
4 facing higher expectations (own and others)
5 losing enjoyment of success
6 experiencing tangible costs (e.g. slumps, injuries, loneliness)
7 experiencing jealousy and interpersonal rivalry
8 experiencing increased recognition and appreciation
9 not receiving support from others
10 losing or not increasing motivation
11 becoming overconfident.

With high levels of fear of success, people may sabotage their opportunities for success by engaging in disparaging self-talk (Conroy & Metzler, 2004). This self-talk may direct attention from the instrumental behaviors that lead to success, and make success less likely.

Social-Cognitive Approach

Research in the **social-cognitive paradigm** of achievement motivation is consistent with the expectancy value models of Atkinson and his colleagues. From this perspective, the behavior of some people may be more determined by a **promotion focus** or a focus on approaching opportunities, advancement, and accomplishment and a relative lack of attention to potential risks and losses (Higgins, 1997). People with a promotion focus appear to be primarily motivated by the motive for achievement. They seek accomplishments and attempt to avoid the experience of nonfulfillment. They attempt to reduce the discrepancy between their current position in life and desired end-states or goals. People who are primarily concerned with avoiding negative outcomes, mistakes, and losses demonstrate a **prevention focus**. They are primarily motivated by the motive to avoid failure. These individuals seek safety and attempt to avoid danger. They seek to increase the distance between their current condition in life and undesired end-states or outcomes.

It is theorized that early socialization experiences with caretakers contribute to these differences in regulatory focus (Higgins, 1997). Children with a promotion focus are more regularly rewarded and encouraged for accomplishments or positive outcomes, while the attention of children with a prevention focus is directed toward avoiding parental reproach.

Adults with a promotion focus demonstrate a risky bias in decision making or a tendency to insure against errors of omission. Those with a prevention focus demonstrate a conservative bias or an effort to avoid errors of commission or false alarms. When tasks become increasingly difficult, promotion-focused individuals are more persistent and successful because of their bias toward avoiding errors of omission or overlooking solutions to problems. Prevention-focused people quit more readily on difficult tasks in an effort to avoid mistakes. The commitment of promotion-focused people to goals is determined by the interaction of their expectancy of achieving the goal and the degree to which they value the goal. The greater and more likely the payoff, the harder they work to achieve it. With a prevention focus, the likelihood of goal attainment is less important. Prevention-focused people focus on the value of a goal and pursue goals as if they were necessities regardless of the likelihood of success or a payoff.

Research concerning promotion and prevention focuses has relevance in evaluating the hedonic principle (Higgins, 1997). The pleasure and pain sought and avoided are different depending on the regulatory focus. The stronger the promotion focus, the greater is the feeling of cheerfulness upon achieving goals and dejection after failure. The more pronounced the prevention focus, the greater is the sense of quiescence, calm, and relief upon goal attainment and the more the feeling of agitation and anxiety upon falling short of goals. Those with a promotion focus might experience pleasure upon the realization of a goal and those with a prevention focus upon the successful avoidance of an outcome. Pain may be appreciated after an unsuccessful pursuit of a goal or after the failed avoidance of an

Hedonic Principle?

"There are parts unknown with regard to human performance, and those are the parts when it's just about pain and forfeit. How do you make yourself do it? You remind yourself that you're fulfilling your obligation to get the best from yourself, and that all achievement is born out of sacrifice." (Armstrong & Jenkins, 2003, p. 222) outcome, depending on the presence of promotion or prevention regulatory focuses, respectively.

Members of national junior and senior (ages 16 through 21) hockey squads in Australia were shown to differ in terms of their tendencies to approach opportunities for success or avoid chances of failure (Watson, 1986). Those with approach orientations were motivated to capture the rewards of success, had high achievement motivation, had intrinsic motivation for involvement in hockey, and experienced low levels of anxiety. Athletes with avoidance orientations were prone to anxiety, were more concerned with social approval and disapproval, and were motivated more forcefully to avoid the sting of failure. Players with avoidance orientations demonstrated more anxiety, and more trait anxiety (anxiety that was stable over time and across situations).

Hedonic principle? (Photo © Pres Panayotov.)

Goals

The findings concerning motives for achievement and avoiding failure continue to influence the direction of current research. These motives have recently been conceptualized as more abstract motivational dispositions that have less direct influence on behavior related to achievement than on **achievement goals**. Achievement goals appear to be the channel or portal through which the underlying motives of achievement motivation or fear of failure have their effects on observable behaviors such as graded performance and intrinsic motivation. Achievement goals are viewed as more phenomenologically or psychologically available to people than traits such as the motives for success and to avoid failure. Goals are psychological constructs that have a more concrete presence to people, as they are commonly understood as the standards by which they regulate their behavior (Elliot & Church, 1997).

Three types of achievement goals have been identified: **mastery, performance-avoidance**, and **performance-approach** goals. The antecedents and consequences of these three types are different. Both mastery and performance-approach goals orient individuals toward the obtainment of positive outcomes (Elliot & Harackiewicz, 1996). The distal, underlying motive disposition of those with mastery goals is solely achievement motivation, and that for people with performance-avoidance goals is fear of failure. People with performance-approach goals have both achievement motivation and fear of failure. Expectations of competency or success are also antecedents of mastery and performance-approach goals, and those that expect failure adopt performance-avoidance goals.

These types of goals are referred to as **goal orientations**. As will be described in Chapter 8, there are multiple systems for classifying goal orientations. Several of these systems have wider use in sport settings. However, comprehensive models of goal orientations, such as that provided by the mastery, performance-approach, and performance-avoidance models, have been seen as offering important new directions for the development of sport psychology (Duda & Hall, 2001), and recent research demonstrates that fears of failure are direct antecedents of performance-avoidance goals in sport settings and mastery orientations may even insulate people from developing fear of failure and self-consciousness during sport performance (Conroy & Elliot, 2004; Conroy, Elliot, & Hofer, 2003).

Those with mastery goals demonstrate high levels of intrinsic motivation, but their keen interest in topics does not always result in the highest levels of graded performance (Elliot & Harackiewicz, 1996). This may be due to their attention to details that are of greatest interest to them rather than to the rehearsal of tasks and acquisition of information on which they will be evaluated (Figure 2.1). People with performance-approach goals may have less intrinsic interest in topics than those with mastery goals, but have been shown to achieve higher grades in college classrooms. The

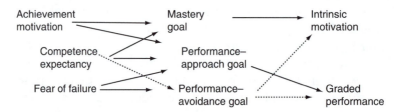

FIGURE 2.1. Goal orientations, achievement motivation, and performance. Solid arrows indicate facilitation; broken arrows indicate inhibition. Adapted from Elliot, A. J., & Harackiewicz, J. M. (1996). Approach and avoidance achievement goals and intrinsic motivation: A mediational analysis. *Journal of Personality and Social Psychology, 70*, 461–475.

concurrent motives to demonstrate performance superior to others and to avoid failure or poor performance motivate strategies that result in the best performance for college students on tests. The least adaptive achievement goal was the performance-avoidance goal. College students with performance-avoidance goals were shown to achieve the lowest grades on tests and to have the least interest in the subject matter.

The nature of the task on which individuals are being evaluated may influence both intrinsic motivation and graded performance (Elliot & Harackiewicz, 1996). Mastery goals may result in superior performance when the subject and the means of evaluation are not imposed on individuals. Mastery goals may also be particularly influential in sustaining high levels of task involvement and commitment in the pursuit of career goals that take years to fulfill. For example, it takes years to become a first-class skater. However, few people are entirely free to pursue their own interests and most are faced with demands to perform well on graded tasks such as tests and work assignments that are not of high intrinsic interest. Optimal performance on both interesting and uninteresting tasks may be best facilitated by the simultaneous maintenance of mastery and approach-performance goals. The presence of both types of goals results in higher levels of intrinsic motivation and graded performance.

Achievement tendencies that are dominated by performance-avoidance goals are not adaptive. Avoidance goals have global consequences on performance and phenomenological wellbeing; they result in less persistence in the face of failure, less task involvement, less intrinsic motivation, and poorer academic performance. Performance-avoidance goals influence the focus of attention during evaluation tasks, as people are more likely to focus on themselves and question whether they will be capable of achieving standards. This focus on oneself directs attention away from the specific activities necessary to achieve goals. Avoidance goals motivate people to shy away from difficult challenges, and to attribute responsibility for success and failure to forces outside of themselves (Elliot & Harackiewicz, 1996; Elliot & Sheldon, 1997). Performance-avoidance goals also have an inimical effect on overall personal adjustment and wellbeing, and contribute to decreased self-esteem, personal control, and life satisfaction.

Attribution Theory

Attributions are the explanations or reasons that people give for events such as successes and failures that occur in their lives and the lives of other people (Biddle & Hanrahan, 1998; Graham & Weiner, 1996). With attribution theory, people are understood as active in construing the causes of their experiences (Heider, 1958; Jones & Davis, 1965; Kelley, 1967, 1972). People are especially motivated to understand the causes of failures in achievement domains, and often interpret failures to result from causal factors that are to varying degrees **internal** or **external** to themselves (locus), **global** or **specific, stable** or **unstable** over time, and **controllable** or **uncontrollable**. For example, if a sportsperson ascribes failure at a competition to an internal cause that is global, stable, and uncontrollable, such as a lack of talent, then that person will be more likely to experience shame and give up. A second person might also experience failure, but explain it as a result of a lack of effort. Effort is not stable over time and is controllable. The second sportsperson may therefore experience guilt, redouble his or her practice efforts, and continue to think of himself or herself as a capable athlete.

Global, internal, stable, and uncontrollable attributions for negative events are associated with a "depressive attributional style" (Seligman, Abramson, Semmel, & von Baeyer, 1979). Tennis players who attributed losses to internal, stable, and global factors were also more likely to show helplessness, or attributions that they could not control the causes of success and failure (Prapavessis & Carron, 1988). Fortunately, sportspersons more commonly demonstrate a self-serving bias in interpreting the causes of success and failure. That is, they attribute success to stable, internal, and controllable factors (Biddle, Hanrahan, & Sellars, 2001). If success is attributed to stable factors, such as talent, then success will be expected in the future. Failure is less demoralizing when it is attributed to controllable factors that are unstable, such as a lack of effort.

A lack of belief in one's abilities has a detrimental effect on a range of tasks in which performance is evaluated (Thompson, Davidson, & Barber, 1995). Performance on tasks involving evaluative threat, such as intellectual aptitude, deteriorates after failures for those who lack confidence in their abilities; this is because they withdraw effort. Additional poor performances can then be attributed to the withdrawal of effort rather than to their lack of ability. The withdrawal of effort preserves the self-esteem of the person with low confidence at the cost of even poorer performance on the evaluative task. Self-esteem refers to self-worth or how people value themselves, and is distinct from confidence in abilities in areas such as academics and athletics.

Even people who lack confidence in their ability can show improvements in performance on evaluative tasks following failures if the environment provides a ready explanation or excuse for failure. Students who attribute failure to unfair tests and runners who point to rainy weather as the cause of poor times in races attribute poor performance to environmental conditions. In effect, the environmental explanation or external attribution for failure removes the evaluative threat from the task and therefore the threat to self-esteem or self-worth.

People who have high levels of confidence in their abilities appear to interpret successes and failures in a manner that is most beneficial to the preservation of their confidence (Thompson et al., 1995). That is, success is attributed to internal, stable factors such as their talent, and failure is explained by external, unstable factors such as bad luck. Regardless of whether they experience success or failure, those with high confidence retain the belief that they can control the factors that lead to success or failure. As stated above, people with little confidence in their abilities may also attribute failures to environmental or external factors. However, they differ from those with high self-confidence in that they also attribute the causes of success to external factors and have less belief in their control of the factors leading to successes and failures.

The coaching staff of the 1973 soccer team at the University of California at Los Angeles (UCLA) demonstrated attributional patterns that supported the confidence of their team (Lefebvre & Cunningham, 1977). This team came within one goal of winning a national championship. Coaches communicated to starting players that their successful performances were the results of internal factors such as ability and effort and that failures were due to external, unstable factors such as luck. These attribution patterns were more pronounced when evaluating the performances of the most talented starting players. The most talented soccer players attributed their successes to ability, a stable internal factor, and their failures to bad luck and a lack of effort. Less talented, but still starting soccer players were more likely to attribute success to an unstable, internal factor – effort – and failure to a lack of effort and ability.

Attributions in Childhood and Adolescence

As described in the previous section, sportspersons and students may conclude that their successes and failures reflect their ability and effort. Alternatively, they may attribute successes and failures to the difficulty of tasks or to luck. Success that is attributed to ability has a more beneficial effect on confidence, mood, and future effort and success. Children younger than about 12 do not reliably differentiate the concepts of ability, effort, task difficulty, and luck (Nicholls, 1992). With the capacity to differentiate ability from effort, adolescents become uncomfortable demonstrating incompetence in sport, and are more prone to withdraw effort or drop out if they perceive their athletic ability to be low.

Motivational Orientation: Intrinsic and Extrinsic Motivation

Intrinsic motivation has been defined and discussed at various points in this chapter. Intrinsic motivation relates to the pursuit of activities and interests that are of an individual's own choosing and that are largely free of internal or external pressure and control. Three forms of intrinsic motivation have been identified: intrinsic motivation for accomplishment; learning and knowledge; and experiencing stimulation of excitement (Vallerand, 2001; Vallerand & Losier, 1994). Intrinsic motivation for accomplishment is not dependent on outcomes or results, as it is the experience of attempting to accomplish a goal or to surpass oneself that provides the rewards (Vallerand & Rousseau, 2001). All three forms of intrinsic motivation may come into play in the course of sport activities as participants may find the mastery of difficult skills, the process of learning new skills, and the fun and excitement of sport to be rewarding.

The experience of external or internal regulation to engage in activities is referred to as **extrinsic motivation**. Behavior is externally regulated when it is controlled by external factors such as rewards and punishments. For example, athletes realize that prestige and honors accrue when they are successful and that coaches will penalize them for skipping practices. Athletic participation may also serve as extrinsic motivation for academic achievement. That is, students must attend school and maintain minimum grade point averages (GPAs) to remain eligible for athletics (Jordan, 1999). Sometimes sportspersons engage in practices that they do not enjoy but believe that they "should" pursue. These sportspersons have introjected or internalized external regulations, and experience guilt when they violate these regulations. For example, soccer players who despise distance running and interval training may be faithful to these forms of training during off seasons if they have internalized and honor the training regimen of their coach.

A third motivational orientation is **amotivation**, or the relative absence of motivation. Sportspersons who quit intensive training because they do not believe that it will result in improved athletic performance in competitions demonstrate amotivation. Amotivated sportspersons may feel incompetent and directionless.

People are sometimes motivated by different forms of motivation in different situations. For example, athletes may be intrinsically motivated to play their sport, but attend class and complete schoolwork only when extrinsically controlled. Considering motivation at a more specific level, sportspersons may relish and show intrinsic motivation for competition but loaf and require extrinsic control for practice (Vallerand & Rousseau, 2001).

Athletes who are intrinsically motivated enjoy sports to a greater degree. Intrinsically oriented athletes are more likely to experience **flow** – a state of wellbeing and efficiency that will be described later in this chapter (Kowal & Fortier, 1999). Extrinsically motivated athletes experience more anxiety and disruptions of concentration, perhaps because they are focused on the results of their performances. Extrinsically motivated athletes are more likely to "choke" under pressure or to perform poorly when optimal performance is most necessary (Baumeister, 1984; Baumeister, Hamilton, & Tice, 1985; Baumeister & Steinhilber, 1984). Intrinsically motivated athletes and people engaging in exercise programs are less likely to quit, and this issue is especially important when considering athletic participation among children.

Intrinsically motivated athletes demonstrate more sportspersonship or respect and concern for other participants, rules, and fair play. For example, intrinsically motivated, elite male adolescent Canadian hockey players were more likely to demonstrate good sportsmanship throughout a hockey season (Vallerand & Losier, 1994). With intrinsic motivation, efforts are made to outdo oneself, and poor sportspersonship and cheating do not bring a sportsperson closer to this objective.

Intrinsic Motivation and Extrinsic Rewards

The experience of *external* or *internal regulation* may diminish intrinsic motivation, at times even if this regulation consists of rewards for achievement. This effect is paradoxical in that the activity becomes less rewarding in and of itself as a result of receiving rewards for engaging in the activity. For example, the interest of children between the ages of nine and 11 in playing with the stabilometer, an interesting motor activity, decreased when they were given a reward to play with it (Orlick & Mosher, 1978). This paradoxical effect has also been reported for collegiate male and female athletes (Kingston, Horrocks, & Hanton, 2006) and football players (Vallerand, Deci, & Ryan, 1987). The athletes with scholarships reported less intrinsic interest in their sport than players who did not receive scholarships.

However, external rewards do not always diminish intrinsic motivation. External rewards only decrease intrinsic interest in activities when the reward is interpreted as an attempt to coerce and control behavior. Scholarship status did not diminish the intrinsic interest of female and male collegiate athletes in a range of sports (Amorose & Horn, 2000). Apparently, they considered the scholarship to be positive feedback that they had achieved a high level of competence, and evidence of competence may enhance intrinsic motivation. Rewards also did not diminish intrinsic motivation among elite athletes who finished in the top ten at major championships in track and field, as they likely also interpret awards and cash prizes as proof of competence (Mallett & Hanrahan, 2004).

Intrinsic Motivation and Feedback

Failure and feedback that performance is poor undermine intrinsic motivation. Activities that promote feelings of competence, autonomy, or control over one's life, and connectedness to others, tend to be intrinsically rewarding (Conroy, Poczwardowski, & Henschen, 2001; Deci & Ryan, 1987; Ryan & Deci, 2000). Feedback indicating failure separates sportspersons from these intrinsic rewards (Vallerand & Rousseau, 2001). Negative feedback diminishes the belief of athletes in their competence or ability; subsequently their intrinsic interest in sport diminishes. Positive feedback or evaluation of athletic performance enhances feelings of competence and intrinsic motivation in males. Female sportspersons may interpret even positive feedback as interpersonal control, and it may thus undermine intrinsic motivation (Vallerand, Deci, & Ryan, 1987).

Intrinsic Motivation and Competition

The effect of competition on intrinsic motivation is determined by whether the participant freely chose to compete. If athletes are obliged or coerced to compete, intrinsic motivation is likely to diminish. However, if athletes decide to engage in competition, it can enhance intrinsic motivation (Vallerand & Rousseau, 2001). Intrinsic motivation increases when sportspersons believe they have done well in competition.

If athletes engage in competition with a focus on "beating" others, then failure undermines intrinsic interest. As will be explained in Chapter 8, attention to improvement in relation to one's baseline of prior performance and to the technical aspects of skilled performance serves to shield performers from the negative effects of failure on intrinsic motivation (Fox, Goudas, Biddle, Duda, & Armstrong, 1994; Horn, Duda, & Miller, 1993). Elite performers often endorse multiple goals for competition (Jones and Hanton, 1996). Goals to beat competitors do not undermine intrinsic motivation and performance if athletes simultaneously endorse goals to improve and demonstrate technical mastery (Burton, Naylor, & Holliday, 2001).

Intrinsic and Extrinsic Motivation and Goals

Athletes with higher levels of intrinsic motivation have been seen as having task goals or to be task-oriented (Nicholls, 1989). With **task orientations**, athletes focus on skill acquisition, self-improvement, and exerting effort; sports are an end in themselves in that their practice is inherently rewarding. Female and male high school athletes with task orientations viewed sports as ways of learning good citizenship, realizing one's potential, learning to cooperate, and building self-esteem and fitness (Duda, 1989a).

Athletes with extrinsic motivation or **ego orientations** focus on the extrinsic reward that can be realized through sports, such as status and material gains. For example, English soccer players with ego orientations were most concerned with the financial remuneration that could be realized through their sport (Carpenter & Yates, 1997). With ego orientations, attention is directed to beating others with a minimum of effort. Male and female high school basketball players with ego orientations were more comfortable with cheating and unsporting play (Duda, Olson, & Templin, 1991). Males who play sports for high school teams and who play recreational sports were shown to be higher in ego orientations than their female counterparts as they focused on the results of play and competition (White & Duda, 1994).

Intrinsic and Extrinsic Motivation and Coaching

As mentioned above, coercion undermines intrinsic motivation. Not surprisingly, coaches who are coercive encourage less intrinsic motivation in athletes than coaches who are more supportive and encourage autonomy. Athletes report less autonomy, competence, and relatedness to teammates when coaches are excessively coercive (Vallerand & Rousseau, 2001). Coaches tend to be more coercive when their jobs depend on the performance of their athletes, and with athletes who do not appear to be intrinsically motivated to reach their full potential. Paradoxically, the efforts of coaches to coerce greater effort from athletes often result in a slackening of effort, as people of all ages resist efforts to limit their autonomy (Vallerand, Deci, & Ryan, 1987). Intrinsically motivated athletes are more often "left alone" or supported in their development of competence.

The influence of coaching interventions on intrinsic motivation appears to be indirect, or mediated through the fundamental needs of perceived competence, autonomy, and relatedness (Deci & Ryan, 1985). For example, democratic coaching behaviors – such as allowing team members to participate in decision-making – increased feelings of autonomy, which in turn enhanced intrinsic motivation among Division I collegiate athletes.

Autocratic coaching behaviors had the opposite effects and led to decreased feelings of relatedness (Hollembeak & Amorose, 2005).

Coercion has a greater effect when athletes or students are younger. Interventions designed to promote autonomy and to decrease coercion from coaches have reduced dropout rates in athletic programs with children. Children tend to respond to interventions supporting autonomy by showing up for more team practices and performing better (Vallerand & Losier, 1999).

This does not mean that coaches should adopt a *laissez-faire* approach and keep a distance from athletes. The intrinsic motivation of athletes is enhanced by the skillful intervention of coaches. For example, novice golfers developed higher intrinsic interest when coaches taught them mental skills such as stress management, goal setting, and self-monitoring (Beauchamp, Halliwell, Fournier, & Koestner, 1996). Novices who learned mental skills were more interested in golf than those who were given instruction only in the physical skills of golf or who were given little instruction. Perceptions of autonomy were enhanced among golfers who learned mental skills. Mental skills training will be discussed in Chapters 3, 4, and 5.

Before concluding this section, note that it is unlikely that sports-persons can find strong intrinsic motivation for all aspects of physical and mental training. As mentioned above, athletes may enjoy their sport but dislike aspects of training such as running distances or intervals. Introjected or internalized external regulations may be helpful to motivate adherence to these unpleasant or uninteresting aspects of training. The internalization of external demands does not make these aspects of training more interesting or rewarding, but it motivates adherence with the threat of guilt.

Achievement, Life Satisfaction, and Flow

Theory notwithstanding, achievement affects life satisfaction (Myers & Diener, 1995). This finding is certainly reasonable, given the portion of life devoted to activities related to achievement (Rain, Lane, & Steiner, 1991). Achievement contributes to a person's identity and to his or her network of supportive relationships. It provides a sense of meaning to life.

People who can become absorbed in their life's pursuits may experience a joyous state described as flow (Csikszentmihalyi, 1990). Flow occurs when people are engaged in optimal challenges, or when they work at tasks that are not so difficult that they exceed their capacities or so easy that they become bored. This is referred to as the **challenge–skills**

balance. This flow experience has resulted not only in productive achievement, but also in happiness. Absorption in meaningful activities, whether at work or play, is associated with greater happiness than passive and mindless inactivity. Achievement, task absorption, and doing one's best are not the only factors associated with life satisfaction. Happy people also have high self-esteem, a sense of personal control over the factors that influence their lives, optimism, and extraversion. As will be described later in this book, these factors are also associated with optimal achievement and performance.

Flow is associated with optimal athletic performance (Jackson, 1995; Jackson & Roberts, 1992; Krane & Williams, 2006; Stavrou & Zervas, 2004). Flow and optimal performance are more likely with careful and exhaustive preparation. Elite international male and female athletes from Australia and New Zealand rated thorough *pre-competitive* and *competitive preparation* and *planning* as the factors most influential in leading to flow (Jackson, 1995). These preparations consisted of developing "game plans" and following pre-competitive routines. With thorough preparation, athletes were able to relax active monitoring of the impending performance and were more likely to engage in the *automatic* execution of actions during performances. With the automatic execution of actions there is less representation of actions in conscious thought, and automatic functioning is associated with elite performance and flow states.

An equally important theme associated with flow was the maintenance of *self-efficacy* – confidence that one is at least equal to the challenge. High perceived ability and self-efficacy has been demonstrated to be critical to flow experiences not only with elite athletes, but also with Division I collegiate athletes (Jackson & Roberts, 1992) and with older non-elite athletes (Jackson, Kimiecik, Ford, & Marsh, 1998). Faith in oneself, or self-efficacy, without action in the form of physical preparation is unlikely to lead to flow. These elite athletes recognized that optimal conditioning and pre-competitive *routines* including proper rest, hydration, and nutrition were necessary if flow was to be experienced during competitions. Deviations from this preparation disrupted flow, as did physical events such as *injuries*. Achieving optimal *arousal* or physiological preparation was often associated with flow; for some athletes this consisted of relaxation and for others it involved becoming more energized. Interference due to excessive arousal or anxiety was more frequently disruptive than excessive relaxation. High motivation was important, especially the establishment of *goals*. *Mastery* goals or full attention to the instrumental behaviors necessary for good performances were a component of flow experiences. *Performance* goals or a focus on the outcome of performances is seldom a part of flow experiences (Jackson & Roberts,

1992). It was often necessary for athletes to feel that performances were going well for them to experience flow. *Concentration* was important to the elite athletes, and during flow task absorption is sometimes so complete that people are unaware of the passage of time (Csikszentmihalyi, 1990). Concentration and self-efficacy limit *cognitive interference* in the form of worries about the results or outcome of performances, about competitors, or about what others think of a performance. Cognitive anxiety or interference "is the antithesis of flow" (Jackson et al., 1998, p. 373) and cognitive interference disrupted performance to a greater degree than *physiological anxiety* with the elite and older non-elite athletes.

Optimal environmental and situation conditions relate to flow, and *familiar* environments often seem less daunting or unfriendly. Prior experience in venues where competitions occur is especially helpful and serves to limit the influence of hostile crowds. Other environmental factors that disrupted flow states among the elite athletes were the behavior of competitors and bad calls from referees. When athletes' attention was given to the assertive play of competitors or other environmental disturbances, performances suffered and flow stopped (Jackson & Csikszentmihalyi, 1999).

If attention is not rapidly directed away from environmental disturbances and internal thoughts that disrupt concentration, performance can deteriorate to the degree that *choking under pressure* occurs. This refers to performance that is significantly below one's average level of performance at times when optimal performance is most important. Excessive self-consciousness is also associated with choking under pressure, and flow is related to the loss of self-consciousness.

The factors that are italicized above and that contributed to flow are topics for examination in the chapters of this book. A review of the table of contents reveals that additional topics will be presented, especially about factors that disrupt performance. Perhaps the latter factors are least understood, as elite athletes believed the factors that led to flow were controllable and that the factors that disrupted flow were uncontrollable (Jackson, 1995).

Summary and Conclusions

Motivation for achievement has been established as an essential element of adaptive human behavior, and work satisfaction is an important contributor to life satisfaction. Indeed, vocational and academic inhibitions are criteria for the identification of mental disorders (American Psychiatric Association, 2000). Achievement motivation has been understood in the context of the hedonic principle or the assumption that people strive to maximize rewards or pleasure and minimize losses and pain. The hedonic principle is an assumption contained in most of the theories reviewed in this chapter. However, people experience rewards and losses in different ways. With a promotion orientation there is an emphasis on the realization of rewards, and with a prevention orientation there is a focus on relief from tension when loss is avoided (Higgins, 1997). A focus on accomplishment or the realization of outcomes or goals rather than the avoidance of failures or mistakes is adaptive.

People also differ in terms of achievement motivation. Recent research has indicated that the motives for achievement and to avoid failure also contribute to the development of achievement goals, and that achievement goals have a more direct effect on graded performance and intrinsic motivation than the motives for achievement and to avoid failure (Elliot & Harackiewicz, 1996).

Self-confidence and good performance are sustained by the attribution of the causes of success to internal factors, such as talent and effort, and of failure to external, unstable factors, such as bad luck. Views that aptitudes are more innately determined and immutable foster withdrawal from problem solving activities when solutions are not readily apparent (Dweck & Leggett, 1988). The optimal state of flow is more likely when self-efficacy and confidence are high and when people are optimally challenged. Optimal challenges are often associated with a balance between skills and challenges.

It should be noted that the causal pathways for constructs such as achievement goals, intrinsic and extrinsic motivation, causal attributions, and perceived competence have not been determined conclusively. In other words, there is disagreement among researchers in psychology about which of these constructs lead to or cause other constructs, which then contribute most directly to achievement behaviors. For example, Dweck (1986) maintained that people with intrinsic or mastery orientations are more likely to adopt learning or mastery goals, whereas Elliot and colleagues (Elliot & Harackiewicz, 1996) maintained that the causal pathway was in the opposite direction, i.e. from mastery goals to intrinsic motivation.

In conclusion, considering the recent empirical literature, how do adaptive orientations toward achievement develop? The caretakers of children with a promotion focus encourage the value of proactively seeking accomplishments and realizing goals. The attention of children with a prevention focus is directed toward avoiding failures, mistakes, and the accompanying disapproval of caretakers. Intrinsic motivation is fostered by environments that allow for greater autonomy and choice and less coercion concerning the selection of activities. Perhaps these environments would provide clever ways of piquing the interest of children to master academic, interpersonal, and athletic skills necessary for adaptive functioning. Confidence and self-efficacy grow incrementally when youngsters are introduced to optimal challenges.

Key Terms and Names

Max Weber

Protestant work ethic

Hedonic principle

Sigmund Freud

Psychoanalysis

Id
Pleasure principle

Ego

Superego

Ego ideal

Alfred Adler

The power motive

Abraham Maslow

Self-actualization

John Atkinson

Achievement motivation

Motive for achievement

Motive to avoid failure

Motive to avoid success

Social-cognitive approach

Promotion focus

Prevention focus

Achievement goals

Mastery goals

Performance-avoidance goals

Performance-approach goals

Goal orientations

Attributions theory

Internal or external attributions

Global or specific attributions

Stable or unstable attributions

Controllable or uncontrollable attributions

Motivational orientation

Intrinsic motivation

Extrinsic motivation

Amotivation

Task orientations

Ego orientations

Flow

Challenge–skills balance

Suggested Readings

Atkinson, J. W. (1978). The mainsprings of achievement-oriented activity. In J. W. Atkinson & Joel O. Raynor (Eds.), *Personality, motivation, and achievement* (pp. 11–39). Washington, DC: Halsted Press.

Conroy, D. E. (2004). The unique psychological meanings of multidimensional fears of failing. *Journal of Sport & Exercise Psychology, 26,* 484–491.

Conroy, D. E., & Elliot, A. J. (2004). Fear of failure and achievement goals in sport: Addressing the issue of the chicken and the egg. *Anxiety, Stress, and Coping, 17,* 271–285.

Deci, E. L., & Ryan, R. M. (1985). *Intrinsic motivation and self-determination in human behavior.* New York: Plenum Press.

Jackson, S. A., & Csikszentmihalyi, M. (1999). *Flow in sports.* Champaign, IL: Human Kinetics.

Maslow, A. (1973). Deficiency motivation and growth motivation. In D. C. McClelland & R. S. Steele (Eds.), *Human motivation: A book of readings* (pp. 233–251). Morristown, NJ: General Learning Press.

Vallerand, R. J. (2001). A hierarchical model of intrinsic and extrinsic motivation in sport and exercise. In G. C. Roberts (Ed.), *Advances in motivation in sport and exercise* (2nd ed., pp. 263–319). Champaign, IL: Human Kinetics.

Weber, M. (1930). *The Protestant work ethic and the spirit of capitalism* (T. Parsons, Trans.). New York: Scribner. (Original work published 1904.)

PART II
PERFORMANCE ENHANCEMENT

Optimal Levels of Anxiety, Intensity, or Arousal 3

Welsh golfer Ian Woosnam entered the final round of the 2001 British Open tied for the lead. He drove his first shot within six inches of the hole and scored a birdie 2 on the par-3 first hole of the final round. Prior to the start of the second hole, he was informed that he would be assessed a two-shot penalty for having 15 clubs in his bag, one over the limit. Earlier that day, he experimented with two drivers, and his caddy neglected to remove the extra club prior to the start of play. When informed of the penalty, Woosnam said he "went ballistic," and later explained: "At the moment, it felt like I had been kicked in the teeth. It's hard enough to be level with the best players in the world. To give them a two-shot advantage wasn't something I was feeling too good about" (Sherman, 2001, p. C7).

Woosnam pared the second hole but made bogeys on holes three and four. He said, "It took me a few holes to recover" (Sherman, 2001). He did make an eagle on the sixth hole and birdies on holes 11 and 13. His final round score was 71; four strokes behind the tournament champion, David Duval. This unfortunate incident caused Woosnam to state: "I didn't really get it out of my head all the way around" (Shain, 2001, C1).

Mental skills and practices that promote and sustain optimal performance are the subjects of Chapters 3, 4, and 5. These techniques are intended for use during and immediately prior to competition, performances, and practice. However, just as physical skills must be practiced frequently and conscientiously, mental skills must be mastered during practice if they are to be useful during competition. The regular practice of mental skills also promotes better general wellbeing or psychological adjustment. Psychological skills that are practiced at times more distal to performances, such as goal setting and the promotion of self-efficacy, also foster better psychological adjustment, and are the subjects of Chapters 7, 8, and 9. Performance suffers if general wellbeing is poor, if thinking is dysfunctional, and if mental disorders are present.

Stress and Performance

Performances, competitions, examinations, and evaluations are often stressful. Although there is no universally accepted definition of stress, the **cognitive-relational theory** of Lazarus and Folkman (1984, p. 19) has proven heuristic and influential:

> Psychological stress is a particular relationship between the person and the environment that is appraised by the person as taxing or exceeding his or her resources and endangering his or her well-being.

Stress is therefore understood to involve a source of threat or challenge from the environment and the person's cognitive appraisal of the environmental challenge or threat (Folkman, Chesney, McKusick, Ironson, Johnson, & Coates, 1991; Lazarus & Folkman, 1984). This appraisal process begins with an interpretation of whether the sources of stress (stressors) impact important areas of functioning and whether the person has resources adequate to cope with the magnitude of the stress.

To illustrate, anticipated evaluations, performances, and competitions may be interpreted as threatening and sources of stress to the unprepared sportsperson. However, the same competitions might be welcomed as opportunities for advancement, recognition, and fun by the prepared sportsperson who feels equal to the challenge. When sportspersons interpret the stress of competition as a challenge, they are more likely to maintain confidence that they can control the action (Anshel, Kim, Kim, Chang,

Optimal levels of intensity (photo courtesy of Western Connecticut State University).

& Eom, 2001). Very important competitions, such as championship games, may be sources of both high risk and opportunity as the threat of loss and opportunities for advancement and recognition are heightened.

The cognitive appraisal of sources of stress is accompanied by emotional responses. Feelings of sadness, anger, guilt, and relief often occur with appraisals of loss. Anxiety, worry, and fear may be generated by appraisals of threat. Feelings of excitement, eagerness, and hopefulness may result from appraisals of challenge.

Stress and Coping

There are different ways of coping with situations that are seen as taxing or exceeding the resources of the person. **Coping** consists of what a person thinks or does in response to stressors. These thoughts and actions may change as situations unfold, and they may be relatively specific to stressors in specific environments. There are two general categories of coping responses (Compas & Epping, 1993; Lazarus, 1991, 2000). **Problem-focused coping** involves efforts to manage, change, or master the problem or challenge that is the source of stress. There are many examples of problem-focused coping, and those more relevant to the focus of this book include goal setting, following regimens to prepare for evaluations and allowing adequate time for preparations, time management, visualization immediately prior to athletic performance, and self-talk to sustain concentration during competition. **Emotion-focused coping** concerns attempts to regulate emotional responses to the source of stress. Relevant examples of emotion-focused coping include the interpretation of stressors as challenges rather than threats, engaging in relaxation, meditation, and physical exercises, and obtaining emotional support from others. However, in many stressful situations such as elite competition, both problem- and emotion-focused coping are utilized as athletes attempt to manage stress in the environment as well as their emotional reactions. For example, US Olympic wrestlers (Gould, Eklund, & Jackson, 1993) and US national champion figure skaters (Gould, Finch, & Jackson, 1993) simultaneously used problem-focused, such as conscientious practice, and emotion-focused strategies, such as relaxation techniques, for coping with the stress of competition and training.

Emotion-focused coping, such as interpreting the stress of competition as a challenge, may involve a cognitive reframing of experience. Avoidance-focused and appraisal-focused coping also focus on reformulating and reinterpreting experience (Cox & Ferguson, 1991; Krohne, 1993). Avoidance-focused coping consists of efforts to ignore or discount the importance of stressors. It has been seen as desirable when the sources of

Tom Brady: "I got out of touch with myself"

After winning the first of his three Super Bowls in 2002 at age 25, quarterback Tom Brady of the New England Patriots was swamped with the adoration of fans. "Female fans leave him cookies, flowers, cards, soup (yes) and, of course, the usual assortment of thongs, propositions, pictures and marriage proposals" (Wickersham, 2004, p. 43). He flew in Donald Trump's jet to judge the Miss American pageant, golfed with John Elway, and dated supermodels. He was constantly besieged by fans for autographs, and ultimately burnt out by the attention. In the subsequent season he suffered a shoulder separation and the Patriots did not make the playoffs.

During the off-season, Brady decided that he needed help to grow as a person and asked his sister to quit her job in a biotech firm in San Francisco to join him in Boston to help him handle the demands on his time. "She's meant everything to him," says dad Tom Sr., "there's no way he could play as well as he has, or be as happy as he is, without her there" (Wickersham, 2004, p. 43).

stress are uncontrollable and transient, such as a "bad" call from a referee in sport. By ignoring the bad call, sportspersons avoid distractions and focus on aspects of performances that are under their control. Appraisal-focused coping refers to efforts to put current stressors in perspective by using logical analyses. Elite athletes and performance artists handled the stress of performances with not only avoidance-focused and appraisal-focused coping, but also with problem-focused and emotion-focused coping strategies (Poczwardowski & Conroy, 2002). The majority also remembered failing to cope sufficiently with stressors.

People differ in the degree to which they use problem- and emotion-focused coping. Problem-focused coping is also associated with the perception of control, whereas emotion-focused coping is correlated with the opposite (Anshel & Kaissidis, 1997; Daly, Brewer, Van-Raalte, Petitpas, & Sklar, 1995; Gaudreau & Blondin, 2002). In general, responses to problems or challenges that can be successfully resolved or mastered are more adaptive if they involve a greater proportion of problem-focused coping. More specifically, problem-focused coping is preferable when the sources of stress can be identified and controlled, and when it is necessary to stay "on task" for extended periods of time in order to master stressors (Roth & Cohen, 1986). For example, major athletic injuries are very stressful, and successful recovery requires daily physical rehabilitation (Udry, 1997). Problem-focused coping strategies have been seen as adaptive because they involve confronting the source of the stress (Zeidner, 1994). Sources of stress for which there is no solution are responded to more successfully with greater proportions of emotion-focused coping. For example, major athletic injuries prompt worries about whether recovery will be complete, and athletes manage these worries by visualizing full recovery (Udry, 1997). It is clearly important to correctly size up a situation as changeable or uncontrollable and to also have effective problem- and emotion-focused coping skills.

Coping and Mental Skills

Clearly some people are more effective than others in coping with the stresses of examinations and performances. The mental skills and procedures discussed in this and ensuing chapters serve to improve coping strategies in close proximity to competitions. A key to understanding why these mental skills and techniques are helpful is that they increase awareness of phenomenology or psychological states during competition. Psychological states are more readily controlled when they are identified (Ravizza, 2006). This process of identifying psychological states is referred to as **insight** or awareness, and a leitmotiv or theme in psychology, psychiatry, and philosophy is that awareness allows for greater control of thoughts and behavior. Corrective action can follow when problems with arousal level, preperformance preparation, attention, self-talk, concentration, and imagery are identified. The experience of control is fundamental to managing stress and anxiety.

Anxiety, Intensity, or Arousal Levels and Performance

The regulation of anxiety levels is related to optimal performance and doing one's best on tasks involving evaluation. The terms "anxiety," "arousal," and "intensity" have at times been used interchangeably. The practice of equating the terms has been criticized (Zaichkowsky & Baltzell, 2001), but has continued. Some sport psychologists prefer the term "intensity" to anxiety and nervousness because these refer to negative or dysfunctional conditions, and to **arousal** as this has been used to signify sexual responsiveness (Taylor, 1996). However, in terms of sports psychology, arousal has been defined as the activation of the body's resources for intense activity (Landers & Arent, 2006; Landers & Boutcher, 1993). Arousal refers to a general state of alertness, and varies on a continuum from deep sleep to intense excitement (Gould & Udry, 1994). **Intensity** is defined as a condition within people that has an energizing function on the body and mind (Taylor & Wilson, 2002). It affects performance in the physiological, motor, and cognitive domains. The physiological domain consists of the levels of heart rate, glandular and cortical activity, and blood flow. The motor area refers to behaviors such as changes in pace and coordination. The cognitive domain consists of the person's thoughts and emotions.

Descriptions of anxiety also often involve the identification of cognitive and physiological or somatic domains. The **cognitive** component consists of worries and apprehensions about the results of evaluations, potential failures and personal inadequacies. The **physiological** component consists of reactions of the sympathetic nervous system such as muscle tension, elevated heart rate, sweating, and feelings of being keyed up or on edge. Cognitive anxiety is particularly disruptive to athletic performance (Jones, Swain, & Cale, 1991).

Anxiety that is activated in response to specific situations, such as evaluations, has been referred to as **state anxiety**, whereas anxiety that remains relatively stable across situations and over time is considered **trait anxiety** (Spielberger, Gorsuch, & Lushene, 1970). It may also be important to distinguish between the cognitive and physiological activity that occurs when someone prepares for an evaluative event and the cognitive and physiological reactions to external input (Hardy, Jones, & Gould, 1996). In this context, reactions to external input are described as arousal and imply a lack of preparation for the external stimuli. Activation refers to the cognitive and physiological preparation for evaluative events. Not surprisingly, sportspersons with higher levels of trait anxiety are more likely to experience state anxiety prior to competition (Hanton, Mellalieu, & Hall, 2002).

In the pages that follow, the terms "arousal," "intensity," and "anxiety" will be used in discussing the results of research. The use of these terms will follow the practices of the authors of this research, and will generally reflect differences in the measurement of these constructs. For example, questionnaires were used to measure anxiety in some studies and arousal in others. Readers are advised to refer to the definitions of arousal, intensity, and anxiety as necessary to clarify these concepts.

Inverted-U Hypothesis

An early theory for conceptualizing the relationship between arousal and performance was the **inverted-U hypothesis** (Yerkes & Dodson, 1908). The tenet of this influential theory was that performance was poor when arousal was low. Performance improved as arousal rose to moderate levels, but then declined when arousal exceeded an optimal level (Arent &

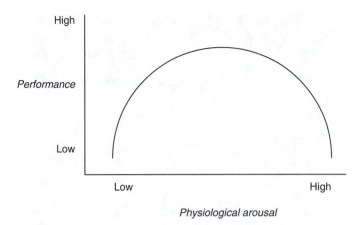

FIGURE 3.1. The inverted-U arousal–performance relationship.

Landers, 2003; Levitt & Gutin, 1971). Therefore a graph of this relationship between arousal and performance was curvilinear, i.e. it had the appearance of an inverted "U" (Figure 3.1).

The effects of arousal on performance differ for tasks that require sustained concentration versus sustained information transfer (Humpreys & Revelle, 1984). Performance on tasks that required sustained concentration was shown to decrease as arousal increased. The human capacity for concentration is limited by the amount of information that can be sustained and processed in working or active memory at any given time. The average limit of working memory is seven units of information, and the active memory of most people falls within a range of five to nine units (seven plus or minus two; Kareev, 2000; Miller, 1956). As will be explained below, arousal may compete with other information for the allocation of the approximate seven units of storage space in working memory and lead to poorer performances as arousal increases.

Performance on tasks that consist of sustained information transfer was shown to improve as arousal increased (Hardy et al., 1996). Sustained information transfer tasks do not require the maintenance of information in working memory or the transfer of information from working memory to long-term memory for permanent storage. Instead, they consist of simply remaining vigilant for signals and producing responses when the signals appear. Many tasks, however, do not simply involve working memory or sustained information transfer, but some combination of these mental processes. For example, a tenacious defender in basketball does not simply respond to the play of opponents. Instead, the defender draws on his or her knowledge of the tendencies of opponents and anticipates their

Physiological arousal and task requirements (photo courtesy of Western Connecticut State University).

play. The relationship between performance and arousal on these complex tasks does appear to correspond to the inverted-U or curvilinear graph. One possible explanation for this is that a moderate amount of arousal provokes optimal working memory capacity and sustained information transfer. Too little arousal results in performance deficits on complex cognitive tasks because of deficient vigilance and preparation to respond (sustained information transfer), and too much arousal erodes performance due to competition for the allocation of working memory resources. Most generally, performance improves when arousal levels match task requirements (Landers & Arent, 2006).

Consistent with the history of science (Kuhn, 1970), there were anomalies that were not explained by the inverted-U hypothesis. Among these was the finding that the levels of intensity that were most facilitative for performance were different for different people (Landers & Arent, 2006; Whelan, Epkins, & Meyers, 1990).

Zone of Optimal Functioning

An understanding that people were different in terms of the level of arousal or anxiety associated with their best performance was integral to the current model of the **individualized zone of optimal functioning (IZOF**; Hanin, 2000b). The IZOF was a refinement of the individual optimum zone model and the zone of optimal function model (Hanin, 1980, 1986). An individual might find his or her IZOF by regularly measuring the level of anxiety and his or her corresponding performances at various tasks. For example, athletes would assess their anxiety levels prior to or after a number of performances, and attempt to replicate the level of anxiety experienced prior to their best performances. This process enhances awareness of emotional states associated with optimal performance, as well as emotional conditions accompanying poor performances. Anxiety level could be assessed empirically by completing a questionnaire such as the State-Trait Anxiety Inventory (STAI; Spielberger, Gorsuch, & Lushene, 1970) or the sport-specific Competitive State Anxiety Inventory-2 (CSAI-2; Martens, Burton, Vealey, Bump, & Smith, 1990). The STAI has been shown to be a particularly reliable measure of anxiety when completed before or after athletic competitions (Annesi, 1997; Harger & Raglin, 1994).

Athletes may also receive counseling and guidance from sport consultants to become aware of the content and intensities of emotions associated with optimal performance. Sport consultants counsel athletes to use mental skills such as self-talk and imagery to reliably achieve optimal preperformance emotional states (Robazza, Pellizzari, & Hanin, 2004).

Successful sportspersons appear more capable of achieving and maintaining their desired level of physiological arousal and of experiencing this arousal as pleasant and not a source of stress (Hanin, 2000c; Kerr, 1997). Arousal levels associated with successful competition are not necessarily low. For example, squash players who competed in city and county teams in England, and members of the England national under-19 squash team who won simulated tournaments experienced high but pleasant levels of arousal throughout the four matches of the tournament (Kerr & Cox, 1991).

The IZOF model has generated a considerable amount of research related to athletic performance. Levels of precompetitive anxiety associated with optimal performances among intercollegiate swimmers (Raglin & Turner, 1996) were shown to vary considerably. Perhaps athletes with higher levels of trait anxiety, or who experience higher levels of anxiety not only prior to competition but also throughout their days, perform more optimally with higher levels of precompetitive anxiety. Also, elite clay-target shooters performed more poorly when levels of anger, depression, and confusion deviated from their own optimal levels (Prapavessis & Grove, 1991).

Elite athletes have been distinguished from non-elite athletes on the basis of performance-enhancing emotions prior to competition (Robazza & Bortoli, 2003). The IZOF model may be less applicable to sub-elite performers than to elite athletes, as the former may be less capable of recognizing their anxiety levels associated with optimal performance (Thelwell & Maynard, 1998). Research with collegiate female varsity softball players called into question the validity of the IZOF and, unlike previous studies concerning the IZOF, measured both cognitive and physiological anxiety (Randle & Weinberg, 1997). Subsequent research with measures of both cognitive and physiological anxiety (CSAI-2) have underlined the importance of identifying optimal preperformance states for individuals rather than groups, because these states differ considerably among athletes (Annesi, 1998). Detailed discussions of how people differ in terms of their reactions to challenges and stress and of the influence of temperament and personality on performance will be presented in Chapter 14.

A further refinement of the IZOF has been to identify a range of emotions in addition to anxiety that are associated with optimal performance (Hanin, 2004; Hanin & Stambulova, 2002; Ruiz & Hanin, 2004). To simplify, emotions are categorized on the bases of hedonic tone (pleasant or unpleasant) and functional impact on performance (optimal or dysfunctional). Separate athletes might perceive the same emotion quite differently. For example, anger might be perceived as pleasant or unpleasant, depending on its functional impact on performance. The athlete who performs well when angry would likely find it to be hedonically pleasing because it serves the purpose of enhancing performance (Robazza, 2006). Athletes with a predominance of functional-pleasant and functional-displeasant emotions are more capable of mobilizing and utilizing energy productively. Conversely, with a predominance of dysfunctional-pleasant and dysfunctional-unpleasant emotions, sportspersons are more likely to be lethargic and distracted (Hanin & Stambulova, 2002).

Catastrophe Theory

Research with the inverted-U theory and early studies of the IZOF model have been criticized because it involved conceptualizations of anxiety or arousal as unidimensional. **Catastrophe theory** was postulated with the understanding that anxiety was a function of both physiological arousal and cognitive anxiety or worry (Gould & Udry, 1994; Woodman & Hardy, 2001). The relationship between physiological arousal and performance was seen to be essentially the same as that outlined by the inverted-U hypothesis when cognitive anxiety was low. However, when cognitive anxiety was high, the deceleration of performance was extreme or catastrophic when physiological arousal (again, some authors refer to this construct as somatic or physiological anxiety) exceeded moderate levels. The question of the ideal level of physiological arousal and cognitive anxiety associated with optimal performance has not been conclusively determined, and may also depend on the nature of the task under evaluation. For example, high levels of physiological arousal have been shown to cause sharp performance decrements in closed skill sports involving fine motor control, such as bowling, golf, and pistol shooting (Gould,

Petlichkoff, Simons, & Vevera, 1987; Woodman, Albinson, & Hardy, 1997). These activities involve closed or fixed skills in that successful performance is a result of executing skills in a prescribed and relatively invariant way. Activities that involve open or generative skills require flexibility in responding to changing conditions and the behavior of competitors.

In general, performance on tasks which require complex motor responses or a great deal of thought or information processing is best under conditions of lower physiological arousal (Billing, 1980; Landers & Boutcher, 1993; Oxendine, 1970, 1984). These complex tasks require sustained concentration, decision-making, multiple cue discrimination, fine motor control, movement fluidity, and manual dexterity. Activities performed best at high levels of physiological arousal involve power, strength, endurance, and speed. For example, high levels of physiological arousal probably facilitate Olympic weight lifting. However, attempts to categorize athletic tasks have been criticized because different activities in the same sport require different levels of complex thought and motor control, and because some athletic tasks require simple skills and complex information processing or complex skills and limited information processing (Hardy et al., 1996).

Identifying Prime Intensity

Finding **prime intensity** requires the assessment of physiological and cognitive intensity as well as the recognition that levels of intensity associated with optimal performance are different for different people. *A person* might find *their* ideal level of intensity by keeping records of their physiological responses, thoughts and emotions, and the social conditions prior to and during competitive tasks (Taylor, 1996; Taylor & Wilson, 2002). People committed to this record keeping become systematic in understanding themselves and their tendencies associated with optimal performance. As sportspersons become more aware of their levels of intensity, they become more capable of controlling intensity levels (Robazza & Bortoli, 1998).

The physical symptoms of overintensity are most apparent. Symptoms include muscle tension, shaking muscles, breathing difficulty, and excessive perspiration. More subtle physical symptoms consist of "butterflies" or feelings of anxiety in the stomach, fatigue, and decreased motor coordination. Overintensity may be revealed by changes in behavior such as an increased pace or rushing during a performance, general agitation, and an increase in performance irrelevant or "nervous" behaviors. Psychological signs of overintensity consist of negative self-talk, irrational thinking, problems with concentration, and the anticipation of poor results (Taylor, 1996; Taylor & Wilson, 2002). An example of negative self-talk is silent or audible criticism of one's performance or ability (e.g. "I'm the worst"). Irrational thinking might consist of all-or-nothing thinking (e.g. if "I can't hit a backhand, I might as well quit") or catastrophizing (e.g. if "I miss this penalty kick I'll go down in history as a choke artist").

Difficulties with overintensity are more common than problems with underintensity. The physical signs of underintensity are low levels of heart rate, respiration, adrenaline, and energy. The person may report feeling lethargic. Behavioral signs include reductions in pace, performance-relevant behaviors (e.g. routines), and increased distractibility. The psychological symptoms include apathy, loss of motivation to compete, and difficulty concentrating on tasks necessary for performance. The causes of underintensity have not been studied extensively. However, among the causes are overconfidence or a belief that one's ability far exceeds the demands of the situation and a lack of interest in competing (Taylor, 1996; Taylor & Wilson, 2002).

Optimal Pressure Model

The **optimal pressure model** (Costanzo, Woody, & Slater, 1992) incorporated concepts from the expectancy-value theory (Atkinson, 1978) described in Chapter 2 and the inverted-U theory (Yerkes & Dodson, 1908). However, this model emphasized situational sources of pressure rather than internal states of arousal or anxiety. Pressure was understood to derive from incentives for optimal performance. These incentives consisted of the intrinsic value of success compared to failure (the importance of the task), the situational consequences of success (social approval or disapproval), and the expectancy of success. High scores in all three of these areas were seen to contribute to pressure, and all three sources were understood to contribute essentially equal amounts of pressure. If attention is directed toward more than one source of pressure or if there are zero sources of pressure, performance suffers.

Doing one's best (at least by one's own estimate) when pressure is greatest may not be the norm. In a study of US Olympic wrestlers at the 1988 Olympic Games, only 20 percent had their all-time best wrestling performance in Seoul (Gould, Eklund, & Jackson, 1992a). Thirty percent of the wrestlers indicated that they had their worst Olympic performance in their most crucial Olympic match.

Anxiety Direction: Facilitative and Debilitative

Efficacy or confidence that one can achieve goals also has a significant influence on the direction of anxiety or how one interprets cognitive and physiological anxiety. People who believe that they exert control over the environment and themselves during evaluative tasks such as academic tests and athletic performances often interpret symptoms of anxiety as **facilitating** performance (Jones, 1995; Jones & Hanton, 2001). For example, almost half of a sample of 91 competitive swimmers between the ages of 14 and 28 reported cognitive and physiological anxiety to be facilitative, and only 23 percent reported both kinds of anxiety as **debilitative** (Jones & Hanton, 1996). Sportspersons at elite, collegiate, and high school levels who believe they will achieve their goals use anxiety as a cue to become more engaged in the task, and show additional persistence and better performance when experiencing anxiety that is interpreted as facilitative (Hanton & Connaughton, 2002; Ntoumanis & Jones, 1998; Wiggins, 1998).

Collegiate athletes who viewed anxiety as facilitative viewed their precompetitive emotional states more positively than their counterparts who considered anxiety to be debilitative (Mellalieu, Hanton, & Jones, 2003). Athletes with facilitative anxiety were more likely to also be excited, focused, motivated, and eager. Heightened levels of physiological and cognitive anxiety are also more likely to be interpreted as facilitative with sports that call for explosive action, such as rugby (Mellalieu, Hanton, & O'Brien, 2004; Hanton, Jones, & Mullen, 2000).

Jones and Hanton (1996) reasoned that swimmers might have interpreted anxiety as facilitative because they had previously experienced success while anxious. Perhaps this successful experience helps to explain why only 16 percent of a group of elite cricket players (Jones & Swain, 1995) and 21 percent of highly advanced tennis players (Perry & Williams, 1998) considered signs of cognitive and physiological trait anxiety to be debilitative.

Success enables sportspersons to interpret signs of anxiety as facilitative. Success does not eradicate the experience of anxiety. For example, the cognitive and physiological anxiety levels experienced by elite and non-elite swimmers (Jones, Hanton, & Swain, 1994), national and club rugby union, soccer, and field hockey players (Hanton, Thomas, & Maynard, 2004), and gymnasts (Jones, Swain, & Hardy, 1993) were of similar intensities. The elite (Jones et al., 1993, 1994) and national level athletes (Hanton et al., 2004) were more likely to interpret this anxiety as facilitative. Professional golfers and rugby players with more experience were also more likely to interpret anxiety as facilitative (Mellalieu et al., 2004).

Sportspersons with lower levels of trait anxiety are also more likely to interpret competitive anxiety as facilitative than those with higher levels of trait anxiety. For example, state anxiety prior to tournaments was experienced as more facilitative and less intense among competitive golfers with lower levels of trait anxiety (Jones, Smith, & Holmes, 2004). Collegiate footballers or soccer players who experienced trait anxiety that disrupted concentration were more likely to report state anxiety, or anxiety within one hour of matches, to be debilitative (Hanton et al., 2002).

As discussed in Chapter 2, some types of goals are more likely than others to facilitate performance. Competitive swimmers did not exclusively identify outcome goals for meets (Jones & Hanton, 1996). With outcome goals, performance is measured in relation to competitors. An example of an outcome goal would be to finish first in a race. Outcome goals were considered to engender debilitative anxiety because the swimmer had no control over the performance of competitors. Most of the swimmers chose a combination of goals that included performance (complete a race under a certain time) and process (attention to the technical elements of the swim) goals (24 percent) or outcome, performance, and process goals (49 percent).

Even the biochemical substrates of anxiety are influenced by the manner in which preperformance anxiety is interpreted. The catecholamine, cortisol, and testosterone levels of elite male marathon canoeists were measured prior to races for selection to the world championships (Eubank, Collins, Lovell, Dorling, & Talbot, 1997). Catecholamine, cortisol, and testosterone levels were measured 24 hours, 2 hours, and 1 hour prior to the start of the races. Elevations in testosterone and catecholamines have been associated with adaptive responses to challenges, and elevated cortisol has been associated with the disruptive effects of stress. Testosterone levels climbed for canoeists who believed that anxiety prior to races facilitated performance and fell for canoeists that interpreted their anxiety before races as debilitating. Cortisol levels increased for the debilitatory and facilitatory groups 1 hour prior to races, but the levels were much lower for the facilitatory group. The catecholamines consisted of epinephrine, norepinephrine, and dopamine; they increased sharply for the facilitatory group, and remained steady or decreased for the debilitatory group. The catecholamines were understood to activate the body to deal with the challenge of competition.

Hanton and Jones (1999a) went on to study how elite male swimmers developed their capacity to interpret cognitive and physiological anxiety as facilitative. Early in their competitive careers, these swimmers experienced cognitive and physiological symptoms of anxiety to be debilitative. For example, some were preoccupied with worry and even vomited before races. They came to take the perspective that anxiety could facilitate performance as a result of mentoring by parents, coaches, and more experienced swimmers. They were mentored to accept anxiety as a natural and necessary reaction to competition and evaluation, and to view anxiety as an aid to optimal performance. These swimmers came to welcome anxiety prior to competition and to try to use it to boost performance and preperformance preparation.

Facilitative and Debilitative Anxiety and Coping

Anxiety has been described as facilitative or debilitative depending on its effects on behavior. Those with facilitative anxiety may also cope more effectively with stressors. For example, college students with facilitative anxiety about impending exams studied more effectively and scored better marks (Raffety, Smith, & Ptacek, 1997). They engaged in problem-focused coping as they began studying well in advance, and sought help from others when help was needed. Collegiate students with debilitative test anxiety were more likely to show avoidant coping, or methods of distracting themselves from the stressor of the test and their anxiety. Students with debilitative test anxiety were also beset with more cognitive anxiety and worries that distracted them from effective study. Students with debilitative and facilitative anxiety experienced physiological anxiety or "butterflies" in their stomachs prior to exams. However, those with facilitative anxiety "shook" these butterflies during exams, whereas students with debilitative anxiety did not. Also, with facilitative anxiety, students were not beset by cognitive anxiety or worry.

Anxiety, Intensity, or Arousal Levels and Performance

The question of the ideal level of physiological and cognitive anxiety associated with optimal performance has not been conclusively determined, and may depend not only on the differences between people, but on the nature of the task under evaluation. For example, high levels of somatic anxiety have been shown to cause performance decrements on complex tasks that require sustained concentration, decision-making, multiple cue discrimination, fine motor control, movement fluidity and manual dexterity. Clearly there are differences in the manner in which people interpret the signs of anxiety, and athletes may learn to interpret signs of anxiety as facilitative. However, not everyone interprets signs of anxiety as facilitative, especially when one doubts one's efficacy to perform successfully (Bandura, 1997). Even some children and adolescents base judgments about their competence in sports on pregame anxiety.

Higher levels of anxiety in these children and adolescents were associated with lower estimates of their sports competence (Weiss, Ebbeck, & Horn, 1997). Finally, the question of when anxiety is experienced is important. The experience of anxiety before evaluations and competitions may facilitate performance if it motivates coping strategies that better prepare a person for the evaluation. However, better results have been associated with decreased anxiety prior to and during evaluations (Giacobbi & Weinberg, 2000) or with the ability to sustain concentration and task-absorption during competitions or evaluations despite some measure of anxiety.

Summary and Conclusions

A considerable amount of research has been devoted to the relationship between levels of arousal, intensity, or anxiety, and performance. Attempts to find universal levels of arousal and anxiety that are most facilitative of performance have not been successful. This appears to be a result of the differences between people in terms of the levels of arousal or intensity that facilitate their best performances. Also, different levels of anxiety and arousal facilitate better performance on different tasks. High levels of physiological anxiety and arousal appear to be more disruptive to performance on tasks that require sustained concentration, complex motor responses, or a great deal of thought or information processing. Higher levels of anxiety may be more facilitative during preparations for performances versus the actual performance. Preperformance anxiety is adaptive to the degree that it motivates the appropriate preparation for the performance or evaluation.

Recent research has emphasized the cognitive and physiological components of anxiety. Heightened physiological anxiety need not disrupt performance so long as a performer interprets it as a factor to facilitate performance. However, all people are not equally intrepid, and the self-efficacy of some people is diminished by the experience of their physiological anxiety. Techniques for gaining control over these physiological responses will be discussed in Chapter 5. These techniques are useful not only for controlling physiological responses proximate to evaluations and competitions, but also for enhancing wellbeing.

Key Terms

Cognitive-relational theory of stress

Problem-focused coping

Arousal

Intensity

Cognitive and physiological anxiety

State anxiety

Trait anxiety

Inverted-U hypothesis

Emotion-focused coping

Insight

Individualized zone of optimal functioning (IZOF)

Catastrophe theory

Prime intensity

Optimal pressure model

Facilitative and debilitative anxiety

Suggested Readings

Hanin, Y. L. (2000b) Individual zones of optimal functioning (IZOF) model: Emotions–performance relationships in sport. In Y. L. Hanin (Ed.), *Emotions in sport* (pp. 65–89). Champaign, IL: Human Kinetics.

Jones, G., & Hanton, S. (1996). Interpretation of competitive anxiety symptoms and goal attainment expectancies. *Journal of Sport & Exercise Psychology, 18,* 144–157.

Landers, D. M., & Arent, S. M. (2006). Arousal–performance relationships. In J. M. Williams (Ed.), *Applied sport psychology: Personal growth to peak performance* (5th ed., pp. 260–284), New York: McGraw-Hill.

Lazarus, R. S. (2000). Cognitive–motivational–relational theory of emotion. In Y. L. Hanin (Ed.), *Emotions in sport* (pp. 39–63). Champaign, IL: Human Kinetics.

Ravizza, K. (2006). Increasing awareness for sport performance. In J. M. Williams (Ed.), *Applied sport psychology: Personal growth to peak performance* (5th ed., pp. 228–239). New York: McGraw-Hill.

Woodman, T., & Hardy, L. (2001). Stress and anxiety. In R. N. Singer, H. A. Hausenblas, & C. M. Janelle (Eds.), *Handbook of sport psychology* (2nd ed., pp. 290–318). New York: Wiley.

Yerkes, R. M., & Dodson, J. D. (1908). The relation of strength of stimulus to rapidity of habit formation. *Journal of Comparative Neurology of Psychology, 18,* 459–482.

Preperformance Routines

4

Tom Brady quarterbacked the New England Patriots to three Super Bowl championships by the age of 27. He attributes his coolness under pressure to his game preparation and practice. In preparing for games, he studies video until 11:00 p.m., and has called offensive coordinator Charlie Weis to his room for late night meetings to share notes. "He's actually getting to the point," Weis said, "where his preparation is so good he's getting to be a pain in the butt" (Greenberg, 2005b, p. C7).

Brady was so well versed in the defensive strategies of the Philadelphia Eagles prior to the 2005 Super Bowl that countermoves were virtually automatic. This bolstered his confidence. "You feel," Brady said, "like you have the answers to the test" (Greenberg, 2005b, p. C7).

Of course, game preparation occurs throughout the week prior to games and throughout athletic seasons. "As strange as it sounds, I enjoy the practices as much as the games," Brady said. "I enjoy the preparation part of it and I take practices very seriously" (Greenberg, 2005, p. C7).

Mental Skills Training

The development of sophisticated preperformance routines is an important aspect of **mental skills training**. As stated in Chapter 3, mental training consists of instruction in developing preperformance routines, anxiety and arousal control, self-talk, concentration, and mental imagery and mental practice. The regular practice and use of these mental skills is directly related to optimal athletic performance (Jackson, 1995; Jackson & Csikszentmihalyi, 1999; Jackson & Roberts, 1992). Elite athletes routinely practice these skills and use them to cope with adversity in the course of competitions (Dale, 2000; Hall, 2001).

Mental skills should be practiced when one is relaxed. Once mastered, they can be transferred to "game conditions" when anxiety is higher (Nideffer, 1985). For example, the practice of mental skills and the relaxation techniques described in Chapter 6 may be practiced within the same period of time.

Like physical practice, mental practice is effective if practiced on a regular – perhaps daily – basis. Simply becoming casually aware of these techniques does not result in appreciable gains in performance. Sportspersons may be much more patient in devoting the time and attention necessary for physical skills than these mental skills (Developing Your Mental Pacemaker, 1989). However, the neglect of mental skills training may inhibit the development of athletic potential. For example, Canadian Olympians and world champions recognized that their ascendancy as elite athletes was delayed by as much as four years because the development of their mental skills lagged behind physical skill development (Orlick & Partington, 1988).

As mentioned above, elite athletes regularly practice and refine their mental skills. Unfortunately, it may be difficult to encourage people who are not self-motivated to regularly practice mental skills. For example, Bull (1991) introduced male and female intercollegiate athletes to the mental skills of relaxation training, visualization, concentration, and positive thinking in eight 1-hour educational sessions across a 4-week period. The athletes were also given reading assignments. In the 8 weeks that followed the 4-week training, the average number of times that mental skills were practiced was 9.7 or i.e. slightly more than once per week. The average amount of time devoted to practicing the mental skills was only 17 minutes per week. Some athletes practiced the mental skills far more than others, and the key factor in determining the frequency and duration of practice was self-motivation or commitment to persevere. Some of the athletes received reminder memos and others engaged in discussion sessions after Weeks 2, 4, 5, and 7 of the 8-week period. The athletes who received the memos and participated in discussion groups did not practice the mental skills any more than a group that received no follow-up after the 4-week training.

As reasons for not practicing mental skills, athletes cited a lack of time, disruptions in their home environments, laziness, and beliefs that mental skills training was of no benefit. Sportspersons without high levels of self-motivation may benefit from individualized training to boost their motivation and mental skills techniques. Athletes may also be more motivated to learn and practice different mental skills. For example, Bull (1991) found that 38.2 percent of the collegiate athletes rated relaxation training, 29.4 percent rated visualization, 11.8 percent rated concentration, and 11.8 percent rated positive thinking to be the most valuable elements of their mental skills training. The remaining 8.8 percent were unable to specify one particular skill.

Research with diverse groups of athletes has demonstrated that attrition rates from psychological skills training programs are approximately 20 to 25 percent (Shambrook & Bull, 1999). It appears that athletes – perhaps especially younger athletes – are least compliant with skills training that must be practiced independently. Athletes may be less compliant with mental as compared to physical training because their primary concern is to advance their physical skills. Young athletes have also been shown to be less compliant when they did not meet regularly with sport psychology consultants. However, some athletes may shy away from mental skills training provided by psychologists because they associate psychological services with psychopathology.

The idea of devoting large blocks of time to mental training may be unappealing, but brief periods devoted to mentally organizing actions necessary for successful performance, and periods of mental practice interspersed with physical practice, can be beneficial (Shambrook & Bull, 1999). Regular mental practice may also enhance motivation for physical practice.

Mental practice is facilitated by the maintenance of daily logs, and some people have to practice this journaling for some time before they experience benefits. The most successful Canadian Olympian athletes refined their mental skills by keeping logs of the mental factors associated with successful and disappointing competitions (Orlick & Partington, 1988). They identified mental states associated with best and unsuccessful performances and tried to assimilate the former and eliminate the latter in subsequent competitions.

Mental preparation (photo © Pétur Ásgeirsson).

In summary, athletes who have the strongest desire to succeed in their sport and who believe that the psychological skills training will enable them to reach their goals are most likely to practice these skills. Individual consultations with sport psychologists sometimes help less motivated athletes discern the benefits of, and become more compliant with, the practice of mental skills. For athletes who are not self-motivated, regular supervised practice of mental skills may be as necessary as the supervision of their physical training and nutritional regimen. With regular practice, mental skills techniques often result in improved performance, and when athletes see these benefits, they are more likely to practice the mental skills.

Preperformance Routines

Preperformance routines are the preparations taken for competition. They facilitate experiences of familiarity, order, consistency, and control (Boutcher & Crews, 1987). Preperformance routines probably should include all aspects that may influence performance, such as sleep, diet, physical and mental practice and preparation, the inspection and preparation of equipment, travel to the venue, mental imagery, and the establishment of prime intensity. Elite athletes practice elaborate preperformance routines that may involve the use of mental imagery, self-talk, goal-setting, managing media relations and the experience of consistent and familiar levels of cognitive and physiological anxiety (Gould, 1999; Hanton & Jones, 1999b; Orlick & Partington, 1988; Thelwell & Maynard, 2002). Mental imagery and self-talk will be discussed in Chapter 5, and goal-setting will be reviewed in Chapter 7. Pre-evaluation routines may extend up to the time of a performance (Taylor, 1996).

An early arrival at athletic venues not only allows for mental and physical preparation, but also facilitates the emergence of pre-evaluative, debilitative anxiety. This anxiety can be recognized and alleviated prior to the actual performance. For example, university athletes in England and Wales rated physical and psychological preparation as more important than other factors such as the strength of competition and expectations for winning in determining cognitive anxiety 30 minutes prior to competitions (Jones, Swain, & Cale, 1991). Female university athletes who believed they were well prepared were more self-confident prior to competition.

Preperformance routines sometimes involve written algorithms or specific steps or procedures that are to be accomplished in a certain order. With written preperformance routines, it is less likely that key aspects will be overlooked. However, routines should allow for some degree of flexibility; otherwise a person may become anxious if their routine is interrupted. For example, it may be difficult to adhere to a routine of going to sleep at 10:00 p.m. on nights before competitions. Sleep may be interrupted by anxiety or by external events such as travel to a venue.

It Weakens Your Legs?

In preparing for the Olympic Games in approximately 444 BC, Ikkos of Tarentum ate large quantities of wild boar, goat meat, and cheese, coated his body with olive oil, and abstained from sex. He won the Olympic Pentathlon, and the tradition of abstaining from sex prior to athletic competition began (Spencer, 2006). US Olympic triathlete Victor Plata abstained from sex for 233 days prior to the 2004 Olympic Games in Athens. Lightweight boxing champion Diego Corrales goes without sex for 11 weeks prior to fights. He reasoned, "if you have sex, you're in a very good mood. That's a problem when you get in a ring" (Spencer, 2006, p. A1). Professional football teams often lodge teams in hotels even before home games to sequester players from wives or partners. Shaun Smith, defensive tackle for the Cincinnati Bengals, noted, "You don't want to feel relaxed, weak and laid back before a football game. You want to be jumpy and excited" (Spencer, 2006, p. A1). Smith's pregame routine includes drinking virgin daiquiris and praying with his mother and wife on the phone from his hotel room.

Athletes abstain from sex prior to competition because they believe that sexual satisfaction will decrease their aggressiveness and cause distraction and fatigue. However, the fatiguing effect of heterosexual coitus among married couples is minimal and results in the expenditure of only 25 to 50 calories, or "the energy equivalent of walking up two flights of stairs" (McGlone & Shrier, 2000). Theories that sexual satisfaction and ejaculation drain testosterone, the hormone associated not only with sex drive but also with muscle development and aggression, are also likely to be false. Indeed, testosterone levels may increase for both men and women who regularly experience sex.

Ultimately, whether performance is disrupted by sexual activity is likely to depend on whether it has been a part of the sportsperson's routine throughout their training and preparation. Disruptions to routines generally impair performance.

Preperformance Preparation at the Site of Competition

Gaining as much experience as possible with the actual competition venues serves to decrease anxiety and increase self-efficacy. The more similar the experience is to the conditions under which the performance will occur, or to actual "game conditions," the more useful it is in diminishing unfamiliarity. Therefore, actual performances, competitions, or evaluations in the same setting are most effective in diminishing unfamiliarity (Menzel & Carrell, 1994). For example, elite divers cited a lack of experience in managing high levels of pressure, such as the pressure

Very Exhaustive Preperformance Preparation or Superstition?

Wade Boggs was inducted into the National Baseball Hall of Fame in 2005 (Doyle, 2005). His insistence on eating chicken before every game is well documented, and he even developed his own chicken cookbook, *Fowl Tips*. His pregame routine extended well beyond his diet, and has been described as **superstitious** (inclined to irrationally believe that actions are related to outcomes). His pregame routine consisted of the following steps (Heyman, 1993).

1 Eats chicken every day.
2 Grows his beard when hitting well; shaves when he hits a slump.
3 Draws the Hebrew letter *Chai* in the batter's box.
4 Does everything at the same time each day. He eats at 2, leaves his house at 3, changes into his uniform at 3:30, goes to the dugout at 4, takes grounders at 4:15.
5 After taking grounders, he ends the drill at 4:40 by stepping on third base, second base and first base, then steps on the foul line and takes two steps in the first base coach's box before heading for the dugout.
6 When he takes his position each inning, he steps over the foul line.
7 Runs wind sprints at 7:17 to signify a 7-for-7 game.
8 Has lucky bats, gloves, and T-shirts. Slumps can make them unlucky bats, gloves, and T-shirts.
9 Throws the ball against the dugout wall for five minutes before each game.
10 Leaves his glove and ball in the same spot in the dugout every game.
11 Arranges pine tar, weighted doughnut, and resin in a precise way in the on-deck circle and applies them in that order.

Although the insistence on this ritual may be seen as superstitious behavior (Heyman, 1993), it may have contributed to his sense of personal control. Boggs maintained that it relieved worry: "All superstition is a positive framework for your mind" (Heyman, 1993). This routine was elaborate but not overly rigid because circumstances probably rarely precluded following this algorithm. Bogg's preparation and consistency are reflected by career statistics. In 1999 he became the 23rd major leaguer to have 3000 hits (*Hartford Courant*, 1999). He had the highest batting average in the American League four times in a five-year period, had seven consecutive seasons in which he had 200 hits, and was an All-Star for 11 consecutive years.

    Perhaps Boggs's extensive preparation shielded him from distractions. In 1986, a year he won a batting title, his mother died in a June auto accident. He also won a batting title in 1988 despite being at the center of a considerable scandal concerning a lawsuit by his traveling companion, Margo Adams. Adams claimed breach of contract after Boggs apparently tried to end their 4-year affair. She pleaded for compensation for wages lost while she accompanied him on road trips (Gammons, 1988; Swift, 1989).

Wade Boggs (photo © Bettmann/CORBIS).

to qualify for national teams, as responsible for their less successful performances (Highlen & Bennett, 1983).

Practice under conditions that approximate game conditions results in the reduction of novelty and provides experience in ignoring distractions. These "dress rehearsals" may include simulations of loud and distracting behaviors by spectators and opponents and practice under the most adverse conditions (Schmid & Peper, 1993). This is referred to as

Preparing for the Weather

From a weather station overlooking the Olympic ski slopes, a team of meteorologists and snow experts provided weather reports at 10-minute intervals during the 2006 Olympic Games in Turin, Italy (Kahn, 2006). The cost for this weather service was an estimated minimum $4.2 million, and yet most Olympics teams used weather information from their own meteorologists because they did not trust the accuracy of the local weather station. In sports such as alpine skiing, the air and snow temperatures and humidity levels determine the composition of waxes that are applied to skis. Optimal waxes allow for reduced friction and faster times. In cross-country skiing, technicians often apply a wax that provides traction when skiers kick or propel themselves forward and a second wax to help skiers glide. Weather conditions influence the delicate mix of the two waxes. Prior to the 2002 Winter Games in Salt Lake City, UT, the Norwegian team requested samples of snow from different months in the year. The snow was then analyzed in labs in Oslo.

simulation training, and has been shown to be a high priority for Olympic athletes (Orlick & Partington, 1988). Simulation training may involve recreating aspects of competitions that have disrupted an athlete's concentration, such as a bad line call in tennis (Hardy, Jones, & Gould, 1996).

> The trash talk, the lewd remarks, the clapping and foot stomping by a hostile crowd, the distance runner's self-doubt, the fear of missing the short field goal in a crucial game . . . all of these distractions, external or internal can be responded to.
>
> A time-tested approach to external distractions is simulating the competitive situation in practice – exposing the athlete to the distractions they can expect to encounter during the game. The more realistic, the better – the less effect they will have during the game.
>
> Probably the simplest example of a simulated situation is scheduling practice to coincide with the actual starting time of the game, especially if it falls at an odd hour.
>
> Perhaps the most elaborate kind of preparation is that practiced by major football and basketball coaches the week before visiting one of those "snakepits" where they will be exposed to torrents of sound – yelling, foot-stomping, whistling, clapping, cacophonic bugle calls, drumming, etc.
>
> Probably the only way to prepare for such nightmares is to simulate them in practice – bring in your own student body and band and cheerleaders to simulate the nightmare and to condition your players for the worst. (Dale, 1997, p. 5)

Even if game conditions cannot be simulated, preperformance simulations are helpful. For example, walking through a performance, such as figure skating, has positive effects on performance and improves confidence and self-efficacy that the performance will be successful (Garza & Feltz, 1998).

The use of mental practice, or just imagining performance in the setting or learning about the setting from others with first-hand experience, is also helpful, especially when actual practice is not possible. An additional level of familiarity is added to mental practice if it occurs in the venue where the competition is to take place, and this mental practice may involve the use of external as well as internal imagery (Nideffer, 1985). Internal imagery is directed toward one's thoughts and emotions and external imagery is focused on outside details. If mental practice at actual competition venues is impossible, familiarity is added to mental practice when athletes are provided with photographs of sites for competition, warm-up areas, and training rooms (Vealey & Greenleaf, 2006).

Deviation from Preperformance Routines

In general, performance is compromised by **deviations from routines** and by the introduction of novelty and unpredictability prior to and during a performance. This may occur even when aspects of preperformance routines consist of superstitious behaviors. Superstitious behaviors do not have technical functions in preparing sportspersons to execute skills, but are associated with better performance (Moran, 1996). For example, free-throw accuracy decreased when collegiate and club basketball players in England where inhibited from engaging in pre-shot superstitious rituals (Foster, Weigand, & Baines, 2006). Perhaps rituals such as "taps own head 3 times prior to shooting" (Foster et al., 2006, p. 171), promoted feelings of emotional stability and control.

One aspect that introduces unfamiliarity and deviations from routines is travel for competition. Individuals and teams perform better, and prefer to compete, at home (Courneya & Carron, 1992; Nevill & Holder, 1999). For example, the performance of professional or college basketball teams is disrupted by travel to other cities for games. Their performance is influenced by unfamiliar living accommodations, court composition and lighting, physical confinement while traveling, and opposing crowds. In the eight seasons between 1987–8 and 1994–5, home teams won 64 percent of the games by an average margin of 4.6 points in the National Basketball Association (NBA; Steenland & Deddens, 1997). Home teams won 65 percent of the games in the Atlantic Coast Conference (ACC) during a 10-year period from 1971 to 1981 (Silva & Andrew, 1987). Visiting teams were less accurate at shooting from the field, turned the ball over more often, and committed more fouls.

Elite adolescent male hockey players in Canada won 58.8 percent of games on home ice (Agnew & Carron, 1994). Countries were more likely to win Olympic medals when they hosted the Olympics (Leonard, 1989). World Cup soccer teams won 63 percent of their games at home, 37 percent away, and 40 percent at neutral sites in 1987 and 1998 (Brown et al., 2002). A home advantage was particularly evident for World Cup or continental championship games, and performance was worse for visiting teams that traveled longer distances. Of the 175 no-hitters thrown by US major league pitchers between 1900 and 1989, 63 percent occurred at home ballparks and 78 percent of the perfect games in this era were thrown at home ballparks (Irving & Goldstein, 1990). Travel between time zones may disrupt the sleep–wake cycle of athletes, especially if there is a change of three hours or more and if travel is eastbound so that the timing of the sleep–wake cycle is advanced (Savis, 1994).

Preperformance Routines and Performance

The establishment of preperformance routines facilitates preparation for and performance in a variety of sports including golf, tennis service, basketball free throws, soccer, volleyball service, bowling, gymnastics, wrestling, skiing, skating, and diving (Taylor, 1996). US wrestlers who won Olympic medals were systematic and highly conscientious in adhering to prematch routines throughout the Olympic tournament, whereas non-medalists and wrestlers who had their worst Olympic performance deviated from routines prior to matches with lowly regarded opponents and when it was inconvenient (Gould, Eklund, & Jackson, 1992a). US Olympic wrestlers were more likely to follow their strategic plans during their best matches (Gould, Eklund, & Jackson, 1992b). They refocused as necessary, and some used breathing techniques as cues to refocus. During best matches, wrestlers maintained concentration throughout, and were highly motivated to put forth their best efforts. By contrast, during their worst matches, wrestlers were distracted, experienced negative emotions, deviated from strategic plans, and reported cognitive interference. The most successful Canadian Olympic athletes also emphasized the importance of remaining focused on the specific components of their strategic plans (Orlick & Partington, 1988). Canadian Olympians who made major changes to preperformance routines and strategic plans for competition immediately before the Olympics were less successful. The topic of cognitive interference will be discussed in Chapter 10; it represents a form of cognitive anxiety that displaces attention to the actions necessary for successful performance.

Wearing Red in Competition

It is widely recognized that Tiger Woods wears red on Sundays or on the final day of golf tournaments. Red is a unique color in the animal kingdom in that intense red hues are associated with male dominance and testosterone levels (Hill and Barton, 2005). At the 2004 Olympic games, contestants in four combat sports (boxing, tae kwon do, Greco-Roman wrestling, and freestyle wrestling) were randomly assigned red uniforms or body protectors. Athletes wearing red won more frequently in all across weight classes, when they were evenly matched with opponents. The same held true at the Euro 2004 international soccer tournament, as teams wearing red had better results largely due to scoring more goals.

Success or failure in sports such as wrestling is determined in a matter of minutes. Given the difficulty of devising a new strategy in such a brief time and with the stress of competition, it is not surprising that deviations from strategic plans were associated with worst performances. Strategic plans probably represented the best thinking of athletes and coaches for exploiting weaknesses and tendencies of opponents and capitalizing on the strengths of wrestlers. Carefully developed plans are therefore more likely to be successful than strategies developed in a matter of seconds during the pressure of competition. When carefully developed strategies prove to be ineffective during competition, sportspersons may consider their "Plan B."

"Plan B"

Unexpected events that occur in the course of competition or evaluative tasks contribute to beliefs that one has little control over the causes of success and failure. Unexpected events are less likely to happen if thorough preparation has been completed prior to the evaluative task. This thorough preparation will likely include predictions about the nature of the evaluation (e.g. what can I expect at tryouts, what questions will be on the test), the competition, the competition's tendencies, and the competition's probable plan of attack (e.g. a scouting report). Unexpected events may still occur, but developing a "Plan B" can minimize their impact (Taylor, 1996). **Plan B** refers to alternative strategies for problem solving, performances, and competitions that are adopted when "Plan A" – the primary strategy or game plan – is not successful. The presence of alternative or B plans facilitates the preservation of self-efficacy in the face of initial failures and unexpected obstacles. For example, US Winter Olympians considered the ability to make tactical adjustments during the course of competition to be an important determinant of performance (Gould, 1999).

The experience of problems and distractions during the course of a performance is not uncommon. For example, elite male decathlon participants who represented the United States in international competition uniformly identified competitions in which they struggled to overcome problems. All the decathletes had struggled with poor weather, pain, fatigue, a poor performance in at least one event, and worries due to comparing themselves to other competitors (Dale, 2000). Performance is disrupted less by unfavorable conditions such as bad weather if preperformance preparation has included practice in inclement weather

(Gould, 1999). With this preparation, athletes can develop tactics suited to particular weather conditions.

It is sometimes difficult to prepare a Plan B for all the things that can go wrong in the course of a competition. As illustrated in the vignette about Welsh golfer Ian Woosnam at the 2001 British Open at the start of Chapter 3, surprises do occur. Perhaps at these points, mental skills and relaxation exercises are especially crucial.

Why Preperformance Routines are Helpful

There are several theoretical explanations for the benefits of preperformance routines involving movement (Cohn, 1990b).

1   *Schema* theory holds that groups of skills (such as a serve in tennis or a jump in figure skating) are stored in permanent or long-term memory in the form of schemas or mental representations. Preperformance routines have the effect of selecting the most appropriate motor schemas and tailoring those schemas for the particular situation. For example, just prior to serving, a tennis player may visualize a flat, wide serve to an opponent's backhand in the deuce court.

2   The *stage* theory of motor learning emphasizes the amount of thinking and attention required to execute newly acquired skills. With practice, the execution of skills require less thought and attention can be devoted to making minor adjustments in the sequence of movements. As skills are mastered, they can be executed with little conscious attention to how they should be performed and sequenced, and this is described as the **autonomous phase**. Skills become autonomous as a result of extensive practice. Practice enhances the organization of skills into an organized schema or mental representation of the skills. This schema can be quickly and directly retrieved from memory and skills are executed automatically. With this automatic execution of skills minimal demands are placed on attentional resources, thus allowing the performer to focus on other information such as tactics or strategy. Preperformance routines may promote the automatic execution of autonomous skills (Singer, 2002). The stage theory has direct implications for routines that occur immediately prior to the execution of skills. If skills cannot be executed automatically, preperformance mental and physical rehearsals should include thought about how to execute the skills and cue words or self-talk to direct attention to the sequence of skills in the performance.

Feel

Golf instructor, analyst, and writer, Dave Pelz's description of "feel" for golf strokes is consistent with the previous explanation of autonomous skills execution (Pelz & Frank, 2001). For example, Pelz maintained that "feel" is based on a great deal of practice that results in memories of actual golf swings and strokes, and the results of these swings. With this practice and these memories, golfers have a basis for predictions and expectations about the likely results of individual swings or strokes. The golfer with "feel" develops expectations about how a golf ball will fly, and where it will land. The putter with "feel" makes predictions about the speed, slopes, and breaks of greens before balls are struck. In effect, Pelz's definition of "feel" melds visualization and automatic execution of skills, and recognizes no clear demarcation between the two.

"Feel" becomes available to golfers after they have mastered the mechanical aspects of various golf strokes, and mechanical shortcomings keep even professional golfers from developing "feel" in some aspects of their game. Once mechanics have been mastered, Pelz encourages golfers to try to remember the results of each swing or stroke. This builds the "memory bank of knowledge and expertise called 'feel' " (Pelz & Frank, 2001, p. 115). He recommends visual and kinesthetic mental practice (see the discussion of mental practice and imagery in the next chapter) prior to every shot in practice and competition as a way of pulling "the right 'feel' out of your memory for the shot at hand" (p. 115). This cueing for the development of "feel" involves visualizing the desired shot and taking practice swings to retrieve the kinesthetic memory of the proper swing.

When the golfer "feels" the perfect swing, she or he is encouraged to visualize the desired result for the ensuing shot. With visual and kinesthetic "feel" for the shot, the golfer is encouraged to take one look at the landing spot and then to swing.

Given this discussion, it appears that "feel" and autonomous skill execution do not occur "automatically," but with strict preperformance routines, visualization, and preparation. Perhaps some elite golfers focus primarily on the mechanical aspects of shot making while their "feel" for shots has a subconscious influence. Others focus more directly and primarily on "feel." Even among golfers who routinely approach the game with "feel," their attention may periodically be directed toward mechanical aspects of their strokes. This focus on mechanics typically occurs when there are flaws in the technical aspects of their strokes.

3 The *set* hypothesis recognizes that preperformance routines facilitate attention to skills, strategies, and tactics and physiological arousal levels associated with good performance. Preperformance routines serve to direct attention to behaviors instrumental to good performance, and away from cognitive anxiety and regret about prior errors in a competition.

4 Finally, the benefits of preperformance routines may be understood to be the results of *mental rehearsal* or practice. This topic will be taken up in Chapter 5, and one theory of the benefits of mental rehearsal is psychoneuromuscular priming – the preparation of muscular groups to react as a result of imagining the execution of skills. Perhaps these routines facilitate a shift in the activation of brain hemispheres prior to actual performance. For example, among highly skilled marksmen, there was a reduction in activation in the left hemisphere (verbal processes) and an increase in activation in the right hemisphere (spatial, nonverbal processes) prior to competition (Hatfield, Landers, & Ray, 1984; Salazar, Landers, Petruzello, Han, Crews, & Kubitz, 1990).

Summary and Conclusions

The establishment of preperformance routines facilitates experiences of familiarity, order, consistency, and control. Practice should occur under conditions that most closely approximate "game conditions." Generally, they should be carefully scripted and followed throughout periods of preparation and up to the time of the actual performance. However, flexibility should be included in preperformance routines because environmental conditions may necessitate changes in routines. Efficacy that is dependent on rigid adherence to preperformance routines and "game plans" may be brittle and easily shattered by environmental conditions that force changes in routines, by unexpected questions on examinations, and by surprising tactics by opponents. By adding flexibility to preperformance routines and to game plans, the experience of control can more readily be maintained. Sportspersons may be advised to develop "Plan Bs" for both preparation and performances.

Preperformance techniques have to be practiced on a regular basis to be effective, as the introduction of novel interventions prior to and during performances is typically disruptive. The benefits of preperformance routines are due in no small degree to the order and control that they bring to the schedules and psychological states of athletes.

Key Terms

Mental skills training

Preperformance routines

Superstitious behavior

Simulation training

Deviation from preperformance routines

"Plan B"

Autonomous phase

Suggested Readings

Carver, C. S., & Scheier, M. F. (1998). *On the self-regulation of behavior*. Cambridge, UK: Cambridge University Press.

Hardy, L., Jones, J. G., & Gould, D. (1996). *Understanding psychological preparation for sport: Theory and practice of elite performers*. Chichester: Wiley.

Orlick, T., & Partington, J. (1988). Mental links to excellence. *The Sport Psychologist*, 2, 105–130.

Shambrook, C. J., & Bull, S. J. (1999). Adherence to psychological preparation in sport. In S. J. Bull (Ed.), *Adherence issues in sport and exercise* (pp. 169–196). Chichester: Wiley.

Singer, R. N. (2002). Preperformance state, routines, and automaticity: What does it take to realize expertise in self-paced events? *Journal of Sport & Exercise Psychology*, 24, 359–375.

Spielberger, C. D., & Vagg, P. R. (1995). Test anxiety: A transactional process model. In C. D. Spielberger & P. R. Vagg (Eds.), *Test anxiety: Theory, assessment, and treatment* (pp. 3–13). Washington, DC: Taylor & Francis.

Mental Imagery, Self-Talk, and Concentration

5

The American golfer Jack Nicklaus won 18 "major" golf tournaments (six Masters, four US Opens, three British Opens, five PGAs), and was placed second 19 times at majors. He won his first major, a US Open, in 1962, and his last, a Masters, in 1986, at age 46. To place this record in context, the players with the next highest numbers of victories of comparable majors are Tiger Woods with 13, and Gary Player and Ben Hogan, each with 10. Bobby Jones won 13 of the 21 majors he entered, but during his era the majors were considered the US and British Opens and Amateurs.

Nicklaus has been meticulous in his practice of mental skills and adherence to mental simulation regimens during golf tournaments:

> Before every shot I go to the movies inside my head. Here is what I see. First, I see the ball where I want it to finish, nice and white and sitting up high on the bright green grass. Then, I see the ball going there; its path and trajectory and even its behavior on landing. The next scene shows me making the kind of swing that will turn the previous image into reality. These home movies are a key to my concentration and to my positive approach to every shot. (Nicklaus, 1976, p. 45)

Elite athletes such as Jack Nicklaus routinely visualize sport skills, strategies, and anticipated tactics of opponents. For example, 90 percent of the athletes at the US Olympic Training Center used mental imagery, and 97 percent of these athletes rated visualization as an extremely effective technique for enhancing performance (Murphy, 1994). Some 99 percent of Canadian Olympians used mental imagery for training and competition (Orlick & Partington, 1988), as did elite athletes in a variety of sports (Cumming & Hall, 2002; Hall, Rodgers, & Barr, 1990), such as soccer (Salmon, Hall, & Haslam, 1994) and female gymnasts (Calmels, d'Arripe-Longueville, Fournier, & Soulard, 2003). Olympic hopefuls who did not use imagery were less likely to qualify for the 1976 US Olympic team than those who did (Mahoney & Avener, 1977). Almost all US Olympic coaches

(94 percent; Murphy, 1994) practiced visualization with athletes, and expert tennis coaches rated visualization as second only to self-talk in its value as a mental training technique (Moran, 1995).

Mental Imagery

The terms "mental imagery," "mental practice," "mental rehearsal," and "mental simulation" are at times used interchangeably. Imagery appears to be the major component of mental practice (Hall, 1985), and the term "mental imagery" will be used in this discussion. **Mental imagery** consists of intentionally bringing images to mind or rehearsing performances without actually physically enacting the performance. Mental imagery is not limited to visualization, and it has been recommended that it involves all the senses (Vealey & Greenleaf, 2006; Vealey & Walter, 1993). This means that imagery should involve mental representations of sights, sounds, smells, touch, and tastes. In addition, imagery should involve representations of kinesthetic or bodily movement, and should include the recall or anticipation of emotional responses during competitions, especially if athletes intend to gain control of these emotional responses.

Mental Imagery: When and Where

The more activities depend on mental operations and the less on physical strength, endurance, and coordination, the greater is the benefit of mental imagery (Driskell, Copper, & Moran, 1994). Athletes use mental imagery in competition and practice (Hall, 2001; Munroe, Giacobbi, Hall, & Weinberg, 2000; White & Hardy, 1998). Mental imagery is more effective if it occurs directly prior to performance, and is unproductive if it extends beyond 20 minutes.

Jyoti Randhawa: Mental imagery.

Mental Practice and Physical Practice

Mental imagery is no substitute for the acquisition of skills through physical practice (Gould & Damarjian, 1996; Noel, 1980). Physical skills are best acquired through physical practice, and physical practice generally has a greater effect on performance than mental practice. However, mental imagery may be substituted for some of the physical practice without decreasing the acquisition of skills (Durand, Hall, & Haslam, 1997). After skills have been developed, the use of imagery supplements regular physical practice (Hall, 2001). The substitution of mental imagery is sometimes welcomed, such as during times of injury, fatigue, and travel.

Mental Imagery and Skill Level

Regardless of skill level, performance improves with the practice of mental imagery in sports such as basketball, football, swimming, track and field, martial arts, skiing, tennis, and golf (Feltz & Landers, 1983; Martin, Moritz, & Hall, 1999; Murphy, 1994; Murphy & Martin, 2002). Athletes who are not elite are less likely to practice visualization (Mahoney & Avener, 1977). Perhaps less elite athletes have less awareness and instruction in the practice of mental skill, despite research on this topic that dates to 1897 (Murphy, 1990). Although some people appear to have more aptitude for visualizing movement than others, visualization abilities improve with practice (Hall, 2001).

Cognitive and Motivational Imagery

Mental imagery may involve the execution of specific sport skills, groups of skills in larger routines, or entire game plans. For example, in soccer, a player might visualize the specifics of a corner kick to deliver a ball to a teammate positioned in front of the goal. Footballers or soccer players might also imagine interactive plays with teammates. Game plans might include strategies to exploit the weaknesses of opposing teams, antici-pation of the tendencies and strategies of opponents, and a "Plan B" should game plans prove ineffective.

Imagery that promotes the acquisition of sport skills is considered to serve a cognitive function related to either specific skills (cognitive specific) or general strategies in sport (cognitive general; Paivio, 1985). Imagery focused on the steps necessary for goal attainment serves more of a motivational function. Motivational general imagery augments affect and arousal; motivational specific imagery focuses on the specific steps for goal attainment. When sportspersons identify goals, they are often moti-vated to develop plans for reaching their goals and managing emotions, such as anxiety, that emerge in the process of pursuing these goals.

Goals motivate people to take the steps necessary to reach objectives and therefore counteract delays and procrastination. When athletes attend to the specific steps necessary for goal attainment, they are also more likely to develop motor skills and reach goals (Martin et al., 1999). Therefore goals may serve cognitive as well as motivational functions. Furthermore, a particular image may have a cognitive function for one athlete and a motivational function for another (Short, Monsma, & Short, 2004).

Productive Mental Imagery

The **direction** of imagery may be toward images of success or failure. The visualization of images of failure – especially immediately prior to performance – is detrimental, and successful images should precede performance. The visualization of failure results in diminished performance and self-efficacy, especially with women (Short et al., 2002). Women tend to be more modest than men in estimating their physical efficacy (Lirgg, 1991). Imagery involving mastery of sport skills bolsters the efficacy of women and can reduce the deleterious effects of subsequent images of failure.

Coping images may be entertained at a time somewhat distant from the actual performance. Coping imaging refers to the consideration of difficulties and setbacks during performance, and how to overcome obstacles.

Generally, more *vivid* mental imagery is more beneficial (Hall, 2001), and therefore ideally, as mentioned above, imagery should involve the five senses and not consist of just visualization. It is also important to be able to *control* the imagery, or to reliably bring the elements of a successful performance to mind in their proper sequence. Without this control, mental imagery might consist of a series of somnambular "bad dreams," as it might bring to mind images of failed or faulty performances (Murphy & Martin, 2002). With practice, imagery generally becomes more controllable and vivid (Evans, Jones, & Mullen, 2004; Rodgers, Hall, & Buckolz, 1991), and Olympians developed this control with persistent and daily practice (Orlick & Partington, 1988).

The use of both **internal** and **external perspectives** may be helpful (Gould & Damarjian, 1996). An internal perspective involves how one might experience the elements of a successful performance; an external perspective refers to how the performance would appear to other people. All but one of the four male and four female archers on the 1996 Italian Olympic archery team visualized prior to their Olympic performance (Robazza & Bortoli, 1998). The mental imagery of the Italian archers involved several senses (e.g. see the target, feel the muscles), took both an internal and an external perspective, and was supported by self-talk in some cases. Similar results were reported for Canadian (Orlick & Partington, 1988) and American Olympic athletes (Murphy, 1994), and perhaps elite athletes are more likely to practice imagery from an internal perspective (Orlick & Partington, 1988; Rotella, Gansneder, Ojala, & Billing, 1980; Salmon, Hall, & Haslam, 1994). Archery is a sport that involves closed or fixed skills, and with closed skill sports, successful performance is a result of executing skills in a prescribed and relatively invariant way. External perspectives have been recommended for closed skill sports. Internal perspectives have been recommended for open skill sports, such as soccer, that demand flexibility in responding to changing conditions and the behavior of competitors (Hardy, 1997; Hardy & Callow, 1999; White & Hardy, 1995). However, athletes in open and closed skill sports make regular use of vivid imagery with internal and external perspectives (Cumming & Ste-Marie, 2001; Highlen & Bennett, 1983; Orlick & Partington, 1988; Robazza & Bortoli, 1998).

Mental imagery is often selected and tailored to fit the requirements of specific sports. For example, divers have been encouraged to focus on the most critical elements of dives in preperformance preparations. They are advised to visualize these elements performed perfectly and to attempt to imagine the kinesthetic experiences of the dive during this visualization. Divers are also directed to use a verbal cue to sustain attention on these performance keys throughout the execution of the dive (Cohn, 1990b).

Effective mental imagery begins with feelings of **relaxation**. This may be difficult at times, and if images associated with stressful competitions are entertained, sportspersons may experience anxiety and excitement. If a person does not feel relaxed prior to the start of imaging, they are advised to practice a technique such as progressive relaxation or deep breathing to bring about relaxation. The topic of progressive relaxation and other methods of inducing relaxation will be discussed in Chapter 6. Perhaps by pairing relaxed states with images of stressful performances, the two become associated so that a person may perform with less anxiety. With Richard Suinn's (1986) **visuo-motor behavior rehearsal (VMBR)**, athletes are taught to relax with a form of progressive muscle relaxation (PMR) and then to practice visualizing successful performance. Athletes also reduce performance anxiety when they visualize themselves successfully handling stressful athletic situations (Martin et al., 1999). The pairing of relaxation and imagery should of course occur during practice and stages of skill acquisition (Murphy & Martin, 2002).

Viewing *videotapes* of oneself during a successful performance or of a successful person to be emulated may facilitate effective visualization. While viewing these "success" tapes, one might listen to favorite music. Replaying that music may then bring associations of the success and facilitate productive mental imagery. Productive mental imagery may also be associated with key words that may be repeated during actual performances. Repeating the key words might facilitate associations to the mental imagery and direct attention to the correct organization and sequencing of behavior during performance.

Athletes have been encouraged to use imagery during *transition points* in practice and athletic contests such as prior to the start of routines in figure skating or springboard dives (Nideffer, 1985). Mental imagery can be integrated with centering at these transition points. Centering is a relaxation technique and is described in greater detail below. By centering, mental imagery can become more vivid. For example, a diver might achieve a calm focus by centering and using imagery prior to initiating dives in practice and competition.

Why Mental Imagery is Beneficial

There are at least 10 explanations for the psychological benefits of mental imagery (Driskell et al., 1994; Gould & Damarjian, 1996), as follows.

- *First*, skills become symbolized or mentally represented and organized in the process of mental imagery. These mental representations or schemas become the standard by which physical practice and performance are evaluated. Skills are refined as athletes shape their performance to match schemas. Conversely, athletes recognize that their internal representations are not adequate when they execute a skill in a manner that comports with their schema and still the performance is not sufficient. This informs the person that they have more to learn and to practice. If novice sportspersons do not have accurate schemas of skills, then their mental imagery may consist of the rehearsal of "bad habits" or the wrong set of skills (Hall, 2001; Noel, 1980). Once a high level of expertise and skill has been established, visualization may serve as a conduit for the transfer of skills from practice to competition.
- Explanations two, three, four, and five are related. The *second* explanation is that sportspersons are more likely to believe that skills will be successfully executed if skills were successfully performed in mental imagery. The *third* is that mental simulation may promote self-efficacy and sport confidence (e.g. Callow, Hardy, & Hall, 2001; Evans et al., 2004; Mamassis & Doganis, 2004; Short et al., 2002), and self-efficacy competes with feelings of helplessness and anxiety. Of course, if imagery is to enhance efficacy beliefs, it must include images of success, competence, and confidence (Moritz, Martin, Hall, & Vadocz, 1996). *Fourth*, mental imagery may divert attention from questions about the likelihood of successful performance and

direct attention to the behavioral elements that will result in success-ful performance (Bandura, 1997; Calmels, Berthoumieux, & d'Arripe-Longueville, 2004). *Fifth*, mental simulations may lead people to place greater value on their goals, and to believe that their goals are more proximal or close to being realized.

- *Sixth*, the automation of complex skills occurs during the process of mental and physical practice. Automation occurs as discrete skills become organized into integrated routines, as specific courses of action are developed for particular situations, and as sportspersons become more efficient in using feedback to correct actions during the process of a performance.
- *Seventh*, in the course of forming mental simulations, people can anticipate problems and "think through" their solutions.
- *Eighth*, mental simulations may evoke anxiety, but by mentally repre-senting realistic and successful mastery in these situations, anxiety can be diminished (Page, Sime, & Nordell, 1999; Taylor, Pham, Rivkin, & Armor, 1998). Anxiety is reduced as people reinterpret their anxiety and understand it as controllable and manageable, and as they are more effective in obtaining support and emotional solace from other people, and as plans for coping with stressors are developed.
- *Ninth*, the benefits of mental imagery that occurs immediately prior to performances may also be due to psychoneuromuscular "priming" or activation of the muscular groups that are responsible for the actual performance (Vealey & Greenleaf, 2006; Vealey & Walter, 1993). The empirical support for the psychoneuromuscular theory is uneven and limited (Moran, 1996; Murphy & Martin, 2002).
- *Finally*, mental rehearsal appears to be an efficient way of invoking a state of intensity or arousal that corresponds to the state of intensity that occurs during actual physical practice (Hardy, Jones, & Gould, 1996). Mental rehearsal is therefore an efficient way of maintaining intensity levels and attentional focus during delays in the action of athletic contests (Moran, 1996).

Mental Imagery Controversies

Mental imagery that consists simply of imagining the fruits of success has been criticized as little more than wishful thinking (Taylor et al., 1998). There is even evidence that devoting time to imagining successful results is detrimental. Levels of aspiration and performance decreased for college students who devoted their attention to the joy they would experience after achieving high grades. Their wishful thinking was pleasant but did not motivate more study (Taylor et al., 1998). The time that could have been given to preparing for exams may have been squandered on the pleasant experience of imagining success.

These criticisms of the visualization of successful outcomes notwithstanding, highly skilled athletes devote time to visualizing successful performances. Elite female netball players were likely to visualize sporting success and to report high levels of sport confidence (Callow & Hardy, 2001). The association of images of success and sport confidence was not as strong for less skilled female netball players. The less skilled players were more likely to report sport confidence when their visualization focused on technical aspects and persistent effort in the practice of netball. This pattern of visualization may support skill acquisition among the athletes that are in need of additional instruction and practice in order to achieve their goals.

However, visualization of specific successful performance has been shown to be helpful even for novices. Beginning golfers who visualized successful putts set higher goals and practiced more than beginners who just visualized perfect putting strokes (Martin & Hall, 1995).

Clearly Iatrogenic Mental Imagery

As discussed above, negative imagery such as unsuccessful putting is detrimental to performance (Short et al., 2002). Attempts to suppress negative images are also detrimental. For example, when instructed to be careful to not undershoot the target, putting accuracy at golf decreased, even when putters tried to suppress the images (Beilock, Afremow, Rabe, & Carr, 2001). Persistent attempts to suppress negative thoughts and images can have the ironic effect of increasing the likelihood that these thoughts and images will impact performance.

Self-Talk

Self-talk is what people say to themselves. It may be silent or audible to others. Audible self-talk is more likely among children, and with maturation self-talk becomes more covert. Sport psychologists have studied self-statements that direct attention (e.g. what to expect next from an opponent), provide motivation (e.g. "I can"), label oneself or others (e.g. "I don't perform well under pressure"), judge performance (e.g. "I'm the worst"), and enhance or undermine performance (Williams & Leffingwell, 1996). Self-talk is used for skill acquisition (point the toe down and strike the soccer ball with the instep), self-instruction (chop steps as necessary to plant your take-off foot), and breaking bad habits (follow the ball all the way to the racket; Landin & Hebert, 1999).

Self-talk that supports a positive self-concept and self-confidence, directs attention to the tasks necessary for successful performance, and diminishes self-doubt and anxiety (Hardy et al., 1996; Highlen & Bennett, 1983) is adaptive. Self-talk that diverts attention away from task-absorption and to questions about whether performance will be successful or the reaction of others generally inhibits performance and is referred to as **negative self-talk**. Negative self-talk may also focus on past mistakes or direct attention to the future, such as whether one will win or lose a competition.

Self-talk. Andy Roddick (photo © 2004 Judy Hedding, licensed to About.com).

Unfortunately, the self-talk of junior tennis players during competition was sometimes balanced toward self-critical and judgmental statements (Van Raalte, Brewer, Rivera, & Petitpas, 1994). The self-talk of skilled adult tennis players was also negative in tone. Negative self-talk as frequent as six times in a match was demonstrated by 94 percent of competitors, whereas comparable frequencies of positive self-talk were recorded by only 11 percent (Van Raalte, Cornelius, Hatten, & Brewer, 2000). Additionally, self-talk was often in response to prior action in the match and did not appear to systematically direct attention to actual match play or to the anticipation of opponents' play. All the competitors complimented their opponents at least twice. Although compliments may demonstrate sportspersonship, they may also be distracting during the course of play and may best be reserved until the end of matches.

This negative self-talk was recorded in actual tennis matches. When asked on questionnaires about their self-talk, collegiate athletes reported that their self-talk was more positive than negative (Hardy, Gammage, & Hall, 2001). Perhaps athletes understand the benefit of positive self-talk, but have difficulty maintaining a positive focus during the stress of competition.

Motivational self-talk is intended to enhance confidence, inspire a greater expenditure of effort, and develop a positive mood. For example, football players might augment intensity levels and prepare for especially aggressive play with exhortations of "this is my kind of party."

Instructional self-talk facilitates concentration as well as the development and deployment of sport skills and strategies. An example of instructional self-talk is the self-instructions that are rehearsed by more successful elite divers prior to and during competition (Highlen & Bennett, 1983). Motivational and instructional self-talk appear to do equally well in facilitating performance at tasks that predominantly require muscular strength and endurance (Theodorakis, Weinberg, Natsis, Douma, & Kazakas, 2000). Instructional self-talk enhances performance to a greater degree on tasks that require fine motor movements, sustained concentration, anticipation, planning, and the flexible selection and application of strategies. For example, instructional self-talk was associated with enhancing the performance of figure skaters (Ming & Martin, 1996; Siri & Martin, 1996), hockey goaltenders (Rogerson & Hrycaiko, 2002), elite sprinters (Mallett & Hanrahan, 1997), elite skiers (Rushall, Hall, Roux, Sasseville, & Rushall, 1988), novice basketball players (Perkos, Theodorakis, & Chroni, 2002), and beginning (Ziegler, 1987) and skilled (Landin & Hebert, 1999) tennis players.

Some authors encourage the use of instructional self-talk during the acquisition of skills. For example, while learning to strike soccer balls, young footballers might recite instructions for placement of their plant foot, striking the ball with their instep, and keeping their eyes on the ball to the point of contact. As skills become automated, self-talk may refer to more global aspects of sports skills such as how to "set up" or trick defenders (Zinsser, Bunker, & Williams, 1998). The development of automated skills will be discussed below. However, even skilled athletes benefit from instructional self-talk that directs attention to specific techniques. For example, elite, under-14 female soccer players fired shots on goal more accurately when they used the cue word "downlock" to direct their attention to proper technique involving pointing their toe down and locking their ankle (Johnson, Hrycaiko, Johnson, & Halas, 2004). Collegiate, Division I female tennis players demonstrated improved volleying with the use of the cue words "split" and "turn" to direct their attention to optimal techniques (Landin & Hebert, 1999). Cue words such as "downlock" also enhance the competence of sportspersons.

Positive self-statements can be a part of an adaptive preperformance routine, and may be helpful in focusing attention in the course of performance. The practice of keeping a log of thought patterns prior to and during performances can help to identify self-talk that has accompanied satisfactory and unsatisfactory performances. Efforts can then be made to initiate patterns of self-talk that have been historically associated with good performances during and prior to competitions and practice.

Negative Self-Talk or Cognitive Interference

As mentioned above, negative self-talk disrupts concentration and performance. It may involve doubts and questions about the likelihood of success and the reactions of spectators. Negative self-talk diverts attention from the skills and strategies necessary for optimal performance and is detrimental to performance. A general term for thoughts such as this negative self-talk is **cognitive interference** (Yee & Vaughan, 1996), and cognitive interference will also be discussed below.

Sportspersons may be unaware of negative self-talk as it may occur automatically or unintentionally. The effects of these automatic thoughts are insidious as they direct attention away from the task at hand and toward concerns about the adequacy of performances.

Concentration may be disrupted and cognitive interference may increase during the course of performance. This occurs because of expected events or obstacles (e.g. a particularly tough opponent or surprising tactics by an opponent), or because of anxiety that occurs prior to or during a performance. Recall that anxiety has physiological and cognitive dimensions, and cognitive anxiety in competition often includes worries about success and expectations of failure (Baumeister & Showers, 1986; Humphreys & Revelle, 1984; Sarason, Pierce, & Sarason, 1996).

The degree to which people can become absorbed in tasks is relative, and athletes may question whether they will be successful during the course of a performance. However, intrusive and repetitive thoughts about the adequacy of one's performance are likely to adversely affect performance. Furthermore, the more often the person queries themselves about whether they will be successful, the more likely it is that they will answer "no" (Carver, 1996, p. 38).

Self-Talk, Cognitive Interference, and Self-Efficacy

People with high **self-efficacy** and confidence are more capable of maintaining positive self-talk and focused attention in the course of evaluations and in the face of adversity. With traits of confidence and self-efficacy, athletes can remain task-focused and, to relative degrees, ignore setbacks and their own fears and uncertainties in the pursuit of goals. If the attention of confident people is directed to questions of whether they will accomplish goals, they show even greater task absorption and persistence because they believe they have the capacity to reach the goals. In addition, the process of sustaining attention on the elements of one's performance is likely to enhance efficacy because the sportsperson is focused on events in their control (Bandura, 1997). The behavior of observers and competitors is less under a person's control.

With high self-efficacy, sportspersons also more quickly rid themselves of ruminations about mistakes and failures that inevitably occur during the pursuit of difficult goals. They are more likely to attribute mistakes to external and unstable factors such as bad luck, and are less apt to exacerbate the effects of setbacks by getting "down on themselves" or by judging themselves harshly and having punitive self-reactions. They learn, perhaps with the help of mentors, to identify and modify the specific elements in their performance that led to lack of success, and do not make global judgments about their competency.

When self-efficacy is shaky, people more frequently brood about mistakes and feel lousy about them. As attention is drawn to self-judgments and self-reactions and away from the elements in a performance, performance suffers further and people with low self-efficacy may judge that they are having a "bad day" or that momentum has shifted in the favor of an opponent. The attention of doubtful people is captured by concerns that they will not be equal to tasks and their fears will be realized.

The effects of efficacy and performance interact, so that lowered efficacy disrupts performance and problems with performance lower efficacy. If this cycle of declining performance and efficacy is not interrupted, the quality of performance will diminish rapidly (Lindsley, Brass, & Thomas, 1995). When this focus on past mistakes extends past a single performance, the person may believe they are in a "slump." A slump consists of a period of substandard athletic performance.

The performance of sportspersons that lack confidence suffers as they disengage mentally or physically from challenges. As they engage in off-task behaviors such as procrastination, daydreaming, and negative and perhaps self-deprecatory ruminations, time that could be devoted to mental and physical practice is lost.

Disengaging Cognitive Interference

It may be difficult to disengage from this cycle of cognitive interference in the course of a performance. To do so requires an interruption in the process of critically evaluating oneself and a return of attention to the present moment of the contest (Zinsser, Bunker, & Williams, 2006). Sophisticated preparations for performances should probably include cue words or techniques for interrupting performances that deteriorate in this manner. For example, sportspersons may slow themselves down between parts of their performance, become aware of their critical self-focus, and redirect attention to the current moment. Self-talk or cue words can be rehearsed during physical practice, mental practice, and preperformance preparation, and repeated during performances to sustain concentration and to re-direct concentration when cognitive interference occurs (Developing Your Mental Pacemaker, 1989). For example, the word "anticipate" might be a cue word in tennis to sustain attention. This may cue a player to predict likely shots from opponents and to attend to their own game plan. Generally, cue words direct attention to the process of performance and away from attention to outcomes. Cue words should be brief and easy to pronounce and the number of cue words should be kept to a minimum (Landin & Hebert, 1999). Self-talk or written notes can serve as reminders of the key components for successful performances.

Athletes also counter negative self-talk by reminding themselves that difficult conditions are even more detrimental to the performance of com-petitors (Suinn, 1986). For example, in her semifinal tennis match in the 1999 US Open, Martina Hingis was exhausted and trailing 3 games to 2 in the third set, after losing her serve. She recalled matches with Steffi Graf, who presented an image of impeccable conditioning and composure. She initiated the self-talk: "She must get cramps, too. She can't be so fresh. It paid off. It was a mental game" (Jacobs, 1999). Hingis prevailed over Venus Williams 6–1, 4–6, 6–3.

Athletes who are losing in competition may counter negative self-talk by reminding themselves that opponents are unlikely to perform flawlessly throughout matches, and that they may have opportunities to capitalize on the errors of opponents (Williams & Underwood, 1970). As mentioned in Chapter 4, careful preparation sometimes includes the development of a Plan B or alternative if a primary game plan fails to produce the desired results. With a Plan B, sportspersons are more likely to sustain belief that they have control over the outcome of competitions and are less likely to experience cognitive interference and debilitating anxiety.

The effects of symptoms of physiological and psychological anxiety can be mitigated if they are interpreted as likely to facilitate performance (Hardy et al., 1996), or at least as expectable reactions to stressors and not signs that one is "choking" or that performance is about to rapidly deteriorate. As has been emphasized throughout this text, careful and exhaustive preparation is associated with optimal performance. For example, elite swimmers were more likely to interpret signs of anxiety as facilitative if they followed precompetitive routines that included goal setting, imagery, and self-talk (Hanton & Jones, 1999a, 1999b).

As previously mentioned, people may interpret symptoms of anxiety more benignly if they have received direct and empathic instruction that anxiety commonly accompanies performances. An instructor, a coach, or a more experienced performer who has already "been there" or experienced similar anxiety reactions prior to and during performances might provide this mentoring.

People who have not had the benefit of mentoring or coaching to interpret signs of anxiety as facilitative can benefit from psychological interventions. For example, Hanton and Jones (1999b) intervened with elite swimmers who interpreted cognitive and somatic anxiety as debilitating. The swimmers were provided with instruction in goal setting, mental imagery, preperformance regimens, positive thinking and self-talk, and self-talk and reminder cue cards. The cognitive and somatic anxiety of the swimmers did not decrease, but they learned to interpret their anxiety as facilitative and demonstrated improved swimming performances. Swimmers reported improved confidence, probably because they felt more comfortable with their thoughts and bodily reactions prior to competitions. Alternatively, the confidence of swimmers may have improved because they actually were swimming faster due to the psychological interventions. Sportspersons may not be able to rid themselves of "butterflies" in their stomach, but by interpreting them as facilitative, they can make them "fly in formation" (Hanton & Jones, 1999a, p. 19).

Taking time off and regaining focus on the process of performances may interrupt slumps. Strategies for coping with slumps that are problem-focused, or that identify and correct flaws in performance, are also helpful in resolving slumps and increasing self-efficacy (Hardy et al., 1996). Guidance and information from knowledgeable and supportive people such as mentors are also helpful in resolving slumps. Strategies that involve avoiding thoughts about slumps, engaging in less corrective practice, and wishful thinking are not adaptive.

Concentration and Attention

Concentration has been described as a learned skill of becoming absorbed in tasks and not reacting to or being disturbed by irrelevant stimuli (Schmid & Peper, 1993). This process has also been described as *attentional control*, and it is a process by which individuals selectively attend to stimuli in the environment or to their own thoughts (Kane & Engle, 2003). External stimuli such as the efforts of other people to interfere with concentration, novel environments and situations, pressure in the form of daunting challenges and pressure for exceptional performance can disrupt concentration. Elite athletes are often adept at blocking both internal and external distractions and at directing attention to the specific skills necessary for successful performances (Robazza & Bortoli, 1998). High levels of self-confidence and concentration have been described as two factors that differentiate successful from unsuccessful elite athletes (Highlen & Bennett, 1983; Moran, 1996). Intense concentration is a cardinal feature of flow experiences (Jackson & Csikszentmihalyi, 1999), and flow is associated with optimal performance and wellbeing.

The capacity for concentration is limited to the amount of information that can be sustained and processed in working or active memory at any given time. The limit of active memory is approximately seven plus or minus two units of information (Kareev, 2000; Miller, 1956). That is, at any given time, people attend to approximately seven bits or units of information from the environment or their own minds and bodies and screen out any number of other stimuli.

Concentration and Automated Skills

With practice, skills may become more **automated** in that they can be performed without attention to the specific procedures necessary for their execution (Logan, 1988). Highly skilled and elite performance is associated with autonomous skills execution. However, skills that have this automatic quality are not as easily altered or adjusted in the course of a performance as skills that are consciously controlled and that place demands on attention. The development of autonomous skills involves three processes. The first, *mergerization*, consists of merging progressively larger segments of a skill into a single integrated routine. The entire routine is thereafter represented as a single cognitive unit rather than the individual segments and the linkages of the segments. The second process consists of *automation* or the immediate execution of certain skills in certain situations. For example, hockey players may always shoot when positioned in the goalmouth. The third process consists of a *shift in attention* from the execution of skills to strategies concerning when to use the skills (Bandura, 1997). For example, a tennis player may decide to serve to an opponent's backhand on crucial points.

Less of the limited capacity of working memory is occupied during the execution of skills that have this over-learned or automatic quality (Hardy et al., 1996). Additional active memory resources are therefore available during the execution of autonomous skills. These resources can be put to good use in monitoring environmental conditions such as the behavior of competitors or teammates. Expert athletes attend to and extract more information from advance behavior "cues" that are unwittingly provided by opponents (Abernethy, 2001; Moran, 1996). Experts are more efficient in recognizing the relevant behavioral cues that "give away" their opponents' next move. In this way, experts are more generally prepared for ensuing action in competitions, are less frequently "fooled," and more frequently "get the jump" on opponents. For example, skilled tennis players are more adept at detecting subtle cues about the direction of forehand and backhand shots by detecting shifts in the head, shoulders, and hips of opponents (Williams, Ward, Knowles, & Smeeton, 2002b). Elite soccer players as young as age nine also demonstrate this advanced skill at recognizing patterns of play based on the position of players on the field and on the postural position of opposing players (Ward & Williams, 2003). Elite footballers or soccer players are also more selective in focusing on the players who are most likely to initiate or respond to action. Expert athletes use these cues to anticipate actions, and prepare to respond to these actions. The action in sport is often so rapid that decisions about how to respond to the actions of opponents must be made prior to as opposed to after the action.

With experience, athletes gain understanding about where to direct their focus to pick up cues about ensuing action. For example, expert karate performers focus more on the torso area of opponents and detect information about movements of opponents' hands and feet with peripheral vision (Williams & Elliott, 1999; Williams, Janelle, & Davids, 2004).

Expert athletes appear to have a **quiet eye period** prior to the initiation of closed motor skills. For example, prior to shooting free throws in basketball (Vickers, 1996) and shots in billiards (Williams, Singer, & Frehlich, 2002), skilled players focus their vision on targets for longer

Concentration and Batting

Ted Williams was rated as the third best baseball player of all time and was the last Major League Baseball player to hit over .400 (*Hartford Courant*, 1999). He opined that hitting a baseball was the most difficult skill in sport. A Major League Baseball pitcher delivers a baseball to the strike zone in 0.40 seconds. Batters must recognize whether the pitch is a fastball, slider, curve, or changeup within 0.10 seconds. Williams concluded that even superior baseball players must anticipate or guess what pitch will be thrown next if they are to be able to respond in this amount of time. He maintained that "proper thinking" was 50 percent of effective hitting and that guessing or anticipating what pitch a pitcher would throw was essential for every plate appearance (Williams & Underwood, 1970).

periods of time than less skilled players. During this time, experts fine-tune motor responses. More difficult shots require longer quiet eye periods (Williams et al., 2002).

Concentration and Distraction

The additional attentional resources that are available with automization of skills can also be captured by distractions. Distractions divert attention from the instrumental tasks necessary for skilled performance, and include internal thoughts or worries and stimuli from the environment. They compete for attentional resources in working memory. Distractions can also disrupt the flow of automatic actions and cause sportspersons to become more self-conscious. With "deautomation," performances become clumsy.

Cognitive interference is a form of **internal distraction** and was described as a form of negative self-talk. With increasing worry, less attention is given to tasks necessary for successful performance and more attention is given to a self-conscious focus on oneself (Baumeister & Showers, 1986). The topic of cognitive interference will be reviewed in Chapter 10, and it will be shown to be a primary determinant of "choking under pressure." Optimal performance occurs when athletes are "in the moment" or when their attentional resources are fully focused on each moment of play. Choking under pressure is more likely when distractions about the results of competitions occupy the attention of sportspersons. Distracting thoughts about the results of a match are apparently not uncommon because teams in sports such as hockey and soccer may concede a goal soon after having scored one due to this lapse of concentration.

Another form of internal distraction is regret about poor performances or missed opportunities earlier in a match or competition. In addition, some athletes find it difficult to concentrate when they are pitted against an opponent they clearly outmatch.

Examples of **external distraction** are noise or unwanted sound, weather and playing conditions, and visual distractions. Given the discussion of the importance of preperformance routines in Chapter 4, it comes as no surprise that unfamiliar venues and atmospheric conditions disrupt concentration and performance. Unexpected changes in ambient noise are often distracting – they may increase athletes' arousal levels and result in a narrow attentional focus. There are many opportunities for visual distractions. Athletes lose concentration when they attend to visual cues such as members of the audience or scoreboards listing their performance in relation to competitors.

> ## Gamesmanship
>
> The eccentric billionaire, Howard Hughes, was recognized as an aviator and movie producer. As a young man, he had the goal of being the "best golfer in the world" (Hack, 2005, p. 88). He practiced forms of gamesmanship on the golf course: "Sometimes, as opponents got ready to putt on the eighth green a few paces from his villa, Hughes would give a cue and a naked ingénue would appear on his balcony to distract his rivals" (Hack, 2005, p. 90).

Opponents' behavior is sometimes a form of external distraction. The deliberate effort to disrupt the attention of opponents is known as "gamesmanship" (Potter, 1947). Gamesmanship may take many forms. For example, if a pseudo-compliment is rendered to an opponent, the opponent may become overly self-conscious and automatic execution of skills may be disrupted. Comments masquerading as altruistic may also represent subtle forms of gamesmanship. For example, a diver may caution an opponent to be careful when taking off from a springboard because of its slippery surface (Nideffer, 1985). Another form of gamesmanship is to call a time out prior to an opponent's free throw in basketball in an effort to cause cognitive interference and worries about missing the free shot. It is unlikely that this practice will abate despite empirical evidence that it does not decrease the accuracy of free throws (Kozar, Whitfield, Lord, & Mechikoff, 1993). Gamesmanship may also be far less subtle and may consist of deliberate intimidation through verbal or physical means.

Attentional Width and Direction

The influential **Nideffer** (1981a) **model of attention** in athletic activities maintained that attentional style varies along the dimensions of width and direction. Attention can be given to a *broad* or *narrow* range of cues or information. The direction of attention can range from an internal focus on one's thoughts and emotions to an external focus on outside details. Therefore the direction of attention could be **internal–broad, internal–narrow, external–broad, external–narrow**. A narrow focus of concentration is appropriate when strength and intensity are key elements of a successful performance. Tasks such as auto racing are performed best by maintaining a broad and external focus of attention as drivers have to attend to their own driving, the positions of other drivers, information from their crew, and the condition of their car and the track. Successful diving might demand a narrow and internal focus, as performers would optimally

Materazzi to Zidane: "The mother is sacred"

Zinedine Zidane was the captain of the French soccer team. At age 34, he played his final match before retiring after the 2006 World Cup. He was International Footballer of the Year in 1998, 2000, and 2003, and scored two goals in the final of the only World Cup won by France, in 1998. He scored France's only goal in the 2006 World Cup final and won the Golden Ball as the outstanding player in that World Cup. He was also given a red card (sent off) in the 110th minute of the 120-minute overtime final for head-butting Italy's Marco Materazzi. With the match tied 1–1 after 90 minutes and two 15-minute overtime periods, the game was decided with penalty kicks. Italy won, five kicks to three. France's coach, Raymond Domenech, commented: "He was missed in the last 20 minutes tonight. It weighed heavily in the outcome" (Top of the World: Italy Wins Shootout with France for Fourth Cup Title, 2006).

A "Paris-based advocacy group" cited "several very well informed sources from the world of football" in alleging that the provocation for the head-butt was that Materazzi called Zidane a "dirty terrorist" (Butt Why?, 2006). Zidane's parents had emigrated to France from Algeria. Materazzi denied calling him a terrorist: "I'm not cultured and I don't even know what an Islamic terrorist is" (Italian Admits to Insult, 2006). Materazzi acknowledged insulting Zidane – "It was one of those insults you've told tens of times that always fly around the pitch" – denied saying anything about race, religion, or politics. Ultimately, Zidane said that the insult concerned his mother and sister (Zidane: "I don't regret anything that happened," 2006); a charge that Materazzi also denied: "The mother is sacred" (Italian Admits to Insult, 2006).

Two months after the World Cup, the mystery was revealed. After Materazzi held his opponent's shirt, Zidane said: "If you want, I'll give you the jersey later." "I responded that I preferred his sister's, it's true," Materazzi said (Italian Player Ends Mystery, 2006).

attend to their self-talk or visualization related to the elements of their dive. Some distance runners maintain a broad and internal focus as they ration energy and monitor fatigue throughout their bodies. Hitting a baseball requires a narrow and external focus on the behavior of the pitcher and the flight of the ball.

Efficient *control* of attention often requires the capacity to adjust both the width and the direction of focus to adapt to the requirements of given situations (Nideffer & Sagal, 2006). For example, when planning a golf shot, golfers must attend to the characteristics of a particular hole, such as distance; the placements of hazards like sand traps; and atmospheric

Motor sports place extreme demands on attention (photo © Tan Kian Khoon).

conditions, such as the direction of the wind. Efficient golfers then shift to a broad–internal focus, as they recall prior shots in similar situations and select the proper club. When golfers engage in visualization and mental imagery prior to striking the ball, attention is directed efficiently if it has an internal–narrow focus. Finally, when swinging, attention is on the ball itself, and is focused externally and narrowly.

Attentional Width and Direction, and Anxiety

People may differ in their capacities to sustain the various widths and directions of attentional focus (Nideffer, Sagal, Lowry, & Bond, 2000). As anxiety and pressure increase, people may rely more strongly on their preferred widths and directions of attention. High levels of physiological arousal can result in a perceptual focus that is overly narrow and internal and cause deficits for performances that require a broad and external attentional focus (Moran, 1996; Nideffer, 1993). Anxiety and pressure also interfere with the flexibility with which attentional focus may be adjusted. If the width and direction of attention do not fit well with the task at hand, performance suffers (Smith, 1996).

In addition to physiological arousal, cognitive anxiety results in **attentional narrowing**. With cognitive or physiological anxiety, drivers respond more slowly to signals in the periphery of their visual field, and more frequently misidentify signals (Janelle, Singer, & Williams, 1999). Paradoxically, with high anxiety and attentional narrowing, drivers spend more time gazing in the periphery of their visual fields, as it takes them longer to identify and respond to signals in the periphery. Of course, time given to hunting and responding to peripheral information is taken from attention to the central peripheral field where most of the information relevant for fast and skilled driving is to be found, and the anxious drivers are slower in races. The attention of the anxious drivers is therefore deployed inefficiently in the periphery and center of their visual fields. English karate performers also directed a greater proportion of their attention to the periphery when experiencing anxiety (Williams & Elliott, 1999). Anxiety was also shown to disrupt the performance and attentional processes of tennis players (Williams, Vickers, & Rodrigues, 2002a). However, their attentional deficits appeared to be due to excessive tracking of the ball flight with the fovea or central area of their visual field. Anxiety appears to disrupt the functional connection between perception and action by reducing the sportsperson's capacity to identify relevant visual information.

Sarah Learns to Drive

On her 16th birthday, Sarah received her driving permit. Immediately thereafter, she practiced driving on the roads in her neighborhood. With a brave smile, her father took a position next to her in the passenger's seat. Sarah's capacity for steering the automobile was advanced, but her grasp of the motor skills necessary for the operation of a manual transmission was rudimentary. Her attention was given almost exclusively to the operation of the clutch and shifting gears. She was determined to avoid stalling the automobile. Since she did not have a "feel" for when the clutch would engage, she compensated by watching the tachometer as she found it would "jump" just prior to the point when the car began moving. Sarah's attention to the clutch and tachometer was not disturbed by the smell of the clutch burning. This odor made it a bit more difficult for her father to keep a stiff upper lip.

Skilled driving requires a broad and external attentional focus so as to respond to changing road conditions, traffic signs and signals, pedestrians, and other vehicles. The focus of Sarah's attention was external but narrow. She remained focused on the clutch and tachometer but did not notice oncoming vehicles. Soon the smell of burning rubber commingled with the clutch odor as her father steadily yanked on the emergency brake.

Potential Techniques for Improving Concentration

Sport psychologists and coaches have identified techniques for focusing attention during athletic performances. The efficacy of some of these techniques rests on lore rather than empirical proof. In addition, there have been no empirical determinations of which techniques are most effective. It is necessary to practice and refine these techniques prior to actual performances, and they will be more effective if they become a part of practice and preperformance routines. As people come to recognize when attention is compromised, they can develop strategies for refocusing on the factors that support good performance.

First, fatigue compromises concentration, and therefore maintaining *optimal physical fitness* enhances concentration. This includes the maintenance of *sleep hygiene*, as sleep deprivation results in impaired concentration. Athletes can use fatigue as a cue that they are vulnerable to distractions, and consciously redouble efforts to concentrate (Moran, 1996).

As mentioned in Chapter 4, practice under conditions that approximate game conditions results in the reduction of novelty and provides experience in ignoring distractions. These "dress rehearsals" may include simulations of loud and distracting behaviors by spectators and opponents and practice under the most adverse conditions (Wilson, Peper, & Schmid, 2006; Schmid & Peper, 1993). This is referred to as **simulation training**, and has been shown to be a high priority for Olympic athletes (Orlick & Partington, 1988). Simulation training may involve recreating aspects of competitions that have disrupted an athlete's concentration, such as a bad line call in tennis (Hardy et al., 1996).

Mental rehearsals of performances also provide opportunities for recognizing cognitive interference and redirecting attention to the elements responsible for good performances. Mental imagery may include visualizations of the novel aspects of venues, and athletes may post photographs of athletic venues at home and at practice so that the venues appear less foreign.

Careful preparation before performances and game plans that focus on the details in the performance that are under the control of the performer facilitate concentration. Detailed competitive plans may direct or lead attention in that they create states of preparedness to implement responses or strategies at specific times during a competition, in certain situations, or when opponents give certain responses. For example, runners may plan to run splits or segments of the race in certain times, and may have strategies for responding to surges or bursts of speed by competitors. Athletes may also prepare for responding to their mistakes in the course of competition, and immediately mentally rehearse executing skills perfectly after errors (Wilson, Peper, & Schmid, 2006).

Less experienced athletes and test-anxious students may profit from observing how experienced and skilled athletes and students screen out distractions. *Social support* has been empirically demonstrated to diminish self-preoccupation and enhance performance. For example, performance improved when greater cohesiveness was developed among youthful athletes and between athletes and coaches, and when students experienced empathic understanding of and solutions to evaluation anxiety (Moran, 1996).

Athletes have been trained in adjusting the width and focus of their attention during the course of a competition. This training is informed by the understanding that an intense and narrowed focus of attention cannot be maintained indefinitely. Athletes are therefore trained to *"soften"* – maintain a relaxed external focus – during times when performances are interrupted, but then to "zoom in" on critical stimuli at critical moments. It may be speculated that this process of hardening and softening attentional focus serves to maintain self-efficacy as athletes may come to understand that they can control their attention. Behavioral routines that occur during the time that attention is softened may not be trivial because they may suppress cognitive interference and cue sportspersons to harden their focus. The elaborate routines of Wade Boggs, which were described in Chapter 4, may facilitate this hard focus. Boggs maintained that when batting, his attention was so focused on the point at which the ball was released from the pitcher's hand that he could see the spin on the ball as it left the pitcher's fingers.

More generally, training to improve perceptual focus and attention in actual game conditions appears to hold promise for improving the attentional efficiency of even elite athletes during competition. Midfield soccer players from the Norwegian World Cup team were trained to develop and rehearse personalized imagery scripts whereby they imagined game sequences such as receiving the ball and moving their bodies and heads to scan for opportunities (Jordet, 2005). Two of the three midfielders improved their visual exploration of the soccer pitch by improving their scanning of play to their rear. This pair also demonstrated improvement by continuing to focus on their surroundings until literally the last second prior to receiving the ball. English recreational tennis players were trained to anticipate the direction of serves in tennis with on-court instruction and practice (Williams, Ward, Smeeton, & Allen, 2004). This training allowed the tennis players to pick up cues about the flight of serves by "reading" postural cues of the server, and to more quickly initiate moves to the right or left to return serves.

Anticipation skills may also be honed with video-based instruction. English recreational tennis players positioned themselves to return fore-hand and backhand shots with greater speed and accuracy after viewing videotapes and receiving instruction about how to "read" the postural cues of opponents (Williams et al., 2002b). These recreational players benefited from implicit instruction concerning body cues and from instruc-tion consisting of a guided discovery technique about where to look for these cues.

A number of exercises developed to improve concentration among athletes have not been reviewed because empirical and anecdotal evidence of their usefulness is lacking (Moran, 1996). These exercises include watch-ing the face of a clock (Albinson & Bull, 1988), focusing on an object related to sport (Burke, 1992), or rapidly scanning grids of numbers (Harris & Harris, 1984). The grid consists of two-digit numbers from 00 to 99, and the objective is to mark a slash through as many sequential numbers as possible during a period of one to two minutes. Athletes have also been trained to recognize task-irrelevant thoughts, to label them as "TICs," and then to develop a "TOC" or task-relevant focus (Burns, 1993).

Focusing Concentration with Centering

A technique that has been empirically related to improved performance is centering (Nideffer, 1993). It has been described by some martial arts experts as a way of controlling anxiety and concentration under pressure. **Centering** involves directing the focus of attention to a point immediately below the navel, or the body's center of gravity. This focus is paired with recommendations to let one's mind rest on the experience of strength and balance. With centering, attention is briefly directed inward to check one's pattern of breathing and muscular tension. In preparation for per-formances, this centering focus should be associated with deep, abdominal breathing, so that under pressure an athlete can very quickly control both his or her focus and breathing. Shallow, thoracic breathing has been associated with anxiety and muscle tension. The process of checking the pattern of breathing has the secondary benefit of interrupting cognitive interference.

It is beneficial to learn to center from the standing position because athletes are often standing in competition and because it is most difficult to control breathing and muscular tension from this position. From the standing position, athletes are directed to spread their legs to shoulder width and to flex slightly at the knees. Then inhaling deeply, athletes should scan for tension in arms, shoulders and neck muscles, and con-sciously let these muscle groups relax. When exhaling, athletes allow the muscles in their thighs and calves to relax, permit their knees to bend slightly and their hips to lower. Thoughts of relaxation, heaviness, and the purging of anxiety are associated with exhalation (Nideffer, 1985). With practice, the purpose of centering is to shed excessive physiological anxiety and muscle tension in a single breath. It is a technique for gaining momentary control over physiological anxiety or arousal and concentration. It is recommended for use just prior to crucial points in a match or competition when anxiety is likely to be highest. Its practice is also recommended during natural pauses in competitions, prior to the start of a performance, and after its completion.

After centering, it is necessary to quickly pull oneself away from the centering exercise and back to the action of the competition. Athletes may pull concentration back to internal or external and narrow or broad stimuli, or they may take stock of their performance, strategies, and tactics. As is true with all the strategies discussed in this chapter, centering will be more helpful to athletes if they incorporate it into their daily practice as a method for controlling physiological anxiety. A more detailed discussion of techniques for controlling cognitive and physiological anxiety and reducing cognitive interference will be provided in Chapter 6.

Centering, along with other mental skills such as self-talk, is often used by professional hockey players (Botterill, 1990; Halliwell, 1990). They are seen as an effective way of refocusing and remaining confident after bad shifts. The play of hockey goaltenders in the elite Canadian junior A league improved after they were taught a mental skills "package" consisting of centering and self-talk (Rogerson & Hrycaiko, 2002). These goaltenders, who were between the ages of 16 and 18, improved their save percentages or the number of shots stopped when they engaged in centering with self-talk during league games. A mental skills package consisting of relaxation, imagery, self-talk, and goal setting improved the times of an elite male runner and three male triathletes in 1600 meter runs (Patrick & Hrycaiko, 1998). Collegiate midfield soccer players benefited from a mental skills package consisting of relaxation, imagery, and self-talk (Thelwell, Greenlees, & Weston, 2006).

Comparing Forms of Mental Skills Training

There has been some inquiry regarding whether certain psychological skills are more effective and appropriate for particular types of performance. For example, Lohasz and Leith (1997) evaluated the effects of self-talk, self-determined mental preparation strategies, and efforts to enhance and sustain attentional focus, on the reaction times of college athletes. The athletes were required to attend to the center of a computer monitor and to press a series of buttons when a signal was flashed in the periphery of the monitor. All the mental preparation strategies were equally effective in decreasing the reaction times of athletes. In addition, efforts to systematically identify people more comfortable with visualization or self-talk and then tailor training to enhance their preferred mode of mental preparation have not yet been successful. This has led to suggestions to offer training in both self-talk and visualization so that sportspersons can use either or both techniques (Thomas & Fogarty, 1997). It is also not surprising that research has not proved one form of mental preparation to be superior, because the same person commonly uses more than one form prior to and during performances. For example, professional tennis players consistently use a variety of mental preparation techniques such as self-talk and visualization prior to serving and returning a serve (DeFrancesco & Burke, 1997). Given that sportspersons exchange one skill for another during competition, future research may evaluate the efficacy of mental skills "packages" as opposed to individual mental skills (Rogerson & Hrycaiko, 2002; Thelwell & Greenlees, 2003).

Summary and Conclusions

Five components of proximal preparation for optimal performance have been discussed in Chapters 3, 4, and 5: the control of arousal, anxiety, or intensity; preperformance preparation; self-talk; concentration; and mental imagery. All have been shown to enhance athletic performance, and there is every reason to incorporate them in preparation for competition and training. There are no empirical or scientific bases for emphasizing certain techniques or of determining which techniques work best for which people, and readers may be comfortable with some techniques and not with others (McKenzie & Howe, 1997). Successful athletes often use these techniques in combination (Patrick & Hrycaiko, 1998), and different athletes select different combinations. Clearly, all the techniques have to be practiced on a regular basis to be effective, as the introduction of novel interventions prior to and during performances is typically disruptive.

Mental imagery is most productive when it is vivid or involves all the senses, takes an internal and external perspective, and is under the control or direction of the sportsperson. The benefits of visualizing successful results are controversial. The visualization of success has been criticized as a waste of time that could be devoted to productive mental or physical practice. However, successful athletes imagine victory, and novice golfers who visualized success set more demanding goals for putting accuracy.

Self-talk or self-statements that direct attention to the tasks necessary for successful performance are adaptive. Self-talk that promotes a focus on the results of a performance, the reactions and judgments of others, and doubts about whether goals will be accomplished inhibits performance and is consistent with cognitive interference.

Concentration can be maintained during performances by remaining focused on one's game plan or strategies and tactics; anticipating obstacles, challenges, and initiatives of opponents; and quickly recognizing cognitive interference and physiological anxiety. The execution of automatic or over-learned skills and responses demands less of people's limited attentional resources. The unused attentional resources can be utilized to focus on strategies and tactics that will augment performance. For example, if tennis skills are automated, less attention is required to execute specific shots, and additional attentional resources may be devoted to how an individual shot sets up future shots, how to best attack an opponent, and anticipating the tactics of opponents.

With the systematic application of these techniques discussed in Chapters 3, 4, and 5, order, predictability, and control are imposed on training schedules and performances, and performance is enhanced. The techniques advance greater awareness and control over one's psychological states or phenomenology.

Key Terms

Mental imagery

Direction, vividness, control of mental imagery

Internal and external perspectives of mental imagery

Visuo-motor behavior rehearsal (VMBR)

Self-talk

Negative self-talk

Motivational self-talk

Instructional self-talk

Cognitive interference

Self-efficacy

Concentration

Automated skills

Quiet eye period

Internal distraction and concentration

External distractions and concentration

Nideffer model of attention

Internal–broad, internal–narrow, external–broad, external–narrow attention focuses

Attentional narrowing

Simulation training

Centering

Suggested Readings

Hall, C. R. (2001). Imagery in sport and exercise. In R. N. Singer, H. A. Hausenblas, & C. M. Janelle (Eds.), *Handbook of sport psychology* (2nd ed., pp. 529–549). New York: Wiley.

Moran, A. (1996). *The psychology of concentration in sport performers.* Hove, UK: Psychology Press.

Murphy, S. M., & Martin, K. A. (2002). The use of imagery in sport. In T. S. Horn (Ed.), *Advances in sport psychology.* Champaign, IL: Human Kinetics.

Nicklaus, J. (1976). *Play better golf.* New York: King Features.

Taylor, S. E., Pham, L. B., Rivkin, I. D., & Armor, D. A. (1998). Harnessing the imagination: Mental simulation, self-regulation, and coping. *American Psychologist, 53,* 429–439.

Zinsser, N., Bunker, L., & Williams, J. M. (2006). Cognitive techniques for building confidence and enhancing performance. In J. M. Williams (Ed.), *Applied sport psychology: Personal growth to peak performance* (5th ed., pp. 349–381). New York: McGraw-Hill.

Relaxation Training: Calming the Physiology

Standing on the platform, Karen prepared for the most difficult dive in her program. She was too nervous to visualize the elements of the dive and she noticed that she was shaking. She thought of how disappointed spectators and teammates would be with a poor dive. Fortunately, she recognized this anxiety and had a routine for disengaging it. She stalled for time by adjusting the springboard, not once, but twice. Breathing deeply, she noticed muscle tension and a nervous stomach. She focused on a point immediately below the navel or at the body's center of gravity. Flexing at the knees she took a deep breath and while exhaling she experienced a release of tension and anxiety. She thought, "Now I'm in control."

In Chapter 3, the inverted-U hypothesis, individualized zone of optimal functioning (IZOF) model, catastrophe theory, and prime intensity were discussed. Each hypothesis or theory evaluates the effects of the physiological or somatic aspects of anxiety, and presents data indicating that either alone or in some combination with cognitive anxiety, heightened levels of the physiological aspects of anxiety disrupted performance. Some researchers have minimized the importance of physiological anxiety on sport performance. These studies indicate that the effects of physiological anxiety have less influence on performance than the interpretation of that anxiety (Jones & Hanton, 1996; Raffety et al., 1997). However, even if anxiety is interpreted as facilitative (Jones & Hanton, 1996; Raffety et al., 1997), the evidence does not indicate that high levels of physiological anxiety are associated with better performance; indeed, relaxation is a characteristic of peak performance in athletics (Hardy, Jones, & Gould, 1996; Roberts, Spink, & Pemberton, 1999). Further, there are significant differences between individuals in their capacity to interpret signs of physiological anxiety as facilitative. Prior experience in performing well while experiencing heightened arousal, and perhaps empathic mentoring, may be necessary to interpret heightened physiological anxiety as facilitative (Hanton & Jones, 1999a).

The experience of the physiological aspects of anxiety may be distracting, as attention is diverted from the performance to bodily signs of anxiety. As performers focus on their physiological responses, they miss critical environmental cues that determine optimal performance (Nideffer, 1993).

Physiological anxiety also leads to fatigue. People with high anxiety have more unnecessary muscle activity and wasted energy before, during, and after athletic activities. They simultaneously contract agonist and antagonist muscle groups, and this **bracing** contributes to wasted muscular activity and inhibited coordination (Weinberg, 1977).

Physiological anxiety has less impact on performance that requires strength, speed, and power, but a greater and detrimental influence on tasks that call for decision-making and fine motor control (Jones & Hanton, 1996). Athletes may attempt to increase somatic anxiety or arousal prior to sport requiring explosive power through "psyching-up" procedures. However, these procedures may easily become detrimental and result in "psyching-out" performers (Hardy, 1997). Superior performance often requires sustained practice across the course of years, and factors that contribute to overall adaptive functioning, such as the control of physiological anxiety, eventually influence performance on specific tasks.

Benefits of Controlling Anxiety

Gaining control of physiological anxiety contributes to self-efficacy (Bandura, 1997), enhanced sport performance (Greenspan & Feltz, 1989; Meyers, Whelan, & Murphy, 1996), and improved control of cognitive anxiety. For example, the practice of progressive muscle relaxation (PMR; Jacobson, 1938) produced significant reductions in cognitive anxiety among semiprofessional soccer players (Maynard, Hemmings, & Warwick-Evans, 1995). PMR will be discussed in this chapter and is a technique for reducing physiological anxiety. True to its design, PMR had a greater impact on the physiological than on the cognitive anxiety of the soccer players. However, the players with PMR training came to interpret signs of physiological anxiety as facilitative, perhaps because they developed a greater belief in their ability to control arousal levels.

The control and management of cognitive anxiety appears to be an additional benefit of the reduction of physiological anxiety. Techniques that target cognitive anxiety have the greatest impact on reducing and managing this anxiety (Lehrer, 1987; Norton & Johnson, 1983). For example, among the semiprofessional soccer players (Maynard et al., 1995) the practice of a cognitive treatment for anxiety (positive thought control; Suinn, 1987) reduced both cognitive and physiological anxiety, but the reduction in cognitive anxiety was more marked. With positive thought control, the players were more likely to interpret symptoms of cognitive and physiological anxiety as facilitative.

All findings considered, learning to control or contain physiological anxiety is adaptive. The focus of this chapter will be the most reliably validated psychological interventions for reducing physiological anxiety or arousal. Although these interventions are useful at a time proximal to evaluations, they require daily practice to be effective prior to and perhaps during evaluations. The regular practice of these techniques contributes to general wellbeing, as they serve to diminish the physiological and psychological reactions to chronic stress.

Pharmacological interventions have also been used to reduce forms of anxiety. Of course the use of medications requires the supervision of physicians, and the potential for side effects may outweigh their benefits (Lehrer, 1987). Beta blockers and other drugs for controlling anxiety are banned substances in many athletic venues such as the Olympic Games (Voy, 1991). At some point after strenuous exercise, anxiety is reduced (Landers & Petruzzello, 1994), but this of course would be impractical before and during athletic competition as it would deplete physical resources.

The relaxation methods in this chapter may appear to be in conflict with many of the other recommendations discussed in this book. Most of these other recommendations involve active and goal-directed strivings and require analytic thought, awareness, and insight. Relaxation occurs when goal-directed activity ceases. Paradoxically, the harder one works to be relaxed, the less it occurs. Relaxation is more likely the result of "trying without trying" (Smith, 1990, p. 43). However, consistent with the

Relaxation training (photo © Alexander Motrenko).

techniques for mental proximal preparation discussed in Chapters 3, 4, and 5, the methods for realizing relaxation require systematic and regular practice.

Progressive Muscle Relaxation

Edmund Jacobson, an American physician and psychologist, developed **progressive muscle relaxation (PMR)** in the 1930s (Jacobson, 1938). The purpose of training in progressive relaxation is to recognize and eliminate tension in skeletal muscles (Lehrer & Carr, 1997). Jacobson conceptualized relaxation as a method of preserving adenosine triphosphate (ATP), one of the body's principal energy sources, avoiding deterioration of the skeletal muscles, and limiting fatigue. The theoretical rationale for PMR was that one of the routes by which brain structures, or specifically the ascending reticular activation system and the hypothalamus, receive information about environmental stress is through the skeletal muscular system. When the skeletal muscles are relaxed, the ascending reticular activation system and hypothalamus receive less information that the sympathetic branch of the autonomic nervous system should be activated to prepare the body for emergencies (Carlson & Bernstein, 1995). It has also been proposed that the effects of PMR are due to the activation of the parasympathetic branch of the autonomic nervous system, which then inhibits the sympathetic branch. Nerve fibers run from the ascending reticular activation system to the cortex, or the center for higher thinking. Therefore, skeletal muscle tension results in activation of the reticular action system, which then contributes to increased alertness and nervousness.

To review (Carlson & Bernstein, 1995), the peripheral nervous system comprises the autonomic and somatic nervous systems. The central nervous system consists of the brain and the spinal cord. The somatic nervous system allows for voluntary muscle control and regulates the functioning of the internal organs. Historically, the somatic nervous system has been labeled the voluntary peripheral nervous system, and the term "involuntary nervous system" has been applied to the autonomic nervous system. The latter terms reflected the assumption that the functioning of the autonomic nervous system could not be consciously controlled, and did not require conscious, volitional regulation. This belief in the uncontrollability of the autonomic nervous system waned after research with biofeedback demonstrated that voluntary regulation of autonomic processes was possible.

The **autonomic nervous system** consists of two branches, which to some degree are mutually inhibitory, such that the activation of one branch inhibits the activation of the other. Given optimal functioning of the autonomic system, the **sympathetic** and **parasympathetic** branches would be mutually self-regulatory. Under these conditions, optimal states of arousal would be maintained, the sympathetic branch would increase arousal in preparation for stressors ("fight-or-flight"), and the parasympathetic branch would decrease arousal levels when external threats or challenges were no longer present. Examples of sympathetic activation include increased heart rate, respiration, sweating, blood pressure, and other physiological components of arousal.

Instruction in PMR is available to the public without professional consultation. For example, Roberts et al. (1999) provided a script for the induction of PMR and recommended that individuals make a tape-recording of the script and then play the tape to induce relaxation. PMR training provided by audiotape has been shown to result in significant reductions in somatic or physiological arousal (Lehrer, 1982). However, the originator of PMR and other psychologists have subsequently cautioned that PMR should be taught by clinicians (Borkovec & Sides, 1979; Carlson & Bernstein, 1995; Jacobson, 1938; Lehrer, 1982; Lehrer & Carr, 1997), and medical clearance has been considered a prerequisite for relaxation-based therapy (Carlson & Bernstein, 1995). There are several reasons for this caution. First, people may differ in their capacity for observing and reporting on muscle tension. It is necessary for the person undertaking PMR training to be capable of observing and reporting on muscle tension. Second, PMR training by clinicians is probably more effective, as the training can be tailored on the basis of the trainee's responses and progress (Borkovec & Sides, 1979; Lehrer, 1982). For example, a trainee may have difficulty relaxing certain muscle groups and may require additional time and instruction before they experience tension reduction in that muscle group. Third, sympathetic nervous system overactivation will probably remit more slowly in response to PMR if it is a chronic condition. Self-diagnosing sympathetic nervous system overactivation without medical consultation may also be risky, as forms of medical pathology may be overlooked or misdiagnosed. The symptoms of medical disorders such as hyperthyroidism, nerve root compression, and cardiovascular disorders may mimic symptoms of sympathetic overactivation. Finally, relaxation-induced anxiety may result from the practice of PMR and other forms of relaxation.

Relaxation-induced anxiety is rare and occurs most frequently in people who have preexisting anxiety disorders or significant anxiety problems (Carlson & Bernstein, 1995). Relaxation-induced anxiety has occurred with relaxation techniques that have cognitive (e.g. transcendental meditation, TM) or somatic (PMR) focuses, but appears more common for techniques with cognitive focuses (Heide and Borkovec, 1983; Norton, Rhodes, & Hauch, 1985). Indeed, a suggestion for counteracting this ironic process of becoming more anxious when attempting to relax is to downplay the importance of mental control and highly motivational instructions about how to achieve relaxation (Wegner, 1994; Wegner, Broome, & Blumberg, 1997).

There are several explanations for the mechanisms underlying relaxation-induced anxiety. Relaxation may increase anxiety in people who try to insure their wellbeing by continuously monitoring factors related to their safety. If they decrease these efforts at monitoring and vigilance, anxiety may increase due to their fear of losing control of themselves and their environment. Relaxation-induced anxiety may also result from increased attention and awareness of existent physiological anxiety, or sources of cognitive anxiety or worry. Sequelae of parasympathetic nervous system dominance during relaxation can be frightening for chronically tense people, as they might experience heaviness, tingling, heat or cold, numbness, and even sensations of floating. Relaxation-induced panic and perhaps relaxation-induced anxiety have also been associated with hyperventilation, especially in persons prone to hyperventilation.

With these cautions in place, the procedures for PMR, visuo-motor behavior rehearsal, autogenic training, TM, the relaxation response, and centering will be outlined for the purpose of academic instruction. Readers interested in practicing these techniques may seek appropriate consultation.

The PMR Technique

PMR is a skill that improves with practice. People learning PMR begin by tensing and rapidly releasing tension in muscle groups. In this way muscles become deeply relaxed, and awareness about the sensations associated with tense versus relaxed muscles increases. There are 16 basic muscle groups and a sequence of tensing each of them is as follows (Carlson & Bernstein, 1995, p. 25):

1 dominant hand and forearm – make a tight fist
2 dominant upper arm – push elbow down against chair
3 nondominant hand and forearm – same as dominant
4 nondominant upper arm – same as dominant
5 forehead – raise eyebrows as high as possible
6 upper cheeks and nose – squint and wrinkle nose
7 lower face and jaw – clench teeth and pull back corners of mouth
8 neck – pull chin toward chest and try to raise it simultaneously

9 chest, shoulders, upper back – pull shoulder blades together
10 abdomen – make stomach hard
11 dominant upper leg – tense muscles on upper side and lower side
12 dominant calf – pull toes toward head
13 dominant foot – point toes downward, turn foot in, and curl toes gently
14 nondominant upper leg – same as dominant
15 nondominant calf – same as dominant
16 nondominant foot – same as dominant.

Each muscle group is tensed for 5 to 7 seconds and relaxed for 30 to 40 seconds. Muscle groups should not be flexed to the point of pain, and the presence of injuries may necessitate the omission of a muscle group from this sequence or a reduction in the time it is flexed. Muscle spasms may occur, and are interpreted to trainees as signs of deep muscle relaxation. PMR is typically practiced in a seated position with eyes closed, and with support for the head and spine; a reclining chair often provides optimal seating. Even with a reclining chair, trainees may be more comfortable if they are able to support body parts with pillows. Trainees adjust clothing and make visits to the restroom prior to initiating PMR so as to become as comfortable as possible. A minimum of muscle contractions, movements, and vocalizations should occur prior to initiating PMR. People with bronchial problems may have difficulty breathing or may cough frequently. Adjustments in seating positions may alleviate bronchial problems, but severe difficulties may necessitate postponement of PMR training.

Clinicians instruct trainees to tense and relax each muscle group twice. After the second time, trainees signal by raising the index finger on the dominant hand only to indicate that the muscle group is completely relaxed. Trainees try not to move muscle groups after they have been relaxed with this procedure, and try to remain silent except for the abovementioned finger signals. This emphasis on stillness is intended to encourage relaxation and attentional focus on the muscle groups that are sequentially relaxed. Breathing should be slow and rhythmic. As muscles are tensed and relaxed, the trainee focuses on the difference in sensations. After the sequence of 16 exercises, trainees are asked to indicate with their index finger if their entire body is relaxed. If muscle groups are still tense, the appropriate exercise should be used to induce relaxation.

This entire sequence of 16 exercises comprises an abbreviated version of PMR, and can be completed in a training session of approximately 45 minutes. If trainees faithfully practice this PMR on a twice-daily basis for 15 to 20 minutes, they will probably be capable in realizing deep relaxation with the 16-muscle-group procedure after approximately three training sessions. From this point, the PMR procedure can be abbreviated in a number of steps. The goal of abbreviating the induction of PMR is to induce relaxation rapidly, without the necessity of muscle contractions, and in a range of venues.

First, the 16 exercises can be condensed to a group of seven exercises. These are conducted in the same manner as the original 16, and are as follows (Carlson & Bernstein, 1995, p. 28):

1   dominant hand, forearm, and upper arm
2   nondominant hand, forearm, and upper arm
3   all muscles in the face
4   neck
5   chest, shoulders, upper back, and abdomen
6   dominant upper leg, calf, and foot
7   nondominant upper leg, calf, and foot.

With approximately 2 weeks of practice, most trainees are able to experience deep relaxation with this seven-step procedure. Some may have difficulty combining certain steps, and it may be necessary to separate and individually practice the components of the steps that cause difficulty. When the seven-step process has been mastered, the process can be condensed to the following four steps (Carlson & Bernstein, 1995, p. 28):

1   both arms and both hands
2   face and neck
3   chest, shoulders, back, and abdomen
4   both legs and both feet.

With mastery of these four steps, relaxation can be induced in approximately 10 minutes. Throughout this process, PMR is practiced twice daily.

The next step in the process of condensing the PMR process is to achieve relaxation by simply recalling the sensations in the each of the four muscle groups included in the four steps above. Trainees are first asked to recall the sensations in both the arms and hands after they were first tensed and then relaxed. Trainees direct their attention to these sensations with the cue words "OK, relax." If this "relaxation by recall" has been successful, attention is directed to the face and neck, and the same cue words are used to initiate relaxation in those regions. If muscle groups are not relaxed with this recall procedure, attention is redirected to the sensations of releasing tension from the muscle groups with the same cue words. If the muscle groups remain tense, the process of tensing and relaxing each of these muscle groups is repeated. This process continues for Steps 3 and 4, and this relaxation by recall is practiced at home on a twice-daily basis.

Once the recall procedure has been developed to reliably induce relaxation, adding a counting procedure deepens relaxation. At the end of a relaxation by recall procedure, the trainee is encouraged to relax more deeply as the therapist or trainer counts from 1 to 10. A number is recited at each exhalation, and the trainee may imagine descending to deeper relaxation as the numbers increase.

The last step in the process of streamlining PMR, to make it as rapid and portable as possible, consists of inducing relaxation with only the "counting from 1 to 10" procedure. If the trainee is unsuccessful in realizing relaxation with just this counting, he or she is instructed to recall muscle relaxation in the four muscle groups. If the trainee remains tense, then one or more tense–release–relax cycles with the four muscle groups are initiated. After relaxation is reliably achieved by counting alone, the relaxation by counting alone procedure should be practiced at least once daily.

PMR has been used successfully with athletes. For example, after PMR training, the accuracy of serves increased and anxiety decreased among female, high school varsity volleyball players (Lanning & Hisanaga, 1983).

Visuo-motor Behavior Rehearsal

A procedure similar to the final step in the streamlined PMR procedure described above has been used in athletic venues (Suinn, 1986). This on-site relaxation does not appear to be as streamlined as the PMR described above. In addition to focusing on breathing and using cue phrases such as "OK, relax," the visualization of relaxation in muscles is encouraged. Trainees are encouraged to visualize each muscle group loosening up "like light bulbs being turned off one by one" (Suinn, 1986, p. 9).

Whether mastery of PMR would strengthen the capacity to relax on cue and accomplish relaxation during competitions remains an open question. Despite the similarities between the two approaches, this question has not been answered with empirical research.

This discussion has focused on streamlining PMR so that relaxation can be realized more rapidly and during performances. Relaxation has also been coupled with mental rehearsal, mental practice, and visualization in **visuo-motor behavior rehearsal (VMBR**; Suinn, 1986). VMBR calls for the induction of relaxation and then mental practice. The objective of these exercises is to transfer the relaxation experienced during mental practice to conditions of actual practice and competition (Suinn, 1986), and it has been shown to enhance athletic performance at karate (Weinberg, Seabourne, & Jackson, 1971), tennis serving (Noel, 1980), and pistol marksmanship (Hall & Hardy, 1991).

Relaxation has also been combined with the recall of successful performances to encourage the emergence of the IZOF (individualized zone of optimal functioning). Of course the mental practice during relaxed states should emphasize competence, mastery of challenging situations, and self-efficacy in competitions. Mental practice of this sort may not only lead to the emergence of optimal states of intensity, but also make it more likely that intensity is interpreted as facilitative of good performance (Hale & Whitehouse, 1998).

VMBR has been used to decrease daily stress among NCAA Division II swimmers and NCAA Division I football players. A correlate of stress is susceptibility to injuries, and injuries among swimmers and football players were reduced by 58 percent and 33 percent, respectively, during the years VMBR was instituted (Davis, 1991). The competitive records of both teams improved dramatically during the same years. This was not an experimental study, and the degree to which VMBR contributed to these results is not entirely clear. As explained in Chapter 5, visualization and mental practice is not a substitute for physical practice. Further, mental practice is unlikely to bring improvements in performance if the skills that are visualized have not already been mastered physically (Noel, 1980).

Autogenic Training

Although the title of this chapter mentions "Calming the physiology," the techniques to accomplish this calming or reduction in anxiety or arousal are generally described as having more wide-ranging benefits. For example, **autogenic training (AT)** has been described as a physiological self-control therapy and a psychophysiologic form of psychotherapy (Linden, 1990). The benefits of AT have been shown to extend beyond the acute reduction of arousal. People trained in autogenic techniques demonstrated less cortisol production in response to stress. Cortisol has routinely been identified as a hormonal correlate of stress reactions. Patterns of brain waves are routinely altered during the practice of AT. Typical changes include increased synchronicity of brain waves and predominance of alpha waves during AT practice. Alpha waves have been reliably associated with deep relaxation. Respiration decreases during AT practice, and skin temperature increases during the warmth formula, which will be described below.

The term "autogenic" is derived from Greek, and AT is defined as a type of self-induced therapy. It is a method by which people can gain greater control of their autonomic nervous system, and has been proposed as a method to maintain optimal homeostasis or balance of the autonomic system; this may often involve decreasing the activation of the sympathetic branch. AT involves a passive focus on bodily sensations and elements of a self-hypnotic trance. Johann H. Schultz, a German neurologist, developed AT, and his first book on the topic was published in 1932. AT is probably the most widely practiced self-regulation therapy in the world, but it is infrequently applied and studied in English-speaking countries. AT may be conducted individually or in groups. AT instruction should be provided by experienced therapists (Linden, 1990; Pikoff, 1985).

AT has been shown to be efficacious in the treatment of disorders such as insomnia, migraine headaches, and Raynaud's disease (Linden, 1994; Pikoff, 1985). Raynaud's disease is a functional disorder of the cardiovascular system involving intermittent vasospasms, or constriction of the blood vessels causing restricted blood flow to the hands, feet or face on exposure to low temperatures or stress.

AT is also rightly described as a method of calming the physiology, as – unlike most psychological interventions – it has a direct effect on physiological functioning (Linden, 1994). AT is not considered appropriate for young children or people with mental retardation or acute central nervous system disorders. The minimum age necessary for trainees to benefit from AT has been estimated to be between 6 and 10 years. The cautions described in the section in PMR above about relaxation-induced anxiety pertain. Trainees' concerns about loss of control may be mitigated if they understand relaxation training as another method for controlling themselves.

The degree to which these techniques can be self-taught has not been determined. There may be a risk in attempting AT without the supervision of a therapist in that "autogenic discharges" or anxiety may be precipitated by AT. Clearly AT will be more effective if practiced regularly (Linden, 1994).

Due to space limitations, the following is an abbreviated description of AT. AT consists of instruction in six standard formulas or exercises. In the first formula, trainees are taught to focus on muscular relaxation, which is experienced as heaviness. Unlike PMR, there is no instruction to flex muscle groups and attention is focused on just the experience of heaviness in the dominant arm. The specific procedures for the first formula are as follows.

1 The trainee assumes a comfortable sitting or lying position. With eyes closed, attention is given to bodily reactions for a period of two minutes.

2 The first formula consists of silently repeating, "My right (left) arm is very heavy" (Linden, 1990, p. 27) six times and for a duration of approximately 1 minute.

3 The trainee is then instructed to direct attention from the arm, to silently repeat, "I am very quiet" (Linden, 1990, p. 28) and to enjoy the experience of relaxation for a duration of approximately 2 minutes.

4 Procedure 2 is repeated.

5 Procedure 3 is repeated.

6 A "take back" procedure is initiated. This allows for a gradual emergence from the autogenic state of relaxation. It consists of four steps, and a waiting period of 15 seconds precedes each step.

7 The trainee is instructed to make several fists with their hands in rapid succession to "get the blood pumping."

8 The arms are bent inward several times.

9 A few deep breaths are taken and the lungs are filled with air.

10 The trainee opens his or her eyes and is instructed to feel relaxed and alert.

The focus of the second formula is the entire peripheral cardiovascular system. It involves the same six procedures as the first formula, with the exception that the formula "My arm is very warm" (Linden, 1990, p. 30) replaces "My right (left) arm is very heavy" on Procedures 2 and 4. All the formulas are silently repeated six times. This formula results in an increase of at least 1 degree Celsius in body warmth after it has been mastered. It relies on vascular dilation and should be attempted only by individuals without cardiovascular impairment.

Perhaps in the third of eight training sessions, the first and second formulas are combined. The formula "My right (left) arm is very heavy" is used on Procedure 2 and "My arm is very warm" is repeated on Procedure 4. The remaining four procedures are identical to those described in Exercise 1.

The focus of the third formula is the regulation of the heart. This begins with an awareness of the heart beating. Some may be able to feel their heart beating, and others may become aware of their heart beating by monitoring their pulse. Still others may be instructed to lie flat on their back with their right hand placed over their heart so that they can monitor their heartbeat. When trainees can recognize and monitor their heartbeat, Formula 3, "My heartbeat is calm and strong" (Linden, 1990, p. 33), is introduced and repeated on Procedure 4. The formula "My arms are very heavy and warm" (Linden, 1990, p. 27) is repeated on Procedure 2. The purpose of this formula is not to reduce the heart rate, because this could lead to damage.

Formula 4 concerns the regulation of breathing. This does not result from intentional changes in the rate of breathing, as breathing in AT is to function autonomously and in a self-regulatory manner. The fourth formula, "It breathes me" (Linden, 1990, p. 34), reflects this passive focus on breathing. Trainees are encouraged to find their own breathing rhythm. The fourth formula is introduced as Procedure 6, and Procedures 1 through 5 are the same as described above.

The focus of Formula 5 is the regulation of the visceral organs and especially the area of the solar plexus. The solar plexus is located halfway between the navel and the lower end of the sternum. The sternum is also referred to as the breastbone and is located by tracing a line from the navel upward to the bone from which the ribs arch. The fifth formula is "Warmth is radiating over my stomach" (Linden, 1990, p. 36), and the trainee is encouraged to think of solar plexus as a sun that sends warm rays to other areas of the body. The fourth formula is introduced as Procedure 8, and procedures 1 through 7 are the same as described above.

The goal of Formula 6, "The forehead is cool" (Linden, 1990, p. 38), is the regulation of the head. The trainee might imagine that a cool cloth has been placed on the forehead or that they experience a cool breeze. This formula involves vasoconstriction and occasionally has resulted in migraine headaches or fainting. The fourth formula is introduced as Procedure 10, and Procedures 1 through 9 are the same as described above.

Transcendental Meditation

PMR and AT target peripheral manifestations of arousal or anxiety, such as muscle tension, breathing, and heartbeat. Forms of meditation emphasize the importance of achieving states of mental stillness, and decreased arousal or anxiety occurs in the process of quieting thought. Decreased arousal is considered a necessary but not sufficient condition for meditation, as the latter requires an alertness associated with coordinated or organized neuronal functioning in the brain (Jevning, Wallace, & Beidebach, 1992). **Transcendental meditation (TM)** is a widely practiced relaxation method. Consistent with other techniques reviewed in this chapter, the regular practice of TM produces additional health benefits, such as the treatment and prevention of hypertension (elevated systolic and diastolic blood pressure; Schneider, Alexander, & Wallace, 1992).

TM History

TM has probably existed for thousands of years, but its current form was widely disseminated by Maharishi Mahesh Yogi (Russell, 1976). According to TM teachings, Maharishi acquired the TM technique from the Indian sage Brahmananda Saraswati, who spent most of his life living in solitude in the Himalayas and was referred to as the "Divine Teacher." Maharishi brought the TM technique to western nations from India, and the first permanent western teaching center was established in California in 1959. To facilitate the rapid growth of TM, Maharishi trained instructors, and by 1975 approximately 10,000 people were qualified to teach TM. The Beatles focused international attention on TM as a result of their training at the Maharishi's training center or ashram in Rishekesh in north India in 1968 (Brown & Gaines, 1983). The Maharishi International University was established in Iowa to integrate the study of TM with conventional academic disciplines and the Foundation for the Science of Creative Intelligence was built to offer TM services to business and industry. By 1975, TM was estimated to be the fastest growing organization in the world, as approximately 35,000 people per month were trained. By 1975 there were an estimated 550,000 trainees in the United States and one million worldwide. Today, it is practiced by as many as four million people worldwide (www.tm.org). In excess of 500 studies concerning the effects of TM have been conducted in 33 countries around the world and in over 100 peer-refereed journals (Orme-Johnson, Zimmerman, & Hawkins, 1997).

TM training has been standardized and is provided only by certified instructors. The standard fee for adults for TM training is $2500. The Maharishi has been adamant that there be no alteration in the TM technique. It is provided in four lessons on four consecutive days. Three additional sessions are then provided to determine that the meditation is progressing properly. The novice at TM checks with the instructor after approximately 2 weeks to evaluate progress, and this process of checking on the progress of trainees becomes less frequent with the passage of time.

The TM Technique

Essentially, the goal of TM is to achieve a state of mental stillness. TM trainees are assigned **mantras**, or words that carry no meaning but that are phonetically soothing or pleasant sounding. Mantras serve as vehicles for directing attention inward and ferry thought to deeper levels that are quiet or relatively devoid of conscious meaning. Indeed, TM has been labeled transcendental because it was considered to allow for transcending the usual forms of conscious thought and to foster the experience of the source of human thought, or pure consciousness.

This diminution of mental activity is considered to be eminently satis-fying, rewarding, and charming (Orme-Johnson et al., 1997). Therefore, meditators did not have to make efforts to rid their minds of distracting thoughts, as they would seek this self-reinforcing state of pure conscious-ness once they were provided with TM instruction.

Realizing this state of mental stillness is a result of a paradoxical tech-nique of not trying to rid the mind of distractions, but rather of passively allowing attention to move toward the satisfying state of stillness. This technique may be counterintuitive for many people concerned with achievement, as it operates on the basis of "the less effort the better" (Russell, 1976, p. 43). The Maharishi taught that this technique was so surefire, it would inevitably carry meditators to states of mental silence regardless of whether they believed that TM was worthwhile.

Effects of TM

Physiological changes in the activity of the brain occur during the practice of TM. Brain activity during TM is similar to that during the transition from waking to sleeping, and brain waves consisting of theta-alpha and delta waves are often recorded. Alpha waves are associated with an alert mind that is not focused on solving problems and delta waves have been associated with deep sleep. The presence of theta-alpha and delta waves has been interpreted by advocates of TM as an indication of transcendental consciousness (Travis, 1994). Brain waves appear to show synchrony across sections of the cortex during TM, and advocates of TM interpret this synchrony as an indication of intellectual flexibility and efficiency (Orme-Johnson et al., 1997).

The effects of TM that are most central to the focus of this chapter are the degree to which TM reduces somatic arousal during meditation and whether the regular practice of TM allows one to respond more adaptively to stressors. It is unlikely that TM practice reduces physiological arousal more than simply resting with eyes closed (Holmes, 1984). At most, TM practice in comparison to resting with eyes closed may result in greater reductions in somatic arousal as measured by skin resistance, respiration rate, and plasma lactate, but not heart rate and spontaneous skin resistance (Dillbeck & Orme-Johnson, 1987). Simple rest may lower these physio-logical measures sufficiently that additional decreases in arousal are unlikely regardless of the technique utilized to reduce arousal (Morrell, 1986). There is no evidence that the practice of TM is associated with less somatic arousal or release of stress hormones in response to threatening situations (Dillbeck & Orme-Johnson, 1987; Holmes, 1984; MacLean et al., 1997).

> ## TM and Golf
>
> The members of the golf team at Maharishi High in Fairfield, Iowa practiced an advanced form of meditation known as TM-Sidhi. This form of TM is also known as yogic flying. The distinguishing feature of yogic flying is levitation during the practice of TM (alltm.org/flying.html). A member of the Maharishi High golf team levitated by bouncing "on his bum like a human Super Ball," and experienced "a zap of bliss" (Lidz, 1996, p. 123) when in the air.
>
> Fairfield, Iowa is also the home of the Maharishi University of Management, and the golf coach at Maharishi High, Ed Hipp, was also a TM instructor. For these golfers and coach Hipp, TM presented a unifying principle for practice, competition, and the conduct of their daily lives: "Our whole lives are a preshot routine" (Lidz, 1996, p. 123). In just his third year as coach, Hipp's Maharishi Pioneers won the Iowa state 1A golf championship by 19 strokes.

In the interest of fairness it should also be noted that TM has been evaluated more thoroughly than other relaxation techniques; there is no proof that the regular practice of other techniques prepares athletes to respond more adaptively to stressors. Furthermore, the physiological and psychological effects of TM and PMR are similar (Lehrer, Woolfolk, Rooney, McCann, & Carrington, 1983; Throll, 1982; Zuroff & Schwarz, 1978).

The Relaxation Response

The concepts of minimizing conscious thought and movement, utilizing mantras, and descending to transcendental states of consciousness are not unique to eastern cultures. Christians in the fourteenth century utilized meditative practices to achieve unity with God, and suggestions for mantras included the words "love" or "God" (Benson, 1983). Examples of Jewish mysticism date to the second century BC. Early Islamic mysticism also involved the repetition of the name of God as well as rhythmic breathing. However, mysticism has not been as integral to western religious practices and to everyday life in the west as has been the case in the east. Benson noted that in the sixth century BC, Indian scriptures outlined the basic principles of meditation, and that meditative practices are outlined in Zen Buddhism, Shintoism, Taoism, and Shamanism.

The American cardiologist Herbert Benson studied forms of meditation and relaxation (e.g. Wallace & Benson, 1972) and argued that a common variable accounted for the physiological benefits and altered states of consciousness associated with these meditation techniques and with TM, AT, and hypnosis. Benson (Benson, Greenwood, & Klemchuk, 1975) and independent researchers (Lehrer, Carr, Sargunaraj, & Woolfolk, 1994) described this variable as the **relaxation response**. The relaxation response was seen to be responsible for parasympathetic nervous system activation and inhibition of the sympathetic nervous system, and decreased oxygen consumption and carbon dioxide elimination. Altered states of consciousness associated with the relaxation response were a result of cortical activity or brain waves associated with relaxation and wellbeing. This activity consists of increased slow alpha waves and occasional theta waves and decreased beta waves (Jacobs, Benson, & Friedman, 1996). Consistent with other methods of calming physiological arousal, practice of the relaxation response is helpful for decreasing blood pressure, hypertension, cardiac arrhythmias (Everly & Benson, 1989), and the number of premature ventricular contractions (a risk factor for mortality in patients with ischemic heart disease). Benson (1983) described the relaxation response as a simple non-religious technique, and it is the simplest method described in this chapter. The abovementioned changes in alpha, theta, and beta waves were observed with volunteer subjects during their first exposure to the relaxation response technique, and this exposure consisted of listening to tape recorded instructions (Benson, 1983). There are four steps for realizing the relaxation response.

1 Sit quietly in a comfortable position with eyes closed.
2 Deeply relax all of the muscle systems, beginning with the feet, and progressing to the face. Maintain this relaxation in the muscle systems.
3 Breathe through the nose. During exhalation, silently repeat the word *one*. Continue this process of silently repeating the word *one* during exhalation for approximately 20 minutes. After 20 minutes sit quietly for a few minutes, first with eyes closed and then with eyes open.
4 Maintain a passive attitude about whether a state of deep relaxation is realized. That is, do not worry about or become concerned about

The many pathways to the relaxation response (photo © Phil Date).

whether one is "getting it right" or achieving a state of deep relaxation. Allow relaxation to occur at its own pace. Also, do not attempt to fight off intrusive thoughts so as to focus solely on the word *one*. Ignore distracting thoughts by thinking "Oh well" (Benson et al., 1975), and continue to repeat the word *one*. Practice the relaxation response once or twice daily, but not within two hours of eating because digestive processes may interfere with the subjective experience.

Centering

In Chapter 5, centering was discussed as a relaxation technique for use not only before but also during athletic performances (Nideffer, 1993). To review, **centering** involves directing the focus of attention to a point immediately below the navel, or the body's center of gravity. This focus is paired with recommendations to let one's mind rest on the experience of strength and balance. With centering, attention is briefly directed inward to check one's pattern of breathing and muscular tension. In preparation for performances, this centering focus should be associated with deep, abdominal breathing, so that under pressure an athlete can very quickly control both his or her focus and breathing. Shallow, thoracic breathing is associated with anxiety and muscle tension.

Centering has the secondary benefit of interrupting cognitive interference. It is beneficial to learn to center from the standing position because athletes are often standing in competition and because it is most difficult to control breathing and muscular tension from the standing position. From the standing position, athletes are directed to spread their legs to shoulder width and to flex slightly at the knees. Then, inhaling deeply, athletes should scan for tension in arms, shoulders and neck muscles, and consciously let these muscle groups relax. When exhaling, athletes allow the muscles in their thighs and calves to relax, and permit their knees to bend slightly and their hips to lower. Thoughts of relaxation, heaviness, and the purging of anxiety are associated with exhalation (Nideffer, 1985). With practice, the purpose of centering is to shed excessive physiological anxiety and muscle tension in a single breath. It is a technique for gaining momentary control over physiological anxiety or arousal and concentration. It is recommended for use just prior to crucial points in a match or competition, when anxiety is likely to be highest. Its practice is also recommended during natural pauses in competitions, as well as before and after performances.

Characteristics of centering are similar to those of the relaxation response. Both emphasize attention to breathing and techniques are straightforward. Centering offers the considerable promise of being maximally "portable" in that it can be practiced before, after, and during competitions.

Summary and Conclusions

Has one form of relaxation been proved to be superior in decreasing somatic anxiety or arousal? In a word, no. However, there are at least eight factors to consider in evaluating the practicality of relaxation techniques for sportspersons.

First is a consideration of whether professional instruction is necessary for a form of relaxation training. Forms of relaxation training such as AT and TM require formal instruction that must be purchased from qualified instructors. The relaxation response can be acquired through self-instruction, but medical clearance is suggested. Professional instruction is generally recommended for PMR, but there are many examples of PMR training through self-instruction.

Second, some forms of anxiety or arousal reduction may require less skill and practice than others. Proponents of TM maintained that the process of maintaining attention on mantras was surefire and effortless (Russell, 1976). However, meditation may effectively reduce arousal only for those with the capacity to focus or maintain attention on simple stimuli for extended periods of time (Smith, 1990). This skill in focusing may be refined with practice (Davidson, Goleman, & Schwartz, 1976), but PMR appears to be more effective in reducing anxiety for people who have difficulty focusing and becoming absorbed in mental stimuli (Weinstein and Smith, 1992). Under conditions of situational stress, PMR may be preferable as stress might interfere with absorption with mantras (Tellegen, 1981).

The third consideration may be which intervention seems most creditable or likely to produce positive results (Kirsch & Henry, 1979). A creditable intervention is likely to be practiced more regularly and to lead to self-efficacy or confidence that arousal can be brought under conscious control. In the future it may be possible to recommend relaxation techniques on the basis of demographic or personality characteristics (Friedman & Berger, 1991). However, at present, that time appears far in the future, and such tailoring of relaxation techniques would also require additional consultation with professionals.

Fourth, consistent and even daily practice appears to be the critical variable in determining the effectiveness of relaxation techniques (Kirsch

& Henry, 1979; Throll, 1982). Techniques that can be practiced in the least amount of time in the greatest variety of settings may be more attractive for the greatest number of people.

Fifth, if relaxation-induced anxiety occurs during the practice of one technique, it is recommended that it be replaced by another relaxation method. Relaxation-induced anxiety has been shown to be somewhat specific to the particular form of relaxation (Heide & Borkovec, 1983).

Sixth, if the primary purpose for practicing a relaxation technique is to gain control over arousal during challenging performances, then a technique that is portable or capable of being practiced prior to and during the course of performances should be selected (Schwartz, Davidson, & Goleman, 1978). For example, jogging reduces arousal, but it would be impractical during competitions such as archery. Jogging and other forms of exercise would also deplete physical resources prior to performances that are physically demanding such as athletic events.

A related and seventh concern is whether the cognitive skills and structures associated with particular relaxation techniques compete with the attentional focus necessary for optimal performance during the evaluation or competition. Relaxation techniques differ in the degree to which they place demands on the cognitive skills of focusing, passivity, and receptivity (Smith, 1990). As previously stated, focusing refers to the maintenance of attention on simple stimuli, such as mantras, for extended periods of time. The ability to stop unnecessary goal-directed activity and analytic thinking is the definition of passivity, and receptivity concerns openness to uncertain, unfamiliar, and paradoxical experiences. Forms of meditation such as TM are most dependent on these cognitive skills whereas PMR places minimal demands on these mental resources (Smith, Amutio, Anderson, & Aria, 1996). It appears obvious that the practice of TM during the course of a challenging evaluation would be impractical, as concentration on a mantra would compete with the task absorption necessary for optimal performance.

As mentioned above, one relaxation technique has not been shown to be more effective than others. It is still important to demonstrate that relaxation techniques are efficacious in sport settings, and this is consideration eight. PMR and AT are the relaxation techniques that are most widely practiced in athletic, academic, and musical settings (Kirkcaldy, 1984). AT is frequently practiced in continental Europe, whereas PMR is utilized most frequently among English speakers in athletic (Onestak, 1991), academic, and musical settings. In sporting contexts, PMR may be more effective in reducing physiological anxiety and cognitive interventions may more effectively relieve cognitive anxiety (Maynard, Hemmings, & Warwick-Evans, 1995). Perhaps both interventions reduce both cognitive and physiological anxiety because they enhance self-efficacy (Hamann, 1985; Kirsch & Henry, 1979) and prompt athletes to interpret signs of anxiety as facilitative to performance.

Given these eight considerations, PMR appears most relevant to the largest number of people. PMR has been identified as the treatment of choice for reducing physiological anxiety among athletes (Onestak, 1991), and is the most widely utilized technique among professional psychologists who consult with elite athletes (Ogilvie, Haase, Kranidiotis, Mahoney, & Nideffer, 1979).

Centering has been developed specifically for use in athletic contests and also serves to focus attention and inhibit cognitive interference; with practice, it is seen to reduce arousal and inhibit cognitive interference with just a single deep breath. Centering (Nideffer, 1993) was developed more recently and has less empirical background than PMR (Jacobson, 1938), but it is perhaps the most portable and its cognitive demands are perhaps the least.

Given this portability and simplicity, centering may be the technique of choice if it is proved to be as effective as PMR. Even if PMR is proved to be superior, it may be reasonable to explore integrating centering with PMR. This process might involve moving the practice of counting from 10 to 1 to the penultimate step in the PMR streamlining process and making the centering exercise the final step. This integration process might be facilitated if athletes are taught to take a deep and relaxed inhalation and exhalation when relaxing muscle groups (Suinn, 1980). Whether the integration of centering with PMR is superior to retaining the abovementioned procedure with the practice of counting from 10 to 1 as the final step remains an empirical question.

It is probably unrealistic to expect that PMR or other relaxation techniques will relieve all somatic anxiety, and as discussed in Chapter 2, the objective is to induce an optimal level of arousal for the task at hand. As discussed earlier in this chapter, PMR can assist in both inducing an optimal level of activation or arousal and helping performers to interpret somatic and cognitive anxiety to be facilitative to performance. Finally, PMR and other relaxation techniques are best utilized in combination with the other strategies for proximal and distal preparation for evaluations and performances. To some degree, somatic and cognitive anxieties are related reciprocally. The management of somatic anxiety contributes to the preservation of confidence or self-efficacy during performances, and self-efficacy leads to the management and control of somatic anxiety (Hamann, 1985; Kirsch & Henry, 1979).

Key Terms and Names

Edmund Jacobson

Progressive muscle relaxation (PMR)

Autonomic nervous system

Sympathetic and parasympathetic
Nervous system

Visuo-motor behavior rehearsal
(VMBR)

Autogenic training
(AT)

Transcendental meditation
(TM)

Mantras

Relaxation response

Centering

Suggested Readings

Benson, H. (1983). The relaxation response: Its subjective and objective historical precedents and physiology. *Trends in Neurosciences, 6,* 281–284.

Carlson, C. R., & Bernstein, D. A. (1995). Relaxation skills training: Abbreviated progressive relaxation. In W. O'Donohue & L. Krasner (Eds.), *Handbook of psychological skills training: Clinical applications and techniques.* Boston: Allyn & Bacon.

Linden, W. (1990). *Autogenic training: A clinical guide.* New York: Guilford.

Suinn, R. M. (1980). *Psychology in sport: Methods and applications.* Minneapolis, MN: Burgess.

Suinn, R. M. (1986). *Seven steps to peak performance: The mental training manual for athletes.* Toronto, Canada: H. Huber.

Williams, J. M., & Harris, D. V. (2006). Relaxation and energizing techniques for regulation of arousal. In J. M. Williams (Ed.), *Applied sport psychology: Personal growth to peak performance* (5th ed., pp. 285–305), New York: McGraw-Hill.

Goals

After winning his first major golf tournament – the 1997 Masters – by a record 12 strokes, Tiger Woods, at age 21, concluded "My swing really [is bad]" (Goodgame, 2000, p. 57). Woods concluded that his Masters victory was a result of accurate putting, and that excellent timing compensated for flaws in his swing. Woods set about not only reconstructing his swing, but also improving his strength and conditioning, adding 20 pounds through weight training. With the help of his coach, he practiced his new swing and reviewed videotape of his swing until it became automated. He became an obsessive student of the game and spent hours reviewing old videotapes of tournaments for clues about how to play each hole. In short, Woods strives for continuous improvement, or what the Japanese call *kaizen*.

Goals motivate preparation for competitions at times distal to actual performances, and also direct attention and guide behavior prior to and during performances. Simply put, a goal is what a person attempts to accomplish. Goals represent a person's current concerns, and can be as general and abstract as one's "life tasks" or as specific as getting a haircut (McIntosh, 1996). Goals regulate performance by directing activity toward objectives that have been prioritized in relation to less important activities. Goals identify benchmarks or standards for evaluating performances and judging accomplishments. They have been described as the minimal level of performance with which a person will be satisfied with himself or herself. Given that goals reflect a standard to be obtained in the future, movement from one's current situation is necessary to reach the goals.

Theories of the definition and function of goals have evolved over the past century, and there are approximately 31 theories that posit goal-like constructs. In the mid-1960s, goal-setting theory developed with the premise that human behavior is purposeful and directed by conscious goals (Locke & Latham, 1994). This theory has influenced much of the analysis in this chapter. The focus of this chapter will be on goals that people set for themselves as opposed to goals that are assigned by outside parties, and on the ways in which goals relate to performance.

Goals regulate behavior throughout the lifespan, and even young children demonstrate the ability to plan and organize their behaviors to achieve goals. For example, Bauer, Schwade, Wewerka, and Delaney (1999) found that children as young as 21 months were capable of completing three steps to build objects when they were shown an example of the completed object. The completed object represented the goal that the children were to achieve by sequencing the three steps. These very young children were apparently able to think for themselves in determining what steps to take to reach these goals.

Goal Dimensions

Goals are a source of motivation and an incentive for action. The establishment of a goal often stimulates planning to reach that goal. People consistently work faster, harder, and for a longer duration when their behavior is guided by goals. Relevant dimensions of goals are content, intensity, and difficulty. The **content** of a goal is the object of an action. **Intensity** refers to the degree of effort exerted to reach a goal, the importance of a goal, and the **commitment** to achieving a goal (Locke, Latham,

Goals direct and motivate (photo © Gregory Kendall).

& Erez, 1988). As demonstrated in industrial and sporting venues, goal commitment increases when goals are determined more by individuals and less by outside coercion. When people are committed to **difficult** goals, they are more tenacious in pursuing those goals. Goals are often adopted in the absence of instructions or training to set goals. Some (Sheldon & Elliot, 1999) argue that when people are motivated to action, they always pursue goals, even when they are not explicitly aware of these goals.

Difficult Goals

Over 400 research studies have demonstrated that higher achievement results from setting more **difficult** goals, provided that people possess the requisite ability and knowledge to reach the difficult goals (Locke & Latham, 1994). People with difficult goals exert greater effort at physical tasks such as lifting weight and pedaling a bicycle. They also exert more effort at cognitive tasks such as mental arithmetic and solving puzzles; they work longer and rest less. Effort is roughly proportional to the difficulty of goals, and greater persistence is demanded to reach difficult goals. However, when someone reaches the limit of his or her skill and ability, there is little room for improvement regardless of the level of goal difficulty.

People come to realize how to regulate the expenditure of effort to reach difficult versus easy goals. People realize that to reach a goal, they have to direct their attention to that goal to the exclusion of activities that would compete with the realization of that goal.

Goals serve as standards for satisfaction with oneself. People who set higher goals demand more of themselves (Locke & Latham, 1994). More intense feelings of satisfaction and failure result from attaining or failing to reach more important goals.

When goals are assigned by outside sources, it is important to determine whether individuals actually accept the assigned goals. For example, Weinberg, Bruya, Jackson, and Garland (1987) demonstrated that the level of difficulty of assigned goals was not related to the performance of college students on sit-up tasks in physical education classes. The number of sit-ups was closely related to the internal goals of the students. However, an independent study of male college students in physical education classes demonstrated that personal goals are influenced by assigned goals. When these students were assigned difficult goals for the number of sit-ups to achieve in one minute, their personal goals for sit-ups also increased (Lerner & Locke, 1995).

The performance of novice athletes, who may not be intrinsically motivated to perform at a high level, may be best motivated by goals that are assigned by experts. For example, college students enrolled in beginning tennis classes showed more rapid progress in serving accurately when assigned goals by instructors (Boyce, Wayda, Johnston, Bunker, & Eliot, 2001).

Goals and Self-Efficacy

People are more likely to expect that they are capable of reaching difficult goals if they observe people similar to themselves reach equally difficult goals. However, observing others is not always influential, and its influence decreases as people learn by experience what they are capable of achieving (Weiss, Suckow, & Rakestraw, 1999). **Self-efficacy** – confidence that one can accomplish a range of related goals – has a direct and stable effect on self-set goals in that those that have high self-efficacy set higher goals and expect more of themselves. Higher self-efficacy and higher self-set goals are both related to higher performance (Phillips & Gully, 1997). High **self-esteem** or a global sense of self-worth has also been associated with setting higher goals and better performance (Martin & Murberger, 1994; Tang & Reynolds, 1993).

Setting the level of goal difficulty beyond the limits of one's abilities has not been recommended, as people tend to reduce effort or give up when goal attainment appears impossible. Repeated failures to reach goals that exceed one's abilities are demoralizing and decrease self-efficacy (Bandura, 1989b).

Goal Specificity

In addition to goal difficulty, higher performance has consistently been related to the specificity of goals. However, specific goals are likely to lead to higher performance only when the goals are difficult. Goal **specificity** is obtained primarily by quantifying goals (e.g. improve by 10 percent) or by enumeration (e.g. a list of tasks to be completed on a given day). Specific goals are also more likely to lead to greater consistency across performances. Greater variability occurs with vague goals because the standards for good performances are never clear. Specific goals designate the amount and type of effort necessary for their attainment, and allow for self-satisfaction upon reaching goals (Bandura & Simon, 1977). Vague goals, such as just doing one's best, have little effect on performance. Vague goals can be redefined after the fact to accommodate low performance. If specific standards are not set for goals, people are more likely to be satisfied with modest performances.

Goal Commitment

Specific and difficult goals lead to higher performance if people are committed to these goals, but not when goal commitment is low, and commitment to easy goals does not lead to higher performance (Klein, Wesson, Hollenbeck, & Alge, 1999). Goal **commitment** refers to one's determination to reach a goal. It is a function of one's conviction or belief that the goal is important or attractive, that it is attainable, and that progress toward its attainment is possible. With histories of attaining similar goals and challenges, and with the requisite ability, experience, and training, people are more likely to believe that their goals are attainable.

Goal commitment is a dynamic process in that it involves more than making an initial decision to reach a goal. Consciously recalling goals and reminding oneself of commitments to goals enhances goal commitment. This involves consciously reviewing the importance of specific goals and how specific goals are integrated with long-range goals, objectives, and values. Goal commitment is also enhanced by analyzing or taking stock of the training and knowledge that must be obtained to make goal attainment possible. Bringing goals to mind is an effective way to blunt the demoralizing effects of setbacks. Noting progress toward goal realization or toward reaching **subgoals** also enhances maintaining commitments to goals.

Goals and Feedback

Feedback about progress toward goals contributes to effective goal setting. It provides information about whether performance standards have been met. If feedback indicates that performance standards have been met, then the behavior and effort exerted in pursuit of a particular goal is often sustained. Information that performance falls beneath standards motivates improved performance. The effects of explicit feedback are enhanced if clear goals have been established and if self-efficacy for realizing goals is high (Cervone & Wood, 1995).

Proximal and Distal Goals

Feedback is more abundant if difficult end goals or omnibus goals are divided into subgoals. Goals that are structured with difficult end goals and progressively more difficult subgoals provide the most specific information about what is necessary to reach both the end goal and subgoals (Bandura & Simon, 1977). If subgoals are also **proximal** (to be accomplished in the near future), then an almost constant stream of feedback is available about whether current behavior is leading to goal accomplishment. Explicit, proximal goals lead to better performance in sport and other settings (Gould, 2006; Kyllo & Landers, 1995), and when people are simply provided with end goals, they often develop their own proximal goals. For example, people spontaneously developed subgoals when assigned distal goals for weight loss (Bandura & Simon, 1977) and daily study habits (Morgan, 1985).

A focus on **distal goals** may contribute to procrastination, because distal goals provide less information about what immediate action is necessary. Distal goals do not provide adequate markers against which a person may gauge his or her progress, and demoralization and negative emotions often occur when progress seems minimal (Kanfer & Ackerman, 1989).

Proximal goals are especially important in the early stages of work on complex tasks because progress can be gauged against the marker of the subgoal. If timely progress does not occur in relation to subgoals, alternative strategies can be tried while there is still time to reach the distal goal. Self-efficacy is also enhanced with the attainment of proximal goals, as people become more convinced that the attainment of the distal goal will result from the orderly process of reaching the proximal goals (Latham & Seijts, 1999).

Proximal goals not only guide the behavior necessary for the accomplishment of distal goals, but also provide **incentives**. Self-satisfaction or dissatisfaction in relation to the proximal goals provides a chain of incentives in the process of working toward the accomplishment of the ultimate goal. This discussion of proximal and distal goals assumes that the person has understood the adoption of the goals to serve their self-interest, and that external forces did not impose the goals.

Goals are most motivating when they are proximal or just beyond a person's reach. In fact, people may be expected to work approximately twice as hard when they are approaching their goal as when they have exceeded it. This finding is consistent with the frequently reported result that difficult and challenging goals evoke better performance. If a goal is difficult and challenging, it is less likely to have been met and greatly exceeded. Goals are less influential when they are distal, when they have already been met, and especially when they have been greatly exceeded (Heath, Larrick, & Wu, 1999).

Goals in Sport: Controversies

Approximately 90 percent of the studies conducted in industrial and business settings were consistent with the findings reported above about the benefits of specific and difficult goals. The effects of goals on sport and exercise performance have been more equivocal. It has been reasoned that goals may be less necessary in sport environments because athletes are typically already highly motivated, and because their performances are judged against objective standards such as time or scores.

An important limitation of some of the studies in sporting contexts is that they did not evaluate the goals that athletes set for themselves. In some studies, goals were assigned by experimenters, and in others, participants set their own quantitative goals, but only within parameters defined by experimenters (e.g. Lerner & Locke, 1995; Weinberg et al., 1987). As described above, goal commitment is an important determinant of the influence of goals in motivating behavior. People are more committed to goals that are important to them and that are self-selected. It is reasonable to question the motivating effects of assigned goals such as to perform a given number of sit-ups (Weinberg, Bruya, & Jackson, 1985) or to complete coordination tasks (Smith & Lee, 1992).

This controversy about the influence of goals in sporting contexts has been at least partially resolved in a study that statistically aggregated the body of research concerning goals and sport performance (Kyllo & Landers, 1995). Moderately, but not extremely, difficult goals led to better sport and exercise performance. More precisely, if participants in the sport and exercise studies were assigned goals that were achieved by no more than 10 percent of the participants, there was no improvement in performance. The assignment of goals that were accomplished by no more than 25 percent of participants contributed to improved performance. The motivating qualities of goals diminish if participants do not have the ability to reach goals, and the participants in these sporting studies may have realized that the extremely difficult goals were unrealistic. Moderately difficult goals are more motivating in sport and exercise settings if they are specific and if short- and long-term goals are used in combination.

The effects of goals are as great for endurance tasks as for skill-related tasks such as archery. Skilled and experienced athletes perform better when they set their own goals or cooperate with mentors in setting goals as opposed to receiving assigned goals. Sportspersons may be in the best position to evaluate their ability and to set a standard for an optimal performance.

Goals Set by Athletes and Coaches

The actual goals set by athletes have been studied. Consistent with research in industrial settings, college athletes indicated that goals influence performance by directing attention toward their attainment. College athletes have identified this as the primary purpose for setting goals (Weinberg, 1996). Goals also channel effort, and provide information about progress toward goals.

Better performance is associated with difficult and specific goals. For example, following the completion of a summer wrestling camp, male high school wrestlers described goals for the upcoming preseason and wrestling season, and long-term goals (Kane, Baltes, & Moss, 2001). The wrestlers with difficult and specific goals for their preseasons (such as bench press double my weight) tended to have more difficult and specific goals for their wrestling seasons (such as win over 25 matches and better on my feet [takedowns]). Wrestlers with more specific and difficult goals for the preseason and season showed more improvement as rated by their coaches.

Short-term (proximal) goals are especially useful in providing feedback about progress. Goals also foster problem solving because after setting a goal it becomes necessary to figure out how to reach it. Perhaps more successful athletes set more specific proximal goals. For example, the most successful Canadian Olympic athletes set specific, daily goals (Orlick & Partington, 1988). These Olympians established what they wanted to accomplish each day and in each workout.

Most athletes set their own goals. For example, a survey of 578 college athletes (321 males, 249 females, and eight who reported no gender) representing 18 different sports demonstrated that almost all (96.4 percent) set goals (Burton, Weinberg, Yukelson, & Weigand, 1998). Most of the athletes rated their goals as only modestly effective in motivating their behavior, perhaps because they were referenced with only moderate frequency. That is, athletes evaluated goal effectiveness, wrote goals, publicly disclosed goals, and developed action plans to reach goals with only moderate frequency. It appeared that many athletes had only a vague idea of how to set goals and use them as reference points to guide behavior and gauge progress. They may not have understood how to set short- and long-term goals, and how to organize goals in hierarchies. The more effective athletes took the abovementioned action to commit themselves to public goals, frequently evaluated goal effectiveness, developed action plans to reach goals, and developed short- and long-term goals for practice and competition.

Athletes' Goals

Goals of improving overall performance, winning, and having fun with others were most important to Division I college athletes (Weinberg, Burton, Yukelson, & Weigand, 1993). These were also rated as most important by 187 male and 151 female US Olympic athletes representing 12 different individual and team sports (Weinberg, Burton, Yukelson, & Weigand, 2000). Given the emphasis on winning medals in Olympic competition, it was notable that 42 percent of the athletes rated improving overall performance as their most important goal, whereas 25 percent rated winning and 15 percent rated having fun as their most important goals. Perhaps the Olympians perceived these goals to be interrelated, such that improvement accompanied winning and enjoyment.

Highly skilled young athletes also rated improving performance, having fun, and winning as their most important goals (Weinberg, Burke, & Jackson, 1997). The goals of younger athletes are more likely to focus on skill acquisition; the goals of more advanced athletes are more focused on skilled performance. For example, the most effective goals for younger athletes such as tennis players appear to focus on physical conditioning, practice, and the refinement of skills and techniques (Weinberg et al., 1997).

Only One Gold

The sporting press hyped Michael Phelps as a likely candidate for eight Olympic gold medals in men's swimming at the 2004 Olympic Games in Athens, Greece – one more than Mark Spitz's record of seven gold medals at the 1972 Olympics in Munich, Germany. Phelps' goal was to win one gold medal: "That's the only goal I have. Bringing back one Olympic medal to the US would be an honor for me" (Hine, 2004b, p. E10). "It becomes more about finishing and skating through a program. It's the feeling you have after you've accomplished something and knowing that after the days and days of hard work, you just skate the way you've always imagined" (Hine, 2004a, p. C2).

Phelps did not win eight gold medals. Still, his haul of six gold and two bronze medals matched the most won by any Olympian (Dillman, 2004).

The Olympic athletes and college athletes set realistic goals. Notwithstanding the level of Olympic competition, 52 percent of the Olympians reported that they set moderately difficult goals, with 25 percent reporting very difficult goals. College athletes (Weinberg et al., 1993) and young athletes (Weinberg et al., 1997) are also more likely to set moderately difficult goals.

Coaches' Goals

Comparable surveys of the percentages of coaches who make use of goals are not available. However, information about the goal-setting techniques of eight male and six female high school coaches is available (Weinberg, Butt, & Knight, 2001). These coaches had reputations for integrating goal setting in their coaching practices. They were shown to set goals for individual athletes, for teams, and for themselves. There was wide variability in the degree to which goal-setting techniques were systematically applied. More specifically, there was variability with regard to writing down goals, measuring progress toward goals, and having practice time available for the review of goals.

There was greater agreement between coaches regarding the importance of short-term goals, as most coaches set individual and team short-term goals. The coaches appreciated the value of measuring progress and motivating athletes with proximate goals, and understood the position of short-term goals in goal hierarchies with long-term goals. The coaches set goals to provide direction to athletes, teams, and coaches, and valued goals as sources of feedback. The high school coaches estimated that a lack of cohesion or agreement among teammates was the primary barrier to achieving team goals. They recognized the hazards of setting unrealistically high goals, as they believed that this would lead to demoralization. However, the coaches tended to set very difficult goals, and this is at variance with the information presented earlier indicating that moderately difficult goals were most motivating (Kyllo & Landers, 1995).

Goal Hierarchies

Goals are often organized not only on the basis of standards that are distal and proximal, but also in **hierarchies**. Goals for the most discrete and concrete actions are at the bottom of these hierarchies, and omnibus, abstract goals are at the top. Goals at higher levels in the hierarchy relate to "why or for what effect" (Brett and VandeWalle, 1999, p. 864) one engages in activities. Goals at lower levels relate to how particular actions are accomplished. The pursuit and accomplishment of lower-order goals is instrumental in attaining higher-order goals.

For example, readers of this book may have the abstract, omnibus goal of doing their best in situations where performance is evaluated. Beneath that goal might be less abstract but still broad goals such as to achieve the highest grades possible in college. Beneath that level of abstraction might be goals for grades in a particular class in which this textbook is used. Next down in the hierarchy would be goals for daily and weekly strategies for budgeting time for study. Additional goals at this level of abstraction might include the adoption of principles for managing one's own behavior described in this chapter. The most concrete and discrete goals in the hierarchy would concern behaviors immediately prior to and during examinations. For example, students might attempt to practice the principles detailed in Chapters 3, 4, and 5 to control anxiety in evaluations. Goals that have a higher order in the hierarchy set the standards for the goals at the next lower level. An example of a goal hierarchy is represented in Figure 7.1.

Abstract Goals

With clear linkages between lower- and higher-order goals, progress toward **abstract goals** is more discernible. However, when this linkage is apparent, there is more negative affect when progress toward lower-order and concrete goals is poor, because of the realization that the attainment of omnibus goals is also threatened (McIntosh, 1996).

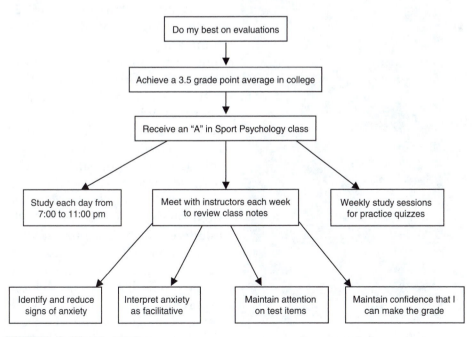

FIGURE 7.1. Goal hierarchy example.

Not all people strive for equally abstract goals. Goals that are more abstract are less manageable and more difficult to accomplish than more concrete goals. The pursuit of higher-level goals typically results in more negative affect because progress toward their realization is often slower. Conversely, people directed by lower-level goals may not pursue aspirations that provide as much fulfillment and meaning in their lives. They experience less negative affect at the cost of avoiding very difficult and challenging projects (Emmons & Kaiser, 1996).

Abstract goals that are of intrinsic interest are more likely to lead to life satisfaction, and these activities often provide the experiences of competence, autonomy, and interpersonal relatedness (Deci & Ryan, 1987). People limit their potential life satisfaction when they pursue abstract goals that are not concordant with their intrinsic interests (Sheldon & Elliot, 1999). In place of the selection of goals that will lead to the most life satisfaction, they may adopt the goals assigned by others. Goals that are concordant with intrinsic interests are likely to be enduring and to sustain effort over time. Goals that are pursued due to external pressure or to introjected guilt or shame have less capacity to sustain effort over time. For example, children may halfheartedly cooperate with parents by attending sport practices and camps, and later drop the sport because it did not capture their interest.

Goals sustain effort (photo © Glenda M. Powers).

When abstract goals are in conflict, people spend more time ruminating about goals and less time in the productive pursuit of these goals. Goals are in conflict when the attainment of one goal interferes with the attainment of another. For example, a student may be conflicted about playing a collegiate club sport such as rugby because time spent at practice, competition, and travel is taken from study time and potentially interferes with her pursuit of a superior GPA (grade point average). When there is a great deal of goal conflict, people seldom experience psychological well-being because they almost always feel they are not making adequate progress toward at least one of their goals. People with a high degree of goal conflict do not have a coherent structure for directing their activities and for rendering meaning to their lives.

Why Goals Are Motivating

When goals are set at a level above one's current level of performance, people deliberately establish a state of internal **disequilibrium**. This disequilibrium creates self-dissatisfaction because one's current status falls beneath goals, and it is only ameliorated when goals are reached. Positive and negative emotions are experienced not only at the time of goal attainment or nonattainment, but also during the pursuit of goals. If progress toward goals is rapid, positive emotions are experienced. Positive emotions can therefore be experienced even when the discrepancy between one's current status and goals is large, so long as the rate of movement or velocity toward the reduction of this discrepancy is rapid. Conversely, if the rate of movement toward goals is slower than one's expectations or nonexistent, negative emotions are experienced. Negative emotions could therefore be experienced even when goals are close at hand if progress toward these proximal goals is slow or nonexistent. Extremely rapid progress produces a rush of excitement, and rapid deceleration produces a "sinking feeling" (Carver, Lawrence, & Scheier, 1996).

Is movement toward goals motivated more by efforts to capture positive emotion or to avoid negative emotion? Perhaps ironically, it appears to be the latter. The amount of dissatisfaction and negative emotion experienced when goals are not realized is significantly greater than the amount of positive emotion and self-satisfaction experienced when one exceeds a goal (Heath, Larrick, & Wu, 1999). Therefore, negative emotions and dissatisfaction – and to a lesser extent the anticipation of self-satisfaction – drive people toward goals.

Negative emotion may provide information that goal attainment is threatened, whereas positive emotion may signal that one can "coast" or take it easy and still reach goals on schedule. When satisfied with goal attainment, people may divert attention and energy to collateral goals and pursuits and lose momentum toward goal attainment. This satisfaction with goal attainment may be temporary, as people with high self-efficacy set new goals for themselves after goals are realized.

When performance falls short of goals, sportspersons experience negative emotions (Graham, Kowalski, & Crocker, 2002), and self-dissatisfaction motivates corrective action (Bandura & Simon, 1977). People with higher self-efficacy are more dissatisfied when they do not

Coasting after Goal Attainment

After winning the state open tennis championship as a sophomore, Brian seemed to lose direction. He avoided tennis camp in the summer, and joined his high school swim team. Although rusty at the start of the tennis season in his junior year, he was certain that he would come into form by the time of the state open tournament. With an early round loss, he was almost inconsolable. He realized that he had been coasting, and that a single-minded commitment to tennis would be necessary to return to championship form.

reach goals, and they also demonstrate a greater intensification of effort to reach goals after learning that they have fallen short of standards (Bandura & Cervone, 1986). Negative emotions motivate not only efforts to reach goals but also reconsiderations of strategies for goal attainment and goal reprioritization.

Intercollegiate athletes were shown to set goals for performances in track and field events at levels higher than their best previous performances. They almost always "raised the bar" in this fashion as prior to 98 percent of individual events in track and field competitions, athletes set goals that were above their best previous performances during the season. Athletes adjusted goal difficulty and set proximate goals that were reasonably above their current levels of performance. Goals that were too difficult were adjusted downward, and when goal realization was at hand, goal difficulty was increased. If athletes concluded that they could not control the factors related to the realization of their goals, goal difficulty was adjusted downward. If they believed that they controlled the factors that determined the realization of goals, they set goals at higher levels and were more persistent in attempting to reach these goals (Williams, Donovan, & Dodge, 2000).

Iatrogenic Effects of Goals

There are **iatrogenic** or negative effects of working to achieve goals. People that are unable to relinquish goals that are unattainable are likely to experience depression. An additional iatrogenic effect occurs when goals are conceptualized in an all-or-none fashion such that if goals or subgoals are not met, the goal is renounced. Goals are more likely to be conceptualized in an all-or-none manner when they refer to behaviors that people are trying to avoid instead of behaviors to be increased. Often, "slips" in these **inhibitional goals** of abstaining from certain behaviors are seen as losses because the goal requires perfection or total abstinence.

An example of an inhibitional goal is to keep the daily consumption of calories beneath a certain limit. Exceeding the calorie limit may be perceived as a failure and a loss of the daily subgoal, and the person may subsequently greatly exceed their daily calorie limit and demonstrate the "What the hell effect" (Cochran & Tesser, 1996, p. 101). The "what the hell effect" or the renunciation of goals appears to be the result of monitoring inhibitional behavior with proximal subgoals. Applying these findings to the problem of weight loss, the maintenance of optimal health and weight is more likely if inhibitional goals such as calorie limits are combined with positive goals such as frequent or daily exercise.

Goals that call for positive action or increased behavior to reach a standard allow for the perception of incremental advancement toward the standard. Goals that simply refer to avoiding behavior are more likely to promote all-or-none thinking because lapses are readily equated as a loss of the goal or the subgoal. Failure to make progress toward a goal that one wishes to achieve is less likely to be perceived as such a loss because the person has not yet achieved the goal and so cannot lose it.

Acquisitional or positive goals direct attention toward the correct actions for goal realization. Inhibitional goals direct focus to behaviors to be decreased and to one's errors. Focusing on the negative aspects of one's behavior increases anxiety and leads to avoidance of feedback or of monitoring progress toward goals. As feedback is avoided, behavior becomes less regulated by goals, and self-confidence and self-efficacy are eroded. Focusing on behaviors to be avoided can also foster negative emotions and cognitive interference, and these reactions compete with attention to the tasks necessary to accomplish goals (Cervone & Wood, 1995).

An excessive focus on inhibiting behavior can also produce a rebound effect and actually result in a greater production of the behavior that was to be inhibited. For example, numerous studies have demonstrated that when people try to suppress a certain thought, they cannot get that thought out of their mind (e.g. avoid thinking of a pink elephant; see Wegner, 1994).

In short, frequent monitoring of progress toward inhibitional subgoals has the opposite effect of frequent monitoring of progress toward acquisitional goals. It erodes confidence and performance because the feedback often reflects failure. Goals should be framed in terms of what to do, not what not to do.

Recommendations for a Goal-setting Process in Sport

A comprehensive goal-setting process involving seven steps has been recommended for sportspersons (Burton, Naylor, & Holliday, 2001).

1 Establish a hierarchy of long-term and short-term goals. There should be goals for practice and competition.
2 Enhance commitment to reaching goals. Commitment is enhanced when athletes collaborate with others such as coaches in setting goals, when goals are self-set, when there are external rewards such as championships, and when reaching goals is supported by others. Writing down and publicly posting goals also enhance commitment.
3 Evaluate barriers to goal attainment. Barriers may involve conditions that are internal to athletes such as inadequate knowledge, skill, and conditioning, and external factors such as family commitments.
4 Construct a plan of action to reach goals.
5 Monitor feedback about progress toward goals.
6 Evaluate goal attainment. This is considered crucial in sustaining motivation and confidence to reach goals; the topic of why goals are motivating was discussed earlier in this chapter.
7 Reinforce goal attainments. As mentioned above, with short-term and proximate goals, there are abundant opportunities for feedback and rewards *en route* to the attainment of long-term and distal goals.

Athletes are also more likely to set effective goals when they establish **SMARTS goals** (Smith, 1994):

- **S**pecific, precise performance standards
- **M**easurable or quantifiable standards
- **A**ction-oriented goals that indicate what is to be done, as opposed to inhibitional goals
- **R**ealistic or reachable goals as opposed to impossibly difficult goals
- **T**imely goals, achievable in a reasonable period of time
- **S**elf-determined or established by the participant or with input from the participant.

Summary and Conclusions

People become more productive when they establish goals. The most effective goals establish not only what is to be accomplished but also when the task should be completed. In athletic and other venues, goals serve to direct attention toward standards. Goals sustain the behavior and effort necessary to reach standards, and provide feedback about progress. With this feedback, athletes can more readily recognize when techniques and strategies must be altered or improved if goals are to be accomplished.

Goals identify what current behaviors are necessary to reach standards that are either proximal or distal. Difficult and specific goals direct and require effort for their realization, but they have this effect only when people accept assigned goals or establish them themselves and when they have the requisite skill to reach the difficult goals.

Goals that are self-selected or to which there is a high degree of commitment, and that represent highly important accomplishment, are more likely to motivate higher performance in sporting venues. If coaches or other mentors assign goals, commitment can be enhanced if athletes cooperate in the goal-setting process.

Not surprisingly, people with high self-efficacy (belief in their capacity to reach goals) establish more challenging goals for themselves. However, even those with unshakable self-efficacy are ill advised to underestimate the effort and resources necessary to reach difficult goals.

Goals are often organized in hierarchies of long- and short-term goals. Long-term goals provide coherent structures for activities and, in the most general sense, can provide a sense of purpose in life. However, distal or long-term goals provide little information about whether current efforts are likely to be sufficient to reach them. It is difficult to gauge progress toward distal goals, whereas proximal goals allow for a steady stream of feedback about whether current behaviors are successful in reaching short-term standards.

By setting proximal and distal goals, people create a state of internal disequilibrium because one's current state is beneath the proximal or distant standard for satisfactory attainment. Dissatisfaction drives people to reach their goals, and goals that are just beyond one's reach are most motivating. The pursuit of goals is not accompanied by unremitting negative emotion, as positive emotions are experienced if progress toward goal attainment is satisfactory. However, as the trajectory of movement toward goal attainment flattens and reverses, the emotional experience becomes increasingly unpleasant.

The body of information about goals has practical applications in sport settings. A process of seven stages has been recommended. It is important for sportspersons not only to establish goals, but to nest short-term goals in hierarchies, identify action necessary to realize goals, remove barriers to goal attainment, and continually monitor progress toward goals.

Key Terms

Goal dimensions: content,
intensity, commitment

Difficult goals

Goals and self-efficacy

Goals and self-esteem

Goal specificity

Goal commitment

Subgoals

Goals and feedback

Proximal goals

Distal goals

Goal incentives

Goal hierarchies

Abstract goals

Disequilibrium

Inhibitional goals

SMARTS goals

Suggested Readings

Burton, D., Naylor, S., & Holliday, B. (2001). Goal setting in sport: Investigating the goal effectiveness paradox. In R. N. Singer, H. A. Hausenblas, & C. M. Janelle (Eds.), *Handbook of sport psychology* (2nd ed., pp. 497–528). New York: Wiley.

Carver, C. S., Lawrence, J. W., & Scheier, M. F. (1996). A control-process perspective on the origins of affect. In L. M. Martin, & A. Tesser (Eds.), *Striving and feeling: Interactions among goals, affect, and self-regulation* (pp. 11–52). Mahwah, NJ: Lawrence Erlbaum Associates, Inc.

Gould, D. (2006). Goal setting for peak performance. In J. M. Williams (Ed.), *Applied sport psychology: Personal growth to peak performance* (5th ed., pp. 240–259). New York: McGraw-Hill.

Heath, C., Larrick, R. P., & Wu, G. (1999). Goals as reference points. *Cognitive Psychology, 38,* 79–109.

Locke, E. A. (1996). Motivation through conscious goal setting. *Applied and Preventive Psychology, 5,* 117–124.

Weinberg, R. S., Burton, D., Yukelson, D., & Weigand, D. (2000). Perceived goal setting practices of Olympic athletes: An exploratory investigation. *The Sport Psychologist, 14,* 279–295.

Zimmerman, B. J. (2000). Attaining self-regulation: A social cognitive perspective. In M. Boekaerts, P. Pintich, & M. Seidner (Eds.), *Self-regulation: Theory, research and application* (pp. 13–39). Orlando, FL: Academic Press.

Goal Orientation and Self-Regulation

8

Michelle Kwan won her eighth national title at the US Figure Skating Championships in January 2004. She trailed Sasha Cohen after the short program and commented: "Titles are just titles, I gain so much more from skating than just medals."

Sasha Cohen rarely looks at hers. "My medals are in a shoebox in my garage," said Cohen. "Each year, I'm learning a little bit more about what Michelle has learned over her career. It becomes less and less about winning titles and medals. It becomes more about finishing and skating through a program. It's the feeling you have after you've accomplished something and knowing that after the days and days of hard work, you just skate the way you've always imagined." (Hine, 2004a, p. C2)

In the mid-to-late 1970s, it became increasingly clear to psychologists at the University of Illinois that people differed in terms of **goal orientation** or the types of goals they pursued (Roberts, 2001). The conceptualizations of Carol Dweck and John Nicholls have been particularly influential in explaining why people strive for achievement in areas such as athletics and academics (Elliot, 2005). Nicholls' formulation has been most influential in athletic settings. A basic distinction in both conceptualizations is whether competence is *defined* in relation to self-referenced versus external standards. Learning goals (Dweck) and task orientations (Nicholls) orient individuals to self-referenced progress, intrinsic interest in tasks, and a range of positive outcomes. Performance goals (Dweck) and ego orientations (Nicholls) measure performance normatively or in relation to others. Normatively referenced goals lead to a range of negative outcomes, especially when people judge their ability to be inferior to that of competitors.

The models of goal orientations from these and other research traditions will be examined and compared in this chapter. Comparisons of such models are controversial, and the foremost experts disagree about their similarities and differences (Duda, 1997; Duda & Hall, 2001; Hardy, 1997; Treasure, Duda, Hall, Roberts, Ames, & Maehr, 2001). Although readers are advised to regard these comparisons with caution, they help to organize information from the different models.

Task and Ego Orientations

Task orientations focus on self-referenced mastery or improvement in relation to one's personal standards. With task orientations, success is perceived when learning, improvement, and mastery are achieved (Williams, 1994). Athletes with **ego orientations** are concerned with gaining favorable judgments from others and compare their performance to that of competitors (Nicholls, 1989). With ego orientations, ability is perceived when performance exceeds that of others, especially when less effort is exerted. Task and ego orientations do not simply influence how progress and success are measured in discrete settings or situations. For example, adolescents who endorsed task or ego orientations in athletic venues were more likely to measure their school progress with the same orientation (Duda & Nicholls, 1992).

Athletes with ego orientations are vulnerable to cognitive and somatic anxiety before and during performances if they rate their ability as inferior to that of competitors. With ego orientations and low estimates of abilities, people are more likely to drop out of competitions or performances, rate evaluations or competitions as unimportant, and set standards for their performance that are unrealistically high or very low. By setting extremely high or low standards, performers essentially avoid or escape comparing their performance to others, as neither provides a fair comparison of performance.

Ego orientations are also associated with pressure from parents and coaches to reach exacting goals, and with concern over making mistakes. With task orientations, sportspersons may set exacting goals, but these goals conform to the athlete's own standards (Dunn, Dunn, & Syrotuik, 2002).

People with ego orientations are also more likely to view ability as a fixed, innate quality, so that a failure at any point in time signals a future of failures. However, if sportspersons withhold effort and do not try to do their best during competitions and evaluations, failure is less diagnostic of inadequate ability and can be attributed to a lack of effort. Failure is most threatening to those with ego orientations when they put forth maximum effort because it can then be attributed only to insufficient ability (Duda & Hall, 2001). With ego orientations and performance referenced in relation to others, failure is more threatening because it threatens self-esteem (Dweck & Leggett, 1988). As described in Chapter 9, self-esteem and competence are abstract goals and likely to occupy higher-order positions in goal hierarchies. Threats to higher-order goals evoke powerful, negative emotional reactions.

Athletes who adopt task orientations have less vulnerability to cognitive and somatic anxiety. They have more control over the factors that lead to success and failure, whereas with performance orientations, sportspersons have little control over the performance of others. Control over the standards of success and failure also contributes to heightened intrinsic interest in sport (Duda & Hall, 2001).

Junior fencers of approximately 13 years of age with task orientations were shown to be more confident and reported less somatic anxiety prior to competitions regardless of whether they perceived themselves to be talented fencers (Hall & Kerr, 1997). Young fencers, high school varsity athletes, intercollegiate athletes, and college-age recreational athletes (White & Zellner, 1996) with ego orientations were more likely to experience cognitive anxiety prior to and during competitions.

Ego orientations are particularly problematic for athletes when they perceive their talent to be inadequate to win. In these competitions they are more likely to experience cognitive interference, to be less flexible in selecting strategies during the course of a performance, and to wish to escape or withdraw from competition. For example, British club snooker and tennis players who were an average of 30.4 years of age with ego orientations wanted to escape competition when they thought they were unskilled in comparison to opponents. Adult club athletes with task orientations recorded little cognitive interference during competition and few wishes to avoid competition (Hatzigeorgiadis & Biddle, 1999). The performance of athletes with ego orientations was considered to be more "fragile" or dependent on confidence that their ability was superior to that of competitors.

Young sport participants of approximately 11.5 years of age were more likely to perceive sports as a means of enhancing self-esteem, developing good citizenship, developing increased skill and cooperation, and being physically active when they endorsed task goals (White, Duda, & Keller, 1998). Adolescent female soccer players in Norway were more likely to emphasize companionship, loyalty, and constructive relationships with friends on their team when they also endorsed task orientations (Ommundsen, Roberts, Lemyre, & Miller, 2005). With high task orientations and low ego orientations, Norwegian adolescent soccer players were more likely to endorse aspects of sportspersonship such as respect for social conventions, rules and officials, and opponents, and to make a full

> ## Joe Torre's* Take on Success
>
> "... in my book, success and winning are not always one and the same ... To me, success is playing – or working – to the best of your ability. And winning is a by-product of living up to your highest standards for yourself, getting the most out of your natural talents, reaching down and rooting out your own drive, courage, and commitment. In other words, if you succeed in realizing your own abilities, the chances that you'll be a winner in objective terms – with all the rewards – are maximized" (Torre & Dreher, 1999, p. 7).
>
> * Manager of four New York Yankees World Series Championship Teams.

commitment to their sport. Soccer players with high ego orientations and high perceived soccer ability endorsed one aspect of sportspersonship, respect for rules and officials (Lemyre, Roberts, & Ommundsen, 2002). Task orientations have also been associated with good sportspersonship, greater respect for social conventions in hockey, and greater respect for the rules and officials (Dunn & Dunn, 1999) among elite male hockey players of approximately 13 years of age in Canada. Young hockey players with ego orientations were more comfortable with aggressive play. Similarly, high school basketball players with ego orientations were more likely to endorse the use of aggression and unsporting behaviors in games (Duda, Olson, & Templin, 1991). Male high school basketball players were more likely than females to demonstrate ego orientations.

Measurement of Goal Orientations

The most extensively employed questionnaires for assessing goal orientations are the **Task and Ego Orientation in Sport Questionnaire (TEOSQ**; Chi & Duda, 1995; Duda, 1989b; Duda & Nicholls, 1992) and Perceptions of Success Questionnaire (POSQ; Roberts, Treasure, & Balaguer, 1998). Both assess task and ego orientations, as does the Goal Orientation in Exercise Scale, a questionnaire recently developed for measuring goal orientation in exercise venues (Kilpatrick, Bartholomew, & Riemer, 2003). Clearly defined cutting points or scores for identifying individual task and ego orientations have not been established with the TEOSQ and POSQ (Harwood, 2002; Lemyre, Roberts, & Ommundsen, 2002). Further, although goal orientations have been shown to be stable (Treasure & Roberts, 1998), they are still influenced by situational pressure, such that in actual competition, elite sportspersons are likely to focus more on ego and less on task orientations (Harwood, 2002). A measure of clinical judgment is therefore necessary in assessing goal orientations among individual athletes (Harwood, 2002).

Task and Ego Orientations and Motivational Climates

Goal orientations of young athletes correspond with their perceptions of the goal orientations of their parents (Escarti, Roberts, Cervello, & Guzman, 1999). Peers also influence goal orientations, especially during adolescence (Carr & Weigand, 2002). Parents and other important adults create **motivational climates** that encourage the development of task and ego orientations. For example, child athletes with task orientations are more likely to play for coaches who emphasize mastery of skills and the enjoyment of sport. Elite adolescent athletes who trained in climates encouraging task orientations experienced less performance anxiety and greater satisfaction about being members of their teams. In environments that encourage task orientations, young athletes indicate that effort is the primary cause of success. In motivational climates that prompt ego orientations, young athletes rate normative ability and deception as the most important causes of success (Treasure & Roberts, 1998).

Task-involving team environments also promote satisfaction with personal and team improvement and results and with coaches. For example, elite Spanish handball players between the ages of 17 and 34 were more satisfied with their individual and team improvement and with their coaches when these coaches created motivation climates that encouraged task orientations (Balaguer, Duda, Atienza, & Mayo, 2002). In

Motivational climates, goal orientations, and fun.

motivational climates that are more task-involving and less ego-involving, elite Spanish handball and tennis players were more likely to view coaches as closer to their "ideal" coach, or someone who was helping them to improve and do their best (Balaguer, Duda, & Crespo, 1999). Experienced Catalan (Spain) soccer players between the ages of 10 and 14 were satisfied with their soccer experience and referenced internal standards to evaluate their ability when motivational climates were task-involving (Boixados, Cruz, Torregrosa, Valiente, 2005). Further, task-involving motivational climates were more likely to promote cohesion on elite French female basketball and handball teams (Heuze, Sarrazin, Masiero, Raimbault, & Thomas, 2006), and constructive relationships among adolescent female adolescents on Norwegian soccer squads (Ommundsen et al., 2005).

Ego-involving team environments prompt sportspersons to consider unproductive strategies for enhancing skills such as the avoidance of practice, and with ego orientations and low perceptions of ability, young sportspersons avoid objective feedback about their progress (Duda & Hall, 2001). Adolescents in ego-involving climates were more likely to acknowledge anxiety about the adequacy of performances and less contentment with team membership (Walling, Duda, & Chi, 1993). Adolescents are more likely to drop out of sports when the motivational climates are highly ego-involving and when they judge their athletic ability to be low (Duda & Hall, 2001).

Sportspersonship and moral behaviors such as considering the impact of one's behavior on others are influenced by motivational climates. Norwegian collegiate athletes who perceived the environment of their teams to be highly ego-involving were less likely to view athletic participation as a means for the development of social responsibility and skills for use throughout their lifetimes (Ommundsen & Roberts, 1999). Experienced Norwegian male soccer players between the ages of 12 and 14 with coaches who emphasized performance-oriented goals were likely to

---

Dirtiest Teams at the 2006 World Cup

The British office of Information Builders created the Foul Play Index (FPI) as a measure of the dirtiest teams in the 2006 World Cup soccer tournament. Teams were assigned points for dirty play for yellow (major foul) and red (expulsion) cards, dives (exaggerating contact from another player in an effort to be granted a free kick or penalty kick), faked injuries, tantrums, and bullying referees. Prior to the final, Paraguay led the tournament with an FPI of 45, followed by Italy (40), the Netherlands, Ivory Coast, and Portugal (37) (Ranking the Dirtiest Teams, 2006).

Poor sportspersonship (photo © Matthew Jacques).

use whatever means were necessary to pursue victory, including aggressive and cheating behaviors (Ommundsen, Roberts, Lemyre, & Treasure, 2003). Youthful soccer players who played for coaches who nurtured mastery climates demonstrated respect for game rules and officials and opponent players. Similarly, experienced Catalan male soccer players between the ages of 10 and 14 who played on teams that emphasized ego-involving and de-emphasized task-involving motivational climates were more likely to endorse rough play and cheating (Boixados et al., 2005).

Motivational climates, along with task or ego orientations, contribute to intrinsic interest in sport. Climates that encourage task orientations foster intrinsic interest in sport. Perhaps these climates provide opportunities for experiencing competence, self-determination, and relatedness to others – characteristics that are considered primary motives for investment in sport (Duda & Hall, 2001). Climates that emphasize mastery and task-involvement also teach metacognitive strategies, which provide individuals with cognitive frameworks or models for evaluating current skills and for future self-regulated learning. People with metacognitive learning strategies have "learned how to learn." Examples of metacognitive strategies in evidence among adolescent physical education students include procedural knowledge (knowing how to sequence motor skills), self-monitoring (determining whether a skill was performed precisely), and debugging (identifying and correcting mistakes). Students with internalized task orientations also demonstrate these metacognitive cognitive processes (Theodosiou & Papaioannou, 2006), and both task orientations and task-involving climates predispose physical education students to engage in sport and exercise in out-of-school settings (Papaioannou, March, & Theodorakis, 2004).

Goal orientations become more internalized and entrenched or fixed with experience, and therefore the influence of internal goal dispositions is less for children than for adults. However, by adolescence, internal goal orientations are stable internal characteristics, and both goal orientations and motivational climates influence the beliefs of adolescents about what leads to athletic success and failure. For example, the perceptions of female basketball players of approximately 14 years of age about the motivational climates of summer basketball camps as well as their goal orientations influenced their beliefs about the causes of success and failure (Treasure & Roberts, 1998). Task orientation was the most important factor in determining efforts for mastery in comparison to one's own baseline, and the influence of this internal disposition was augmented when the basketball players thought that coaches created mastery environments. The striving for social approval of adolescents with ego orientations was decreased by motivational climates that encouraged mastery. However, it appears that motivational environments must be salient or highly noticeable if they are to influence the beliefs of adolescents about the causes of success and failure. Coaches and other influential adults and adolescents who consistently emphasize mastery criteria as standards of success create salient environments.

Motivational climates are subject to change. The motivational climates of adolescent, elite tennis players in England were influenced by interventions with the players and their coaches and parents (Harwood & Swain, 2002). This intervention encouraged self-directed goals consisting of demonstrating improvement in relation to the adolescents' baselines of prior tennis skills, as well as goals to prevail in individual matches. Intervention also de-emphasized attention to gaining social approval and encouraged self-efficacy.

Simultaneous Task and Ego Orientations

Sportspersons may approach competitions and practice with multiple goal orientations. That is, sportspersons with high, moderate, or low task orientations may have high, moderate, or low ego orientations, and vice versa.

Optimal performance may result from the endorsement of moderate to high levels of task and ego orientations (Barron & Harackiewicz, 2001; Horn, Duda, & Miller, 1993). Athletes who finished in the top 10 in major track and field championships were driven by both task (e.g. producing a perfect performance) and ego (beating opponents) goals (Mallett & Hanrahan, 2004), as were the most mentally tough English cricketers during the 1980s and 1990s (Bull, Shambrook, James, & Brooks, 2005). The negative effects of high ego orientations may be buffered by concurrent high task orientations (Hodge & Petlichkoff, 2000).

Situational pressure or demands for competent performance may also determine how influential a goal orientation is during a particular competition or at specific times in a competition (Harwood, Hardy, & Swain, 2000; Harwood & Swain, 2002). With both task and ego goals, athletes may also default to task goals when they perform poorly in relation to competitors (Duda, 2001). When people respond to situational pressure by attending to outside factors such as the behavior of competitors or to audiences, "choking under pressure" or performance inhibition is more likely. Choking under pressure will be discussed in detail in Chapter 10.

Goal orientations also influence the mental imagery of athletes. The imagery of competitive, adolescent Canadian swimmers corresponded somewhat to their goal orientations, as swimmers with moderate-task/ high-ego orientations focused more of their mental resources on imagining themselves besting others (Cumming, Hall, Harwood, & Gammage, 2002). Elite, adolescent British athletes in a broad range of sports who maintained high-task/high-ego goal orientations were more likely to use imagery than counterparts with combinations of moderate and low task and ego goal profiles (Harwood, Cumming, & Hall, 2003). Elite, British adolescent athletes with higher-task/moderate-ego goal orientations also use more imagery and self-talk than counterparts with lower-task/higher-ego and moderate-task/lower-ego goal orientations. With higher-task/moderate-ego goal orientations the adolescent athletes engaged in more goal-setting in practice and competition than counterparts with lower-task/higher-ego profiles and more goal setting in competition than counterparts with moderate-task/lower-ego profiles (Harwood, Cumming, & Fletcher, 2004).

Mastery, Performance-Approach Goals, Performance-Avoidance Goals

To this point, goal orientations have been distinguished on the basis of how competence is defined; self- or other-referenced. Goals may also have different underlying motives or different *valences*. As discussed in Chapter 2, the underlying motive for **performance-avoidance goals** is the fear of failure. With performance-avoidance goals, people are likely to become anxious and self-conscious, and to question their competence in the face of difficult tasks (Cury, Da Fonseca, Rufo, Peres, & Sarrazin, 2003; Cury, Elliot, Sarrazin, Da Fonseca, & Rufo, 2002; Elliot & Harackiewicz, 1996; Elliot & Sheldon, 1997). Not surprisingly, performance-avoidance goals have an inimical effect on wellbeing and performance in the classroom and in sport contexts (Conroy & Elliot, 2004; Conroy, Elliot, & Hofer, 2003; Duda & Hall, 2001).

The underlying motives for **performance-approach goals** are the fear of failure and achievement motivation, or the concurrent motives to demonstrate performance superior to others and to avoid failure. Performance-approach goals are associated with high achievement (Elliot & Harackiewicz, 1996). Indeed, students with performance-approach goals are more likely to achieve higher grades than those motivated solely by achievement motivation and **mastery goals**, perhaps because those with mastery goals pursue topics that relate more directly to their intrinsic interests rather than studying information that is likely to appear on tests. Mastery goals have been seen as similar to learning goals and task orientations, and performance goals as similar to ego orientations (Ames & Archer, 1987, 1988; Duda, 2005; Elliot, 2005).

Norwegian Olympic-level athletes who acknowledged fear of failure were more likely to endorse performance-avoidance goals (Halvari & Kjormo, 1999). When performance-avoidance goals were fostered, adolescent French physical education students experienced heightened anxiety prior to an evaluation of their competence at dribbling a basketball, and indicated that their performance was of less importance (Cury et al., 2002, 2003). This anxiety and discounting of the importance of the dribbling evaluation probably interfered with their preparation, as they spent less time practicing. With mastery and performance-approach goals, the physical education students did not experience this anxiety, discounting of task importance, and avoidance of practice.

As discussed in Chapter 11, people who expect to perform poorly sometimes engage in self-handicapping, such as the avoidance of practice. Handicaps provide explanations for failure and poor performances other than a lack of ability.

Outcome, Performance, and Process Goals

Another convention in athletic settings is to categorize goals into **outcome, performance, and process** types. The focus of outcome goals is the results of a performance and is usually based on social comparisons such as to beat others in a competition. Performance goals refer to an end product of a performance, but the end product is a self-referenced standard. For example, a swimmer might try to swim seconds faster than her personal best time. Process goals refer to the actions necessary to reach an outcome.

British competitive swimmers between the ages of 14 and 28 have been shown to rarely endorse outcome goals (Jones and Hanton, 1996), such as winning a race or beating opponents. Goals of this sort are more likely to engender debilitative, cognitive anxiety because one is not able to control the performance of competitors. Most of the swimmers choose a combination of goals that include performance (complete a race under a certain time) and process (attention to the technical elements of the swim) goals (24 percent) or outcome, performance, and process goals (49 percent). Perhaps the goal orientations of these competitive swimmers were shaped by experience and mentoring from coaches. For example, high school coaches have been shown to use all three types of goals, and to focus on performance and process goals, especially when setting individual goals for athletes (Weinberg, Butt, & Knight, 2001). In addition, swimmers with less adaptive goal orientations, such as outcome goals, may not have reached the competitive level of the swimmers in this sample.

The advantages of multiple goal orientations were also demonstrated with British college students who were studying for sport related degrees (Filby, Maynard, & Graydon, 1999). Students with multiple goal strategies were more accurate in kicking soccer balls both during practice and competition. Students with multiple goals prioritized process goals (proper techniques for ball striking) immediately prior to practice. Outcome goals or the awareness that they would be competing against others may have inspired additional effort during practice. Students with only process goals did no better than students with no goals. Perhaps goals that focused simply on the proper techniques for ball striking did not motivate students to exert sufficient effort to practice and execute optimally. Students with only outcome goals were significantly less accurate in their ball striking during competition than the students with no goals, probably because the diversion of attention to the performance of competitors resulted in debilitative anxiety.

The adaptability of multiple goal orientations has been demonstrated in other sporting contexts. For example, young athletes in a variety of sports with both mastery and competitive goal orientations were more skilled at their sport and found it to be more enjoyable than athletes with just one of these goals (Fox, Goudas, Biddle, Duda, & Armstrong, 1994; Horn et al., 1993). Mastery goals are similar to task orientations and competitive goals are similar to ego orientations. Athletes with multiple goal orientations also show greater persistence in the pursuit of their sporting interests. With both mastery and competitive goals, amateur athletes participated in their sport for greater numbers of years (Duda, 1988, 1989a).

College students in introductory golf classes put in more practice and enjoyed golf more when assigned mastery and competitive goals. They practiced almost twice as much as students with just mastery or competitive goals, and their performance also showed the most improvement (Steinberg, Singer, & Murphey, 2000).

Outcome, Performance, and Process Goals and Proximity to Competition

Various combinations of performance goals have been recommended at times distal and proximal to performances. Athletes have been encouraged to make explicit outcome goals several weeks prior to competitions. Public commitments, such as to win a competition, have been seen to motivate greater efforts to prepare for competitions and for the development of sophisticated strategies for competition. Athletic performance and process goals are recommended to support practice and training for competitions. Athletic performance goals have been shown to support self-confidence and self-efficacy, as athletes record progress in relation to their baseline of prior performance. Process goals are effective in directing attention to instrumental behaviors necessary for good performances. Athletes have been advised to focus on outcome and performance goals immediately prior to competition, and to attend to process goals during competition. These process goals should include holistic aspects of techniques such that the automatic execution of skills is not disrupted (Hardy, Jones, & Gould, 1996). Motor skills achieve automaticity when they are capable of being executed without conscious attention to the motor elements that compose the overall motor skill.

Shaq and Process Goals

Perennial All-Star, three-time NBA Champion, and future NBA Hall of Fame basketball player Shaquille O'Neal was shooting 38 percent from the free throw line in the playoffs of the NBA (National Basketball Association). His coach, Phil Jackson, gave him an article written by an 80-year-old man who made more than 3,000 straight free throws. Following the advice of the octogenarian, O'Neal hit nine of 11 free throws in his next game against the Minnesota Timberwolves.

    "I've just really been focusing on my routine," O'Neal said. "The article said that if you focus too much on the result, you fail" (Shaq, Lakers Play It Cool, 2004).

The influence of performance and process goals was studied with British male amateur golfers across a duration of 54 weeks. Golfers who set either performance or process goals showed more improvement across the 54 weeks (as measured by handicap) and less anxiety than golfers who did not set goals (Kingston & Hardy, 1997). Golfers who were guided by process goals had the additional advantages of gaining in self-efficacy and concentration during golf rounds. Complex tasks such as golf involve the development of many different skills and strategies, and process goals guide attention to the development of these facets. As mentioned above, process goals do not necessarily disrupt the automaticity of over-learned actions, such as a golf swing, because attention may be given to key global components rather than the swing's minor elements.

Kitsantas and Zimmerman (1998) reported that process goals were particularly influential in the successful acquisition of novel motor skills such as throwing darts. They reported that process goals directed the attention of female high school students to the elements of the skill that is to be mastered, and skill acquisition is enhanced further if athletes self-monitor or record their progress in skill acquisition.

This self-monitoring consists of keeping a record of the motor skills that produced good results and the motor actions that resulted in faulty performance and were in need of adjustment. Therefore, effective process goals direct attention to what actions need to be continued, changed, adjusted or tweaked to produce optimal results.

The process of self-monitoring served to sustain the students' self-efficacy because it directed their attention to the contributions of improper technique and practice to poor performance (Kitsantas & Zimmerman, 1998). They were therefore less likely to attribute poor performance to a lack of ability. The maintenance of self-efficacy was important because higher self-efficacy was associated with better subsequent performance at dart throwing. The students who self-monitored were also more satisfied with their efforts and results, and self-satisfaction led to greater interest in improving their performance at dart throwing. Performance on athletic tasks may be enhanced further if athletes shift to performance goals or a combination of performance and process goals after automaticity for the motor task has been obtained.

Goals and Proximity to Competition

Less than 24 hours after losing in the second round of the state soccer championship, Tommy was in his backyard working on his skills. It was not too soon to prepare to make good on his promise, "next year we'll win the state." Mindful of this goal and the formidability of his rivals, he left nothing to chance in refining techniques, and building anaerobic power and aerobic fitness. Although he was shy by nature, soon everyone knew that this training was directed by the goal of a championship.

Tommy realized that he would not make good on this pledge if he did not improve his striking capacity with his head and left foot. His technique was adequate but his skills did not have automaticity. He visualized proper techniques and used cue words to direct the execution of skills. When heading he repeated, "Just nod – eyes open," and when striking with his left foot he said, "Toe – head down." Skills became more automatic, but he found this self-talk helped him concentrate, so he continued with it throughout the season.

Preparing for games in the season, Tommy collaborated with coaches and teammates to develop their game plans and exploit the vulnerabilities of opposing teams. Once games began, he tried to ignore the intentions of opponents and focus on what his team intended to accomplish.

Performance-Oriented, Success-Oriented, and Failure-Oriented Goals

Still another way of categorizing goals in athletic settings is to define performance-oriented, success-oriented, and failure-oriented goals (Burton, 2002). With **performance-oriented goals**, athletes focus on learning, mastery, and improvement, and the demonstration of competence through social comparison is a secondary concern. These goals appear similar to task orientations and process goals, because they help athletes focus on increasing skills and on problem-solving, and the process of goal attainment is emphasized rather than the results of a performance. Athletes with performance-oriented goals demonstrate persistence in the face of adversity, have less anxiety about the prospects of failure, set difficult goals, and demonstrate self-confidence. Athletes with **success-oriented goals** focus on beating competitors. Failure is more daunting because it shows that they did not reach their goal. They set only moderately difficult goals, as these are more likely to be achieved, and they are less persistent to avoid failure. With success-oriented goals, self-confidence fluctuates greatly depending on the strength of the competition. With **failure-oriented goals**, the emphasis is on avoiding failure and not demonstrating a lack of competence. This goal orientation does not protect people from failure, but it does allow them not to take responsibility for failures. This responsibility is avoided by setting unrealistically high goals, exerting limited effort during preparations and performances, and avoiding effective problem-solving.

Female gymnasts between the ages of 12 and 14 with failure-oriented goals rarely participated in gymnastic competitions during an eight-week season (Pierce & Burton, 1998). They avoided trying out for positions in competitive lineups, and their practices were devoted more to off-task behaviors than to practicing competitive routines. When involved in practice, they worked on single tricks as opposed to an integrated routine that would be displayed in competition. Gymnasts with performance-oriented goals demonstrated the greatest improvement across the course of the season. They were persistent in working toward difficult goals, whereas the success-oriented gymnasts only performed routines when their coaches watched.

Self-Regulation

Goals have been understood to compose an element of a larger process of **self-regulation** (Zimmerman, 2000). Self-regulation refers to processes by which people manage their own behavior in the absence of external controls or constraints. This self-management involves not only the identification and pursuit of goals, but also resisting temptation to engage in activities that compete with the pursuit of these goals (Kirschenbaum, 1984). Competing activities may offer rewards and gratification that are more immediate, and the pursuit of difficult and long-term goals often requires delaying gratification (Anshel, 1995).

Goals are established during a **forethought** phase of self-regulation. These goals include process and performance goals. With the development of athletic expertise, more specific performance and process goals are set. For example, expert male high school basketball players and female collegiate volleyball players (Kitsantas & Zimmerman, 2002) set more specific technique or process goals than did less skilled teammates. Expert athletes also demonstrate higher levels of intrinsic motivation and expectations for reaching higher performance standards.

In a **performance control** phase, strategies such as self-instruction, imagery, and attentional focusing are used to optimize performance. Not unexpectedly, expert athletes use these strategies more frequently and effectively. Experts self-monitor and observe their athletic responses in "real time" or in the process of athletic performances. For example, during practice, expert collegiate female volleyball players more frequently monitored process goals (the technical aspects of serves) as well as performance goals (where the serves landed; Kitsantas & Zimmerman, 2002).

The last phase of this self-regulation process is **self-reflection**. In this phase, performance is compared to goals, and adjustments necessary to direct performances nearer to goals are identified. Expert athletes are more accurate and objective in scrutinizing aspects of performances that are in need of improvement and refinement. They more readily identify techniques in need of modification, whereas less skilled sportspersons are less likely to know what to do to improve. Experts are also more adept in recognizing when they need help and coaching and in soliciting this assistance.

In addition to this model with the phases of forethought, performance control, and self-reflection, a five-stage model has been identified. The stages are problem identification, commitment, execution, environmental management, and generalization (Kirschenbaum, 1984). Consistent with the three-stage model (Zimmerman, 2000), this model emphasizes the importance of self-monitoring. Continuous and even unremitting or "obsessive-compulsive" (Kirschenbaum, 1984, p. 163) monitoring of sport performance has been associated with elite performance.

When learning new skills, improvement is most rapid when sportspersons focus on their successes and maintain positive expectations. For example, unskilled bowlers and golfers marked better scores when focusing on the positive than on the negative aspects of their form (Kirschenbaum, Ordman, Tomarken, & Holtzbauer, 1982; Johnston-O'Connor & Kirschenbaum, 1986). After skills have been mastered, negative self-monitoring – attention to areas in need of improvement – has been associated with skill enhancement.

Summary and Conclusions

There are differences between people in terms of the types of goals they pursue. An extensive research tradition has examined the effects of goals that compare behavior to self-referenced standards versus external standards or norms. Self-referenced goals have been identified as task orientations, athletic performance or process goals, and performance-oriented goals. Goals that determine success in relation to the performance of others have been defined in the same research traditions as ego orientations, outcome goals, and success-oriented or failure-oriented goals. Initially, goals that defined success in relation to others or to norms were seen to impede achievement, persistence at difficult tasks, and intrinsic interest in activities, and to result in higher levels of anxiety during performances. This finding was of course ironic, as the focus on winning in relation to others resulted in impaired performance.

Goal orientations that emphasized mastery in relation to one's own baseline were seen to encourage the development of self-esteem and good sportspersonship. This finding had direct applications, especially with young students and athletes. For example, with the understanding that parents, coaches, and adolescent peers contribute to motivation climates for athletic performance, efforts might be made to develop climates that encourage task orientations.

Subsequent studies demonstrated that goals that measured performance in relation to others did not always impede achievement. In athletic venues, high ego orientations are not iatrogenic if athletes also maintain high task orientations. Almost half (49 percent) of a sample of competitive adolescent and adult British swimmers endorsed goals of winning in relation to other swimmers, as well as goals of improving performance in relation to their baselines of prior performances, and of focusing on the process of skilled swimming. Successful athletes may learn by experience to develop combinations of goals and to avoid goals that simply focus on performance in relation to others.

Exclusive attention to winning in relation to others competes with concentration on technical skills necessary for skilled performance. This is especially true in the face of superior competition. If competitors are seen to be more formidable than oneself, anxiety increases, and attention is directed away from the technical aspects of skilled performances. However, it should be emphasized that although anxiety about the formidability of competitors may serve as an impediment during performances, it may motivate thorough preparation for performances. "Healthy respect" for opponents may motivate exhaustive practice and preparation for performances. "Healthy respect" or outcome goals facilitate preparation at times distal to competition, and performance during competition is better directed by a combination of goals that are to some degree self-referenced.

Goals have been understood to be a part of a larger process of self-regulation. Self-regulation involves at least three phases: the forethought phase; the performance control phase; and the self-reflection phase. In the forethought phase, goals are established. In the performance control phase, skills are deployed to optimize performance and athletes monitor progress toward goals. Sportspersons evaluate progress during the self-reflection phase, and identify areas in need of improvement.

Key Terms

Goal orientation

Task orientation

Ego orientation

Task and Ego Orientation in Sport
Questionnaire (TEOSQ)

Motivational climates

Performance-avoidance goals

Performance-approach goals

Mastery goals

Outcome goals

Performance goals

Process goals

Performance-oriented goals

Success-oriented goals

Failure-oriented goals

Self-regulation

Forethought

Performance control

Self-reflection

Suggested Readings

Duda, J. L. (2005). Motivation in sport: The relevance of competence and achievement goals. In A. J. Elliot & C. S. Dweck (Eds.), *Handbook of competence and motivation* (pp. 318–335), New York: Guilford.

Duda, J. L., & Hall, H. (2001). Achievement goal theory in sport: Recent extensions and future directions. In R. N. Singer, H. A. Hausenblas, & C. M. Janelle (Eds.), *Handbook of sport psychology* (2nd ed., pp. 417–443). New York: Wiley.

Filby, W. C. D., Maynard, I. W., & Graydon, J. K. (1999). The effect of multiple-goal strategies on performance outcomes in training and competition. *Journal of Applied Sport Psychology, 11*, 230–246.

Harwood, C., Hardy, L., & Swain, A. (2000). Achievement goals in sport: A critique of conceptual and measurement issues. *Journal of Sport & Exercise Psychology, 22*, 235–255.

Treasure, D. C., Duda, J. L., Hall, H. K., Roberts, G. C., Ames, C., & Maehr, M. L. (2001). Clarifying misconceptions and misrepresentations in achievement goal research in sport: A response to Harwood, Hardy, and Swain. *Journal of Sport & Exercise Psychology, 23*, 317–329.

Self-Efficacy and Sport Self-Confidence 9

Prior to becoming a leading box office attraction as a movie star and the governor of California, and after winning six Mr Olympia and three Mr Universe bodybuilding championships, Arnold Schwarzenegger described his belief that he would be the world's best bodybuilder:

> I always had a positive attitude about going to the top. Never was there even the slightest doubt in my mind that I would make it. And this helped me keep training and trying. I was determined and constant. I never wanted to pause or stop training. I trained twelve months of the year, really hard, with no letup. Most of the bodybuilders didn't do that. I sacrificed a lot of things most bodybuilders didn't want to give up. I just didn't care, I wanted to win more than anything. And whatever it took to do it, I did. (Schwarzenegger & Hall, 1977, p. 67)

Self-efficacy has been referenced in five of the seven preceding chapters. Its influence on performance begins at points distal to competition and evaluations and continues throughout competition and practice. It is a concept that is highly relevant to the topic of performance enhancement because it relates to efforts to control the circumstances and events in one's life.

In a larger sense, people influence the course of their lives by exerting control over their pursuits. With high self-efficacy, people are more likely to take action to control their environment and less likely to disengage from challenges and the stress of competition (Haney & Long, 1995). With stronger and sturdier efficacy beliefs, people tackle more difficult projects, and overwhelming evidence is necessary before they admit defeat. This belief that one has the capacity to organize and execute the actions necessary to realize attainments or goals in particular areas or domains of functioning is referred to as **self-efficacy**. The concept of self-efficacy was developed by Albert Bandura, and has influenced research not only in

Self-efficacy and striving for difficult goals (photo © Alan C. Heison).

sport psychology but also in social, clinical, industrial, and health psychology (Bandura, 1997).

Self-Efficacy and Expectations about Future Success

Self-efficacy reflects expectations about future success. It is an especially important determinant of performance when people compete in unfamiliar venues and against unfamiliar opponents. In these situations, performers are uncertain about their chances of success. Competitors are also likely to be uncertain of their chances of success when they are evenly matched. Relative physical equality is not uncommon at elite levels of athletic competition. Among elite, collegiate, and high school athletes, self-confidence distinguishes more and less successful counterparts (Covassin & Pero, 2004).

For example, the physical skills of wrestlers in overtime matches are roughly equivalent. Perceived efficacy was the sole determinant of success in wrestling matches with high school boys that extended into overtimes (Kane, Marks, Zaccaro, & Blair, 1996). As will be discussed later, an important source of self-efficacy is one's history of prior success at similar tasks. However, self-efficacy reflects more than just memories of prior won–loss records because it represents expectations about success with new and evenly matched opponents. High and sturdy efficacy sustains belief in successful outcomes when clear information about one's likelihood of success is unavailable.

The importance of self-efficacy in estimating future success was also demonstrated with female athletes learning to execute back dives (Feltz, 1982; Feltz & Mugno, 1983). During the early stages of skill development, efficacy for diving was the most important determinant of their actual performance. As skill in diving was developed, prior success at diving became a more critical determinant of additional progress. Similar results were observed with female basketball, field hockey, and soccer players from university and community teams and between the ages of 16 and 28 (Haney & Long, 1995). Self-efficacy was a stronger predictor of performance at shooting free throws and penalty shots during a first round of competition than during a second round. Success in the second round was best estimated by first round performance, as in the latter stages of skill development, actual success at diving and free throw or penalty shooting is a more accurate predictor of additional gains.

Optimistic Self-Efficacy Beliefs

Both in athletic venues and more generally, people do not always make accurate determinations of their capabilities. Inaccurate determinations occur when new tasks are undertaken and feedback about progress is not forthcoming. Self-efficacy judgments are often derived from assessments of performances on similar tasks, and of course these assessments may be faulty because of differences in the tasks, misinterpretations of the similarities of the tasks, and faulty judgment of one's success at the similar task. Underestimating efficacy results in the avoidance of activities that could lead to advancement and greater life satisfaction, whereas overestimating efficacy on tasks that involve considerable risk can easily result in loss or injury. Significant personal, scientific, and athletic advancements often involve the acceptance of risk, because they require prolonged effort for an uncertain reward. With optimistic self-efficacy beliefs, people are more willing to take these risks because they have a sturdy belief in their ability to prevail in advance of proof that they will be successful.

Optimistic assessments of efficacy can be detrimental not only when dangers are ignored, but also when the difficulty of acquiring new skills and knowledge is underestimated. As described in Chapter 4, it is adaptive to be realistic about the necessity of thorough and even exhaustive preparation for optimal performances. It is unlikely that even elite athletes can ignore the challenge of highly difficult athletic accomplishments. For example, male and female divers from the US national team were acutely aware of the difficulty of the dives in their programs. They were more cautious in their efficacy assessments prior to the execution of the more difficult dives (Slobounov, Yukelson, & O'Brien, 1997). Still, efficacy increased over the course of a program with the successful execution of difficult dives. Of course it is important to maximize efficacy from the first moment of competitions, and the strategies for optimal proximal preparation make this more likely.

During performances, self-doubt undermines the execution of the skills acquired during preparation. In extreme sports, such rock climbing without ropes, whitewater kayaking, and skiing on terrain so dangerous that "If you fall you die" (Slanger & Rudestam, 1997, p. 359), both efficacy and preparation must be very high because there is no room for error. So long as dangers and thorough preparation are not ignored, optimistic efficacy beliefs allow people to do their best with the talent and skills they possess.

Self-Efficacy and Persistence

Disappointments and setbacks often occur in the pursuit of significant accomplishments, and therefore efficacy beliefs must be sturdy so that optimism is quickly restored after discouragement. Innovative and creative artistic and scientific work is routinely received, at least initially, with disinterest or rejection, perhaps because it provides a paradigm or worldview that is unlike what exists at its time. Truly creative work is "outside the box" of conventional thinking, and therefore the self-efficacy of innovators must be especially sturdy as they must believe that not only can they reach a standard necessary for success, but they can also establish a new standard.

Efficacy beliefs can shape the course and direction of people's lives. With higher efficacy beliefs, people are more likely to consider a wider range of career options. These career options are more likely to be available to them because efficacy for academic achievement resulted in greater academic competency, and because they are more likely to persist throughout difficult education programs to realize career goals.

Higher self-efficacy leads to higher levels of motivation and effort persistence at difficult tasks and higher achievement at sports such as cricket, tennis, gymnastics, diving, and endurance exercises with adults and children (Bandura & Cervone, 1983; Bull, Shambrook, James, & Brooks, 2005; Wurtele, 1986). It sustains performance under pressure, in the face of stiff competition, adversity, and setbacks, and is particularly influential in face-to-face competition. In the vernacular of sport, participants with very high self-efficacy are said not to "have an ounce of quit" in them. Efficacy beliefs are vital not only during performances or the dem-

Self-Efficacy and Persistence

As a Black South African lawyer and political activist in the African National Congress (ANC), Nelson Mandela devoted his adult life to ending apartheid and gaining legal and political equality for Black South Africans. He was convicted of conspiracy, which was similar to treason, and for which he could have received the death penalty. He served 27 years in prison. After his release, he was awarded the Nobel Peace Prize in 1993. After helping to develop a new constitution and obtain the voting franchise for South Africans of all races, he was elected president in 1994.

Reflecting on his odyssey from a childhood in a traditional African tribe, to imprisonment, and to the presidency of South Africa, at age 76, Nelson Mandela wrote:

> I have walked that long road to freedom. I have tried not to falter; I have made missteps along the way. But I have discovered the secret that after climbing a great hill, one only finds that there are many more hills to climb. I have taken a moment here to rest, to steal a view of the glorious vista that surrounds me, to look back on the distance I have come. But I can rest only for a moment, for with freedom comes responsibilities, and I dare not linger, for my long walk is not yet ended. (Mandela, 1994, p. 544)

onstration of acquired skills, but also during the acquisition or learning of skill. Sustained effort is often necessary to master the skills and subskills necessary for successful performances.

Heightened self-efficacy is associated with improved problem-solving, heightened physical stamina, and increased pain tolerance. In the face of difficulties or obstacles, people with lower efficacy reduce their efforts and settle for mediocre results, whereas those with high efficacy intensify their efforts to reach goals. The persistence of people with high efficacy may be due to their commitment to reach goals. With higher goal commitment and higher self-efficacy, people set loftier goals for performance (Theodorakis, 1995, 1996). People with high self-efficacy do not become satisfied and quiescent upon reaching a goal, but instead set additional and higher goals.

Nelson Mandela (photo © Reuters/CORBIS).

Self-Efficacy and the Use of Skills

Efficacy beliefs are not a substitute for skill, as without the skills and training necessary for successful performance, unshakable efficacy may be little more than wishful thinking. But **self-efficacy and the use of skills** are linked in that efficacy beliefs allow people to make optimal use of their acquired skills. Skills often have to be selected, organized, and integrated in novel ways during performances, and efficacious beliefs allow for this flexibility. With heightened self-efficacy, people make optimal use of the skills they have mastered, and more quickly acquire new skills and knowledge.

With high self-efficacy, skills can be applied flexibly and in various combinations, and performance is more consistently excellent. For example, female and male divers from the US national team with higher self-efficacy were more consistent in performing key elements of dives such as the placement of feet on the board and the angle of takeoff (Slobounov et al., 1997). These elements occurred near the point of takeoff from the board. There was more flexibility and variability in the movements of the most efficacious divers prior to the point of takeoff. Variability in preparatory movements apparently offers divers ways of self-regulating performance and finding the combination of movements that leads to optimal dives.

Self-Efficacy and Anxiety

People with high self-efficacy are not easily daunted by difficult tasks and initial failures in problem solving. Perhaps this is due to their tendency to attribute initial difficulties to insufficient effort rather than to inadequate talent. Without high efficacy beliefs, the same initial difficulties prompt doubts about whether one has the skills to perform successfully. Self-doubts and concerns about the consequences of failure compete with the planning and execution of skills necessary for success at the task. When self-efficacy is low, difficult tasks are more readily seen to be threats rather than challenges, and unsuccessful performances cause demoralization that is enduring.

As will be discussed in Chapter 10, a firm belief that one has the capacity to reach standards necessary for successful performances serves as a powerful source of psychological insulation against cognitive interference and cognitive anxiety during performances. **Self-efficacy and anxiety** are linked; for example, male high school wrestlers with higher self-efficacy had less anxiety prior to matches and more positive emotions (Treasure, Monson, & Lox, 1996). The wrestlers with higher self-efficacy also had better won–loss records and scored more points during matches.

Self-Efficacy and Realistic Assessment

After he was unanimously named the Most Valuable Player in the National League in 1994, Jeff Bagwell, first baseman of the Houston Astros, commented: "I don't think I can play much better. I'm almost worried about if I can do it again" (O'Connell, 1994, p. C1). Bagwell's response demonstrated a realistic uncertainty about reaching an extremely difficult goal. He has probably maintained his self-efficacy as a baseball player, as he was a National League All-Star in 1996, 1997, and 1999. However, he was also correct in assessing the difficulty in repeating as Most Valuable Player. In 1995 he missed one month of baseball due to a broken hand, and in 1998 the National League All-Star first basemen were Mark McGwire (who of course set the then single season home run record with 70 in 1998) and Andres Galaraga.

Among male university athletes in England and Wales, expectations for winning were the most important determinants of cognitive anxiety measured 2 hours and 30 minutes before competitions (Jones, Swain, & Cale, 1991). Those who expected to win experienced less cognitive anxiety.

There is a place for self-doubt in the course of evaluations, performances, and competitions, and it is in the preparatory stage. Realistic evaluations of areas in need of improvement and strategies to counter strengths of opponents promote better preparation for performances (Bandura, 1997). Motivation might best be maintained by combining a resilient sense of efficacy with realistic appraisals of the likelihood of accomplishing difficult tasks.

Generalizability of Efficacy Beliefs

Efficacy beliefs pertain to domains of functioning such as academic or athletic aptitude. For example, efficacy for math performance predicts higher achievement in mathematics across ability levels for college students. With high efficacy for math performance, children complete more math problems correctly, and rework problems they missed. Children with higher academic self-efficacy are more conscientious and effective in completing homework assignments and in working at their classroom desks, and achieve higher grades (Pajares, 1996).

However, some people have efficacy beliefs that are quite general so that they believe they can function successfully in a wide range of domains. Sometimes these domains are only superficially dissimilar and rely on similar subskills. For example, a coach and university professor might have efficacy for her facility to provide lectures to college students and effective coaching to her soccer team. Both tasks may rely on similar subskills such as skill in public speaking and sensitivity to the reactions of others. Self-efficacy about public speaking and responding empathetically to others may further generalize to beliefs about her capacity to conduct workshops for high school coaches; hence the **generalizability of efficacy beliefs**.

Efficacy beliefs also generalize when facilities in different domains are developed contemporaneously. Continuing with the previous example, efficacy beliefs in functioning as a professor and coach could be the result of gaining competency as a graduate assistant coach and scholar during graduate school training.

Generalizability of Efficacy Beliefs

American cyclist Lance Armstrong won the Tour De France a record seven times. Four others have won the Tour five times. In October 1996 he was treated for testicular cancer that had metastasized to his lungs and brain. A testicle was removed, he received chemotherapy for 12 tumors in his lungs, and tumors were surgically removed from his brain. After he won the Tour in 1999, his oncologist Dr Craig Nichols confided that his cancer was so advanced that he estimated that Armstrong had a 3 percent chance of survival.

Armstrong's victory over cancer was so meaningful and poignant that it probably increased his already powerful and generalized self-efficacy. He led the 1999 Tour entering the ninth of 20 stages, but the ninth stage was a climb of 213.50 kilometers through the Alps. At 2,645 meters, Col du Galibier was one of three mountains in this stage, and the highest peak in the Tour. Prior to cancer, Armstrong was considered too heavy at 175 pounds to be a world-class climber. He entered the 1999 Tour at 158 pounds and was a more efficient climber. The ninth stage is considered a turning point in the Tour, and Armstrong's victory in this stage was decisive in his overall Tour win. He recounted his thoughts as he neared the finish:

> I faced forward again. Now I could see the finish line – it was all uphill the rest of the way. I drove toward the peak. Was I thinking of cancer as I rode those last few hundred yards? No. I'd be lying if I said I was. But I think that directly or indirectly, what had happened over the past two years was with me. It was stacked up and stored away, everything I'd been through, the bout with cancer, and the disbelief within the sport that I could come back. It either made me faster or them slower, I don't know which. As I continued to climb, I felt pain, but I felt exultation, too, at what I could do with my body. To race and suffer, that's hard. But it's not being laid out in a hospital bed with a catheter hanging out of your chest, platinum burning in your veins, throwing up for 24 hours straight, seven days a week. (Armstrong & Jenkins, 2000, p. 243)

The development of metastrategies also leads to the generalization of efficacy beliefs. Metastrategies are skills that can be used in a variety of situations. For example, techniques to control somatic or physiological anxiety were discussed in Chapter 6. These techniques could be practiced in a range of settings, such as prior to athletic competitions and prior to tests in school. The successful deployment of techniques to control somatic anxiety would foster a generalized belief in the controllability of anxiety (Smith, 1999). Efficacy beliefs are also generalized from experiences in which fears are mastered. For example, upon the mastery of snake phobias, people were emboldened to tackle other fears such as fear of public speaking (Bandura, Jeffery, & Gajdos, 1975).

Highly salient or meaningful mastery experiences are more likely to result in heightened general or widespread self-efficacy. For example, women who obtain training in self-defense are likely to view personal safety as an important issue. The amelioration of this vulnerability was shown to have more general effects among college women who were taught methods of physical self-defense (Weitlauf, Cervone, Smith, & Wright, 2001; Weitlauf, Smith, & Cervone, 2000). This training included

the use of verbal resistance and persuasion, and physical resistance. The physical resistance techniques were based on the Japanese martial arts of Shotokan karate and aikido. With these techniques, women were trained to free themselves from assailants and to disable opponents with punches and kicks to vulnerable areas of the body. These women gained self-efficacy not only in the domain of self-defense, but also for their capacity to master other physical skills and demands, and most generally for their ability to master challenges in areas of life not related to physical functioning. They appeared to have gained confidence in their capacities to channel anger and aggression in adaptive ways.

Enactive experience and self-efficiency (photo © Marc Pagani Photography).

Self-Efficacy versus Self-Esteem

Self-efficacy is not synonymous with **self-esteem**. Self-esteem refers to self-worth or how people value themselves; self-efficacy relates to convictions that one can initiate and sustain sufficiently skilled actions to realize a range of goals in domains of functioning. High self-esteem may be unrelated to high achievement because this self-esteem may be dependent on sources other than high achievement and people may be satisfied with low levels of achievement. For example, the high self-esteem of college students was unrelated to setting goals for high grades in college courses and to the realization of high grades in college courses (Mone, Baker, & Jeffries, 1995).

Conversely, high achievement does not inevitably lead to high self-esteem. This is because self-worth may be dependent on realizing standards that are impossibly high and that have been internalized in the context of important relationships, such as the relationship between a child and his or her parents. The internalization of impossibly high standards has been associated with relationships with parents who almost chronically reflect a degree of disappointment in their children and who do not set clear and attainable standards for their children. With lofty and "fuzzy" internal standards, dissatisfaction with oneself may persist because external accomplishments are unlikely to match internal standards for self-satisfaction. These children strive to escape feelings of disappointment but do not experience increased self-worth after reaching goals because the standards for self-satisfaction are not clear. The topic of striving for impossibly high standards and perfectionism will be explored further in Chapter 12.

Failure appears to decrease self-efficacy to a greater extent among sportspersons with lower self-esteem. Following a loss in a tiebreak, adolescent and young adult national standard tennis players with lower self-esteem reported larger decreases in self-efficacy compared to their counterparts with higher self-esteem (Lane, Jones, & Stevens, 2002).

Sources of Self-Efficacy

Self-efficacy develops from successful experience at related tasks or **enactive attainments**, from watching a person similar to oneself accomplish a task (**observational learning**), and from encouragement and persuasion from others (**feedback**). Self-efficacy is also judged on the basis of one's thoughts and emotional reactions, especially the reactions that occur in the process of performances and competitions (**physical and emotional** states). Finally, **childhood experiences** form the basis of judgments about self-efficacy.

Enactive Attainments

The actual experience of success is the most persuasive source of self-efficacy. For example, the United States Tennis Association (USTA) ratings of adult league tennis players strongly predicted the perceived tennis abilities of these tennis players (Sheldon & Eccles, 2005). The USTA ratings were assigned by certified teaching professionals. High self-efficacy then makes future success more likely, and the ensuing experiences of success further augment self-efficacy (Bond, Biddle, & Ntoumanis, 2001). Resilient self-efficacy requires experience in overcoming obstacles and learning to persist in the face of difficulties. If self-efficacy has been built on experiences of easy successes, it is vulnerable under conditions in which success depends on sustained effort and initial failures are experienced. Experience in overcoming adversity is beneficial in that it teaches that success at difficult tasks requires sustained and sometimes extraordinary effort, and provides information about how to hone and organize skills to reach difficult goals (Bandura, 1997).

It is not the experience of success that influences self-efficacy, but how the person understands his or her contribution to the success. Success that is attributed to internal and stable characteristics, such as talent and ability, augments efficacy beliefs (Bond et al., 2001). For example, confidence in tennis abilities is built not just on USTA ratings but also on confidence in one's psychological skills and knowledge of strategy (Sheldon & Eccles, 2005).

If self-efficacy for functioning in particular domains is low, success experiences in those domains can be readily discounted, attributed to luck or to inordinate effort rather than talent. These success experiences may also be ignored because people selectively attend to information that is consistent with their self-efficacy beliefs and ignore disconfirming information. If experience is to alter low efficacy beliefs, the discordance between the experience and the beliefs must be confronted and reconciled. The resiliency of efficacy beliefs is advantageous when self-efficacy is high as failures do not easily deflate efficacy and are attributed to inadequate effort or preparation, and external factors such as luck. Efficacy beliefs are reinforced and strengthened by selectively recalling successful performances.

Success that is largely due to the help or efforts of others does little to enhance self-efficacy. Failure is less likely to diminish efficacy if little effort is exerted and if it is attributed to environmental conditions rather than to talent. However, the withdrawal of effort when one is confronted with challenges is hardly an adaptive strategy, and if adopted routinely leads to a pattern of **self-handicapping** that will be discussed in Chapter 11. By self-handicapping, people are spared failure experiences at the cost of avoiding opportunities in which success is not assured. To try hard and fail under optimal conditions undermines efficacy beliefs, especially if failure occurs prior to a pattern of successes in a realm of functioning and prior to the establishment of a sturdy sense of efficacy.

Observational Learning

The adequacy of a performance is often evaluated in relation to the performance of others. People estimate their efficacy by evaluating the competence of people to whom they are similar, and the successes and failures of similar other people increase and decrease efficacy, respectively. For example, the self-efficacy and performance of female college students on a muscular endurance task was increased when they observed females like themselves perform the task. Observing models similar in terms of age, gender, and lack of athletic experience was more beneficial than viewing a male physical education teacher at the same task (Gould & Weiss, 1981). Female college students also persisted at a leg-extension endurance task longer when they observed nonathletic male or female models perform the task than when athletic models were watched (George, Feltz, & Chase, 1992). College women were better at a balancing task when they believed that a model had no prior experience than when they were told the model was experienced at balancing tasks due to experience as a gymnast and dancer (McCullagh, 1987).

The influence of this vicarious experience is greatest when people have little prior experience in the realm of functioning and when the models are highly similar to the observer. In effect, with little prior experience, the results obtained by the model present the best information about the probable results of one's own performance. If one model of similar status is convincing, then observing several similar models is even more convincing to the observer that they can also execute that function.

Vicarious experience not only affects efficacy beliefs, but also provides instruction about the skills necessary for successful performance (Bandura, 1997). The observer forms a mental representation of action that serves both to initiate imitation and as a reference for judging the correctness of motor actions (McCullagh & Weiss, 2001). Some models also provide information about the influence of efficacious beliefs, as they voice their determination to surmount obstacles. Models can also verbalize problem-solving strategies to the benefit of observers. Instructive models help observers to predict threats that may occur in the course of a performance, and also to respond to and control these sources of threat.

People who have serious doubts about their ability to function in various domains may find a **coping model** most similar. Coping models do not demonstrate initial proficiency in domains such as academic problem solving, but demonstrate a process by which they build competence. This process may involve learning general rules for solving problems, and techniques for managing anxiety. The observer learns that he or she will also have to learn new skills and techniques for managing anxiety. The coping model demonstrates that successful performance is due to effort and persistence rather than to initial talent.

Coping models have been seen to be preferable to mastery models for the acquisition of novel motor skills. Girls in the ninth grade who learned to throw darts by observing an adult coping model achieved higher dart scores and self-efficacy, and gained greater intrinsic interest in darts than girls who observed an adult mastery model (Kitsantas, Zimmerman, & Cleary, 2000). In the coping condition, girls learned to identify subskills necessary for good throws and how to correct errors in their throws. Feedback improved the girls' identification of proper skills and subskills, self-efficacy, and intrinsic interest in throwing darts. Exposure to the coping model appeared to teach the ninth graders that missed shots were due to strategy limitations and limited experience and effort. These limitations are subject to remediation and do not result in demoralization and decreased intrinsic interest in darts. Training with the mastery model was more likely to lead to attributions that misses were due to inadequate ability.

Similar models also help children overcome anxiety and develop self-efficacy. For example, children who were fearful of swimming were less fearful, made more progress with swimming lessons, and developed greater self-efficacy when observing peer models (Weiss, McCullagh, Smith, & Berlant, 1998).

Coping and **mastery models** – models that demonstrate skills proficiently and with limited anxiety – are most effective to the degree that they explicitly demonstrate and verbalize the step-by-step actions that the observer must follow to perform competently. It may also be unnecessary to demonstrate initial ineptitude such as would be the case in true coping modeling to foster feelings of similarity between the observer and model. In place of enacted ineptitude, the model can simply detail their historical difficulties and demonstrate the skills that allow them to master problems. By verbalizing their conviction that solutions to problems are found after the expenditure of sufficient effort, models encourage observers to be persistent and to not attribute difficulties to insufficient talent.

Regardless of whether models demonstrate coping or mastery, they are most influential if they demonstrate **competence**. For example, sixth-grade girls observed skilled or competent or unskilled peers or teachers climb a ladder. The observation of the competent model resulted in higher ladder climbing and higher efficacy, regardless of whether the model was an adult or child (Lirgg & Feltz, 1991). The benefits of observing competent models are especially apparent when observers have much to learn and models have this knowledge, and if the observer believes they are similar to the competent model.

Observing a videotape of oneself – **self-modeling** – is also informative. For example, by viewing a tape on one's golf swing, flaws can be detected and modified. Commentary and direction from an expert can facilitate this process. Progress can be recorded on tape, and this data enhances self-efficacy.

Feedback

The comments of others can augment or erode self-efficacy and performance. For example, the self-efficacy and performance of experienced weightlifters was influenced not simply by the actual amount of weight they lifted, but how much they believed they lifted. When feedback exaggerated the amount they actually lifted, their efficacy and performance increased (Fitzsimmons, Landers, Thomas, & Van der Mars, 1991). Similar findings were reported with adults between the ages of 45 and 65. The middle-aged participants pedaled at submaximum intensity on a bicycle ergometer and were given feedback that exaggerated their performance. This feedback lifted their efficacy for walking, cycling, and doing push-ups (McAuley, Duncan, Wraith, & Lettunich, 1991). Further, in a study involving Spanish college students and performance in the track and field event of hurdling, feedback influenced not only self-efficacy and performance, but also decisions to participate in more difficult hurdling events in the future (Escarti & Guzman, 1999). Feedback was altered to reflect slower or faster times for the completion of a 70-meter hurdle event with seven hurdles. Self-efficacy, subsequent hurdling times, and decisions to tackle difficult hurdle events in the future were all influenced by feedback.

Adults are sensitive to encouraging feedback that does not sound **authentic**. Faint praise may or may not be damning, but it does erode efficacy, as people interpret it as indicating that little is expected of them. Feedback that focuses on progress toward goals enhances efficacy and performance, whereas feedback about shortfalls has the opposite effect. Criticism about shortfalls offers little information about how to correct or improve performance.

Feedback is more persuasive if it comes from **experts**. Experts may have mastery of the skill they are evaluating, and may also be qualified on the basis of their training, credentials, and experience. Persuasive feedback is also **believable**. For example, feedback that performance can improve moderately is more believable than advice that rapid, huge improvements can be easily realized. Feedback that raises expectations to unrealistic levels is likely to be discounted soon after sportspersons follow instructions and do not realize rapid gains.

With feedback and verbal persuasion, people can recognize when they have the requisite skills for success and when these skills must be developed. In the former case, the skills may be misapplied. In the latter, the missing skills are identified, performers are persuaded to believe that they have the ability to acquire the skills, and a competent model demonstrates the execution of the skills. New skills are best acquired if they are deconstructed and taught as a series of subskills. Attempts to master subskills are more likely to result in success, and with this success and confirmatory feedback, performers develop efficacy that all of the skills and the ultimate goal will be mastered (Bandura, 1997; Smith, 2006a).

Feedback and Coaches

In many instances the influences of verbal persuasion, vicarious experience, and enactive attainments interact. For example, effective coaches diagnose skills that require refinement or development, develop practice that make it likely that skills and subskills are mastered, model the execution of skills, recognize when skills as misused, and provide feedback that focuses on attainments rather than deficits. Effective coaches recognize that that this is a daily process and that passing comments and random critiques are of little benefit.

Effective coaches understand that the self-efficacy of their athletes is strengthened when they model confidence and make liberal use of praise, when athletes engage in positive self-talk, and then skills are refined with drilling and instruction. American coaches of collegiate wrestlers and Olympic athletes (Gould, Hodge, Peterson, & Giannini, 1989) and male and female high school tennis players (Weinberg & Jackson, 1990), and Western Australian coaches of high school tennis recognized these sources of self-efficacy for athletes (Weinberg, Grove, & Jackson, 1992).

Physical and Emotional States

Physical and emotional states also provide information about efficacy. Physiological anxiety, physical dysfunction and fatigue, and emotional dysphoria provoke doubts about competence. However, as discussed in Chapter 3, physiological anxiety or arousal can be interpreted as facilitative or debilitative to performance. As will be explained in Chapter 10, conviction that one can achieve goals and standards for performance, regardless of arousal and environmental disruptions, is a critical element for minimizing the disruptive effects of physiological arousal and concomitant cognitive interference. Confidence in the capacity to control one's emotions is also associated with less physiological anxiety during athletic performance (Haney & Long, 1995).

Childhood Experiences

Adults contribute to the efficacy of children by providing challenges that are just beyond a child's current level of competency, so that with effort and guidance, successful performance is likely. These adults recognize when children need more and less help, and withdraw assistance as children become more capable of completing tasks on their own. They avoid offering challenges that are too difficult or too easy, as the former are likely to result in failure, the latter in no new learning, and both in the diminishment of self-efficacy. When adults respond contingently to the skill levels of children, they demonstrate an intense interest in the well-being of children and this interest is expressed in an ongoing process of hypothesis testing about the nature of optimal challenges that children might enjoy and master. With stable, supportive attachment to competent adults, children develop psychological resiliency that contributes to efficacy and recovery after setbacks (Bandura, 1997).

When adults offer feedback that links the successes of children to abilities, they provide greater support for efficacious beliefs than when they extol the virtues of work for the attainment of future success (Schunk, 1989). In effect, efficacious beliefs develop more reliably if children are taught that achievement is due to their abilities. As is true with adults, if children consider success to result only from extraordinary effort, they may harbor doubts about their talents. Virtuosity is likely to be the result of talent and hard work, and the families of US Olympic champions communicated confidence in their athletic children's capacities, but also emphasized hard work and persistence (Gould, Dieffenbach, & Moffett, 2002).

Efficacy can be promoted throughout school if efforts are made to compare sportspersons and students to their own baselines of performance rather than to the performance of other children. Frequent social comparisons encourage students to think of ability as fixed or stable rather than malleable and emerging. By focusing on improvement relative to one's baseline, learners are more likely to emphasize personal improvement and skill mastery and to focus on the intrinsic rewards of learning (Duda & Hall, 2001). Similarly, when college students were led to believe that a cognitive task was a test of native ability, their persistence in problem solving declined when solutions were not readily apparent. Conversely, when the college students were instructed that success at the cognitive task was an acquired skill, self-efficacy and performance were more resilient when sustained effort was necessary for success (Wood & Bandura, 1989). Similar results have been reported for tasks that measured motor skills, as atmospheres that identify skill development as the result of effort and learning foster the development of self-efficacy (Kavussanu & Roberts, 1996).

Intrinsic interest in learning and other accomplishments accompanies increased efficacy. Bandura (1986) maintained that practically any task could become intrinsically interesting. Intrinsic interest develops when people assign performance standards or goals to tasks. When reaching these standards, people experience satisfying self-reactions. Meeting goals and achieving a level of competency at tasks contributes to feelings of self-efficacy, and a threshold of competency is necessary prior to the experience of intrinsic interest. For example, competition in a five-day wrestling camp in which high school wrestlers competed in the equivalent of one third to one half of a season's matches may appear more like work than fun. However, wrestlers who were pleased with their performances and who had high efficacy for their wrestling competence discovered intrinsic interest and satisfaction with the camp experience (Kane et al., 1996).

Handling Failure

Despite the best preparation and sturdy self-efficacy, failures occur. The effects of failure on self-efficacy are substantially determined by how the failure is interpreted. When failure is ascribed to stable, internal factors, such as a lack of "natural ability," people are more likely to avoid future opportunities for failure. When interpretations of failures focus on inadequate preparation, execution of skills, and premature efforts to execute complex skills without first mastering subskills, failures are not interpreted as the "final word" about whether skills and anxiety will be mastered. Therapists, coaches, teachers, and mentors help people resolve anxiety about performances by modeling subskills and skills, by identifying the subskills in complex skills, and by correcting trainees' dysfunctional attributions of failure to stable, internal characteristics. This guidance is particularly helpful when provided in the setting where the actual performance will occur. Once complex skills have been performed successfully, it is important to practice variations of the skills in a variety of situations. Skill should be practiced under diverse conditions, and resilient skills can still be properly executed after setbacks and with adversity (Bandura, 1997).

Sport Self-Confidence

Recall that self-efficacy pertains to confidence for reaching goals in domains of functioning. The domain of greatest interest in this book is sport. The concept of **sport self-confidence** was developed specifically to measure confidence for successful athletic performance (Vealey, 2001). With high sport self-confidence, athletes are more capable of successfully deploying their skills to reach goals.

Theory and research about sport self-confidence has accounted for unique social and cultural factors that affect confidence in sport venues. Aspects of sport venues that affect confidence include the level of competition, coaching behavior, and motivational climates. Athletes are sometimes acculturated to participate in certain sports on the basis of gender and ethnicity, and dissuaded from participation in other sports. For example, ethnic minorities and women are infrequent drivers in certain motor sports.

The sources of sport self-confidence have been reliably measured with the Sources of Sport Confidence Questionnaire (SSCQ; Vealey, Hayashi, Garner-Holman, & Giacobbi, 1998). The SSCQ identifies nine specific sources of sport self-confidence: *mastery, demonstration of ability, physical/ mental preparation, physical self-presentation, social support, vicarious experience, coach's leadership, environmental comfort, situational favorableness.*

The nine categories form three larger domains of sport self-confidence. The first domain involves sport self-confidence from actual *achievement. Mastery* and *demonstration of ability* are sources of confidence in this domain. Sport self-confidence is increased when skills are mastered or improved. Sportspersons also obtain confidence from the demonstration of ability and when they show off or demonstrate more skill than opponents. Mastery and demonstration of ability are the two most important sources of self-confidence for high school and college athletes. As was demonstrated with self-efficacy, nothing builds confidence like success. Sport self-confidence is unlikely in the absence of quality training, practice, and skill development. Coaches rate physical conditioning and practice as the most important sources of self-confidence, and athletes also recognize the importance of physical preparation.

The second domain is *self-regulation. Physical/mental preparation* and *physical self-presentation* are sources of confidence in this domain. With proper physical and mental preparation for performances, confidence increases. The physical self-presentation of athletes or how the athlete believes that he or she looks to others is a source of confidence for some. Physical self-presentation is a more important source of confidence in individual sports and for female athletes, perhaps due to the societal focus on the appearance of women.

The third domain is the *social climate*. The sources of confidence in this domain are *social support, vicarious experience, coach's leadership, environmental comfort*, and *situational favorableness*. Coaches, family, and teammates are potential sources of social support. Vicarious experience can enhance confidence when others such as teammates perform successfully, as can confidence in the leadership of coaches. Environmental comfort often is the result of familiarity with venues such as with home fields. Situational favorableness occurs when athletes believe that the "breaks" or luck are in their favor.

As was the case with high self-efficacy, with high sport self-confidence, athletes are less vulnerable to cognitive interference during competition and are more likely to interpret physiological anxiety to be facilitative of athletic performance (Cresswell & Hodge, 2004; Hanton, O'Brien, & Mellalieu, 2003; Jones & Hanton, 1999; Jones, Hanton, & Swain, 1994; Jones & Swain, 1995). Confident athletes establish more difficult goals and show greater persistence in pursuit of these goals. Confident athletes more frequently establish athletic performance goals. With these performance goals, athletes compare progress against their baseline of prior performance, and they have greater control over factors contributing to success. US Olympic athletes at the winter games in Nagano, Japan in 1998 rated self-confidence and confidence in teammates as the most influential factors in determining performance (Gould, 1999).

Summary and Conclusions

Self-efficacy consists of beliefs that one can exert sufficient control over the environment and oneself to realize goals. Self-efficacy refers to convictions that one will obtain future goals, and it motivates behaviors that make actual goal attainment more likely. With higher self-efficacy, effort is sustained despite difficulties and obstacles. Effort is also deployed in purposeful ways, as people with higher self-efficacy are flexible in their selection, organization, and integration of skills. Difficult and even unyielding problems do not daunt people with high self-efficacy, as they persist in the application of sophisticated strategies to solve difficult problems. With beliefs that one can reach goals, failures provide information that one must both try harder and think better to discover an answer or solution that is already in one's repertoire, or to learn new skills to solve problems. Efforts to master difficult tasks have the effect of "keeping you humble" because this task mastery requires sustained effort. A realistic appreciation of the difficulty in reaching certain goals is not inconsistent with high self-efficacy, and it motivates the preparation necessary to acquire skills.

The cliché "nothing builds confidence like success" has been shown to be accurate. That is, the most convincing source of self-efficacy is actual success in similar domains of functioning. The development of resilient self-efficacy does not occur with singular success experiences, but is the result of mastering increasingly difficult tasks and of sustaining effort to accomplish complex tasks and reach long-term goals. Mentors such as parents, coaches, teachers, therapists, and senior colleagues can facilitate the development of efficacy by providing encouragement and support, and modeling behaviors that will likely lead to success. Sensitive mentors patiently build self-efficacy in others by issuing challenges that are neither so difficult as to result in consistent failure and weakened self-efficacy or so easy that trainees do not learn how to sustain effort. Efficacy also grows and develops when success is attributed to skill and talent and failure to inadequate preparation and execution of skills. Little is accomplished by noticing unfavorable comparisons between oneself and others with greater endowment, and efficacy is fostered when progress is noted in relation to a baseline of one's own behavior. Progress or enactive attainments enhance efficacy, which then leads to additional progress and a cycle of continuing achievement and confidence that additional achievement is within one's grasp.

Sport self-confidence is similar to self-efficacy for achieving goals in sport. The study of sport self-confidence has emphasized the sources that are unique to athletic settings. For example, sport self-confidence is influenced by the leadership of coaches, by comfort and familiarity with athletic venues, and by belief that the breaks will fall in one's favor. Sport self-confidence is not a substitute for the training and practice that are necessary to become highly skilled at sport. Indeed, the development and demonstration of ability are the most influential sources of sport self-confidence. With sport self-confidence, athletes can more successfully deploy existing skills and abilities to reach goals.

Key Terms

Self-efficacy

Optimistic self-efficacy beliefs

Self-efficacy and persistence

Self-efficacy and the use of skills

Self-efficacy and anxiety

Generalizability of efficacy beliefs

Self-efficacy versus self-esteem

Sources of self-efficacy: enactive attainments, observational learning, feedback, physical and emotional states, childhood experiences

Coping models

Mastery models

Self-modeling

Sport self-confidence

Suggested Readings

Bandura, A. (1997). *Self-efficacy: The exercise of control.* New York: Freeman.

Kane, T. D., Marks, M. A., Zaccaro, S. J., & Blair, V. (1996). Self-efficacy, personal goals, and wrestlers' self-regulation. *Journal of Sport & Exercise Psychology, 18,* 36–48.

Sheldon, J. P., & Eccles, J. S. (2005). Physical and psychological predictors of perceived ability in adult male and female tennis players. *Journal of Applied Sport Psychology, 17,* 48–63.

Smith, R. E. (2006). Understanding sport behavior: A cognitive-affective processing systems approach. *Journal of Applied Sport Psychology, 18,* 1–27.

Vealey, R. S. (2001). *Understanding and enhancing self-confidence in athletes.* In R. N. Singer, H. A. Hausenblas, & C. M. Janelle (Eds.), *Handbook of sport psychology* (2nd ed., pp. 550–565). New York: Wiley.

Vealey, R. S., Armstrong, L., Comar, W., & Greenleaf, C. A. (1998). Influence of perceived coaching behaviors on burnout and competitive anxiety in female college athletes. *Journal of Applied Sport Psychology, 10,* 297–318.

Zimmerman, B. J. (2000). Attaining self-regulation: A social cognitive perspective. In M. Boekaerts, P. Pintich, & M. Seidner (Eds.), *Self-regulation: Theory, research and application* (pp. 13–39). Orlando, FL: Academic Press.

PART III
PERFORMANCE INHIBITION

Choking Under Pressure and Performance Anxiety 10

As soon as Dominick saw the seedings for the state championship soccer tournament he realized that a high school championship game between Xavier and Trinity was very likely. The traditional powers had the best records in the regular season, and were placed in opposite brackets. The rivalry between the schools was beyond bitter. As teammates realized the implications of the seedings, a spontaneous cheer swept across their group. The cheer betrayed exhilaration and anxiety. Xavier had lost 3–1 to Trinity during the regular season.

True to expectations, Xavier and Trinity met in the championship match. Almost as soon as the game began, all of the physical and psychological preparation of Dominick, and perhaps most of Xavier's team, seemed moot. They seemed to be more spectators than players as they watched Trinity's front line and central midfielder move effortlessly toward their goal. In the first 12 minutes, Trinity's all-state forward, Kevin Strauss initiated four breakaway scoring opportunities, or chances to score when the number of offensive players exceeded the number of defenders. He scored, assisted halfback Kenny Chung's score, sent a shot off the goal post, and had a shot blocked by Xavier's goalie, Henry Strohbler. Dominick didn't have a Plan B for winning as the presence of Xavier's all-state sweeper, Paul Geiss, usually made concerns about the offense of opposing teams a non-issue.

As the final 12 minutes of the game began, Dominick looked to the stands. He imagined the disappointment in the faces of classmates, the "soccer groupies," and his parents. He knew they would be thinking, "X chokes again." He didn't know how he could face them. Xavier's sophomore phenomenon, Wayne Bleighley, had other things on his mind. He simply picked up a free ball and scored. It was almost as if he said, "I'm not waiting for you guys." The game mind had changed. The attention of Trinity's players was turned to attempts to counter Xavier's initiatives. Within minutes, Dominick found himself in front of Trinity's goal with a ball presenting itself for a volley. In an instant it was in the back of the goal, the equalizer.

Performance and pressure (photo courtesy of Western Connecticut State University).

Readers who have practiced the techniques in Chapters 3, 4, 5, and 6 prior to and during evaluations and performances and have found themselves to be entirely focused and free of debilitative anxiety may be uninterested in this chapter. For the rest of us, Chapter 10 is the first of eight chapters devoted to the exploration of the psychological factors that impede performance. In some ways Chapter 10 is a companion chapter to Chapters 3, 4, 5, and 6 because the proximal factors that impede performance are often countered by the techniques described in those chapters. As will be explained in ensuing chapters, people differ in their psychological and physiological reactions to the stress of evaluations and performances. However, most people find evaluations and performances to be stressful. Readers interested in additional information about how anxiety impairs performance are referred to the discussion in the Appendix. Like choking, test anxiety is paradoxical because it impairs performance when people are highly motivated to perform optimally. The literature about test anxiety is largely consistent with that of choking and in addition there is information about how to ameliorate test anxiety that may have applications in sport settings.

As explained in Chapter 3, stress can be conceptualized as a relationship between the person and the environment in which the person evaluates the stressor or the source of stress as exceeding his or her coping resources and endangering his or her wellbeing (Lazarus & Folkman, 1984). The process of comparing the source of threat to one's capacity to handle and master that source is accompanied by emotional responses. If one's coping resources are appraised to be inadequate to handle the stressor, the experience of anxiety, worry, and fear is likely. Conversely, if coping resources are seen to be adequate, the stressor may be seen as a stimulus for excitement, eagerness, and hopefulness. These positive emotions are also more likely if the stressor is interpreted as an opportunity for advancement (Burton & Naylor, 1997).

Anxiety Direction: Facilitative and Debilitative

As described in Chapter 3, anxiety does not always result in performance deficits and may be interpreted as facilitative or debilitative. In everyday life, anxiety is adaptive or useful to the degree that it serves as an internal signal of future danger. Anxiety that is **facilitative** motivates forward planning and preparation for activities such as performances and evaluations. In this context anxiety facilitates problem-focused coping strategies that confront the source of the stress (Zeidner, 1994). Students and athletes who experience facilitative anxiety are not free from physiological anxiety, but their anxiety serves as a signal to prepare for the stress of an evaluation or performance, and they interpret the physiological anxiety as an indication that they are ready to do their best. Students with low debilitating test anxiety are more likely to reduce their levels of physiological anxiety or "shake their butterflies" when it matters most – during exams (Raffety, Smith, & Ptacek, 1997). Athletes with facilitative anxiety have confidence that they can control themselves and the environment, and that they will realize their goals (Jones & Hanton, 1996, 2001). Anxiety is debilitative if it disrupts preparation and planning to resolve or master the sources of stress and threat.

Anxiety that is **debilitative** often orients people to the protection of their wellbeing at the expense of goal-directed behavior. This may involve the protection of their personal safety or of their reputation or image in the eyes of others (Carver & Scheier, 1992; Tallis & Eysenck, 1994). Preoccupation with one's personal wellbeing interferes with attention to the tasks necessary for optimal performance.

Trait and State Anxiety

The focus of this chapter will be the debilitative effects of anxiety on performance. To review, anxiety has *cognitive* and *physiological* manifestations. The physiological component consists of reactions of the sympathetic nervous system such as muscle tension, elevated heart rate, sweating, and feelings of being keyed up or on edge. The cognitive aspect of anxiety has been referred to as cognitive interference, and will be discussed at length in this chapter. Anxiety that is activated in response to specific situations, such as competitions and evaluations, has been referred to as **state anxiety**, whereas anxiety that remains relatively stable across situations and over time is considered **trait anxiety** (Spielberger, Gorsuch, & Lushene, 1970).

Specific questionnaires have been developed to measure competitive trait anxiety and competitive state anxiety in sport settings, such as the Sport Competition Anxiety Test (SCAT; Martens, 1977), the Sport Anxiety Scale (SAS; Smith, Smoll, & Schultz, 1990), and the Competitive State Anxiety Inventory-2 (CSAI-2; Martens, Burton, Vealey, Bump, & Smith, 1990).

Cognitive Interference

High levels of anxiety lead to performance deficits on a wide range of cognitive tasks. These deficits are more marked for tasks that are demanding versus simple (MacLeod, 1996). The capacity of active or **working memory** is limited, as people can keep a limited amount of information in mind at one time. As discussed in Chapter 5, the average limit of active memory is seven units of information, and the active memory of most people falls between a range of five and nine (Kareev, 2000; Miller, 1956). This information is short-term in that it is kept in mind temporarily or only so long as other information does not crowd it out and capture the seven units of space. Units of active memory are occupied with the task-irrelevant and intrusive thoughts concerning danger and risk in highly anxious people. Perhaps this is why tasks that require complex motor control, higher-level mental processes and decision-making are more negatively affected by high levels of anxiety (Taylor, 1996). Tasks that require only sustained vigilance, such as to respond whenever a particular sign or signal is detected, are not as adversely affected by anxiety (Humphreys & Revelle, 1984). In general, higher levels of cognitive and physiological anxiety lead to greater distractibility (Yee & Vaughan, 1996).

Cognitive interference refers to intrusive thoughts that compete for the attentional resources that would ideally be devoted to other tasks such as problem solving, decision-making, anticipating the responses of opponents, and integrating automatic skills during evaluations and performances (Pierce, Henderson, Yost, & Lofreddo, 1996). Although the execution of over-learned or automatic skills requires little attentional storage space, cognitive interference is still disruptive to their execution. This is because forms of cognitive interference can occupy the space in working memory that is not required to execute the automatic skills. Working memory space that is available during the execution of automatic skills is usually needed to sequence and organize the automatic skills, to anticipate the next moves of opponents, and to respond to opponents and situations with the selection and performance of the most appropriate skill. Further, these forms of cognitive interference can disrupt automatic behavior so that the performer thinks about the execution of skills that have previously been executed automatically. As mentioned in Chapter 4, automatic execution of skills is associated with elite performance. Cognitive interference may also affect the flexibility of performers in adjusting the breadth and direction of attentional focus and in adjusting from soft to hard attentional focuses (Nideffer, 1993).

Forms of Cognitive Interference

Cognitive interference can be seen as a loss of control over one's thoughts, as **emotionally valenced thoughts** take precedence over attention to tasks and skills necessary for optimal performance (Sarason, Pierce, & Sarason, 1996). Thoughts are emotionally valenced when associated with the experience of emotion. Two forms of emotionally valenced thoughts are worry about the consequences of unsuccessful performance and the reactions of spectators. A third form of cognitive interference is **preemptory thoughts**, or thoughts related to general themes that color the manner in which a person views themselves and their potential for achievement and happiness. An example of a preemptory thought is "I don't perform well under pressure," and this theme might influence performance across venues. A fourth form of cognitive interference is **self-doubts**. People with self-doubts lack confidence to realize goals that are within their range of abilities. Consequently, self-doubters set less challenging goals and underachieve (Schwarzer, 1996).

The forms of cognitive interference are influenced by the age and sport of participants. For example, the cognitive anxiety of collegiate Canadian hockey players was shown to form four categories (Dunn, 1999). The hockey players were fearful of: (1) injury and physical danger, (2) performance failure, (3) negative evaluation by others such as teammates, coaches, and spectators, and (4) the unknown, such as the strengths and weaknesses of opponents. Not surprisingly, younger athletes are more concerned about the reactions of parents. For example, male wrestlers and soccer players between the ages of 9 and 14 worried about: failure, evaluations by parents and coaches, and pleasing oneself and others (Scanlan & Lewthwaite, 1984; Scanlan, Lewthwaite, & Jackson, 1984). The worries of young wrestlers prior to a tournament consisted of: concern about pleasing oneself and others, about negative evaluations from the father of the wrestler, and about failure and negative evaluations from other adults (Gould, Eklund, Petlichkoff, Peterson, & Bump, 1991).

Fear of Failure and Cognitive Interference

The **fear of failure** in sport has five dimensions: "(a) fears of experiencing shame and embarrassment; (b) fears of devaluing one's self-estimate; (c) fears of having an uncertain future; (d) fears of important others losing interest; and (e) fears of upsetting important others" (Conroy, 2004, p. 484). Four of the five dimensions of fear of failure have been associated with hostile forms of self-talk and cognitive interference among students and athletes. Examples of hostile self-talk include self-blame and self-attack. Fears of upsetting important others were not associated with hostile self-talk, but still were related to diminished self-esteem.

Those who fear failure view athletic competition as a threat, as they dread "the agony of defeat" (Smith, 2006a, p. 43). Attention that is captured by fears of failure is taken from concentration on the instrumental behaviors necessary for skilled performance, and choking under pressure is more likely. Such fearful athletes are also more vulnerable to injury (Smith, Smoll, & Passer, 2002).

Trait Anxiety and Cognitive Interference

Environmental stressors such as evaluations, competitions, and performances cause a measure of situational or state anxiety in most people. State anxiety is more likely to escalate and leads to cognitive interference among people who are generally anxious, or who have high levels of trait anxiety. People with trait anxiety and with anxiety disorders have a particular sensitivity to processing information that relates to the primary domain of their worry. For example, students with test anxiety have high levels of intrusive and threatening thoughts concerning poor performance when working on demanding intellectual tasks. College students who experienced cognitive interference during one examination were likely to report cognitive interference on other examinations (Pierce, Henderson, Yost, & Lofredo, 1996). College football players who reported cognitive interference during examinations were also likely to report cognitive interference during football games. Thoughts concerning imminent danger and threat are also characteristic of people with anxiety disorders such as generalized anxiety disorder (physiological and cognitive components of anxiety almost always present), claustrophobia (fear of being trapped in a place where escape would be difficult), simple phobias (excessive fear of discrete things), and panic disorders.

It is difficult for people with anxiety disorders and trait anxiety to ignore signs of threat in their environment and to devote their attention to thoughts related to problem solving on intellective tasks. They encode or bring information related to threat into their active memory. People with high levels of trait anxiety and people with anxiety disorders are also likely to selectively impose threatening interpretations on ambiguous information from the environment. This interpretation results in cognitive interference because the outcomes of performances are often ambiguous. For example, opponents in competition may be relatively evenly matched, and success or failure may only result from prolonged effort and prolonged concentration on the tasks necessary for successful performance. An athlete with high trait anxiety might prematurely conclude that they are beaten by an opponent if they do not experience easy success.

The interpretive bias of anxious people to selectively encode information related to threat occurs *automatically* (at a level outside their conscious awareness). This automatically encoded information becomes in effect the raw material for their thoughts. They may engage in self-talk that consists of blaming themselves for poor performances, and ironically, this blaming may be what they fear most (Conroy & Metzler, 2004). State anxiety caused by evaluations is often not disruptive to the performance of people with low levels of trait anxiety, as they demonstrate a bias toward automatic attentional avoidance of the sources of stress and threat in the environment. Clearly the latter attentional bias is adaptive, as environmental stress is largely inevitable.

People high in trait anxiety have an overly pessimistic assessment of future outcomes. They expect the worst, and to be less successful than others (Eysenck & Derakshan, 1997).

Why Cognitive Interference Exists

Why does cognitive interference exist? Perhaps because it represents deviations of normal, adaptive patterns of thought. The average amount of time that college students kept any single thought in mind was shown to be five seconds. In a 16-hour day, these undergraduates shifted the content of their thought 4000 times (Klinger, 1996). Attention shifts whenever a person encounters an environmental cue or has a thought that arouses emotion because of its relation to one's current concerns. A current concern is what is important to someone. The more closely an environmental cue or thought relates to one's current concerns, the more likely it is that thoughts will shift to that current concern. For example, if a golfer is concerned about the strength of an opponent, seeing that opponent's name at the top of the leader board is likely to augment cognitive interference about the strength of the opponent. Cognitive interference occurs when a cue initiates emotional responses and patterns of thought that compete and interfere with the behaviors necessary for successful performances.

This cognitive interference may be unwanted and puzzling because it occurs automatically when cues are encountered. That is, a cue may initiate a shift in thought content even though a person does not intend to think about the subject of that cue. Indeed, if people receive spoken cues related to their concerns while they are sleeping, the content of their dreams will correspond to the spoken cues. It is therefore more difficult to keep one's mind on the tasks necessary for successful performances in environments rich with cues related to important concerns or while experiencing strong emotion that prompts internal thoughts.

Cognitive interference in the form of fear of failure occurs when athletes have been punished excessively for mistakes. For example, some coaches infrequently reinforce success, growth, and effort, and are relentless in chastising sportspersons when they make errors. Under these circumstances, athletes become afraid of taking risks of any sort in competition, and ironically, are more likely to make the same errors for which they were chastised (Petri & Govern, 2004).

Choking under Pressure

"**Choking**" is a term that is widely recognized in the vernacular of sport and refers to inferior performances under pressure. Performances that do not measure up to a person's acquired skill level are considered inferior. **Pressure** refers to the conditions or factors that increase the importance of performing well. Pressure is increased when the rewards for superior performance are high, when an evaluating audience is present, when competition is stiff, when the outcome of a performance is especially important, and when there is only one chance to be successful (Baumeister & Showers, 1986). For example, championships are often contested on a yearly basis, and opportunities to win a championship may occur only once in a lifetime. Pressure may also increase when the costs of failure are high.

Choking is paradoxical because performers are often most highly motivated to do their best when the stakes or consequences of performances are highest. However, choking does not occur as a result of insufficient effort, but rather because pressure impairs skilled performance. Skilled responses are likely to be automated (see Chapter 5), effortless, and executed without conscious attention to composite elements. Conscious attention and effort to the component elements disrupts their automatic and skillful execution (Beilock & Carr, 2001; Beilock, Carr, MacMahon, & Starkes, 2002; Jackson, Ashford, & Norsworthy, 2006; Singer, 2002; Smith, 1996).

Choking occurs when physiological anxiety or arousal increases and attention is involuntarily directed inward and to a narrow range of topics (Nideffer & Sagal, 2006), and when thoughts turn to the result of a performance rather than the process. These topics include self-conscious concerns that one cannot meet a standard of performance or cannot measure up to a competitor, which constitute cognitive interference because they compete with attention to the details necessary for successful performances. These thoughts are emotionally valenced in that they prompt cognitive and physiological anxiety. They capture attention and take it from the cues in the environment that require recognition. With attention captured by emotionally valenced thoughts and the experience of physiological anxiety, the execution of automated skills is inhibited. As stated above, efforts to consciously control automated elements of a performance also disrupt their automatic execution.

Under pressure, athletes may become impulsive and abandon game plans or strategies for performances. Game plans typically represent strategies that present the greatest opportunities for optimal performance. In lieu of these carefully crafted game plans, pressured athletes may become hurried and impulsive and adopt high-risk, high-reward strategies. For example, a basketball team's game plan may call for initiating offensive sequences by "working the ball into the paint" or looking for scoring opportunities near their basket. This presents a low-risk strategy because a player may become open for a high percentage shot, a player may be fouled and have the opportunity to shoot free throws, or the ball may be passed to a player on the perimeter for an open and high percentage shot. Under pressure and with high anxiety, this game plan may be abandoned as a player takes a three-point shot as soon as the ball enters their half of the court. The three-point shot is a low percentage shot because it must be shot from at least 25 feet from the basket in American professional basketball. It provides a one-point bonus over the two points of other baskets or field goals. Therefore, taking the first available three-point shot is a high-risk, high-reward option that is unlikely to lead to success (Leith & Baumeister, 1996).

Not everyone becomes impulsive under pressure; in fact some become overly deliberative or slow in making decisions (Butler & Baumeister, 1998; Heaton & Sigall, 1991). These sportspersons may be overly cautious and in effect play to avoid losing rather than to win (Wallace, Baumeister, & Vohs, 2005). Perhaps both disruptions to tempo impair the automatic execution of skills.

As mentioned above, trait anxiety places one at risk for cognitive interference, distraction, and strategies that are risky and have low probabilities of success. Trait anxiety also results in doubts that one will be capable of reaching standards necessary for success and in beliefs that competitors are superior. Lacking confidence that one can perform to a level necessary for success, choking is more likely.

Clearly thoughts, emotions, and performance are interrelated. They interact so that cognitive interference and negative emotions disrupt performance and poor performances augment cognitive interference and negative emotions. It may be difficult to interrupt this **downward cycle** in the course of a performance, as the thoughts and emotions may be cued automatically by internal or external stimuli. Physiological anxiety may contribute to this downward cycle. High levels of physiological anxiety disrupt performance on tasks that require sustained concentration, decision-making, multiple cue discrimination, fine motor control, movement fluidity, and manual dexterity. As stated in Chapter 5, if this cycle is not interrupted, performers may withdraw effort and resign themselves to "having a bad day." If the cycle is extended past a single performance, performers may see themselves as being in a slump.

Choking and Self-Esteem

Choking is also more likely when attention is directed away from the performance and toward the preservation of one's self-esteem. As previously mentioned, self-esteem refers to liking for oneself. People with high self-esteem generally set more challenging goals and accomplish more than people with low self-esteem. Self-esteem also makes positive contributions to wellbeing, mental health, and adjustment. However, people with high self-esteem may be more vulnerable to distractions that challenge their self-esteem prior to and during performances. For example, when college students with high self-esteem were challenged to prove that they would not choke and were capable of competing at challenging video games, they performed quickly but inaccurately (Baumeister et al., 1993). By choosing the most difficult games, college students with high self-esteem took a high-risk, high-payoff strategy. Their attention may have been diverted from pursuing strategies more likely to lead to success, and captured by efforts for self-enhancement as a result of realizing a glorious success. Those with high self-esteem may have put too much pressure on themselves in service of self-enhancement.

Perhaps the students with high self-esteem recognized that the realization of their lofty goals was beyond their reach, or at least that a flawless performance would be required to realize a glorious success. Consistent with the leitmotiv of this section on choking, a lack of confidence that one can reach a standard necessary for successful performance is a critical aspect of choking. Their performance also shared characteristics with that of people who become anxious or experience negative emotions during performances (Leith & Baumeister, 1996), in that they took high-risk strategies that were unlikely to be successful.

The Effects of Pressure

Pressure often disrupts the performance of not only average adults but also elite athletes (Wang, Marchant, & Morris, 2004). For example, Lewis and Linder (1997) described the effects of pressure on the putting accuracy of college students. A condition of moderate pressure was created by informing students that they would receive twice the usual class credit if they could place 10 putts within an average of 5 cm from the putting target. Putting accuracy decreased under pressure as the average distances from the target for the low-pressure and high-pressure groups were 55.5 and 81.5 cm, respectively. Of interest, some of the students spontaneously verbalized "Don't choke!," "The pressure's on now!," and "The pressure's getting to me!" (Lewis & Linder, 1997, p. 941).

Among elite athletes ranked in the top four for their sport in the USA, 13.7 percent acknowledged being panic-stricken prior to performances, 18.4 percent acknowledged intense panic while performing, and 49.6 pecent indicated that they became very anxious during performances if they make mistakes (Mahoney, Gabriel, & Perkins, 1987). As mentioned in Chapter 3, 30 percent of the US wrestlers at the 1988 Olympic Games in Seoul said that their worst Olympic performance was in their most crucial match (Gould, Eklund, & Jackson, 1992a).

Even the most elite performers acknowledge choking. For example, after his record-tying seventh singles title at Wimbledon and record-breaking 13th Grand Slam singles title in the open era (seven Wimbledon, four US Open, and two Australian Open), Pete Sampras acknowledged choking at a critical juncture in the first set of the match. Despite Sampras' dominating serve, his opponent, Patrick Rafter, won five of his 12 points in a first set tiebreaker on Sampras' serve. Regarding his erratic play in the tiebreaker, Sampras reflected "We all choke . . . The title could be won or lost in a matter of a couple shots" (Hersh, 2000, p. C2). Sampras went on to win a 14th Grand Slam singles title at the 2002 US Open.

Elite athletes learn to perform well under pressure. Members of the Professional Golfers' Association Tour (PGA Tour), Ladies' Professional Golfers' Association Tour (LPGA Tour), and Senior Professional Golfers' Association Tour (Senior PGA Tour) generally won top-tier tournaments (such as the four majors) and second-tier tournaments when leading and within one stroke of the lead after three of four rounds (Clark, 2002).

Choking on the Threshold of Victory

Is victory more difficult to grasp when it is close at hand? Baumeister and Steinhilber (1984) maintained that professional baseball players more often "choked" or began to perform poorly when victory was close at hand and when they began to imagine themselves as champions. This choking process was seen to be more likely in front of supportive home crowds and in final or deciding games of championship series. The support of the home crowd was understood to intensify the ball players' focus on themselves as impending champions, and to distract attention from the hitting and fielding necessary to win. This self-attention or daydreaming about oneself was maintained because it was pleasant. However, this self-attention also disrupts the automatic and unselfconscious execution of skills that characterize elite performance. Perhaps similar processes occurred among British golfers in the final round of the British Open Golf Championship, as their performance was inferior to that of foreign golfers on final rounds (Wright, Jackson, Christie, McGuire, & Wright, 1991). Home field was not a disadvantage for major league baseball players in championship games only when the victorious team was a decided underdog, perhaps because the players were less likely to be drawn to fantasies about their status as champions.

These findings of Baumeister and Steinhilber (1984) were derived from the archival statistics of the World Series of Major League Baseball in the USA, and were counterintuitive and inconsistent with a larger body of research conducted in controlled, laboratory settings. This laboratory research demonstrated that self-attention disrupted performance when stakes were high and when performers expected failure. Self-attention facilitated performance when the level of pressure was high and when success was expected. The findings of Baumeister and Steinhilber were also inconsistent with evidence summarized in Chapter 4 that home teams are advantaged in terms of won–loss records. For example, World Cup soccer teams won 63 percent of their games at home, 37 percent away, and 40 percent at neutral sites in 1987 and 1998 (Brown, Van Raalte, Brewer, Winter, Cornelius, & Andersen, 2002). A home advantage was particularly evident for World Cup championship games, and performance was worse for visiting teams that traveled longer distances.

In addition, independent analyses of archival data from the World Series of Major League Baseball revealed that home teams won 60 percent of the decisive sixth or seventh games in the World Series between 1924 and 1993 (Schlenker, Phillips, Boniecki, & Schlenker, 1995). Further, during the seventh games of World Series, fielding errors were made three times as often when the home team was behind rather than ahead in the score. Therefore, Schlenker et al. attributed choking to self-attention concerning failure rather than to self-attention regarding the anticipation of success. The combination of wanting to impress the hometown fans and having self-doubts about the likelihood of success apparently impaired the performance of the professional baseball players. Expectations of success and self-efficacy facilitate performance, even when the expectations of others are high and when a public performance is important. Schlenker et al. considered the essential ingredients of choking in athletic and other venues to be self-doubts and high motivation to impress others.

In the sixth and seventh games of World Series, it is reasonable to assume that opponents are somewhat evenly matched. Competition with individuals or teams that are equal or superior in skill can cause performers to question whether they have the capacity to prevail over these competitors (Baumeister, 1984; Gould et al., 1992). These questions erode confidence that one can reach a standard necessary for success and allow for involuntary surrender of storage capacity in working memory to cognitive interference. Self-efficacy or confidence that an individual or team can prevail when evenly matched is a vital determinant of performance under conditions of high pressure and intense competition (Bandura, 1997). Efficacy beliefs are especially important in determining the results of face-to-face competition. For example, self-efficacy was shown to be the most influential factor in containing cognitive anxiety among adolescent male wrestlers during a tournament (Gould et al., 1991). Efficacy beliefs may also be influenced by the behavior of teammates. Observing ineffective performances of teammates with equal or superior ability may diminish the efficacy of other teammates and inflate perceptions about the superiority of opponents. Teams with high collective efficacy are resilient in the face of pressure and are not easily daunted by defeat.

On the Threshold of Victory

John McEnroe was ranked number one in professional men's tennis from 1981 to 1985. He won 77 career singles titles and 77 doubles titles, more than any other tennis professional. In 1984, he won 13 of the 15 tournaments he entered, including the Masters and the Grand Slams of Wimbledon and the US Open. Yet his loss in the final of the 1984 French Open, a Grand Slam event, still causes him sleepless nights and days of nausea when he returns to the site of the French Open to do commentary for television (McEnroe & Kaplan, 2002). McEnroe considered this loss to be the worst in his life and to have cost him a legitimate claim to being the best player ever.

McEnroe won the first two sets of the French Open final from Ivan Lendl, and was leading 4–2 in the third set; he thought he could read the facial expressions of friends in the audience. He imagined that they were thinking that he had essentially won the tournament and that it would be a *fait accompli* in a half hour. He found himself wondering: "I've been playing so amazingly. How can I keep it up?" (McEnroe & Kaplan, 2002, p. 177). A squawking headset from a television cameraman also distracted him. He lost his composure and complained throughout the remainder of the match. A largely supportive crown turned hostile. McEnroe lost in five sets.

The Kinder and Darker Forms of Choking on the Threshold of Victory

Whether choking on the threshold of victory is due to a "**dark form**" of belief that standards for success and expectations of others will not be met, or a "**kinder form**" of pleasant fantasies about an impending change in status to that of champions, has not been conclusively determined (Baumeister, 1995). Both the dark and kind forms of choking divert the limited attentional resources of performers to conditions in the future rather than to the skilled and sometimes automatic execution of tasks in the here-and-now (Sanders, Baron, & Moore, 1978). However, both forms of choking appear to be more than just forms of distraction, and both represent cognitive interference in that they are emotionally valenced.

Audience Effects

Supportive audiences communicate their interest in seeing a performer do well. They may identify with performers and may experience gains and losses in self-esteem and moods as a result of the successes or failures of the performers. The supportive audience may experience the glory reflected from their favorite successful performers. Supportive audiences have a strong interest in how performers do, whereas neutral audiences have little or no stake in the results of performances. Hostile audiences root for poor performances. Supportive audiences may provide an emotional buffer for performers so that their attention is not captured by negative emotions and so that efficacy is preserved under adverse conditions. Perhaps performers believe that they will not lose the esteem of supportive audiences because the members of supportive audiences are aware of their past histories of competent performances. However, supportive audiences may also hold high expectations for performers, and therefore make success seem more difficult to achieve. Supportive audiences tend to scrutinize performers more closely, and this may increase the self-consciousness of the performers. Performers sometimes demonstrate higher levels of physiological anxiety before supportive audiences.

Performers generally prefer a supportive audience, but its presence is not necessarily associated with better performance. This is especially true when the standards for a successful performance are high, and success is far from assured. Supportive audiences have detrimental effects on performance when students and athletes lack confidence that they will be successful (Butler & Baumeister, 1998) and athletes have both self-doubts and high motivation to impress others (Schlenker et al., 1995). When performers lack confidence, the presence of a supportive audience may increase the pressure to reach a goal that they considered to be beyond their reach (Baumeister, Hamilton, & Tice, 1985), and contribute to choking.

The effects of audiences: Cheeky fans (photo © Reuters/CORBIS).

Audience Effects and Self-Consciousness

Individuals low in **self-consciousness** typically focus their attention on factors external to themselves. They are therefore more likely to make judgments about themselves on the basis of this information from the external world. They are more sensitive to external sources of pressure such as the responses of an audience. With low self-consciousness, people tend to perform well when they expect to please an audience, and struggle when their performance does not conform to the expectations of the audience. This struggling or choking includes performing more slowly when they expect to fail before a supportive audience and also when they expect to succeed before a hostile audience. People who are more self-conscious are less concerned with the responses of audiences, and more likely to concentrate on their own standards of success (Heaton and Sigall, 1991).

Choking is Not Inevitable

To this point, choking has been described as somewhat normative. It is not inevitable, and clearly some sportspersons choke or respond less favorably to pressure than others (Wang et al., 2004). With experience in actual competition and with simulation training, sportspersons and performers learn to perform well and optimally under pressure (Thomas, 1996). For example, in the Lewis and Linder (1997) study cited earlier, some college students practiced putting while being videotaped. These students expected that sport psychologists, coaches, and the golf team would examine the films of their putting. These students were in effect "inoculated" to putt accurately under conditions of heightened self-awareness, and the high-pressure condition did not interfere with their accuracy. Sportspersons also learn to manage the disruptive effects of supportive and unsupportive audiences with experience (Wallace et al., 2005).

As mentioned in Chapter 4, ideal preperformance planning involves developing game plans and anticipating problems, impediments, and the tactics of opponents. Thorough preperformance preparation may also involve strategies for interrupting cognitive interference and choking. Cue words and breathing exercises are examples of strategies for interrupting cognitive interference. If cognitive interference and emotionally valenced thoughts are interrupted, performance is likely to improve, even if the disruption is distracting. For example, in the Lewis and Linder (1997) study, collegiate putters who were required to count aloud backward from 100 by twos were relatively unaffected by the high-pressure condition.

Worst Choke in Golfing History?

In 1996, the world's top ranked golfer, Greg Norman, said, "One of my great motivations in life is a fear of failure" (Garber & Berlet, 1996, p. K1). In that year, Norman "suffered the worst collapse in major tournament history" (Reilly, 1996, p. 24) at the Masters golf tournament. He entered the final day of this tournament leading the field by six strokes and ended the day five strokes behind the eventual winner, Nick Faldo. News reports did not provide information about whether Norman may have adopted performance-avoidance goals (such as not to lose; Elliot & McGregor, 1999), but there was evidence of state anxiety: "His routine is so different," said Faldo's coach David Leadbetter. "He's standing over the ball an *incredible* amount of time. I'd say he's spending six, seven seconds longer per shot, fidgeting, moving around in ways I've never seen him do" (Reilly, 1996, p. 26).

In a list of the "top 10 chokes in majors" in *Golf Magazine* this performance was rated as the worst choke in golfing history (Top 10 Chokes in Majors, 2002). Norman entered the final round with the lead in seven of golf's major tournaments. He lost the 1986 Masters to Jack Nicklaus on the final hole. He entered the final round of the 1986 US Open with a one-stroke lead and finished six shots behind winner Ray Floyd. He led starting the final round of the 1986 British Open and won by five shots. He started the final round of the 1986 PGA Championship with a lead of four shots, but lost by two strokes. In the 1987 Masters, he started the final round with a one-stroke lead and lost on a second playoff hole. Norman was tied with Faldo as they entered the final round of the 1990 British Open, but lost to Faldo by nine shots. By 1996, Norman was well aware that he had been identified in the press as a choke artist. The degree to which he internalized choking as a stable, internal charac-teristic is open to speculation. However, in 1996 he defended himself to the press: "I know I'm not a loser. There's a lot of golf left in me. They'll call you a choker, and a gagger. But it's only a game. I'm a better person for it. I will achieve my goals in life" (Garber & Berlet, 1996, p. K1).

Perhaps more than any golfer prior to Tiger Woods, Greg Norman had been considered the heir apparent to golf's greatest champion, Jack Nicklaus (McDermott, 1986). He was a crowd favorite due to his skill and finesse, power, and good looks. Galleries and audiences were supportive, but their expectations were high. These high expectations may have placed additional pressure on Norman, especially if he had doubts about whether he was a winner. His career has been far from unsuccessful, as he has been named as the 22nd best golfer of all time (Yocom et al., 2000).

Their putting was roughly as accurate as students in low-pressure conditions without distractions, and far more accurate than the putting of students in high-pressure conditions that were not counting backward. The explanation for this curious finding was that students in the high-pressure condition were less able to focus on themselves because their attention was occupied by the task of counting backward. Do the results of this study suggest that people should look for distractions such as counting backward when attempting expert performance? No. This form of distraction disrupted performance under low-pressure conditions and attenuated the inoculating effects of practice under conditions of heightened self-awareness.

It is also not recommended that sportspersons simply attempt to suppress cognitive interference by simply making efforts to block these thoughts from conscious awareness. Intentional efforts to suppress thoughts may activate two cognitive processes: an "intentional operating process" and an "ironic monitoring process" (Wegner, 1994, 1997a, 1997b). The intentional process consists of a conscious, effortful search for a desired mental state, such as a focus on a game plan. The ironic monitoring is an unconscious and automatic search for mental contents that indicate that one has mentally strayed from the desired mental state, such as thoughts about getting nervous and choking under pressure. Under stress and pressure, the ironic monitoring process may supersede the intentional operating process, causing the unwanted thoughts about choking to come to mind with even greater frequency.

Instead of focusing on thoughts to suppress, sportspersons are better served by preparing to focus, and refocus as necessary, their attention to task-relevant cues throughout competitions and practices (Dugdale & Eklund, 2002; Martens, 1987). For example, cue words may be used to disrupt choking and refocus attention. Cue words and other strategies are most useful when they promote concentration on the instrumental behaviors responsible for optimal performance. Attention will therefore be directed toward the sportsperson's intentions, plans, strategies, and tactics at specific points in contests and in response to the play of opponents. Allocating attention to the execution of highly skilled motor responses is likely to disrupt their automatic execution. The downward performance spiral of choking may also be disrupted by decreasing the attendant physiological anxiety or arousal. For example, athletes may use the centering technique (described in Chapter 5) to reduce tension during practice and competition (Nideffer & Sagal, 2006).

Perhaps choking under pressure is also less likely in sports that generally require a broad and external attentional focus and almost constant action and movement. For example, evidence of home-ice disadvantage in championship matches in the National Hockey League is at most equivocal (Gayton, Matthews, & Nickless, 1987; Wright & Voyer, 1995).

Most generally, the detrimental effects of anxiety and pressure on performance are not all-or-none phenomena. Anxiety and pressure may engender cognitive interference and distraction and interfere with performance during one point in a performance, but not at others. For example, collegiate wrestlers experienced some doubts before peak performances (Eklund, 1994). These wrestlers transformed doubts into states of confidence during their matches. In the 2001 US Open in golf, the three leaders three-putted the final hole of the tournament. It can easily be argued that the eventual winner, Retief Goosen, choked when he three-putted from 10 feet, and missed his second putt from 3 feet – a putt that would have won the championship. The somewhat universal recognition of the effects of anxiety on performance and choking under pressure was reflected in the title of a newspaper article about this match, "Gag Order" (Berlet, 2001, p. C1). Goosen may have gagged when victory was within 3 feet, but this gagging was short lived. He won the US Open in a playoff on the next day.

Performers regain their concentration and composure by redirecting attention to their game plans or strategies for performances (Eklund, 1994, 1996), by reestablishing efficacy or conviction that their performance will exceed standards necessary for success, and by controlling their physiology. Efficacy may also be restored if opponents are recognized to be vulnerable.

Nagging doubts about being a "choker," "gagger," or "choke artist" are likely to be highly detrimental to performance. To see oneself as a choke artist implies that choking is a stable, internal characteristic, and that performance is likely to be impaired across venues or situations and over time (Elliot & McGregor, 1999). In effect, the conviction that one is a choke artist means that there is no end to one's choking. The recognition that choking during performances and on examinations is a common characteristic is helpful if it contributes to convictions that choking is relatively universal and situational.

Summary and Conclusions

Choking occurs when external pressure for skilled performance has the paradoxical effect of producing inferior performances. Choking happens when attention is captured by concerns that one cannot measure up to a criterion necessary for success or to competitors. In the course of a competition, the likelihood of victory or defeat becomes more apparent.

Choking is more likely if the attention of performers is captured by these potential outcomes and diverted from the skilled execution of tasks in the here-and-now. Performers may be distracted by pleasant fantasies of an impending change in status to that of a champion, or by aversive thoughts of lacking what it takes to win. Supportive audiences comfort performers, but if they lack confidence that they can reach standards necessary for success this standard is raised by the presence of an audience. If negative emotions such as fear or embarrassment are experienced during a performance and perhaps if the opportunity for success is believed to be slipping away, performers may engage in novel and untested strategies that have little chance for success. For example, performers may attempt high-risk strategies, and may also become overly impulsive or deliberate.

The recognition of cognitive interference is an important step in its amelioration. Recognition serves to interrupt the automatic occurrence of interfering thoughts and provide a greater sense of control of these thoughts. With guidance, social support, and coaching, cognitive interference and physiological anxiety can be recognized and interpreted as facilitative anxiety. Attention can be directed to the elements of a performance that will lead to an optimal or at least satisfactory performance. An effective method of providing guidance and coaching is to model or demonstrate effective problem solving in response to obstacles and to enunciate the strategies used in surmounting obstacles.

The importance of confidence that one can realize standards necessary for success has been emphasized throughout this chapter. In keeping with this theme, choking is less likely if goals are not set beyond one's capabilities. Efficacy and confidence are more likely to be maintained if goals are attainable with some margin for error. Focusing on aspects in a performance over which one has control also supports efficacy beliefs. Repeated queries to oneself about whether goals will be realized during the course of a performance are not helpful. These queries compete with attention to the planning, ordering, and execution of elements of a performance. They can take the form of cognitive interference, as a performer may conclude that he or she will not reach standards necessary for success.

Effective control of debilitative anxiety and cognitive interference during evaluations and performances begins with the conscientious practice of the techniques described in Chapters 3, 4, 5, and 6. This preparation provides performers with direction and solutions to obstacles that occur during the course of a performance. Well-prepared performers are more likely to believe that they are equal to challenges and opponents and to maintain self-efficacy when success is not readily achieved.

Careful preparation should probably include measures to "inoculate" performers against the disruptive effects of audiences. Without this inoculation, the presence of an audience may cause greater self-consciousness and prompt overly expeditious or deliberate performance in place of the execution of automatic skills. The importance of preparing to perform under conditions that are similar to "game conditions" was discussed in Chapter 4. This discussion can now be expanded to physical and mental practice with friendly, hostile, and neutral crowds.

Key Terms

Debilitative and facilitative anxiety

Trait and state anxiety

Working memory

Cognitive interference

Emotionally-valenced thoughts

Choking under pressure

Kinder and darker forms of choking on the threshold of victory

Audience effects

Self-consciousness

Suggested Readings

Baumeister, R. F. (1995). Disputing the effects of championship pressures and home audiences. *Journal of Personality and Social Psychology, 68*, 644–648.

Baumeister, R. F., & Steinhilber, A. (1984). Paradoxical effects of supportive audiences on performance under pressure: The home field disadvantage in sports championships. *Journal of Personality and Social Psychology, 47*, 85–93.

Dugdale, J. R., & Eklund, R. C. (2002). Do *not* pay attention to the empires: Thought suppression and task-relevant focusing strategies. *Journal of Sport & Exercise Psychology, 24*, 306–319.

Lewis, B. P., & Linder, D. E. (1997). Thinking about choking? Attentional processes and paradoxical performance. *Personality and Social Psychology Bulletin, 23*, 937–944.

Nideffer, R. M., & Sagal, M.-S. (2006). Concentration and attention control training. In J. M. Williams (Ed.), *Applied sport psychology: Personal growth to peak performance* (5th ed., pp. 382–403). New York: McGraw-Hill.

Petri, H. L., & Govern, J. (2004). *Motivation: Theory, research, and applications* (5th ed.). Belmont, CA: Wadsworth/Thomson Learning.

Schlenker, B. R., Phillips, S. T., Boniecki, K. A., & Schlenker, D. R. (1995). Championship pressures: Choking or triumphing in one's own territory. *Journal of Personality and Social Psychology, 68*, 632–643.

Self-Handicapping  11

As a six-time US champion and four-time world champion, 21-year-old Michelle Kwan was the favorite for the gold medal in women's figure skating at the 2002 Winter Olympics in Salt Lake City, Utah. A scant five months prior to these Olympic Games, Kwan fired her highly regarded longtime skating coach Frank Carroll. In a move widely interpreted as desperation if not outright insanity (Starr, 2002a), Kwan trained and competed without a coach, an endeavor unprecedented in Olympic competition. Elite coaches are instrumental in supervising the training of skaters, organizing their skating programs, and advancing the interests of their skaters with judges and other officials in backroom wheeling-dealing. After firing Carroll, she was accompanied only by her father, described as a cheerleader but without technical knowledge of elite figure skating.

With reasoning that was described as "dreamy" and "New Age," Kwan maintained that this solo act was motivated by a desire to "listen to the voice inside of me" and "take control of my life" (Howard, 2002a). This reasoning was questioned in the sporting press, with suggestions that fears of failure were behind this move that appeared to make success less likely or at least more difficult. More specifically, it was described as "a move by a worried woman locked in a quixotic chase that's ended with her falling short of gold once before" (Howard, 2002a).

In 2002, Kwan led the Olympic women's figure skating competition after the short program on the first day of competition, and it appeared as if she would fulfill expectations as the Olympic favorite. Despite skating a conservative program without the technical difficulty of her closest competitors, Kwan could not muster a critical triple-triple jump, and "doubled" the second jump by landing on two blades rather than one blade (Starr, 2002b). She later put a hand to the ice to avoid falling on a triple flip. She finished third and won the bronze medal.

If competing without a coach represented a form of self-handicapping, it did not "work" or was not successful in excusing her below par Olympic performance in the eyes of others. In the sporting press, her performance was seen as an example of "her self-inflicted history of Olympic mishaps – nearly all of them brought on by a lack of guts" (Howard, 2002b).

Kwan hired Scott Williams as her coach in September 2002 (Hine, 2003a). She won her seventh US Figure Skating Championship in January 2003 (Hine, 2003b), and her fifth world championship in March 2003 (Hine, 2003c). By 2005, she won a record-tying nine US Figure Skating Championships (Associated Press, 2005, January 16).

The gold medal winner, 16-year-old Sarah Hughes, went to the 2002 Olympics with her coach Robin Wagner. The two became particularly close in 1999 when Hughes' mother was receiving treatment for breast cancer, and Wagner was described as a best friend and second mother (Starr, 2002b). Six times weekly, the two would drive 90 minutes to practice from Hughes' home on Long Island, NY to an ice rink in Hackensack, NJ.

Hughes was in fourth place after the first day and short program of Olympic competition. Working with Wagner, Hughes boldly changed the final 90 minutes, or last third, of her long program to ratchet up its technical difficulty and artistic merit. A second triple-triple jump combination was added and a triple jump was fitted in at the end to provide a bigger finish. On the day of the long program, Wagner kept her skater to her normal routine of morning practice, lunch, light walking, afternoon nap, and a snack prior to competition. Hughes slept in her good-luck Peggy Fleming (former Olympic champion figure skater) pajamas. In preparing for the Olympics, Wagner oversaw every detail of preparation including custom skates, skating outfits, coiffure, and even the sharpening of Hughes' skates. "Team Hughes" won out.

Choking under pressure and performance anxiety were examined in the previous chapter and shown to inhibit performance during evaluations and competitions. Sources of performance inhibition that have a negative effect on performance and wellbeing at times distal and proximal to competitions are described in Chapters 11 through 17.

To this point in this book, the literature presented has rested on the assumption that people are motivated to do their best, or by the hedonic principle. The basis of the hedonic principle is that human motivation is determined by efforts to maximize pleasure and minimize pain. As described in Chapter 2, the hedonic principle has dominated the understanding of human motivation from the time of the ancient Greeks to the present day. It is the basic motivation assumption in psychological theories as diverse as emotion in psychobiology, behavioral psychology, decision-making, and social psychology (Higgins, 1997). The focus of this chapter is self-handicapping, which has the paradoxical effect of making success less likely. A key to understanding this paradoxical behavior is that under some circumstances, people avoid diagnostic information about their own capabilities and talents. They avoid knowing precisely what they are capable of accomplishing at their best, perhaps because they doubt their abilities (Jones & Berglas, 1978). Indeed, those prone to self-handicapping experience anxiety and cognitive interference after non-contingent success or success that is not due to their efforts and abilities (Thompson, 2004). They are more likely to attribute their success to luck and to doubt the likelihood of future success.

The first of these paradoxical dispositions or tendencies was first described in 1978 by Edward Jones and Steven Berglas. They identified people who created or claimed impediments prior to performance that made their success less likely. Since these people performed with handicaps, their failures could be excused and attributed to the handicaps and their successes could be seen as truly extraordinary. This strategy was described as **self-handicapping**, and it had the effect of attributing failure in athletic and academic settings to external, unstable, and specific factors, such as drunkenness, illness or injury, or inadequate practice, and avoiding internal, stable, global, and uncontrollable attributions for failure, such as a lack of talent (Arkin & Oleson, 1998; Greenlees, Jones, Holder, & Thelwell, 2006). Self-handicaps are anticipatory excuses that are presented to obscure the link between performance and ability. Self-handicaps protect people's images of self-competence in the event of poor performances.

Other forms of self-handicapping include reduced effort and academic underachievement, choosing to perform under adverse conditions, and laziness. Symptoms of anxiety, physical illness, and depression (Baumgardner, 1991; Ferrand, Tetard, & Fontayne, 2006) have also been cited as self-handicaps (Riggs, 1992). As explained in Chapter 9, failure provides information about one's competence to the degree that one prepared optimally and attributes failure to internal, stable, and uncontrollable factors. If success occurs despite the presence of handicaps, the self-handicapper can claim and receive additional credit for overcoming obstacles. If one imposes handicaps such as a lack of preparation, tasks become more difficult, and failing at a highly difficult task is less damaging to self-esteem than failure on tasks of moderate difficulty.

By avoiding "fair" tests of their competence, self-handicappers defend beliefs in their abilities and bolster their self-esteem at the cost of optimal performance and achievement. Indeed, if success occurs despite the presence of a handicap, not only may performers claim exceptional talent, but others may also concede that the handicapped person possesses exceptional talent. **Acquired handicaps** such as drunkenness and an actual lack of preparation both serve as an excuse for poor performance and decrease the chances for a successful performance. **Claimed handicaps** such as anxiety, depression, illness, fatigue, and stress serve to excuse poor performances but do not necessarily lessen the chances for success.

Self-handicapping and sport (photo © Zaichenko Olga).

Perhaps a fundamental self-handicap is the claim of being unconcerned about doing one's best in an event or competition that is of critical importance (Kuczka & Treasure, 2005).

Self-Handicapping and Sport

Jones and Berglas (1978) estimated that self-handicapping was common in sport and athletic venues. Claimed handicaps have been seen as most influential in explaining a lack of adherence to exercise regimens of adults. Handicaps that are routinely claimed to interfere with exercise are difficulties incorporating exercise into daily routines or accessing adequate exercise facilities, and poor health/physical ailments (Shields, Paskevich, & Brawley, 2003).

Competitive athletes both cite and acquire handicaps. Sportspersons cite handicaps such as a lack of preparation, competing school, work, and family obligations, injuries and illness, and conflicts with teammates and coaches (Prapavessis, Grove, & Eklund, 2004). Such cited handicaps served to obscure the relationship between an unsuccessful competition and perceived judo ability among nationally ranked male judo players. Further, the athletes perceived greater increments in judo talent after successful matches (Greenlees et al., 2006).

Athletes withdraw effort and acquire handicaps when they avoid optimal practice and training. For example, male college swimmers who were high in trait self-handicapping practiced less than low self-handicappers and were rated by their coach as putting less effort into practice before important swim meets (Rhodewalt, Saltzman, & Wittmer, 1984). Professional golfers who competed at the state level and who were high in trait self-handicapping also spent less time practicing than low self-handicappers before important golf tournaments. High self-handicappers practiced less on average than low self-handicappers. With both the swimmers and the golfers, the high self-handicappers did not decrease their preparation time prior to important performances, but they did not increase the amount of practice before these performances as much as the low self-handicappers.

Perhaps the handicaps identified by female and male athletes differ. For example, the disruptions in training and practice identified by late adolescent and young adult, elite male and female athletes who competed in basketball, volleyball, swimming, rowing, wrestling, and track and field were different (Hausenblas & Carron, 1996). Female athletes more frequently cited handicaps related to the sport itself, such as cancelled practices, illness and fatigue, and problems with family and friends. Both females and males frequently cited school commitments as handicaps.

Acquired Handicap?

Pedro Martinez finished second to Barry Zito in the 2002 voting for the Cy Young award as the best pitcher in the American League of Professional Baseball. As a two-time Cy Young winner, Martinez believed that he deserved the honor in 2002. Martinez claimed that baseball writers made excuses for not giving him the most votes, such as not facing as many tough teams as Zito. He stated that bias was the real reason for his second place finish, in that baseball writers did not want to give all of baseball's awards to Dominican players. Martinez also claimed that this bias victimized him in 1999 when he should have received the league's most valuable player award in addition to the Cy Young.

Given Martinez's expectation that writers would search for excuses to support their bias, it is difficult to explain why he delivered a convincing reason for judging his record to be second to that of Zito. After getting his 20th victory on September 22, 2002 and with his team, the Boston Red Socks having no chance for the playoffs, Martinez declared himself through for the season even before his manager made a decision about his last start. Baseball writers went on record to attribute Martinez's second place finish to his decision to skip his last start of the season, as well as Zito's superior season (Heuschkel, 2002). Zito also made all of his 35 starts and compiled a record of 23 wins versus five losses, and an earned run average (ERA) of 2.75. Zito helped his team, the Oakland Athletics, win the American League West – the strongest division. His peers voted Zito as the winner of the Players Choice Award, and *The Sporting News* named him the top pitcher.

Audience for Self-Handicapping

The audience for self-handicapping is apparently both the self and other people (Prapavessis et al., 2004). That is, self-handicappers do not want to discover and reveal a lack of ability to themselves and to others. Handicapping is probably augmented in the presence of other people, but the public value of handicapping has been considered secondary to its importance in protecting the self-handicapper's private conception of self-competence.

Self-handicapping "works" or has the desired effects in so far as self-esteem is preserved following failure and enhanced after success. As explained in previous chapters, self-esteem refers to how well or badly people regard themselves. Without handicaps, failure is more detrimental to, and success less bolstering of, self-esteem (Feick & Rhodewalt, 1997). This self-esteem protection comes at the cost of achievement in areas such as college grades and physical fitness. Self-handicapping also provides a buffer to negative affect or mood following poor performances (Drexler, Ahrens, & Haaga, 1995). Handicappers even claim altruism when they lessen their chances of success by providing opponents with an advantage in competition. Perhaps the self-handicapper limits the sting of under-achievement with thoughts of the future successes that will result from the application of their innate talent.

Self-handicapping "works" not only to protect self-esteem, but also to preserve intrinsic interest in tasks. Intrinsic interest in activities is typically lessened after failure, but not if failure is attributable to handicaps. For example, male college students who handicapped by not availing them-selves of practice prior to competitive pinball games performed worse than those who practiced (Deppe & Harackiewicz, 1996). However, the handicappers responded with a measure of indifference to feedback that they had failed in competition. Failure sapped the enjoyment of those who practiced for the pinball competition and they practiced less for future games. The college students who self-handicapped in many situations involving evaluation, i.e. high dispositional or **trait self-handicappers**, stated that they enjoyed and were more absorbed in the pinball games than the men who seldom self-handicapped. They apparently believed they had little to lose, since failure could be blamed on the handicaps rather than on their ability at pinball. High self-handicappers did indeed blame failure on their lack of practice and were still able to see them-selves as "good" pinball players after not practicing and failing. Men who were high in the self-handicapping trait and who practiced prior to the competition did not enjoy the competition. Men with low self-handicapping traits enjoyed the competition more and were more absorbed in the game when they prepared thoroughly and less when they did not practice.

Despite the performer's claim of exceptional talent, success that occurs with the presence of a handicap does not resolve the handicapper's uncertainty about their ability and efficacy. This is because self-handicapping blocks the attribution not only of failure but also of success to internal factors. High self-handicappers experience less happiness, satisfaction, relief from anxiety, and feelings of control as a result of their successes (Thompson & Richardson, 2001). Self-handicappers may want to believe that at some point they can remove the handicap and demonstrate their potential. Perhaps that is why withholding effort and not trying to do one's best is a frequently observed handicap. It can be readily removed and it is not a permanent impediment. Of course until the impediment is removed and the self-handicapper succeeds in fair competitions, uncertainty persists.

Recognition of Self-Handicapping

People who cite handicaps to excuse poor performance may be quite unaware that they engage in a consistent pattern of behavior that spares them attributions about inadequate abilities and also results in under-achievement. At other times, people may be quite aware of their self-handicapping and consciously adopt strategies that will provide viable excuses for poor performances. For example, female college students claimed the handicap of test anxiety to avoid responsibility for poor performances on intelligence tests. However, when test anxiety was dis-counted as a viable excuse for poor performances, these students simply identified another handicap, a lack of effort (Smith, Snyder, & Handelsman, 1982). Similar results have been demonstrated with high school students (Riggs, 1992). **Recognition of self-handicapping** varies, even on the part of the person involved.

Self-handicapping is not routinely recognized by others. Others do not hold people as responsible for irresponsible behaviors when they have handicaps such as drunkenness. Just as the handicapper does not attribute failure to a lack of ability, the presence of a handicap convinces outside observers that failures do not reflect inadequate ability. For example, if a runner performs badly at a race but does not train properly, outside observers are less likely to judge the failure as a reflection of ability. Out-sider observers generally do not recognize that the self-handicapper is doubtful about his or her abilities and is using a strategy to protect self-esteem. Some observers are impressed that handicapping techniques such as not studying for tests are a reflection of confidence or cockiness.

Men are more likely to confuse handicapping with confidence, but self-handicappers spot handicapping in others and do not associate it with confidence or cockiness.

Observers do, however, have less favorable impressions of self-handicappers. If outside observers believe that handicaps are self-imposed, such as inadequate preparation or drunkenness, then the handicapper may be seen as lazy and weak. People who cite self-handicaps that appear to be under their volitional control, such as putting forth little effort in training, are viewed less favorably than people who present handicaps over which they have less control, such as anxiety (Rhodewalt, Sanbonmatsu, Tschanz, Feick, & Waller, 1995). Another handicap that appears to be outside the handicapper's control is the pursuit of an extraordinarily difficult goal. Observers do not ascribe negative attributes to handicappers who strive to reach extraordinarily difficult goals.

Observers may be relatively sympathetic to self-handicapping because it is a way of offering excuses before rather than after performances take place. Excuses for failures that are given after performances receive a less favorable reception if a handicap has not been claimed or imposed prior to the performance (Crant, 1996).

Etiology of Self-Handicapping

Why do people undermine their chances for success? In terms of the **etiology of self-handicapping**, Berglas and Jones (1978) stated that handicapping begins with a hunch that success is uncertain in situations and on tasks. For example, people who suspect that prior successes and accomplishments were not due to their talent and abilities avoid future evaluations for fear that their suspicions will be confirmed. Male college students who believed that their high scores on intelligence tests were due to luck were more likely to self-handicap prior to taking a second test of intelligence. These students handicapped by taking apparent performance-inhibiting drugs as opposed to performance-enhancing drugs prior to the second test. Self-handicapping is also more likely after success that was not contingent on or the result of a person's effort. Since the person does not understand what they did to achieve this success and doubts that the success can be repeated, they fear another evaluation.

Jones and Berglas (1978) reasoned that self-handicappers somehow believe that love is conditional on performance and ability. They concluded that some children are placed in emotional binds in which their parents expect the demonstration of high ability, yet still do not provide a

> ## No Need for Self-Handicaps
>
> The Australian tennis professional Patrick Rafter provided a lesson about how to face the possibility of defeat without being daunted. He was two points from defeat in a match with American Andre Agassi in the semifinals of the 2001 men's final at Wimbledon. He recalled his thoughts at that juncture: "Just give it a go and see what happens. When you walk off, you hold your head up high. Bad luck, gave it my best shot, lost 6–4 in the fifth. Instead, here I am with a big smile on my face" (Bricker, 2001, p. C2).
>   Rafter won the match 2–6, 6–3, 3–6, 6–2, 8–6.

high degree of warmth and acceptance after ability has been demonstrated. Under these circumstances, the child learns that success does not ensure unconditional love. By withholding effort, they protect themselves from the demonstration of average or below average ability as well as from the realization that unconditional acceptance will not be provided by their parents if they actually demonstrate good ability. Therefore, self-handicapping keeps hope alive that parents will deliver the longed for, unconditional love in the future. Under these conditions, it is understandable that fair tests of ability would threaten those prone to self-handicapping. It may appear ironic that self-imposed handicaps are more likely when evaluations are most important. However, it is on these tasks that ability is revealed and imagined unconditional love is at risk. Although the self-handicapper has doubts about his or her abilities, by avoiding fair tests, they sustain uncertainty about their talent and their likelihood for success.

Self-handicapping and self-esteem are related. Given that a primary motivation for self-handicapping is to protect self-esteem, it is understandable that it occurs when people are faced with evaluations that are important to their self-image (Martin & Brawley, 2002). For example, college students were more likely to self-handicap when taking tests of verbal intelligence compared to tests of hand–eye coordination and fine motor control (Tice, 1991).

As mentioned above, self-handicapping serves not only to protect self-esteem but also to enhance one's image by the overcoming of handicaps. People with high self-esteem have been shown to be concerned with *enhancing* their public image and self-image, and they engage in self-handicapping as a means of making their successes appear truly outstanding. People with low self-esteem self-handicap to *protect* against the esteem-threatening implications of failure. For example, college students with high self-esteem were more likely to self-handicap by not practicing for tests of verbal intelligence when successful performances were seen to reflect superior ability (Tice, 1991). College students with low self-esteem were more likely to avoid practice for tests of verbal ability when failure was shown to indicate poor aptitude.

Paradoxically, the collegians prepared more optimally when tasks were less important and relevant to their self-esteem. College students with high self-esteem practiced more in preparation for tests of hand–eye coordination and fine motor control when they understood practice to enhance their chances of performing outstandingly. Students with low self-esteem practiced more on the same tasks when they understood practice to lessen their chances of failure.

Over time, self-handicapping contributes to lower self-esteem, poorer moods, and decreased wellbeing. Of course, lower self-esteem and performance uncertainty makes self-handicapping more likely, and thus a cycle is created in which self-handicapping, poor performance, and decreased self-esteem all become more likely (Zuckerman, Kieffer, & Knee, 1998).

Stability of Self-Esteem and Self-Handicapping

Self-esteem is more **stable** in some people than in others, and daily successes and failures have a greater influence when self-esteem is unstable. Those with unstable and high self-esteem are more dependent on activities that enhance their image than are those with stable, high self-esteem. People with unstable and low self-esteem are more active in avoiding activities that will confirm their low self-regard than are those with stable, low self-esteem. People with unstable self-esteem are somewhat more likely to self-handicap than college students with stable self-esteem. When taking nonverbal intelligence tests, college students with unstable, high self-esteem were more likely to self-handicap to enhance the impressiveness of their performance, and students with unstable, low self-esteem were more prone to handicap to avoid the embarrassment of failure (Newman & Wadas, 1997).

Trait Self-Handicapping and Self-Esteem

Self-handicapping is also more stable in some people than in others, and trait self-handicapping refers to a disposition to handicap in different situations and over time (Rhodewalt, Morf, Hazlett, & Fairfield, 1991). With both high self-esteem and high trait self-handicapping, people are more likely to invent handicaps to enhance attributions about ability. Low self-esteem and high trait self-handicapping increase the likelihood of creating handicaps to avoid attributing failure to ability (Rhodewalt, Morf, Hazlett, & Fairfield, 1991).

Highly skilled male golfers who frequently engage in self-handicapping were shown to have lower self-esteem (Prapavessis & Grove, 1998). Perhaps the self-handicappers were more uncertain about the outcome of tournaments. Of course, the question of whether athletes and performers with high self-esteem claim or acquire handicaps to enhance the impressiveness of performances would be of interest, especially among elite athletes.

People with low self-esteem who seldom handicapped may attribute failure to inadequate ability and thus further decrease their self-esteem. This attributional style resembles the style of people with depression in that negative outcomes are ascribed to stable, internal factors and positive outcomes to external, unstable factors.

Gender and Self-Handicapping

Are **gender and self-handicapping** related? There has been a debate about whether men and women are equally likely to *acquire* handicaps. For example, preliminary research demonstrated that both women and men who characteristically self-handicapped claimed stress as a handicap for poor performance, but only men avoided extra practice when they were informed that practice would improve their chances for success (Hirt, Deppe, & Gordon, 1991). It was reasoned that these gender differences were due to socialization practices. That is, failure in boys tends to be attributed to a lack of effort, whereas failure in girls is attributed to a lack of ability. Therefore, effort withdrawal may not "work" as an effective

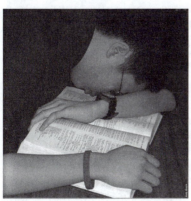

Reduced effort and self-handicapping.

excuse for poor performance in females since their failure is already more likely to be attributed to a lack of ability. If effort withdrawal is not considered a reasonable excuse for failure, women are better off practicing as much as possible to improve their chances for success.

Another explanation for the gender difference in acquired versus claimed handicaps is that certain handicaps simply involve behaviors that are more common in males. For example, in the initial studies of self-handicapping, men were shown to more frequently acquire the handicap of debilitating drug use (Berglas & Jones, 1978). Substance use and abuse is far more common in males than females (Kessler et al., 1994).

Gender does not generally influence the **number** of claimed handicaps or the attributional benefits of the claimed excuses. For example, both college women and men claimed handicaps such as having a heavy course load, sickness, lack of sleep, having other exams for which to study, and having studied the wrong material, prior to taking college tests. With handicaps, both males and females discounted failure as reflective of their ability and claimed extra talent when they performed well with handicaps (Feick & Rhodewalt, 1997).

The differences between genders with regard to claimed versus acquired handicaps may be **historical**. Research demonstrated that when men and women who were high in trait self-handicapping were given the opportunity to both claim stress and acquire a handicap by avoiding practice, both the women and men selected the claimed handicap (Thompson & Richardson, 2001). These high self-handicappers availed themselves of an excuse for poor performance but did little to sabotage their chances for success, as they practiced as much as the low self-handicappers for the evaluations. The claimed handicap appeared to have all of the "benefits" of the acquired handicap in that it excused failure. In addition, the claimed handicap did not disrupt performance and therefore offered the additional benefit of enhancing attributions about talent when they performed well. Perhaps women and men would more readily acquire handicaps if they sensed that claimed handicaps would not "play well" or be believable to skeptical audiences.

Perhaps most generally, there are likely no gender differences in claimed, situational self-handicaps when competitions are equally important or ego-relevant to female and male athletes. For example, prior to a prestigious national intercollegiate NCAA Division I golf tournament, the number of claimed situational handicaps was essentially equivalent for male and female golfers (Kuczka & Treasure, 2005).

Self-Handicapping and Goals

Self-handicappers tend to regard characteristics such as talent, ability, and intellect as **fixed** and **immutable entities**. Failure is seen to be highly threatening because it is seen to reveal permanent deficiencies in academic (Covington, 1992; Midgley, Arunkumar, & Urdan, 1996) or athletic talent (Ommundsen, 2001). Despite histories of exceptional achievement, self-handicappers are inclined to doubt their ability on the basis on one unambiguous failure or one failure that cannot be attributed to handicaps. On the other hand, this understanding occurs quite early, as ninth-grade physical education students in Norway (Ommundsen, 2001) and American eighth-graders (Midgley et al., 1996) who viewed abilities as fixed were prone to self-handicapping, especially when they doubted their abilities.

Self-handicappers are also more likely to pursue **performance** or **ego goals**, which focus on the demonstration of competence in comparison to others (Midgley et al., 1996; Rhodewalt, 1994). By contrast, people with **mastery, learning**, or **task goal orientations** (the three refer to similar goal orientations) to achievement regard ability as a mutable characteristic that is built by their efforts to develop and refine their skills (Dweck & Leggett, 1988). With mastery or learning goals, people are more prone to strive for incremental development of their skills in relation to their own baseline of prior performance. Failure is less threatening with these orientations, because deficits are understood to be subject to remediation. For example, failure might indicate that additional training and practice is necessary to master aspects of a particular element in sport performance. Given that failure denotes inadequate effort rather than inadequate ability, people with mastery goal orientations are not particularly vulnerable to threats to their self-worth, and are therefore less likely to self-handicap (Martin, Marsh, & Debus, 2001). With mastery or task orientation people are less likely to have negative expectations about performance, and to spend more time and effort on reflecting on or thinking about what needs to be done to prepare optimally for performances.

Self-handicapping was more prevalent among boys and girls between the ages of 10 and 17 who played recreational and competitive soccer when the children had performance goals and played on teams in which children were commonly compared to each other (Ryska & Yin, 1999). The children with performance goals were prone to using self-handicapping strategies such as making excuses and effort reduction as protection from threatening attributions about their abilities. Environments in which there is an emphasis on performance relative to others, such as classrooms and intercollegiate teams, foster performance goals and self-handicapping (Kuczka & Treasure, 2005; Urdan, Midgley, & Anderman, 1998).

Examining performance goals more closely, physical education students with **performance-avoidance goals** were likely to endorse self-handicapping, whereas **performance-approach goals** and task orientations were not associated with self-handicapping (Ommundsen, 2004). Seventh-graders with performance-avoidance goals were also prone to self-handicapping (Midgley & Urdan, 2001). Performance-approach goals refer to the attainment of competence in relation to norms or to other people, and performance-avoidance goals refer to orientations to avoid demonstrating incompetence in relation to norms or in the eyes of others (Elliot, 1999). With mastery or task and performance-approach orientations, people strive to grasp possibilities. With both performance-approach and performance-avoidance orientations, success is measured in relation to others. However, with performance-avoidance goals success involves avoiding mistakes and failures and dodging blunders. The distal, underlying motive disposition of those with mastery goals is solely the motive for achievement, and that for people with performance-avoidance goals is the motive for avoiding failure (Atkinson, 1957, 1964). The underlying motives for people with performance-approach goals are both the motive for achievement and the motive for avoiding failure (Elliot & Harackiewicz, 1996).

Norwegian male and female 10th-grade physical education students who endorsed performance-approach and task orientations also considered themselves to be competent at athletics (Ommundsen, 2004). With expectations of competence, there was less endorsement of self-handicapping or strategies to excuse athletic inadequacies. Additionally, when the 10th-graders held task orientations in combination with either performance-approach or performance-avoidance goals, they were less likely to acknowledge self-handicapping. Apparently, the emotional valence of efforts to avoid failure (as with performance-avoidance goals) is countered by the positive emotional valence associated with striving for success and with intrinsic interest in athletic tasks.

Self-Handicapping and Coping

People who engage in self-handicapping have been seen to engage in **emotion-focused coping** (Lazarus & Folkman, 1984). As discussed in Chapter 3, emotion-focused coping consists of managing emotional responses to stressors such as competitions and evaluations, and **problem-focused coping** involves taking action to master or resolve the source of stress. College students with high dispositional or trait self-handicapping demonstrated emotion-focused coping prior to tests and evaluations (Zuckerman et al., 1998). Their emotion-based coping strategies consisted of withdrawing from the challenge of preparing optimally for examinations. They studied less and were less efficient in studying for tests.

Emotion-focused coping may temporarily ease the stress of evaluations and soothe the sting of poor performances. This soothing comes at the cost of lower achievement (Martin et al., 2001; Zuckerman et al., 1998). Further, emotion-focused coping does not spare people from ruminations or intrusive and repetitive thoughts about poor performances. Perhaps difficulties in accepting the consequences of performances motivated their involvement in self-handicapping. That is, if people with high disposi-tional self-handicapping cannot accept and move on after performances, having excuses for poor performances may make their ruminations about poor performances less painful.

Australian athletes who were prone to self-handicapping were also more likely to use emotion-focused coping when experiencing slumps or prolonged periods of poor performance (Prapavessis, Grove, Maddison, & Zillmann, 2003). As was the case for college students, emotion-focused coping may promote disengagement from active problem solving and pro-long slumps. Self-handicapping tendencies did not spare recreational and elite athletes from the experience of cognitive and somatic anxiety prior to competitions, and self-handicapping tendencies were also associated with lower self-esteem.

Team Cohesiveness and Self-Handicapping

Team cohesiveness and self-handicapping are related in that athletes who are high in trait self-handicapping are more likely to claim handicaps when they are members of cohesive teams. Female and male athletes high in the trait of excuse making rated disruptions in training and practice schedules as unimportant when team cohesion was low, but as highly disruptive when the team cohesion was high (Carron, Prapavessis, & Grove, 1994). Athletes who were low on the self-handicapping trait of excuse making rated disruptions to practice and training as trivial regard-less of whether team cohesion was low or high. Perhaps cohesiveness provides reassurance that claimed self-handicaps will be received sympa-thetically. Alternatively, athletes may experience more responsibility to the group and cite handicaps to excuse disappointing the cohesive team.

Summary and Conclusions

The literature about self-handicapping demonstrates that some people will go to considerable lengths to avoid diagnostic information about their own capabilities and talents and a precise understanding of what they are capable of accomplishing at their best. Self-handicappers have an accurate, naïve understanding that failure under ideal conditions is highly diag-nostic about their abilities. With self-handicaps they forward antici-patory excuses that obscure the link between performance and internal, stable attributions about their ability. The benefits of claimed or acquired handicaps are the protection of self-esteem, mood, and intrinsic interest in tasks. These benefits are realized at the price of lower achievement. Self-handicappers preserve faith in their potential ability but are unlikely to be entirely free of self-doubts because they have not actually demonstrated this ability. As discussed in Chapter 9, the most convincing source of self-efficacy is enactive attainments or actual successful performance. Other people generally do not recognize the defensive qualities of self-handicapping and may even consider it to reflect cockiness. Other people do not attribute poor performance to insufficient ability in the self-handicapper, but are likely to attribute unfavorable qualities to the handi-capper, such as laziness, if the handicaps are self-imposed.

At times the motivation for self-handicapping is not to breach the connection between performance and ability, but rather to enhance the impressiveness of accomplishments. People with high self-esteem are more likely to self-handicap to embellish their achievements and attributions about their abilities.

Failure is more threatening if ability is considered to be innately determined and immutable, and people with performance or ego goals often hold this view of talent. People with this goal orientation are at risk for self-handicapping because task difficulty signals inadequate ability. By withdrawing effort, or engaging in some other form of self-handicapping, those with performance goals attempt to break the link between perform-ance and ability and avoid attributions that their innate or genetic talent is puny. With performance-avoidance goals, self-handicapping is especially likely because these goals focus attention on avoiding failure. With learn-ing, mastery or task goals, ability is considered to be acquired and success to be a result of effort. Stubborn problems are expected to yield to per-sistent effort. Since failure is considered to be subject to remediation, it is far less threatening. Success is marked in relation to one's baseline of prior performance, and therefore improvement and effort are more likely to be counted as successes, and these successes can enhance confidence in one's abilities.

Self-handicapping allows for the avoidance of unfavorable attribu-tions about one's ability. Of course, competitions, performances, and evaluations cannot be avoided, and it is necessary to remove self-handicaps to realize one's full potential. The systematic application of the principles described in Chapters 3 through 9 serve to inhibit self-handicapping. As discussed in this chapter, self-handicapping is less likely with the adoption of mastery or performance-achievement goals and the relinquishing of performance-avoidance goals.

If Jones and Berglas' (1978) explanation for the etiology of self-handicapping is accurate, then the renunciation of archaic wishes for unconditional parental love and prizing with extraordinary success may be necessary. This process of relinquishing the unfinished business of childhood may be difficult because it implies going on with life without capturing coveted parental supplies of unconditional love, and it may be necessary to consult sophisticated counselors and therapists to resolve resistance to this process. However, with both self-handicapping and procrastination, which will be discussed in the next chapter, action is not taken and opportunities are lost. Squandered and lost opportunities are regretted most with the passage of time (Gilovich & Medvec, 1995).

Key terms

Self-handicapping

Acquired handicaps

Claimed handicaps

Trait self-handicapping

Etiology of self-handicapping

Recognition of self-handicapping

Self-esteem and self-handicapping

Stability of self-esteem

Stability of self-handicapping

Self-handicapping and self-esteem

Gender and self-handicapping

Self-handicapping and goals

Mastery, learning, or task goal orientations

Performance-avoidance goals

Performance-approach goals

Emotion-focused coping

Problem-focused coping

Team cohesiveness and self-handicapping

Suggested Readings

Berglas, S., & Jones, E. E. (1978). Drug choice as a self-handicapping strategy in response to noncontingent success. *Journal of Personality and Social Psychology, 36*, 405–417.

Ommundsen, Y. (2004). Self-handicapping related to task and performance-approach and avoidance goals in physical education. *Journal of Applied Sport Psychology, 16*, 183–197.

Prapavessis, H., Grove, J. R., Maddison, R., & Zillmann, N. (2003). Self-handicapping tendencies, coping, and anxiety responses among athletes. *Psychology of Sport and Exercise, 4*, 357–375.

Ryska, T. A., & Yin, Z. (1999). The role of dispositional goal orientation and team climate on situational self-handicapping among young athletes. *Journal of Sport Behavior, 22*, 410–425.

Thompson, T., & Richardson, A. (2001). Self-handicapping status, claimed self-handicaps and reduced practice effort following success and failure feedback. *British Journal of Educational Psychology, 71*, 151–170.

Procrastination and Perfectionism 12

Herb decided that he would reach his goal of bench pressing 225 pounds for 12 repetitions during the summer before his senior year in high school. He was also determined to start the wrestling season at 147 pounds and to be first in his weight class. Since he could only press 155 pounds for 12 repetitions, he knew he had to get busy. He took advantage of a Memorial Day sale and purchased four new 45 pound plates, which he neatly arranged in his basement with the other weights. He decided that he did not want to do a "halfway" job of weight training, so he planned to delay weight training until school ended on June 22. After all, the body builders in *Muscle and Fitness* trained for at least six hours per day. Just when he was ready to start, he remembered that his family was going to the beach for the 4th of July week. "Oh well," he reasoned, he still would have a good seven weeks of summer after that week.

In July, Herb was offered a landscaping job at which he would earn $10 per hour. He could work 10-hour days and save quite a bit of money. He remembered his goals for weight training, but figured the manual labor would also be a good form of training. Besides, he read an article in *Popular Psychology Journal* that said that athletes should not be too perfectionistic or else they will burn out. He convinced himself that he would know the right time to start training if he adopted an "Eastern philosophy" of "letting the weights come to him."

As August approached, the weights had still not "come to" Herb, and he began avoiding the basement and a visual sighting of his weight bench. At the preseason meeting for the wrestling team, Herb weighed in at 162 pounds. He wondered if the extra weight would contribute to his bench press.

Procrastination

As described in Chapter 11, procrastination with regard to studying was identified as the most prevalent form of self-handicapping among students. It is a form of withholding effort, and also prevalent among sportspersons. As an acquired handicap, it not only obscures the link between performance and ability but also erodes actual performance and achievement. Procrastinators are also at risk for acquiring and claiming other handicaps. Procrastination and other forms of self-handicapping are more likely to occur when one is facing tasks that threaten self-esteem, such as competitions and tests (Ferrari & Tice, 2000). Procrastination involves an unusual form of self-handicapping in that it extends over a period of time, and compromises optimal preparation at times both distal and proximal to performances and competitions. Given that optimal athletic performance typically requires discrete periods of overtraining and tapering, procrastination may be especially disruptive to sportspersons (Raglin & Wilson, 2000). It may therefore be surprising that it has been studied less extensively than other forms of self-handicapping in sport venues. The review of procrastination in this chapter will be brief and will focus on its etiology and its theoretical similarities with perfectionism.

The term "procrastination" is derived from the Latin verb *procrastinare*, which is defined as putting off, or postponing until another day (De-Simone, 1993). It has been described as an irrational tendency to delay tasks that require completion. Procrastination may occur when tasks are considered important but unattractive. The unattractive tasks are avoided in favor of more enjoyable activities. Interest in overcoming procrastination is due to the long-term rewards that will follow the execution of aversive or unattractive actions or work.

Procrastination has been a concern in modern times and in technologically advanced countries where timeliness and punctuality is emphasized. Approximately 20 to 30 percent of college students identified themselves as "problem procrastinators" in that postponing tasks decreased both their academic achievement and their enjoyment of life. Among adults in the general population, 25 percent acknowledged that procrastination was a significant problem and 40 percent allowed that procrastination had caused them financial loss during the past year. Procrastination is most prevalent at approximately ages 20 and 25 for women and men, respectively in the general population (Ferrari, Johnson, & McCown, 1995). Forms of frequent or chronic procrastination are referred to as **trait procrastination**.

Costs of Procrastination

It is not uncommon for procrastinators to discount the **costs** of their dawdling. For example, some procrastinators say that they do their best work under the pressure of deadlines, and that when squeezed by deadlines they experience excitement. They might also argue that by delaying the start of work projects, they preserve leisure time and increase their quality of life. This view that dawdling is adaptive or at least not harmful does not withstand scientific scrutiny (Steel, Brothen, & Wambach, 2001). College student procrastinators receive lower grades on term papers and on exams (Tice & Baumeister, 1997) and experience higher levels of worry about tests (Flett, Blankstein, & Martin, 1995). During the early portions of college semesters, procrastinators experience lower levels of stress and have fewer physical illnesses and problems, perhaps because they avoid the stress of preparing for classes. However, at the end of the semester and in total, procrastinators reported more physical symptoms, experienced *more stress*, and made more visits to healthcare professionals than nonprocrastinators (Tice & Baumeister, 1997).

Collegiate sport administrators reported experiencing guilt when procrastinating, perhaps because they also associated procrastination with laziness, lack of confidence, and poor time management skills (Parsons & Soucie, 1988). These administrators also attributed procrastination to institutional problems such as having too much work and too little direction.

It is even more difficult to rationalize procrastination as beneficial to athletic training. Athletic and mental skills are often developed incrementally and maintained through regular practice. As described in Chapter 4, extensive and regular practice is necessary for athletic skills to become autonomous or capable of execution with little conscious attention and regulation. Skills and fitness also develop over time with the systematic management of overtraining, staleness, and tapering (Raglin & Wilson, 2000). Delays in the initiation or maintenance of athletic training cannot be remediated with feverish last-minute preparations.

Procrastination and Coping

Procrastination is associated with more stress in the form of daily hassles or problems and annoyances, depression, negative self-concepts, and lower self-esteem and self-efficacy (Lay, 1995). Because of their tendency to avoid the sources of stress in their lives, procrastinators use coping strategies that are far less effective in mastering the sources of stress. Procrastination involves an *emotion-focused coping* response to the stress of accomplishing a difficult or unpleasant assignment (Lazarus & Folkman, 1984). As mentioned above, these avoidance behaviors serve the short-term purpose of reducing anxiety but incur considerable long-term costs. When they are procrastinating, it is sometimes difficult for people to completely rid their mind of thoughts about what they are avoiding or what they should be doing. They live with the knowledge that adverse

Martina Navratilova Was a Procrastinator

"Or maybe you're a born procrastinator. Okay, I'll admit it, so am I – or I was. Procrastination is an old habit that many times in my life kept winning out. I'd let problems slide and slide, mostly because I needed shelter from them when I was playing tennis. Conflict, for example – I tried to avoid it at all costs. I would just let things build, and they'd get worse. But just imagine what might happen if you let your health slide. Who wants to hear a doctor say, 'If you don't stop smoking, you'll be dead in 6 months' or 'If you don't stop drinking, your liver will give out in 2 years'? Don't let things deteriorate into a life-or-death situation. Please! I learned to deal with problems head on, and sooner rather than later. You can as well." (Navratilova, 2006, p. 13)

consequences loom and they do not control aversive stimuli, such as deadlines. Like the self-handicapper, the procrastinator lives with pervasive and consistent doubts about their ability.

Procrastinators also live with disappointment about lost opportunities and regret how they waste time. This regret does not typically teach people to stop procrastinating. Instead, people try to avoid future experiences of regret, and therefore demonstrate even greater avoidance of the challenges in the future (Van Eerde, 2000).

As has been mentioned at several points in this book, *task-focused coping* strategies are more effective in reducing the effects of stressors that must be faced and mastered. **Task-focused** coping refers to rational preparation and responses to stressors, such as the use of the strategies for optimizing performance that were discussed in Chapters 3 through 9.

Procrastination and inadequate preparation (photo © Spauln).

Theoretical and Scientific Explanations for Procrastination

Psychoanalytic

Procrastination has been explained in the contexts of some of the most influential paradigms in psychology. The **psychoanalytic** paradigm began with Sigmund Freud and was introduced in Chapter 2. In Freud's model of the psyche, the ego conducts executive functions such as the detection of anxiety. The ego employs a variety of methods for reducing anxiety; these include intrapsychic defenses, which push the causes of anxiety out of conscious awareness. For example, thoughts that cause anxiety are repressed and tasks that cause anxiety are avoided by procrastination. Although difficult to validate empirically, the psychoanalytic perspective has fostered research. For example, procrastination has been seen to reflect an unconscious preoccupation with death, in that tardiness reflects an attempt to put off death until a later date (Blatt & Quinlan, 1967).

Psychodynamic

From a **psychodynamic** perspective, procrastination is understood to be a result of childrearing practices. For example, parents of procrastinators have been shown to make love and approval contingent on achievement, to set unrealistically high goals for their children, and to be overly coercive in emphasizing achievement. As described in Chapter 11 in the context of self-handicapping, these experiences place the child and later the adult in a bind that encourages procrastination. Task avoidance allows for avoidance of anxiety related to fear of failing to achieve the lofty goals and also keeps alive hope of obtaining parental love in the future. Excessive parental coercion also fosters **reactance**, or efforts to reestablish autonomy and independence, and dawdling demonstrates that the child will not be pushed at the parents' schedule.

Children who are involved in struggles about achievement with parents may also procrastinate as a passive aggressive way of expressing anger at the parents. Passive aggressive behaviors typically frustrate and anger the other person without a direct display of aggression. There is a certain naïve genius to procrastination in response to an authoritarian parent who pushes for the accomplishment of unrealistic goals. There are probably few other responses available to the child that would cause equal frustration to the parent and also sustain the parent's belief in the child's abilities. College students with trait procrastination report conflict not only with their parents but also with best friends of the same sex (Ferrari, Harriott, & Zimmerman, 1999).

Developmental Psychology

A related explanation from **developmental psychology** regards pro-crastination as originating in a context of high levels of parental criticism and expectations. These parents may respond with harsh criticism when their children fail to meet their expectations. Given all the learning that occurs throughout development, there are practically unlimited oppor-tunities for authoritarian parents to see their children as falling short. Children form primary attachments to these critical parents, and must accommodate their behavior and manners of viewing themselves and others to fit these relations or attachments to their parents. These children may therefore come to judge themselves in overly harsh and critical ways, and expect the same judgments from people outside of their family of origin. Expecting harsh judgments, these children are less likely to turn to others when they need help, and more likely to compare their performance to that of others in achievement contexts (Flett et al., 1995). These children often compare their academic or athletic ability to that of their most capable peers, and feel dumb or clumsy in comparison. Children escape from these negative social comparisons by avoiding competitions and evaluations, and one form of this avoidance is procrastination.

An assumption of the psychoanalytic and psychodynamic perspec-tives is that procrastination is a trait or characteristic that appears con-sistently over time and across situations. This assumption is almost certainly correct. Empirical research has demonstrated that trait pro-crastination can be reliably and validly measured (Lay, 1986; McCown & Johnson, 1989), and that these measures of procrastination predict tardi-ness in completing assignments across settings (Tice & Baumeister, 1997).

Behaviorism

The psychological perspective that is perhaps the most theoretically opposed to psychoanalytic and psychodynamic paradigms is **behaviorism**. Behavioral psychologists have also reported that people procrastinate prior to initiating and completing tasks that are unpleasant, difficult, or boring. Such tasks are often put aside in favor of activities that appear to have more immediate rewards and fewer aversive characteristics. People procrastinate when faced with such tasks because it is often difficult for them to sustain effort until these tasks are completed. If difficult and boring tasks are to be completed, people must inhibit interference from competing thoughts and activities. Similarly, when frustrated, it is neces-sary to inhibit behaviors that are more rewarding and less frustrating. Sometimes people are frustrated and resentful when others impose tasks and jobs on them. With resentment, people may procrastinate as a means of reacting against the imposition of duties by others (Blunt & Psychl, 2000).

From a behavioral paradigm, a key to overcoming the tendency to avoid the difficult and seek the easy tasks is to follow **Grandma's Law** – "First clean up your plate, then you may have your dessert" (Homme, 1970, p. 17). Applying Grandma's Law to academic venues, students would be advised to study first and play later. Athletes will be far more successful if they practice or train first and relax afterwards. Continuing with the analogy, procrastinating athletes and students may be as likely to do their work after "goofing off" as the grandchildren are to eat broccoli after ice cream.

Fear of Failure

Another explanation for procrastination that is consistent with behavioral paradigms is that procrastination is a result of **fears of failure**. For example, students who fear failing on tests avoid the stimulus for their fear, the test, by procrastinating. Anxiety is thus reduced. Despite the intuitive appeal of this explanation, empirical studies demonstrate that only a small proportion of procrastination is due to fears of failure (Schouwenburg, 1995).

Cognitive Psychology

Cognitive psychology examines the beliefs that lead to procrastination. From this perspective, procrastinators often hold unreasonably high standards for their performance (Ferrari et al., 1995). This perspective is consistent with the discussion of self-handicapping in Chapter 11 in that by withdrawing effort and delaying the initiation of tasks, individuals provide themselves with excuses for not reaching their extreme standards for performance. It is also consistent with a discussion of perfectionism that will follow, as perfection is the highest goal for a performance.

Personality Traits and Procrastination

A number of **personality traits** are associated with procrastination. Procrastinators often show low levels of **conscientiousness**, and conscientiousness and procrastination are negatively correlated for children as young as eight (Lay, Kovacs, & Danto, 1998). With low levels of conscientiousness, people lack self-discipline, dutifulness, achievement striving, orderliness, and strong commitments to reach their goals. Procrastinators underestimate the amount of time necessary to complete assignments. Trait **neuroticism** also appears to be higher among procrastinators. Neuroticism refers to depression, self-consciousness, impulsiveness, anxiety, somatic concerns, and social discomfort. The influence of neuroticism has been more equivocal than that of conscientiousness (Steel et al., 2001).

Procrastination and Self-Esteem

The self-esteem of procrastinators is lower than average, and therefore more easily threatened. Like self-handicappers, procrastinators avoid fair tests of their ability and prefer to work on easy, unchallenging tasks. Because of their difficulty in starting and finishing tasks, they live with any number of unfulfilled ambitions, intentions, and dreams. For procrastinators, it is sometimes preferable to do nothing than to risk failure and look foolish (Ferrari & Tice, 2000). Like self-handicappers, procrastinators protect their self-esteem at the cost of underachievement, unrealized goals, and wasted potential. Perhaps ruminations about "what might have been" sustain hope in abilities, but again this comes at the considerable cost of regret regarding lost and squandered opportunities.

Summary and Conclusions

Procrastinators avoid the stress, anxiety, and work of challenges during times that are distal to evaluations and performances. Since they do not prepare optimally during distal times, they perform more poorly and underachieve. After evaluations, they are left with disappointment and ruminations about lost opportunities. The cumulative effects of procrastination are lower self-esteem and self-efficacy and higher risks for depression. At times proximal to evaluations, stress, anxiety, and somatic or physical symptoms accelerate and become intrusive as procrastinators can no longer avoid and deny the impending evaluation and their lack of preparation.

In a review of the factors that inhibit optimal performance, two themes will persist. First, the conscientious practice of the techniques for optimal proximal and distal preparation competes with and counteracts the inhibiting factors. The preparation of procrastinators for performances is faulty at times distal and proximal to evaluations. It is likely necessary to identify optimal but realistic challenges, and to be systematic in establishing timetables for accomplishing goals and subgoals. Competing goals may be prioritized so that procrastination is recognized when time is given to or wasted on tasks that are not of a high priority. It is often important to schedule adequate chunks of time to muster the concentration necessary to accomplish difficult subgoals. Intrinsic interest in tasks can be strengthened and boredom decreased when efficacy for the accomplishment of the task is increased. Almost any task can be interesting or rewarding if one is good at it. Efficacy builds with the experience of successfully realizing goals.

The second theme that will be present in many reviews of the factors that inhibit performance is that in some instances, it will be necessary to consult mentors who are knowledgeable about these issues for advice, coaching, guidance, counseling, or therapy. This process of gaining help from others may be accomplished with formal or informal mentoring relationships. Formal mentoring relationships often occur with recognized professionals such as coaches, teachers, and psychologists.

Perfectionism

The hockey performance of the University of Minnesota defenseman Keith Ballard was impaired by perfectionism: "not being good all the time was something I couldn't handle" (Blount, 2004, p. 10C). His coach, Don Lucia, commented, "In the past, if he made a bad play in the first period, it would affect him the whole game. He was a guy who felt he had to hit a home run all the time" (Blount, 2004, p. 10C).

Ballard's game improved when he accepted that perfection was impossible on a daily basis, and when he shouldered more responsibility for the entire team's performance as an assistant captain. Coach Lucia noted, "Keith has become more mentally mature this year, and he's able to move on after a mistake" (Blount, 2004, p. 10C).

Definitions of perfectionism are influenced by the theories and empirical research of teams of psychologists, and therefore are not identical. As is often the case with complex psychological phenomena, alternative viewpoints or explanations for these phenomena are not necessarily in competition, and at this point can be understood to be heuristic. Moreover, different teams emphasize several common dimensions. Most theoretical and empirical discussions of perfectionism emphasize the setting of *extreme standards* for performance. As discussed in Chapter 7, setting difficult and even extreme goals is not dysfunctional and leads to higher achievement. Perfectionism associated with very high standards for performance is normal to the degree that one does not feel compelled to perform flawlessly on unimportant tasks, and that efforts to excel are saved for situations when excellence is warranted and rewarded (Rehm,

1982). **Normal perfectionism** is distinguished by lofty but achievable goals, intrinsic pleasure in tasks, and satisfaction upon reaching goals (Rehm, 1982). Exacting and adaptive goals allow for some margin of error during performances and competitions. Normal perfectionists sometimes experience facilitative anxiety or excitement prior to evaluations and performances.

Neurotic Perfectionism

Neurotic perfectionists differ from normal perfectionists in a number of important ways. First, their perfectionism does not motivate higher performance and achievement. Ironically, with goals of perfection, people try harder but do worse (Frost & Marten, 1990), because their attention is given to detecting flaws in their performances and avoiding mistakes. In effect, neurotic perfectionists "worry about their deficiencies and concentrate on how to avoid doing things wrong" (Hamachek, 1978, p. 28). Attention to flawlessness is excessively self-focused, and self-focused attention frequently gives way to cognitive interference and performance inhibition and deterioration (Anshel & Mansouri, 2005). Examples of this cognitive interference are self-derogatory or self-critical internal monologues (Cervone, 2000), and it may slow performance on tasks requiring speed and precision (Rheaume et al., 2000). These monologues also are distracting and neurotic perfectionists sometimes miss important feedback about progress toward their goals. This feedback provides information about whether efforts are producing desired results and is essential for understanding when efforts, such as training regimens, should be altered. Neurotic perfectionists are prone to "end-state" daydreaming about the consequences of reaching goals. As discussed previously in the context of mental practice, this kind of daydreaming interferes with the instrumental behaviors that make goal attainment more likely.

Neurotic perfectionism directs attention to the negative aspects of performance and allows for little satisfaction with the results of performances. It is generally not sufficient for neurotic perfectionists to be perfect in one domain of life functioning, as they often strive toward perfection in other domains (Flett, Sawatzky, & Hewitt, 1995). Given that this perfection is largely unattainable, neurotic perfectionists remonstrate with themselves that their performances should have been better. Neurotic perfectionists are harsh in their self-criticism when they make mistakes and especially when they fail. The thinking of perfectionists is often dichotomized such that they regard themselves as perfect or as failures. Since perfection is all but unattainable, this all-or-nothing thinking often leaves the neurotic perfectionist feeling like a failure.

Neurotic Perfectionism and Depression

Feeling that they are lacking, being angry with themselves for their lack of perfection, and seeing themselves as failures, neurotic perfectionists are vulnerable to depression (Flett, Hewitt, Blankstein, & Gray, 1998). This type of depression tends to be characterological or long-standing (Hewitt, Flett, Ediger, Norton, & Flynn, 1998), and its amelioration requires an extended course of psychotherapy (Blatt, 1995). In cases of extreme perfectionism, failure and humiliation can foster suicidal thoughts and behavior.

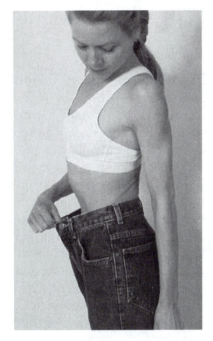

Neurotic perfectionism impairs performance and is associated with eating disorders.

Paradoxically, depression may contribute to the further elevation of self-set standards because depressed people may achieve high goals and still feel depressed rather than feeling a measure of self-satisfaction upon realizing goals. In effect, the depressed person makes a tacit assumption that the relief from depression will result from the realization of even more difficult goals. Of course, the realization of extreme goals is unlikely, and as the depressed person experiences fewer successes in relation to their self-set goals, negative moods are likely to deepen (Cervone, Kopp, Schaumann, & Scott, 1994).

The impossibility of reaching standards of perfection serves only to increase the likelihood of rumination about the perfectionistic goal. Ruminative thinking and depression commonly result when unattainable goals are not renounced (McIntosh, 1996). Perfectionists have a difficult time disengaging from unattainable goals and brood about "what might have been" if they were perfect. This thinking brings to mind depressing thoughts about the gulf between the standards of perfection and the neurotic perfectionist's current status and level of functioning.

Theoretical and Scientific Explanations for Perfectionism

Psychoanalytic Theory

Psychoanalytic theory identified a harsh and punitive superego as the source of perfectionism. As indicated in Chapter 2, Sigmund Freud determined that the dynamic structures of the psyche were the superego, ego, and id. The superego was seen to be the moral seat of the psyche and to contain the equivalent of the conscience and the standards for performance also known as the **ego ideal** (Freud, 1917/1957; 1923/1961). Metaphorically speaking, the superego and ego ideal sit in judgment of the individual and her or his accomplishments. If the standards of the superego and ego ideal are too extreme, people may incessantly push themselves toward perfection, but never experience satisfaction with their accomplishments. People with these extreme superegos may experience a need to maintain a personal and public image of strength and perfection and feel as if they are always on trial and in need of proving themselves. This need for perfection may also inhibit them from turning to others when help is needed (Blatt, 1995).

Multidimensional Perfectionism: Flett and Hewitt

Contemporary psychologists have determined that perfectionism is a **multidimensional** construct or psychological trait, and that it has adaptive features. Perfectionism may simply consist of high personal standards, and it is associated with ambitiousness and conscientiousness. With this **self-oriented** perfectionism, people tend to focus on the rewards associated with realizing goals rather than the punishments and losses that may result from failed performances. Learning or mastery goals and intrinsic motivation are more likely associated with self-oriented perfectionism. Perhaps intrinsic motivation and efficacy for reaching extreme goals shield those with self-oriented perfectionism from procrastination. In fact, greater procrastination occurs when self-oriented perfectionism and standards are low and when expectations for success are low (Flett, Hewitt, & Martin, 1995).

It appears that self-oriented perfectionism is adaptive under conditions of low stress. With the experiences of high levels of stress and negative life events, the belief of self-oriented perfectionists in their personal control is shaken, and they are at risk for depression (Flett & Hewitt, 1995) and cognitive and physiological anxiety (Flett & Hewitt, 1994). Self-oriented perfectionists are especially prone to experience anxiety prior to and during important evaluations and performances. For example, dancers with high self-oriented perfectionism and low personal control experienced debilitating anxiety during performances (Mor, Day, Flett, & Hewitt, 1995). Self-oriented perfectionists are also prone to self-handicapping (Hobden & Pliner, 1995). They bombard themselves with criticism following imperfect performances, and over time these negative, global, and stable attributions take their toll in the form of depression (Hewitt, Flett, & Ediger, 1996).

Perfectionism is **other-directed** when individuals expect and demand that others perform and behave perfectly. Other-directed perfectionism often sparks hostility because other people do not meet standards of perfectionism, and this promotes efforts to dominate and control the people who are not performing perfectly.

A third kind of perfectionism occurs when people believe that others expect them to reach standards that are difficult or impossible to achieve, and that acceptance and approval are dependent on achieving these standards. This **socially prescribed** perfectionism probably originates with expectations of perfectionism imposed by significant others. It promotes excessive attention to the reactions of others and fears of their negative evaluations. With socially prescribed perfectionism there is a pervasive fear of failure and negative evaluations and feelings of failure, anxiety, anger, and helplessness are common. Given that these perfectionists anticipate negative reactions from others, it is not surprising that they keep their emotional reactions under control and are careful not to upset others (Flett, Hewitt, & De Rosa, 1996).

Socially prescribed perfectionism is associated with performance goals and less intrinsic interest in tasks. Socially prescribed perfectionists lack efficacy and confidence that externally imposed goals will be realized and are prone to attribute their successes and failures to external factors (Flett & Hewitt, 1998). Such perfectionism promotes efforts to avoid challenges and potential failures rather than to approach opportunities and potential gains. It is also associated with procrastination (Flett, Blankstein, Hewitt, & Koledin, 1992) and a lack of conscientiousness.

As with self-oriented perfectionism, socially prescribed perfectionism is associated with cognitive and physiological anxiety (Flett & Hewitt, 1994). It inhibits performance and promotes self-handicapping. Finally, perfectionism has been associated with eating disorders in women, and this association appears stronger for socially prescribed perfectionism (Hewitt, Flett, & Ediger, 1995).

Multidimensional Perfectionism: Frost et al.

An independent research team also determined that perfectionism is multidimensional. The dimensions, however, are determined not by whether perfectionism is directed at the self or at others, but by the manner in which the self is evaluated and judged. These dimensions of perfectionism are: **personal standards, organization, parental expectations, parental criticism, concern over mistakes, and doubts about actions** (Frost, Marten, Lahart, & Rosenblate, 1990). The dimensions of personal standards and organization are associated with high levels of achievement, effective work habits, a lack of procrastination, and normal perfectionism (Brown, Heimberg, Frost, Makris, Juster, & Leung, 1999). Organization is also related to neatness, efficiency, and order.

Concern over mistakes, excessive parental expectations, and doubts about actions are associated with procrastination, fear of failure, and depression and anxiety. The doubts about actions dimension relates to a vague sense of doubt about the quality of one's performance. With high levels of doubts about actions, people have a pervasive sense that something is wrong, but they cannot identify specific mistakes or correct what is considered to be wrong. Concern over mistakes disposes people to lack confidence during evaluations when mistakes are likely and to experience negative moods during these tasks. With high concern over mistakes, people are more concerned that other people will think they lack intelligence during these evaluations and they are grudging about sharing the results of their performances with others (Frost, Turcotte, Heimberg, Mattia, Holt, & Hope, 1995).

Correlations between the Two Multidimensional Perfectionisms

Both of the abovementioned characterizations of multidimensional perfectionism identified adaptive and maladaptive aspects and these aspects are statistically related. Socially prescribed perfectionism is maladaptive, and it correlates highly with concern over mistakes, excessive parental expectations, and parental criticism (Frost, Heimberg, Holt, Mattia, & Neubauer, 1993). High parental expectations and socially prescribed perfectionism are also related to wishes for perfect interpersonal relationships (Flett et al., 1995).

Dimensions of Perfectionism in Sport

Both of the multidimensional models apply to perfectionism across domains or situations. However, perfectionistic tendencies for some intercollegiate athletes are higher in sport than in the classroom (Dunn, Gotwals, & Dunn, 2005). Perfectionism that is specific to athletic domains has also been measured, and consists of the dimensions of personal standards, concern over mistakes, perceived parental pressure, and perceived coach pressure (Dunn, Dunn, Gotwals, Vallance, Craft, & Syrotuik, 2006). The dimensions of **sport multidimensional perfectionism** overlap with those of the abovementioned models of Flett and Hewitt and Frost et al. For example, concern over mistakes is correlated with Flett and Hewitt's self-oriented perfectionism and socially prescribed perfectionism. One advantage of the sport multidimensional perfectionism model is the possibility of identifying perceived demands for flawlessness from both coaches and parents.

Etiology of Perfectionism

Neurotic perfectionism is more likely to result when people have histories of high levels of parental criticism and parental expectations. As explained above, these parental characteristics are also associated with procrastination (as well as fear of failure in sport [Conroy, 2003]). Children who receive little parental love and approval, and who lose these short supplies when they do not perform successfully, fear initiating tasks and chancing failure. These parents may be overly controlling and authoritarian, and appear to value performance above closeness and affection. They may readily provide criticism when the child behaves in ways that are considered unacceptable, and fail to provide clear standards for behavior and direction about how to reach acceptable standards. In these environments children can only escape criticism if their performance is flawless, but they experience performance inhibition because they are never sure what constitutes a flawless performance. When parents chronically withhold approval and urge their children to do better, they provide a model that when internalized results in the child's chronic dissatisfaction with his or her performance. With this implicit model, children "see themselves through their parents' eyes." In adulthood these models exist in abstract or metabolized forms, not necessarily as expectations of parental responses, but as perfectionistic standards for judging oneself and others (Pacht, 1984).

It has also been hypothesized that neurotic perfectionists have histories of **insecure attachments** to parents and caregivers. Consistent with the previous theorizing, these parents are understood to make approval conditional on the child's performance and to impose harsh criticism when performance has flaws. In response to the harsh and punitive responses of these parents and caregivers, their children learned to avoid others when

> ### Normal Perfectionism
>
> In 2001 and 2002, Annika Sorenstam was the most dominant golfer in the world. She may be seen as a normal perfectionist in that she constantly strives to improve all aspects of her game, as well as her physical fitness. Her perfectionism did not derive from parental pressure: "My parents are more laid back, more social, more party people than I am. I've always been a perfectionist in whatever I do and think when I see the results, I get more into it. I really want to see how good I can be" (Farrell, 2002, p. 23).

they experienced distress (Flett et al., 1995). Children with insecure and ambivalent/anxious attachments are quite dependent on caretakers, but are also vigilant to avoid this criticism. These children are more likely to compare their performance to that of others in achievement contexts, and often compare themselves with people who set the standard for performance in their sphere. For example, a child who is uncertain about her or his athletic ability may compare herself or himself to the swiftest runner in her or his class, and as a result experience demoralization and inadequacy.

The parents of perfectionists may also be perfectionistic in their own right, and model or demonstrate perfectionism in their own behavior. The concordance of perfectionism between generations has been studied more extensively with female than with male college students. High neurotic perfectionism among college women was associated with high perfectionism in their mothers but not their fathers (Frost, Lahart, & Rosenblate, 1991). Mothers who set high standards for their daughters believed that their parents set high standards for them. High personal standards and organization in parents were correlated with the same dimensions of normal perfectionism in their daughters.

Perfectionism and Sport

Neurotic Perfectionism

Research about the **impact of perfectionism on sport** performance has emphasized the effects of neurotic or maladaptive perfectionism (Flett & Hewitt, 2005). For example, neurotic perfectionism was shown to be higher among runners who felt "obliged" to run, or who were excessively uncomfortable with the idea of skipping a day's run (Coen & Ogles, 1993). The obliged runners experienced more fear of making mistakes and performance anxiety. They had high levels of trait anxiety, and experienced intense state anxiety when their self-esteem was threatened. More generally, perfectionism is associated with exercise dependence (Hagan & Hausenblas, 2003; Hausenblas & Symons Downs, 2002). Aspects of exercise dependence include the experience of anxiety if one cannot exercise and the organization of one's life around exercise.

Neurotic perfectionism is also associated with anxiety about the appearance of one's physique. This finding was reported with elite male and female Australian athletes (Haase, Prapavessis, & Owens, 2002). Among the elite female Australian athletes, neurotic perfectionism and anxiety about the appearance of one's physique was associated with negative eating attitudes. Neurotic perfectionism has also been described as negative perfectionism, and positive and negative perfectionism have been measured with the Positive and Negative Perfectionism Scale (Terry-Short, Owens, Slade, & Dewey, 1995), which has been validated with elite athletes from Australia and New Zealand (Haase & Prapavessis, 2004).

Perfectionism and Anxiety

Perfectionism has consistently been associated with cognitive anxiety in groups of athletes. This finding was reported with female softball players and male baseball players in high school (Castro & Rice, 2003), and female and male high school runners (Hall, Kerr, & Matthews, 1998). With the high school runners, higher levels of perfectionism were associated with higher levels of cognitive anxiety when both were measured 1 week, 2 days, 1 day, and 30 minutes prior to cross-country meets. Higher levels of perfectionism were related to higher somatic anxiety when they were measured one week prior to competition. Perfectionism was more closely related to anxiety than perceived ability and goal orientation. However, maladaptive perfectionism is related to ego orientations, and perhaps both direct the attention of athletes to external standards for measuring performance (Dunn, Dunn, & Syrotuik, 2002).

In terms of the dimensions of perfectionism identified by Frost and colleagues (Frost et al., 1990), high levels of concern over mistakes and doubts about actions were associated with higher levels of cognitive and somatic anxiety among current or potential Olympic athletes in Sweden (Koivula, Hassmen, & Fallby, 2002). Concern over mistakes was associated with anxiety, and concern over mistakes and doubts about actions were associated with less self-confidence during athletic competition among intercollegiate Division II female athletes (Frost & Henderson, 1991). Concern over mistakes, doubts about actions, and parental criticism were associated with lower general self-esteem and self-esteem in sport among female and male intercollegiate athletes (Gotwals, Dunn, & Wayment, 2003).

As mentioned above, concern over mistakes and parental criticism are correlated with socially prescribed perfectionism, and both relate to expectations that others expect perfection and will not brook blunders (Frost et al., 1993). Athletes with high levels of perfectionism on the dimensions of concern over mistakes and doubts about actions apparently view competition as an opportunity for failure.

Perfectionism and Cognitive Interference

With high levels of concern over mistakes, doubts about actions, and parental criticism, athletes experienced cognitive interference when they made mistakes (Frost & Henderson, 1991; Koivula et al., 2002). This cognitive interference consisted of worries about disappointing coaches and teammates, focusing attention on the mistake, self-talk about the mistake, experiencing pressure to make up for the mistake, having difficulty forgetting about the mistake, and having intrusive images about the mistake. Even the coaches of these athletes were aware of their difficulties in recovering from mistakes during the course of performances.

High levels of concern over mistakes, doubts about action, and parental criticism are likely to foster attention that is self-focused rather than task-focused. As explained in the discussion of choking under pressure (Chapter 10), with self-focused attention there is a greater risk for cognitive interference and questioning whether one has the capacity to reach standards necessary for success. If the standard for success is perfection, then the answer will usually be "no" (Carver, 1996). With this answer, anxiety and cognitive interference are likely to rise and self-efficacy is likely to shrink.

Perfectionism and Relationships with Teammates

Maladaptive perfectionism has also been associated with a reduced quality of relationships with teammates among experienced adolescent female and male Norwegian soccer players (Ommundsen, Roberts, Lemyre, & Miller, 2005). The maladaptive perfectionism of the adolescent males appeared to stem from excessively high parental criticism and expectations and criticism and concern over mistakes. Perhaps the perfectionistic footballers become impatient and critical with teammates who do not perform to their excessively high standards. Alternatively, the perfectionistic adolescents may withdraw from more interactions with teammates as they expect that the judgments of peers will be as harsh as their own self-criticism.

Alex Rodriquez's Normal Perfectionism?

Despite winning the Most Valuable Player award for the American League in 2005, Alex Rodriguez finds it difficult to accept imperfection in himself. This concerned his manager Joe Torre. "He doesn't think he should do anything wrong, ever. We can't live our lives that way" (Amore, 2006, p. C2). This drive for perfection motivates Rodriguez to tirelessly train and practice. Torre observed, "He's here most days before most of the coaches. He's always out there trying to make himself better, and over 162 games, that takes its toll, the brow-beating he gives himself" (Amore, 2006, p. C2).

Normal Perfectionism

Athletes who endorsed the high personal standards factor of perfectionism were more likely to enjoy thoughts concerning the opportunities for success in competitions. Canadian high school footballers that recorded high personal standards also endorsed task orientations (Dunn et al., 2002). It has been speculated that task orientations provide a buffer against maladaptive perfectionism (Dunn et al., 2002); however, athletes with high personal standards were still concerned about avoiding failure (Frost et al., 1993). US Olympic champions recorded high levels of personal standards and organization, and low levels of concern over mistakes, doubts about actions, parental expectations, and parental criticism (Gould, Dieffenbach, & Moffett, 2002).

Perfectionism and Burnout

Perfectionism is recognized as one reason why junior tennis players lost interest in and became apathetic about playing tennis, or "burned out" (Gould, Tuffy, Udry, & Loehr, 1996a). Burned-out juniors recorded significantly higher scores for parental criticism, parental expectations, concern over mistakes, and personal standards and organization than juniors who were enthusiastic about tennis. Some burned-out juniors became immobilized and withdrew from competition.

What to Do about Perfectionism

Neurotic perfectionists have been encouraged to accept imperfection as a goal (Pacht, 1984), and to essentially work toward becoming normal perfectionists. As normal perfectionists they can strive for excellence, but also relax their standards when situations warrant. Neurotic perfectionists have also been advised to limit their perfectionism to one or two important areas of life functioning, and to give themselves permission to be less than perfect in other areas. They were encouraged to set reasonable goals and to develop at least one area in which they can function without any self-evaluation (Hamachek, 1978).

The adaptive aspects of normal perfectionism notwithstanding, performance may improve if all perfectionism is removed and replaced with exacting proximal and distal goals, mastery and performance-approach goals, and high and sturdy self-efficacy. This conclusion is based on the observation that aspects of perfectionism, with the exceptions of high personal standards and organization, interact with situational pressure to erode performance (Frost & Henderson, 1991). For example, high levels of stress and negative life events disrupt the self-efficacy and sense of personal control of normal perfectionists and place them at risk for depression (e.g. Blatt, 1995). The stress of very important evaluations provokes self-handicapping and vulnerability to anxiety among normal perfectionists. The tendency to compare performances to standards of perfection represents a specific vulnerability to cognitive interference (Frost & Henderson, 1991; Koivula et al., 2002).

Optimal athletic performances often have dynamic and creative qualities, whereas perfectionism implies that performance will be compared with an abstract, static and pre-established standard. This suggests that rather than attempting to replicate perfect performances that have somehow been identified by others, athletic performers should attempt to stamp performances with their unique signature while staying within the boundaries of the competition. This advice might hold even for a closed skill sport that appears to allow for little creativity, such as archery. It might be quite different for an athlete to enter a competition with the goal of having every one of *their* arrows hit *their* bull's-eyes, and believing that they have the efficacy and the competence to control the flight of each of *their* arrows. Conversely, greater anxiety may result if archers believe that their performance must not deviate from a standard of perfection that has been established or imposed by others.

Replacing perfectionism with self-efficacy and optimally adaptive goals is not necessarily accomplished with minimum effort. Altering perfectionism is especially difficult if it developed in the context of relationships with parents and important attachment figures throughout childhood. These important relationships form the basis for implicit models by which the self and others are judged and evaluated. Their entrenched nature makes them difficult both to recognize and to change. In addition to self-exploration and introspection, guidance from highly skilled mentors such as coaches and psychologists (Blatt, 1995) may be necessary to alleviate the dysfunctional aspects of perfectionism.

Summary and Conclusions

Perfectionism is "normal" so long as it facilitates setting realistic and achievable goals, even if the goals are lofty and perhaps extreme. It is also normal if it does not involve a somewhat compulsive drive to behave perfectly in all situations and at all times. High personal standards and organization direct people to higher levels of achievement.

With neurotic adherence to perfectionism, performance and wellbeing suffer. The neurotic perfectionist demonstrates a slavish adherence to perfectionism such that they appear subject to the extreme goals rather than the goals being under their direction and control. The neurotic perfectionist asks a lot of herself or himself, and does not excuse imperfect performances. They count themselves as total failures when they are unsuccessful, and do not credit themselves for improvements that occur within the context of unsuccessful performances. They are unlikely to hold mastery, learning, or task goals. They develop performance-avoidance goals as they focus on avoiding mistakes and unfavorable comparisons to others. Goals of flawlessness provoke all-or-nothing thinking, and neurotic perfectionists frequently see themselves as having "nothing" of the perfection they desire. With the recognition of imperfections, they can be harshly critical and remonstrate with themselves as failures. To regard oneself as a failure and devoid of good qualities is to make stable, internal, and global attributions that are starkly negative, and that lead to depression.

The self-efficacy of the neurotic perfectionist is flimsy under the pressure of important performances, and they are vulnerable to cognitive interference and anxiety during performances. The attention of the neurotic perfectionist is excessively self-focused during performances as they direct attention away from the instrumental behaviors necessary for optimal performance and toward comparisons of their performance to an ideal standard.

Some psychologists have suggested guiding neurotic perfectionists to a form of normal perfectionism. Another suggestion is to replace perfectionism with a focus on exacting proximal and distal goals, mastery and performance-approach goals, and resilient self-efficacy. This refocusing may require guidance from highly skilled mentors.

Key Terms

Trait procrastination	Ego ideal
Costs of procrastination	Multidimensional perfectionism (Flett & Hewitt): self-oriented, other-directed, socially prescribed
Theoretical and scientific explanations for procrastination: psychoanalytic, psychodynamic, developmental psychology, behaviorism, fear of failure, cognitive psychology	
	Multidimensional perfectionism (Frost et al.): personal standards, organization, parental expectations, parental criticism, concern over mistakes, doubts about actions
Personality traits: conscientiousness, neuroticism	
Reactance	Sport multidimensional perfectionism
Grandma's Law	
Normal perfectionism	Insecure attachments
Neurotic perfectionism	Perfectionism and sport

Suggested Readings

Blatt, S. J. (1995). The destructiveness of perfectionism. *American Psychologist, 50,* 1003–1020.

Ferrari, J. R., Johnson, J. L., & McCown, W. G. (1995). *Procrastination and task avoidance: Theory, research and treatment.* New York: Plenum.

Flett, G. L., Hewitt, P. L., & De Rosa, T. (1996). Dimensions of perfectionism, psychosocial adjustment, and social skills. *Personality and Individual Differences, 20,* 143–150.

Flett, G. L., Hewitt, P. L., & Martin, T. R. (1995). Dimensions of perfectionism and procrastination. In J. R. Ferrari, J. L. Johnson, & W. G. McCown (Eds.), *Procrastination and task avoidance: Theory, research and treatment* (pp. 113–136). New York: Plenum.

Frost, R. O., Marten, P., Lahart, C., & Rosenblate, R. (1990). The dimensions of perfectionism. *Cognitive Therapy and Research, 14,* 449–468.

Haase, A. M., & Prapavessis, H. (2004). Assessing the factor structure and composition of the Positive and Negative Perfectionism Scale in sport. *Personality and Individual Differences, 36,* 1725–1740.

Haase, A. M., Prapavessis, H., & Owens, R. G. (2002). Perfectionism, social physique anxiety and disordered eating: A comparison of male and female elite athletes. *Psychology of Sport and Exercise, 3,* 209–222.

Hamachek, D. E. (1978). Psychodynamics of normal and neurotic perfectionism. *Psychology, 15,* 27–33.

Koivula, N., Hassmen, P., & Fallby, J. (2002). Self-esteem and perfectionism in elite athletes: Effects on competitive anxiety and self-confidence. *Personality and Individual Differences, 32,* 865–875.

Learned Helplessness  13

The Futility Index was developed to provide an answer to questions about which sport teams were the biggest all-time failures. It is a mathematical measure of the likelihood of a team not winning a championship over consecutive years. "In math terms, the probability of a team not winning a championship in a given season is $(n - 1)/n$, where n equals the number of teams in the league. Multiplying that fraction over and over for every year a team doesn't win and then taking the reciprocal yields the Futility Index" (Fatsis, 1998, p. B1).

Among American professional sport teams, the Chicago Cubs took the Futility Index prize as they did not win a World Series in over 95 years. "'It's nice to know you're No. 1 in something,' says Ed Cohen, founder of Cubs Anonymous, a group of long-suffering fans. 'And yet it's very sad'" (Fatsis, 1998, p. B1).

The essence of **learned helplessness** is the conviction that one has little or no control over events in one's life. It is the converse of self-efficacy in that it refers to beliefs that one cannot accomplish tasks and goals (Seligman, 1975). Martin Seligman, an American psychologist, developed the concept of learned helplessness.

Learned helplessness refers to the debilitating consequences of uncontrollable events, and it has been studied extensively with humans and infrahuman species such as dogs, cats, and rats (Abramson, Seligman, & Teasdale, 1978). An outcome is uncontrollable when its occurrence is not related to the responses of the person or animal. For example, college students exposed to uncontrollable loud noise in a first condition tended to do nothing to turn off loud noise in subsequent situations where the termination of the noise was under their control. These students did not flip a switch that was in plain view and that would have terminated the noise. Conversely, students who were exposed to loud noise that could be terminated by pressing a button in the first condition were quick to flip

Lacking control over the environment (photo © Roger Devenish Jones).

the switch to turn off the noise in the second condition. Students who received no noise in the first condition were also quick to switch off the noise in the second condition. Humans, but not animals, can also acquire helplessness by observing the helplessness of others (Peterson, Maier, & Seligman, 1993).

The experience of uncontrollability produces expectations that future outcomes will be uncontrollable, and voluntary responses to exercise control on the environment are inhibited. With helplessness, little effort is exerted to control events and situations that are truly uncontrollable. Helplessness is associated with a belief that current and future success is not contingent on effort. For example, French adolescents of approximately 14 years of age practiced less by taking fewer shots at a target in a pistol shooting task after first taking a test of pistol shooting accuracy in which their performance was unrelated to outcomes. In the first test of pistol shooting accuracy, signals to indicate hits on target were unrelated to actual shooting accuracy (Gernigon, Thill, & Fleurance, 1999).

Helplessness and Cognitive Bias

More than just exposure to uncontrollable events and unsolvable problems is necessary for the development of learned helplessness. People must attribute their lack of control to their inadequacies, and in this way develop a **helpless cognitive bias** (Peterson et al., 1993). For example, a sportsperson may attribute failure to their lack of athletic aptitude. This interpretation or attribution is *internal* in that it refers to a stable character- istic that is likely to be expressed in future situations. Athletic aptitude also refers to a *global* ability that would be expressed in diverse sports and exercises. Athletic aptitude is likely to be seen as *chronic* (similar to the stable dimension discussed in Chapter 2), and perhaps *uncontrollable*, or not subject to change with practice and training.

A second sportsperson might consider failure at a competition to be an unfair and biased reflection of their ability. This attribution is *external*, and this sportsperson would be less likely to believe that they are helpless to influence their future athletic achievements. The attribution is also *specific* (in that it refers to a particular competition), *transient* (subject to change in the future), and *controllable*. Failure is also attributed to external sources when people fail at impossibly difficult goals that others also fail to achieve. For example, not running 100 meters in less than nine seconds is unlikely to be demoralizing because no one has run that fast.

The attribution of failures to internal, stable, and global causes, such as a lack of athletic talent, results in the greatest amount of helplessness (Mikulincer, 1986). To the degree that uncontrollability is attributed to external, specific, and transient factors, helplessness beliefs will be brief or time-limited and relegated to specific domains of functioning.

For example, elite male and female tennis players between the ages of 11 and 25 who demonstrated a helpless pattern during performances and matches attributed failure to internal, stable, and global factors (Prapavessis & Carron, 1988). They doubted their ability and capacity to control the factors leading to success or failure. Helplessness was equally distributed among male and female tennis athletes. As is true for self- efficacy, attributions of helplessness are independent of actual skill level. Some players with the highest level of skills thought and behaved as if they could not control the outcome of matches, and some with lesser skills stubbornly believed that they held the keys to success and failure. The athletes who attributed success and failure to external, unstable, and specific factors showed little helplessness.

Learned Helplessness, Depression, and Trauma

Depressed mood is sometimes a result of beliefs that one cannot control the occurrence of untoward or bad events. It is therefore not surprising that **helplessness is associated with depressed mood**. Depressed mood is not the first emotion that occurs when people are placed in uncontrollable situations; they first experience anger and anxiety.

The association between helplessness and depression is also not surprising because people with depression tend to attribute their failures to internal, stable, and global factors and their successes to external, specific, and unstable factors. If failures result from actions or a lack of actions that were controllable, a greater amount of self-criticism, self-blame, and guilt often ensues. Depression and decreased self-esteem are more likely when people experience helplessness in areas of functioning that are particularly important to their wellbeing.

Traumatic, uncontrollable events that affect the lives of children for long periods of time, such as the death of a parent, are also associated with depression in children. These traumatic events may provoke pessimistic explanatory styles, which then lead to entrenched negative moods (Nolen-Hoeksema, Girgus, & Seligman, 1986). Indeed, traumatic events have been shown to be most influential in predicting future depression for third graders in a 5-year longitudinal study (Nolen-Hoeksema, Girgus, & Seligman, 1992).

Success experiences tend to decrease the degree to which helplessness attributions are global. Success experiences are more influential if they occur prior to the development of a helpless cognitive bias, as early successes serve to inoculate people against attributions of global helplessness. Further, self-efficacy is likely to be enhanced if success is attributed to ability rather than to effort and persistence, and if failure is attributed to a lack of effort rather than to ability (Bandura, 1997; Miserandino, 1998).

Learned Helplessness and Optimism and Pessimism

The helpless cognitive bias has also been described as **pessimism**. Like depression, pessimism is associated with the attribution of difficulties and failures to internal characteristics that are stable over time, and with the attribution of successes to external, unstable, and specific factors. The opposite pattern of attributions holds for **optimists** (Helton, Dember, Warm, & Matthews, 1999).

Pessimism and optimism predicted the number of poor swimming performances among nationally ranked collegiate swimmers at the University of California at Berkeley (Seligman, Nolen-Hoeksema, Thornton, & Thornton, 1990). The pessimists had more poor or disappointing swims during their collegiate swim seasons. Also meriting notice was the finding that the women swimmers were far more pessimistic than the males. These elite women swimmers were no more optimistic than typical college women. The men were as optimistic as any group tested by the authors, and their scores were comparable to the scores of insurance salesmen.

After the season, a subset of the most elite swimmers participated in a second experiment. They were timed at their best event and then given a false and disappointingly slow time. After a 30-minute rest, they swam the event again. The swimmers with the optimistic style were unfazed by their apparent poor performance and swam times that were at least as fast as their first efforts. The performance of the pessimists deteriorated after the apparent defeat. It should be noted that the participants in the second experiment had remained on campus to prepare for the 1988 Olympic trials, and were therefore seasoned performers who had experienced a high level of success. Pessimism is not simply determined by one's history of successes and failures, but also reflects one's attributions about the causes of success and failure.

The performance of pessimistic French high school students on a test of dexterity at dribbling a basketball deteriorated following failure feedback. They also expected to do more poorly on their next evaluation of this basketball skill, and their elevated heart rate suggested heightened anxiety. Their optimistic counterparts dribbled with greater dexterity, expected better results, and did not evince state anxiety at such high levels (Martin-Krumm, Sarrazin, Peterson, & Famose, 2003).

The effects of team optimism and pessimism have also been demonstrated to affect team success after losses. Press reports of the statements of members of the five teams of the Atlantic Division of the National Basketball Association were rated for optimism and pessimism. Teams that explained bad events such as losses and slumps in an optimistic manner during the 1982–1983 season were more likely to perform better during the 1983–1984 season. The optimistic teams were significantly more likely to beat the Las Vegas point spread for the games following losses (Rettew & Reivich, 1995). Press reports of player statements were also rated for optimism and pessimism for the 12 teams in the National Baseball League during the 1985 and 1986 seasons. Team optimism in 1985 and 1986 after bad events was a powerful predictor of team winning percentage during the 1986 and 1987 seasons, respectively. Team optimism predicted performance for these professional basketball and baseball teams even after controlling statistically for the abilities of team members.

Failure may not demoralize optimistic teams and people because they attribute it to external, unstable, and situational factors. Pessimists do not have this form of attributional protection, as they take the blame for their failures. Optimists are more likely to believe that challenges will be mastered, and are more likely to use what Lazarus and Folkman (1984) have described as *problem-focused coping* strategies. As explained in Chapters 3 and 11, problem-focused coping consists of initiatives for confronting and finding solutions to stressors such as evaluations. Examples of problem-focused coping strategies include planning, seeking social support, interpretation of failures as a result of situational and environmental events, acceptance of occasional poor performances, and suppression of competing activities when training. Pessimists are more likely to practice *emotion-focused coping* or to be sensitive to their emotional reactions when confronted by stressors. Emotion-focused coping is more likely to involve passive strategies or ways of tolerating conditions that are considered to be beyond one's control.

The trait of optimism (Norlander & Archer, 2002) appears similar to that of sport confidence among athletes (Grove & Heard, 1997). Both are positively related to problem-focused coping and negatively related to emotion-related coping. They are also negatively related to avoidance-oriented coping – the tendency to deny and avoid stressors.

Alternative Theories of Learned Helplessness

There are **alternative views** of the processes responsible for learned helplessness. One view is that repeated failures, rather than merely the disconnection between responses and outcomes, are necessary for helplessness. For example, in groups of French adolescents who practiced a pistol shooting task, failure, along with a disconnection between shooting accuracy and signals that targets were hit, appeared to be more influential in lowering self-efficacy expectations and influencing future shooting accuracy (Gernigon, Fleurance, & Reine, 2000). Conversely, adolescents who received success feedback that was contingent on actual shooting performance were subsequently more accurate in pistol shooting.

Another view is that helplessness emerges in uncontrollable situations because people cannot find solutions to problems. According to this view, when faced with problems, people generate hypotheses about potential solutions. Solvable problems provide clues about which hypotheses are likely to be successful. These clues may emerge quickly, as with easy problems. Difficult problems yield clues only after extended study and hypothesis generation. Unsolvable problems provide no information about potential solutions, and people spin theories about the solutions but come no closer to them. This condition of hypothesis generation without reductions in uncertainty about problem solutions is uncomfortable, and after a period of time most people give up trying. They experience cognitive exhaustion and "stop thinking" (Sędek & Kofta, 1990, p. 730) of potential solutions. With cognitive exhaustion, people do not generate hypotheses about solutions to new and solvable problems, performance deteriorates, the sophistication of hypotheses suffers, people have difficulty concentrating on problems, and intrinsic interest in problems decreases. People may then not have the energy to think carefully about problems and challenges and develop novel and creative hypotheses and solutions. Instead they may adopt strategies that they have used in the past because, pulling up "ready-to-use" (Sędek & Kofta, 1990, p. 741) strategies requires less energy. This "tired" thinking may be implicated in depression because the attribution of misfortunes to internal, global, and stable factors requires little exertion of mental energy.

With helplessness, adaptive responses to failures are derailed. Failure signals that one's knowledge and behavioral repertoires are insufficient to meet the demands of the environment. Adaptive responses to failures are to learn more, try harder to solve problems, and even to ruminate about problems and the causes of failures (Mikulincer, 1996). This rumination involves the active search for solutions to problems, and interrupts perseveration (the repetition of failed solutions).

If failure continues despite continued efforts to solve problems, people often begin off-task rumination. People who are depressed may engage in off-task rumination after a single failure, while those with high self-efficacy are resistant to off-task rumination. Off-task rumination often includes automatic, intrusive thoughts concerning failure, and this cognitive interference was discussed in Chapter 10. Off-task ruminations also consist of thoughts that are simply irrelevant to the evaluation.

Some people cope with the threat of failure by attempting to avoid or suppress the source of threat of failure. This strategy is unlikely to be successful when failure threatens important goals, as thoughts related to failure are readily cued by associated thoughts or environmental stimuli. In effect, the person fighting off these thoughts of failure has lost a measure of control over his or her thoughts, as ruminations of failure spring to mind automatically when cued in the abovementioned manner. When one is preoccupied with off-task ruminations or automatic thoughts about failure, attention is diverted from problem solving.

Ruminations may be disrupted by interventions such as aerobic exercise, guided imagery, and ingesting sugar (Weisenberg, Gerby, & Mikulincer, 1993). Aerobic exercise and ingesting sugar in the form of chocolate reduce anxiety and task-irrelevant cognitions, and guided imagery decreases anxiety related to the experience of helplessness. With the reduction of anxiety and cognitive interference, performance improves.

Learned Helplessness and Achievement

The **effects of helplessness on academic achievement** are in some ways the converse of self-efficacy. Students with helplessness beliefs are not persistent in working to solve difficult problems and to remove barriers to their success. College students with helplessness beliefs had lower grades point averages (GPAs) than college students of equivalent ability with optimistic attributional styles. College students with helplessness beliefs were more passive than peers with efficacious beliefs in that they sought out less help from academic advisors (Peterson & Barrett, 1987). College freshmen with helplessness attributional styles made internal, stable, and global attributions for poor academic performances, such as a lack of ability; and external, stable, and specific attributions for their academic successes, such as "the course was easy" (Kamen & Seligman, 1986).

The effects of helplessness beliefs are evident in elementary and middle school students, and their helplessness beliefs are reflected in physical education and other classes (Martinek, 1996; Walling & Martinek, 1995). Children with helplessness beliefs attribute failures to internal and stable factors such as a lack of ability or to internal and unstable factors such as a loss of ability (Diener & Dweck, 1978; Fincham, Hokoda, & Sanders, 1989). As was the case with their older counterparts (Mikulincer, 1996), young students with helplessness beliefs avoid grappling with difficult problems, engage in daydreaming when they are faced with failure and difficult problems, and are prone to depression (Nolen-Hoeksema et al., 1986).

Helplessness, a lack of control (photo © Junial Enterprises).

Athletes with helpless beliefs and pessimism are less persistent in learning new athletic skills and improving performance. This lack of persistent effort has been demonstrated with young elite Canadian tennis players (Prapavessis & Carron, 1988), British college students with majors in sport studies (Johnson & Biddle, 1989), and American collegiate swimmers (Seligman et al., 1990). The presence of helpless orientations among elite athletes is perhaps surprising given their histories of high achievement (Hale, 1993; Prapavessis & Carron, 1988).

Athletes with helplessness beliefs attribute failure to internal, stable characteristics (Prapavessis & Carron, 1988). They have expressed less confidence in their ability to control and change the factors that led to disappointing performances.

Mastery Orientations and Helplessness

By the age of 10, children differ in their response to failure. Some show a helpless pattern with negative affect, negative thoughts about themselves, and a tendency to give up easily. These children tend to avoid challenging tasks on which failure is possible (Dweck & Leggett, 1988). By the same age, children may also show a mastery-oriented pattern, which consists of persistence in attempting to solve difficult problems, the maintenance of positive affect, and high expectations for success (Heyman, Dweck, & Cain, 1992).

Children with mastery orientations simply count failures as "mistakes" (Dweck, 1980). Children and adults with mastery orientations are optimistic, intrinsically motivated, and measure performance against their own baseline of prior performances. They experience less pressure and anxiety when performing because of their stable, internal attributions about their competence. With this stable, internal foundation of confidence, individual successes and failures are less threatening, as their efficacy is not dependent on singular performances. With mastery orientations, children are able to look past singular failures and expect stubborn problems to yield to their problem-solving efforts. With helplessness orientations, children are able to look past successes and expect future failures.

Even at an early age children hold theories about the nature of their abilities. The young children who do not view ability as a malleable quality demonstrate the helpless pattern because failures demonstrate that problems exceed their capacities. These children view abilities as stable and uncontrollable. They are concerned with the adequacy of their abilities and seek to avoid public recognition of their shortcomings. Young children who view abilities as mutable qualities are persistent in study and practice because they view intelligence and achievement as a reflection of effort (Sarrazin, Biddle, Famose, Cury, Fox, & Durand, 1996). They seek to master challenges because they have faith that their efforts will be sufficient to solve problems and that they will improve their abilities and aptitudes as a result of their efforts to solve problems.

When engaged in a challenging task, the attention of children with mastery orientations is devoted primarily to the task rather than to questions of whether they have the ability to meet the challenge. They are more capable of thinking of ways of meeting the challenge or resolving the problem and their optimism leads to enhanced performance.

Etiology of Helplessness and Efficacy

The **seeds of self-efficacy and helplessness** are first sown in infancy. Infants develop beliefs in their personal efficacy by recognizing that their behaviors influence the things and people in their world (Bandura, 1997). They learn this most readily if the environmental influences occur soon after their actions. If the effects or actions are separated by some period of time, infants will not recognize that their action caused the effect because they cannot sustain mental representations of their actions and the effects of actions due to their limited working memory capacity. For younger infants to recognize the connection between their behavior and its effect, the effect must be produced in the vicinity of their action. For example, it would be difficult for a young infant to learn the association between moving a rattle and the noise it produced if the rattling sound emerged from an area distant to the rattle.

An especially important source for the development of personal agency in infants is the contingent responses of adults. Attentive adults who take interest and delight in studying the behaviors of infants, attempting to discern the meaning of the infants' actions, and then responding contingently, provide clear evidence to the child that his or her behaviors are efficacious.

Very young children do not have conceptualizations of specific traits such as ability and effort. Instead, they think of human characteristics in global terms. The dichotomy of "good" and "bad" is perhaps the most basic and global distinction by which very young children categorize other people and themselves. These very young children may judge their goodness and badness on the basis of the reactions of important others, such as parents, and also on the basis of their performances in venues such as school. Children just starting school may interpret their successes or failures on achievement tasks as reflections of their goodness or badness. Children who have routinely experienced **punitive responses** to their failures are more likely to lack persistence in attempting to solve problems, and to show passivity and helplessness (Boggiano, Barrett, & Kellam, 1993; Heyman et al., 1992). These children are sensitive to criticism from adults. In response to adult criticism they are more likely to rate themselves as not good at a task, not smart, not a good person, not nice, and to view their imagined deficiencies as unchangeable.

The development of helpless versus mastery achievement patterns is influenced more by the consistent responses of parents than of teachers (Hokoda & Fincham, 1995). For example, children who demonstrate help-lessness in the classroom more commonly have parents who attribute their children's failures to the children's lack of ability. Children's explanations of their failures correspond with their parents' explanations, and parents who ascribe failure to their children's inability commonly have children who attribute their failures to internal and stable traits. Mothers of helpless children are sometimes not subtle in discouraging self-efficacy, as they have been shown to make derogatory comments about their children's ability and to encourage them to quit when working at difficult problems. These mothers were also more likely to foster the development of per-formance goals, or achievement measured in relation to the performance of others.

These mothers responded to the negative moods of their children with their own negative moods, and this may have validated feelings of demoralization in their children. Mothers of helpless children may have modeled passivity and a lack of productivity in response to difficulties, because they often did nothing in response to their children's requests for help. This lack of parental responsiveness may augment helplessness, as the child's effort to elicit help is unrelated to receiving help. In this context of help-seeking, the child is exposed to another uncontrollable situation.

Etiology of Helplessness and Mastery Orientations

Children that are bathed in parental attentiveness are more likely to develop **mastery motivation**, perhaps because they form global images of themselves and the world as good. These parents reflect warmth and a positive mood toward their children. Responsive parents are attentive and provide help to children when it is needed. The help they provide directs children's attention toward the technical aspects of problems and does not impart beliefs that the child is incapable at sport and in school.

Mothers of children with mastery orientations frequently compliment their children for having high ability. They maintain a positive affect or mood, even as the children struggle with difficult problems. These mothers encourage their children to find solutions to difficult problems, and they do not lose confidence in their children as they struggle with difficult puzzles (Hokoda & Fincham, 1995). They discourage helplessness and conclusions that failures reflect inadequate ability, and redirect their children toward strategies for mastering difficult tasks. They even contradict statements from their children that reflect discouragement with reminders of their children's high ability.

Etiology of Helplessness and Traumatic Events

It should be noted that the reactions of parents are but one – albeit a very important one – of the potential causes for helplessness and depression in children. **Traumatic, uncontrollable events** that affect the lives of children for long periods of time, such as the death of a parent, are also associated with depression in children. These traumatic events may provoke pessimistic explanatory styles, which then lead to entrenched negative moods (Nolen-Hoeksema et al., 1986). Indeed, traumatic events have been shown to be most influential in predicting future depression for third-graders in a 5-year longitudinal study (Nolen-Hoeksema et al., 1992). Depressive symptoms also lead to pessimistic attributional styles, and these pessimistic attributions persist even after depressions have subsided.

Etiology of Helplessness and Classroom, Physical Education, and Recreation Environments

The responses of teachers are also important in the development of helplessness in children. In **classroom, physical education, and recreational settings** (Boggiano et al., 1992; Robinson, 1990, 1993) where the greatest efforts are made to exert external control of students' learning through the use of rewards, punishments, and pressure from instructors, children are oriented toward extrinsic or external learning orientations. In these environments, children tend to focus on pleasing others and avoiding their displeasure. This motivational orientation results in decreased intrinsic interest in learning, and places children at greater risk for helplessness because desired outcomes, such as praise from instructors, are to some degree outside of their control. Indeed, children with strong **extrinsic motivation** may credit powerful others, such as teachers, with successes that are entirely due to their own efforts and abilities.

Children who pursue activities because the activities are inherently satisfying have **intrinsic motivation**, and are less vulnerable to experiencing helplessness. These children attend more to internal standards for determining their successes and failures, and to some degree these factors remain under their control even if others do not recognize their accomplishments. Intrinsic motivation is more likely in environments that promote mastery orientations.

Children and adults with intrinsic orientations are more likely to attribute the results of evaluations to their self-initiated and self-regulated efforts. People with extrinsic orientations are more likely to attribute their successes and failures to the reactions of others (Boggiano et al., 1992). For example, children with intrinsic orientations might consider attempts to solve problems to be successful if they credited themselves for the amount of effort expended and with the acquisition of knowledge, even if efforts to solve specific problems were unsuccessful. Extrinsically motivated children are more interested in the demonstration of ability to others, and therefore are more likely to experience helplessness when their efforts do not result in notices of approval from the others.

Children with intrinsic orientations not only are undaunted by failures to solve problems, but also develop more sophisticated strategies to solve problems after experiencing failure (Boggiano, 1998). The opposite trend has been demonstrated for children with extrinsic orientations, as their sophisticated problem solving deteriorated after their first experience of failure.

Gender Differences and Helplessness

The question of whether girls or boys are more susceptible to helplessness remains equivocal. Some researchers have argued forcefully that girls more often demonstrate helplessness than boys, and that girls also more frequently blame failure on their lack of ability and show negative affect after failure information (Boggiano & Barrett, 1991). An influential hypothesis for these **gender differences** is that "socializing agents," such as teachers and parents, have different expectancies for boys and girls in academic and competitive arenas. They expect helpless behaviors from girls because they are consistent with stereotypes of females as dependent. The socializing agents expect mastery-oriented responses from boys, as these responses are deemed consistent with stereotypes of males as independent. The different expectancies of parents and teachers motivate differential treatments of boys and girls. Girls receive more support when they behave in dependent and helpless ways, and boys are supported more when they act in independent and mastery-oriented fashions. Adults respond more stridently to control and limit mastery-oriented and independent behaviors in girls and helpless and dependent responses from boys.

Gender differences have also been demonstrated among athletes. Female Japanese intercollegiate swimmers endorsed higher levels of helplessness related to daily life and competitive life (Yasunaga & Inomata, 2004).

Research with adults has identified differences in the attributional styles of men and women. Women have been seen to be more pessimistic in their explanatory styles in that they more often attribute failures to internal and stable factors. As discussed earlier in this chapter, nationally ranked collegiate female swimmers at the University of California at Berkeley were far more pessimistic than their male counterparts (Seligman et al., 1990). Men more commonly consider failure to result from external factors. With tendencies to make internal attributions and to ruminate or have repetitive thoughts about failures, women have been seen to be prone to depression (Nolen-Hoeksema, 1990; Nolen-Hoeksema, Parker, & Larson, 1994; Seligman, 1990).

Perhaps the gender of the person providing failure feedback is important. Fifth-grade girls have shown more helplessness when females as compared to males provided failure feedback (Dweck & Bush, 1976). When the girls received failure feedback from adult males, they more frequently attributed failure to effort rather than ability, and performance subsequently improved. These findings were considered to reflect tendencies of female teachers to provide less explicit feedback to students about the causes of incorrect responses on evaluations or to ask additional questions so that students can respond correctly. The pursuit of correct solutions following failure may discourage internal attributions for failure, such as ascribing failure to inadequate ability. College students have also demonstrated less helplessness when males delivered failure information (Rozell, Gundersen, & Terpstra, 1997).

Several studies have identified limited gender differences regarding helplessness. For example, Farmer and Vispoel (1990) asked high school students to recall failure experiences and their responses to the failures. They identified attributional patterns that were characteristic of helplessness after failures, and determined that high school boys and girls are highly similar with regard to attribution patterns characteristic of helplessness. Confidence in the results of this study is limited by its design, as the recollections of high school students may be susceptible to a variety of distortions and biases. Both boys and girls most frequently recalled school failures, and boys more frequently recalled athletic failures and girls more often remembered failures in their families.

In other studies, attributional patterns were evaluated immediately after actual failures (Eccles, Adler, & Meece, 1984). Boys and girls were shown to respond similarly after the failures in terms of the time spent trying to solve problems and actual successful performance. There were differences in attributions immediately after failure, as the girls' expectancy of success dropped lower than the boys'. However, after completing all of the problems in the experiment, the expectancies of success of the two genders were equivalent.

Summary and Conclusions

Learned helplessness is described as the converse of self-efficacy because it refers to stable beliefs that one has little or no control over events in one's life. With helplessness, people believe that stable, global, and internal qualities such as a lack of talent make control over events in the future unlikely, and they do not put forth the efforts that lead to successful performances and achievements. Helplessness is associated with pessimism, whereas efficacy corresponds to optimism or beliefs that challenges will be mastered and difficulties will yield given sufficient effort. With optimism, efficacy is shielded from the effects of failure, as failures are blamed on external, unstable, and situational factors. Helpless people not only "give up trying" to perform successfully, but they give up the difficult work of thinking of complex and novel ways of solving problems and reaching goals. Instead of selecting strategies and skills to meet the demands of a specific situation, they show a form of prolonged mental exhaustion by attempting solutions to problems that have already been shown to fail.

There is evidence that helplessness and pessimism develop early in life. If young children are consistently exposed to harsh criticism of their work products by parents and teachers, they internalize helplessness and passivity. Children who attribute their failures to their lack of ability often have parents who attribute the children's failures to the same stable and internal traits. Mastery motivation, which consists partially of resistance to helplessness, is associated with parental confidence in children's abilities and with their empathic support of children's efforts to achieve. Empathic support implies that parents make accurate judgments about when to provide help and when to let children work independently when no help is needed. The parents of helpless children are more likely to be passive as their children struggle with problems, thus their children learn that they are helpless to solve problems and helpless in gaining assistance from their most important attachment figures.

Children who are consistently exposed to classroom environments that emphasize external control of students' learning place children at greater risk for helplessness and extrinsic motivation for achievement. These children focus to a greater extent on eliciting favorable responses from others, something that they can control only partially. Conversely, when children are aware of the intrinsic benefits of achievement pursuits, they are more likely to compare progress and success against their own internal standards or baseline. Efficacy is more likely to be preserved when progress is measured in relation to one's baseline.

The question of whether girls or boys are more susceptible to help-lessness remains equivocal. The evidence that girls blamed failure on a lack of ability and showed negative affect after failure is stronger than the evidence that girls spent less time trying to solve problems and actually solved fewer problems after failures on problems. The effects of socialization practices may accumulate or have differential effects at different stages in life, as adult women demonstrate more pessimism than men.

Key Terms

Learned helplessness

Helpless cognitive bias

Learned helplessness and depression

Learned helplessness and optimism and pessimism

Alternative theories of learned helplessness

Learned helplessness and achievement

Mastery orientations and helplessness

Helpless is stable but not immutable

Etiology of helplessness and efficacy: punitive responses

Etiology of helplessness and mastery orientations

Etiology of helplessness and traumatic events

Etiology of helplessness and classroom environments

Extrinsic and intrinsic motivation

Gender differences and helplessness

Suggested Readings

Abramson, L. Y., Seligman, M. E. P., & Teasdale, J. D. (1978). Learned helplessness in humans: Critique and reformulation. *Journal of Abnormal Psychology*, 87, 49–74.

Gernigon, C., Fleurance, P., & Reine, B. (2000). Effects of uncontrollability and failure on the development of learned helplessness in perceptual-motor tasks. *Research Quarterly for Exercise and Sport*, 71, 44–54.

Gernigon, C., Thill, E., & Fleurance, P. (1999). Learned helplessness: A survey of cognitive, motivational and perceptual-motor consequences in motor tasks. *Journal of Sports Sciences*, 17, 403–412.

Helton, W. S., Dember, W. N., Warm, J. S., & Matthews, G. (1999). Optimism, pessimism, and false failure feedback: Effects on vigilance performance. *Current Psychology: Developmental, Learning, Personality, Social*, 18, 311–325.

Peterson, C., Maier, S. F., & Seligman, M. E. P. (1993). *Learned helplessness: A theory for the age of personal control*. New York: Oxford University Press.

Seligman, M. (1975). *Helplessness: On depression, development, and death.* San Francisco: Freeman.

Seligman, M. E. P. (1990). *Learned optimism.* New York: Pocket Books.

Seligman, M. E. P., Nolen-Hoeksema, S., Thornton, N., & Thornton, K. M. (1990). Explanatory style as a mechanism of disappointing athletic performance. *Psychological Science, 1,* 143–146.

Performance Inhibition Due to Personality Factors

14

At age 20, Mike Tyson was the youngest heavyweight champion in boxing history. Six years later, in 1992, he was convicted of raping the 18-year-old beauty contestant, Desiree Washington, and served three years in prison. Tyson was required to undergo a psychological evaluation in 1998 to regain his boxing license that was revoked when he bit off a piece of Evander Holyfield's ear during a boxing match (Smith, 1998). The evaluation identified difficulties with impulse control, inhibition of behavior, judgment, anger, low self-esteem and depression.

Although he earned nearly $400 million in prize money, by age 38, in 2004, he was bankrupt and owed $23 million to creditors. He reflected that when he was flush with money, "I was an animal. I was so belligerent. I was so cantankerous, so persistently disregardless. I wasn't that nice of a person." He recognized, "I don't have nothing. I don't have nobody, my life has been a total waste" (Gray, 2004, p. D7).

The focus of this chapter will be the personality characteristics that inhibit performance. In addition, personality traits associated with optimal sport performance will be described. As is true for most topics in psychology, a definition of personality that is universally accepted does not exist. Rival theories of personality were reviewed in Chapter 2. These include the psychoanalytic and neo-analytic viewpoints, humanistic theories, and social-learning approaches such as self-efficacy theory. The influence of self-efficacy on sport performance was considered in Chapter 9, and the inhibiting influence of the related construct of helplessness was addressed in Chapter 13. The number of pages devoted to self-efficacy and helplessness reflects the amount of empirical research that was inspired by these theories.

Another paradigm or theoretical model that has generated a body of research in sport psychology is trait theory. With this model, personality is conceptualized as a composite of a number of discrete traits or enduring characteristics. Hans Eysenck's model of personality (Eysenck & Eysenck,

1985) has influenced the greatest number of empirical studies. The five-factor model is another trait approach to personality that has influenced research in sport psychology.

The Profile of Mood States (POMS; McNair, Lorr, & Droppleman, 1971) and the Athletic Coping Skills Inventory (ACSI; Smith, Schutz, Smoll, & Ptacek, 1995) will be reviewed in this chapter. Neither measures dimensions of behavior that are as broad and stable over time as traditional personality traits. Nevertheless, tradition dictates that the POMS and ACSI are examined in treatments of personality and sport psychology (Cox, 2002; Gill, 2000; Pragman, 1997; Weinberg & Gould, 2007), as the ACSI was developed specifically for differentiating more and less successful athletes, and the POMS has been utilized extensively in sport settings. The topic of temperament will also be examined in this chapter. Temperament, especially biological vulnerability to experience anxiety, is related to Eysenck's theory of personality and provides useful information for understanding performance under pressure.

Trait Theories of Personality

Regardless of theory, trait approaches identify major dimensions of behavior that are consistent over time and in different situations. These traits or enduring characteristics are distributed normally in human populations. Normal distributions form a bell curve, such that the mean (average score), median (point that divides the population evenly) and modal (most frequent) scores are the same. Normal distributions and bell curves are symmetrical so that 68 percent of the scores of the entire population fall within plus and minus one standard deviation from the mean. Fully 95 percent of the normal distribution falls within plus or minus two standard deviations from the mean.

Theory and data indicate that personality traits in the five-factor and Eysenck models are not only normally distributed, but also orthogonal (Costa & McCrae, 1992; Eysenck, 1992). Traits are orthogonal when they are statistically independent. In other words, knowledge of whether someone is high or low on a trait such as neuroticism provides absolutely no information about whether that person will be high or low on either of the other two traits in Eysenck's model or any of the other four traits in the five-factor model.

Even extreme scores on these dimensions of personality do not guarantee that behavior consistent with the particular dimension will be expressed in a given situation and at a given time. Instead, high scores on personality traits produce a statistical likelihood or greater probability that the behavior in question will occur. Behavior is often understood in terms of diathesis and stress. These dimensions of personality create a **diathesis** or likelihood that characteristics are expressed in response to certain environmental **stressors**. Common stressors in sport psychology are the demands of competition, especially pressure for optimal performance during critical times in crucial competitions. To complicate matters further, the behavior of some people is more consistent than that of others (Mischel & Shoda, 1995; Smith, 2006b). In general the behavior of adults is more consistent than that of children and adolescents.

Finally, although the focus of this chapter will be the effects of personality on performance, sport and exercise have an influence on

Personality traits influence sport participation (photo © Emmanuel R. Lacoste).

personality (Furnham, 1990). Sport and exercise may influence personality as a result of their influence in diminishing anxiety and depression and improving mood (International Society of Sport Psychology, 1992). Anxiety and depression are important components of personality traits such as neuroticism, which will be described later. Exercise and sport may also improve fitness and appearance, and physique improvements may lead to improved self-esteem. As described in Chapter 9, mastery in the areas of sport and exercise may foster improved self-efficacy. Sport and exercise regimens may result in patterns of socialization, and the influence of other people may alter personality.

Hans Eysenck's Theory of Personality

Hans Eysenck at the University of London developed the most influential of the trait theories in terms of generating scientific research in sport psychology. Eysenck was a student of Sir Cyril Burt, and Eysenck's theorizing about personality reflects Burt's emphasis on the genetic influences on behavior. Eysenck identified three major dimensions or traits in personality: **neuroticism**, **psychoticism**, and **extraversion** (Eysenck, 1994). People who demonstrate high levels of the psychoticism, neuroticism, and extraversion dimensions do not necessarily evince these characteristics at all times. As mentioned above, high levels of traits represent dispositions to demonstrate certain behaviors when these behaviors are elicited by environmental conditions.

These traits are bipolar, such that the opposite pole of extraversion is introversion, the opposite pole of neuroticism is stability, and the opposite pole of psychoticism is superego or a strong conscience. Extraversion is characterized by the adjectives sociable, lively, active, assertive, sensation-seeking, carefree, dominant, surgent, and venturesome. Primary characteristics defining neuroticism are: anxious, depressed, guilt feelings, low self-esteem, tense, irrational, shy, moody, and emotional. Psychoticism is defined by the characteristics: aggressive, cold, egocentric, impersonal, impulsive, antisocial, unempathic, creative, and tough-minded. True to the name of this trait, Eysenck (1992) also argued that the psychoticism dimension represented a continuum of mental disorders. At the extreme of this continuum were people prone to severe mental illness such as bipolar, schizoaffective, and schizophrenic disorders, with schizophrenic disorders occupying the most extreme position and representing the most severe disturbance.

People with extreme scores on Eysenck's personality dimensions are more likely to demonstrate a wider range of the behaviors characteristic to that dimension and to demonstrate these behaviors more forcefully. People with moderate levels of these traits may show fewer of the characteristic behaviors and demonstrate less extreme characteristic behavior, but moderate levels of these traits still contribute to important differences in behavior. Given that these traits are normally distributed, most people have moderate levels of introversion or extraversion, stability or neuroticism, and superego or psychoticism.

Extraversion and Cortical Arousal

Eysenck maintained that these traits were largely determined by genetic factors. For example, introverts were seen to have a higher level of **cortical arousal** than extraverts and to have stronger and more labile autonomic nervous system responses. Cortical arousal level was seen to be a function of the activity level of the **ascending reticular-activating system** (ARAS). Extraverted behavior patterns are produced by a relatively under-reactive ARAS and therefore higher levels of environmental stimulation are necessary for extraverts to realize an optimal hedonic level. The tension and excitement of sport afford means for augmenting cortical activation. Exercise and movement may also augment cortical activation, as the ARAS receives proprioceptive feedback from the muscles and somatic or peripheral nervous system. Conversely, introverts have an overactive ARAS, and realize optimal hedonic tone with limited environmental input.

The cortical activation of extraverts is lowest in the morning and increases during the day, perhaps due to the effects of environmental stimulation (Kirkcaldy, 1980). State anxiety is experienced as increasingly facilitative of performance with the nearing of competition (Cerin, 2004). Extraversion also diminishes with increasing age so that it is generally lower in older than in younger people.

This conceptualization of cortical arousal is overly simplified by modern neurophysiological standards (Rammsayer, 1998). The activation of the brain involves a number of cortical structures and neurotransmitters. Neurotransmitters are chemicals responsible for communication between neurons – the tiny structures that provide for information processing in the brain. The neurotransmitter dopamine has been identified as important in cortical activation, and it appears that introverts have dopamine in greater abundance than extraverts or that introverts are more responsive to dopamine.

Extraverts tend to habituate to environmental stimuli more quickly than introverts. Habituation is measured by both the amplitude of cortical arousal and the degree to which people continue to pay attention to input from the environment. Extraverts lose interest quickly in redundant stimuli and seek out novel experiences. Extraverts are therefore more easily distracted by environmental stimuli. Introverts demonstrate a more narrow focus of attention and are more likely to sustain their attentional focus and inhibit responses to environmental stimuli. Extraverts are also more likely to respond physically to the stimuli. Because of the relative hunger of marked extraverts for external stimulation, they are less precise at some tasks that call for sustained vigilance and responding to feedback in the environment. For example, extraverts have more accidents while driving automobiles as their attention wanders from vigilance for danger.

People tend to seek out environments that provide for an optimal level of stimulation. Environments that introverts find optimal are counted as boring to extraverts, while extraverts are most comfortable in situations that cause anxiety to introverts. Introverts are less "hungry" for environmental stimulation than extraverts because of their higher level of cortical stimulation. Extraverts are far more comfortable than introverts in situations involving risk and danger. For example, extraverts are far happier when working at dangerous jobs in a steel mill such as that of a crane driver or operator (Farthofer & Brandstatter, 2001).

Both introverts and extraverts will try to place themselves in environments that provide for the optimal hedonic tone or the optimal amount of cortical arousal. Therefore introverts may seek to avoid too much stimulation from the environment, whereas extraverts are more willing to take physical and social risks for varied, novel, and complex sensations and experiences that are stimulating, exciting, and even thrilling.

Research indicates that extraverts are more motivated by the possibilities of realizing gains and rewards and introverts are more sensitive to avoiding loss and punishment. Eysenck's theorizing (1952) anticipated this research, and also anticipated by perhaps 40 years sophisticated recent research concerning people who were motivated primarily by the opportunities for gains versus the avoidance of loss. For example, and as discussed in Chapter 2, people with a *promotion* focus attend to opportunities for accomplishments and are relatively unconcerned with potential risks and losses (Higgins, 1997). They seek to avoid the experience on nonfulfillment. Those with a *prevention* focus seek safety and attempt to avoid danger.

Eysenck's Theory and Sport

Perhaps the most widely reported finding concerning Eysenck's theory of personality and sport is that athletes are likely to be **extraverted**. Competitive sports often produce a high level of stimulation and excitement, and extraverts may be especially drawn to sports that involve risk, excitement, and aggression (Eysenck, Nias, & Cox, 1982). Athletes have also traditionally been shown to have relatively low levels of neuroticism and high levels of psychoticism, although the latter finding is less well established.

The Eysenck Personality Questionnaire and Sport

The Eysenck Personality Questionnaire (EPQ; Eysenck & Eysenck, 1994) was developed to measure the traits of extraversion, neuroticism, and psychoticism, and differences between groups of athletes and non-athletes have been estimated with the EPQ. For example, Italian high school students who played competitive tennis scored higher on extraversion and lower on neuroticism, psychoticism, anxiety, and depression than classmates who did not participate in sport (Daino, 1985). Australian high school athletes in the 11th and 12th grades demonstrated higher extraversion, and lower neuroticism scores on the EPQ, as well as lower state and trait anxiety, depression, and confusion than classmates who were not athletes (Newcombe & Boyle, 1995).

The male athletes in this Australian sample endorsed less trait anxiety, extraversion, and neuroticism, and more psychoticism than their female counterparts. Comparing female athletes and nonathletes, female athletes typically show higher extraversion and psychoticism scores, perhaps reflecting traits that have been identified as masculine or androgynous (e.g. Bem Sex Role Inventory; Bem, 1974, 1978) in groups of female athletes (Francis, Kelly, & Jones, 1998).

Not only have the traits of extraversion, neuroticism, and psychoticism been shown to distinguish between sportspersons and nonathletes, but also more successful and elite sportspersons demonstrate higher levels of extraversion and psychoticism and lower levels of neuroticism than average sport performers. These results have been reported among Olympic athletes, college football players, elite swimmers, and international table tennis and badminton players. Small differences of this nature were reported among collegian athletes versus athletes who competed at national or professional levels in Canada (Davis & Mogk, 1994). Extraversion appears to be particularly sensitive in differentiating elite from sub-elite athletes. For example, among candidates for the male 1974 US Heavyweight Rowing Team, extraversion was more accurate than measures of state and trait anxiety, a measure of bodily perception during stressful situations, and the tension, depression, anger, vigor, fatigue, and confusion scales of the POMS (McNair et al., 1971) in identifying oarsmen who made the team (Morgan & Johnson, 1978). Among candidates for the 1974 US Lightweight Rowing Team, higher levels of extraversion and vigor differentiated the oarsmen who made the team.

It should be noted that these findings hold true for groups of elite performers, and that individual elite athletes sometime have higher levels of neuroticism and lower levels of extraversion. For example, tennis players of Wimbledon standard have been identified with levels of neuroticism that exceed the mean of psychiatric patients with depressive disorders (Eysenck et al., 1982).

It should also be noted that athletes represent only a small minority of the international populations that are high on the dimensions of extraversion, perhaps high on psychoticism, and low on neuroticism. For example, measures of extraversion, neuroticism, and psychoticism were comparable for sports enthusiasts who were fans, sports participants at the recreational level, Canadian professional athletes, athletes on national teams, and collegiate varsity athletes (Davis & Mogk, 1994). Perhaps the common interest in sport among these Canadian fans and athletes was responsible for the pattern of high extraversion and psychoticism and low neuroticism. Because of its physical nature, extraverts tend to be drawn to sport to a somewhat greater degree than some other leisure activities. For example, extraverted adult male and female residents of Oxfordshire in England were more likely to participate in sport clubs than to engage in church activities, participate in musical groups such as choruses, or regularly watch television soap operas (Hills & Argyle, 1998).

More on Extraversion and Sport

The acceptance of risk among the highly extraverted is rewarded in sports where explosive actions and very rapid decisions are necessary. Whether extraverts are more likely to participate in team sports is open to question (Newcombe & Boyle, 1995). Extraversion and a lack of neuroticism may contribute to team cohesion, at least in the workplace (van Vianen & De Dreu, 2001).

Participants in "extreme" sports such as hang gliding, powerboat racing, whitewater canoeing, parachuting, and mountaineering have been shown to be particularly extraverted and to show low levels of neuroticism (Watson & Pulford, 2004). Consistently high scores on the psychoticism dimension have not been reported for athletes who engage in extreme sports (Egan & Stelmack, 2003). Mountaineering involves extreme risks and consists of mountain climbing, mountain skiing, and alpinism (climbing at altitudes greater than 8000 meters). The death rate for athletes in the Spanish Federation of Mountaineering was 15 percent in 1988 (Freixanet, 1991). Alpinists have been considered to take the greatest risks of any of the extreme athletes, and they have been shown to achieve the most extreme elevation on the extraversion dimension. The marked extraversion of extreme athletes reflects their seeking of risk, but not impulsiveness (failure to plan and tendency to act without forethought). Consistent with the earlier discussion of extraversion, extreme athletes are motivated more by the opportunities for rewards such as thrill and adventure seeking than by the threat of punishment. Alpinists were least influenced by the potential for punishment (Freixanet, 1991).

Participants in high-risk sports have been shown not only to be willing to assume risks, but also to be drawn to activities that provide intense, complex, and novel sensations. This tendency to seek intense experiences that may present risk has been identified as the trait of **impulsiveness–sensation seeking** by the American psychologist Marvin Zuckerman (1994). People high on this trait are willing to take not only physical risks, but also social, financial, and legal risks in order to capture intense, novel, and complex sensations. Participants in high-risk sports have consistently demonstrated higher levels of this trait than athletes in low-risk sports. For example, female and male athletes in New Zealand between the ages of 13 and 76 who engaged in the high-risk sports of hang gliding, mountaineering, skydiving, and automobile racing demonstrated higher levels of the impulsiveness–sensation seeking quality than athletes involved in the low-risk sports of swimming, marathon running, aerobics, and golfing (Jack & Ronan, 1998). However, consistent with Freixanet's results with Spanish alpinists, athletes in high-risk sports did not demonstrate higher levels of impulsiveness or lack of planning than low-risk athletes.

Long-distance runners are more likely to be introverted and to demonstrate less sensation seeking than athletes who engage in high-risk sports and athletes who engage in the low-risk sports of swimming, aerobics, and golf (Jack & Ronan, 1998). They are not, however, more introverted than general populations of people who do not exercise regularly or engage in sports (Egloff & Gruhn, 1996). It is not surprising that distance runners are not markedly introverted given that their training requires a high level of activity, some socialization, and a willingness to tolerate pain – all characteristics associated with extraversion (Eysenck et al., 1982). Participants in sports involving explosive action are more likely to be mesomorphic or muscular, and mesomorphy is associated with extraversion. Distance runners are more likely to have ectomorphic or thin physiques, and ectomorphy is associated with introversion.

Extraverts are less deterred by potential adverse consequences in sport such as failure, and are less fazed by the disapproval of others. Extraverts worry less about the prospect of aversive encounters with others, and maintenance of harmonious relationships is not particularly appealing to them. Extraverts find competition with others to be less aversive than introverts (Graziano, Feldesman, & Rahe, 1985). Indeed, extraverts find competitive situations to be more arousing, rewarding, interesting, and likable (Wolfe & Kasmer, 1988).

As explained in Chapter 10, the presence of an audience creates additional pressure for performance, and this is often accompanied by increased levels of cortical arousal. Given the higher levels of resting cortical arousal among introverts, it is not surprising that their performance erodes markedly with the presence of an audience. Conversely, the performance of extraverts is enhanced by the presence of an audience, as the additional pressure may bring their cortical arousal to optimal levels. For example, the accuracy of serves in table tennis was evaluated in a group of English male college students with majors in sports studies and physical education. The students who were clear extraverts served far more accurately in the presence of 12 male peers as well as a table tennis coach. The accuracy of the serves of the introverts decreased dramatically in the

TABLE 14.1
Mean Scores and Standard Deviations (SD) on Points Scored for Introverted and Extraverted Groups in Audience and No Audience Conditions

	Audience		No audience	
	Mean	SD	Mean	SD
Extravert	23.9	7.5	18.1	7.6
Introvert	18.1	4.5	26.3	4.2

From Graydon, J., & Murphy, T. (1995). The effect of personality on social facilitation whilst performing a sports related task. *Personality and Individual Differences, 19*, 265–267.

presence of this audience (Graydon & Murphy, 1995). The debilitative effects of the audience on the performance of introverts may have been due to excessive levels of cortical arousal, or the introverts may have been more distracted by the audience. If the short-term or active memory resources of the introverts were captured by attention to the behavior of the audience, then fewer resources would be devoted to the instrumental behaviors necessary for skilled performance.

The tendency of introverts to sustain attention may provide them with an advantage at sports such as rifle shooting and archery, which call for deliberate preparation and execution of skills. Extraverts tend to trade vigilance and accuracy for speed, and their records for automobile accidents reflect this orientation. However, many sports reward partici-pants for initiating action and anticipating the responses of others, espe-cially in open skill sports such as tennis. The attention of the extravert is given more to anticipating and predicting changes in sporting and other environments, whereas introverts are less proactive and focused more on reacting to changing environmental conditions and the reactions of others.

More on Neuroticism and Sport

A primary aspect of the **neuroticism** trait is the experience of **anxiety**. The relationship between anxiety, arousal, or intensity and performance was discussed in Chapter 3. Distinctions between cognitive and physio-logical, trait and state, and facilitative and debilitative anxiety were identified. Neuroticism has aspects of trait anxiety, and performance on tasks that require complex motor actions, thought and decision-making is likely to be negatively affected by high levels of neuroticism and high state and cognitive anxiety. For example, male British squash players who were winners in a tournament were much lower in the trait of neuroticism than counterparts who were losers (Cox & Kerr, 1990; Kerr & Cox, 1991). Differences in the traits of psychoticism and extraversion were not evident for winning and losing squash players who competed at city, regional, or national levels. With high levels of neuroticism, people may avoid competition and athletic activity (Davis, Elliott, Dionne, & Mitchell, 1991).

Higher levels of neuroticism have also been related to the experience of state anxiety and negative mood states among female and male adults who competed in a national rifle-shooting championship in Australia (Prapavessis & Grove, 1994). The rifle shooters with higher neuroticism experienced higher levels of tension, depression, anger, fatigue, confusion, and vigor prior to competition.

Anxiety is experienced as increasingly debilitative with the nearing of competition among athletes with high levels of neuroticism. For example, cognitive anxiety was experienced as increasingly debilitative in the week prior to competition among Tae Kwon Do practitioners high in the trait of neuroticism (Cerin, 2004). Levels of somatic anxiety were comparable 1 week prior to competition among practitioners high and low in neuroticism. However, practitioners who were low in the neuroticism trait experienced this anxiety as increasingly facilitative as they approached competition.

People with high levels of neuroticism often display cognitive anxiety or cognitive interference during complex motor tasks such as sport and automobile driving. Cognitive interference occupies attentional resources that can be put to best use focusing on motor tasks and changing environmental conditions, and people who are both highly neurotic and extraverted have been shown to have particularly poor driving records (Shaw & Sichel, 1971).

Even athletes with low neuroticism scores experience anxiety in situations involving pressure for optimal performance. However, as explained in Chapter 9, self-efficacious beliefs that one can control the aspects of a competition or a performance that lead to success, and reach standards necessary for success, contain anxiety during performances. More successful athletes such as US Olympic gymnasts are quite successful at controlling anxiety during performances, despite experiencing high anxiety 1 hour prior to competitions (Mahoney & Avener, 1977).

More on Psychoticism and Sport

People with high **psychoticism** traits are more likely to be **aggressive** and comfortable with behavior that violates social norms or that is even anti-social. Eysenck et al. (1982) maintained that this trait was adaptive in sport. Psychoticism and extraversion are associated with Machiavellianism or taking every opportunity to advance personal interests (Allsopp, Eysenck, & Eysenck, 1991). More specifically, psychoticism is associated with the Machiavellian attitudes of deceitfulness, cunning, manipulation, ruth-lessness, and power seeking. Extraversion is more closely related to a Machiavellian focus on social influence and power.

Aggression and Sport

Aggressive behavior is integrated into the flow of sports such as ice hockey, where aggressive acts in various levels of European male hockey have been shown to occur every third minute (Isberg, 2000). Very few of these aggressive acts in hockey games resulted in penalties, and coaches and other players encouraged players to commit aggressive acts during the game. Youth hockey players have discriminated good from bad penalties on the basis of whether the penalized player's team gained an advantage or avoided a disadvantage as a result of the illegal action.

Aggression in hockey that resulted in penalty minutes has not con-sistently proved to be adaptive in terms of producing victories in the National Hockey League (McGuire, Courneya, Widmeyer, & Carron, 1992). This is reasonable since the penalized team plays for a period of time with a dis-advantage in terms of the number of skaters while the penalized player sits in the penalty box. There was also no significant correlation between penalty minutes and team victories among male participants in the Ontario University Athletic Association (Widmeyer & Birch, 1979). All-stars in this University Athletic Association were penalized less than non-all-stars.

When attentional resources are occupied with concerns about opponents, fewer attentional resources are free for a focus on instrumental behaviors that contribute to optimal performance. Anger and hostility directed toward opponents or toward oneself serve as a source of this distraction (Silva & Conroy, 1995).

Five-Factor Model of Personality

Eysenck's model of personality was discussed in detail because it has generated the greatest amount of research concerning personality and sport. Other influential theories of personality propose a greater number of traits or dimensions of personality. Raymond Cattell identified 16 personality factors, and some research with this model has been conducted in sport settings (e.g. Schurr, Ashley, & Joy, 1977). The most influential five-factor model (Costa & McCrae, 1992), in addition to the abovementioned traits of **neuroticism** and **extraversion**, identifies traits of **agreeableness**, **conscientiousness**, and **openness to experience**. The authors of this model maintained that it provides a broader description of personality than that of Eysenck (Costa & McCrae, 1995). Eysenck and others (Draycott & Kline, 1995) demonstrated that agreeableness and conscientiousness were not independent traits, but rather were negatively correlated with psychoticism. Costa and McCrae (1995) countered that psychoticism was an arbitrary conflation of two independent dimensions, agreeableness and conscientiousness. Openness to experience has also been shown to share characteristics of extraversion.

Perhaps it is useful to consider that the EPQ contains 100 questions and the questionnaire used by Costa and McCrae to measure the five factors, the NEO-PI-R, contains 240 questions. The NEO-PI-R measures aspects of personality that are not included in the EPQ.

There has been far less research with the five-factor model in sporting contexts. However, consistent with research with the EPQ, participants in a 100-mile ultra-marathon conducted in Alaska during February recorded higher scores on the extraversion scale (Hughes, Case, Stuemple, & Evans, 2003). They also endorsed higher levels of openness to experience.

The usefulness of this model of personality in predicting performance in soccer matches and coaches' ratings was also evaluated with female Division I collegiate soccer players (Piedmont, Hill, & Blanco, 1999). The trait of conscientiousness or tendency to fulfill responsibilities was the only factor to predict aspects of performance during the soccer matches of women at four universities. These aspects consisted of scores, assists, shots on goal, and the number of games played. The more conscientious players delivered more in all of these areas during collegiate matches. These variables were of a summary nature and did not capture qualities of the performances of defensive players such as fullbacks, sweepers, and goalkeepers. Conscientiousness and neuroticism predicted coaches' ratings of players. Higher levels of neuroticism were related to lower levels of coachability, athletic ability, game performance, and "team playerness." Higher levels of conscientiousness were related to higher coaches' ratings of coachability, game performance, and work ethic. Coachability refers to the athlete's response to the instructions and directions of coaches. The combination of low neuroticism and high conscientiousness has been associated with high achievement in a variety of settings. This combination is associated with setting high standards and sufficient

Boris Becker and Personality Traits

Boris Becker was the youngest ever men's champion at Wimbledon in 1985. He won the tournament at 17 years of age, and was also the first unseeded winner and the first from Germany. He won an additional two titles at Wimbledon, two at the Australian Open, and one at the United States Open, for a total of six major tennis titles. Yet he expressed conflicting reactions to competition. He compared tennis matches to gladiatorial contests in which one wins and the other "dies" (Atkins, 1990). He explained:

> My opponents are human beings, not enemies. In order to survive a tournament you have to be some kind of beast. You have to beat your opponent psychologically. After tough tournaments I frequently go through phases of deep depression and see no reason to go on. I can't bear to go out and be among people who touch me and ask how I am, especially after a big success like Wimbledon. (Atkins, 1990, p. 5)

He also likened competitive tennis to art and sex:

> That Sunday afternoon: You're in the Wimbledon final, it's the third set, and you're about to win . . . This is something I miss. Because even with a great business deal, it's not the same sensation. Tennis is an art form. I feel as if I'm performing on a stage in front of millions of people, and I was sometimes able to fascinate them for two weeks. This culminates with a Sunday final, match point, and then all the celebrations. It's like a long foreplay that ends with a huge orgasm. That's what it is. (Price, 2001, p. 90)

Becker was also acutely uncomfortable with the understandable adulation of German fans, and appeared to associate expressions of national pride with Nazi fanaticism. He commented, "When I looked into the eyes of my fans I thought I was looking at monsters. When I saw this kind of blind, emotional devotion I could understand what happened to us a long time ago in Nuremberg" (Atkins, 1990, p. 5). Of course, the emotional devotion of fans "comes with the territory" of sporting virtuosity, perhaps especially with tall, powerfully built prodigies who are "strikingly handsome" (Atkins, 1990, p. 3). This adulation is independent of ethnicity or country of origin.

emotional stability and self-confidence to withstand setbacks and frustration in the pursuit of long-term goals.

People generally recognize that competition is not all "fun and games." For example, college students understood competitive situations to involve fewer friendly interactions and harmonious relationships than situations requiring cooperation with others (Graziano, Hair, & Finch, 1997). Competitive situations were seen as more challenging, difficult, and enjoyable, and to cause more anxiety. However, competitive situations are seen to be even more problematic by people who are high in the trait of *agreeableness*, who are more highly motivated to maintain harmonious relationships with others and to avoid competitive interactions. Competition may present a greater conflict for highly agreeable people because their victories often involve defeating others and disrupting interpersonal harmony. It may be difficult to reconcile defeating an opponent with wishes for interpersonal harmony because the agreeable person recognizes that opponents also want to win.

Still, competitiveness can be elicited in highly agreeable people. Situations and other people that are highly competitive elicit competitive reactions from even highly agreeable people. Highly competitive people expect other people to be competitive and actually elicit more competition from others.

Narcissism

Narcissism is a trait that refers to an excessive focus on oneself, and a relative lack of concern for others except as sources of admiration. Narcissists may believe that they are special human beings who are capable of accomplishing special things. With this trait, people tend to focus on gaining glory and therefore put forth greater effort and are at their best in the presence of an audience and under pressure. They perform equally well in the presence of supportive and unsupportive audiences, as they focus on demonstrating their superiority rather than on the responses of the audience. Their objective is to gain the admiration, not the affection, of the audience. They perform beneath their capabilities when an audience is not present, as they put forth less effort when there are no opportunities for self-enhancement (Wallace & Baumeister, 2002).

Readers will recall that the performance of extraverts is enhanced in the presence of an audience (Graydon & Murphy, 1995). However, this is likely due to the augmented cortical arousal perpetrated by environmental pressure. The traits of psychotism (high) and agreeableness (low) are also associated with a lack of empathy or concern with the welfare of others, and narcissism is associated with low levels of agreeableness (Bagby, Costa, Widiger, Ryder, & Marshall, 2005) and high levels of psychoticism and extraversion (Raskin & Hall, 1981).

Temperament

Theories of personality, such as Eysenck's, that hypothesize and to some degree document associations between traits and brain functions are consistent with theory and research on temperament. **Temperament** refers to inherited or genetically determined, physiological and psychological processes that are apparent early in life or in very young children. Temperament creates biases or tendencies to behave in certain ways, but does not guarantee that this behavior will occur. Conversely, without a temperamental bias, behaviors such as excessive fearfulness are far less likely, even in environments that provoke this fearfulness. An analogy for the relationship between a particular bias and the expression of corresponding behavior is the relationship between temperatures under 32 degrees Fahrenheit (0 degrees Celsius) and the likelihood of a blizzard. Blizzards often do not occur when the temperature is below 32 degrees, but if they are to occur, chances are that the temperature will be below 32. Blizzards never occur when the temperature is above 50 degrees Fahrenheit (10 degrees Celsius; Kagan, 1994).

Jerome Kagan (1994), an American psychologist, asserted that temperamental differences were due to inherited differences in the levels of norepinephrine, a primary neurotransmitter in the brain and sympathetic nervous system, and corticotrophin releasing hormone (CRH). Higher levels of norepinephrine result in greater activation of the parts of the **amygdala** associated with fear and anxiety. The amygdala is a part of the limbic system – the brain structure most responsible for the experience of emotion. CRH contributes to the bodily or physiological experience of anxiety. CRH production leads to the production of cortisol, which has been described at several points in this text as a sign of stress. With this constellation of norepinephrine and CRH, children have a more reactive circuit from the limbic system to the sympathetic nervous system. Perhaps because the amygdala has neuronal projections to the frontal lobes of the cerebral cortex, higher levels of activation of the amygdala are associated with higher levels of beta wave activity and lower levels of alpha wave activity, especially in the right frontal cortex. This pattern of beta and alpha wave activity is associated with unpleasant and anxious feelings (Kagan, Snidman, McManis, & Woodward, 2001).

Children with this biochemical diathesis are more likely to be inhibited, withdrawn, and shy, especially when faced with unfamiliar situations. They resemble Eysenck's introverts. They are prone to experience heightened states of anxiety when faced with unfamiliarity and challenges, and in response they have difficulty processing information and remembering new information. They also show less willingness to take risks. For example, when given the opportunity to throw balls into baskets and to determine the distance they would stand from the basket, inhibited children stood approximately one and one half feet from the basket. Uninhibited children stood about five feet from the basket. Inhibited children were also less willing to chance errors by guessing about the source of recorded familiar sounds; they demonstrated the largest heart accelerations under stress and generally had more muscle tension.

Approximately 10 to 15 percent of children are inhibited types. A small group of inhibited children may also experience high physiological reactivity, but not subjective feelings of anxiety or disruptions in their motor behavior. Perhaps these children demonstrate the physiological but not the cognitive aspects of anxiety.

The diathesis for inhibition is particularly evident in novel situations and in social settings, and is therefore relevant to the issue of performance anxiety and choking under pressure. For example, children classified as inhibited in the second year of life are more likely to develop social anxiety

Ectomorphy and Inhibition

Kagan reported that the biochemical predisposition to inhibited and fearful behavior was not democratically distributed. He found that about 60 percent of inhibited children had blue eyes and 60 percent of uninhibited children had brown eyes. He also discovered that 60 percent of ectomorphic boys with thin faces were inhibited. The combination of ectomorphy and blue eyes resulted in the greatest chance for behavioral inhibition. Placed in a larger context, approximately 20 percent of Caucasian children begin life with this inhibited disposition, and 40 percent begin with the uninhibited characteristic. These dispositions are to a large degree determined by genetic factors, but are influenced by experience. For example, parents who understand when inhibited children profit from a bit of a nudge to master tendencies to withdraw, help their children become less fearful. Parents who place demands on uninhibited children to follow rules assist these children to rein in their fearlessness.

Women and girls are also more likely to demonstrate inhibition and anxiety. This may be due to differences in the norepinephrine, CRH, and cortical and peripheral structures. Alternatively, these differences may be due to greater environmental demands on women, especially well-educated women in the USA and Europe. These women commonly experience pressure to meet high standards of beauty, success in sustaining relationships and attachments, and vocational competence. Believing that they fall beneath standards in one or more of these areas, women may respond with social anxiety and withdrawal.

Temperament and sport.

or to become anxious and inhibited in the presence of others, especially strangers, at age 13. Indeed, 61 percent of a group of 13-year-olds who demonstrated withdrawal during their second year of life demonstrated social anxiety, whereas 27 percent who were uninhibited in their second year demonstrated this later social anxiety (Kagan et al., 2001).

The Profile of Mood States

There are alternative models of psychological factors associated with enhanced versus impaired athletic performance. These models are commonly referred to as personality theories, even though they do not refer to stable dimensions of behavior that are consistent over time and across situations. For example, the American psychologist William Morgan developed the mental health model for differentiating more and less successful athletes. Athletic performance was seen to rise and fall in relation to the mental health of athletes. Successful athletes were seen to experience fewer psychological problems than less successful athletes. For example, elite senior male weightlifters, junior male weightlifters, and female weightlifters that were ranked in the top three of their weight categories by the US Weightlifting Federation had fewer psychological problems than their counterparts who were ranked lower than eleventh or were unranked (Mahoney, 1989). The elite weightlifters had less depression, less psychoticism, and fewer overall problems.

Working within this model, mental health was commonly measured with the **Profile of Mood States (POMS)**. The POMS is a self-report questionnaire designed to measure the mood states of tension, depression, anger, fatigue, confusion, and vigor. It was created in 1971 as a measure of reactions to current life situations. The POMS was specially designed to measure progress in psychotherapy or counseling in outpatient settings (McNair et al., 1971). It was also developed for use in measuring mood states among normal subjects of at least 18 years of age, and has been used extensively in exercise and sport settings. The POMS had been used in at least 258 published studies by 1998 (LeUnes & Burger, 2000), and in over 1400 studies that were listed on PsycInfo by 2006.

The POMS Iceberg Profile

The POMS has been shown to be sensitive to fluctuation in the moods that influence athletic performance. This quality has been demonstrated most convincingly among groups of athletes that were homogenous with regard to skill level and physical conditioning (Terry, 1995). More successful athletes have traditionally been identified by the "**iceberg profile**" on the POMS, which consists of a high level of vigor or an abundance of energy, and low levels of tension, depression, anger, fatigue, and confusion (Figure 14.1). The term "iceberg" refers to the graphic picture that is created when this configuration of scores is plotted on a POMS profile sheet rather than to predictions that these successful athletes would be cool under pressure. In the vernacular of sport, athletes who are cool under pressure and unlikely to choke are referred to as having "ice water" in their veins. With the iceberg profile, the tension, depression, anger, fatigue, and confusion scales are suppressed beneath the "water line" or the average scores for these scales (broken line in Figure 14.1), and there is a sharp spike for the vigor scale.

The POMS was seen as a technique for predicting successful performances among elite athletes. Wrestlers who qualified for the 1976 US Olympic team demonstrated this iceberg profile, whereas wrestlers who were not selected for the team demonstrated less vigor and more depression, anger, fatigue, and confusion (Morgan, 1980). Similarly, wrestlers and speed skaters from the 1972 US Olympic team, international rowers, and international runners also gave iceberg profiles on the POMS. Collegiate tennis players who won matches at a NCAA regional (VII) tournament were more likely to evince the iceberg profile than counterparts who lost (Covassin & Pero, 2004).

Successful competitors for the 1972 Olympic Freestyle Wrestling team scored lower on tension and confusion and higher on vigor than wrestlers who did not make the team (Nagle, Morgan, Hellickson, Serfass, & Alexander, 1975). The authors did not provide statistical tests to

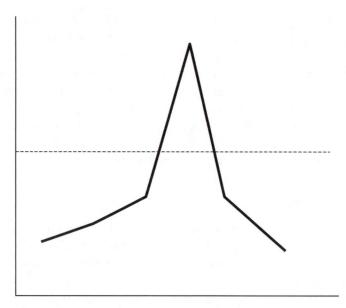

FIGURE 14.1. Example of an iceberg profile. Adapted from Terry, P. (1995). The efficacy of mood state profiling with elite performers: A review and synthesis. *The Sport Psychologist, 9,* 309–324.

demonstrate that differences between successful and unsuccessful wrest-lers were significant, and readers have wondered if these differences were substantial (Renger, 1993). Australian high school athletes demonstrated higher levels of vigor and lower levels of depression and confusion than classmates who were not athletes (Newcombe & Boyle, 1995). The ice-berg profile was even more in evidence for elite Australian high school athletes.

The success of the POMS in differentiating elite and non-elite athletes has not been consistent. The male candidates for the 1974 US Heavyweight and Lightweight Rowing teams that were previously described (Morgan & Johnson, 1978) also showed less tension, depression, anger, fatigue, confusion, and more vigor than college norms, but the POMS did not differentiate between successful and unsuccessful candidates for the teams. The POMS profiles of distance runners who ran world-class times were indistinguishable from those of high-caliber college runners (Morgan & Pollock, 1977). The runners who ran world-class times had superior aerobic power and lower submaximal lactate levels than the runners who were simply of a high caliber. Both groups of runners differed from college norms by scoring lower on the POMS scales of tension, depression, fatigue, and confusion, and higher on vigor. There were small differences on the POMS between groups of rock climbers who competed at moderate and advanced levels (Feher & Meyers, 1998). These groups included male and female American rock climbers, and the advanced group demonstrated more mood disturbance than the moderate climbers. In a sizeable number of studies involving marathoners, field hockey players, basketball and football players, and ultra-marathoners, the POMS did not differentiate between elite and non-elite athletes (Prapavessis, 2000).

It is somewhat unreasonable to expect that the POMS or any measure of mood or personality will always distinguish between winners and losers at extremely elite levels of competition. For example, the POMS did not identify World Netball Championship titleists (Miller & Miller, 1985). In some extremely elite competitions it is reasonable to expect that there is not only little physical difference but also little psychological difference between competitors.

How the Moods Measured by the POMS Affect Performance

Little is known about how the moods measured by the POMS affect athletic performance. For example, do high levels of confusion and depression impair attentional control? Does tension lead to difficulties with fine muscle control, and do moderate levels of tension contribute to the ideal level of arousal? Fatigue would be expected to reduce physical capacity, but might it also decrease self-efficacy? Anger may impair attention, but might it also enhance determination and pain tolerance (Terry, 1995)?

The POMS and Satisfactory Performances

Precompetitive moods, as measured by the POMS, differentiate between athletes who are satisfied and dissatisfied with performances. Athletes with POMS profiles that approximated the iceberg profile were far more likely to report that their performance in competition met their expectations. For example, the iceberg profile consistently identified athletes in rowing and bobsledding Olympic and World competitions who were satisfied with performances. Similarly, satisfied oarsmen at the 1993 World Rowing Championships and participants in the 1993–1994 Bobsled World Cup event were distinguished by the iceberg profile (Terry, 1995). The greatest differences for athletes who were satisfied with performances versus those who believed they had underperformed were on the vigor scale of the POMS.

The POMS was not effective in predicting self-rated satisfactory performances in national and world championship cricket and netball competitions. Perhaps this is due to the fact that mood states fluctuate and may therefore change across the 60 minutes of a netball match or the (up to) five days of a cricket test match. Similar findings were reported with elite and non-elite marathoners, as at best an elite marathoner could complete a race in approximately 2 hours and 10 minutes (Durtschi & Weiss, 1986). Competition in wrestling, rowing, and bobsledding occurs in a duration of less than 10 minutes, and moods prior to these competitions are therefore more likely to persist throughout the competition. Further, the POMS appears more predictive of performance in sports that involved closed skills and that are self-paced. In open skill sports, there are more external factors that influence performance.

Individual Differences in POMS and Optimal Performance

As explained in Chapter 3, sports that require precision, fine motor control, and higher-order thinking are performed optimally when arousal or state anxiety levels are moderate. Events requiring explosive power require higher levels of arousal for optimal performance. Similarly, the optimal POMS differs by sport (Terry, 1995). Performance in cross-country running and karate has been shown to improve with elevated anger scores on the POMS. Higher anger scores have also been recorded for sports that are more violent. For example, the anger scores were almost twice as high for steer wrestling compared to roughstock, roping, and barrel racing participants at a collegiate rodeo competition, and steer wrestling involves the most violent interaction between human and animal (Meyers & Sterling, 1990). More elite collegiate rodeo athletes demonstrate greater skill in anger management, as well as anxiety management, concentration, and confidence (Meyers & LeUnes, 1996).

Further, as has been emphasized throughout this book, people are different. Up to 26 percent of successful performances in Olympic and world championship competition occurred with athletes who did not show the iceberg pattern prior to competition. Conversely, 54 percent of these elite athletes produced these iceberg profiles and subsequently had unsuccessful performances (Terry, 1993). The understanding that the POMS profile associated with optimal performance may be different for different athletes has led to suggestions that athletes learn from experience what POMS "works best" for them, and then attempt to reproduce that POMS prior to competitions.

Deviations from this pattern of moods and POMS may serve as warnings to athletes that they are not emotionally prepared to perform, and they may then take action to alleviate negative moods. For example, athletes in the closed skill sport of clay-target shooting recorded POMS profiles prior to competition for a period of 12 months (Prapavessis & Grove, 1991). When POMS scores prior to acceptable and worst performances were compared, the POMS scores for acceptable performances were far closer to each athlete's optimal POMS profile. POMS profiles that are stable for days prior to competition suggest a better impending performance than POMS reflecting fluctuating moods.

The Inverse Iceberg Profile

An **"inverse iceberg"** POMS profile has been considered to reflect staleness, especially low scores on the vigor factor. Staleness is a state of psychological and physical fatigue that results in impaired sport performance and an inability to train at customary levels (Morgan, Brown, Raglin, O'Connor, & Ellickson, 1987). Staleness is often the result of overtraining, but overtraining or progressively increasing training loads is necessary to improving performance with endurance sports. Staleness is most likely during cycles of intense training, and is represented on the POMS by increased fatigue and global mood disturbance, and decreased vigor. The inverse iceberg profile may also present after an athlete is injured. A return to an iceberg profile may coincide with the physical recovery of injured athletes and tapering or reducing the training load of fatigued athletes.

The POMS in Practice

It appears that the POMS should be used as a suggestion of readiness to do one's best rather than an absolute sign of impending difficulties. It is not sufficiently accurate for use in selecting members to teams. The influence of preperformance mood as measured by the POMS on athletic performance is small in comparison to the importance of other psychological factors, physiological characteristics of athletes, training schedules, and histories of prior athletic success. Sophisticated statistical analyses have demonstrated that less than 1 percent of athletic performance was predicted by preperformance POMS (Rowley, Landers, Kyllo, & Etnier, 1995). Of course, if outcomes of athletic events were 100 percent predictable on the basis of prior information it would be unnecessary to hold actual competitions. This being said, the remaining 99 percent of the factors that determine outcomes of athletic events remain to be determined if only preperformance POMS scores are available. Information about the many other psychological factors, physiological characteristics of athletes, training schedules, and histories of prior athletic success would be referenced to make more accurate predictions about athletic performances.

As has been emphasized throughout this book, it is unrealistic to expect that one will feel full of vigor and self-efficacy if proper physical training has been neglected. Athletes with the iceberg profile are prepared to do their best in competition, and a history of success in competition and excellent preparation, training, and the development of superior skills are likely to lead to the development of the iceberg profile. For example, successful athletes who produced iceberg profiles prior to competitions had better records throughout the athletic season, more experience, and superior training facilities and programs (Heyman, 1982).

Athletic Coping Skills Inventory

The **Athletic Coping Skills Inventory (ACSI)** was originally developed in the mid-1980s in context with research about psychological resiliency and vulnerability to athletic injury. The scales of the ACSI measured factors such as social support, psychological coping skills, and life stress, and these scales were implicated in explaining resiliency and injuries. The ACSI was refined and the most recent and scientifically sound version consists of 28 questions that compose seven scales: **coping with adversity**, **peaking under pressure**, **goal setting/mental preparation**, **concentration**, **freedom from worry**, **confidence and achievement motivation**, and **coachability** (Smith, Schutz, Smoll, & Ptacek, 1995a).

The ACSI-28 and other psychological tests were given to large groups of male and female high school varsity athletes (Smith et al., 1995a). The freedom from worry scale correlated negatively with measures of anxiety in sporting contexts. Concentration, confidence and achievement motivation, coping with adversity, goal setting/mental preparation, and peaking under pressure were all highly correlated with general self-efficacy. A composite score of the ACSI items was shown to correlate .58 with a measure of general self-efficacy. Similar, albeit slightly less robust, correlations were seen between these ACSI-28 scales and a measure of self-esteem.

Contrary to arguments about the POMS, the ACSI is not considered to measure mental health problems or wellbeing. The ACSI-28 is unrelated to coaches' ratings of high school athletes' athletic performance. Significant, although small, differences on the coping with adversity and concentration scales and on composite ACSI-28 scores were recorded for high school athletes who underachieved versus overachieved. The performance of underachievers and overachievers was inferior and superior, respectively, to what was expected given their physical talent.

The ACSI-28 was also used to predict the performance of professional minor league baseball players (Smith & Christensen, 1995). The confidence, coping with adversity, and total or composite score for the ACSI-28 predicted the batting averages of position players. The confidence and peaking under pressure scales were significant correlates of low earned run averages (ERAs) among pitchers. As mentioned above, the confidence scale resembles self-efficacy, and this factor predicts both hitting and pitching skill. Information from the ACSI-28 allowed for significantly more accurate predictions of batting averages for position players and ERAs for pitchers than was possible solely on the basis of the ballplayers' physical talent. In fact, coaches' estimates of pitchers' physical talent (e.g. velocity, control, movement of fast ball, adequacy of breaking ball and changeup) were practically unrelated to ERAs. The ACSI-28 was seen to be at least as accurate in predicting baseball performance as tests of intelligence (IQ tests) were in predicting academic performance for college students.

Composite ACSI-28 scores also allowed for more accurate predictions of which minor league players would still be in baseball after two and three years. Estimates of physical talent were also accurate predictors of the players who would avoid being cut after two and three years. Competition in professional baseball is so keen that only 74 percent survive after two years and only 26 percent have managed to stick with their team after three years.

Summary and Conclusions

Hans Eysenck proposed that personality consists of three large dimensions or traits that are at least somewhat determined by genetic inheritance. Traditionally, athletes have been seen as high in the traits of extraversion and psychoticism and low in neuroticism. Of course, athletes are not the only people with this profile of traits – for example, sports fans show similar profiles. Because of higher levels of cortical and sympathetic nervous system arousal, introverts are more reactive to environmental stress than are extraverts. Given that introverts might choose to shun environments that include tension and excitement, their comfort in many sports may be problematic. This was forcefully illustrated in the study of English college students with majors in sports studies and physical education (Graydon & Murphy, 1995). The presence of an audience eroded the performance of introverts when the accuracy of table tennis serves was measured. Extraverts "came alive" in the presence of an audience, and the accuracy of their table tennis serves improved relative to their accuracy when serving in solitude. Extraverts habituate or stop attending to environmental stimuli quickly, and their poorer performance without an audience may be because table tennis serving in solitude is not sufficiently exciting to sustain their attention. Competition may also be more aversive to introverts because of their concerns about maintaining harmonious relationships with others. Extraverts count competition as arousing, interesting, and rewarding.

Jerome Kagan's descriptions of withdrawn children were similar to Eysenck's characterizations of introverts. These children became behaviorally inhibited when stressed or anxious. This temperamental bias for inhibition and withdrawal was seen to be the result of highly reactive amygdalas and, more generally, limbic systems and sympathetic nervous systems.

With high levels of neuroticism, people may also avoid competition and athletic activity. Neuroticism has characteristics of trait anxiety, and those high in neuroticism are prone to state anxiety during performances of complex motor tasks.

The five-factor model was discussed and compared to three factors of Eysenck. The trait of agreeableness partially reflects low scores on the psychoticism dimension. Those high in the agreeableness trait are more uncomfortable with interpersonal conflict. Competition often presents a form of conflict in that achieving victory and protecting opponents from the sting of defeat are mutually exclusive goals.

Should introverts be consigned to sports that do not involve explosive action and are better suited to ectomorphic physiques, such as distance running? Given their capacity to sustain attention, are they better candidates for closed skill sports such as target shooting? These questions cannot currently be answered on the basis of empirical evidence. However, given that marked extraversion is a statistical rarity, to reserve competition, especially with audiences and pressure for optimal performance, to these extraverts with "ice water in their veins" would be to deny the majority the benefit of competition and sport. Further, many factors such as physical talent determine performance, and elite athletes such as tennis players of Wimbledon standard have been identified with levels of neuroticism that exceed the mean of psychiatric patients with depressive disorders (Eysenck et al., 1982).

Research with the POMS has traditionally indicated that athletes with the iceberg profile were prepared to do their best in competition. The iceberg profile reflects high level of vigor or an abundance of energy, and low levels of tension, depression, anger, fatigue, and confusion. It appeared that the vigor scale was most sensitive in predicting satisfactory performances. However, the finding that POMS profiles associated with optimal performance may be different for different athletes led to suggestions that athletes learn from experience what POMS is associated with best performances, and then attempt to reproduce that POMS prior to competitions. When moods are clearly different from these optimal profiles, athletes may be warned that they are not prepared to do their best.

Other deviations from profiles that are optimal for performers, such as the inverse iceberg, may indicate staleness or injury.

The POMS measures psychological states whereas the Eysenck and five-factor models describe traits or stable characteristics. The Athletic Coping Skills Inventory (ACSI-28) was developed specifically for use in sporting contexts and offers the promise of measuring skills that are closely related to performance. For example, a composite score from the ACSI-28 was shown to correlate with a measure of general self-efficacy.

Ancient Greek philosophers encouraged people to "know yourself," as armed with self-knowledge people were better able to predict their own responses and tendencies. With self-knowledge, people can build on their strengths and work around their weaknesses (Eysenck & Wilson, 1976). These themes have been consistently presented throughout the chapters of this book. A greater understanding of one's psychology serves to take the mystery out of the factors that relate to performance.

It may also be difficult to determine one's personality based on the descriptions provided in this book, and personality can certainly be evaluated more precisely by a professional psychologist. However, the descriptions provided in this chapter may at least stir the curiosity and provide insight to those troubled by performance inhibition.

Whether traits are as genetically determined and relatively immutable as argued by Eysenck is a matter of controversy. However, the traits of extraversion and neuroticism have been shown to influence performance in sporting contexts, and knowledge of one's tendencies to respond with anxiety or enthusiasm to situational pressure during performances appears useful. Scientific research is necessary before clear directions can be provided about how to use information about personality to enhance performance.

The influence of personality traits on performance is probably best considered at times distal to performances and competitions. Information about traits may provide performers with information about their tendencies. This information may be integrated into training regimens and preperformance routines. For example, knowledge that one is likely to respond with cognitive and physiological anxiety, perhaps due to introversion or neuroticism, may signal that techniques described in previous chapters to control anxiety and choking under pressure are especially relevant. Athletes who are excessively agreeable may consider whether their overly empathic responses to the psychological wellbeing of competitors is unreasonable under rules of fair play.

Key Terms

Diathesis and stress

Hans Eysenck's theory of personality: neuroticism, psychoticism, and extraversion

Extraversion and cortical arousal

Ascending reticular-activating system

Extraversion and sport

Impulsiveness-sensation seeking

Gamesmanship

Neuroticism, anxiety, and sport

Psychoticism, aggressiveness, and sport

Five-factor model of personality: neuroticism, extraversion, agreeableness, conscientiousness, openness to experience

Temperament

Amygdala

The Profile of Mood States: tension, depression, anger, fatigue, confusion, vigor

The POMS iceberg profile

The inverse iceberg profile

Athletic coping skills inventory: coping with adversity, peaking under pressure, goal setting/mental preparation, concentration, freedom from worry, confidence and achievement motivation, coachability

Suggested Readings

Costa, P. T., Jr., & McCrae, R. R. (1995). Primary traits of Eysenck's P-E-N system: three- and five-factor solutions. *Journal of Personality and Social Psychology, 69*, 308–317.

Eysenck, H. J., & Eysenck, M. W. (1985). *Personality and individual differences.* New York: Plenum.

Kagan, J. (1994). *Galen's prophecy: Temperament in human nature.* New York: Basic Books.

Prapavessis, H. (2000). The POMS and sports performance: A review. *Journal of Applied Sport Psychology, 12,* 34–48.

Smith, R. E., Schutz, R. W., Smoll, F. L., & Ptacek, J. T. (1995). Development and validation of a multidimensional measure of sport-specific psychological skills: The Athletic Coping Skills Inventory-28. *Journal of Sport & Exercise Psychology, 17,* 379–398.

Van Vianen, A. E. M., & De Dreu, C. K. W. (2001). Personality in teams: Its relationship to social cohesion, task cohesion, and term performance. *European Journal of Work and Organizational Psychology, 10,* 97–120.

Substance Abuse 15

Jennifer Capriati was described as "tennis' new legend in the making" (Scheiber, 1990), the "The Can't Miss Kid," and "eighth-grade wonder of the world" (Leerhsen & Barrett, 1990). At age 12, she won the US Tennis Association 18-and-under competitions on clay and hard courts, and was named junior Player of the Year by *Tennis* magazine. At age 16, she won an Olympic gold medal as the women's singles champion.

Capriati turned pro as a tennis player on her 14th birthday in 1990, the first day she was eligible for professional status. At age 14, she became the youngest woman to be ranked in the top 10 of women's professional tennis and the youngest to reach the semifinals of a Grand Slam tournament, at the French Open. As a 14-year-old, she earned in excess of four million US dollars, primarily from endorsement contracts such as racketmaker Prince and Italian apparel maker Diadora. The figure was estimated to be six million when she was 15. Renowned sport psychologists described her as having an almost insatiable hunger for practice and training, and as earning highest marks for psychological fitness. At age 14, the press gushed that she "represents an evolutionary advance, a superior approach to the game" (Leerhsen & Barrett, 1990, p. 63).

In December 1993, Capriati was arrested for shoplifting a $15 ring from a shopping mall. Soon after, she underwent inpatient treatment for substance abuse. She withdrew from tennis and from other professionals on the women's tour, gained approximately 20 pounds, and described herself as self-loathing and suicidal. On May 16, 1994, Capriati was arrested for marijuana possession. She had funded a 36-hour party at a Coral Gables, FL motel. A 19-year-old at the party was arrested for possession of crack cocaine and drug paraphernalia, a 17-year-old was charged with possession of heroin, and two teenagers at the motel party accused Capriati of using both substances (Jenkins & Whiteside, 1994). Endorsement deals with Prince tennis rackets, Diadora, Oil of Olay and others stopped after the arrest. Capriati received inpatient treatment for substance abuse for the second time after this arrest (Wertheim, 2001b).

The prevalence or frequency of substance use and abuse among sports-persons is comparable to that of the general population. Among athletes and the general population, substance abuse results in interpersonal and vocational dysfunction and decreases wellbeing. Substance use and abuse may also directly impair motor and cognitive performance. Performance suffers from substance abuse at times proximal and distal to performance. Due to the focus on performance impairment in this part of the book, the topic of performance-enhancing or ergogenic substances will be addressed more briefly and with a focus on associated health hazards.

The most widely abused drugs are alcohol, nicotine, cannabis, and cocaine/crack. Due to space limitations, this chapter will concentrate primarily on a review of the effects of alcohol and cannabis. Cannabis is most often consumed in the form of smoked marijuana. Alcohol use has been studied in greatest detail, perhaps because it is a legal substance and the most widely used. Far more people use tobacco than cannabis, but the effects of tobacco on performance are less immediate. However, tobacco use has profoundly negative effects on health such as increased risks for bronchitis, obstructive lung disease, cardiovascular disease, and forms of cancer. Tobacco users become profoundly dependent on nicotine, and experience painful withdrawal symptoms when its use is stopped. Cocaine/crack is a powerfully addictive drug that also pro-motes dependence and painful withdrawal. Its use is far less frequent than alcohol and cannabis. Both nicotine and cocaine/crack are stimulant drugs.

Problems Caused by Substance Abuse

The abuse of alcohol and other drugs **leads to problems** and untoward events. Alcohol is involved in 40 percent of deaths among adolescents and young adults, mainly in automobile accidents (Pollack, Franklin, Fulton-Kehoe, & Chowdhury, 1998). The likelihood of suicide attempts increases with drug use and abuse. The odds of suicide for current heroin users was six times as great as for people who do not abuse drugs, and at least twofold greater for cocaine users. The risk of first suicide attempts increased as the number of substances currently used increased (Borges, Walters, & Kessler, 2000).

People with substance abuse and other mental disorders are more likely to drop out of high school and college (Kessler, Foster, Saunders, & Stang, 1995). Among college students, increasing alcohol use is related to lower average grades and a contributing factor in 28 percent of all college dropouts. Alcohol use is involved in about 80 percent of campus

---

Nate Newton up to 388 Pounds – of Pot

Six-time All-Pro lineman Nate Newton was a bedrock of the Dallas Cowboys professional football team that won three Super Bowls in the 1990s. In December 2001, he was arrested for the second time in five weeks for marijuana possession. Police found 213 pounds of pot in Newton's van in the first bust and 175 pounds of weed in the second arrest. Together, the 388 pounds of pot approached Newton's playing weight of 350 pounds (Newton up to 388 Lbs. – of Pot, 2001).

---

vandalism, 95 percent of campus violence, and two thirds of campus suicides (Bower & Martin, 1999).

Teenage females with substance abuse and other mental disorders are more likely to give birth, and to give birth prior to marriage (Kessler et al., 1997a). Alcohol use and abuse also contribute to sexual aggression, unintended sexual liaisons and pregnancies, and infections from sexually transmitted diseases including HIV (Centers for Disease Control and Prevention, 1998).

Substance abuse and other mental disorders lead to absences from work and decreased work productivity (Kessler & Frank, 1997). The annual medical costs for people in the USA with substance abuse or depressive disorders are $1766 higher than that for people without these mental disorders (Druss & Rosenheck, 1999). The total US healthcare cost for treating substance abuse disorders was $32.1 billion in 1998. Drug abuse cost the US economy an additional $98.5 billion in lost earnings due to absenteeism and lost productivity. Crime-related expenses caused by drug use totaled $88.9 billion, and these costs included property damage, police expenses, and criminal justice expenses (Report Finds Economic Cost of Substance Abuse Exceeds $143 Billion, 2002).

These costs would be considerably higher if everyone in need of treatment obtained it. National surveys demonstrated that 50 percent of Canadians, 60 percent of Mexicans, and 72 percent of Americans with substance abuse or dependence disorders seek help for their addictions (Kessler et al., 2001a). However, on average there is a lag of 10 years between the occurrence of their substance disorder and this help seeking. Unfortunately, people who begin substance abuse at a younger age are less likely to seek treatment.

Scope of Substance Use in the USA

The best estimates of substance use in the USA are provided by national surveys conducted by the Substance Abuse and Mental Health Services Administration (SAMHSA, 2006). In 2005, this survey was conducted with 68,308 people. Among the results were that 20.1 percent of the population 18–25 years old were current illicit drug users, meaning that in the month prior to the interview, they used an illicit or illegal drug. The most commonly used illicit drug was marijuana, as 16.6 percent of the sample used it during the month prior to the survey. Prescription-type drugs that were consumed nonmedically were next most frequently used, with 6.3 percent of young adults acknowledging their use. A sizable percentage of young adults, 2.6 percent, also used crack/cocaine. Tobacco products were used by 29.4 percent in the prior month. Considering ethnic differences, among Americans 12 and older, 8.1 percent of Caucasian, 9.7 percent of African American, 12.8 percent of Native American, 3.1 percent of Asian, and 7.6 percent of Hispanic respondents were current illicit drug users.

Of the population who were 12 and older, 51.8 percent were current alcohol users and heavy drinking was reported by 6.6 percent. Heavy drinking consisted of drinking five or more drinks on the same occasion on at least five days in the past month. Binge drinking consisted of drinking five or more drinks on the same occasion on at least one day in the past month, and 22.7 percent of this sample of Americans met this criterion. Males (58.1 percent) are more likely to be current users than females (45.9 percent) and to be binge and heavy users. Ethnic differences in alcohol consumption are summarized in Table 15.1.

Alcohol consumption reaches its peak among Americans between the ages of 18 and 25, and many of the studies in sport psychology involve

---

TABLE 15.1 Alcohol Use for Americans 12 Years Old and Older (%)

	Use in past month	Binge use	Heavy use[1]
Caucasian	56.5	23.4	8
African American	40.8	20.3	3
Native American	42.4	32.8	11
Asian	38.1	12.7	2
More than one race	43.7	20.8	4
Hispanic	42.6	23.7	4

From Substance Abuse and Mental Health Services Administration (2006). *Results from the 2005 national household survey on drug abuse: National findings* (Office of Applied Studies, USDUH Series H-30, DHHS Publication No. SMA 06-4194). Rockville, MD.
[1] Figures are approximate.

college-age participants who are in this age group. Binge drinking occurred among 41.9 percent of those in this age group, and heavy drinking was reported by 15.3 percent of these young adults; each percentage is approximately double that of the entire population. Males – and especially Caucasian males – are the largest consumers of alcohol.

Diagnoses of Substance Abuse

Substance abuse and dependence disorders are classified as mental disorders in the *Diagnostic and Statistical Manual of Mental Disorders, Fourth Edition* (DSM-IV-TR; American Psychiatric Association [APA], 2000). The DSM-IV-TR is the essential nosology or classification of mental disorders in the USA. The terms of the DSM-IV-TR are compatible with the terms and codes in Chapter V, "Mental and Behavioural Disorders" of the *International Classification of Diseases and Related Health Problems*, Tenth Revision (ICD-10; WHO, 2007). The ICD-10 was developed by the World Health Organization and is the classification system for diseases throughout much of the world. All mental disorders identified in the DSM-IV-TR significantly disrupt functioning, adjustment, and wellbeing in **interpersonal**, **vocational**, or **intrapsychic** spheres.

In the DSM-IV-TR there are 11 classes of substance-related disorders: alcohol, amphetamine (e.g. methamphetamine, Dexedrine), caffeine, cannabis (e.g. marijuana), cocaine, hallucinogen (e.g. LSD), inhalant (e.g. paint, glue), nicotine, opioid (e.g. heroin), phencyclidine (e.g. PCP), and sedative, hypnotic or anxiolytic (e.g. barbiturates such as secobarbital and benzodiazepines such as Valium). Obviously people use legal drugs such as alcohol and caffeine in ways that do not impair their functioning. However, the use of alcohol and any of the other classes of substances warrants a DSM-IV-TR diagnosis if this use significantly impairs interpersonal or vocational functioning or intrapsychic wellbeing. There are two general categories of diagnoses for significantly problematic use of the 11 classes of substances, **Substance Abuse Disorders** and **Substance Dependence Disorder**s.

Substance Abuse Disorders and Substance Dependence Disorders

Briefly, diagnoses of Substance Abuse Disorders refer to recurrent patterns of substance use that result in significant problems in a person's life. Diagnoses of Substance Dependence Disorders imply even more serious impairment. The substance-dependent person has for practical purposes lost control of their use of substances or of their ability to use the substance in moderation. This loss of control is reflected in their use of larger amounts of substances over a longer period of time than intended. There may also be repeated, unsuccessful efforts to limit or stop substance use. A great deal of time may be devoted to finding, obtaining, or "scoring" the substance, and recovering from its intoxicating effects. The substance may be used despite clear knowledge that this use results in physical or psychological damage. For example, an athlete might drive while drunk, despite knowledge that he or she will lose a scholarship if caught.

With substance dependence disorders, there is often more chronic or habitual use of substances over an extended period of time. With habitual use, **tolerance** develops for most of the abovementioned 11 classes of substances. Tolerance consists of the need for increasing amounts of the substance to achieve the desired level of intoxication. This of course promotes the use of the substance in increasing amounts, as intoxication does not occur if the substance-dependent person continues to use the same amount of the substance.

With substance dependence disorders, **withdrawal** may be experienced when the use of the substance is terminated. In general, withdrawal consists of physical and psychological reactions that are the opposite of those produced by the consumption of the abused substance (APA, 2000). For example, amphetamines are stimulant drugs and their use results in the speeding up of thought, action, and the sympathetic nervous system, decreased need for sleep and possibly euphoria. Amphetamine withdrawal includes fatigue, dysphoric mood, and often slowing of movement. Alcohol is a depressant drug and results in disinhibition and sedation. Alcohol withdrawal includes motor agitation and sympathetic nervous system overactivity.

Prevalence of Substance Abuse in the Americas, Europe, and New Zealand

Prevalence rates for alcohol and drug disorders are **high in the USA in comparison to other countries**, as illustrated in Table 15.2. There is also evidence of substantial substance use that is not reflected in this table. Approximately 52 percent of New Zealanders who were 21 years of age used cannabis in 1992, and 9.7 percent met DSM-III-R criteria for cannabis dependence (Poulton, Brooke, Moffitt, Stanton, & Silva, 1997). High school students in Spain consume considerable amounts of alcohol (Lopez-Frias, De La Fe Fernandez, Planells, Miranda, Mataix, & Llopis, 2001). Spanish males between the ages of 14 and 19 consume an average of 15 drinks per

TABLE 15.2 Lifetime Prevalence Rates by Country		
	% Lifetime dependence – alcohol	% Lifetime dependence – all other drugs
Germany	6.2	2.1
Mexico	6.7	0.7
Netherlands	5.5	1.8
Ontario, Canada	9.1	3.2
USA	14.3	7.5

From Merikangas et al. (1998). Comorbidity of substance use disorders with mood and anxiety disorders: Results of the international consortium in psychiatric epidemiology. *Addictive Behaviors, 23*, 893–907.

week, and more than half of the drinks are consumed on Saturday. Spanish high school girls drink about eight drinks per week; again, more than half are consumed on Saturday. Spanish adolescents who consumed more alcohol were more likely to drop out of school. These Spanish teenagers drank more beer than wine or distilled spirits, and this preference for beer has also been reported among French teenagers. Spanish adolescents who do not attend school consume even more alcohol.

Prevalence of Alcohol Use among Athletes

In terms of **alcohol use among athletes**, college students are more likely to be current, binge, and heavy drinkers than their nonmatriculated peers (Wechsler, Davenport, Dowdall, Grossman, & Zanakos, 1997). Among the initiatives to prevent underage drinking have been efforts to engage young people in sport. Ironically, college athletes drink more than peers who are not athletes. Students who were collegiate athletes were more likely to drink on a twice-weekly basis (39.6 percent) than college students who played sports in high school (35.9 percent), and college students who did not compete at the high school or college level (21.2 percent; Hildebrand, Johnson, & Bogle, 2001). The college athletes were more likely to average three or more drinks per sitting (65.8 percent) than the students who played sports in high school (52.4 percent) and the collegians who were not sportspersons (44.4 percent). Indeed, there is evidence that alcohol abuse increases with increasing involvement in athletics, in that team leaders were more likely to engage in binge drinking (five or more drinks in a sitting) than other teammates (Leichliter, Meilman, Presley, & Cashin, 1998). Athletic leaders were also more likely to experience negative consequences as a result of drinking, such as hangovers and arguments. Similar findings were reported for French adolescents, as males and females who participated in team sports reported more alcohol use

(Peretti-Watel, Beck, & Legleye, 2002). Collegiate swimmers and divers reported at least one more episode of heavy drinking than athletes in baseball, softball, basketball, and volleyball. It has been speculated that these relatively high levels of alcohol consumption are due to a tradition of male and female swimmers and divers socializing and "partying together" (Martens, Watson, & Beck, 2006).

These results (Leichliter et al., 1998) held true for male and female athletes, but female athletes demonstrated fewer negative consequences and less binge drinking than male athletes. Still, female athletes demonstrated significantly more binge drinking and negative consequences than college women who did not participate in sport.

Among African American intercollegiate athletes, 14 percent reported drinking at least four drinks per sitting during athletic seasons and 46 percent reported drinking at this level out of season (Bower & Martin, 1999). Consistent with the larger literature about alcohol use, binge drinking was most common among Caucasian male athletes, or athletes who smoked marijuana or cigarettes.

College students who were both athletes and members of fraternities or sororities drank more than any other identifiable college group, and sorority and fraternity members who were not athletes drank more than athletes who were not fraternity or sorority members. Perhaps involvement in social activities where alcohol is typically consumed is responsible for these differences in alcohol consumption among these groups of collegians (Meilman, Leichliter, & Presley, 1999).

American high school athletes who participated in two or more sports drank more often and were more likely to drink in binges than classmates

Alcohol use is not uncommon among college athletes (photo © Galina Barskaya).

Heavy Drinking among Athletes Is Nothing New

The association between drinking and athletics is not a recent phenomenon. The sportswriter Dick Schaap spent a week in the 1961 NFL (National Football League) season chronicling the activities of Paul Hornung. Hornung was a Heisman Trophy winner and an NFL all-pro halfback for the Green Bay Packers. Hornung began drinking martinis at about three in the afternoon. Martini time was over at about six, when it was time for Scotch before dinner and wine with dinner. After-dinner drinks were brandy, and then it was back on scotch. Schaap was not able to determine the exact number of drinks consumed by Hornung during the week, but estimated it to be in excess of 60, a number nowhere near the club record (Maraniss, 1999).

---

who were not athletes. This pattern was not repeated among young and high school athletes in Italy, who drank less than peers who were not sportspersons (Gutgesell & Canterbury, 1999). About one fourth of high school athletes tried beer and cigarettes prior to the seventh grade, and consistent with older groups, high school sportsmen were more likely to drink alcohol than sportswomen (Mikow & Raven, 1993, cited in Stainback, 1997).

American college and former high school athletes were more likely to engage in sexual intercourse under the influence of alcohol. Intercollegiate athletes have been shown to more frequently drive while under the influence of alcohol, ride with intoxicated drivers, and have more sexual partners as well as more sexually transmitted diseases than nonathletes (Nattiv & Puffer, 1991).

Prevalence of Cannabis Use among Athletes

In terms of **cannabis use among athletes**, intercollegiate athletes were less likely to have used marijuana in the past 30 days than nonathletes (Wechsler et al., 1997). Twelve and 10 percent of male and female intercollegiate athletes used cannabis whereas 16 and 11 percent of male and female college students who did not participate in athletics used marijuana. The finding that collegiate athletes use less cannabis than college students who do not engage in sports has been consistently reported, and athletes have also been shown to use less cocaine and crack (Anderson, Albrecht, McKeag, Hough, & McGrew, 1991). Adolescents who use substantial quantities of cannabis are less likely to engage in conventional tasks such as athletics and extracurricular sport activities, and are more frequently involved with delinquent or substance-using peers (Brook, Kessler, & Cohen, 1999; Lynskey & Hall, 2000).

Those who regularly use cannabis may be less likely to engage in athletic or other effortful activities. Cannabis has a direct effect on decreasing motivation and attention to study and training, a condition referred to as **amotivational syndrome**.

Marijuana and the NBA

Major new sources have consistently reported that American professional basketball players in the National Basketball Association (NBA) routinely smoke marijuana. The extent of marijuana use in the NBA has not been established by scientific surveys, but the *New York Times* cited sources such as two dozen active players, former players, basketball agents, and basketball executives in estimating that 60 to 70 percent of NBA players smoked marijuana (Roberts, 1997). The NBA's drug policy does not list marijuana as a prohibited substance, and therefore differentiates between cannabis and other illegal substances such as cocaine, heroin, amphetamines, and LSD. The current NBA policy states that teams *may* drug screen rookies once during training camp and no more than three times during the regular season. Veterans face random testing no more than one time during the regular season or during the first 15 days in which they report to their team, typically training camp (Wise, 2000). League policy calls for a ban of players guilty of a crime involving cocaine or heroin, and this policy was developed in response to arrests of NBA players involving these drugs in the 1970s and early 1980s.

The NBA initiated a screening program for cannabis during training camps in 2000. They boasted that only 2.8 percent of the players tested positive for cannabis (Wise, 2000). The players were aware when they would be tested, therefore the "hit rate" of 2.8 percent reflects less a true survey of cannabis use in the NBA and more the percentage that were "extremely stupid or really dependent on the drug" (Keteyian, 1999) so that they were unable to stop prior to the drug test. Players cannot be dismissed from the league for testing positive for cannabis, but can be banished for a single positive test of the other illegal drugs.

NBA players and their union president Billy Hunter have defended their resistance to more frequent and unannounced screening with the argument that the cannabis use in the NBA mirrors its use in society. Of course, this argument is spurious, as about 4.8 percent of the US population smoke marijuana as frequently as monthly (SAMHSA, 2006).

How is it that there is such a potential disparity between the levels of cannabis use among college athletes and the potential use among professional athletes? One explanation is that the wealth and influence of professional athletes provide access to almost unlimited party scenes. With average salaries in excess of two million dollars in the NBA, plenty of free time, and little mentoring by senior adults, players accept this access.

Motivation for Substance Use

It should come as no surprise that the primary **motivation for using cannabis and alcohol** is to experience their effect. Cannabis users report a "high" that includes feelings of intoxication and pleasure. However, some experience anxiety and even paranoia when trying cannabis (Ashton, 2001). Drinkers find the sedating effects of alcohol to be rewarding. Some experience disinhibition and report they are better able to enjoy themselves after using alcohol.

The motivation for alcohol use has been studied more extensively than the use of other substances, perhaps due to the greater prevalence of alcohol use and the fact that it is a legal substance. In surveys of the populations in Alaska (Segal, 1986) and Buffalo, NY (Cooper, 1994; Cooper, Russell, Skinner, & Windle, 1992) three factors have been shown to motivate the drinking of adults and adolescents. First, the drinking of some adolescents and adults is determined primarily by peer-related or **social** motives. These people consider drinking to be the thing to do when socializing, at parties, or when celebrating. A second group is primarily motivated by sensation-seeking or efforts for **enhancement** of phenomenological states. This group is more likely to be extraverted and interested in exciting and even risky activities. Tension-reduction or **palliation** motives are primary when alcohol is used for self-medication of depression and anxiety or to palliate or reduce anhedonia (an absence of pleasure).

Drinking that is primarily determined by social motives has been shown to be least related to excessive drinking and difficulties controlling drinking. The social use of illicit drugs by adolescents may be a different matter. Approximately 90 percent of adolescent substance abusers have friends that use the same drugs (Dinges & Oetting, 1993). Alcohol use that is motivated by enhancement and palliation motives is more likely to be problematic (Cloninger, 1987; Gallucci, 1997; Kessler et al., 1997b; MacAndrew, 1980, 1981; Merikangas et al., 1998; Mezzich, Tarter, Kirisci, Clark, Buckstein, & Martin, 1993; Schuckit, 1994).

Athletes' Motivation for Substance Use

Collegiate athletes use alcohol and other drugs for exactly the same reasons as do adults and adolescents from the general population. The motives of athletes and representative samples of Americans for alcohol and other drug use are for facilitating social interactions and celebrations, to enhance phenomenology or feeling states, and to palliate or self-medicate unpleasant feelings (Evans, Weinberg, & Jackson, 1992). The athletes who used alcohol scored higher on the anger, fatigue, and vigor scales of the Profile of Mood States (POMS). Males who used alcohol reported more pressure from coaches to perform well at their sport.

Potential Etiology of Jennifer Capriati's Substance Use

The etiology and causes for Jennifer Capriati's descent were pieced together by her recollections at age 18. Substance abuse may have been secondary to self-loathing and feelings of failure due to not confirming predictions that she would be an evolutionary advance in women's tennis. Capriati experienced unprecedented pressure to win tournaments at a young age, and experienced disappointment such as in her semifinal loss in the US Open when she was age 15. As an 18-year-old Capriati commented on depression:

> I was always expected to be at the top, and if I didn't win, to me that meant I was a loser. The way I felt about myself had to do with how I played, and if I played terrible, allowed that pressure to win I'd say, yes, I can handle it, but really I couldn't; I felt like no one liked me as a person. I felt like my parents and everybody else thought that tennis was the way to make it in life, they thought it was good, but I thought no one knew or wanted to know the person who was behind my tennis life. (Finn, 1994, p. C2)

This provoked Capriati to spend one week in bed and to experience such self-loathing that she wished to kill herself. Although she did not kill herself, she did inflict a great deal of damage. The arrests for shoplifting and cannabis possession followed, and her public image and endorsements died. Perhaps Capriati sought, at least unconsciously, to escape from obligations and expectations over which she experienced little control.

The pressure of achieving in the world of professional tennis was compounded by the complications of progressing through adolescence. Capriati was separated from, but wanted the approval of, adolescent peers in high school, and felt the academic pressure of high school.

Family therapists might wonder if generational boundaries and lines of authority with parents were complicated by her wealth. Her father was described as a former athlete, stuntman, and tennis pro, and her mother was an airline stewardess. Their hierarchical roles in relationship to their daughter may have been compromised by her role as the primary breadwinner, and by the degree of autonomy and adulation given to her on the professional tour.

After 11 years, and this travail, Capriati overcame the tag of tennis' prodigal daughter. She took the first two Grand Slams of tennis in 2001 by winning the Australian and French Opens. She won the Australian Open in 2002. After winning her first Grand Slam at the Australian Open in 2001 she remarked, "I just hope people who are down or don't feel good about themselves can see this and use it as inspiration" (Wertheim, 2001b, p. 77). "Who would have ever thought I would have made it here after so much has happened?" said Capriati. "Dreams do come true" (Wertheim, 2001a, p. 56).

Acute Effects of Alcohol on Psychomotor Performance

Alcohol has **acute effects on psychomotor performance**. A universally recognized psychomotor task that is influenced by substance use is automobile driving. In the USA, blood alcohol concentrations (BACs; grams of alcohol per 100 milliliters of blood) of 0.08 or 0.1 are commonly recognized as the standard for determining illegal driving under the influence of alcohol. The National Highway Traffic Safety Administration determined that BACs as low as 0.02 impaired driving performance (Tests Show Impairment at Low BACs, 2000). Compared to drivers who did not drink alcohol, the risk of fatal accidents for drivers with BACs from 0.05 to 0.09 is approximately 11 times greater; it is 48 times greater for drivers with BACs between 0.1 to 0.14, and 385 times greater for drivers with BAC levels of at least 0.15 (Zador, 1991). BAC levels as low as .05 are more generally associated with lowered alertness, impaired judgment, and disinhibition. At higher levels, motor coordination and reaction times become increasingly impaired.

Given the increased likelihood of automobile accidents after drinking alcohol, it is no surprise that skills necessary for safe driving such as sustained attention and low reaction time are negatively affected by alcohol. The same issues extend to flying aircraft (Stainback, 1997). Sports that involve complex motor skills, sustained attention, and complex decision-making are more likely to be negatively affected by recent alcohol use. Skills that are automatic are also more likely to be negatively affected.

Gender Differences and Alcohol

Alcohol causes **more cognitive impairment in women than men**. This impairment is apparent on tasks that require working memory, reaction time, and hand–eye coordination. This impairment has a negative effect on driving, and piloting a commercial aircraft with

Test to measure psychomotor impairment (photo © Frances Twitty).

even trace amounts of alcohol in one's bloodstream is forbidden. With driving and flying, the ability to attend to two or more sources of information is especially important and easily disrupted by alcohol consumption. Women have proportionally more body fat and less water in the body than men of equivalent body weights. Alcohol is dispersed in the water in the body, and women reach higher levels of BAC with equivalent amounts of alcohol and adjusting for body weight. These gender differences in response to alcohol do not appear to result from changes in levels of sex steroid hormones throughout the menstrual cycle of women (Mumenthaler & Taylor, 1999).

Acute Effects of Cannabis on Psychomotor Performance

In terms of the **acute effects of cannabis on psychomotor performance**, driving is affected less by cannabis use than by alcohol, but driving skills decrease with higher doses of cannabis (Schwenk, 1998). Apparently drivers are capable of suppressing the "high" from cannabis intoxication while driving, because cannabis intoxication has consistently been associated with decreased sustained attention and concentration.

In addition to disrupting attention and concentration, cannabis intoxication is traditionally correlated with difficulties in working memory or with learning new information, and with distorted estimates of time. While intoxicated, the cannabis user estimates that more time passed than actually has.

Traditional correlates of cannabis use notwithstanding, the influence of cannabis on performance has been controversial, with some scientists maintaining that the effects are relatively benign. This controversy has prompted rigorous studies of the acute effects of cannabis in laboratories. This research has typically required subjects or participants first to smoke sufficient amounts of marijuana to become intoxicated (stoned), and then to complete cognitive and psychomotor tests.

For example, smoking a marijuana cigarette or drinking enough alcohol to reach the legal limit of drunkenness impaired the accuracy of adult males in matching geometric patterns with numbers during a span of 90 seconds. This task measures visual-motor speed and accuracy, as participants are required to identify geometric patterns that correspond to numbers, and then to copy the patterns in boxes beneath the numbers. Performance was also impaired after this smoking and drinking when they were asked to recall lists of words (Heishman, Arasteh, & Stitzer, 1997).

In another study, the effects of substances on psychomotor performance were studied by supplying eight healthy men with alcohol, marijuana, stimulants, and opiate drugs. A general finding was that as the intellectual demands of tasks increased, performance was impaired with lower doses of drugs. Examples of psychomotor tasks included: locating six letters from a random string of 24 letters, mental addition or subtraction, and sorting playing cards by color and category. Alcohol impaired performance on all of these tasks and marijuana slowed mental addition and subtraction by 46 percent (Pickworth, Rohrer, & Fant, 1997). The effects of marijuana on psychomotor performance were in general less than those for alcohol and the influence of amphetamines or stimulants was seen as minimal.

In another study, the influence of marijuana on cognitive and psychomotor performance was considered to be minimal (Hart, van Gorp, Haney, Foltin, & Fischman, 2001). However, the debilitating cognitive and psychomotor effects of cannabis were probably minimized in this study by two factors. First, the participants were chronic marijuana smokers who averaged four marijuana cigarettes per day. The active ingredient of cannabis, tetrahydrocannabinol (THC), has a half-life of about 19 hours. That is, after 19 hours, half of the THC in the bloodstream from a given dose of cannabis has been eliminated or deactivated by the liver (Ray & Ksir, 2002). The participants in this study may have smoked marijuana before arriving at the clinic for the study. By smoking a single marijuana cigarette prior to the experimental tasks, THC was added to prior amounts of THC that were already circulating in the bloodstream, and these prior amounts were likely to be substantial. Second, these experienced "tokers" had almost certainly developed a tolerance to THC so that a dose larger than a single marijuana cigarette would be necessary to greatly alter their cognitive and psychomotor responses. People who have not developed a tolerance to cannabis show larger performance decrements after marijuana use (Haney, Ward, Comer, Foltin, & Fischman, 1999). Still, after smoking the marijuana cigarette, the male and female participants in this study demonstrated impairment on tasks requiring the inhibition of responses before more than one dimension of a problem is analyzed (Hart et al., 2001).

Independent research has demonstrated that tolerance to the cognitive and psychomotor effects of cannabis almost surely occurs. Even with tolerance, performance on some tests of visual-motor coordination, such as matching geometric patterns with numbers during a span of 90 minutes, is impaired (Haney et al., 1999). However, among cannabis users, it is not only the acute effects of cannabis intoxication on performance that are of concern, but also the effects of withdrawal from cannabis. In a sample of adult males who smoked about six marijuana cigarettes per day (Haney et al., 1999), performance was actually impaired on a task requiring sustained concentration following abstinence from cannabis, and these effects were seen even on the fourth day of abstinence.

Abstinence from cannabis affects not only performance but also mood, food intake, sleep, and social behavior. Heavy cannabis users report heightened anxiety, stomach pain, and irritability after abstinence. They also eat less often and socialize less. The withdrawal symptoms are most severe on about the fourth day of abstinence, but persist after the fourth day. For example, aggressive behavior and irritability persist for at least seven days.

Cannabis Use and Long-Term Impairment

Does heavy and frequent use of cannabis lead to **impairment in cognitive functioning that persists** beyond the time of acute intoxication? Historically, studies have yielded minimum evidence of cognitive impairment among chronic cannabis users. As the sophistication of scientific inquiries has increased, the effects of cannabis on the brain have been shown to be far from harmless.

The finding that long-term cannabis use results in subtle impairments in verbal memory has been consistently reported. For example, comparing males who used cannabis almost every day of the month, memory functions were impaired for a group using for an average of 23 years but not for a group with 10 years of use (Solowij et al., 2002). The group with 23 years of cannabis abuse demonstrated impaired attention, and was more easily distracted. Independent research has also demonstrated that the total lifetime consumption of cannabis was important in determining not only cognitive impairment but also impairment in hand–eye coordination (Croft, Mackay, Mills, & Gruzelier, 2001). **Memory impairment** is not unique to cannabis use, and the memory deficits that result from long-term MDMA (ecstasy) are more severe (Rodgers, 2000).

Smoking cannabis causes pathological changes to the lungs that are similar to those caused by smoking tobacco. However, the pathological changes occur more rapidly with cannabis due to the respiratory burden of inhaling large puffs of cannabis and holding the smoke in the lungs. The effects of daily or almost daily marijuana smoking on the respiratory system was studied with a large sample of 21-year-old New Zealanders. Marijuana smokers had significantly more wheezing apart from colds, shortness of breath caused by exercise such as climbing hills, production of sputum in the morning, and nocturnal wakening with chest tightness (Taylor, Poulton, Moffitt, Ramankutty, & Sears, 2000). Many of the marijuana smokers also smoked tobacco. Smoking both tobacco and cannabis produced more respiratory symptoms than smoking either alone. The magnitude of these respiratory symptoms caused by cannabis dependence was similar to smoking up to 10 cigarettes per day.

Alcohol Use and Long-Term Impairment

The **long-term effects of alcohol** are less controversial than those of cannabis. Most dramatically, alcohol has been shown to be the third leading external or nongenetic contributor of death, trailing only tobacco use and diet and activity patterns (Grant, DeBakey, & Zobeck, 1991; McGinnis & Foege, 1993). Cirrhosis of the liver due to alcohol abuse usually occurs after approximately 10 years of drinking about a pint of whiskey per day. With such heavy and prolonged alcohol consumption, Wernicke-Korsakoff syndrome may also occur. This syndrome includes loss of many important brain functions including memory (Ray & Ksir, 2002).

Chronic exposure to alcohol produces diffuse brain dysfunction in that many areas of the brain may be impaired. The severity of this function varies from mild to severe, with perhaps 50 percent demonstrating significant impairment. Chronic alcoholics lose mental efficiency or the facility to identify important and accurate information and ignore irrelevant and inaccurate information. Deficits with cognitive efficiency are especially apparent on timed tasks or when jobs and performances must be completed by deadlines or during discrete periods of time (Nixon, 1999).

Chronic alcoholism does not appear to cause muscle atrophy and diminished muscle size, but does result in decreased speed and force of muscle movements. Deficits in the speed and force of muscle contractions due to alcoholism have been considered small because they were less than 10 percent (York, Hirsch, Pendergast, Glavy, 1999). However, in competitive athletics, differences of this magnitude are enormous. Muscle energy is partially recovered within two weeks of abstinence from alcohol among chronic alcoholics.

Alcohol and Sport

The American College of Sports Medicine (1982) took a position in 1982 that the use of **alcohol was of no benefit for sport**, and that its use may be detrimental for athletes. It should be obvious that the acute effects of alcohol on sport performance are detrimental. As discussed above, with recent alcohol consumption, reaction time, eye–hand coordination, and accuracy and balance are compromised. Alcohol use among young leisure sport participants contributes to serious injuries in activities such as cycling, boating, swimming, snow skiing, and ice-skating. These injuries result from impaired psychomotor functioning and judgment. Approximately half of the victims of fatal leisure boat accidents were intoxicated. About half of the people who suffered spinal cord injuries when diving into pools and more than half of young adult drowning victims were using alcohol at the time of their accidents.

Alcohol provides no benefit in terms of increasing stored energy sources such as glycogen that can be converted to glucose and used to fuel muscle performance. The typical increase in glucose levels in the blood that occurs with exercise is inhibited after the consumption of alcohol. Alcohol consumption, even on the night before competition, contributes to dehydration due to the suppression of antidiuretic hormones which results in increased volume of sweat and urine. This loss of fluid has an especially deleterious effect on endurance performance. Alcohol also disrupts performance in cold weather. With alcohol use, peripheral veins and arteries become dilated (increase in diameter). This results in excessive heat loss, which interferes with the normal vasoconstriction of blood vessels in cold weather. Also, the use of alcohol during competition is banned by the International Olympic Committee.

Alcohol and Sleep

Alcohol has been used since ancient times as a folk remedy to facilitate **sleep**. About 15 percent of the US population use alcohol to induce sleep at least 30 times in one year, and 6 percent drank to go to sleep 180 times or more in the course of a year (Johnson, Roehrs, Roth, Breslau, 1998).

In actuality, alcohol consumption worsens sleep quality. People who use alcohol to induce sleep are more tired and less alert during the day. Perhaps the appeal of alcohol as a sleep tonic is due to its sedating effects. Drinking even a small amount of alcohol, such as one to three drinks, prior to bedtime provides sedation, an immediate enhancement of slow-wave sleep, and a concurrent suppression of REM or rapid eye movement sleep (Castaneda, Sussman, Levy, O'Malley, & Westreich, 1998). Slow-wave sleep is associated with deep sleep, and dreaming occurs during REM sleep. With the metabolization of alcohol, blood alcohol levels reach 0 after approximately two to three hours. At that point a rebound effect occurs that consists of elevated heart rate and a greater likelihood of awakening. With this rebound, the drinker is not only no longer sedated, but also more alert than would be the case without alcohol.

With nightly use of alcohol and alcohol tolerance, these disruptions of the sleep cycle may diminish, but rebound effects and sleep disruptions will recur with the discontinuation of alcohol use. Indeed, insomnia is a symptom of alcohol withdrawal (American Psychiatric Association, 2000).

Alcohol consumption serves to obstruct airflow during sleep. Normal sleepers who consume a single large alcoholic drink can develop sleep apnea or obstructions of airflow when trying to breathe. Chronic snorers are likely to develop frank apneas during the first hours of sleep when alcohol levels are highest, and airflow is decreased further for those with preexisting sleep apnea. With sleep apnea air flow to the brain is decreased.

People who have at least two drinks per day have more restless sleep. They are especially likely to move their legs about during sleep. About the same amount of alcohol also suppresses melatonin. Melatonin is a pineal hormone, and its secretion prompts drowsiness and sleep. Regular schedules of bedtime capitalize on the secretion of melatonin and allow for easy transitions to sleep and more restful sleep. With the regulation of sleep, circadian rhythms – patterns of wakefulness and drowsiness – are predictable, and more under the control of athletes. Inadequate sleep impairs performance and may result in lethargy, fatigue, difficulties with concentration, and depressed mood.

Growth hormone or somatomedin is released during the first hours of sleep, and is also suppressed by a few drinks prior to bed. Of course, growth hormone stimulates growth during childhood and adolescence, the latter being a time when drinking is not uncommon. In adults, growth hormone plays a role in sustaining the health of aging body tissues.

Cannabis and Sleep

Regular cannabis users **fall asleep more quickly** after smoking marijuana (Chait, 1990). Abstinence from marijuana following prolonged heavy use is associated with sleep disturbances. Sleep disturbance occurs even with abstinence after smoking five marijuana cigarettes per day for three days. With abstinence, it takes longer for marijuana users to fall asleep and to begin the REM or dream cycle of their sleep.

Doping

The use of drugs to enhance sport performance is referred to as **doping** or ergogenic substance use, and both licit and illicit drugs are used in doping (Voy, 1991). This topic may appear disconnected to the previous examination of substances that inhibit or impair performance. However, athletic careers and the physical wellbeing of athletes are imperiled by ergogenic substance use. For example, Tim Montgomery was banned from track competition by the Court of Arbitration for Sport for two years when it was determined that he used an anabolic-androgenic steroid (AAS; Litsky, 2005). He was also stripped of honors and prize money acquired after March 31, 2001, as well as his former world record of 9.78 seconds in the 100 meters. The former president, Manfred Ewald, and chief sport physician, Dr Manfred Hoppner, of the former East German Sports Federation were convicted of causing bodily harm to minors as a result of secretly mixing anabolic-androgenic steroids such as Turinabol in the sports drinks of adolescent and preadolescent athletes (Ungerleider, 2001). This illegal doping produced dramatic results such as in the 1976 Olympics when the East German female swimmers swept 11 of 13 gold medals. Bodily harm included clitoral enlargement, excessive body hair, deepened voice, and damage to the liver and heart. Of course, the use of ergogenic substances is not only illegal in most sport venues but also provides an unfair advantage and violates the basic principles of fair athletic competition.

The most common licit drugs used in doping are caffeine and creatine and, although licit, the use of creatine (and extreme amounts of caffeine) is banned in many sport venues. AAS; growth hormone (GH) derived from human, animal, or synthetic sources; amphetamines; blood doping; and EPO are illicit forms of doping. Creatine, androstenedione, AAS, and GH are used to build muscular strength, power, and endurance. Caffeine, ephedrine, and amphetamines are central nervous system stimulants and used in doping to decrease fatigue, increase aggressiveness, and enhance confidence: Supplements with ephedrine became illicit after a series of legal actions that ended in 2006. Blood doping consists of adding red blood cells to the blood stream of athletes so as to augment the amount of oxygen that can be carried to muscles. With greater availability of oxygen, muscular fatigue is decreased. EPO is the body's hormone that stimulates the production of red blood cells.

Creatine and caffeine are legal, readily available, and increasingly sanctioned for performance enhancement. For example, the visibility and possible acceptance of the use of substances for doping such as androstenedione and creatine increased after 1998 when Major League baseball's then home run champion, Mark McGuire, publicized his use of androstenedione. The use of increasing amounts of caffeine as a stimulant has recently been publicized in the popular press: Androstenedione was classified as a steroid and a controlled substance by the Food and Drug Administration in 2004, and currently cannot be sold without prescription. Caffeine is currently delivered not only from traditional sources such as coffee, but also in bottled water and soap. "Shower Shock" is a soap that is advertised to deliver 250 milligrams of caffeine per soaping. Soft drinks such as "Whoop Ass" have been "enriched" with large doses of caffeine (Shea, 2002).

Serious health hazards are associated with the use of these drugs, with the possible exception of caffeine (Kuhn, Swartzwelder, & Wilson, 2000). The medical and psychiatric complications of AAS use include hepatic or liver abnormalities such as peliosis hepatis, cholestasis, and benign and malignant tumors. AAS use also results in changes in cardiovascular risk factors such as increased low-density lipoprotein and decreased high-density lipoprotein cholesterol levels and hypertension. Endocrinologic effects resulting from AAS use include decreased plasma testosterone and gonadotropin levels, testicular atrophy and gynecomastia in men, and inhibition of ovulation, hirsutism, deepened voice, and acne in women (Bahrke, Yesalis, & Brower, 1998; Hallagan, Hallagan, & Snyder, 1989; Voy, 1991). Aggressive behavior (Bahrke, Yesalis, & Wright, 1996) and mood disorders with depressive and manic features are also associated with the use of and withdrawal from AAS (Copeland, Peters, & Dillon, 2000; Malone, Dimeff, Lombardo, & Sample, 1995; Pope & Katz, 1994).

Summary and Conclusions

Alcohol and cannabis use is not infrequent in the general population and among athletes. For example, 12 and 10 percent of male and female intercollegiate athletes, respectively, used cannabis whereas 16 and 11 percent of male and female college students who did not participate in athletics used marijuana on a monthly basis. Collegiate athletes have been shown to be almost twice as likely to drink on a twice-weekly basis as college students who did not play sports at the high school or college level. Americans of European descent and who are not Hispanic have been shown to consume more alcohol than Native, African, Asian, and Hispanic Americans. Women of all ethnic groups drink less than men.

The prevalence of alcohol and other drug dependence disorders is high in the USA in comparison to other countries. However, 9.7 percent of New Zealanders who were 21 years of age were found to have cannabis dependence disorders. Considering that Spanish males and females between the ages of 14 and 19 average at least 7.5 and four, respectively, drinks on Saturday, many of these teenagers would meet the SAMHSA standards for heavy or binge drinking.

Drinking motivated by efforts to palliate anxiety and depression or to enliven oneself is more problematic than drinking in the context of socialization. Moderate drinking in the context of social rituals is less likely to lead to substance abuse or dependence disorders.

The importance of preperformance routines was discussed in Chapter 4. Readers were encouraged to simulate "game conditions" during all phases of preperformance preparation and training. Unnecessary deviations and disruptions in preperformance routines are to be avoided as they counter the benefits of systematic preparation to do one's best. With this in mind, the use of any psychoactive drugs other than small amounts of alcohol and prescription medications cannot be defended, and even small amounts of alcohol can disrupt sleep.

The use of substances may impair performance in at least three ways. First, if alcohol and cannabis are routinely used during training and preperformance preparation, psychomotor skill acquisition may be delayed, concentration disrupted, and sleep impaired. Hormonal disruptions secondary to sleep changes, and muscular impairments are potential consequences of chronic alcohol abuse. Chronic marijuana smoking compromises the respiratory system. Moreover, the time wasted while high or drunk is taken from purposeful activities such as physical and mental practice, and an amotivational syndrome that contributes to inadequate effort and poor school performance may also erode motivation for optimal training and sport performance. Second, athletes are likely to experience disequilibrium if psychoactive drugs are routinely used during training and discontinued prior to competition and performances. In effect, these athletes would train with some measure of alcohol or cannabis in their bodies or in some state of withdrawal, and then compete with less alcohol or cannabis in their systems and in perhaps heightened states of withdrawal. These differences in physiology and phenomenology could range from subtle to very noticeable, and would be contrary to the best preperformance preparation strategies. The most extreme form of disequilibrium would be diagnosable alcohol or cannabis withdrawal, which would involve insomnia, irritability, lethargy, anxiety, sympathetic nervous system overactivity, and changes in appetite and food intake. Third, athletes may routinely use alcohol and cannabis during training and competition. These steady substance users avoid the abovementioned disruptions in equilibriums at the cost of the acute effects of alcohol and cannabis on psychomotor performance. These acute effects include decreased visual-motor speed and accuracy, and impaired concentration and memory.

The benefits of preperformance routines are due largely to the order and control that they bring to the schedules and psychological states of athletes. Perceived control and self-efficacy are vital ingredients for sustaining effort in the face of obstacles and across years of practice and preparation. Self-efficacy – belief that one is equal to challenges – is also crucial in limiting choking under pressure. The most convincing source of efficacious beliefs is enactive attainments or actual successful experience. The self-efficacy and confidence of a team is influenced by the skillful performance of its members. With substance abuse, there are fewer opportunities for successful training experiences and less potential for the establishment of sturdy self-efficacy.

Among the recognized costs and consequences of substance abuse are family dysfunction, injuries, stunted academic achievement, and even suicide. Doping or ergogenic substance use imperils the physical well-being of athletes as well as the integrity of sport.

However substantial the recognized costs, the loss of human potential due to substance abuse is probably underestimated. Teenage substance abusers miss important social experiences with peers and family and academic training during the brief time of their adolescence. Once past, opportunities for these experiences cannot be retrieved, but perhaps social and academic skills can be remediated at a later point in life. Squandered opportunities for achievement are even more damaging in athletic venues because the time available for athletic careers is limited and often discrete, as in collegiate athletics. With poignancy and scientific accuracy it can be said that lost opportunities are a primary source of life's disappointments.

Key Terms

Problems caused by substance abuse

Diagnostic and Statistical Manual of Mental Disorders, Fourth Edition: interpersonal, vocational, or intrapsychic impairment

Scope of substance use in the USA

Substance Abuse Disorders

Substance Dependence Disorders

Tolerance

Withdrawal

International prevalence of substance abuse

Prevalence of alcohol and cannabis use among athletes

Amotivational syndrome

Motivation for substance use: social, enhancement, and palliation motives

Acute effects of alcohol on psychomotor performance

Gender differences and alcohol

Acute effects of cannabis on psychomotor performance

Cannabis use and long-term impairment: memory impairment

Alcohol use and long-term impairment

Alcohol and sport   **Cannabis and sleep**

Alcohol and sleep   **Doping**

Suggested Readings

Castaneda, R., Sussman, N., Levy, R., O'Malley, M., & Westreich, L. (1998). A review of the effects of moderate alcohol intake on psychiatric and sleep disorders. *Recent Developments in Alcoholism, 14*, 197–251.

Cloninger, C. R. (1987). Neurogenetic adaptive mechanisms in alcoholism. *Science, 236*, 410–416.

MacAndrew, C. (1980). Male alcoholics, secondary psychopathy, and Eysenck's theory of personality. *Personality and Individual Differences, 1*, 151–160.

Schuckit, M. A. (1994). Low level of response to alcohol as a predictor of future alcoholism. *American Journal of Psychiatry, 151*, 184–189.

Substance Abuse and Mental Health Services Administration (2006). *Results from the 2005 national household survey on drug abuse: National findings* (Office of Applied Studies, USDUH Series H-30, DHHS Publication No. SMA 06-4194). Rockville, MD.

Ungerleider, S. (2001). *Faust's gold: Inside the East German doping machine.* New York: Thomas Dunne.

Voy, R. (1991). *Drugs, sport, and politics.* Champaign, IL: Human Kinetics.

Burnout 16

Dick Vermeil became the head coach of the Philadelphia Eagles National Football League (NFL) team in 1976 at age 39. His philosophy was emblazoned on a sign in the Eagles' locker room: "The best way to kill time is to work it to death" (Coates, 1997, p. 3C). He became known as the "poster boy of coaching burnout" (Coates, 1997, p. 3C), as he worked from early morning to past midnight and often slept on a cot in his office. He considered an average workweek for NFL coaches to be 96 hours, and he tried to squeeze as much work as possible in each 24 hours. He kept a notebook by his bed to record the thoughts that woke him during the night, and interviewed his first assistant coaches during his spare hours between midnight and 3:00 a.m. Vermeil took the Eagles to the Super Bowl in 1981, losing to the Oakland Raiders 27 to 10.

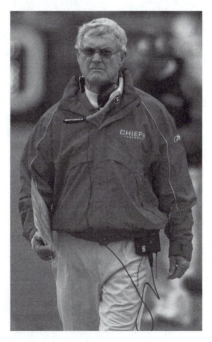

After the 1982 season and at age 46, Vermeil resigned and admitted that he was burnt out. He recognized that he continued to add hours to his workweek in order to be the best in his profession until he finally ran out of hours. He pushed himself and his team to be the best until "I finally ran out of things to push with. I couldn't relax. I couldn't turn it off" (Coates, 1997, p. 3C).

Vermeil sought psychotherapy for burnout, and spent several years dealing with issues such as anger and perfectionism. The influence of his relationship with his father remained with him in his

Coach Dick Vermeil acknowledged burnout (photo © Mike Simons/Corbis).

adult life. His father was a perfectionist, and although Vermeil acknow-ledged his love for his father, he stated that this relationship left him with emotional scars. Vermeil said that his father invented the phrase "verbal abuse." and that "I was 16 before I realized my real first name wasn't Dumb Bastard" (King, 2000). This therapy was successful and he reasoned, "There's such a stigma in this country about seeking help like that, but I can tell you it's one of the best things I've ever done. It really helped me in this job" (King, 2000).

After 14 years and at age 60, Vermeil returned to the NFL as the head coach of the St Louis Rams in 1997. The Rams won the Super Bowl in 2000.

Burnout is a syndrome of mental, physical, and emotional fatigue and even exhaustion. It is characterized by psychological, emotional, and sometimes physical withdrawal from activities, such as sports, that were previously enjoyable. Accompanying burnout may be chronic fatigue, sleep disturbances, susceptibility to illness, and even depression. The term was originally applied to the emotional depletion of volunteers in an alternative health agency in the USA in the mid-1970s (Freudenberger, 1974, 1975). More generally, it has referred to the emotional depletion that occurs in the practice of human service and helping professions. These volunteers gradually lost their motivation and commitment and became more cynical and less idealistic and productive (Farber, 1983). Burnout has been seen as a response to prolonged work stress that overwhelms the coping resources of employees (Maslach & Schaufeli, 1993).

Although initially coined to describe employees, the concept of burn-out has achieved wide recognition in the world of sport (Goodger, Lavallee, Gorely, & Harwood, 2006). Highly motivated athletes have sometimes been described as "burning" with competitive desire, and burnout occurs when these flames are extinguished. It has commonly been seen to be the result of too much work for too long a time with too little rest. It is a malady of those with high levels of achievement motivation, conscientiousness, and idealism, especially if their hard work is devoted to pursuits that are unrewarding. With burnout, people lose their energy and purpose, and perceive that they are accomplishing little. It becomes more difficult to sustain lofty goals and single-minded devotion to these goals. Athletes may develop a reduced sense of accomplishment and lowered athletic efficacy as a result of burnout (Cresswell & Eklund, 2006c; Henschen, 1998).

With burnout, athletes often develop negative attitudes toward their sport and question whether it is still "worth it" to engage in sport (Smith, 1986). There is often a reduced sense of accomplishment, as for example athletes report that they are making little progress and that their efforts are a waste of time (Raedeke & Smith, 2001). The rewards or benefits of sport and other activities seem to be outweighed by the costs or unpleasant aspects. There are intrinsic rewards, such as the sheer enjoyment of sport and competition, the experience of gaining mastery or improving, and self-approval or feeling good about one's progress. Extrinsic rewards include trophies, money, privileges, and the admiration of others. Intrinsic costs include the time, effort, and pain necessary to reach high levels of fitness and skill, and self-derogation and disappointment after poor per- formances. Extrinsic costs include the disapproval of others after failure, and sometimes enduring unpleasant coaches, parents, teammates, and spectators. In general, burnout is less associated with intrinsic motivation and more associated with amotivation (Cresswell & Eklund, 2005a, 2005b; Lemyre, Treasure, & Roberts, 2006).

A sportsperson might pursue athletics even if the costs outweighed the benefits if they decided that they had nothing better to do. However, if they identified competing activities that were more rewarding, such as goofing off, they might drop the athletics in pursuit of the activities that seem to offer more at less cost. It is also possible that a sportsperson will have a difficult time making up their mind about what to do at a particular time because two activities are relatively equal in terms of costs and benefits. Using the same example, a sportsperson might realize that the eventual benefits of proper training are far greater than the benefits of goofing off, but the immediate costs of goofing off are minimal and it is fun. Children often drop out of sports because they find competing activities to be more rewarding.

Measuring Burnout

Burnout has been reliably measured in workplace and sport settings. The Maslach Burnout Inventory (MBI; Maslach & Jackson, 1981, 1986) became the most widely utilized measure of burnout in workplaces. It has also been used to measure burnout among athletic personnel (e.g. Hendrix, Acevedo, & Hebert, 2000; Kelley, Eklund, & Ritter-Taylor, 1999; Martin, Kelley, & Eklund, 1999). A modified version has been validated with athletes (Cresswell & Eklund, 2006b). The **Athlete Burnout Questionnaire** (**ABQ**; Raedeke, 1997; Raedeke & Smith, 2001) was developed specifically for use in sport settings. It measures three dimensions of burnout among sportspersons: (1) emotional and physical exhaustion, (2) reduced sense of accomplishment, (3) sport devaluation.

Stress and Burnout

How is it that the flames of competitive desire burn brightly for years in some sportspersons, whereas others burn out? Clearly, burnout is not simply the result of a great deal of intense practice and competition. For example, elite junior tennis players may believe that 35 hours per week of practice is not enough (Gould, Tuffey, Udry, & Loehr, 1996a). One important part of this answer is the individual's response to the **stress** of competition and training. The reader is reminded of the definition provided by Lazarus and Folkman (1984, p. 19) and first mentioned in Chapter 3: "Psychological stress is a particular relationship between the person and the environment that is appraised by the person as taxing or exceeding his or her resources and endangering his or her well-being." Psychological stress is therefore determined not only by the demands and challenges of particular situations and conditions, but also by the athlete's determination of whether their skill and will are equal to the challenge.

Forms of external challenges or stressors in athletic settings include severe practice conditions, inadequate social support, poor coaching, strength of opponents, and, as discussed in Chapter 10, pressure in competition. An athlete's determination of their internal resources is influenced by factors such as self-efficacy and helplessness, expectations about choking under pressure and anxiety, perfectionism, procrastination, and self-handicapping (Smith, 1986). When perceived internal resources balance environmental challenge, athletes do not feel stressed and drained by pressure and are unlikely to experience burnout.

The importance of **self-efficacy** in influencing performance has been emphasized throughout this book, and it is a vital determinant of burnout. Athletes with burnout often lack self-efficacy or conviction that they will work their way through external challenges and reach their goals. A devotion to unrealized or unrealistic goals is also associated with burnout. **Unrealistic goals** are often overly **narrow, intense**, and established at a very early age. With a narrow focus, an athlete judges himself or herself exclusively or largely on the basis of his or her success in competition, and this focus is overly intense if athletes devalue themselves when performance is flawed. Not surprisingly, athletes with **perfectionistic goals** are more likely to experience burnout. Goals of perfection in all areas of functioning are unachievable, and unattained goals lead to burnout. Athletes who are especially sensitive to the reactions of others, who find criticism especially painful, and who are overly concerned with pleasing others, are also more vulnerable to burnout.

Burnout and Persistent or Chronic Stress

Burnout does not occur overnight. If the imbalance between environmental challenge and internal resources persists, burnout is likely to ensue. With burnout there is a downward cycle of demoralization, diminished performance, withdrawal from practice and preparation, and, at worse, helplessness. This cycle is perpetuated by increased anxiety, depression, and sleeplessness, and withdrawal from and alienation of sources of social support.

Coping with Stressors

There are different ways of coping with situations that are seen as taxing or exceeding the resources of the person. Coping consists of what a person thinks or does in response to stressors. These thoughts and actions may change as situations unfold, and they may be relatively specific to stressors in specific environments. As explained in Chapter 3, there are two general categories of coping responses. **Problem-focused coping** involves efforts to manage, change, or master the problem or challenge that is the stressor. There are many examples of problem-focused coping, and those most relevant to the focus of this book include: goal setting; following regimens to prepare for evaluations and allowing adequate time for preparations; time management; problem solving and decision-making; information gathering; and advice seeking. **Emotion-focused coping** concerns attempts to regulate emotional responses to the source of stress. Relevant examples of emotion-focused coping include the interpretation of the stressor as a challenge rather than a threat, engaging in relaxation, meditation, and physical exercises, and obtaining emotional support from others. In many stressful situations both problem- and emotion-focused coping are utilized. People differ in the degree to which they use the two forms of coping. In general, responses to problems or challenges that can be successfully resolved or mastered are more adaptive if they involve a greater proportion of problem-focused coping. Problem-focused coping strategies have been seen as adaptive because they involve confronting the source of the stress (Zeidner, 1994). Sources of stress for which there is no solution are responded to more successfully with greater proportions of emotion-focused coping. It is clearly important to size up a situation correctly as changeable or uncontrollable, and to have effective problem- and emotion-focused coping skills.

Measurement of Sport Stress

The **Recovery–Stress Questionnaire for Athletes** (RESTQ-Sport; Kellmann & Kallus, 2001) was developed to measure current sources of stress in the lives of athletes and current activities that promote the reestablishment of psychological and physical resources. The athlete rates sources of general life stress, sport-specific stress, and recovery activities that have occurred during the past three days. The recovery process occurs over time and involves an alleviation of stress. Recovery entails psychophysical regeneration or a systematic, planned, and intentional process for creating the best possible conditions for recovery and preparation for upcoming stressors such as competitions (Kellmann & Kallus, 2001).

Recovery is not a passive process as athletes take action, such as attending to needs for sleep, hydration, nutrition, and reinforcing relationships with others, to speed it along. In the time between two competitions, three phases have been proposed to facilitate optimal recovery. During the *evaluation* phase, sportspersons evaluate results from the first competition or match. In the *transition* phase athletes tailor restful activities to regenerate physical and psychological energy. The *final* phase is the preparation phase for the next competition, and this involves mental and physical preparation.

The scales of the RESTQ-Sport are listed in Table 16.1. Sources of stress

---

TABLE 16.1 Scales of the Recovery–Stress Questionnaire for Athletes

1 General stress: mental stress, imbalance, depression, listlessness
2 Emotional stress: frequent irritation, anxiety, inhibition
3 Social stress: interpersonal conflicts and annoyances
4 Conflicts/pressure: unresolved conflicts, goals not achieved
5 Fatigue: time pressure at work, training, school, overfatigue, lack of sleep
6 Lack of energy: ineffective work due to inability to concentrate, lack of energy, inefficient decision-making
7 Physical complaints: bodily complaints
8 Success: success, pleasure, and creativity at pursuits
9 Social recovery: pleasurable social contacts
10 Physical recovery: restoration of physical vigor
11 General wellbeing: good moods and contentment
12 Sleep quality: absence of sleep disorders and sleeping through the night
13 Disturbed breaks: interruptions during recovery periods
14 Burnout/emotional exhaustion: athletic burnout
15 Fitness/injury: vulnerability to injuries
16 Fitness/being in shape: fitness, efficiency, vigor
17 Burnout/personal accomplishment: function in team context and enjoyment of sport
18 Self-efficacy: optimal preparation and resources sufficient for challenges
19 Self-regulation: mental resources to meet goals

From Kellmann, M., & Kallus, K. W. (2001). *Recovery–stress questionnaire for athletes: User manual.* Champaign, IL: Human Kinetics.

that are specific to sport settings are described in seven scales and more general sources of stress are detailed in the remaining 12. This empirically derived instrument provides sportspersons with an estimate of stress and burnout, recovery and wellbeing, and preparation for performance and competition.

Burnout and Dropout

The terms "burnout" and "**dropout**" are not synonymous. Athletes may continue with a sport even when burnt out if they do not believe that there are better alternative activities available to them and if they have invested a great deal of time and effort in attaining proficiency in their sport (Butcher, Lindner, & Johns, 2002; Schmidt & Stein, 1991). Other athletes may feel "entrapped" in that they do not believe quitting is an option and they feel obligated to participate, perhaps due to pressure from parents and coaches. These athletes may not *want* to continue in sport but believe they *have* to. For example, female and male adolescent competitive swimmers who felt entrapped or obligated to train and compete were relatively burnt out but swam on (Raedeke, 1997). Some of these teenagers were very negative on competitive swimming, as they experienced minimal rewards and high costs. Other burnt-out teenagers did not find swimming to be equally aversive, but did not rate it as particularly rewarding. They were emotionally and physically exhausted, but continued out of a sense of obligation. Both groups of burnt-out swimmers "went through the motions" of training and competing and endured burnout because their sense of obligation prohibited quitting. Swimmers who did not rate themselves as obligated to swim were free either to participate for the rewards of training and competition or to quit if they did not find swimming sufficiently enjoyable or if alternative activities were preferred.

With a large investment of time and effort, athletes are more likely to stick with sports that have temporarily become unrewarding. People often expect return on investments, and sportspersons who have invested a great deal of time and energy in training may expect to reap intrinsic and extrinsic rewards in the future.

Social Ties

Social support is often seen as a way of blunting the effects of stress and preventing burnout. This view assumes that the comments and reactions of others are uniformly positive. Of course this is not the case, as the reactions of others can do more harm than good, and serve to increase one's sense of isolation. Elite male and female junior or late adolescent tennis players who identified themselves with burnout recognized that the influence of their parents and coaches was sometimes negative (Udry, Gould, Bridges, & Tuffey, 1997b). These tennis players said that parents and coaches actually created a high-stress environment by emphasizing ego or performance goals such as winning and comparing their perform- ance to other junior players. The tennis juniors responded negatively to excessive coercion by their parents to practice and compete in tourna- ments. Parental criticism that ascribed internal, global, and stable negative attributes, such as being a weakling, was demoralizing to the young tennis players. Some players complained that coaches were not sensitive to their performance anxiety and lack of self-efficacy. These players thought that their coaches expected them to be uniformly confident in matches.

It is probably helpful for parents to recognize when to push their children and when to back off, as the juniors found "**pushing in a good way**" (Udry et al., 1997b, p. 376) to be helpful and supportive. This supportive pushing involved providing the resources necessary for elite participation and avoiding excessive pressure for winning performance. The juniors also felt supported by the empathetic responses of coaches and when coaches expressed confidence in them.

The parents of Olympic champions exerted little pressure to win (Gould, Dieffenbach, & Moffett, 2002). They emphasized discipline and hard work and probably "pushed in a good way" in that they would at times challenge their children while remaining supportive and empathic. These parents also provided the resources necessary for athletic participation.

It is reasonable to assume that the parents and coaches of the juniors with burnout were well intentioned in encouraging and even pushing them to perform at a high level. These efforts did not, however, have their desired effect, as the juniors described the influence of coaches and parents as more negative than positive. Coaches and parents may not have understood that interventions such as comparing players to others were harmful. However, insensitivity to the causes of burnout may not be the rule among coaches. Male coaches of late adolescent swimmers with an average of 19 years of coaching experience demonstrated an accurate understanding of the causes of, and potential ways of avoiding, burnout (Raedeke, Lunney, & Venables, 2002).

The Influence of Coaches

As mentioned above, the **behavior of coaches influences burnout** in athletes. Burnout was more likely among female intercollegiate basketball and softball players when their coaches lacked empathy and were auto-cratic, critical, and preoccupied with winning (Vealey, Armstrong, Comar, & Greenleaf, 1998).

Male and female coaches (of female high school soccer players) who demonstrated the emotional exhaustion feature of burnout were less active in coaching (Price & Weiss, 2000). Their players said that they provided less instruction and training and less social support. These emotionally exhausted coaches may have relinquished tight and effective control of their teams. Consistent with the findings with college basketball and softball players (Vealey et al., 1998), athletes reported more burnout and anxiety about competition and less enjoyment and belief in their abilities when their coaches were burnt out and made decisions autocratically or with little input from players, and when coaches gave minimal training, positive feedback, and social support.

Burnout is not uncommon among coaches. Estimates of burnout include 43 to 63 percent of high school and college coaches admitting to burnout (Vealey, Udry, Zimmerman, & Soliday, 1992). Over half of a group of college tennis coaches also acknowledged aspects of burnout including emotional exhaustion, depersonalization, and a reduced sense of personal accomplishment (Kelley, Eklund, & Ritter-Taylor, 1999). The coping resources of coaches with burnout are not equal to the external demands of coaching such as the pressure to win, and to interact successfully with administrators, parents, the media, and the members of the team. Coaches with burnout reported less autonomy and control in their coaching roles and fewer meaningful accomplishments as coaches. Coaches without social support were more vulnerable to burnout.

Coaches who experienced a sense of commitment to their teams and families and who viewed the tasks of coaching as challenges rather than stressors were less likely to report burnout (Kelley et al., 1999). Some coaches were also undaunted by recruiting and time pressures and were less likely to report burnout.

There are various types of commitment to coaching. For example, among swim coaches, there are those who coached primarily because of their attraction to the actual tasks of coaching such as teaching sport skills, developing programs, and developing the sportspersonship and character of athletes. Others were less attracted to these aspects of coaching but felt relatively entrapped or obliged to continue in their roles as coaches (Raedeke, Granzyk, & Warren, 2000). These coaches reported decreasing satisfaction with coaching and increasing exhaustion over the course of one year. These coaches may have been overly stressed as the time and energy demands of coaching may have exceeded perceived resources. A third group was less interested in coaching. The relative disinterest of this group increased over the course of a year, and perhaps they became less committed to coaching and more drawn to competing activities (Raedeke, 2004).

Sociology and Burnout

In this discussion of stress and burnout, the balance between environmental stressors and pressure and internal coping resources was considered. So long as internal coping resources were seen as sufficient to handle the environmental stressors, burnout was not likely. The **sociological approach** of Jay Coakley to burnout takes issue with the emphasis on individual coping resources. From this vantage point, burnout is not due to individual coping limitations, but instead to the organization of athletic institutions. These institutions were seen as "disempowering" athletes from meaningful control over areas of their lives (Coakley, 1992). Sport institutions were criticized as emphasizing competition at the expense of providing opportunities for the overall social development of young sportspersons. This emphasis on competition encouraged athletes to develop identities that are relatively dependent on successful athletic performance rather than on competence in a wider range of roles.

Coakley also hypothesized that families tightly and excessively controlled the lives of burnt-out young athletes. He conjectured that families that were capable of providing more time and money to support the athletic careers of their children were more likely to encourage a unilateral focus on athletic performance, and that children in these families were prone to participate in sport out of a sense of obligation.

Staleness

As mentioned above, burnout does not occur overnight. It is the result of the cumulative effects of emotional and physical exhaustion. **Staleness** is a related concept, but refers to the acute rather than long-term effects of physical and emotional fatigue and exhaustion. The psychological aspects of staleness are the same for both genders. Staleness results in impaired sport performance and an inability to train at customary levels. It is not uncommon, with about 10 percent of college athletes experiencing it every year and more than 50 percent of elite distance runners reporting it at some point in their careers (Raglin & Wilson, 2000). Staleness is often accompanied by physical complaints such as body aches, headaches, and stomach aches. It has been seen as an early warning sign of burnout: If the signs of staleness are not heeded, burnout will likely follow.

Jennifer Capriati and Burnout

Jennifer Capriati's fall from tennis eminence was described in Chapter 15. It has been attributed to a variety of sources, but a prominent cause was burnout. The expectations and pressure foisted on her by the media, sponsors, and tournament promoters were excessive. The pressure of being the "most hyped tennis player of all time" (Starr & Reiss, 1994) probably contributed to her sense of failure when her career stalled. She did not make the predicted meteoric ascent to the top of professional women's tennis, and discovered that becoming "number one" was more difficult than anticipated. Perhaps this was due to the fact that young Grand Slam winners such as Steffi Graf and Monica Seles were not easily pushed aside by 16-year-old prodigies. At age 15, Capriati reached the semifinals of two Grand Slam events, but she won only one title as a 16-year-old, and described 1992 as a waste. She was plagued by tendonitis and bone chips in her elbow and suffered a first round loss as a 17-year-old in the 1993 US Open. Prior to the Australian Open in January 1992, Capriati complained openly and often about "a lot of pressure from everyone" (Harwitt, 1992).

At age 18, Capriati confirmed that this pressure led to burnout (Finn, 1994). Signs of mental and physical exhaustion were evident prior to her 16th birthday in 1992. She was pushed to compete in so many tournaments that tennis was no longer fun (Jenkins, 1992). She had so little fun playing tennis in 1992 that she simply went through the motions, perhaps because her career was so important to others such as her parents, sponsors, and tennis fans. She was also the primary breadwinner in her family.

Capriati returned to tennis eminence and in 2001 won the Australian and French Opens. In 2002 she won the Australian Open for the second time. This return was possible when she rediscovered intrinsic motivation for playing, training, and competing.

Readers may also recall that the topic of staleness was introduced in Chapter 14 in the discussion of the "inverse iceberg" POMS (Profile of Mood States; McNair, Lorr, & Droppleman, 1971) profile. The inverse iceberg profile consists of low levels of vigor or energy and high levels of tension, depression, anger, fatigue, and confusion (Morgan, Brown, Raglin, O'Connor, & Ellickson, 1987), and this profile identifies staleness. The inverse iceberg profile may also present after an athlete is injured. A return to an iceberg profile may coincide with the physical recovery of injured athletes and tapering or reducing the training load of fatigued athletes. More complete rest is necessary if tapering does not alleviate staleness (Raglin & Wilson, 2000). Ironically, some athletes respond to staleness by training harder.

Staleness is often the result of **overtraining**, but overtraining is necessary to improve physical performance (Raglin & Wilson, 2000). Overtraining is a prescribed period of the most intense training during a training cycle; its goal is to provide maximal training stress without injury. Overtraining is a positive training stress when it leads to improved performance over time. Physiological adaptations to increasing training loads are necessary to improve performance with endurance and other sports. With the development of increasingly scientific training regimens, training loads are increasingly markedly. For example, Mark Spitz reportedly swam 9000 meters per day in preparation for his seven Olympic gold medals in the 1972 Olympics; the training load of some current Olympic swimmers exceeds 18,000 meters per day.

Overtraining is typically followed by brief tapering periods during which training volume, but perhaps not intensity, is decreased. As training intensity increases, additional recovery time is necessary, and overtraining and tapering periods can be balanced to optimize performance and improvements (Kellmann & Kallus, 2001).

Overtraining has not been balanced with tapering when there is excessive difficulty in recovering from fatigue and regaining vigor between workouts, and inability to return to former levels of performance (Hollander & Meyers, 1995). At times it may be difficult to distinguish appropriate levels of the fatigue that accompanies overtraining from staleness. However, careful record keeping provides unambiguous evidence of inability to reach prior performance levels and the necessity of adjustments in training schedules. There is no single biological marker that reliably identifies staleness, but increases in heart rate during rest, exercise, and recovery, and decreases in testosterone and increases in cortisol, a marker of stress, suggest that overtraining has not been balanced with rest (McKenzie, 1999). Overtraining for endurance sports results in an increased susceptibility to upper respiratory tract infections and in less production of a hormone, IgA, that provides resistance to such infections.

Long and indeed continuous athletic seasons are a contributor to staleness. This source of staleness is difficult to reverse, as in many US universities athletes are expected to practice and train formally and "informally" for about 12 months of the year (Henschen, 1998).

Boring practices and training regimens also lead to staleness. Practice that consists of simply "going through the motions" is more likely to lead to staleness, and the antidote to meaningless practice may be to develop specific long- and short-term goals for practice. As explained in Chapter 7, goals that are just beyond one's reach are most motivating, and a sense of purpose is established by organizing proximal goals within a hierarchy.

Proximal goals allow for a steady stream of feedback about whether current behaviors are successful in reaching short-term standards. The adequacy of current training and technique mastery can be estimated by determining whether short-term goals are accomplished, and strategies can be altered in time to achieve distal goals.

Burnout is also less likely when coaches allow athletes some measure of control over practice and training regimens, schedule mental practice sessions, and attend to post-competition tension in their team (Dale & Weinberg, 1989). Post-competition tension is likely to consist of dejection, elation, or aggression that is directed toward oneself or others. Coaches attend to these emotional responses, place the performance in a realistic

Sources of Burnout (Gould et al., 1996a; Henschen, 1998; Kellman & Kallus, 2001; Raedeke & Smith, 2001; Raglin & Wilson, 2000; Smith, 1986; Udry et al., 1997b)

1 Imbalances between internal coping resources and environmental challenges
2 Fatigue, staleness, sleeplessness, anxiety, and depression
3 Alienation from sources of social support
4 Participation in sport because of perceived social pressure rather than because you *want to*
5 Parents and coaches emphasize performance goals such as winning
6 Coercive and authoritarian coaching and parenting styles
7 Training for 12 months of the year
8 Boring practices
9 See the Recovery–Stress Questionnaire for Athletes

Recommendations for Avoiding Burnout

1 Systematically manage overtraining and tapering (reducing training load, rest)
2 Set realistic (not perfectionistic) goals for training, practice, and competition
3 Set short- and long-term goals for training, practice, and competition
4 Develop intrinsic interest in sport
5 Make training, practice, and competition fun
6 Do not isolate athletes from friends and sources of social support
7 Avoid parental overinvolvement
8 More democratic and less dictatorial coaching and parenting styles
9 See the Recovery–Stress Questionnaire for Athletes
10 Overtraining

perspective, and help athletes to move on with preparation for future competitions.

Overtraining

Definitions of staleness and overtraining are not consistent. As mentioned above, overtraining is recognized as a contributor to and precursor of staleness. Alternatively, staleness has been defined as the psychological component of physical overtraining (Hollander & Meyers, 1995). A third alternative considers staleness, overtraining, and burnout to all represent forms of negative responses to training stress (Silva, 1990). In this formulation, overtraining is distinguished from training overload, and the term "overtraining" is reserved for maladaptive responses to proscribed training overload. The definition of training overload in this formulation is similar to that given earlier for overtraining. It is a period of progressively increased training loads during which the volume and intensity of training are maximized in an effort to produce physical improvements. Staleness is then defined as the initial failure to respond adaptively to progressive training loads (Silva, 1990). In this context, staleness is considered an expectable response as mental and physical adjustments are made to increasing training stress. During this "lag period," sportspersons experience **training plateaus** and show no improvements, or perhaps some slippage in performance.

With this definition, approximately 73 percent of male and female collegiate athletes experience staleness during athletic seasons, and many notice it at the midpoint and end of their seasons (Silva, 1990). Athletes either "train through" this plateau and prepare for new and additional cycles of training, or make adjustments to training schedules, such as tapering, to provide for rejuvenation and a return to physiological homeostasis. The

Staleness, a state of emotional and physical exhaustion (photo © Junial Enterprises).

athlete that accomplishes neither in response to staleness is at risk for the overtraining response. This response consists of physical and mental exhaustion, and this fatigue is entrenched and longstanding. It is not uncommon among female and male collegiate athletes, with about 66 pecent experiencing the overtraining response during athletic seasons. The athlete unable to train through or taper and recover from overtraining is more likely to progress to burnout. Intercollegiate athletes identified burnout as the most unfavorable response to training stress. The most common response to burnout was the wish to quit playing their sport. Recovery from burnout was seen as less likely and to predispose athletes to drop out of their sport or to fail to realize prior levels of performance.

Summary and Conclusions

The concept of burnout is well established in sport. It describes the mental, physical, and emotional fatigue that results from the experience of excessive stress and pressure. The experience of psychological stress is only partially determined by situational or environmental demands for training and practice and pressure for skilled performance. These situational stressors are balanced by the coping strategies and resources of individual athletes. Athletes who confront situational pressure with well-established and highly functional coping strategies are likely to be undaunted, and may interpret pressure as a source of excitement and heavy training loads as means of advancement. Emotion- and problem-focused coping strategies are useful for mastering stressors, and problem-focused strategies are especially useful if it is necessary to take action to master environmental demands and pressure. Coping strategies concern not simply what individuals do to address sources of stress, but also the solicitation of information and help from others.

Burnout does not occur overnight, but is the result of a persistent imbalance between internal coping resources and the stressors of training and competition. Athletes with certain characteristics are more or less likely to successfully cope with the pressure of competition and training loads of practice. With high self-efficacy for athletic competence, sportspersons persist in training and competition and remain confident that goals will be obtained. Lacking this confidence, athletes may question whether the time, effort, discomfort, and inconvenience of training, practice, and competition are "worth it." Athletic participation is more likely to be worth it if intrinsic rewards, such as having fun and self-improvement, and extrinsic rewards, such as approval and occasional "pats on the back" from important others, are realized. Coercion for athletic participation from parents and coaches and the establishment of ego or performance and perfectionistic goals diminish intrinsic rewards and increase the likelihood of burnout.

Levels of self-efficacy and goals notwithstanding, burnt-out athletes often question whether the sacrifices and costs of athletic participation are worth the intrinsic and extrinsic rewards. When the costs predominate, athletes may wish to drop out. However, burnout does not always result in dropping out of athletic participation, especially when athletes feel an obligation to others, such as parents and coaches, to continue. Athletes may also continue in their sport when burnt out if there are no preferable alternative activities and if they have already invested a great deal in gaining proficiency.

Sociological theories of burnout de-emphasize individual coping strategies and focus on the stress placed on athletes by athletic institutions. These institutions have been seen as fostering the development of identities that are overly narrow and determined primarily by continuing athletic participation. Institutions have been criticized as disempowering burnt-out athletes and limiting the overall social development of sportspersons.

In responding to these criticisms of athletic institutions, the question arises of whether the correction of these problems will require a radical reworking of athletic institutions – hardly a likely outcome – or whether parents and coaches should be encouraged to limit or stop interventions that are not helpful. For example, burnt-out junior tennis players complained when coaches and parents pressured them to win and compared their performance to that of other juniors. Derogatory comments about mental toughness and talent of juniors had a detrimental effect. Juniors complained if tennis dominated their lives to the degree that socialization with peers was prevented, and multifaceted identities may be developed if competent peer and academic functioning is emphasized.

The topics of staleness, overtraining, and training overload were also addressed in this chapter. There is a lack of agreement on the precise definition of these terms, but definitions that are best integrated with the larger topic of burnout were emphasized. In this context, staleness refers to the acute effects of physical and emotional fatigue and exhaustion. Staleness is often the result of overtraining, or cycles of intense training intended to advance the physical status of athletes. Staleness is distinguished, however, from normal levels of fatigue that result from overtraining. One reliable measure of staleness is diminished performance, and accurate record keeping provides unambiguous evidence of impaired performance.

Staleness is a harbinger of burnout, and efforts to identify and reverse staleness are therefore useful. The most direct way of reducing staleness is to determine whether overtraining is balanced with periods in which training is tapered. Tapering may involve reducing the volume or intensity, or both, of training exercise. Establishing proximal goals for practice and integrating proximal goals in hierarchies also help to make training meaningful, interesting, and challenging, and counteract staleness. Practice is also less likely to be meaningless if athletes adhere to the techniques presented in Chapters 3, 4, 5, and 6, and understand practice as a time not only for physical training but also for mental preparation for competition.

Key Terms

Burnout

Athlete Burnout Questionnaire (ABQ)

Stress

Self-efficacy

Unrealistic goals: narrow, intense, perfectionistic

Burnout and chronic stress

Problem-focused and emotion-focused coping

Recovery–Stress Questionnaire for Athletes

Burnout and dropout

Social support and "pushing in a good way"

Coaches and burnout

Sociology and burnout

Staleness

Overtraining

Training plateaus

Suggested Readings

Cresswell, S. L., & Eklund, R. C. (2006a). Athlete burnout: Conceptual confusion, current research and future research directions. In S. Hanton & S. D. Mellalieu (Eds.), *Literature reviews in sport psychology* (pp. 91–126). New York: Nova Science Publishers.

Freudenberger, H. J. (1974). Staff burnout. *Journal of Social Issues*, 30, 159–165.

Henschen, K. P. (1998). Athletic staleness and burnout: Diagnosis, prevention, and treatment. In J. M. Williams (Ed.), *Applied sport psychology: Personal growth to peak performance* (3rd ed., pp. 398–408). Mountain View, CA: Mayfield.

Kellmann, M., & Kallus, K. W. (2001). *Recovery–stress questionnaire for athletes: User manual.* Champaign, IL: Human Kinetics.

Raedeke, T. D., & Smith, A. L. (2001). Development and preliminary validation of an athlete burnout measure. *Journal of Sport & Exercise Psychology*, 23, 281–306.

Raglin, J. S., & Wilson, G. S. (2000). Overtraining in athletes. In Y. L. Hanin (Ed.), *Emotions in sport* (pp. 191–207). Champaign, IL: Human Kinetics.

Smith, R. E. (1986). Toward a cognitive-affective model of athletic burnout. *Journal of Sport Psychology*, 8, 36–50.

Sport Injuries

About half of the players in the National Football League (NFL) retire because of injuries (Nack, 2001). Disabilities due to athletic injuries are common among players who did not retire due to injuries. Injuries to major weight-bearing joints are common due to the size and power of modern players and to the violent nature of the game. Degenerative arthritis is five to seven times more likely after these injuries to joints. Spinal arthritis is also common as lesions caused by collisions heal with scar tissue. These collisions sometimes cause concussions, and postconcussion syndrome can result from repeated concussions. Postconcussion syndrome consists of headaches, forgetfulness, and blurred vision.

Johnny Unitas was selected as the greatest quarterback in the first 50 years of the NFL (Greenberg, 2001b). He threw a touchdown pass in 47 consecutive games and was known as the Golden Arm. Due to an athletic injury, he could no longer rotate his thumb and grasp objects, or use his right hand to comb his hair or brush his teeth. With two knee replacements, he played golf by strapping his right hand to a golf club with a Velcro strip. Unitas died of a heart attack in 2002 at age 69.

Most NFL players understand the risk of injury but focus on the current rewards of playing professional football rather than future pain and disability. Dr Anthony Tucker, the team physician for the Baltimore Ravens, provides players with lists of their injuries and the long-term consequences of continuing to participate in the NFL. He finds few quitting due to the future consequences of injuries.

Athletic injuries are not uncommon. There are about 17 million sport injuries per year in the USA. Athletic participation accounts for 44 percent of the injuries that occur to students 14 years of age and older (Boyce & Sobolewski, 1989). As many as 750,000 or 30 percent of the athletes who play for US high school and college teams are injured in a given year. Over three million injuries that require emergency room treatment occur yearly during recreational activities such as sport, horseback riding, and

Athletic injuries (photo courtesy of Western Connecticut State University).

skateboarding (Bergandi, 1985; Meeuwisse & Fowler, 1988; National Collegiate Athletic Association, 1992; National Safety Council, 1993; Requa, 1991). Hundreds of millions of dollars are allocated for the treatment of these injuries.

Predicting Athletic Injuries

Injuries do not occur randomly. The likelihood of injuries increases when training and practice, biomechanics, coaching, equipment, playing and practice venues, and luck are less than optimal. Psychological and social factors also increase the chances of athletic injuries, and the relationship between these variables is probably best explained in the following model.

The **stress and injury model** (Figure 17.1) is consistent with the cognitive-relational theory (Lazarus & Folkman, 1984) of stress that has been described throughout the chapters of this book. Athletic competitions and practice that are demanding and that involve pressure are environmental stressors that affect sportspersons differently depending on their personalities, history of stressors, and coping resources. Athletic stressors will produce more intense stress responses in the forms of threatening cognitive appraisals, physiological anxiety, and attentional disruptions if *personality* factors augment the effects of the stressors, if there is a *history of* exposure to *stressors*, and if there are few *coping resources*. Without intervention, the highly stressed athlete is at greater risk for injury (Williams,

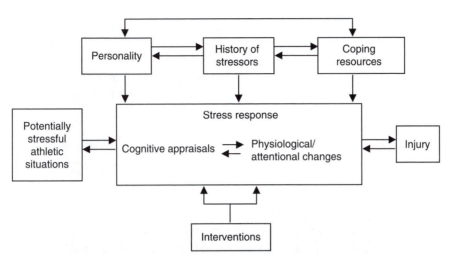

FIGURE 17.1. Stress and injury model. From Williams, J. M. (2001). Psychology of injury risk and prevention. In R. N. Singer, H. A. Hausenblas, & C. M. Janelle (Eds.), *Handbook of sport psychology* (2nd ed., pp. 766–786). New York: Wiley.

2001). In general when internal and external resources are seen to be insufficient to meet challenges presented by environmental pressure, stress responses increase and vulnerability to injury increases.

Depending on a sportsperson's *cognitive appraisal*, environmental stressors may be seen as a source of excitement and attraction or as a source of danger to be avoided. When stressors are seen to be sources of danger, cognitive appraisals can serve as cognitive interference and disrupt *attention*, and also increase *physiological anxiety* (Kerr & Goss, 1996). These responses can accompany unwanted simultaneous contraction of agonist and antagonist muscle groups, a response referred to as **bracing**. This bracing leads to fatigue, reduced flexibility, and decreased motor coordination and fluidity of motion, and consequently to increased risk of injury.

When athletes take the field with cognitive interference and physiological anxiety, they have fewer attentional resources available to focus on sources of danger from opponents and to anticipate action and avoid sources of injury. Not concentrating fully, athletes are less able to make split-second decisions and physical maneuvers to avoid musculoskeletal trauma. Peripheral narrowing may also occur so that athletes focus less attention on action in the periphery of their visual fields (Williams, Tonymon, & Andersen, 1991). Prior physical injuries also create risk factors for future injuries because they potentially represent physical vulnerability as well as a psychological vulnerability if the athlete fears reinjury (Petrie & Falkstein, 1998).

How is it that some athletes appraise environmental challenges as dangerous whereas others find them exciting? In the model under discussion, the answer is found by considering the athlete's personality characteristics, history of stressors, and coping resources. As mentioned throughout this book, personality characteristics refer to stable internal traits. One's history of stressors is determined by identifying major life events, daily hassles or problems, and previous injuries. Coping resources include skill in handling stress and interpersonal resources or help from others.

History of Stressors

Negative major life events are a category of *stressors* or stress that has a dramatic effect on athletic injuries in sports such as football, wrestling, gymnastics, and alpine skiing, with most studies showing that highly stressed athletes are two to five times as likely to incur injuries (Williams, 2001). Examples of negative major life events include poor performances in major competitions, problems maintaining academic eligibility, and conflicts with coaching staff. In fewer studies it was found that injuries were more likely among athletes with higher levels of total life stress, or both positive and negative major life events, and in fewer still injuries were associated with positive life stress. This relationship between stress and injuries holds across competitive levels and from youth to elite levels.

There has been less research about the relationship of daily hassles and prior injuries and future injuries. An example of a daily hassle is an inconvenience such as having to drive 1 hour for swim practice at 5:00 a.m. However, there is evidence that athletes who have more current hassles in their life (Fawkner, McMurray, & Summers, 1999) as well as prior injuries (Williams, Hogan, & Andersen, 1993) are more susceptible to injury.

Personality

Personality factors serve to augment or blunt the effects of stressors. For example, competitive trait anxiety or anxiety that occurs during most competitions is associated with higher injury rates. The combination of competitive trait anxiety and high life stress made starting collegiate football players particularly susceptible to injury (Petrie, 1993). The trait of sensation seeking was discussed in Chapter 14 and seen as similar to extraversion. Male and female high school varsity athletes low in sensation seeking were seen to be at risk for injuries when they also had high levels of negative life events (Smith, Ptacek, & Smoll, 1992). Intercollegiate athletes in football, volleyball, and cross-country who maintained positive states of mind were less likely to sustain injuries. These positive states served to keep athletes focused and concentrating and relaxed, and fostered social support (Williams et al., 1993). Positive mood states appear to buffer the stress of competition and training. Negative mood states such as anxiety and depression increase risks for injury. With negative mood states, athletes appear to have fewer resources available to cope with the stress of competition.

Self-handicapping and defensive pessimism have also been cited as personality factors related to injuries. Intercollegiate female field hockey players with low self-concepts were shown to be more likely to sustain injuries on the day before competitions. These injuries offered excuses for the avoidance of competition or at least for poor play (Lamb, 1986). With defensive pessimism and high life stress, athletes have been shown to be injury prone. Defensive pessimists also took few days' rest, especially under high stress conditions, and even when injured (Williams, 2001).

Coping Resources

Coping resources serve to blunt environmental stress. There are three forms of coping resources (not surprisingly, higher levels of these are associated with fewer injuries). **General coping behaviors** relate to sleep patterns, nutritional habits, and reserving time for recreation. **Psychological coping skills** include the techniques for controlling physiological anxiety and preparing for competitions that were presented in Chapters 3 through 8. Social support is a form of **interpersonal coping** and consists of well-intentioned actions from other people. Social support has been seen as a buffer to stress, and athletic injuries are less frequent when stress is reduced. For example, collegiate football players in the starting lineup who experienced high stress and negative life events were more likely to sustain an athletic injury only when they had little social support (Petrie, 1993). Similar results were found with adult male and female ballet dancers affiliated with a major ballet company in the western USA. Dancers with little social support were vulnerable to the effects of negative life events and especially negative daily hassles (Patterson & Smith, 1998). They were more frequently injured.

Moderate or high levels of either psychological coping skills or social support insulate athletes against the effects of athletic stressors. Varsity male and female high school athletes who were low in both psychological coping skills and social support were shown to be at greatest risk for injury when hit with negative life events (Smith, Smoll, & Ptacek, 1990a). Athletes who were unable to call on internal coping resources or help from other people apparently had no strategies to reduce arousal and physiological anxiety and to sustain attention and avoid harm during practice and competition. Despite the young age of these high school athletes, it appears that if they felt equal to athletic challenges, negative life events did not distract them or produce unremitting physiological anxiety sufficient to lead to injury.

Intervention to Reduce the Risk of Injury

Intervention prior to injury is recommended to lessen the risk of injury (Williams, 2001). This intervention is directed at faulty cognitive appraisals as well as excessive physiological anxiety. The techniques and interventions discussed in Chapters 3 through 8 are useful in helping athletes form realistic evaluations of athletic stressors and of their capacities to master the stressors. Perceived stress and pressure may also diminish if there is team cohesion and helpful communication between athletes and coaches. Physiological anxiety is reduced by the regular practice of the techniques described in Chapter 5, i.e. **psychological skills training**.

Stress inoculation training produced good results in preventing injuries with gymnasts who competed at national and international levels (Kerr & Goss, 1996). In a course of stress inoculation training that consisted of 16 one-hour training sessions, gymnasts learned techniques for mental practice, interrupting negative thoughts, and rational evaluation of the sources of stress and their capacities to master these sources. The benefits of stress inoculation training began to accrue at midseason or about 4 months after the start of practice, and persisted through the second 4 months of the gymnastic season. The gymnasts reported less total and less negative stress in their lives. The gymnasts who practiced stress inoculation training spent about half as many days injured, 5 versus 10, as the gymnasts who did not practice. Less injury time during the second half of the season was important for these gymnasts because national championships were held at the season's end. A form of stress inoculation training was also shown to be effective in reducing the prevalence of injuries and illnesses among male and female collegiate rowers (Perna, Antoni, Baum, Gordon, & Schneiderman, 2003).

Intercollegiate swimmers and football players had significantly fewer injuries during seasons in which they practiced **progressive muscle relaxation** (PMR) and mental practice and rehearsal (Davis, 1991). Similar results were reported for US alpine skiers who were trained in mental practice, attention control, communication skills, team building, and crisis intervention (May & Brown, 1989).

Highly competitive to elite female and male Swedish soccer players who received training to manage stress were less likely to be injured than their untreated counterparts. Those who received the stress management intervention recorded 0.22 injuries during the intervention period that lasted through the first half of their spring competitive season, whereas the untreated players had 1.31 injuries per person (Johnson, Ekengren, & Andersen, 2005). The reduction in injuries may have been the direct result of instruction in somatic and cognitive relaxation, stress management, goal setting, and attribution and self-confidence training. The athletes also kept a critical incident diary, and this may have heightened their awareness of stress and allowed them to better prepare for practice and competition and avoid unnecessary stress at work or school.

After the Occurrence of Injuries

Not only is stress a predictor of the occurrence of injuries, but injuries are also an ongoing source of stress. Stress has been seen as deriving from three potential sources: **major life events**, **chronic stress**, and **daily hassles**. Sport injuries are serious sources of stress because they meet all three criteria. Injuries threaten or postpone advancement in the athlete's area of primary interest and threaten potential careers and livelihoods. They linger for a period of time and are sources of ongoing pain. They are bothersome on a daily basis as athletes adjust their routine to cope with disabilities and limitations.

Serious, season-ending injuries are common among elite skiers. Male and female members of the US ski team identified stress caused by season-ending injuries (Udry, Gould, Bridges, & Beck, 1997a). The majority of the injuries were to the anterior cruciate ligaments (ACLs) of knees. Psychological worries and concerns were a source of stress for all of the injured skiers. They worried that they would never be the same, that they would lose their spot on the team, that teammates would surpass them, and that they would be re-injured. About two thirds felt socially isolated, and found the lack of attention by coaches and teammates to be a source of stress. Many found the

After the injury (photo © James Steidl).

physical limitations caused by the injury to be stressful, and some also worried about the adequacy of medical and rehabilitation care. Rehabilitation consists of the retraining or reconditioning of the musculoskeletal system to return to preinjury levels of physical fitness. The suspension of financial support and career opportunities during injury was an additional source of stress. Prior physical injuries appear to create risk factors for future injuries because they represent potential physical vulnerability as well as a psychological vulnerability if the athlete fears reinjury (Petrie & Falkstein, 1998).

Sport Injury and Grieving

Grief can be defined as an emotional response to a loss. It is often understood to occur in response to the loss of a loved one or someone to whom one has formed an emotional attachment. Injuries result in losses and sometimes grief. As athletes invest more effort, time, and aspects of their identity in their sport, the greater is the loss due to injury.

The losses from injuries include restricted athletic participation, career opportunities, status, playing time, and attention from coaches, teammates, and the media. Athletic injuries portend a loss of independence, mobility, vitality, and control. Additional losses occur with physical separation from teammates, coaches, and training routines, and loss of opportunities for athletic achievement during physical primes. If injuries are career ending, athletes may experience losses to vital aspects of their identity and to their purpose in life (Evans & Hardy, 1995). Grief responses are more likely when injuries are serious and irreversible (Johnston & Carroll, 1998).

Over the past 50 years there has been a considerable amount of theorizing about the process of resolving grief. Although not proven scientifically, it has been almost axiomatic that there are several stages of the grieving process. Kubler-Ross (1969) advanced the most widely recognized **stage theory** of grief. She recognized five stages in the grief process of dying patients: **denial**, **bargaining**, **anger**, **depression**, and **acceptance**. That is, when confronted with the likelihood of death, patients first responded with disbelief or an unwillingness to accept the news. As denial eroded, patients were seen to try to bargain or make deals about what they would offer in exchange for their life being spared. For example, dying patients might promise God to make amends if they survived. The bargaining phase was followed by anger about their fate, and depression when the loss of life appeared inevitable. With acceptance, patients acknowledged and accepted the inevitability of death.

Stage models have been developed to describe responses to athletic injuries. McDonald and Hardy (1990) advanced a two-stage process. The first stage involves an intense emotional experience of shock, panic, disorganization, and helplessness. In this stage the athlete is faced with accepting the reality of the injury. In the second stage, athletes mobilize their energy for the rehabilitation process. Heil (2000) described three components in a cyclical process of recovering from injury. In the first, athletes experience distress in the form of anger, depression, anxiety, guilt, bargaining, complaining, and self-doubt. Second, athletes are seen to engage in denial or unwillingness to accept the severity of injuries. Third, athletes begin determined coping responses and get on with the effort of rehabilitation. In the determined coping stage, athletes seek out and evaluate resources, clarify goals, learn new skills, and commit to rehabilitation plans. Athletes may cycle through the three components several times before completing rehabilitation, but successful rehabilitation implies progress toward the determined coping component.

There are other stage theories that are less widely recognized (Rose & Jevne, 1993). These stage models focus on the psychological reactions to injuries. Medical and psychological stages in the injury process have also been described: preinjury, immediate post-injury, treatment decision and implementation, early postoperative/rehabilitation, late postoperative/rehabilitation, specificity, return to play (Heil, 2000).

The responses of athletes to severe injuries have been evaluated to determine whether they conform to stage theories of grief. For example, male and female members of the US ski team were interviewed to evaluate their reactions to season-ending injuries (Udry et al., 1997a). The majority of the injuries were to the ACLs of knees. The elite skiers recalled the acute and persistent pain of their injuries. They often engaged in a process of attempting to rapidly determine the severity of their injuries. Soon thereafter, they came to appreciate the costs of their injuries, in terms of both lost potential and the inconvenience of rehabilitation. The injured skiers experienced emotional upheaval. They were frustrated and angry, and often had no clear direction for this anger. Some were anxious and scared to the point of panic. Dejection, depression, and disappointment were expectable. Some felt disconnected from teams and alone in hospitals. Despite initially responding with denial and disbelief, many came to accept their injuries and to focus on rehabilitation.

Upon reflection and over time, most of the skiers came to appreciate opportunities for growth that resulted from their injuries. For example, some gained perspective on the importance of skiing and clarified their priorities. Some also thought they matured as a result of their injuries and came to be more empathic to others with injuries. Others attempted to improve other aspects of their life such as academics (Udry, 1999). Other benefits included increased mental toughness and self-efficacy due to successful rehabilitation. Finally, the work ethic, physical fitness, and skiing techniques of some athletes improved as a result of their experience with rehabilitation. In general, athletes are better able to cope with career-ending injuries when they focus on the social and personal growth obtained in sport and when they have the opportunity to remain involved with their sport in some way post-injury.

Consistent with the Kubler-Ross stage theory of response to loss, the injured skiers experienced anger, depression, and acceptance (Udry, 1999; Udry et al., 1997a). They did not, however, engage in denial and bargaining. The responses of the skiers appeared consistent with the stages of distress and determined coping in the Heil stage theory, but not with the denial stage of this theory. Initial emotional upheaval followed by adaptive responses such as getting on with the job of rehabilitation were common reactions of the skiers. This two-step process was consistent with a two-stage model described by McDonald and Hardy, but skiers also emphasized their intense interest in finding out all that they could about their injuries.

Moreover, the grief reactions of athletes often involve a complex pattern of emotional responses that do not fit neatly into a stage model. For example, injured athletes may experience anger, depression, and anxiety simultaneously, and they may not pass through sequential stages in recovering emotional homeostasis (Gould, Udry, Bridges, & Beck, 1997b). Just as people in general are different, injured athletes are different in their emotional responses to injuries. When injuries are severe and status as an athlete is very important, sportspersons experience strong and negative emotional reactions. The cognitive-appraisal model outlined below appears a better fit for these findings.

Cognitive-Appraisal Models and Injuries

The responses of athletes to athletic injuries appear to fit reasonably well with the **cognitive-appraisal model** (Figure 17.2). This model is also consistent with the cognitive-relational theory of stress and the stress and injury model discussed above. This model understands reactions to injuries to be due to preinjury characteristics such as personality, coping resources, history of stressors, and interventions such as stress inoculation training. Post-injury responses involve the personal attributes of the injured athlete as well as the resources in the rehabilitation setting, and social support.

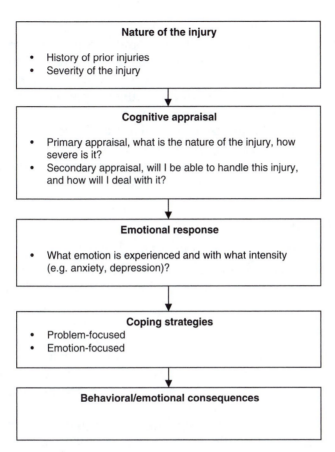

FIGURE 17.2. Cognitive appraisal of injury. From Udry, E. (1997). Coping and social support among injured athletes following surgery. *Journal of Sport & Exercise Psychology, 19,* 71–90.

Following injuries, athletes evaluate the *nature* and severity of the injury. They evaluate their capacity to *handle* the injury and the rehabilitation process, and the amount of social support available for rehabilitation. To the degree that athletes believe that they have suffered irreversible losses and that their self-esteem and wellbeing depend on their athletic status, negative *emotional responses* are likely to be greater. Injuries present a much greater threat to self-esteem and wellbeing when an individual's identity is woven to their role as an athlete (Brewer, 1993; Green & Weinberg, 2001) and when sportspersons have aspirations of becoming a professional athlete (Kleiber & Brock, 1992). These negative emotional reactions may include diminished self-esteem and confidence about athletic abilities, and in some cases, depression. Athletes are most likely to experience depression after severe injuries, when they fail to return to preinjury levels despite working hard in rehabilitation, and when their futures as elite athletes are threatened by injury. About half of a group of Division I collegiate athletes showed mild depression after injuries (Leddy, Lambert, & Ogles, 1994). It is likely that many of these athletes were not seriously injured, as athletes were counted as injured if physiological damage of body pain due to athletic participation warranted medical attention and caused athletes to miss a practice or game. About 12 percent of the injured athletes recorded clinical depression or depression sufficiently severe to qualify for a psychiatric diagnosis. Other studies demonstrated that clinical depression and emotional disturbance were experienced by 5 to 24 percent of injured athletes (Brewer, 2001).

Nature of the Injury

Efficacy and confidence are more likely to be shaken if injuries are severe. For example, beliefs in full recovery are more likely following ankle sprains than tears to the ACL (Wiese-Bjornstal, Smith, Shaffer, & Morrey, 1998).

In general, negative emotional responses decrease across the course of rehabilitation (Brewer, 2001), but may not be transient. Negative emotional responses are likely to decrease when confidence in recovery is higher and to increase when the athlete is presented with evidence that they may be left with limitations. For example, after ACL reconstructive surgery, mood was initially negative, improved for several months and then again turned more negative (Wiese-Bjornstal et al., 1998). Perhaps athletes' optimism and self-efficacy (Quinn & Fallon, 1999) post-surgery was difficult to sustain when they tested their injured knees in their sports and experienced frustration with their initial performance post-injury. The most productive channel for frustration and anger post-injury may be especially conscientious adherence to the rehabilitation process.

Coping Strategies

Athletes recovering from severe or season-ending injuries use a range of coping strategies to handle the loss caused by the injuries and the stress of rehabilitation. For example, the male and female members of the US ski team who experienced season-ending injuries used a number of *coping strategies* (Gould et al., 1997b). As described in Chapter 3, coping strategies can be categorized as problem-focused or emotion-focused. The former involves taking action to handle the sources of stress; the latter consists of managing one's emotional reactions to the sources of stress. Approximately 90 percent of the injured athletes used some form of problem-focused coping during rehabilitation. These strategies included attempting to keep to daily schedules and doing things for themselves. They also refocused their determination to compete again, set new goals, and devoted themselves to rehabilitation exercises and training. Some athletes did new and useful activities, such as going to college to occupy free time during the rehabilitation process. About half of the skiers sought support from others, and the female skiers were twice as likely as the males to utilize this resource.

The majority also used emotion-focused strategies to manage emotions and thoughts. Emotion-focused coping has previously been seen to be less important in the rehabilitation process, but skiers whose performance post-injury equaled or exceeded preinjury performance were more likely to actively manage their emotions and use visualization techniques. It may be that diverse and varied coping strategies are required to meet a major stressor such as a season-ending injury. However, coping that consists primarily of emotion-focused or palliative coping is associated with poorer adherence to rehabilitation schedules (Udry, 1997).

Integrated Model of Psychological Response to Injury

At the risk of overwhelming and confusing the reader, one final model for understanding psychological responses to injuries is presented (Figure 17.3). This **integrated model** (Wiese-Bjornstal et al., 1998) is similar to the cognitive-appraisal model presented above in that appraisals or interpretations of injuries influence behavioral responses, emotional responses, and recovery outcomes. It includes aspects of the stress and injury model that was also previously discussed in this chapter. The stress and injury model organizes the factors that represent vulnerabilities for injuries. The integrated model takes in more of the variables that influence an athlete's response to injuries. Of particular interest for the ensuing discussion in this chapter are the situational, behavioral response, and cognitive-appraisal factors in the integrated model. In the original model (Wiese-Bjornstal et al., 1998), there are longer lists of examples of personal and situational factors. For the sake of clarity, these lists have been abbreviated to include the items discussed in this chapter.

Goals and Rehabilitation (Cognitive Appraisal)

Athletes have been encouraged to establish **goals for physical rehabilitation** post-injury (Gilbourne & Taylor, 1998). As explained in Chapters 6 and 7, behavior that is goal-oriented is likely to be more productive and successful, and athletes who set goals for rehabilitation are more likely to

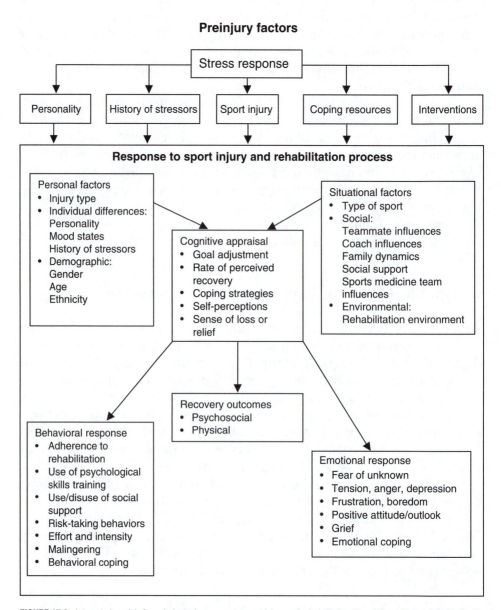

FIGURE 17.3. Integrated model of psychological response to sport injury and rehabilitation. From Wiese-Bjornstal, D. M., Smith, A. S., Shaffer, S. M., & Morrey, M. A. (1998). An integrated model of response to sport injury: Psychological and sociological dynamics. *Journal of Applied Sport Psychology*, *10*, 46–69; abbreviated to account for variables discussed in this chapter.

adhere to rehabilitation regimens both at home and in clinics (Scherzer et al., 2001), and to develop greater efficacy that they can realize rehabilitation goals (Evans & Hardy, 2002a, 2002b).

With social support, athletes are more likely to establish task goals for their rehabilitation (Magyar & Duda, 2000). Task goal orientations are likely to be most adaptive, with athletes measuring progress in relation to their own baseline and persisting throughout the difficult process of rehabilitation. With ego goals, competence is measured in relation to others, and the injured athlete will certainly function at a level beneath healthy peers. Injured athletes with ego orientations may also compare rehabilitation progress to that of other injured athletes. Injuries are not identical, and further injury can result from trying to outdistance other injured athletes rather than simply attempting to improve one's health status. Ego goals for performance are also problematic during the rehabilitation process, because they sustain effort and confidence when athletes believe that their competence is high. When competence is thought to be suspect, as during rehabilitation, maladaptive behaviors such as becoming discouraged, not putting forth maximum effort, missing rehabilitation appointments, and dropping out of rehabilitation are likely. Athletes with ego orientations may also try to return to action prior to full recovery so as to reestablish their position on teams. Task goals concern standards that are under the control of the athlete. By keeping written records, athletes more accurately measure progress toward task goals.

Some athletes with ego orientations adopt task orientations during the process of rehabilitation. For example, some injured collegiate athletes with ego orientations adopted task orientations by the midpoint of treatment (Magyar & Duda, 2000). Perhaps the atmosphere in training rooms clearly encouraged athletes to measure progress in relation to their own baselines.

Athletes with task orientations are more likely to enhance the rehabilitation process by engaging in mental imagery and positive self-talk. The use of imagery during rehabilitation may augment motivation and confidence (Sordoni, Hall, & Forwell, 2000).

Recall that there are several nosologies for categorizing athletic goals. Athletic performance goals refer to an end-product of a performance, but the end-product is a self-referenced standard. Process goals refer to the actions necessary to reach an outcome. Both process and athletic performance goals are seen to be helpful during rehabilitation from season-ending injuries (Evans, Hardy, & Fleming, 2000). With athletic performance goals, sportspersons are able to structure the rehabilitation procedure, and process goals direct attention to the specific behaviors necessary to reach these goals.

Injury Rehabilitation (Behavioral Response and Situational Factors)

Adherence to sport injury *rehabilitation* is more likely when athletes believe that their health status is subject to their personal control and when they have higher tolerance for pain (Brewer, 2001). Adherents to rehabilitation processes have confidence that following treatment regimens will lead to recovery (Brewer et al., 2000, 2003).

Psychological Skills Training (Behavioral Response and Situational Factors)

Regardless of goal orientation and self-efficacy, *training in psychological skills* helps injured athletes in rehabilitation. Athletes make more productive use of the rehabilitation process when they understand the purpose of rehabilitation exercises and procedures and the likely duration of the rehabilitation process (Williams & Scherzer, 2006). Consultation with rehabilitation professionals is helpful in understanding whether pain is a necessary aspect of rehabilitation exercises or whether it is a sign of further injury. Without this form of social coping, athletes may skip painful exercises that will return a full range of function to an injury site or persist at procedures that will cause further damage. Athletes are encouraged to express negative emotions to rehabilitation personnel, and athletes with more serious injuries may profit from sharing negative emotions and learning from the successful rehabilitation experiences of other seriously injured athletes. Professional counseling or therapy has been recommended for athletes who remain despondent and hopeless after injury.

Examples of specific psychological intervention techniques are the use of mental imagery and mental practice. In addition, the use of techniques to control physiological arousal or anxiety such as progressive muscle relaxation (PMR) and guided imagery designed to parallel the rehabilitation process has been encouraged. The use of PMR and guided imagery with athletes recovering from ACL reconstruction produced more rapid rehabilitation, less reinjury, and less anxiety (Cupal, 1998). With less anxiety and higher motivation, athletes may participate more fully in physical therapies.

An example of an integrated psychological intervention for injured athletes was the stress inoculation training provided to adult male athletes who received arthroscopic surgery to repair a torn meniscus in one knee (Ross & Berger, 1996). The stress inoculation training consisted of information about emotional responses such as anxiety and pain. This was given to forewarn the injured athletes that these responses were likely and to prepare them for their management. They were advised to monitor themselves for pain and anxiety responses, and were taught deep breathing exercises and progressive muscle relaxation, positive self-talk, and visualization strategies to decrease pain and anxiety responses. The athletes who practiced this stress inoculation reported less pain and anxiety during rehabilitation, and returned to preinjury levels of fitness more rapidly. An understanding of how the stress inoculation training helped is subject to speculation. For example, by the induction of relaxation, vasodilation may have occurred and allowed greater quantities of blood to flow to injured knees. Alternatively, athletes may have been better able to understand and control their emotional responses so that self-efficacy was not shaken and so that they were able to comply more fully with rehabilitation recommendations.

Social Support (Behavioral Response and Situational Factors)

Social support consists of well-intentioned interactions between people. For example, when a coach calls an injured player to inquire about progress, the coach implicitly communicates that she or he is a caring person who cares about the athlete, and that the athlete is of value (Bianco & Eklund, 2001). In providing social support, people intend or try to do something, such as providing practical help or emotional support, that will benefit the recipient. Three categories of social support have been identified. **Emotional support** consists of nonjudgmental listening, expressions of concern about the wellbeing of others, and sometimes challenging others. **Informational support** consists of clarifying similarities and differences in how people understand problems, acknowledging the effort of others, and challenging others to work harder and be more creative. Social support may also involve **tangible assistance** such as money and other help.

Social support facilitates emotion- and problem-focused coping in the injured and stressed athlete. Of course, social support also serves to enhance relationships. With social support people may become more resourceful in responding to stressors and less likely to simply brood about negative life events. This brooding and self-preoccupation can disrupt attention and increase bracing during competition and performances, both of which are discussed above as representing risk factors for injury.

When people grow up in environments rich with social support, they develop expectations that stress is manageable and that they will be equal to many of the stressors they face. With this background people have a degree of inoculation against the effects of stress. Regardless of inoculation, when social support is accessed in times of stress, the effects of stress are mitigated. People with low self-esteem are in greater need of social support and less likely to ask for it. Those with low self-esteem do not risk losing face and appearing weak and incompetent. For example, injured skiers who had not proved themselves to coaches were less likely to seek the support of coaches (Bianco & Eklund, 2001).

The presence of a support network or a group of people capable of providing support is a necessary but not sufficient condition for the receipt of social support. Those in the network must deliver it. Injured athletes receive more help with feelings of anxiety and frustration when supported by family or friends with whom they have a degree of emotional intimacy. In general, intimate relationships, such as those with spouses, have the largest impact on mental health.

Support in the form of information is most helpful when provided by those who know what they are talking about. For example, physicians best provide medical reassurance, and injured athletes often are in need of information about the severity of injuries and the duration of rehabilitation. People knowledgeable about sport are also more likely to be on target in recognizing what type of support is needed, and injured athletes are

---

Confidence in Medical and Coaching Staff

Brittany Hunter was perhaps the most highly recruited female high school basketball player in the USA when she accepted an athletic scholarship to Duke University in 2003. Playing as a freshman, she had a tear in her lateral meniscus. She resumed play four weeks after arthroscopic surgery, but the knee kept swelling and did not feel stable. The knee was drained of fluid repeatedly and she received three cortisone shots in the joint. There was a second operation after the basketball season.

Hunter lost confidence in the medical, training, and coaching staff, commenting, "There were no lines of communication." Her mother stated: "I had a problem with her being brought back after she was injured. I said I thought she should have sat down. I'm pretty bitter. I think that bringing her back exacerbated the injury and prolonged her healing" (Riley, 2005, p. C3).

Hunter transferred to the University of Connecticut (UCONN), and still the knee continued to swell from basketball practice. She underwent a third operation in which the meniscus was replaced with the meniscus of a cadaver.

At peace at UCONN, she commented: "I've got more drive than I've ever had. Even when I first got hurt, I was like, I'm going to come back, I'm all right. And when I didn't, I was kind of sulking about it. There's a drive to me now. Like there's no doubt in my mind that I'm going to come back the same way. I think that helps you a lot" (Riley, 2005, p. C3).

likely to seek support from knowledgeable people (Bianco, 2001). However, injured athletes will avoid knowledgeable people such as coaches if these people have proved to be unhelpful and uncaring in the past.

Sometimes the social support is well matched to the needs of the recipient. For example, an injured athlete in a grieving process may benefit more from emotional support, whereas an athlete who is focused on physical rehabilitation may find information about the restoration of physical function to be most supportive. Even if the social support offered is not a good match to the needs of the recipient, it is still likely to be helpful if it communicates concern about the recipient's wellbeing (Rees & Hardy, 2000). Sportspersons' need for social support wanes somewhat as they move closer to recovery.

Social Support and Adherence to Rehabilitation

Social support facilitates rehabilitation. With social support from others such as sports medicine providers and teammates, injured athletes are more likely to adhere to rehabilitation programs and realize more complete recoveries (Udry, 1996).

Injured intercollegiate athletes who felt they had the support of parents, teammates, and trainers continued to look to others for guidance and comfort throughout the rehabilitation process (Magyar & Duda, 2000). They were also open to guidance from trainers during rehabilitation. Guidance and feedback from coaches, athletic trainers, and medical personnel provide important information to injured athletes about their progress in rehabilitation. Without this guidance, athletes may underestimate the rate of their progress. This feedback enhances and sustains the self-confidence or self-efficacy of rehabilitating athletes, and this sustains the effort necessary for good results in rehabilitation.

In addition to feedback from trainers, athletes are sensitive to feedback from other rehabilitating athletes, and they learn by watching others in rehabilitation. Athletes also size up their prospects for good recoveries on the basis of their experience during the first days of rehabilitation. If they are assigned exercises and tasks at which they are likely to be successful, they will more likely be successful at later points in the rehabilitation process.

Lacking Social Support

To this point, this discussion of social support has assumed that the comments and reactions of others are uniformly positive. Of course this is not the case, as the reactions of others can do more harm than good, and serve to increase one's sense of isolation. For example, members of the US ski team who sustained season-ending injuries, most of which involved ACL damage, did not find the social support from family, teammates, and coaches to be uniformly positive (Udry, Gould, Bridges, & Tuffey, 1997b). Family and teammates most often provided emotional support in the form of understanding, reassurance, and supporting the decisions of athletes such as to return to skiing. Family and teammates were also supportive in encouraging the injured skiers throughout rehabilitation, and by providing transportation and help with daily living. Coaches who remained in contact with injured skiers, supported and encouraged the skiers, and consulted about rehabilitation provided injured skiers with positive emotional support.

All of the injured skiers experienced some form of this positive support, but a minority reported negative experiences with family and teammates. These negative influences included losing contact with teammates and friends, and not receiving support from family with decisions to return to skiing or to retire from skiing. Injured skiers also identified a lack of contact with coaches as a negative influence. Some complained that coaches did not call until they were back on the snow. Some injured skiers also wanted coaching advice and guidance throughout the rehabilitation process. In general, the injured skiers in this study and athletes from other sports (Brewer, 2001) viewed the social influence of coaches as more negative than positive and the influence of family and teammates as more positive than negative. Injured female intercollegiate athletes from other sports also were more critical of the quality and quantity of social support they received from coaches (Granito, 2002).

Career Termination

Athletes forced into retirement by serious athletic injuries often report low life satisfaction. This is particularly true if their identities are closely and exclusively tied to their sport in that they see themselves only as athletes and without other purposes in life. Some have chronic pain and a physical restriction, but the most important source of their unhappiness appears to be unresolved feelings of loss and inadequate career planning.

However, there is little reason to believe that adjustment problems are the norm after retirement from high school and college athletic careers. Indeed, high school athletes are more likely to attend college, graduate from college and have greater occupation success than classmates who did not play sports. Life satisfaction is generally not less for collegiate athletes and nonathletes at the time of graduation from college (Perna, Ahlgren, &

Zaichkowsky, 1999). Collegiate athletes and elite junior athletes may miss the excitement, camaraderie, and fun of their playing days, but they have been shown to be no less satisfied with or successful in careers. Transitioning from involvement in sport at this level is similar to the transitions and adjustment to new roles in young adulthood such as to work careers after college and to marriage after being single. Life satisfaction is lower for athletes who have not developed career plans and for African American athletes.

Professional and elite amateur athletes may have a more difficult adjustment. There are varying estimates of the percentage of elite athletes that experience significant adjustment problems after retirement, with perhaps the best estimate at 19 percent experiencing serious adjustment problems (Grove, Lavallee, Gordon, & Harvey, 1998). The highest estimate of adjustment difficulties among elite athletes was 70 percent of elite female gymnasts (Kerr & Dacyshyn, 2001). These gymnasts had difficulties with self-identity and body image and felt a general void in their lives. Of course, distress is not universal, as for example 50 percent of recently retired female tennis professionals were relieved to be free of the pressure and grind of competition and available for more traditional lifestyles (Allison & Meyer, 1988).

There are several issues to be considered in predicting adjustment to retirement among elite and professional athletes (Taylor & Ogilvie, 2001). The first concerns the causes of career termination among athletes. Retirement is often the result of aging, and the erosion of speed, strength, and coordination, and sometimes the desire to intensely train and compete. Retirement may also be due to being deselected or cut from teams, or to injury. Sometimes athletes decide to retire because they have had enough of the training and lifestyle demands of their sport and they have reached their goals. Retirement is far more aversive if it is not the athlete's choice.

A second important issue in evaluating adjustment after athletic careers is the degree to which athletes define their self-worth and social identity on the basis of accomplishment and participation in sport (Brewer, Van Raalte, & Petitpas, 2000; Grove et al., 1998; Pearson & Petitpas, 1990). Elite athletes with the most serious adjustment problems after retirement based their identities exclusively on sport and had few other competencies and sources of life satisfaction, and, as mentioned above, this is true for athletes in general. Retiring athletes with few other social and vocational competencies experience marked drops in status and show awkwardness in functioning outside the role of an athlete.

> ## "At 39, you wouldn't think you'd be lost, but you are"
>
> Mike Richter made this comment after retiring from a professional hockey career that spanned 15 years in the National Hockey League (NHL) and included four all-star selections and a Stanley Cup championship (Hine, 2005, p. C2). Richter continued, "In the locker room, there are 20 guys. There's a support group. It's your life, and all of a sudden, it's just gone. You're very much alone for the first time. You've lost your support group" (Hine, 2005, p. C2).
>
> Richter was more fortunate than many athletes in that he had two important support groups outside of hockey: one at home with his wife and three children, and the other at Yale University where he was enrolled as a student at age 39. Richter described the support from Yale faculty and advisors as "unbelievable," and accepted the challenge of disciplining himself to a schedule of study and family responsibilities. He reflected: "But playing hockey doesn't mean you retire and do nothing the rest of your life. You can, but I'd like to develop the different aspects of my personality" (Hine, 2005, p. C2).

Career Transitions

European nations took the lead in the development of programs to assist elite athletes in career transitions. The Canadian Olympic Athlete Career Centre was launched in 1985 to prepare athletes for life after elite competition. The Career Assistance Program for Athletes was initiated by the US Olympic Committee in 1988 and the Lifeskills for Elite Athletes Program was established in Australia in 1989, both for the purpose of assisting elite athletes with career transitions (Taylor, Ogilvie, & Lavallee, 2006).

Athletes make better adjustment after retirement when they redirect time and energy to new concerns and develop new routines or rhythms to their days. If retired athletes have not established webs of social support outside of their former athletic organizations, then support from these organizations is important in facilitating their transition. Some athletes resist occupational planning because they do not want to look to a future after sport that will have less financial remuneration and status. As mentioned above, career preparation is a vital determinant of life satisfaction after athletic careers.

Professional Athletes and Financial Planning

NFL football players are more successful after retirement if they have prepared for post-NFL careers. Despite average salaries of $1.25 million in 2003 (Heath, 2004), many NFL athletes need to generate income after retirement and in addition need to "downsize" or reduce their levels of spending (Wethe, 2004). Organizations such as the Sports Professionals Foundation and the NFL Players Association have been established to promote this career development among NFL players. Nevertheless, it is difficult for some NFL players to plan for a future that portends fewer rewards and less adulation. For example, the NFL Players Association has established off-season internships in corporations to provide job training and assistance in making transitions to jobs post-NFL. Perhaps 30 of the 1600 NFL players participated in these internships in 2001 (Greenberg, 2001a).

Individual NFL athletes have embraced the world of work after retirement. Former Dallas Cowboys wide receiver Raghib "Rocket" Ismail is the owner of a hip-hop record company in Dallas and a performer in the 3 Dot and 3 Pieces ensembles. Former Dallas Cowboys defensive back George Teague developed new skills running Touch of Lace, a lingerie shop in North Richland Hills, TX (Wethe, 2004).

Careful financial planning during peak earning years as an athlete also makes retirement more comfortable. Rod Smith, wide receiver for the Denver Broncos, banks about $1 million of his $2.5 million pretax annual salary. He saved almost half of his $11 million signing bonus. Brad Daugherty lived in an apartment that rented for $625 per month during his playing days with the Cleveland Cavaliers of the NBA. He saved $5 million in his first four years and began investing in car dealerships. He is estimated to be worth tens of millions of dollars (Heath, 2004).

Summary and Conclusions

Injuries often occur in the course of athletic participation. There are about 17 million athletic injuries annually in the USA. There are many factors associated with athletic injuries, such as inadequate training and practice, poor athletic techniques and equipment, and bad luck. The psychological factors associated with the prediction of sport injuries and with optimal rehabilitation have been emphasized in this chapter.

Athletic competition and practice are environmental stressors, especially when they are demanding and involve pressure. However, the degree to which they produce stress responses in sportspersons is explained by the sportspersons' personalities, history of stressors, and coping resources. Athletes coping with a greater number of stressors, with fewer resources for coping with stress, and with personality characteristics such as trait anxiety, experience more intense stress responses from athletic stressors. These stress responses result in cognitive interference as athletes are more likely to interpret pressure as a source of threat. Cognitive interference and physiological anxiety disrupt attention and produce bracing – the simultaneous contraction of agonist and antagonist muscle groups. Athletes are then less able to anticipate and respond fluidly and automatically to the flow of competitions and more likely to become exposed to musculoskeletal trauma.

Coping resources provide an important function in moderating cognitive interference, physiological anxiety, and attentional impairment. Psychological coping skills such as techniques for controlling physiological anxiety and preparing for competitions, and interpersonal coping skills such as accessing social support, provide a buffer to stress responses. Athletes who can access at least one form of coping resource have strategies for reducing stress responses and the chance of injuries. Coping resources can be developed. Athletes who were taught stress inoculation training and PMR had fewer injuries.

After the occurrence of injuries, the injuries are a source of stress. Injuries are potentially major negative life events, sources of chronic stress, and negative daily hassles. Negative emotional reactions commonly occur with injuries. Psychologists have given considerable thought and energy to the question of whether these negative emotional reactions follow a sequential pattern consistent with stage theories of grief. As emphasized throughout this book, people are different. There are some common reactions to injuries, but there is not enough consistency between athletes to maintain that athletes invariably move through stages of grief such as the five-stage theory of Kubler-Ross.

The responses of athletes to injuries are determined not only by the stressor of the injury itself, but also by their cognitive appraisal. This appraisal includes consideration of their ability to cope with the rehabilitation process, the amount of social support available, and the likelihood of recovery. Severe injuries are major negative stressors, and negative emotional responses are more likely if athletes believe their internal and external resources are not sufficient for rehabilitation. If injuries are seen to present irreversible losses and if an athlete's wellbeing is dependent on their status as an active athlete, negative emotional responses are likely to be greater. Such responses are understandable following severe injuries. Mood is seen to brighten as rehabilitation progresses, but mood and self-efficacy are sensitive to the full return of function. The recognition of limitations or incomplete recovery of function is associated with persistent negative emotional responses or diminished efficacy. Athletes handle the stress of injuries by engaging problem-focused coping strategies, such as adhering to rehabilitation programs, and also handle negative emotional responses with emotion-focused coping.

During rehabilitation, sportspersons call on not only their own coping resources but also support and help from family, friends, and professionals. The support of others makes injured athletes not only feel better, but also more likely to make productive use of problem- and emotion-focused coping strategies and to adhere to rehabilitation programs. Athletes who receive social support or help from others throughout their development develop confidence in their own capacities to handle difficult situations and in the likelihood that others will deliver help when it is needed. Without development in supportive environments, sportspersons are less likely to ask for help and more likely to need it.

Professional intervention is helpful in the rehabilitation process. This involves not only medical and physical therapy intervention, but also guidance in using techniques for positive self-talk, visualization, and the control of physiological anxiety. Task orientation or athletic performance and process goals are encouraged during rehabilitation from injuries. These goal orientations measure progress against the athlete's baseline of prior functioning. The severity of injuries and rehabilitation schedules are somewhat idiosyncratic and therefore little is to be gained by comparing progress in rehabilitation to that of other injured athletes. Further injury can result from efforts to compete with, and return to play sooner than, other rehabilitating athletes. Ego orientations also sustain effort and confidence when confidence is high, and confidence typically drops after injury. Injured sportspersons are sensitive to guidance and interventions from professionals in rehabilitation settings, and some adopt more adaptive task orientations as a result of their experience in rehabilitation.

Injuries may result in the end of athletic careers. Career termination or retirement is especially difficult if the goals of the athlete have not been met, and if the athlete does not have alternative vocational opportunities and sources of social support. Career termination is also particularly unhappy if the self-worth of athletes is tied exclusively to their playing status. Professional and elite athletes gain more rewards from sport than high school and college athletes, and therefore are likely to experience a greater loss upon career termination. Career termination may bring feelings of loss, but may also provide freedom to pursue other interests and opportunities.

Key Terms

Stress and injury model

Bracing

Sources of stress: major life events, chronic stress, daily hassles

Coping resources: general coping behaviors, psychological coping skills, interpersonal coping

Psychological skills training: stress inoculation training, progressive muscle relaxation

Stage theory of grieving: denial, bargaining, anger, depression, acceptance

Cognitive-appraisal models and injuries

Integrated model of psychological response to injury

Goals and rehabilitation

Social support: emotional support, informational support, tangible assistance

Career termination

Suggested Readings

Smith, R. E., Ptacek, J. T., & Smoll, E. L. (1992). Sensation seeking, stress, and adolescent injuries: A test of stress-buffering, risk-taking, and coping skills hypotheses. *Journal of Personality and Social Psychology, 62*, 1016–1024.

Taylor, J. & Ogilvie, B. C. (2001). Career termination among athletes. In R. N. Singer, H. A. Hausenblas, & C. M. Janelle (Eds.), *Handbook of sport psychology* (2nd ed., pp. 787–809). New York: Wiley.

Udry, E. (1997). Coping and social support among injured athletes following surgery. *Journal of Sport & Exercise Psychology, 19*, 71–90.

Udry, E., Gould, D., Bridges, D., & Beck, L. (1997). Down but not out: Athlete responses to season-ending injuries. *Journal of Sport & Exercise Psychology, 19*, 229–248.

Wiese-Bjornstal, D. M., Smith, A. S., Shaffer, S. M., & Morrey, M. A. (1998). An integrated model of response to sport injury: Psychological and sociological dynamics. *Journal of Applied Sport Psychology, 10*, 46–69.

Williams, J. M. (2001). Psychology of injury risk and prevention. In R. N. Singer, H. A. Hausenblas, & C. M. Janelle (Eds.), *Handbook of sport psychology* (2nd ed., pp. 766–786). New York: Wiley.

PART IV

INDIVIDUALS AND TEAMS

Gender and Sport 18

Like most first graders, Sarah loved to play. Recess always seemed too brief when there was a football game, and she liked nothing better than galloping with the football. Then one day, Eugene transferred to her class. He was nonplussed when he saw her playing football. He grabbed the ball and held her away with his off-hand saying, "Girls can't play football."

After school, Sarah's father arrived as usual to pick her up. An ashen-faced teacher greeted him and said, "I don't know what got into Sarah. She was sent to the principal's office for fighting. She had Eugene down on the ground. We had to pull her off of him!"

Hearing the whole story on the ride home, her father commented: "You don't have to take that from anybody. But, next time you might tell the teacher instead of whipping someone's behind."

The view that women and men are so different that they derive from separate planets was fostered in popular literature with the publication of *Men Are from Mars, Women Are from Venus* (Gray, 1992). Not surprisingly, this view is described as the *difference hypothesis*. Feminist scholars disagree with this view and instead note that practically all physical and psychological human characteristics are distributed among both sexes (Oglesby & Hill, 1993). This view, the *similarities hypothesis*, recognizes that psychological differences are mostly small or nonexistent. For example, a recent review of research concerning gender differences on cognitive, social and personality, communication, wellbeing, and motor variables demonstrated that there were close-to-zero or small differences on 78 percent of the indices (Hyde, 2005). Furthermore, even when gender differences are identified, these differences may be less the result of innate differences between males and females and more the result of the conformity of the males and females to social expectations or gender roles.

Gender and biological sex are not interchangeable terms. Sex refers to biological characteristics such as chromosomes, internal and external genitalia, gonads, hormones, and secondary sexual characteristics. Secondary sexual characteristics appear with the onset of puberty. **Gender** is a psychosocial phenomenon based not only on biological sex, but also on cultural customs, roles, and expectations associated with being female or male.

Biological sex differences for physical characteristics such as muscle strength and maximal oxygen consumption (a measure of endurance) are not categorical such that *all* men have greater strength and maximal oxygen consumption. Instead, there is considerable overlap between the sexes so that groups of women and men have comparable strength and maximal oxygen consumption. On average, adult American males are 50 percent stronger in most muscle groups and their maximal oxygen consumption exceeds that of women by 20 percent (Brooks & Fahey, 1984). Women show greater flexibility and balance (Hudson, 1978).

While these differences might be cited as evidence of biological differences between the sexes, even these differences are influenced by culture and experience as muscles are typically trained differently in male and female sport and exercise. For example, traditional sports for women, such as figure skating, place a greater emphasis on beauty, grace, and flexibility, whereas traditionally male sports, such as Olympic weight lifting, emphasize explosive power. Prior to the different recreational and sport experiences of the genders, there are greater similarities in physical performance. For example, among elementary school children, girls scored only 2 percent lower than boys on a number of motor skills tests. However, by the end of the first grade, girls rated their skills as 14 percent lower than boys (Eccles & Harold, 1991). This is in part because parents encourage boys to engage in sport and physical activity, which in turn leads to higher levels of athletic confidence (Brustad, 1993). Children are rather accurate in perceiving their parents' appraisals of their athletic ability, and these appraisals influence the corresponding self-appraisals of children (Bois, Sarrazin, Brustad, Chanal, & Trouilloud, 2005). Women and men enjoy similar physiological benefits from exercise and physical training including increased muscle metabolism and strength, decreased body fat, and increased maximal oxygen consumption.

Historical Context of Gender and Sport

Gender differences have historically been emphasized to a greater extent in departments of physical education than in departments of psychology because of the belief that curricula for women's physical education were separate from the counterparts for men. Separate curricula were considered necessary because women were thought to be too frail to engage in outdoor play and physical activity. Mary Bissell questioned this assumption about the frailty of women in the late 1800s (Gill, 1998a). Another canard of this era was that women should refrain from physical activity during menstruation, but Mary Putnam Jacobi (1877; cited in Denmark & Fernandez, 1993) argued that there was no scientific basis for this cultural norm.

There were commonalities in the emphases of physical education programs for women and men in the late 1800s; both emphasized physical training as a component in the development of healthy and well-rounded individuals. However, by 1923 the emphases of physical education programs diverged further along gender lines. Men's programs encouraged competitive athletics, whereas an **anticompetitive movement** gained support in women's physical education. This movement was led by the leading women scholars of this era and by organizations such as the Committee on Women's Athletics of the American Physical Education Association (Pfister, 2000). Sportspersonship and enjoyment of physical activity for all women rather than just elite athletes, and the wellbeing of athletes, were emphasized. Women scholars in physical education did not condemn competition; rather they opposed an emphasis on winning at the expense of participation in athletics by greater numbers of women.

Opposition to the participation of women in rigorous athletics and competition persisted. Beginning in the 1920s, in the USA and Europe, theories about the physiological incompatibility of women and athletics were supported by mainstream medicine (Pfister, 2000). A central assumption of these theories was that women were obliged to bear children and that vigorous athletics would compromise their **reproductive fitness**. It was argued that women had only a limited ration of energy, and that this energy would be dissipated in sport and therefore unavailable for childbearing and childrearing. Physicians maintained that the uterus was the most fragile organ in the female anatomy and that it could be displaced and even tilted backward by strenuous activity such as running or the long jump. Medical men pronounced it unwise to firm the muscles of the abdomen and pelvis through training, reasoning that tautening of the muscle fibers would make childbirth difficult or impossible. Sport was feared to masculinize women, disrupt the polarity of the sexes and the social order, and even lead to homosexuality. These myths endured for some time despite abundant scientific evidence as early as the 1930s that sport did not produce these feared consequences.

Competition in women's athletics received a far greater emphasis in the USA with **Title IX**. Title IX was an aspect of the Higher Education Act of 1972 (US Department of Education, 1972), and was probably fostered by the civil rights and women's movements (Gill, 1998b). With its three-part **compliance test**, Title IX required universities that received federal assistance to demonstrate that in all education programs they did not discriminate on the basis of sex. This extended to intercollegiate and intramural sports. The *first* part of the Title IX Compliance Test requires that the number of males and females who participate in athletics must be substantially proportionate to the full-time undergraduate enrollment at a university. Therefore, if approximately 50 percent of the undergraduates are women at a university, the number of female athletes should be 50 percent. Title IX *secondly* requires universities to demonstrate expansion of women's athletic programs, and *thirdly* requires that the interests and abilities of the underrepresented sex be fully accommodated.

As a result of Title IX, the number of women in intercollegiate sports has increased 6- to 10-fold and women constitute approximately one third of the Olympic, college, and high school athletes in the USA (Gill, 1998b). The 2001–2002 Gender-Equity Report of the National Collegiate Athletic Association (NCAA) indicated that 44 percent of Division I athletes were female and 39 percent of the athletes in Divisions II and III were female (Gender-Equity Report, 2002). The increase in spending for women's programs has not been concomitant with the increase in female participation. This disparity is primarily due to the costs associated with football programs for men. Female head coaches at Division I universities received 36 percent of the average salaries of their male counterparts, and the greatest equity in coaches' salaries occurred at Division II schools where women received 47 percent of the salaries of their male colleagues. At Division I and II universities, the recruiting budgets for women's sports were no more than 40 percent of the budgets for male sports.

An unexpected result of Title IX, however, was the exclusion of women from almost all positions of leadership in amateur sports in the USA. This occurred when women's and men's athletic departments and athletic governing organizations merged. For example, the Association for Intercollegiate Athletics for Women (AIAW) was absorbed into the NCAA, which was controlled by men (Fasting, 2000). Prior to Title IX women coached more than 90 percent of women's athletic teams, whereas women today coach less than half. A survey by the NCAA in 2001–2002 demonstrated that athletic directors were female at 6.4 percent of Division I institutions, 12.9 percent of Division II institutions, and 23.8 percent of Division III schools (Gender-Equity Report, 2002). The percentages of women in associate athletic director positions were: 35.4 percent in Division I, 30.7 percent in Division II, and 36.0 percent in Division III.

Some sport governing bodies, such as the International Olympic

Committee (IOC), excluded women from their inception. This was not surprising considering the exclusion of women from Olympic events as described below. Women first joined the IOC in 1981, and in 2007 12.6 pecent (14 of 111) of the members of the IOC are women. The first IOC conference on women and sport was conducted in 1996, and recommendations included providing equal opportunities for women in the athletic, coaching, and administrative ranks.

It has been difficult to increase the number of women in athletic organizations because entrance to these organizations is often determined by relationships with those currently in power (Fasting, 2000). Positions in these athletic organizations are typically filled informally rather than through formal announcements and competitive application processes. A process by which those in power restrict entry into their organizations to people like themselves is referred to as an "**old boys' network**."

Women may have fewer opportunities to cultivate relationships with those in power in athletic organizations because they carry a disproportionate share of domestic duties and responsibilities for the care of children and elderly parents in their households. They are therefore less available for travel and committee meetings. With greater flexibility in terms of the scheduling of meetings and requirements for travel, more women may have more opportunities to cultivate relationships in "old boys' networks" and gain greater access to positions in the hierarchies of athletic organizations.

Women and the Olympic Games

The first modern **Olympic Games** were held in Athens, Greece in 1896. Women first competed in the Olympic Games in 1900, but this participation was limited to seven women in tennis competitions and 10 in golf competitions. Women were also allowed to participate in sailing as members of crews with males. At the 1908 Games in England, women competed in tennis, ice-skating, and archery, and in mixed crews in sailing and motor boating. In the 1912 Games in Sweden, women began competing in swimming events. Resistance to parity between the genders in Olympic participation mirrored resistance to extending equal rights to women in vocational, academic, and political arenas (Pfister, 2000).

Women first competed in track and field at the Olympic Games in 1928. After female competitors in the 800-meter race dropped to the ground in exhaustion, the IOC responded by excluding women from this event in 1932, reasoning that endurance events were not made for them. Even in recent history, women were excluded from events considered too

Women and sport (photo courtesy of Western Connecticut State University).

traumatic for the feminine physique. For example, women did not run the marathon (26.2 miles) until 1984. Surprisingly, women did not compete in the 10,000-meter race (6.2 miles) until 1988. Women began participating in Olympic volleyball in 1964, basketball and handball in 1976, hockey in 1980, and soccer in 1996.

About 40 countries currently do not send women to the Olympic games. Women in these countries do not have opportunities to train and compete due to religious and cultural practices and poverty.

Gender Roles and Participation in Sport

Cultural institutions such as family, school, church, and state shape **gender roles** (Gill, 1998b). These institutions convey information about behaviors, tasks, and attitudes associated with gender in a particular culture (Oglesby & Hill, 1993). Traditional conceptions of femininity include characteristics such as beauty, grace, submissiveness, and passivity. The attributes of strength and aggressiveness are more often associated with **traditional ideas of masculinity** and these characteristics are also often productive in sport (Martin & Martin, 1995). Socialization practices that encourage nurturing, cooperative, and passive behaviors are seen as somewhat inconsistent with sport and more frequent among girls. Perhaps athletic participation has been more consistent with female gender roles in African American communities (Howard-Hamilton, 1993).

Joan Benoit Samuelson and Gender Roles

In 1984, and prior to assuming the name Samuelson with her marriage, Joan Benoit won the first Olympic marathon. She grew up in a loving and supportive family in Maine, but experienced conflict between gender roles and sport:

It seemed to me that almost everything I had dreamed of doing with my life had overtones of boyishness. The climate of the times encouraged revolution, but my friends and I were slow to shoulder the barricades. As far as we could see, girls were supposed to be finished with boys' games when they were eleven. They weren't supposed to dream of careers in athletics. I can still remember watching a friend playing catch with her male teacher and being envious of her, but at the same time being glad I wasn't blatantly advertising my interest in sports. None of the girls I knew would have been flattered if described as "athletic" or (God forbid) "strong." I used to look at my brother's high school yearbooks and hope to make the "senior superlatives" section: not as Most Athletic, but as Friendliest or Most Optimistic.

My love of sports went underground. If I had known that the boys were missing any insights into their future sexuality I would have thought they were lucky. The insights I was having made me sad and uneasy. A girl who wanted to be an athlete was suspect; maybe we could aspire to be doctors and lawyers now, but we shouldn't want muscles. (Benoit & Baker, 1987, p. 43)

Certain sports such as gymnastics and swimming have been seen as more appropriate for women. These sports often emphasize aesthetic qualities and do not emphasize competition. They remain faithful to traditional notions of femininity such as gracefulness, beauty, and a lack of aggression. In a masculinist culture the female body is an object for the aesthetic enjoyment of others, and sports that provide for aesthetic pleasure are consistent with stereotypic ideas of femininity (Koivula, 2001). Sports that call for the use of physical force to overcome an opponent, such as boxing, or to overcome the resistance of a heavy object, such as weightlifting, were considered less appropriate for women (Metheny, 1965; Sage & Loudermilk, 1979). As mentioned above, aggressiveness has been considered especially characteristic of masculinity and male sport. However, these traditions have yielded as women have engaged in a wide range of athletic activities in venues such as the Olympics. For example, ice hockey requires a high degree of aggressiveness, and it became an Olympic sport for women in 1980.

Socialization that builds **confidence in athletic aptitude** is important. Children and adults are more likely to enjoy and participate in sport and exercise if they believe they are competent and reasonably skilled athletically. Guidance to facilitate belief in athletic competence is often necessary because children cannot accurately make assessments of their own athletic ability. Children as old as 13 years of age are inaccurate in judging their athletic ability (Raudsepp & Liblik, 2002). If girls and women perceive themselves to be competent, they are more likely to find sport and exercise intrinsically rewarding. For example, female collegiate athletes demonstrated only slightly less intrinsic interest in sport than their male counterparts (Amorose & Horn, 2000). Both genders may have interpreted their status as scholarship athletes to be evidence of their competence.

Women and girls have received increased social support for athletic participation. Comparing the responses of female, collegiate volleyball players in Division I programs in the years 1979 and 1989, the latter cohort were encouraged to participate in athletics to a greater degree by family members and male and female best friends (Weiss & Barber, 1995). Mothers of athletes were seen to be increasingly influential in fostering interest in athletics.

Safe at home (photo courtesy of Western Connecticut State University).

However, even female collegian athletes may experience conflicts with regard to body types. Western European cultures have increasingly characterized the ideal female body type as quite thin, and the ideal male body type as more **mesomorphic** or muscular (Sheldon, 1940, 1942). Regardless of gender, the mesomorphic body type is likely to be more adaptive in most sports. Female collegian athletes have been shown to have a higher incidence of eating disorders and concerns about weight than their male counterparts. Female athletes more commonly engage in unhealthy eating practices in order to control their weight. Coaches are more likely to believe that female athletes need to lose weight and

Femininity and Strength

With a number one ranking in women's professional tennis, and Grand Slam victories in the French Open, Wimbledon, and the US Open, Serena Williams was the Sportswoman of the Year in *Sports Illustrated*'s annual report of 2002. The bodacious "all-black, one-piece short-shorts catsuit" (*The Queen*, 2002) that she wore at the US Open made it difficult to ignore the symmetry and muscularity of her physique. Standing close to 5 feet 10 inches with wide shoulders and hips, her beauty did not conform to traditional feminine stereotypes and required the incorporation of strength and muscularity into traditional images of beauty.

In 2001 and 2002, Annika Sorenstam was the most dominant golfer in the world. During that time, she reconfigured her physique with a grueling regimen of weightlifting, running, and stretching. This regimen included as many as 1000 sit-ups per day. As she prepared to be the first woman in the modern era to compete in the men's Professional Golf Association (PGA) tour in the USA, she was pronounced "built for battle, with industrial-strength arms, the thighs of a sprinter" (Bamberger, 2003). Perhaps photographs that accompanied this *Sports Illustrated* article were intended to document the results of Sorenstam's training regimen. These photographs captured her golf swing, but she was clothed only in a leotard that resembled a two-piece bathing suit. Perhaps they were also intended to draw attention to Sorenstam's physical attractiveness.

that males need to gain weight, and more male than female coaches attribute being overweight to laziness (Griffin & Harris, 1996).

Gender Role Orientation and Athletes

The study of gender roles progressed rapidly in the 1970s with the development of questionnaires for assessing gender role orientation. Prominent among these was the **Bem Sex Role Inventory** (BSRI; Bem, 1974, 1978). With the BSRI, people are rated for characteristics that are traditionally feminine (sensitive to the needs of others, affectionate) or masculine (willing to take risks, independent) (Table 18.1). People are then identified as feminine if ratings are high on feminine and low on masculine traits, masculine if scored as high on masculine and low on feminine traits, **androgynous** if rated as high on both feminine and masculine traits, and undifferentiated if they score low on both. The Children's Sex Role Inventory (CSRI) was developed to assess gender roles in children (Boldizar, 1991). It is comparable to the BSRI and appropriate for the assessment of sex typing and androgyny from middle school through adulthood.

TABLE 18.1 Items from the BSRI	
Masculine items	Feminine items
Acts as a leader	Affectionate
Aggressive	Cheerful
Ambitious	Childlike
Analytical	Compassionate
Assertive	Does not use harsh language
Athletic	Eager to soothe hurt feelings
Competitive	Feminine

From Bem, S. L. (1974). The measurement of psychological androgyny. *Journal of Consulting and Clinical Psychology, 42,* 155–162.

Another influential model and measure of gender roles was the **Personality Attributes Questionnaire** (PAQ; Helmreich & Spence, 1977). Research with this questionnaire and the BSRI consistently demonstrated that female athletes were either androgynous or masculine, whereas average college women rated as feminine. These findings have been reported for collegiate athletes (Edwards, Gordin, & Henschen, 1984; Gill, 1995; Koca, Asci, & Kirazci, 2005), high school athletes (Andre & Holland, 1995), and younger children (Salminen, 1990). They are not surprising given that athletics is likely to call for assertive and competitive behaviors, and these characteristics are classified as masculine on the PAQ and BSRI.

Gender differences have also been evaluated with the **Sport Orientation Questionnaire** (SOQ; Gill & Deeter, 1988). Men were shown to score higher on scales measuring competitiveness and a focus on winning. Women scored slightly higher on a scale measuring an emphasis on achieving personal goals. Access to and experience with competitive athletics probably influenced the gender differences in competitiveness. These differences all but disappeared when international and collegiate athletes were evaluated (Gill, 1993).

How is it that athletes of both genders endorse masculine or androgynous gender roles? It has been theorized that the experience of sport, with its emphasis on instrumental behavior (initiating action to reach goals), aggressiveness, and competitiveness is responsible for fostering masculine (traditionally or stereotypically) characteristics in both genders. In support of this theory, male athletes have been shown to have more traditional views of the roles of women than male nonathletes. However, if this theory were precise, it would also be reasonable to expect that females who participated in sports that were traditionally defined as more aggressive and therefore more masculine, such as basketball, would have less traditional views of gender roles than their counterparts in traditionally feminine sports such as figure skating. That is, by engaging in activities traditionally identified as masculine, female athletes would adopt androgynous or masculine gender role perspectives. Instead, female and male college (Burke, 1986) and high school athletes (Andre & Holland, 1995) who participate in more aggressive sports, such as males in American football and females in basketball, do not endorse more masculine gender roles than their counterparts in less aggressive sports. An alternative hypothesis is that males with traditional views of gender roles and females who do not carry traditional gender role views choose to engage in sport.

Males have more rigid ideas about sports that are appropriate for each gender. These ideas are likely reified or solidified during childhood and adolescence. For example, children in third grade viewed a range of sporting activities, including weightlifting and cheerleading, as appropriate for both genders. By the eighth grade, 80 percent of a group of boys viewed weightlifting as an activity for boys, whereas 53 percent of the girls saw it as appropriate for both genders (Meaney, Dornier, & Owens, 2002). It is unlikely that these boys in the eighth grade made conscious decisions to adopt stereotypical views of gender roles, and more likely that their perceptions reflected societal expectations of gender-appropriate behavior for males.

Aggression, Sport, and Gender

There are **gender differences** in the expression of **aggression in sport**. Female athletes are more likely to express aggression in socially acceptable ways and in ways that do not violate the rules of their sport. Socialization practices appear to legitimize aggressive behavior to a greater degree in males than females. For example, prior to the start of the basketball season, first year, varsity, female basketball players in high school considered aggression to be more acceptable than experienced female high school basketball players (Ryan, Williams, & Wimer, 1990). Among the aggressive acts that the inexperienced players were more likely to endorse were: verbal intimidation, shoving, knocking the wind out of an opponent so that she would have to leave the game for a few minutes, throwing elbows at opponents with the intention of causing a nosebleed and causing an opponent to leave the game, causing a knee injury and eliminating an opponent from play for an entire season, and inflicting permanent disability. Basketball players who considered these forms of aggression to be more legitimate prior to the start of the basketball season were actually more aggressive during the season.

As a result of actual experience in organized high school athletics, the beliefs of the first-year basketball players about the legitimacy of aggression changed. After the season, the first-year players rated aggression as no more acceptable than their experienced teammates. It has been theorized that without actual sport experience, females may assume that aggression and violence are a part of the experience of sport because of the prevalence of information and media coverage of men's athletics.

Unacceptable Aggression

On March 8, 2004, Todd Bertuzzi of the National Hockey League's (NHL) Vancouver Canucks punched the Colorado Avalanche's Steve Moore in the head from behind and slammed his head in the ice. With two broken vertebrae and a concussion, Moore ended up face-first in a pool of his own blood. The president-elect of the American College of Sports Medicine commented, "It's time to stop these muggings masquerading as sport" (Farber, 2004, p. 56). The NHL suspended Bertuzzi for the remainder of the season and the play-offs, and he forfeited at least $501,926.39 in salary. These penalties to Bertuzzi notwithstanding, the NHL may have a culture of fighting such that "the ultimate game for most players is a Gordie Howe hat trick: a goal, an assist and a fight" (Farber, 2004, p. 59).

The International Society of Sport Psychology has deemed that behavior that is violent and inflicts physical harm and acts that are aggressive and cause psychological injury are unacceptable (Tenenbaum, Stewart, Singer, & Duda, 1996). These forms of aggression bear no direct relationship to the competitive goals of sport, and they are committed with the intention of harming opponents. Athletes may legitimately attempt to dominate opponents and use aggression to realize competitive goals. Aggression that is legitimately channeled within the boundaries of fair play is described as assertive.

Gender and Exercise

Although exercise psychology is beyond the scope of this book, it should be noted that gender differences in the reasons for participation in exercise and sport have been identified. The importance of exercise as an outlet for competition and the demonstration of competence has been emphasized more by young males than by females and older males. The value of exercise for weight control and to enhance appearance is more important for women. There is a question about whether women value exercise as a means to facilitate social interaction to a greater degree than men, as independent research has produced conflicting results.

These gender differences are more pronounced among males that identify more strongly with traditional masculine roles and females that identify with traditional feminine roles. For example, Swedish college students who exercised for the experience of competition were more likely to be males who identified with traditional masculine motives. To a lesser extent, androgynous men and women exercised for the experience of competition (Koivula, 1999). Women and men who strongly endorsed traditional feminine motives said they exercised to enhance appearance.

Similar results have been reported for exercise and sport participation for boys and girls. For example, in the USA, girls emphasized friendship and fitness and boys considered achievement and status as important reasons for participation in sport and exercise (Gill, Gross, & Huddleston, 1983; Gould, Feltz, & Weiss, 1985). Australian boys also rated opportunities for competition and status as important reasons for engagement in sport and exercise, and girls were more interested in learning skills, improving health, and engaging in cooperative activities (Weinberg et al., 2000b).

Girls were also more likely to consider the benefits of physical fitness and playing on a team as reasons for sport participation. Gender differences for sport participation by adolescents between the ages of 13 and 18 appear consistent regardless of whether the adolescents reside in the USA, Australia, or New Zealand (Weinberg et al., 2000b). Adolescent boys were more likely than adolescent girls to say they played sports for the competition and status benefits and because it provided independence, social outlets, and means of releasing tension and energy. The female and male adolescents in all three countries played sports and exercised because they found the activities to be intrinsically rewarding or to provide their own benefits and rewards, and because of extrinsic or external rewards. Examples of the intrinsic rewards for sport and exercise participation were "to have fun" and "improve my skills" (Weinberg et al., 2000, p. 337). The most commonly identified extrinsic benefits were to stay in shape and gain status and recognition.

Intrinsic rewards are proximate or contiguous to the exercise activity and have been associated with the maintenance of exercise programs. The intrinsic reward of exercise enjoyment or fun is an important factor associated with the continuation or maintenance of exercise in African

Physique Enhancement and Competition

Michelle Lombardo is a swimsuit model for *Sports Illustrated* and an actress. She captained her high school volleyball team and played youth travel soccer (elite town team), fast-pitch softball (pitcher), and basketball. At 5 feet 10 inches and 135 pounds, she is anything but a waif-like fashion model. "I'm here to make them see all body types are beautiful. Believe me, I'm not one of those girls who can eat anything. I work for it" (Jacobs, 2005, E14). This work includes weekend soccer games and daily workouts on a treadmill.

American and Caucasian adolescent girls (Motl, Dishman, Saunders, Dowda, Felton, & Pate, 2001). Extrinsic rewards have been more closely related to the initiation of exercise programs. Extrinsic rewards, such as the improvement of appearance, accrue more distally or in the future (Bartlewski, Van Raalte, & Brewer, 1996; Diehl & Petrie, 1995).

Achievement Motivation and Gender

As explained in Chapter 2, Matina Horner (1973) pioneered the examination of gender differences in achievement motivation in the context of Atkinson's expectancy value formula. She maintained that there was a psychological barrier that interfered with the achievement of women, and referred to this as the **motive to avoid success** (MAS). The MAS refers to the belief that negative consequences will accompany success. Horner reasoned that traditional conceptions of femininity involved the suppression of aggressive and competitive impulses. Therefore success and competition would engender anxiety in women, as they would fear social disapproval and a "loss of femininity" (Horner, 1973, p. 223). She (1978) recognized that the tendency to avoid success in a given situation (T-S) was a function of a stable, internal characteristic (MAS), subjective estimates of the probability of success in the situation (Ps), and the negative incentive value for success (Ias):

$$T\text{-}S = MAS \times Ps \times Ias$$

Ias was greater for women in competitive situations, when their competitors were men, and when engaged in tasks considered masculine, such as mathematics.

The tendency to avoid success inhibits competitive and adaptive strivings and adversely affects performance; this tendency was far more frequent in college females than college males. Horner demonstrated that the performance on achievement tests of two thirds of male college students improved in competitive versus noncompetitive conditions, whereas improvements in performance occurred for only one third of female college students. For female students high in MAS, 75 percent achieved at a significantly higher level in the noncompetitive condition compared with 7 percent of the women low in MAS. Women high in MAS indicated that doing well was significantly more important to them in noncompetitive conditions, and doing well was rated as least important in competitive conditions with men. Statistical trends indicated that the motive to avoid success was more influential for college women high in ability and achievement motivation and who had a history of academic success.

Criticism of Horner's Fear of Success Construct

Much of Horner's innovative research was conducted approximately 35 years ago. Despite refinements (Fleming & Horner, 1992), her work came under a considerable amount of criticism due to her research methodology (Metzler & Conroy, 2004; Zuckerman & Wheeler, 1975) and because independent researchers did not replicate her findings. In groups of students in high school, college, and medical school, females did not show higher fear of success than males (Costanzo, Woody, & Slater, 1992; Mednick & Thomas, 1993; Piedmont, 1988). Likewise, college women did not record higher levels of fear of success as they performed motor activities (Conroy & Metzler, 2004).

Other studies have demonstrated that while women had higher scores than men on measures of fear of success, these measures did not predict grade point averages or ACT scores. Further, performance during competition for those high in T-S may be impaired for both sexes, and some adolescent boys are more affected by competition with a girl than with a boy (Graham & Weiner, 1996).

Regardless of whether women are uncomfortable demonstrating prowess in competition with men, women as a whole may be more uncomfortable demonstrating high levels of competence in the presence of men and women who have much less competence (Piedmont, 1988). This finding was demonstrated in a study in which female and male college students with high nonverbal ability completed half of a test of nonverbal ability alone and half with a male or female student of much lower ability. The performance of the women versus the men with high ability was suppressed when they were paired with a student of lower ability, regardless of the gender of the latter. Those that suppressed their performance when paired with the less capable student also had lower college grades, Scholastic Aptitude Test (SAT) scores, need for achievement, and aspirations for higher education. Social needs may be more influential in females such that they suppress their performance if they believe that success will cause discomfort in others or result in their being disliked (Costanzo et al., 1992).

Achievement Motivation and Sport

Expectancy value theories have been shown to be valid for evaluating motivation in sporting contexts, and gender differences have been considered. Males in high school and college were more likely than females to acknowledge an achievement orientation that consisted of a willingness to participate and strive for success in competitive sports (Gill, 1998a). These males said they had more interest in winning and avoiding losing than their female classmates, but the females were as interested as the males in achieving their own goals and in achievement across areas of life functioning. These males also reported more activity and experience with competitive sports.

Differences in achievement motivation between younger girls and boys in athletic contexts have also been demonstrated. Girls have been shown to be more receptive than boys to games with cooperative rules. Boys have been shown to focus more on winning at games. These results hold for Caucasian and Native American children. Native American children were more receptive to cooperative games, perhaps due to cultural influences (Duda, 1986; McNally & Orlick, 1975).

Gender differences in achievement motives are minimal among more accomplished athletes (McElroy & Willis, 1979). Accomplished female athletes have demonstrated no particular vulnerability to be uncomfortable with success, although male collegiate athletes have been shown to rate themselves as having less fear of success than female collegiate athletes and female and male nonathletes (Silva, 1982). Gender differences in achievement orientation were shown to be minimal for college athletes in Iowa and for international athletes and university athletes in Taiwan (Gill, 1998a). Involvement in athletics may foster this achievement orientation, as female college and international athletes scored higher on this achievement orientation factor than male nonathletes. Alternatively, women with higher achievement orientation may be drawn to athletics.

Are audiences uncomfortable with the success of female athletes? This question is reasonable if sport is considered to represent masculine activities and therefore inconsistent with the roles of women. If audiences were uncomfortable in this way, then the success of female athletes might be attributed to luck, cheating, and the lack of serious competition. Regardless of whether sports were seen to be more stereotypically masculine (e.g. handball) or feminine (e.g. figure skating), the success of female and male athletes was considered to be due to talent (Duda & Roberts, 1980).

Stress and Coping

Both female and male athletes use a range of **problem- and emotion-focused coping** strategies to handle stress. The similarities in coping responses of women and men are far greater than the differences, especially for elite athletes. Some gender differences in the coping strategies of sportspersons have been noted. Female athletes who competed at highly skilled to elite levels (Anshel, Porter, & Quek, 1998; Crocker & Graham, 1995), as well as adolescents (Kowalski & Crocker, 2001), were more likely than males to utilize emotion-focused coping by seeking out emotional support from others when their goals were thwarted. Among elite skiers with season-ending injuries, about half sought support from others, and the female skiers were twice as likely as the males to utilize this resource (Gould, Udry, Bridges, & Beck, 1997b). In response to slumps (periods of below-average performance), female elite runners more frequently utilized emotion-focused coping and males preferred problem-focused coping (Madden, Kirkby, & McDonald, 1989). The elite women responded with stronger emotion, such as anger, and accepted sympathy from others, whereas the men attempted more direct solutions to emerge from slumps such as altering their training regimen.

Mental Skills

Gender differences in the amount of cognitive anxiety or worry have been noticed. Female collegiate athletes acknowledged more cognitive anxiety or worry prior to competition, and especially 30 minutes prior to matches (Jones & Cale, 1989). Gender differences in the nature of cognitive anxiety have also been reported. Female collegiate athletes were shown to worry about reaching their personal goals and about whether they were sufficiently prepared for competition (Jones, Swain, & Cale, 1991). Males were more concerned with the strength of competition and the outcome of the competition. Findings that the self-confidence of female as compared to male athletes drops and the somatic anxiety (muscular tension, and elevated heart rate) increases prior to competition (Jones & Cale, 1989) have been less consistent (Jones et al., 1991).

Female and males do not differ in their capacity to interpret signs of cognitive and physiological anxiety as facilitative of their efforts to reach goals. For example, almost half of a sample of 91 competitive swimmers between the ages of 14 and 28 reported cognitive and physiological anxiety to be facilitative, and only 23 percent reported both kinds of anxiety as debilitative (Jones & Hanton, 1996). The swimmers who believed they would achieve their goals used anxiety as a cue to become more engaged and persistent in training and competition.

Negative self-talk interferes with optimal performance. The self-talk of female junior tennis players during competition was weighted toward self-critical and judgmental statements, especially during losing matches (Van Raalte, Brewer, Rivera, & Petitpas, 1994).

Goal Orientations

As discussed in Chapter 8, **goal orientations** refer to the manner by which progress is measured. With task orientations progress is measured in relation to one's baseline of prior performance. Both female and male athletes benefit from task orientations (Petherick & Weigand, 2002). For example, junior elite female gymnasts who trained with coaches who were seen to encourage task orientations demonstrated more enjoyment of their sport, more positive body images, and higher self-esteem (Duda, 2001). The 11-year-old gymnasts in this sample who trained with coaches that encouraged ego orientations were more likely to experience competitive stress. Ego orientations involve measuring performance in relation to external standards, and present an additional threat to female athletes, in that they may encourage body dysphoria or dissatisfaction, perfectionism, and eating disorders. Perfectionism among young, elite female gymnasts is an insidious consequence of coaching that emphasizes ego orientations, and this perfectionism contributes to disordered eating and preoccupation with food (Duda & Kim, 1997).

Sexual Harassment and Abuse

Female athletes are more likely to be coached by males and to experience sexual harassment and abuse from coaches and other sporting officials (Brackenridge, 2000). **Sexual harassment** consists of unwanted attention that is motivated by sexual interest. **Sexual abuse** consists of coerced sexual contact. Coerced sexual contact occurs not only with actual physical force, but also when someone such as a coach uses a position of authority to obtain sexual contact. Athletes are coerced when they believe that they risk alienating coaches and jeopardize their careers by resisting unwanted sexual contact. Sexual exploitation may occur at elite levels of competition (Weiss, Amorose, & Allen, 2000) or at beginning levels where coaches are volunteers and have minimal preparation and screening.

Sexual Harassment

The ethical code of the Association for the Advancement of Applied Sport Psychology (AASP; 1994) is based in large part on the Ethical Principles of the American Psychological Association (2002). Both ethical codes forbid multiple relationships with clients, students, and supervisees. For example, a psychologist would not supervise a student and have that student as a client. A psychologist would also avoid business or financial relationships with clients or students. Both ethical codes forbid sexual relations with students, supervisees, and clients over which the psychologist has authority. These multiple or dual relationships are likely to impair the judgment of psychologists, and most importantly are exploitative.

The subject of sexual relations between coaches and athletes has received attention in the popular press (Wahl, Wertheim, & Dohrmann, 2001). Public statements from governing bodies for coaches are inconsistent in their treatment of this topic, but such affairs are clearly in violation of ethical standards for psychologists. The WNBA (Women's National Basketball Association), WUSA (Women's United Soccer Association), NCAA, USA Track and Field, and USA Soccer organizations have no policies about this issue. USA Soccer does not prohibit coaches and players from dating and considers dating a personal activity. The USA Basketball organization has no written policy, but the federation stated that coaches and athletes are discouraged from dating.

In a survey of 266 Canadian elite athletes, 21.8 percent stated that they engaged in sexual intercourse with a coach or sports authority figure. The majority of the authority figures and coaches were male and 80 percent of the athletes who engaged in sexual intercourse were female. Coaches and tennis athletes spend large blocks of time together, and former player Pam Shriver opined "For every one [that becomes a romance], I'll bet there are sexual feelings in 99 percent of the other player–coach relationships that never surface" (Wahl et al., 2001, p. 68).

Regardless of whether the authority figure is male or female, the effects of such sexual contact on athletes and teams appear similar and detrimental. Coaches or other officials are in a position of authority and make myriad decisions that affect the careers of athletes such as playing time and roles on teams and in individual sports. Because of the power differential in these relationships, there is a question about whether a sexual relationship between an athlete and a coach or other authority figure in sport can be consensual. Team members may wonder if team selections, roles, and playing times were influenced by intimacies between coaches and players.

For example, the US women's volleyball team was described as on the edge of disintegration prior to the 1996 Olympics. Five months before the Olympics, team captain Tammy Liley broke off an affair with assistant coach Kent Miller. Team sources said that Miller became so distraught that he could not function effectively as a coach. The head coach suspended Miller and stripped Liley of her captaincy. These events altered team chemistry to such a degree that a player said, "After this happened, we were toast before we ever set foot on the floor" (Wahl et al., 2001, p. 70).

Women and Coaching

As mentioned earlier, prior to the passage of Title IX in 1972, approximately 90 percent of the coaches of women and girls were women. By 1990 this number was less than half, and dramatically less in collegiate sports such as swimming and diving, track, and soccer (Acosta & Carpenter, 1990; cited in Weiss, Barber, Ebbeck, & Sisley, 1991). With Title IX, the number of collegiate athletic teams for women increased markedly and there was a concordant need for more college coaches. Men filled many of the new coaching positions.

Male athletic directors reasoned that more men were hired as coaches because of a dearth of qualified female applicants, whereas female athletic administrators cited discriminatory hiring practices to be the cause of the declining number of female coaches. The number of women in the upper echelons of athletic administrations is limited, and women may not benefit from the "old boys' club" or assistance from acquaintances to secure coaching jobs (Acosta & Carpenter, 1985). That is, given that the majority of athletic directors are male, they may be more favorably acquainted with coaches of their gender.

Some athletes also believe that female coaches are less qualified than their male counterparts. Female high school athletes demonstrated **gender biases** when estimating the skill of female coaches and the likelihood that a coach would be successful, and when making hypothetical choices about playing for a female or male coach (Parkhouse & Williams, 1986; Williams & Parkhouse, 1988). These biases may have diminished more recently, at least with female swimmers between the ages of 10 and 19 (Medwechuk & Crossman, 1994), and female and male high school track and field athletes (Frankl & Babbitt, 1998). The young swimmers also demonstrated preferences for a same-sex coach, perhaps because of experience with competent female coaches.

Biases about the qualifications of collegiate female head coaches are

Pat Summitt: Most successful basketball coach in NCAA history, coach of six national championship teams, and member of the NCAA Basketball Hall of Fame (photo © AARON JOSEFCZYK/Reuters/Corbis).

unfounded. They are as likely as their male counterparts to have collegiate athletic playing experience, while male coaches are more likely to have experience as a high school athlete. Collegiate female head coaches are more likely to have a professional background in physical education. This professional background may provide a greater amount of training for coaching positions (Hasbrook, Hart, Mathes, & True, 1990). Female high school soccer coaches were shown to have more experience as soccer players than their male counterparts (Millard, 1996).

The decrease in the number of female coaches is due to not only to this influx of men, but also to women dropping out of the profession. Specific training and mentoring in coaching facilitate the entry and retention of women in the coaching profession (Sisley, Weiss, Barber, & Ebbeck, 1990). Even programs that provide limited training in the specifics of how to coach and manage practice, and that do not screen coaching mentors to insure their wholehearted cooperation (Weiss et al., 1991), are likely to markedly improve retention rates for women in coaching. Perhaps novice coaches can profit from instruction about the technical aspects of their sport, training in the management of overly involved and intrusive parents (see Chapter 20), and training in the management of schedules and practices (Sisley et al., 1990).

The ongoing development of **coaching competence** is an important motivator for female and male coaches. There are similarities in the ways by which female and male head coaches of high school girls' volleyball, basketball, softball, and soccer teams evaluate their competence (Barber, 1998). Both genders attend to improvements in their athletes, the emotional tone of their athletes, and their own coaching skills in evaluating their competence and performance. Female coaches may well judge their competence in teaching sport skills to be superior to the male coaches (Barber, 1998). Female coaches with extensive educational backgrounds in physical education are more likely to have more training in teaching sport skills. Both female and male coaches rate time demands as the most important reason for withdrawing from coaching.

If women are to remain in coaching, the **costs** as well as the **benefits of coaching** will be important considerations. For both current and former female high school coaches, the costs of coaching include: time demands, inadequate professional compensation, lack of support, stress, and low perceived competence. The benefits of coaching include: the success of their programs and the opportunity to experience and participate in athletics (Weiss & Stevens, 1993). These costs are balanced by benefits such as the success of the coaches' teams and the experience of athletic competition.

Coaching Interventions and Gender

The topic of effective coaching and leadership will be addressed in greater depth in Chapter 21. In brief summary, positive reinforcement, encouragement following mistakes, technical advice, and avoidance of negative feedback and criticism, have been identified as positive characteristics of coaches (Smith & Smoll, 1990; Smoll & Smith, 1989).

Some differences in the coaching interventions of female and male high school soccer coaches during games were noted. Males were more given to providing technical instruction and females provided more encouragement (Millard, 1996).

Does Gender Influence Reactions to Coaches?

Adult female and male Australian athletes showed similar preferences for coaching interventions (Sherman, Fuller, & Speed, 2000). These athletes consisted of female and male basketball players, female netball players, and male Australian Rules footballers. The coaching responses preferred by both females and males in descending order were positive feedback, training and instruction, democratic behavior, social support, and autocratic behavior. Autocratic behavior often consists of decision-making without input from team members (Chelladurai & Doherty, 1998).

Although this is not unequivocal (Black & Weiss, 1992), perhaps female adolescents and children respond somewhat differently to coaching interventions. For example, Allen and Howe (1998) reported that confidence was higher among female field hockey athletes between the ages of 14 to 18 who played for coaches who emphasized praise and technical information following skilled performance and who made fewer comments in the form of encouragement and corrective information after mistakes. However, these players on regional teams in Canada were more satisfied with their field hockey experience if they perceived coaches as providing praise and information following good performances as well as encouragement and corrective information following mistakes. Feelings of confidence and satisfaction with hockey experiences were influenced by the actual athletic skill of the athletes, and the more skilled players were more confident in and satisfied with their sport.

Collegiate female athletes in a variety of sports appear to respond more unfavorably to **autocratic coaching styles** than their male counterparts (Amorose & Horn, 2000). These women were negatively affected by autocratic behaviors such as punishing feedback and comments from coaches and when coaches ignored their successes and failures. Male athletes were also negatively affected by autocratic coaching styles, but less so than the women. Coaches who manifested aspects of democratic leadership such as praise and recognition after good performance and encouragement and informational feedback after failures enhanced the intrinsic motivation of their athletes. These democratic interventions supported athletes' beliefs in their efficacy and competence at their sport. Democratic coaching interventions also encouraged athletes to think of their athletic experience as being under their personal control. Beliefs in personal control, efficacy, and competence contribute to intrinsic interest in sport.

Women as Sport Psychologists

In the year 2000, 46 percent of the members of the AASP were women, and 43 percent of AASP certified consultants were women. Nevertheless, applied sport psychology has been described as a profession dominated by White, middle-class males (Roper, 2002). **Female sport psychologists** have not been seen to have equal opportunities for consultation with athletes, perhaps because male coaches or athletic administrators are likely to select male consultants (Roper, 2002).

Summary and Conclusions

The benefits of sport and exercise include increased muscle metabolism and strength, decreased body fat, increased maximum oxygen consumption, and improved wellbeing. It is therefore reasonable to encourage children, adolescents, and adults to participate in exercise and sport if they are medically capable. Historically, the participation of women in some forms of sport and exercise has been limited, discouraged, or prohibited. Efforts to exclude women from athletic participation have decreased more recently, as it has been recognized that impediments to their involvement have been due to social constructions rather than physiological limitations. The participation of women in collegiate athletics was enhanced dramatically in the USA with Title IX federal legislation in 1972. However, the representation of women in collegiate and other coaching and athletic administrative positions remains limited. It also appears that social factors continue to influence girls to underestimate their motor skills and to lose confidence and expectations for success in future activities that require these motor skills.

Gender roles that were construed to exclude the involvement of women in sport have also receded and support for the participation of girls and women in sport has increased with the passage of time. However, girls continue to judge their athletic ability more negatively than boys, and their doubts about athletic competence are likely to limit intrinsic interest and involvement in sport. Those women who play sports through their collegiate years show levels of intrinsic interest in sport that are comparable to their male counterparts. They also demonstrate gender-role orientations that are less traditionally feminine. Female athletes continue to have greater conflicts between body images that are conceptualized as ideal for women in general and for women in sport. This conflict is negligible for men, as mesomorphic or muscular physiques are prized aesthetically and athletically.

There are also gender differences in the motivation for exercise, and these differences are more pronounced for males and females that identify with traditional roles. For example, with masculine gender roles, men more commonly pursue exercise for the experience of competition. With traditional feminine gender roles, women exercise to enhance appearance.

The motive to avoid success (MAS) has been evaluated for over 30 years, and reliable evidence that women inhibit achievement in the presence of men is lacking. In athletic contexts, males acknowledged more interest in winning and avoiding losing than females, but these differences are minimal among accomplished athletes. Further, evidence that women suppress their athletic performance in the presence of males or less capable competitors is lacking. However, there was evidence that women were uncomfortable in demonstrating superior intellectual ability in the presence of less capable peers, irrespective of the peers' gender. Perhaps the women were more sensitive to the potential reactions of the peers and suppressed their performance if they suspected that their success would cause discomfort to others.

This interpersonal sensitivity has also been evidenced in the coping strategies of female athletes. They more frequently seek out emotional support from others.

Athletes of both genders are capable of interpreting signs of anxiety as facilitative, and when sportspersons are confident that they will reach their goals, anxiety is more likely to facilitate performance. Female sportspersons may be more vulnerable to disruptive cognitive anxiety prior to performances and to self-critical thoughts during competition. Sportspersons are more likely to adopt task orientations in environments or motivation climates that encourage and support these task orientations.

Parents and coaches make important contributions to the motivational climates of athletes. The conduct of coaches and other sporting officials with female athletes is especially important because of the greater likelihood that males will coach them. The ethical codes of the AASP and APA forbid sexual harassment and relationships between psychologists and clients, students, and supervisees. The governing bodies of other organizations are less decisive.

Training, mentoring, administrative, and interpersonal support are important factors for introducing and retaining women in coaching professions. Athletes respond more negatively to autocratic than to democratic coaching styles. Collegiate women athletes respond more negatively to autocratic coaching interventions than their male counterparts.

Key Terms

Gender

Anticompetitive movement

Reproductive fitness

Title IX

Compliance test

Old boys' network

Women and the Olympic Games

Women as sport psychologists

Traditional ideas of masculinity

Confidence in athletic aptitude

Mesomorphic

Gender roles

Bem Sex Role Inventory

Androgyny

Personality Attributes Questionnaire

Sport Orientation Questionnaire

Aggression, sport, and gender

Motive to avoid success

Achievement motivation and sport

Problem- and emotion-focused coping

Self-handicapping

Goal orientations

Sexual harassment

Women and coaching

Coaching competence

Costs and benefits of coaching

Autocratic coaching styles

Suggested Readings

Conroy, D. E., & Metzler, J. N. (2004). Patterns of self-talk associated with different forms of competitive anxiety. *Journal of Sport & Exercise Psychology*, 26, 69–89.

Gill, D. L. (2002). Gender and sport behavior. In T. S. Horn (Ed.), *Advances in sport psychology* (2nd ed.). Champaign, IL: Human Kinetics.

Oglesby, C. A., & Hill, K. L. (1993). Gender and sport. In R. N. Singer, M. Murphey, & L. K. Tennant (Eds.), *Handbook of research on sport psychology* (pp. 718–728). New York: Macmillan.

Pfister, G. (2001). Women and the Olympic Games: 1900–97. In B. L. Drinkwater (Ed.), *Women in sport* (pp. 3–19). Oxford: Blackwell Science.

Weiss, M. R., Barber, H., Ebbeck, V., & Sisley, B. L. (1991). Developing competence and confidence in novice female coaches: II. Perceptions of ability and affective experiences following a season-long coaching internship. *Journal of Sport & Exercise Psychology, 13,* 336–363.

Ethnic and Cultural Differences and Sport Psychology

19

In effect, 1970 [World Cup; championship of soccer] was the first major confrontation between Europe and South America that the world had had the opportunity to witness. When Czechoslovakia went one up in Brazil's opening game, David Coleman observed that "all we ever knew about them has come true"; he was referring to Brazil's sloppy defense, but the words are those of a man whose job it was to introduce one culture to another.

In the next eight minutes, everything else we knew about them came true too. They equalized with a direct free kick from Rivelino that dipped and spun and swerved in the thin Mexican air (had I ever seen a goal scored direct from a free kick before? I don't remember one), and they went 2–1 up when Pele took a long pass on his chest and volleyed it into the corner. They won 4–1 and we in 2W [in England], the small but significant center of the global village, were duly awed.

It wasn't just the quality of the football, though; it was the way they regarded ingenious and outrageous embellishment as though it were as functional and necessary as a corner kick

Ethnic and cultural differences and sport (photo © Jamie Wilson).

or a throw-in. The only comparison I had at my disposal then was with toy cars: although I had no interest in Dinky or Corgi or Matchbox, I loved Lady Penelope's pink Rolls-Royce and James Bond's Aston Martin, both equipped with elaborate devices such as ejector seats and hidden guns which lifted them out of the boring ordinary. Pele's attempt to score from inside his own half with a lob, the dummy he sold to the Peruvian* goalkeeper when he went one way round and ball went the other ... these were football's equivalent of the ejector seat, and made everything else look like so many Vauxhall Vivas. Even the Brazilian way of celebrating a goal – run four strides, jump, punch, run four strides, jump, punch – was alien and funny and enviable, all at the same time. (Hornby, 1992, p. 37)

As mentioned in Chapter 1, most of the information in this book is presented without reference to gender, ethnicity, culture, or socioeconomic status. This emphasis on universal human responses to competition and training notwithstanding, individual differences that are determined by ethnicity and culture have been identified. The study of these ethnic and cultural differences is in its rudimentary stages (Duda & Allison, 1990). A recent analysis of influential sport psychology journals demonstrated that the cultural background of study participants was identified in only 11.5 percent of the articles published between 1987 and 2000. Furthermore, cultural background was a substantial focus of study in only 1.5 percent of these research articles (Ram, Starek, & Johnson, 2004). It is likely that the study of culture and ethnicity will progress as psychologists attempt to refine their interventions with increasingly diverse and international athletes.

Ethnic and cultural differences may also exist between sport psychologists and clients. There is less cultural and ethnic diversity among sport psychologists than among the sportspersons with whom they are likely to consult. For example, in the USA sport psychologists are predominantly Caucasians (Gill, 1998b; Roper, 2002; Williams & Scherzer, 2003). Psychologists and sport psychologists are also ethically obliged to become educated and sensitive to cultural and ethnic concerns (as well as gender issues), and to recognize and avoid bias in their professional functioning (Association for the Advancement of Applied Sport Psychology, 1994; American Psychological Association, 2002). **Culture** and ethnicity are not synonymous. Cultures share attitudes, beliefs, values, norms for judging behavior, and often geographic regions and languages. Ethnic or racial backgrounds include African or Negroid, Asian/Pacific Island or Mongoloid, and European or Caucasoid. However, the division of people into distinct racial groups is controversial (Cavalli-Sforza & Cavalli-Sforza,

---

* In fact this occurred in Brazil's semifinal against Uruguay.

1995; Helms, Jernigan, & Maschler, 2005). These racial groups have been seen to differ phenotypically (in appearance), but geneticists emphasize the similarities between races as racial groups are genetically 99.9 percent alike (Smedley & Smedley, 2005).

Athletic Participation and Academic Engagement and Achievement

Given the representation of African American athletes in American sports such as the National Basketball Association (NBA) and National Football League (NFL), it might be assumed that higher percentages of African Americans are involved with sport at all levels. However, it is estimated that only 18 percent and nearly 10 percent of African American students participated in team and individual sports, respectively, by the 10th grade (Jordan, 1999); for Caucasian students the corresponding figures were 23 percent and 16 percent. The assumption of higher African American participation has validity in certain sports at elite levels. For example, among National Collegiate Athletic Association (NCAA) athletes, 68 percent of men's basketball players, 57 percent of football players, and 43 percent of women's basketball players were from ethnic minorities (National Collegiate Athletic Association, 1997). These percentages were higher than the corresponding percentage, 29 percent, of US citizens who were not of European descent.

Athletic participation among Native Americans has been limited by factors such as poverty, insufficient athletic equipment and facilities, and inadequate coaching and instruction (Coakley, 2001). Native Americans may also have concerns that athletic participation will result in their cultural alienation.

For African, European, and Hispanic American high school students, athletic participation led to **higher academic achievement** and grades, higher academic self-confidence, and better self-concepts. Participation

---

Hank Aaron and Vocational Advancement for African Americans

Until 2007, Hank Aaron held the Major League Baseball record for home runs (755). As an owner of a BMW dealership in Atlanta, he encouraged BMW to start the MetroSTEP program in 2004. This program provides 7-month, paid internships in automobile technician training for minority-group members. Graduates of this program are guaranteed jobs at BMW dealerships with starting salaries of almost $40,000 a year (Bluestein, 2004).

in sports and other extracurricular activities increases students' interest in school, facilitates positive relationships with coaches, teachers and administrators, and motivates athletes to achieve adequate grade point averages (GPAs) so as to maintain athletic eligibility (Jordan, 1999).

Life Satisfaction

Male African Americans on the verge of graduation from college demonstrated slightly less **life satisfaction** or wellbeing than their male Caucasian counterparts. This relationship held regardless of whether the students were Division I athletes and whether the athletes sustained significant injuries during their college careers (Perna, Ahlgren, & Zaichkowsky, 1999). Further, regardless of athletic participation, students without post-collegiate career plans had less wellbeing.

African American collegiate athletes are more likely to participate in "revenue-generating" sports such as football and basketball (Upthegrove, Roscigno, & Charles, 1999). Graduation rates for African American Division I NCAA male football and basketball players are increasing, but still lag behind the rates for Caucasians (National Collegiate Athletic Association, 2003). As of 2003, 44 percent of African American football players graduated six years after enrolling as freshmen in 1996. By comparison, 59 percent of Caucasian, 45 percent of Asian/Pacific Island, and 47 percent of Hispanic football players graduated in the same period. Considering men's basketball, 36 percent of African American males graduated and 53 percent of Caucasians graduated in this time interval. The graduation rates for women are considerably higher. For example, 58 percent of African American women and 69 percent of Caucasian women graduated from Division I basketball programs during this time period.

African American female collegiate athletes (Howard-Hamilton, 1993), and perhaps African American athletes in general, benefit from experiences with "career" mentors, especially when matched with former athletes or coaches. Educational and vocational advancement may also be facilitated by encouraging African American athletes to keep daily journals of their experiences on college campuses and to meet for monthly workshops to discuss career options. African American female athletes have been encouraged to engage in mock job interviews, seek out vocational internships, and serve as role models for high school athletes. African American athletes may invest sport with a high degree of importance because of its potential to provide professional advancement. Injured athletes are particularly in need of support from consultants, coaches, and mentors.

Motivational Orientation and Ethnicity

The **motivational orientations** of sportspersons of several ethnic groups and cultures differ. Mexican American and Navajo adolescents are more likely to focus on the amount of effort exerted and improvement in comparison to one's baseline of prior performance when evaluating successful performance. This focus is consistent with a task orientation to motivation. Task orientations were discussed in Chapter 8; to review briefly, they refer to evaluating performance in terms of improvement relative to prior performance, the amount of effort exerted, and the fulfillment of individual potential. Navajo and Mexican American adolescents also focus on their contribution to group or team success to a greater degree than American adolescents of European descent. European American adolescents more commonly focus on ego goals or judge success in relation to outperforming others. Evidence of task orientations among Mexican American adolescents contradicts the theory (Ryska, 2001) that a cultural ideal of *machismo* disposes Hispanic males to adopt particularly strong ego orientations in an effort to prove themselves superior to male counterparts. Machismo refers to an exaggerated sense of masculinity stressing attributes such as courage and aggressiveness.

Individual members of ethnic groups within the USA are not monolithic or identical in terms of acculturation (the adoption of values, attitudes, and behaviors consistent with mainstream US culture). Acculturation among Mexican Americans is typically measured on the basis of language use (English versus Spanish), use of media in English versus Spanish, and the ethnic identities of friends and associates (Marin, 1993).

Although it may be expected that Mexican American adolescents who are more acculturated would more strongly endorse ego goals, evidence of this is available only for females. Further, the goal orientations of Latino athletes, like their counterparts in other ethnic groups, are shaped by the experience of athletic participation (Duda, 1985). Motivational climates of athletic teams influence the goal orientations of ethnically diverse sportspersons.

Korean middle school athletes were shown to score higher in ego orientations and lower on task orientations and intrinsic interest in sport than their American counterparts (Kim, Williams, & Gill, 2003). These differences were significant but small, and the motivational climates for sport in the USA and Korea may be different. Admission to high schools is limited in Korea, and athletic excellence provides a route for winning admission. Korean middle school athletes therefore compete for these limited seats in high school.

Ethnicity and Coping Strategies

The strategies used by national level athletes in Korea to cope with the stress of competition overlapped with those of US Olympic wrestlers (Gould, Eklund, & Jackson, 1993) and US national champion figure skaters (Gould, Finch, & Jackson, 1993a). The coping strategy cited most frequently by the Korean athletes (97.2 percent) was mental training, including visualization, meditation, and a category defined as psyching-up that included positive self-talk (Park, 2000). The Korean athletes also cited somatic relaxation, including stretching and sleeping, focusing on training and strategies during competition, hobbies, and prayer, as coping strategies. Meditation techniques such as Zen, breath control, and contemplation are practiced more frequently in eastern countries such as Korea, Japan, India, and China.

Also consistent with the coping responses of Americans, Korean athletes engaged in forms of problem-focused, emotion-focused, and avoidance-focused coping. Additionally, Korean athletes may engage in a form of transcendent coping or give up their own efforts to control events in the face of adversity and turn their destiny over to the course of nature (Yoo, 2000). Both avoidance-focused and transcendent coping are described as indirect and passive ways of managing stress in a detached manner (Yoo & Park, 1998a, 1998b). Elite, as opposed to state and local level, Korean athletes were more likely to engage in transcendent coping, perhaps because the elite athletes practiced Zen meditation or Confucian philosophy (Yoo, 2001).

Attributions and Ethnicity

Navajo and Mexican American adolescents have been seen to be more likely to attribute athletic success to effort and failure to inadequate ability (Duda, 1986; Duda & Allison, 1982). European American adolescents have been seen to be more likely to attribute success to ability and failure to a lack of effort. Native American adolescent athletes may understand the causes of success and failure to be less internal and controllable because of cultural values that define success in terms of group and team performance (Morgan, Griffin, & Heyward, 1996).

Self-Talk and Culture

East Asian and European American students have been shown to differ in the proportion of negative to positive self-talk during a dart-throwing task (Peters & Williams, 2006). East Asian college students engaged in a higher proportion of negative self-talk. However, unlike their European American counterparts, poorer performances were not associated with higher proportions of negative self-talk among the East Asians. Perhaps negative self-talk reflects a fear of future failure that is detrimental to the performance of European Americans and those that emanate from individualistic cultures and beneficial to performance of East Asians and those from a collectivist cultural background. As mentioned above, the culture of European Americans has been said to emphasize individual accomplishments. East Asian culture has been seen to focus on the relationships of individuals within a group.

Stereotypes and Sport

Racial **stereotypes** in sport represent overgeneralized beliefs about the sources of athletic ability or aptitude. Among the problems associated with stereotypes is the fact that they potentially interfere with performance on evaluations (Steele, 1997). This interference occurs when individuals become concerned that their performance will confirm a negative stereotype. That is, individuals develop expectations that their performance is likely to be poor and therefore confirm the negative stereotype that their racial or ethnic group has less ability than others. Negative stereotypes are not confined to explanations of ethnic differences, as concern about confirming negative stereotypes have also been shown to have debilitating effects on the performance of women in areas of mathematical reasoning (Spencer, Steele, & Quinn, 1999).

Theories about ethnic differences in athletic aptitude have been published since the 1880s. Social scientists, medical doctors, biologists, and most notably, coaches have advanced these theories (Wiggins, 1997). Over the years, theory and lore have focused on differences between Black and White athletes, and have forwarded notions that the dominance of Black athletes in some sports was due to genetic advantage. For example, in 1971, Martin Kane, a senior editor of *Sports Illustrated*, wrote "An Assessment of 'Black is Best' " in which he gave voice to lay or unscientific theories of Social Darwinism. According to these theories, the Africans that survived the oppression of slavery in the USA possessed superior physical traits, and the less physically capable were casualties of slavery. Since only the more physically capable and superior survived to produce offspring, it was argued that superior athletic aptitude was genetically transmitted to ensuing generations.

Of course an alternative explanation for the survival of slavery would be that superior intelligence and character were necessary (Edwards,

Hostile Native American Images

The NCAA banned schools with mascots or nicknames deemed hostile or abusive to Native Americans from NCAA championship competitions effective February 1, 2006. Upon appeal, three schools were permitted to continue using nicknames of specific tribes because the affiliated tribes supported the use of these names: Central Michigan (Chippewas), Florida State (Seminoles), University of Utah (Utes; Davis, 2005; Lederman, 2005). The University of North Dakota was denied an appeal to continue using Fighting Sioux as a nickname after it was concluded that the majority of the Sioux tribes opposed its use. The NCAA also denied appeals to use nicknames that referred to Native Americans as a group, such as the Indians (seven colleges), Braves (two colleges), Redmen (Carthage College), and Savages (Southeastern Oklahoma State University). Specific names of tribes were seen to be owned by the tribe, whereas names that made general reference to Native Americans were not considered the property of tribes and were considered to present the potential for hostile and abusive imagery.

1973). Continuing within the context of Social Darwinism, Africans with superior intellect and character would survive slavery, produce offspring, and superior intellect would be genetically transmitted to subsequent generations.

The ascendancy of Black athletes in sport is perhaps best considered in historical context. Black athletes were denied access to sport venues in the USA for much of the 20th century, and the color barrier was only broken in Major League Baseball in 1947 when Jackie Robinson assumed the field for the Brooklyn Dodgers. Even after the introduction of athletes of African descent, an implicit quota called the 50 percent color line existed (Kahn, 1971). This quota limited the number of Blacks to four of the starting nine members of a baseball team. This color line was breached with the Brooklyn Dodgers in 1954. Jim Brown, a member of the National Football League (NFL) Hall of Fame, maintained that when he entered the NFL in 1957 there was a quota of no more than eight Blacks on a team roster (Brown & Delsohn, 1989). A mere 24 years after Black men began playing professional baseball, sportswriters pondered whether "Black is Best" (Kahn, 1971). In the 1984 Summer Olympic Games in Los Angeles, Blacks won 40 of the 49 medals awarded in track and field and 10 of 11 medals in boxing. Women and men of African descent hold world records in track and field events that require speed and explosive power, and have held these records for at least 40 years (Ashe, 1993). Africans have more recently dominated distance running events.

Consumer Discrimination against Black College Basketball Players

Economists have determined that attendance at Division I college basketball games increases with the addition of Caucasian players. In the 1988–89 season, Division I schools had an average of seven African American and six Caucasian players. The addition of one Caucasian player to this average ethnic distribution resulted in the realization of more than $100,000 in additional annual gate revenues (Brown & Jewell, 1994). This consumer discrimination among largely Caucasian audiences may motivate college basketball programs to discriminate against African Americans in awarding scholarships. Denying minority and low-income students college scholarships is particularly harmful, as they already have more limited employment opportunities.

More recently, consumer discrimination was seen to be minimal among NBA fans. However, there is price discrimination among the management of NBA teams, as African American players are paid significantly less than Caucasian players of equivalent ability (McCormick & Tollison, 2001).

Implicit in theories of athletic superiority of Africans is the understanding that other races such as Caucasians or Whites possess less athletic ability. Continuing with these genetic theories or stereotypes, skilled or superior athletic performance among Whites is understood to be more the result of effort, training, and mental preparation and practice rather than natural ability. These concepts have been popularized in films such as *White Men Can't Jump* and *Hoop Dreams*.

These stereotypes are widespread. College football coaches rated

Disrespecting Larry Bird by Guarding Him with White Players

"I really got irritated when they put a White guy on me ... Come on, you got a White guy coming out here to guard me, you got no chance ... As far as playing, I don't care who guarded me, red, yellow, black, I just didn't want a White guy guarding me. Because it's disrespect to my game" (Caesar, 2004).

These comments by NBA Hall of Fame player and president of the Indiana Pacers, Larry Bird, reflect his belief that "the greatest athletes in the world are African American." Bird, who is White, opined that basketball "is a Black man's game, and will be forever" (Caesar, 2004, p. C7).

African American athletes as having better speed, quickness, and achievement motivation, and Caucasians as more reliable and mentally facile (Williams & Youssef, 1975). African and European American college students endorsed similar beliefs (Sailes, 1993). The effects of expectations about athletic ability and race were also illustrated in a study in which White adults listened to the broadcast of a basketball game. Half of the listeners were informed that a very successful player was Black and the other half were led to believe that the player was White. Despite the fact that all the listeners heard the same broadcast, those that thought the player was White attributed success to "court smarts" and "hustle" rather than natural athletic ability. When the player was thought to be Black, success was attributed to natural ability and less to court smarts and hustle (Stone, Perry, & Darley, 1997). Moreover, the player was considered better when thought to be Black.

Negative Stereotypes and Performance

Negative stereotypes have been shown to affect the athletic performance of African Americans. The accuracy of African American college students at putting golf balls decreased significantly when they were prompted to think that putting measured their sports intelligence or even when they were required to indicate their race prior to putting (Stone, Lynch, Sjomeling, & Darley, 1999). Instructions that putting was a measure of natural athletic ability had no effect on putting accuracy. Just the opposite effects were found for White college students when given instructions that putting measured sports intelligence, natural athletic ability, or when just required to indicate race. White college students were shown to hold negative stereotypes about their athletic ability, and this belief diminished their putting accuracy.

Stereotypes about athletic and other abilities only present a threat when ability represents an area that is important to one's self-worth or self-esteem. In the case of the White college students, instructions that putting accuracy was a measure of natural athletic ability impaired the performance of only those whose self-worth was determined partially from their athletic achievement.

Stereotypes?

Despite being drafted in the third round, Bill Romanowski experienced considerable success in the National Football League (NFL). In his 16 years as a linebacker, he played for two Super Bowl Championship teams in San Francisco and two with the Denver Broncos. His effort for a fifth Super Bowl win fell short in 2003 as his Oakland Raiders team lost in the Super Bowl. His commitment to physical training was equaled perhaps only by Jerry Rice, a future Hall of Fame receiver and arguably the best ever at his position. Off-season training was shown to include 3 hours on a track refining sprint mechanics, 30 minutes of swimming, and three hours of weight training (Murphy, 1998).

Efforts to boost performance included more than physical training. Romanowski's regimen of nutritional supplements prompted teammates to nickname him Rx (shorthand for prescription; Yaeger, 2000). On August 9, 2000 a Colorado grand jury handed down a felony indictment charging Romanowski with using family and friends to acquire phentermine, a diet drug. Used in sufficient doses, the effects of phentermine mimic amphetamines. Family and friends acquired upward of 500 phentermine pills, and ephedrine was also delivered to Romanowski's Colorado home. No one denied that the drugs were for Romanowski. He was acquitted of these charges. In November 2003, the NFL notified Romanowski that he tested positive for the steroid THG or tetrahydrogestrinone, and in 2005 he acknowledged that he stayed one step ahead of the NFL drug policy by taking supplements that were not yet banned (Associated Press, 2005, May 18).

Stimulants of this sort mask the experience of fatigue and pain and increase alertness and aggressiveness. Whether stimulant use was related to his fierce demeanor in games is a matter for speculation. Extracurricular aggression in games has included spitting in the face of wide receiver J. J. Stokes, repeatedly kicking running back Larry Centers in the helmet, breaking the jaw of quarterback Kerry Collins with a helmet-to-helmet hit in a preseason game, and tearing the helmet off teammate Marcus Williams and punching him in the face so as to break the left eye socket (Associated Press, 2005, March 23). Romanowski was ordered to pay $340,000 for damages that ended the career of Williams.

A Caucasian teammate maintained that Romanowski reasoned that stimulant use was necessary for him to compete on a level playing field with African American players: "They're faster and stronger, and we have to take advantage of this. It is the only way we can compete with the Black guys" (Yaeger, 2000, p. 28). Romanowski's lawyer denied that his client said anything about Black players. The results of a survey (NCAA Research Staff, 2001) demonstrated similar levels of use of ergogenic substances such as anabolic-androgenic steroids among Caucasian (1.3 percent) and African American (1.6 percent) athletes. Ergogenic substances (see Chapter 15) are taken to enhance performance, and many of these substances, such as amphetamines, violate rules for athletic competition.

Negative stereotypes provoke self-doubts or worries that one's performance will confirm a negative stereotype. This worry represents a form of cognitive interference. As discussed in Chapters 4 and 10, cognitive interference disrupts attention to the tasks necessary for optimal performance.

Coaches' Responses and Ethnic Differences

Do **coaches** demonstrate biases in responding to **athletes of different ethnic groups**? This question has been addressed, but not answered convincingly. For example, the coaching interventions of college coaches of female and male basketball players were studied (Solomon et al., 1996). The gender of the coaches was not specified, and the responses of female and male basketball players were pooled. Coaches provided less praise and more instruction to players of African versus European descent. Technical instruction consists of advice about how to improve action and encouragement involves comments that the athlete can be successful. Whether this difference is due to a stereotype about ethnicity is a matter for speculation. The finding that coaches provided African American players with more technical instruction would appear inconsistent with the stereotype that the skilled performance of athletes of African descent is due to natural ability.

An alternative explanation is that the differences in coaching interventions were stimulated by actual differences in basketball abilities. Coaches provided more instruction to the basketball players whom they rated as having the highest ability. Of the eight players rated with the highest ability, seven were African American (Solomon et al., 1996). Less instruction and praise was given to the less talented players, as coaches rationed disproportionate amounts of time to more talented athletes.

African American Football Players and Reactions to Coaches

The **responses of African American football players to coaches** are not always apparent, as demonstrated at a Division I program in the southwestern USA. The head coach and nine assistant coaches were White, and one assistant coach was African American. The coaches were perceived as insensitive to the individual and socio-cultural interests of the African American athletes, and also as not objectively assessing their skill. The athletes reported a lack of communication and trust. They did not think that their coaches understood their background, family, and culture. There was a suspicion of unfair treatment on the basis of race. The

African American coach was seen as an extension of the White coaching staff.

The African American football players did not respond well to harsh criticism, and wanted coaches to earn their respect. These football players said that a greater portion of their self-esteem was drawn from their athletic performance, and harsh criticism and limited playing time were therefore more threatening to their self-esteem and confidence. These athletes were embarrassed and decreased rather than increased subsequent efforts in response to harsh criticism. As explained by one player, "When the coach yells at me, that's it. I feel no motivation; I don't want to have anything to do with it" (Anshel, 1990, p. 241).

Some believed that personal accomplishments were more important than team accomplishments. They preferred pregame preparation strategies that were subdued and individualized as opposed to their coach's pregame talks and coaching instructions (Anshel, 1990). Compared to White players, African American footballers considered coaches too authoritarian and untrustworthy, and were unhappier if their team won but they played poorly (Anshel & Sailes, 1990).

The mental skills employed by the African American and White players differed. The African American footballers reported that they ignored or minimized the importance of scouting reports, coaching instructions, and pregame talks. They did not want to get caught up in these "head games," and prepared by focusing on their own internal responses rather than the coach's instructions. They believed that coaches underestimated their achievement motivation because they responded to the demands of competition in a less intense and emotionally demonstrative way.

An independent group of African American football players rated mental preparation as less significant in determining the outcome of competition. They emphasized the importance of physical preparation, and showed fewer tendencies to engage in introspection (Nation & LeUnes, 1983). They felt more confident of performing well even when depressed, were less likely to brood over past poor performances, and attributed athletic outcomes to physical rather than psychological factors.

It is unlikely that all or perhaps most of athletes who are members of ethnic minorities are equally uncomfortable and suspicious of White coaches. However, sport psychologists and professional psychologists are ethically obliged to be knowledgeable and sensitive to differences on the bases of ethnicity, culture, gender, physical disabilities, sexual orientation and socioeconomic differences, and to avoid bias on the basis of any of these factors (American Psychological Association [APA], 2002; Association for the Advancement of Applied Sport Psychology [AASP], 1994).

> Ethics and Differences
>
> The ethical code of the AASP (1994) is based in large part on the Ethical Principles of the APA (2002). Both codes of ethics emphasize competence or the limitation of practice to areas in which the psychologist has training, education, or experience.
>
> The ethical codes mandate that psychologists are aware of cultural, individual, and role differences, including those due to gender, ethnicity, race, religion, sexual orientation, language, disability, and socioeconomic status.

Being knowledgeable about and open to the discussion of racial and cultural differences has been seen as important in developing effective working alliances between sport psychologists and clients (Cogan & Petrie, 1996; Petrie, 1998).

African American Athletes and Responses to Sport Psychologists

As mentioned in Chapter 1, African American (and male Division I inter-collegiate) athletes were particularly uncomfortable with the prospect of accessing help from sport psychologists, as they feared being stigmatized (Martin, Wrisberg, Beitel, & Lounsbury, 1997). The stigma consists of being cast or viewed as someone with mental disorders or problems. These athletes estimated that coaches and teammates would think less of them and perhaps harass them if they received the services of a sport psychologist. The African American athletes indicated that they would be more comfortable consulting a sport psychologist of their own race, and African Americans are also more mistrustful of Caucasian counselors (Watkins, Terrell, Miller, & Terrell, 1989). Hispanics, Asian Americans, and Native Americans also tend to access professional counseling to a lesser degree than Caucasian Americans (Kontos & Breland-Noble, 2002).

Becoming Knowledgeable about Ethnic Differences

This issue of becoming knowledgeable about ethnic differences is not straightforward because the scientific basis for this literature is often limited, and therefore students from different cultures are often not certain if the information is accurate, is accurate for subsets of cultural communities, or reinforces stereotypes. For example, in contrast to Anshel's (1990) findings that African American athletes approached competition with less demonstration of emotion, Lee and Rotella (1991) argued that "black expressiveness," "soul," and "core black experience" are characterized by a high degree of emotion expression and a merging of thought, emotion, and movement. Adding to this distinction of emotional expressiveness is the contention that African American athletes have not only the goal of winning, but also the goal of stamping performances with elements of their own individual stylistic flair (Kochman, 1981). Coaches also rated African American athletes higher than Caucasians on exhibitionism and impulsivity, and lower on orderliness, understanding, and abasement (Chu, 1982).

Perhaps both stoicism and emotional expressiveness are integrated among African American male athletes in a "cool pose" (Majors, 1998). The cool pose was seen as a response by African American males to their experience of less socioeconomic status than Caucasians. With the demonstration of both unflappability and expressive styles of demeanor, gestures, and speech, the cool pose was seen to imply strength, uniqueness, and masculinity.

There is also some empirical support for an interest in expression of individual flair in performances among African American high school track athletes, and it does not appear to be in conflict with adaptive motives for achievement (Gano-Overway & Duda, 1999). However, this interest in expressing individual flair is only slightly higher for African American than for European American track athletes, and this interest in stylistic expression was likewise not in conflict with adaptive goals among the European Americans.

The culture of European Americans has also been seen to be consonant with independence, efforts to be unique and distinct from others, and the demonstration of success in comparison to others. Cultural differences between European American and Native Pacific Islanders in Hawaii and European Americans from the mainland of the USA have also been considered. Hawaiians, regardless of ethnic heritage, have been considered to share aspects of culture. The Hawaiian culture was considered to emphasize interdependence, affiliation with others, and harmony

Detroit, Goodyear Tires, and Braids

Richard Hamilton was a member of the 2004 NBA champions Detroit Pistons. Given his success and the fact that Detroit is the home of US automakers, Goodyear Tire & Rubber Company paid Hamilton, an African American, to braid his hair to match the tread of its Assurance Triple/Tred tire (Bloomberg News, 2005).

The shared culture of sport.

within one's reference group (Hayashi, 1996). However, the reasons for recreational weightlifting were much the same among Hawaiian and mainland European American males. They all demonstrated interest in maintaining interpersonal bonds with other weightlifters. They lifted for a variety of goals such as demonstrating improvement in relation to their own baseline of fitness and to look better than others. The Hawaiians were more humble and shunned showing off or "acting."

Perhaps this study also illustrates how shared activities bring together people with similar interests, experiences, and goals, regardless of their ethnic and cultural backgrounds. Alternatively, the common psychological characteristics of these weightlifters may have been shaped by the shared experience of weightlifting. They were approximately 27 years of age, and the average number of years of weightlifting was in excess of 15.

Multicultural Training in Sport Psychology

Multicultural training consists of formal learning experiences for graduate students or professionals in sport psychology or counseling. The goal of this training is to prepare students for more effective counseling and consulting services to clients of different ethnic and cultural groups. Multicultural training may also involve instruction and experience in providing counseling services to lesbian/gay/bisexual and disabled clients.

As mentioned above, it is important that stereotypes are not

> ## Bad Multicultural Training
>
> As the public relations director for the NFL's San Francisco 49ers, Kirk Reynolds produced a video to coach players about how to handle media questions in diverse San Francisco. In the video, Reynolds impersonated San Francisco Mayor Gavin Newsom and officiated at a topless lesbian wedding, and a 49ers trainer traveled to Chinatown to make ethnic slurs about Chinese people. Team owner John York fired Reynolds, calling the video offensive and inexcusable. York stated: "Ostensibly, the video was created to raise player awareness about how to deal with the media and to demonstrate by example how poor conduct can unintentionally make news. Unfortunately, this video is an example in itself" (Associated Press, 2005, June 2).

reinforced in this training. Perhaps one way of accomplishing this is with a formal curriculum in graduate school with textbooks, classroom discussion, and supervised applied experience (Martens, Mobley, & Zizzi, 2000). This curriculum may also involve exercises designed to augment the sensitivity of students to different cultural viewpoints. For example, Caucasian trainees may be asked to attend meetings of African American or Arab American groups.

Practical Advice

Are the methods of sport psychologists dominated by "White middle-class approaches to thinking" (Lee & Rotella, 1991, p. 365), which depend on logical analysis and the isolation of thought and emotion? Do different cultural and racial groups view these methods with suspicion and concern that they will "tie them up in knots" (Lee & Rotella, 1991, p. 365)? Perhaps the best way of answering these questions is to ask the athletes and determine whether the athletes utilize the suggestions of consultants.

To avoid stereotyping, it is important to remember that any of the differences described above pertain only for ethnic or cultural groups as a whole, and not necessarily for the individual members of those groups (Andersen, 1993). For example, while some evidence may exist that European American football players rated mental skills as more important than their African American counterparts, it would be misleading to consider athletes of European descent to be generally interested and conscientious in the practice of mental skills (Shambrook & Bull, 1999).

Regardless of racial, cultural, and gender differences, successful consultations depend on the development of effective working alliances. Such alliances are more likely when an athlete trusts and believes that the consultant's interest is in helping the athlete reach her or his potential. Trust is fostered by efforts to learn about and understand the whole person who is also an athlete, and this includes differences due to culture and gender. There may be more impediments to trust in relationships between White consultants and African American athletes, as the latter may be socialized to expect racism and bias (Butryn, 2002; Peters, 1981). Caucasian consultants are advised to be sensitive to their own biases, such as beliefs that athletes of African descent achieve eminence through natural ability in place of mental skills and effort, and that their own "Whiteness" has no effect on athletes of other ethnic groups (Butryn, 2002; Cogan & Petrie, 2002). Sport psychologists have been encouraged to compare their world-views (understanding of the world) to the worldviews of ethnically diverse athletes (Kontos & Breland-Noble, 2002; Sue & Sue, 1999).

Ethnic and cultural concerns should not obscure the presenting problem or the reason the athlete consulted the sport psychologist (Kontos & Breland-Noble, 2002), but should be considered in context with the presenting problem.

Finally, sport psychologists may advocate within institutions when racism is identified (Cogan & Petrie, 2002). Examples of this advocacy include providing diversity training with coaches and management and working to end discrimination in recruitment and hiring.

Summary and Conclusions

The study of ethnic differences in sport psychology is in its nascent stages. As this study progresses, the responses of sportspersons may be shown to be increasingly similar or dissimilar across ethnic and cultural groups.

The beneficial effects of sport are similar for African American, European American, and Hispanic American high school students. High school athletes realized higher academic achievement and academic self-confidence, and better self-concepts. African American and European American collegiate athletes also demonstrated comparable life satisfaction as they prepared for graduation, and wellbeing was lower for those without plans for careers after college.

Differences in motivational orientations have been noted for Navajo, Mexican, and European American adolescent sportspersons. The Navajo and Mexican adolescents were more likely to acknowledge task orientations. However, they also attributed failure to a lack of ability and success to effort more frequently than their European counterparts. Task orientations are adaptive in sustaining effort as progress is measured in relation to the individual's baseline of prior performance. The attribution of failure to internal, global, and uncontrollable factors such as a lack of talent does not promote persistent effort in response to failure. More recent research indicated that Mexican American males were more likely to endorse ego goals or orientations.

There is little disagreement about the detrimental effects of negative stereotypes on performance in both athletic and academic venues. African Americans and European Americans, as well as women, have been negatively affected by stereotypes. Stereotypes appear to interfere with performance when individuals think that they will perform ineptly and confirm the negative stereotypes. These thought processes resemble cognitive interference, a topic discussed in Chapter 10.

The population of athletes is far more diverse than the population of sport psychologists, at least in the USA. Athletes may be more comfortable consulting with a psychologist of their own race, and sensitivity to these concerns and historical and cultural differences is warranted on the part of Caucasian psychologists. Trust is an essential element of the working alliances between psychologists and clients regardless of ethnicity, culture, gender, and socioeconomic status.

Key Terms

Culture	Coaches and ethnic differences
Higher academic achievement	African American football players and reactions to coaches
Life satisfaction	
Motivational orientation	African American athletes and sport psychologists
stereotypes	Multicultural training

Suggested Reading

Cogan, K. D., & Petrie, T. A. (2002). Diversity in sport. In J. L. Van Raalte & B. W. Brewer (Eds.), *Exploring exercise and sport psychology* (2nd ed., pp. 417–436). Washington, DC: American Psychological Association.

Martens, M. P., Mobley, M., & Zizzi, S. J. (2000). Multicultural training in applied sport psychology. *The Sport Psychologist, 14*, 81–97.

Morgan, L. K., Griffin, J., & Heyward, V. H. (1996). Ethnicity, gender, and experience effects on attributional dimensions. *The Sport Psychologist, 10*, 4–16.

Solomon, G. B., Wiegardt, P. A., Wayda, V. K., Yusuf, F. R., Kosmitzki, C., Williams, J., & Stevens, C. E. (1996). Expectancies and ethnicity: The self-fulfilling prophecy in college basketball. *Journal of Sport & Exercise Psychology, 18*, 83–88.

Smedley, A., & Smedley, B. D. (2005). Race as biology is fiction, racism as a social problem is real: Anthropological and historical perspectives on the social construction of race. *American Psychologist, 60,* 16–26.

Stone, J., Lynch, C. I., Sjomeling, M., & Darley, J. M. (1999). Stereotype threat effects on Black and White athletic performance. *Journal of Personality and Social Psychology, 77,* 1213–1227.

Youth and Sport 20

Ridgeway Rovers was a great time for all of us, not just the players. Our families got involved, whether it was washing uniforms, driving us about, coming on trips or raising funds. That team was together for six years, which meant our families were, too. And you can't spend that amount of time together without becoming pretty close. I remember Micah Hyde's dad, Ken, used to have dreadlocks: him and my dad – short back and sides – would be standing on the touchline together on a Sunday for the Ridgeway game. The parents used to organize dinners and Friday night dances to help raise money to pay for the team. Even though it was Dad who took us for training, my mum probably put in almost as many hours on me and my soccer, despite her job as a hairdresser. She was the only one of the mums who

Youth and sport (photo © photobank.ch).

drove, so if there was a minibus run she always ended up with the job. When Dad was out working, Mum would be the one who got me to where I needed to be, when I needed to be there, with the right stuff ready in the right bag. (Beckham & Watt, 2003, p. 27)

Sport often serves important functions in the lives of children, families, and coaches. Many of the topics reviewed in this book have applications with children and adolescents. Furthermore, the etiologies of the factors that facilitate and inhibit performance were shown to often date to childhood. In this chapter, topics specific to sport participation by youth, or children and adolescents, will be examined. These topics include: the goals of youth sport, factors that promote and inhibit sport participation, stress associated with youth athletics, and coaching and leadership with youth.

Athletic participation is beneficial because it affords children and adolescents with opportunities for physical, psychological, social, and educational growth (Smoll, 1998; Smoll & Cumming, 2006). It may be surprising to realize that athletic participation prior to age 12 was not always considered to be beneficial in the USA. Little League baseball was inaugurated in Williamsport, PA in 1939, and with its success, it was recognized that sport was not overly strenuous for boys who were 12 years of age and younger. Little League is now an international organization with at least 2.5 million participants (Franklin, 1989), and softball programs for girls enroll approximately 400,000 players.

By the 1950s, it was recognized that physical activity programs in the USA were not sufficiently strenuous. American children were shown to be physically unfit in comparison to their European counterparts. In 1955 and during the Eisenhower administration, the President's Council on Youth Fitness was established to promote youth fitness (Kraus & Hirschland, 1954).

Today, many young people play sports and engage in physical activity. Estimates are that 23 million youth in the USA between the ages of five and 16 participate in sports after school and another 6.5 million play sports that are sponsored by their schools (Participation Survey, 1999–2000). The participation of females has increased markedly in the past 30 years, as in 1972–1973, 17.8 percent of young sportspersons were females and in 1999–2000, this figure increased to 40 percent. These youth engage in traditional sports such as baseball, basketball, and swimming, as well as more regional sports such as rodeo and cross-country skiing (Ewing, Seefeldt, & Brown, 1996).

Goals of Youth Sports

A fundamental **goal of youth sport** is to provide an *education experience* for the development of desirable psychological and physical qualities (Smoll, 1998; Smoll & Cumming, 2006). These characteristics are useful not only in childhood and while engaged in sport. Some of these attributes are physical, such as improved fitness and athletic competence. Others are psychological, and these include leadership skills, discipline, respect for authority, and achievement motivation. Sport provides venues for learning social skills, making friends, and spending time with family members. Young people sometimes seek to experience the excitement of sport, and the challenge of competition (Gould & Petlichkoff, 1988). Perhaps the most important reason for youth sport is to have fun. These coaching objectives square with the reasons that youngsters play sports. The top four reasons that young athletes engage in organized athletics are to have fun, to improve athletic skill, to socialize with friends, and to succeed or win (Smith & Smoll, 2002).

In addition to this fundamental goal of youth sport, three additional goals have been recognized (Siedentop, 2002). These are the **public health goal**, the **elite-development goal**, and the goal of **preserving and protecting the sport practices**. Public health is enhanced when youth and adults exercise and play sports, and the practice of vigorous activities serves to prevent health problems. When the most talented and interested young athletes are encouraged to reach their athletic potential, elite-development goals are served. Varsity sport programs in US high schools and colleges pursue elite-development goals in that a select few make prestigious teams such as basketball teams.

Youth sport provides educational and recreational experiences and is differentiated from **professional sport**. The goal of the latter is to entertain and to produce income. Winning is fundamental to professional sport because it delivers an audience and this income. Winning is not the primary goal of youth sport, although success may be conceptualized as striving to win and putting forth maximum effort. The most important product of youth sport is the quality of the experience provided for the participants (Hanlon, 1994). Effective coaching and parental involvement begins with an understanding of the purpose of youth sport and its differentiation from professional sport.

Sport and Peer Relationships

A fundamental goal of youth sport is to encourage the development of social skills and friendships, and children who are competent at sport are more popular with peers. For example, boys in grades four through six rated being good at sports as most important in determining popularity among peers. The boys rated achieving good grades as the next highest determinant of **popularity**. Girls in these grades rated having good grades followed by good sport achievement as most influential in determining popularity (Buchanan, Blankenbaker, & Cotton, 1976). The finding that boys identified sport competence as most important in determining popularity was replicated with boys between the ages of eight and 13 (Chase & Dummer, 1992). Physical attractiveness or good looks and good grades followed skill in sport as the next most important factors. Girls in the same age group rated being pretty as most important, and sport and academic achievement followed good looks in their estimates of the sources of popularity with peers.

Friendships are often forged in the course of athletic participation. Female and male children and adolescents between the ages of eight and 16, who were current or former participants in a university summer sports program, identified 12 dimensions of the relationship with their best friend in sports (Weiss, Smith, & Theeboom, 1996). Almost all of these young sportspersons rated companionship or spending time together as an important quality of this friendship. The friendship boosted the self-esteem of most of the youngsters. Friends helped each other with sport skills and schoolwork, and offered advice. The friends were often prosocial in that they tried to be nice and to avoid being unkind to one another. Friendships had aspects of intimacy in that friends trusted each other with their thoughts and feelings. Best friends were loyal to one another, and like intimacy, loyalty indicates a deep emotional bond. Common interests, such as sports, were aspects of many of the friendships of these sports-persons. Finally, friends were esteemed for attractive psychological and physical qualities, because they provided emotional support, and because disagreements could be resolved with the best friend.

Adolescent soccer players who rated themselves as having positive friendship qualities and peer acceptance also rated themselves as higher on leadership qualities. Coaches rated the most skilled soccer players as having the most leadership ability (Glenn & Horn, 1993; Moran & Weiss, 2006).

Encouraging Children to Participate in Sports

Children come to value athletic participation and to develop confidence in their capacity to function well or adequately as sportspersons as a result of a number of influences. Parents are an important source of encouragement when they communicate their beliefs in the value of athletic participation and their expectations that their children will be competent sportspersons. Parents who enjoy physical activity are more likely to encourage their children to participate in sport, and to provide opportunities for this participation. These encouraged children are more likely to develop confidence in their athletic aptitude. Boys are more likely to receive this encouragement from parents and to develop greater confidence in their athletic aptitude (Brustad, 1993). Parental support buffers stress related to athletic performance (VanYperen, 1995).

The roles of parents in supporting athletic participation may differ at various stages in the athletic development of their children. For example, among elite junior Canadian female and male athletes in rowing and tennis, parents were responsible for getting their children involved with and encouraging the enjoyment of sport during the *sampling* years or prior to adolescence (Cote, 1999). A sampling of extracurricular activities and sports has been encouraged during these years (Carlson, 1988, 1997). Parents of future elite athletes may notice special gifts or natural talents in their children and especially encourage the development of these talents.

Fun and excitement remain important reasons for athletic participation among elite athletes during the *specialization* years or between the ages of 13 and 15 (younger for some sports such as gymnastics; Cote, 1999). However, elite athletes often increasingly focus on one or two sports and make increasing commitments to practice during these years. Parents devote more of their time and financial resources to support the increasing commitment of their children to sport, and mothers sacrifice engaging in competing social activities (Wolfenden & Holt, 2005). Fathers of elite adolescent male soccer players were also important sources of informational support (Holt & Dunn, 2004). Many of these fathers were experienced footballers and were capable of providing their sons with technical advice about soccer.

Athletes who achieve elite status may enter the *investment* years at approximately age 15. This period is characterized by intense commitments to practice and the development of expertise in one sport. This may also be a time of investment for parents and other family members as the adolescent athlete's training and competition requirements may dominate the schedule of the entire family. Parents may need to ration their attention to avoid creating jealousy among siblings.

Mental Skills Training with Children

The development of mental skills promotes the personal development of children and enhances motivation to engage in sport and physical activity across the life span (Weiss, 1991). The range of mental skills was discussed in Chapters 3, 4, and 5, and sport psychologists in Canada, Sweden, and the USA have taught many of these skills to children to help them function more effectively and with less stress and anxiety (Orlick & McCaffrey, 1991). The mental skills are adapted to appeal to children, and are simplified and described in terms that children are likely to understand. As is the case with adults, mental skills must be practiced regularly if they are to be reliable, and their practice is more likely if they are incorporated into practice schedules. The ongoing integration of mental skill and physical skill development is more certain if adults, such as assistant coaches, assume the responsibility of continuously reminding youthful athletes to engage in the practice of mental skills. This training is likely to be more successful if the parents of youthful sportspersons understand and support the procedures, and if they are in positions to prevent or reduce sources of stress in the lives of their children.

An example of a mental skill that was adapted for children is the **spaghetti toes** procedure (Orlick, 1992). This technique is a derivative of Progressive Muscle Relaxation (PMR), a technique described in Chapter 6. To illustrate the concept of tension, children are shown pieces of uncooked and stiff spaghetti. The concept of relaxation is next illustrated with cooked and soft spaghetti. The children are then instructed to wiggle the toes on either foot and to make the toes soft and sleepy and similar to cooked spaghetti lying on a plate. The wiggling is comparable to instructions in PMR to flex muscles, and instructions to imagine cooked spaghetti correspond to directions to relax muscles and experience tension flowing from muscles.

After wiggling and relaxing toes, this procedure is repeated with both legs, and the buttocks. Next, the procedure is applied to either set of fingers, and to either arm. Finally, children are asked to let their entire body become sleepy and warm like soft spaghetti. While relaxed, children are instructed that this relaxation technique may be utilized to respond to cognitive or physiological anxiety. Children are encouraged to think that they can become "the boss of your body by talking to it" (Orlick & McCaffrey, 1991, p. 325). Lastly, children are asked to repeat the flexing and relaxation procedure with their mouth, tongue, and eyebrows.

Why Youth Discontinue Sport Participation

Given that youth participate in sport to have fun, to improve and learn skills, to enhance their fitness, to affiliate with teammates, to experience the excitement of sport, and for the challenge of competition, it is not surprising that they drop out when these interests are not realized (Gould & Petlichkoff, 1988). Further, youth who drop out or do not participate in sport believe that they have less sport competency (Weiss & Chaumeton, 2002). As discussed in Chapter 9, a threshold of competency is necessary prior to the experience of intrinsic interest. Tasks that are intrinsically interesting are fun, and it is difficult to enjoy sport if youngsters believe they have little competency and demonstrate the same.

Efficacy and perceived competency are also supported in atmospheres that identify skill development to be the result of effort and learning (Kavussanu & Roberts, 1996). Coaches and other adults can promote efficacy and perceived sport competence by encouraging young sportspersons to evaluate their performance in relation their own baselines of performance rather than to the performance of other children. By focusing on improvement relative to one's baseline, youngsters are more likely to emphasize personal improvement and skill mastery and to focus on the intrinsic rewards of learning. Frequent social comparisons encourage young athletes to think of ability as reified or innate rather than malleable and emerging.

Burnout

Some youth discontinue sport participation because of burnout. As described in Chapter 16, **burnout** occurs when youthful participants lose interest and find sport no longer enjoyable. With burnout, athletes develop negative attitudes toward their sport and question whether it is "worth it" to engage in sport (Smith, 1986). There is often a reduced sense of accomplishment, and these youth may believe that they are making little progress and that their efforts are a waste of time (Raedeke & Smith, 2001). The rewards or benefits of sport and other activities seem to be outweighed by the costs or unpleasant aspects.

A youthful sportsperson might pursue athletics even if the costs outweighed the benefits if they decided that they had nothing better to do. However, if they identified competing activities that were more rewarding, such as spending free time with friends, they might drop out of athletics in pursuit of the activities that seem to return more at less cost.

Perfectionism has been identified as a precursor of burnout and

dropout among youthful athletes. As discussed in Chapter 12, perfection-ism – efforts to be flawless – inhibits not only performance but also interest and enjoyment in sport. Perfectionism was recognized as an important reason why elite junior female and male tennis players lost interest in and became apathetic about playing tennis (Gould, Tuffey, Udry, & Loehr, 1996a, 1997a). Elite juniors who dropped out of tennis lost motivation to exert the energy necessary for elite play (Gould et al., 1996b). The burnt-out tennis players found it difficult to concentrate. Negative emotions such as anxiety, irritability, and depression accompanied burnout, and athletes often reported low self-esteem. Many became isolated and kept their problems to themselves.

The burnt-out juniors often complained that too much of their time was dominated by tennis. With the demands of training and travel they felt they had too little time for socializing with peers. If young athletes become isolated from peers, they have fewer opportunities for social support to blunt the stress of competition. If they do not have friends with whom to share their tennis experiences, it may become less fun. Com-peting activities that involve peers may also become more attractive if playing tennis requires being cloistered from peers. The importance of balancing sport with social activities during adolescence and keeping sport enjoyable was confirmed with a group of male high school golfers (Cohn, 1990a).

Early Pro

Hall of Fame LPGA (Ladies Professional Golf Association) golfer Nancy Lopez criticized Michelle Wie and her inner circle for the decision to play professional golf at age 14 and for her interest in skipping over the LPGA to play on the professional men's tour.

"I feel bad for her," said Lopez, the mother of three girls. "If I had a daughter that played the type of golf that she's playing, I would have the patience to let her be a little girl for a little while and enjoy that time of her life because she may choose not to play this game. We don't know what kind of pressure she's under, but I saw so many players who were really good amateur players not make it on the LPGA Tour. There was too much pressure behind closed doors, and they ended up really hating the game instead of loving it the way I did" (Berlet, 2005, p. C3).

Six days prior to her 16th birthday, Wie announced that she was turning pro. With the announcement came notice that Nike and Sony would be cor-porate sponsors and would pay her $5 million each for her endorsements (Bonk, 2005).

Some junior tennis players appeared to lack intrinsic motivation for the rigors of training at an elite level, and appeared to endure these demands in order to please their parents (Gould et al., 1996a). Lacking intrinsic motivation, tennis was not fun. Indeed, these juniors said they would advise other juniors to find intrinsic motivation and enjoyment for their game.

The tennis juniors said that they would encourage parents of other juniors to avoid overinvolvement in the tennis careers of their children and suggested that parents not coach their children. They encouraged other parents to try to understand and empathize with the emotions of their children, and to not push their children beyond their limits. These young women and men wished that parents would place less emphasis on winning and the outcome of matches. As discussed in Chapter 2, external pressure and coercion, a focus on outcomes, results or evaluations, and an emphasis on comparing children to others serve to undermine intrinsic motivation. Intrinsic motivation sustains deep interests and enjoyment in activities, as well as the persistence necessary to develop elite skills.

The juniors advised coaches to be less dictatorial and more democratic. This would involve listening and utilizing input from players and trying to empathize with the feelings of players. Some of the burnt-out juniors would also like coaches to intervene with parents who place too much pressure on their children.

Stress and Youth Sport

As explained in Chapter 3, stress originates in the environment or external world, and discrete sources of stress are described as stressors. As is the case for adults, competition is often stressful for youthful sportspersons. For example, among elite American male adolescent wrestlers, common sources of stress associated with competition were not wrestling well, losing, not performing up to their ability, and not improving on prior performances (Gould, Horn, & Spreemann, 1983). The most frequently reported source of acute stress for Australian field hockey players between the ages of 10 and 12 was "bad" calls from umpires (Anshel & Delany, 2001). Making physical errors in games was also a common source of stress for these youngsters. The pain of injury, the sudden success of opponents, and unpleasant comments and cheating from the opposition were also stressors. Female hockey players were more discomforted by hearing unpleasant comments from the sidelines, whereas males found getting bad scores in games to be more frequent sources of stress.

The most frequent coping responses to these game stressors were examples of **avoidance coping** (Anshel & Delany, 2001). These included trying to ignore stressors, forget incidents, and accept that there was nothing they could do in response to stressors. This avoidance coping has been seen as desirable when the sources of stress are uncontrollable and transient. With avoidance coping, attentional resources are directed to aspects of performances that are under the control of youthful athletes.

Sportspersons cope with stress with intrapersonal or individual strategies such as avoidance coping, and with interpersonal strategies such as gaining social support from others. Parental support is an example of **interpersonal support**; it provides a buffer to interpersonal stress from teammates and coaches when young athletes are performing poorly.

The importance of interpersonal support was illustrated with Dutch male soccer players between the ages of 15 and 22 years who were pupils at an elite soccer school from which the majority of the Dutch national team was selected. The soccer players who were rated by coaches as less skilled than teammates experienced less conflict with teammates and disgruntlement about their roles on the team when they had close emotional bonds with parents (VanYperen, 1995). The players with similarly lower levels of skill but also with lower levels of parental support reported less interpersonal support from teammates. Perhaps the latter players were more sensitive to and in need of interpersonal support from teammates because they received less support from their parents.

Players with higher skill levels and with higher parental support reported more interpersonal stress with teammates than their counterparts with higher skill and less parental support (VanYperen, 1995). With high skill and high parental support, players were more attentive to their discontent with the performances of teammates. Perhaps with high skill and low parental support players were more in need of interpersonal support from teammates and less likely to be critical of teammates.

Coaching, Leadership, and Youth Sport

Coaches are influential leaders. Indeed, there is evidence that child athletes rate positive evaluations from coaches as more important than similar parental evaluations (Smith, Smoll, & Smith, 1989). Several interventions by coaches have been shown to have a considerable impact on youthful athletes. These interventions consist of **positive feedback** or recognition and verbal reinforcement for skilled action, **encouragement** or comments that the athlete can be successful, **technical information** or advice about how to improve action, and **negative feedback** or criticism following mistakes.

Coaching and positive control (photo © Adam Tinney).

Male Little League baseball coaches who provided more positive feedback and encouragement following mistakes supported the development of higher general self-esteem among their male players, and coaches who provided more technical instruction or instrumental support encouraged higher levels of athletic self-esteem (Smoll & Smith, 1989). Little Leaguers (ages 12 and younger) also liked coaches more who were supportive and provided technical assistance (Smith & Smoll, 1990). These players responded favorably to coaches who emphasized encouragement and technical assistance, but not to coaches who were punitive or frequently made negative comments or gave correction in a hostile manner. Young baseball and basketball players not only liked their coaches more and had more fun when coaches emphasized positive reinforcement for desirable performance and effort, but also liked their teammates more (Smoll & Smith, 2006).

Young basketball players responded similarly to positive feedback, encouragement, technical instruction, and criticism (Smith, Zane, Smoll, & Coppel, 1983). Athletes on high school female and male basketball teams were more satisfied with the atmospheres of their teams when coaches were more supportive and gave more frequent positive reinforcement and less frequent negative feedback (Fisher, Hirsch, Proulx, & Starowsky, 1982). These basketball players had more verbal interaction with teammates and found their teams to be more cohesive. High school football coaches who were active in providing instruction and training, positive feedback, and social support, and who allowed athletes to participate in decision-making also fostered team cohesion and satisfaction among teammates (Westre & Weiss, 1991). The comments of coaches and other important adults also influence the judgment of children about their athletic ability.

Self-Esteem and Response to Coaches

Children with low **self-esteem** are especially sensitive to the reactions of coaches. With low self-esteem, children are also more likely to interpret the responses of coaches to be punitive. For example, Little Leaguers with low self-esteem judged coaches to be less supportive and more punitive than teammates with high self-esteem (Smith & Smoll, 1990).

Little Leaguers with low self-esteem responded most negatively to coaches who did not provide encouragement and technical support, and most positively to coaches who provided either form of support (Smith & Smoll, 1990). Little Leaguers who had high self-esteem were less influenced by the leadership behavior of coaches.

Athletes and students with low self-esteem are more dependent on support from coaches. They have a shallow reservoir of positive self-regard or positive feelings about themselves (Rogers, 1954; Tice, 1991), and this reserve is apt to be exhausted if they do not receive a regular supply of encouragement and technical advice. When self-esteem is high, youth are affected less by supportive and punitive responses from others because they have internal reserves available for the preservation of positive self-regard. With high self-esteem, people may also be more capable of eliciting support from a greater number of people, and therefore less dependent on the reactions of just one person such as a coach (Smith & Smoll, 1990).

Does Age Influence Reactions to Coaches?

The question of whether age affects the response of sportspersons to coaching interventions remains open. Children between the ages of six and eight versus between 12 and 14 years responded similarly when watching coaches provide feedback to children who successfully batted baseballs and softballs (Amorose & Weiss, 1998). Male and female children in both age groups judged the batters to demonstrate more ability and effort and to be more likely to have future success when coaches praised the batters. Successful batters who received technical or neutral feedback from coaches were judged lower in all three categories. Batters who swung and missed balls were judged by other children to have more ability and to be more likely for future success when they received informational feedback than when feedback was neutral. Unsuccessful batters who received neutral feedback were seen to be more competent and likely for future success than unsuccessful batters who were given criticism.

Several differences in responses to coaches have been recorded for older children and adolescents. With competitive swimmers between the ages of 12 and 14, perceived competence, success, and enjoyment were elevated more when coaches were perceived as providing technical information after desirable performances (Black & Weiss, 1992). Praise alone did little to influence perceived competence, success, and enjoyment. Swimmers between the ages of 15 and 18 reported more perceived competence, success, and effort, when they perceived coaches as delivering praise and technical information following successful performances. Among the swimmers in the 15-to-18 age group, criticism undermined perceived ability and effort, even if criticism was paired with technical information.

Coach Effectiveness Training

Leadership styles are not immutable or unchangeable. Coaches can be trained to provide more encouragement, more technical support, and fewer punitive responses with interventions such as **Coach Effectiveness Training** (CET; Smith, Smoll, & Curtis, 1979). CET is a systematic program of instruction that trains coaches to emphasize principles of positive control and avoid aversive control. Positive control includes reinforcement for good performance, encouragement after mistakes, providing correction in a supportive manner, and technical instruction in the mechanics and strategies of sport. Aversive control includes nonreinforcement or failure to respond to good performance or effort, verbal or nonverbal punishment, and providing instruction in a sarcastic and punitive manner. The motivating factor for aversive control is fear.

There are five core principles of CET. First, winning is defined in terms of the self-referenced goals of giving maximum effort and demonstrating improvement in relation to individual baselines of prior performance (Smith & Smoll, 2002). Coaches are directed to emphasize the values of having fun, taking satisfaction from being a member of a team, learning sport skills, and increasing the self-esteem of team members. Coaches are encouraged to de-emphasize the goal of winning, and certainly not to project a "win at all costs" orientation (Smith & Smoll, 1997). This approach is likely to decrease competitive anxiety (Smoll & Smith, 1988). Fear of failure is reduced when sportspersons are encouraged to separate feelings of self-worth from the results of their sport performance and game outcomes. The importance of winning is not ignored with CET, but it is regarded as subsidiary to the objectives of having fun, increasing self-esteem, and developing skills. CET also emphasizes that success consists of giving maximum effort, demonstrating improvement, and having fun.

The second principle of CET is for coaches to emphasize positive reinforcement, encouragement, and technical instruction and to avoid punitive behaviors and excessive criticism. Reinforcement should not be reserved for the learning and mastery of sport skills; coaches should also reinforce teamwork, leadership, sportspersonship, and especially effort (Smith & Smoll, 2002b). Athletes have control over the amount of effort they exert but only partially control the outcome of competitions. Encouragement is recommended especially after mistakes, and again effort rather than results should be the focus of encouragement. Teammates should be reinforced for encouraging other teammates, and this form of peer support enhances cohesion.

The provision of corrective instruction is seen as consistent with this emphasis on a positive approach. Sportspersons are described as receptive to corrective instruction after mistakes, and coaches are advised to include ample supplies of encouragement and wrap instruction following errors in a **"positive sandwich"** (Smith & Smoll, 1997). The "bread" (the first and third statements by the coach) is reinforcements. For example, a coach might first reinforce a player for effort, and lastly reassure the sportsperson that they will improve with practice. Between the two reinforcing comments, coaches with this positive approach provide the technical correction and emphasize that they expect the player to master the skill in the future.

The use of harsh criticism, punishment, and even sarcasm is strongly discouraged in CET. Such responses are seen to contribute to the decisions of youngsters to drop out of sports, and are regarded as destructive to team cohesion.

Third, coaches are taught to establish norms for their teams that require members to help and support teammates. The purpose of these norms is to build team cohesiveness and commitment. By focusing on the game and supporting teammates, even benchwarmers contribute to the team effort and cohesion. Coaches support "we're in this together" (Smith & Smoll, 1997) team norms when they acknowledge the verbal support of players on the bench and when they give the reserves attention, encouragement, and instruction in practice. Some coaches encourage team cohesion by "buddying" more skilled with less skilled teammates.

The fourth principle of CET is to engage team members in making decisions about team rules and in monitoring compliance with rules. Rules should be established at the start of seasons and should be fair and consistent. If coaches can create an atmosphere in which teammates monitor each other, they remove themselves from the position of exclusively policing their team and responding punitively. If team members have a say in the determination of team rules, then individuals violate team norms, rather than merely the order of a coach, when they break rules.

Fifth, coaches monitor themselves and perhaps seek feedback from others on an ongoing basis to determine if they remain consistent in emphasizing positive reinforcement, encouragement, and technical instruction and de-emphasizing punitive responses.

Empirical Support for CET

At least four training programs are currently available in the USA for coaches of youthful athletes, but CET is the only program that has been systematically evaluated (Smith & Smoll, 2002b). Little Leaguers who played for coaches who completed CET played with less anxiety and had more fun playing (Smith, Smoll, & Barnett, 1995b). They liked their coaches and teammates more, and thought their coaches liked them more. They also rated coaches as better teachers of baseball skills. Their anxiety about making mistakes and not playing well decreased significantly across the course of the Little League season. Players with low self-esteem were especially responsive to the CET coaches, and their self-worth increased across the course of the season.

The leadership provided by the CET coaches also influenced dropout from Little League as 95 percent of the players on teams with CET coaches returned to play the next year, whereas only 74 percent of the players on the teams without CET coaches returned (Barnett, Smoll, & Smith, 1992). The won–loss records of teams did not influence dropout as the teams with and without CET coaches had approximately equal records. Children on teams without CET coaches were more likely to drop out because playing was a bad experience.

More generally, quality leadership from adult coaches is an important determinant of the experience of children and adolescents in sport. Problems and difficulties with coaches are important reasons why children and adolescents drop out of athletics. Dropout is an important concern in that as many as half of the children who begin a sport stop playing.

Coaches and Parents

It is sometimes necessary for coaches of children and adolescents to practice effective leadership with not only the youthful athletes but also their parents (Smoll, 1998; Smoll & Cumming, 2006). At one end of a spectrum of problematic parental involvement are parents who are **disinterested** in the participation of their children in athletics. At the other end of this spectrum are parents who are overly involved. An example of an overly involved parent is the father who is a **"frustrated jock"** and seeks to experience athletic success through his child that he never realized in his own youth. This parent may see the child as an extension of himself, and in some ways define his self-worth in terms of the child's success. Overly involved parents experience losses to their self-image if their children do not perform well and may require that their children excel before they grant their approval. The children of overly involved parents experience pressure to excel and the parents may demonstrate the **reversed-dependency trap** (Smith & Smoll, 2002b) in that their wellbeing is dependent on their children's success.

Effective leadership with overly involved parents involves diplomatic efforts to clarify that youth athletics are for the growth and development of the children. As was described in Chapter 10, simultaneous goals of winning in relation to competitors and winning parental approval are likely to provoke performance anxiety and choking under pressure.

Coaches may also have to intervene with parents in the viewing area that scream to such a degree that they disrupt play, embarrass their children, and represent a nuisance. Parents model self-control and discipline during the athletic contests of their children. Coaches face a more difficult task in teaching good sportspersonship when parents are poor sports and prone to emotional outbursts. Parents who coach from the sidelines or who are overprotective also may require tactful intervention from coaches. Some coaches attempt to limit parental coaching from the sidelines by asking them to not sit directly behind the bench for their child's team (Strean, 1995).

Coaches show leadership with disinterested parents by inviting them to participate and by explaining that their support is of value to their children. Busy parents are often unable to balance other commitments with time to watch their children's matches. Coaches are advised to have parents make reasonable commitments to attend games and practices and to not promise more time than they can actually deliver. Coaches may also explain to their teams that not all parents can attend games and practices due to work and other commitments.

Parents Out of Control

Upset that his daughter, Melanie, received a three-game suspension for missing a softball game to attend a senior prom at North Haven (CT) High School, Mark Picard appealed to coach John Corvo to rescind the suspension and allow Melanie, a senior, to play on seniors' day. Corvo, the softball coach of the all-girls Sacred Heart Academy in Hamden, CT, refused and stated that he did not want Melanie at practice and to take her home. As Corvo walked away, Picard struck him several times about the head and shoulders with an aluminum softball bat (Eagan & Gonzalez, 2005). Corvo sustained injuries to his neck and chest, his ear canal collapsed, and he had severe swelling in his right knee (Gonzalez & Courchesne, 2005). Dave Cypher, the former coach at Sacred Heart Acadamy said that part of the reason he resigned was a run-in with Picard. In 2004, Cypher allowed all the seniors to play as a group on Senior Night. After Sacred Heart was beaten badly, Picard, "was screaming, 'You are the worst coach I've ever seen. You were just sitting on the bench saying nothing' " (Gonzalez, 2005, p. C8). Cypher speculated that the Picards might have been upset with him because he did not choose Melanie to be a team captain. Picard was instrumental in building equipment sheds for the track and softball teams and raised money for athletic programs at Sacred Heart. Picard had taught art and photography at Notre Dame High School in nearby West Haven, CT since 1980.

Regardless of their availability and time constraints, some demands are placed on the parents of youthful athletes. These parents must entrust their child to the guidance of coaches, and accept the coaches' authority in matters relating to sport (Smoll & Cumming, 2006). Disappointment occurs in the course of athletic striving, and children benefit when they can share disappointments with parents. Parents should avoid shaming children about their disappointment and even about crying following poor performances. Parents support their children when they help them to learn from disappointments and losses.

A final demand placed on the parents of youthful athletes is the need to understand when to allow children to make their own decisions about sports. Parents play an important role in motivating children to participate in sports, but some children choose not to participate despite the best efforts of parents.

Preseason Meetings with Parents

Coaches are more likely to be effective leaders with parents when they clarify the roles of parents and coaches in meetings with parents. The roles and responsibilities of coaches, parents, and athletes, and the objectives of the sport program are explained in such meetings. These meetings are considered vital to avoiding misunderstandings and problems with parents such as overinvolvement, sideline coaching, abusive verbal behavior from parents in the stands, and disagreements about the playing time of children.

These goals may best be accomplished in **preseason meetings** with parents. Follow-up meetings may be held at other times in the season. A guide for coaches in planning meetings with parents and in providing effective leadership with parents and athletes is provided in the book *Way to Go, Coach!* (Smith & Smoll, 2002a).

On the Need for Leadership with Parents

In July 2000, Thomas Junta watched his son practice ice hockey at the Burbank Ice Arena in Reading, Massachusetts. Junta complained to the coach, Michael Costin that play was too rough. Costin disagreed and after practice the two scuffled (Campo-Flores & Kirsch, 2002). They were separated by bystanders, but Junta returned within minutes. At 275 pounds, Junta wrestled the 156-pound Costin to the floor. With Costin lying on his back and Junta kneeling over him, Junta pummeled him with from three to 10 punches, and according to several witnesses, slammed Costin's head to the floor. The blows ruptured a vital artery in Costin's neck, and he died after spending two days in a coma. At the ensuing trial a medical examiner testified that Costin's brain was so severely damaged that during the autopsy it "came squeezing out like tooth-paste" (Campo-Flores & Kirsch, 2002). The men's sons and the other children on the hockey team witnessed this fatal dispute about rough play.

Organizers of youth hockey in Massachusetts considered ways of reining in parents and preventing violence in the future, such as holding educational sessions with parents and requiring parents to sign codes of conduct.

Summary and Conclusions

The benefits of youth sport include the enhancement of physical fitness and athletic competence and the development of leadership skills, discipline, respect for authority, and achievement motivation. In the course of athletic participation, children and adolescents learn social skills, make friends, spend time with family members, and have fun. Youth sport also serves a public health interest, preserves the tradition of organized sport, and develops elite athletes. Unlike professional sport, the fundamental goal of youth sport is not winning, but young sportspersons are encouraged to put forth maximum effort and to strive to win.

There are also social benefits for youth sport. Young sportspersons are more likely to be popular with peers. These youth also have opportunities to make good friends during athletic participation.

The benefits and goals of youth sport are more likely to be realized when coaches emphasize positive feedback, encouragement, and technical information, and de-emphasize negative feedback. With this emphasis, the general and athletic self-esteem of young sportspersons is enhanced. Coach Effectiveness Training (CET) is a systematic program developed to teach coaches to emphasize positive feedback, encouragement, and technical information in their interactions with members of their teams. Coaches are even encouraged to wrap corrective feedback in a "positive sandwich." In CET coaches learn to emphasize the goal of giving maximum effort. Youthful athletes enjoy playing for coaches who emphasize positive control; they play with less anxiety and are less likely to drop out of athletics. Effective coaching in youth sport also involves meetings with parents to clarify the roles of coaches, parents, and athletes.

With effective and sensitive coaching, the goals of youth sport are more likely to be realized. Nevertheless, athletic participation is sometimes stressful. Youthful sportspersons are more successful in coping with stress when they practice skills such as the "spaghetti toes" procedure for relaxation. As is true for physical practice, adult supervision of the practice of mental skills is necessary to insure that it is carried out regularly and appropriately.

The benefits of sport accrue for the participants, and therefore the reasons that youngsters drop out or fail to participate are of interest. Youth who do not experience fun, camaraderie, excitement, challenge, and skill enhancement are more likely to withdraw from, or to never initiate, athletic participation.

Burnout develops when the costs of sport participation appear to outweigh the benefits. Alternatives to sport may then be pursued if they appear to offer more benefit at less cost. However, even burnt-out youngsters may not drop out of sport if more attractive alternative pursuits are not available or if they feel "entrapped" or obliged to participate. Interventions from coaches and parents that encourage intrinsic motivation, self-referenced goals, and self-efficacy help athletes to cope with staleness and temporary loss of interest in sport.

Key Terms

Goals of youth sports

The public health goal of youth sport

The elite-development goal of youth sport

The goal of preserving and protecting the practices of youth sport

The goal of professional sport

Popularity and sport

Coaching, leadership, and youth sport

Positive feedback

Encouragement

Technical information

Negative feedback

Self-esteem and response to coaches

Coach effectiveness training

Positive sandwich

Disinterested parents and frustrated jocks

Reversed-dependency trap

Preseason meetings

Avoidance coping

Interpersonal support

Spaghetti toes

Burnout and dropout

Perfectionism

Suggested Readings

Cote, J. (1999). The influence of family in the development of talent. *The Sport Psychologist*, *13*, 395–417.

Smith, R. E. (2006). Positive reinforcement, performance feedback, and performance enhancement. In J. M. Williams (Ed.), *Applied sport psychology: Personal growth to peak performance* (5th ed.; pp. 40–56), New York: McGraw-Hill.

Smith, R. E., & Smoll, F. L. (2002a). *Way to go, coach! A scientifically-proven approach to coaching effectiveness.* Portola Valley, CA: Warde.

Smith, R. E., & Smoll, F. L. (2002b). Youth sports as a behavior setting for psychosocial interventions. In J. L. Van Raalte & B. W. Brewer (Eds.), *Exploring sport and exercise psychology* (2nd ed., pp. 341–372). Washington, DC: American Psychological Association.

Smoll, F. L., & Cumming, S. P. (2006). Coach–parent relationships in youth sports: Increasing harmony and minimizing hassle. In J. M. Williams (Ed.), *Applied sport psychology: Personal growth to peak performance* (5th ed., pp. 192–204). Mountain View, CA: Mayfield.

Leadership and Coaching 21

Joe Torre, manager of four World Series championship New York Yankee teams compared teams to families: "I often make the analogy between teams and families. It's been said before, and it may seem old-fashioned. But no matter how often the analogy is applied, I still see teams in sports and business where upper and middle managers don't pay attention to the needs of their team players and don't treat people with fairness. That tells me that they don't understand the ways in which teams are like families.

Teams are not really families but there are many crucial similarities. Families thrive when members grant one another time; follow agreed-upon rules; treat one another with fairness, respect, and trust; and make togetherness a top priority.

I'm particularly proud of how my Yankee teams ... all of them, but especially the '98 group ... have been a collection of diverse personalities from totally different ethnic and religious backgrounds, who've managed to get along and respect one another. With regard to the 1998 Yankees, I've never seen a team develop such strong bonds of love and cooperation, and I'm certain it helped them to achieve their goals" (Torre & Dreher, 1999, pp. 52–53).

Simply put, leadership consists of influencing others to strive to reach individual and common goals. It concerns building and maintaining effective teams (Hogan & Kaiser, 2005). The early study of leadership focused on the personality characteristics or traits common to successful leaders. This line of research was subsequently criticized as successful in describing the personality characteristics of successful leaders in sport in only the most general terms (Murray & Mann, 2006). However, personality has proved to be highly important in identifying effective leaders in business, and effective leadership results in gains in productivity and employee satisfaction (Hogan & Kaiser, 2005). **Effective leaders** have **integrity, decisiveness, competence, and vision**. Integrity involves keeping one's word and fulfilling promises, not taking advantage of one's position and not playing favorites. Decisiveness consists of making good decisions quickly, especially under pressure. Competence refers to knowledge and skill at a particular enterprise, and it affords legitimacy to leaders. Finally, a leader with vision is skilled at identifying goals and clarifying the roles of team members. Some experts organize these goals in written mission statements (Desjardins, 1996).

The typical interventions of successful coaches are more reliably identified. Effective coaches convince athletes that team and individual goals will be achieved by accepting their leadership. Athletes value the interventions of coaches who know what they are talking about as well as how to communicate this information. These coaches understand the fundamental components of the skills in their sport. They select and demonstrate specific skills in need of improvement, and do not overload athletes with instruction in single practices. Successful coaches often do not treat each athlete in the same way. They attempt to understand what interventions best serve to teach and motivate individual athletes. These coaches are sensitive to the relationships between team members and resolve tensions and animosities.

The success of coaching interventions is also determined by the age and maturity of athletes. More mature athletes are more capable of taking responsibility for and directing their actions. Less mature athletes are in need of more guidance, direction, and emotional support.

Effective coaches build team morale. Positive morale is evidenced by the confidence and willingness of individual team members to perform assigned tasks and by team dedication to common goals. Positive morale exists when players understand that they will be supported but also held to high standards of effort and performance by coaches. Morale is boosted when athletes believe they are part of something larger than themselves that is good.

Relationship and Task Orientations and Leadership

Leaders have different styles or characteristic ways of relating to those under their supervision (Murray & Mann, 2006). Leaders with a **relationship orientation** focus on giving positive feedback after good performance and encouragement following mistakes. Leaders with **task orientations** (see Chapter 8) focus on providing technical instruction and instruction about how to correct errors after mistakes. Often leaders such as coaches are unaware of their characteristic styles of relating to team members. Youthful athletes respond favorably to coaches who provide positive feedback and technical instruction, and these interventions build general self-esteem and athletic self-esteem (Smoll & Smith, 1989). Negative and hostile comments from coaches undermine team satisfaction and cohesiveness among young athletes (Fisher, Mancini, Hirsch, Proulx, & Staurowsky, 1982; Smith, Zane, Smoll, & Coppel, 1983).

College coaches who provide more training and instruction create motivational climates that foster task orientations (Gardner, 1998). Coaches of female high school basketball players encourage task-oriented motivation climates (see Chapter 8) when they emphasize positive feedback and ignore players' mistakes. Ego-oriented motivation climates are associated with punishment-oriented feedback from these high school coaches (Smith, Fry, Ethington, & Li, 2005).

Transformational Leadership

Superior leaders have been described as charismatic or **transformational** in that they inspire others to adopt their vision of common goals. These transformational leaders broaden and elevate the goals and interests of others so that team members adopt not only individual goals, but also shared, group goals. Charismatic leaders inspire and garner the trust of others.

Charismatic and transformational leadership qualities are acquired throughout development. For example, Canadian female and male high school athletes who considered their fathers to be transformational leaders and who were rated by coaches as having high levels of athletic skills were more likely to show transformational leadership qualities (Zacharatos, Barling, & Kelloway, 2000).

Trust, Leadership, and Coaching

Trust is an essential component of effective leadership in business and athletic settings. **Trust** has generally been defined as a belief or expectation that one can rely on another person to fulfill expectations and promises and that the other person has good intentions toward other people. Trust is especially important when one is vulnerable in relation to another person. Athletes are in vulnerable positions in relation to coaches because coaches make important decisions about the roles of athletes on teams. For example, coaches make decisions about starting lineups and playing time. Trust is also very important when people are uncertain if their leader is making the right decisions. For example, athletes are asked to accept or "buy into" the goals and tactics of coaches without knowing in advance if these goals and tactics will lead to team and individual success.

Trust and Communication

Megan Pattyson was a stalwart on the first University of Connecticut (UCONN) team to reach the NCAA final four of women's basketball in 1991. In 2003, she described her former coach Geno Auriemma: "He's the kind of man I could tell, 'I got my period, I got cramps, I'm all bloated'; or 'My boyfriend's acting like a jerk.' You can talk to Geno about anything. How many men can you do that with?" (Deford, 2003, p. 131). Coach Auriemma's UCONN teams won five NCAA national championships in women's basketball.

Athletes are less likely to accept coaching decisions, especially if they are asked to sacrifice individual goals for team goals, if they do not trust coaches. Sportspersons that trust coaches are more willing to accept their individual roles on the team and to work hard to realize the goals and decisions of coaches (Vallee & Bloom, 2005). Teams that trust coaches are also more likely to be successful. For example, male basketball players from 30 National Collegiate Athletic Association (NCAA) Divisions I and II teams who trusted their coaches had higher winning percentages (Dirks, 2000). Trust was measured at the beginning of the teams' conference schedules, which was after the teams had practiced together for 6 weeks. The two teams that recorded the highest levels of trust in coaches were very successful. One was ranked number one in the nation before being upset in the NCAA tournament and the other was defeated in the national championship game. The team with the lowest level of trust in its coach from this sample of 30 teams won approximately 10 percent of

Coaches lead athletes (photo © Joseph Sohm/Visions of America/Corbis).

the games in its conference, and the coach was fired after the season. US Olympic athletes at the winter games in Nagano, Japan in 1998 retrospectively said their performance improved when they trusted their coaches and believed that coaches were totally committed to their success (Gould, 1999).

Leaders and coaches are judged on the basis of the results of their organizations and teams. Coaches of successful teams are often considered good leaders. Coaches with good track records or histories of prior coaching success are expected to be successful in the future. Athletes are more willing to trust and "put themselves in the hands of" coaches who they expect will make them winners. It is more difficult for coaches with poor records of accomplishment to inspire the trust of teams, and without this trust, these coaches are less likely to be successful in the future.

Communication and Coaching

Trust is the foundation for effective **communication** between coaches and their teams (Yukelson, 2006). Coaches judged to be honest, fair, and consistent are seen as good communicators by their teams. Clearly, effective communication involves more than just what is said and how it is said, as athletes take coaches' "body of work" or record as a coach and a person in evaluating their credibility.

As will be described at later points in this chapter, athletes generally respond more favorably to positive reinforcement, support, and technical instruction from coaches. Criticism often undermines morale. Coaches who emphasize positive control and de-emphasize negative control (Smith & Smoll, 2002b) encourage open communication on teams. Positive control includes reinforcement for good performance, encouragement after mistakes, providing correction in a supportive manner, and technical instruction in the mechanics and strategies of sport. Negative control includes nonreinforcement or failure to respond to good performance or effort, verbal or nonverbal punishment, and providing instruction in a sarcastic and punitive manner. The motivating factor for negative control is fear. Coaches are also more likely to develop skill at communication and maintain team harmony when they are committed to the objectives of positive control (Orlick, 1986).

Coaching Efficacy

Coaches who believe they can affect the learning and performance of their teams have coaching efficacy. **Coaching efficacy** consists of four components: **motivation efficacy, technique efficacy, game strategy efficacy, and character building efficacy** (Feltz, Chase, Moritz, & Sullivan, 1999). Coaching efficacy in these areas is developed with successful experience in coaching and with coaching preparation and education. The sources of coaching success are not limited to wins and losses, as coaches focus on improvements in their athletes and in their coaching skills in judging their efficacy (Barber, 1998). Coaching efficacy is enhanced when teams have high ability and when coaches receive social support from school administrators, parents, and the community. Coaching efficacy is also affected by the feedback from players (Malete & Feltz, 2002).

Efficacious coaches excel at developing the talent of their players, and motivating players to believe in themselves and to perform at their highest levels. Efficacious coaches adjust strategies to the talents of their players and the demands of practice and competition.

Coaches have been shown to form expectations for their team's performance (Chase, Lirgg, & Feltz, 1997) based on past performances in games, practices, the injury status of players, the strength of opponents, and the coaches' beliefs about the confidence and efficacy of their players. These coaches' expectations in turn influence team efficacy so that teams with higher efficacy perform more successfully. The performance of teams then ultimately reinforces or supports the original efficacy expectations of coaches.

With higher efficacy, coaches are more likely to be effective, to produce winning teams, and to have players who are confident and satisfied with their coach. Coaches who had higher efficacy beliefs for their teams believed they had more control over the performance of their teams. Not surprisingly, coaches are more likely to discontinue coaching if they no not perceive themselves to be competent, especially female coaches.

Coaches Build the Efficacy of Teams

The strategies of efficacious coaches build the individual and group efficacy of their teams (Bandura, 1997). As described in Chapter 8, enactive attainments are the most convincing sources of self-efficacy, and skilled coaches provide teams with goals in practice and competition that are attainable. With the attainment of progressively more difficult goals, individual and team efficacy increases. These coaches avoid placing athletes in situations where they are likely to fail, such as in pressure situations where they are overmatched.

Despite the best efforts and intentions of coaches, athletes still experience failure. Skilled coaches allow athletes opportunities to get themselves out of trouble in matches and games and avoid pulling players at the first sign of trouble. Successful and efficacious coaches blunt discouragement after losses by directing the attention of athletes to aspects of performance that are under the control of athletes. They help athletes to focus on personal and team improvement regardless of wins and losses, and they provide encouragement, corrective instruction, and feedback to teach athletes the skills necessary for more skillful performance. Coaches also support the efficacy of players when they communicate that they have not lost faith in players after failures and that improvement will occur with technical refinements and training. Players are less likely to lose confidence even in prolonged slumps when coaches communicate that they have every confidence that they will return to form. Repeated failure may result in relegation of players to minor leagues or the bench or a reserve role. Relegation is less likely to impact the efficacy of players if it is interpreted as evidence of the need for skill improvement rather than of evidence of a lack of talent.

Effective coaches support beliefs that necessary athletic skills are acquirable. They also adopt styles of play that capitalize on the strengths and hide the weaknesses of their players.

Coaches of Olympic and national level athletes use many of these techniques to build and sustain high efficacy with athletes. They also emphasize conditioning, set specific performance goals, and encourage positive self-talk (Gould, Hodge, Peterson, & Giannini, 1989).

Effective coaches recognize that the time for teams to doubt their likelihood for success is not immediately prior to and during competition. Doubts about efficacy erode performance during competition. However, skillful coaches deliberately *instill doubts* in their team at times distal to competition so as to motivate teams to train and prepare optimally (Bandura, 1997). These coaches also guard against complacency after successful and triumphant seasons by helping athletes understand that without additional improvement, they are unlikely to be equally successful in the future. Continuous improvement is necessary as prior success may well be due to optimal circumstances for the triumphant team, optimal scheduling, luck, and bad breaks or injuries for opponents. Prior success may have also been partially due to optimal team cohesion at a particular period in time.

Efficacious coaches help athletes to not give up in competition, even when teams are clearly beaten. At these times, athletes are instructed to change the focus of their goals so that they still work on aspects of their games in the losing contests. This refocusing provides opportunities for skill development that are not available in practice against lesser competition.

Improving the Influence of Coaches

Coaches and other leaders interested in enhancing their influence have been encouraged to improve their appearance. By tidying up their attire, eliminating obesity and pudginess, and stopping smoking, coaches may present an image of confidence and control, and inspire these reactions in team members (Murray & Mann, 2006). They are encouraged to acquire necessary expertise in the technical aspects of their sport as well as an understanding of how to motivate individual players (Laios, Theodorakis, & Gargalianos, 2003). Coaches should develop control of their emotions, as athletes often imitate coaches in handling emotions.

Effective Coaches Respond Contingently

Perhaps it goes without saying that effective coaching interventions are given contingently. Comments are *contingent* when they are in response to specific actions or clusters of actions by athletes. Contingent coaching responses are also tailored to fit the level of skill and characteristics of the athlete. Even positive reinforcement that is not contingent on performance does little to enhance feelings of competence (Horn, 1985). In other words, random compliments from coaches have little effect.

Multidimensional Model of Leadership

With experience, it was recognized that a single set of characteristics was not associated with successful leadership in all situations. Settings such as sport venues differ in terms of the age of sportspersons, goals for participation, and type of sport. The **multidimensional model of leadership** (Chelladurai, 1980) was developed specifically for application in sport settings and to account for the interaction of traits and situation factors in explaining effective leadership in sport teams.

The multidimensional model of leadership considers the actual behavior of leaders such as coaches, the style of leadership preferred by subordinates such as team members, and the restrictions placed on leaders by their organizations (Chelladurai, 1980, 1984, 1993). The accompanying diagram (Figure 21.1) was developed to illustrate this model. Boxes 1, 2, and 3 describe antecedents of actual leadership behavior, and consist of the characteristics of situations, leaders, and team members. The arrows depict the influences of these antecedents on behaviors required by sport settings, actual behaviors demonstrated by coaches, and behaviors favored by team members (Boxes 4, 5, and 6). The actual behavior of leaders is

| Antecedents | Leader Behavior | Consequences |

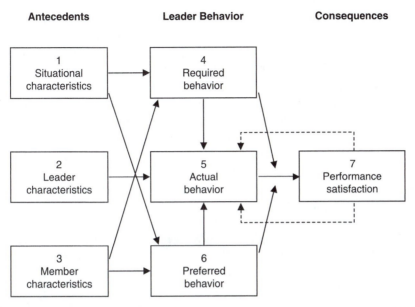

FIGURE 21.1. Multidimensional model of leadership. From Chelladurai, P. (1993). Leadership. In R. N. Singer, M. Murphey, & L. K. Tennant (Eds.), *Handbook of research on sport psychology* (pp. 647–671). New York: Macmillan.

influenced by leader characteristics, such as personality and experience, required behavior (for example, learning plays during a sport season), and preferred behavior (the type of leadership favored by team members). The degree of congruence among the required, actual, and preferred behaviors of coaches is considered to determine the consequences of leadership – the performance of teams and satisfaction of team members with the leadership or coaching (Box 7).

The Leadership Scale for Sport

The **Leadership Scale for Sport** (LSS) was developed to measure the actual leadership behavior of coaches (Chelladurai & Saleh, 1978, 1980). The LSS has five scales. The first scale concerns the degree to which coaches emphasize **training** and **instruction**. This includes strenuous training, providing instruction in the technical aspects of performance in the particular sport, structuring practices, and clarifying roles of team members. A second scale measures the degree to which coaches consider input from team members or allow for **democratic decision-making**. The third and fourth scales measure the interpersonal qualities of **social support** and **positive feedback**. A fifth scale assesses the degree to which coaches make decisions **autocratically** or without input from team members.

Certain styles of decision-making are more appropriate for different situations and different teams (Horn, 1992). There are seven attributes to be considered in matching decision styles to athletic situations (Chelladurai & Doherty, 1998; Chelladurai & Turner, 2006). *First*, when time is limited, coaches are required to be decisive. *Second*, some decisions are more important than others. For example, it is more important to select the most skilled person to be center forward on a soccer team than to select the most skilled player as team captain. Less important decisions

---

A Volatile Mix

Coach P. J. Carlissimo was a highly successful collegiate basketball coach. His collegiate career culminated in 1989 when he brought his Seton Hall Pirates to the championship game of Division One American college basketball. His Pirates lost the championship game by a single point. His skill at recruiting, teaching, and motivating athletes was recognized as responsible for returning the Seton Hall men's basketball program to national prominence, and he was twice recognized as the Coach of the Year in the Big East Conference. In 2002, Carlissimo was inducted in the Seton Hall Athletic Hall of Fame.

Carlissimo left Seton Hall in 1994 to assume the head coaching job of the Portland Trailblazers, a professional basketball team in the NBA. Carlissimo was fired in Portland in 1997 despite three straight winning seasons. Subsequently, he was hired as the head coach of the Golden State Warriors of the NBA, but was fired from that job in 1999.

Carlissimo's style of coaching was seen as confrontational, aggressive, and "incessantly grating" (Rhoden, 1999, p. D1). The mix of these coaching characteristics with the behavior of an aggressive basketball player proved to be combustible. In 1997, Latrell Sprewell responded to Carlissimo's "ranting and raving" (Rhoden, 1999, p. D1) with violence. He choked Carlissimo and attempted several punches. Sprewell was suspended for 68 games and lost $6.4 million in salary plus his endorsement deal with Converse shoes.

Carlissimo experienced far less success as a professional coach than as a collegiate coach. Assuming that his style of relating to players did not change, differences in the players and in the power associated with collegiate versus professional coaching may explain the difference in success. Collegiate coaches are in a position of power in relation to athletes as they allocate team roles, playing time, and scholarships that are renewable on a yearly basis. Professional coaches have far less power over athletes who have typically signed long-term contracts for far more money than the contract of the coach. Professional coaches are accorded power when they earn the trust and respect of players and convince athletes that individual and team goals are achievable if they follow the coach's direction.

can be determined by democratic vote. *Third*, at times coaches have more information about a question, such as the rules of their sport, and in other instances, athletes possess better information. Examples of the latter are questions about athletes' fatigue and injury status. *Fourth*, it is difficult to make complex decisions by committee. The coach or one player is in the best position to make complex decisions such as the sequence of plays in football. *Fifth*, it is more important for teams to accept or "buy into" some decisions than others. Basketball teams are more likely to be successful in applying full-court pressure defense when they agree with coaches that it is an optimal strategy. Group acceptance of the need for sprints to condition them for playing this defense is less important. *Sixth*, teams that are not cohesive have a difficult time with a democratic process of decision-making, as they might have a difficult time agreeing on anything. A democratic process of decision-making might result in a weakening of already fragile team spirit.

Seventh, coaches can impose decisions on teams only when they have power over the group. Many coaches have control of important rewards and punishments such as scholarships, playing time, and practice schedules. This form of power is accorded to coaches as a result of their positions. Coaches earn power in relationship to players when players respect and admire their personal qualities and expertise (Janssen & Dale, 2002). On some teams, such as in the National Basketball Association (NBA), players have more status and power than coaches, and perhaps NBA players respond poorly to autocratic styles (Bandura, 1997).

Autocratic Coaching

Autocratic coaches make decisions unilaterally or without input from team members. The response of athletes to autocratic coaching styles is not clear-cut. Members of team sports such as soccer and basketball appear to prefer decisions rendered autocratically. Canadian female and male basketball players (Chelladurai & Arnott, 1985) and Canadian male soccer players (Gordon, 1988) were not averse to autocratic decision-making by coaches. In fact, the soccer players viewed group decision-making as appropriate for less than 20 percent of coaching decisions. Canadian male and female collegiate and high school basketball players preferred autocratic decisions and were also receptive to processes in which coaches consulted with team members and then made decisions (Chelladurai, Haggerty, & Baxter, 1989; Chelladurai & Quek, 1995).

Athletes in individual sports may be more receptive to cooperative decision-making with coaches (Chelladurai & Reimer, 1998). Male and female Canadian tennis players of international, national, or provincial caliber and between the ages of 12 and 25 rated coaches as more autocratic than was to their liking (Prapavessis & Gordon, 1991). This discrepancy between autocratic styles they perceived in their coaches and what they preferred was unique in relation to corresponding perceived coaching behaviors and preferences on the other four scales of the LSS. That is, they perceived that coaches provided preferred levels of training and instruction, democratic decision-making, social support, and positive feedback.

There is some evidence that male athletes are more receptive to autocratic styles than females (Chelladurai, 1993; Martin, Jackson, Richardson, & Weiller, 1999). However, this evidence is inconsistent, and males and females appear to be more alike than different in terms of the coaching behaviors they prefer (Horn, 1992). In addition, the actual leadership characteristics of female and male coaches appear to be more alike than different (Jambor & Zhang, 1997).

Culture appears to influence the coaching preferences of athletes. For example, Japanese collegiate athletes preferred a more autocratic coaching style and social support than Canadian counterparts. The Canadians recorded preferences for more democratic training and instruction (Chelladurai, Imamura, Yamaguchi, Oinuma, & Miyauchi, 1988).

Mothers prefer more democratic coaching styles for their adolescent sportspersons (Martin et al., 1999). Parents and adolescent sportspersons both opt for positive feedback and technical instruction for skill improvement.

Concordance of Actual and Preferred Leadership Styles

Despite differences in preferred leadership styles among athletes, it is generally true that satisfaction with coaching leadership is greater when the preferences of athletes and the perceived leadership of coaches are in accord. Athletes are generally less satisfied with coaching leadership if there are discrepancies between the levels of training and instruction, social support, and positive feedback that they perceive coaches to supply and the amounts of these resources that they want (Chelladurai, 1990). In addition, satisfaction with leadership is generally higher when the training and instruction of coaches is effective in improving the individual abilities of team members and the performance of the team as a whole, and when coaches provide positive feedback that is contingent on actual good performance (Chelladurai, 1993).

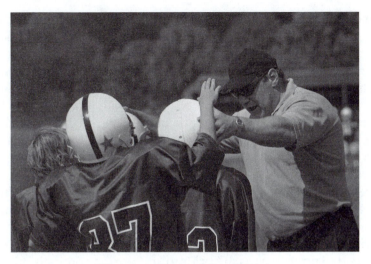

Effective leadership (photo © Suzanne Tucker).

Leadership and Performance

In the multidimensional model of leadership (Chelladurai, 1993) the consequences of leadership are defined as both the satisfaction of subordinates or players and the performance of team members. The relationship between coaching and the satisfaction of players is better understood than the relationship between coaching and performance in the multidimensional model of leadership (Chelladurai & Reimer, 1998). However, athletes held coaches responsible for the performance of their teams and were less satisfied with coaches when teams fell short of goals and expectations (Chelladurai, 1984).

Athletes also consider performance in identifying peer leaders. For example, female collegiate soccer players were more likely to be identified as leaders if they were highly skilled (Glenn & Horn, 1993). Coaches selected the most skilled players as leaders, and these players were more likely to play in the center of the field – on the forward, halfback, or fullback line, or as goalie.

Actual Behavior of Elite Coaches

Perhaps it goes without saying that elite coaches have a great deal of knowledge about evaluating athletic talent, training individual athletes and teams, team organization and administration, and strategies and tactics for competition (Vallee & Bloom, 2005). Expert Canadian gymnastics coaches were shown to develop mental models or plans for developing the potential of elite gymnasts (Cote, Salmela, Trudel, Baria, & Russell, 1995b). With these mental models, coaches determined what interventions during practice and competition were necessary for the development of young gymnasts. Coaches also considered whether young gymnasts were appropriate candidates for competition at elite levels, and whether they themselves had the coaching skills necessary to help the gymnasts reach their potential. Expert coaches altered their mental models or plans for developing elite gymnasts when environmental situations changed or when their coaching was proved to be inadequate to fully develop their gymnasts.

Specific aspects of effective coaching differ depending on the sport. In team sports such as ice hockey, basketball and soccer, coaches are active in providing instruction and motivating athletes immediately prior to and during competition. Expert male and female gymnastics coaches in Canada tend to not "overcoach" prior to and during competitions. Instead, they monitor the degree of anxiety and mental preparation of their elite gymnasts, and intervene when it appears that athletes are overly anxious or not sufficiently focused and motivated for optimal performance (Cote, Samela, & Russell, 1995a). They avoid trying to provide coaching about the technical aspects of routines immediately prior to competition, reasoning that time limitations and stress make it unlikely that this will be helpful (Cote et al., 1995b). Only about one fourth of the coaches attempted to systematically monitor and control aspects of preperformance preparation from the time athletes arrived at competition venues. Coaches exerted control on preperformance preparation when they planned meals, monitored the psychological states of athletes, checked equipment, and anticipated distracting influences prior to and during competition.

During routine practice, gymnastic coaches said that they were supportive, and provided instruction and positive feedback. Coaches of males also acknowledged being dictatorial, demanding respect, and encouraging peer pressure. Coaches of females were more likely to keep an emotional distance and empathize quality training. During practice and training, coaches routinely used simulation training (see Chapter 4) to provide a situation analogous to actual competition.

Elite coaches of adolescent athletes recognize the need to work with parents. For example, Canadian coaches of elite male and female adolescent gymnasts met regularly with parents to explain the roles and expectations for athletes and parents (Cote & Salmela, 1996). These coaches were capable of delegating duty to assistants.

Elite Coaches and Sport Traditions

To this point, the benefits of providing positive feedback, encouragement following mistakes, and technical instruction have been emphasized. Similarly, the liabilities of punitive and negative comments, as well as providing instruction and correction in a hostile and sarcastic manner, have been presented. Regardless of the benefits of the above coaching characteristics, especially with young sportspersons, it would be inaccurate to assume that elite coaches uniformly emphasize them. In addition, routine coaching interventions may differ due to the influences of culture and *traditions* for particular sports (Ryska, Yin, Cooley, & Ginn, 1999). For example, the three male coaches responsible for the preparation of the six-member female 1996 French Olympic judo team were authoritarian, made unilateral decisions, and made frequent use of negative feedback (d'Arripe-Longueville, Fournier, & Dubois, 1998). This authoritarian style is traditional for French Olympic judo coaches, and perhaps for judo coaches and instructors in general (Chelladurai, Malloy, Imamura, & Yamaguchi, 1987). Of the six categories of coaching interaction strategies utilized by these judo coaches, five were confrontational or hostile in tone. These consisted of: stimulating rivalries among the six female athletes; provoking athletes with aggressive and ironic comments and negative feedback; displaying indifference and providing no communication and feedback; engaging in direct conflict and threatening athletes with exclusion from the team; and exhibiting favoritism. The sixth coaching strategy involved developing team cohesion.

The coaches believed that these provocative strategies fostered efforts for continuous improvement and helped athletes to develop mental skills and mental toughness. The coaches did not treat all athletes in the same way. They made observations about the personalities of athletes and tailored strategies – such as provocations with hostile comments – to fit the personalities of athletes. Strategies such as ignoring athletes after injuries or when athletes did not follow instructions in matches were seen not only to be effective but also to comport with judo traditions. The coaches did not believe that selection to an elite athletic team was sufficient to foster team cohesion, and attempted to build cohesion by having the team engage in dangerous tasks. These tasks were intended to promote fearlessness and included driving go-carts, canyoning, and rock climbing.

As they could select athletes for the French Olympic team, these coaches had a great deal of power in relation to the athletes. The responses of athletes to coaches appear to be at least partly determined by their understanding of such power differentials. Judo athletes were diplomatic and made concessions to the coaches. Athletes gained power in relation to coaches by attempting and accomplishing superiority in their weight class. In this way they felt less vulnerable to being cut from the team. Athletes solicited feedback and advice from coaches after poor performances. By initiating this contact, athletes avoided being ignored by coaches, and coaches also hoped that athletes would initiate this movement. Athletes "shopped" for the best coaching and technical information from the three coaches, perhaps demonstrating that just as coaches could make judgments about them, they could also make decisions about coaches. Another effort at self-determination consisted of soliciting training information from sources outside of the coaching ranks, such as athletic trainers or sport psychologists.

Summary and Conclusions

Successful leaders such as coaches know what they are talking about and communicate this understanding to their teams. They appreciate differences among teammates and devise strategies for instructing and motivating them. Effective coaches invest a great deal in teaching and motivating teams and they also hold teams to high standards of effort and performance. Transformational leaders inspire teams not only to improve effort and performance, but also to set higher goals and ask more of themselves.

It is difficult to lead without the trust of team members. Athletes are often asked to put their faith in the decisions of coaches about roles of teams and strategies and tactics for competitions. Sportspersons are less likely to accept coaching decisions that run counter to their individual goals if they do not trust that team goals will be accomplished by co-operating with coaches. It is easier for coaches with a history of success to inspire trust, as athletes expect that they will also become winners if they follow the direction of the successful coaches.

Coaches develop beliefs about the efficacy of their teams and their coaching efficacy. These coaches expect more from their teams, and their teams are more likely to fulfill their expectations. Coaches build the efficacy of teams by setting challenging but attainable goals. With the accomplishment of goals, teams are provided with enactive attainments, the most convincing source of efficacy. Coaches support the efficacy of teams when they monitor the reactions of members to losses and help them to identify unstable factors, such as insufficient practice and skill development that contributed to failures. Coaches intervene when capable athletes become demoralized due to attributing their failures and setbacks to stable, internal factors, such as a lack of talent.

Efficacious coaches dispel doubts about the likelihood for success at times proximal to competition. At times distal, they are vigilant for signs of complacency, and motivate teams to train and practice with a sense of purpose by prompting them to question their readiness for optimal performance.

Coaches often have distinctive styles of relating to players. Coaches with task orientations focus on providing accurate technical information about how to improve athletic skill and performance. With relationship orientations, coaches emphasize positive feedback and encouragement. Coaches are also distinguished on the basis of the degree to which they emphasize positive control or negative control. With positive control, positive reinforcement, encouragement, and technical instruction are predominant. Negative control encourages fear among team members and emphasizes verbal punishment, sarcasm, and efforts to ignore successful performance. Coaches who emphasize positive control support the self-esteem of their players, build team cohesion, and encourage athletes to stick with their sport.

In the multidimensional model of leadership, the characteristics of leaders and subordinates, such as team members, and leadership requirements demanded by particular environments are represented. Styles of leadership have varying degrees of effectiveness in different environments and with different categories of sportspersons. For example, autocratic coaching styles are more likely to be effective when coaches have a considerable amount of power over athletes. Athletes are generally more satisfied with the leadership of coaches when the levels of instruction, social support, and positive feedback that they perceive coaches to supply are approximately equal to the amounts of these emotional resources that they want.

Key Terms

Effective leaders: integrity, decisiveness, competence, vision

Transformational leadership

Communication in coaching

Coaching efficacy: motivation efficacy, technique efficacy, game strategy efficacy, and character building efficacy

Relationship and task orientations and leadership

Multidimensional model of leadership

Leadership scale for sport

Democratic decision making

Autocratic coaching

Suggested Readings

Chelladurai, P., & Reimer, H. A. (1998). Measurement of leadership in sport. In J. L. Duda (Ed.), Advances in sport and exercise psychology (pp. 227–253). Morgantown, WV: Fitness Information Technology.

Cote, J., Salmela, J., Grudel, P., Baria, A., & Storm, R. (1995). The coaching model: A grounded assessment of expert gymnastic coaches' knowledge. *Journal of Sport & Exercise Psychology, 17,* 1–17.

Feltz, D. L., Chase, M. A., Moritz, S. E., & Sullivan, P. J. (1999). Development of the multidimensional coaching effectiveness scale. *Journal of Educational Psychology, 91,* 765–776.

Murray, M. C., & Mann, B. L. (2006). Leadership effectiveness. In J. M. Williams (Ed.), *Applied sport psychology: Personal growth to peak performance* (5th ed., pp. 109–139). New York: McGraw-Hill.

Yukelson, D. (2006). Communicating effectively. In J. M. Williams (Ed.), *Applied sport psychology: Personal growth to peak performance* (5th ed., pp. 174–191). New York: McGraw-Hill.

Team Cohesion, Efficacy, and Goals 22

Gino Auriemma, the coach of the Lady Huskies, or the women's basketball team of the University of Connecticut, led his team to five national championships, two perfect seasons, and a 70-game winning streak. He reflected on teamwork: "I say to my players, the minute you start thinking you play for Connecticut, or you play for Coach Auriemma, or you play for the fans in the building, you could not be further from the truth. I say that the reason you're going to rotate over and take that charge is because your teammate just got beat on a drive and you just bailed them out. The reason you want to block out and get the rebound that saves the game is that when you get in that locker room, your teammates will let you know how they feel about you. You're playing for each other, so forget all the other stuff" (Cyr, 2004, p. 36).

Individuals become members of teams in order to reach certain goals and to affiliate and socialize with others. For example, individuals interested in a *task* such as improving individual skills and winning championships in basketball must become a part of a team. Athletes may also affiliate with teams for *social* reasons such as the enjoyment of the company of teammates. A form of cohesiveness occurs when individuals perceive teams as meeting their interests in achieving task and social goals. This form of cohesiveness is **individual attractions to the group**, and it includes **individual attractions to the group – task (ATG-T)**, and **individual attractions to the group – social (ATG-S)**. Basketball players who join a team that appears most likely to win a championship demonstrate ATG-T, and those that join the same teams as friends demonstrate ATG-S.

Athletes also develop conclusions about the degree to which teammates are united or cohesive in their pursuit of these task and social goals (Carron, Brawley, & Widmeyer, 1998). This form of cohesion is referred to as **group integration (GI)**, and group integration pertains for task **(GI-T)** and social **(GI-S)** goals. Sportspersons who believe that teammates are united in the pursuit of common tasks experience GI-T, and athletes who

Cohesion and performance (photo courtesy of Western Connecticut State University).

find that teammates share their interest in friendship realize GI-S (Carron, Widmeyer, & Brawley, 1985). All four of these forms of cohesiveness (ATG-T, ATG-S, GI-T, GI-S) potentially influence whether sportspersons remain as members of teams. However, the forms of cohesiveness may differ in different situations and age groups (Schultz, Eom, Smoll, & Smith, 1994).

Teams are **cohesive** to the degree that they stick together in pursuit of common goals or for the satisfaction of the emotional needs of the members. Cohesive teams share aspirations, beliefs (Carron, Bray, & Eys, 2002a), and a collective identity (Partington & Shangi, 1992). Shared aspirations and goals and belief in the team's capacity to reach these goals influence team performance to a greater degree than the friendships of teammates. Cohesive teams resist disruptive influences (Brawley, Carron, & Widmeyer, 1988) such as competing privileges and opportunities (Prapavessis & Carron, 1997), and work harder (Bray & Whaley, 2001). Cohesiveness is enhanced when members demonstrate unselfish play and sacrifice for the good of the team (Holt & Sparkes, 2001). Sportspersons approach competition with more facilitative anxiety as members of cohesive teams (Eys, Hardy, Carron, & Beauchamp, 2003).

Athletes are less likely to quit teams when they experience a sense of closeness and belonging to the team. For example, recreational and elite Canadian, female ringette players said they were more likely to return to play for teams with social cohesiveness in the next season (Spink, 1995). Ringette is a sport that is similar to ice hockey, with modified sticks and a ring rather than a puck. Various combinations of the forms of cohesiveness also influence attendance at group exercise programs (Paskevich, Estab-rooks, Brawley, & Carron, 2001). In cohesive exercise groups, members are more likely to not miss classes, arrive on time, resist disruptions to holding exercise classes, and not drop out.

The beneficial effects of team cohesiveness were traditionally considered to be greater for **interacting** as opposed to **coacting sports** (Carron & Chelladurai, 1981). In coactive sports such as gymnastics and swimming, athletes compete individually, whereas in interactive sports, such as lacrosse and basketball, teams compete as a unit and individual success is dependent on team function. However, a recent meta-analysis (statistical integration of extant research) demonstrated that the beneficial effects of cohesiveness were not mitigated by sport type (Carron, Colman, Wheeler, & Stevens, 2002b). Furthermore, even though members of co-acting teams do not coordinate their athletic performances, their inter-actions during competition and practices serve to motivate teammates and foster cohesion (Widmeyer & Williams, 1991).

Cohesiveness is experienced not only in the external interactions between teammates, but also in the individual psychology of team members. Sportspersons incorporate status on cohesive teams and relation-ships with teammates into their personal identities. That is, they come to define themselves partially as a member of a team. If cohesion has been fostered by effective leadership, relationships with coaches are also integrated into the self-definition of athletes (Blanchard, Perreault, & Vallerand, 1998).

Group cohesion does not last forever. It is dynamic or the result of the confluence of the motives, talents, and efforts of team members that exist in certain periods in time or sport seasons (Carron & Dennis, 1998, 2001).

Four Factors Affecting Team Cohesion

At least four factors influence **team cohesion** (Carron & Dennis, 1998). *First*, **situational factors** influence group cohesion. People who spend time in physical proximity have the opportunity for interaction and communi-cation. Sportspersons have opportunities for spending a considerable amount of time together as they share locker rooms, travel together, and may live in common dormitories and eat at training tables. Individuals that share distinctive characteristics are more likely to feel a sense of one-ness and unity. Sportspersons develop this distinctiveness when they earn positions on teams, compete or practice in uniform, and wear clothing such as letter sweaters or jackets that identify them as team members. Coaches and athletic and sport institutions that emphasize the history

Vince Lombardi and Team Cohesion

In 1958, the Green Bay Packers of the National Football League (NFL) "underwhelmed ten opponents, overwhelmed one, and whelmed one" (Maraniss, 1999, p. 191), or achieved a record of 10 losses, one win, and one tie. In 1959, Vince Lombardi was hired as head coach to turn around this professional team. Among his many interventions were efforts to build team cohesion or a sense of family and community. For example, during the final week of training camp, he moved his entire team, including wives and children, to the campus of a suburban Milwaukee boarding school. He instituted a dress code of team blazers and ties for wear on the road, and insisted that team members represent the team in the most dignified manner possible. In a time of segregation in America, he insisted that racial prejudice would not disrupt the cohesion of his team. In a team lecture on racism he stated: "If I ever hear nigger or dago or kike or anything like that around here, regardless of who you are, you're through with me. You can't play for me if you have any kind of prejudice" (Maraniss, 1999, p. 241). Lombardi spread the word in Green Bay that any bar or restaurant that would not serve African American players would also be off limits to his entire team. On road trips, he would not allow his team to stay at segregated hotels, and lodged them at an army post in Fort Benning, GA so that they could stay together prior to an exhibition game.

Lombardi succeeded in turning around the Packers. In 1959, the team had a record of seven wins and five losses. In 1960, they were runners up to the Philadelphia Eagles, losing 17 to 13 in the championship game. They were champions of the NFL in 1961, 1962, 1965, 1966, and 1967. They won the first two Super Bowls that were contested in January 1967 and January 1968. Lombardi retired from coaching the Packers in 1968, having won the NFL championship in 5 of 9 years. He was recognized as a transcendent figure and a symbol of modern football during the time that football became the leading American spectator sport. With no political experience, he was considered as a vice-presidential candidate by both the Democratic and Republican parties. Reflecting Lombardi's place in its history, the NFL named its championship trophy the Lombardi Trophy.

and tradition of their institution encourage feelings of membership in distinctive sororities and fraternities. Coaches also encourage pride in team membership when they work with athletes to establish team goals and instill a sense of responsibility in team members for the overall team success.

A number of studies have demonstrated that cohesiveness is greater in smaller groups (Caron & Spink, 1995; Mullen & Cooper, 1994; Widmeyer, Brawley, & Carron, 1990). Membership of elite teams is very

> ## No-Swear Zone
>
> In American football, cursing or profanity is a part of the culture, except at Vanderbilt and other universities such as Notre Dame, Stanford, Rice, and Furman. At Vanderbilt, coach Bobby Johnson instituted a no-profanity rule that extends to players, coaches, and team managers, games and practice, and all athletic facilities. The penalties for inadvertent swearing are "up-and-down" drills – running in place, dropping to the ground, and jumping up – or pushups. Vanderbilt was considered first in its conference (Southeastern) in decorum (Yantz, 2002).

limited in relation to the numbers of outsiders, and the distinctiveness bestowed by membership of elite teams creates a sense of unity (Carron & Dennis, 1998). Further, members of a starting team or a travel squad (Widmeyer & Williams, 1991) might experience a greater sense of cohesiveness with fellow first team members than with the larger body or reserves and junior varsity players. For example, starting units on collegiate and high school football teams were more cohesive than non-starters (Granito & Rainey, 1988). Regardless of size, cohesiveness is promoted when teammates understand that they must depend on one another for team success (Yukelson, 1997).

A *second* factor demonstrated to influence team cohesion is the **personal characteristics** of the members of teams. Team members may be quite different in terms of socioeconomic background, ethnicity, and athletic experience. These differences need not be divisive, and similarities can be identified. For example, team members may be similar in that they share satisfaction about being a member of a team. Sportspersons are more likely to be satisfied with team membership when relationships with parents, coaches, and other students are positive, and when teammates are showing improvement and committed to common goals.

Third, **effective leadership** fosters team cohesion (Eys, Burke, Carron, & Dennis, 2006). Cohesiveness increases when coaches and athletes pursue common goals and objectives. For example, there was greater cohesiveness on high school basketball and wrestling teams when coaches and athletes were pursuing either team or individual goals, or when both athletes and coaches were focused on maintaining harmonious relationships with teammates (Carron & Chelladurai, 1981). Coaches who are active in providing instruction and training, positive feedback, social support, and who allow athletes to participate in decision-making foster team cohesion (Westre & Weiss, 1991). Task cohesion is encouraged when athletes participate in setting team goals. Teams may also be cohesive and not accept the

Riley's Rules

Pat Riley coached the Los Angeles Lakers to four National Basketball Association (NBA) championships in nine years. A former player, he has also been the head coach of the New York Knicks and the Miami Heat of the NBA. He asked the Lakers to enter with him into a core covenant, or commitment to the welfare of the team (Riley, 1993). He collaborated with players in making decisions, even about personnel. He asked team members to set standards for practice and games and to monitor these standards. Riley enforced the standards by benching players who did not fulfill the covenant. However, peer pressure was the primary resource for enforcing the core covenant, and he maintained that this replaced blaming and finger-pointing. In this process, members of the Lakers came to trust that Riley's agenda represented their individual and group interests.

leadership of coaches. This sometimes occurs when a popular coach is replaced and team members compare the replacement with the predecessor.

Fourth, as teams take shape, members assume roles, acquire status, and develop **norms** – formal and informal rules or standards for behavior. On cohesive teams, members understand and accept their roles (George & Feltz, 1995). They attempt to perform their roles to the best of their ability. Role acceptance is increased when coaches make roles explicit, determine whether athletes accept their roles, emphasize that team success is dependent on the successful role performance of all team members, and when differences in status between roles is minimized. Coaches may also assign team and individual goals to increase role clarity and acceptance.

Cohesiveness and Performance

Better team and individual athletic performances are associated with team cohesiveness. For example, collegiate male ice hockey teams in Canada that were cohesive at midseason were more likely to have successful postseasons (Ball & Carron, 1976). Canadian female and male high school athletes were more likely to recognize social and task cohesiveness on successful teams (Partington & Shangi, 1992). Elite Canadian female and male basketball and soccer players from winning collegiate and club teams reported higher levels of GI-T and ATG-T (Carron et al., 2002a). The individual performances of female and male high school basketball players improved with the development of team cohesiveness (Bray & Whaley, 2001). High school basketball players demonstrated improvement in terms of field goal and foul shot percentages, points per game, rebounds, and assists per game. As they accepted or bought into the goals and objectives of their teams and developed social relations with teammates, their effort, intensity, and productivity increased. US Olympic athletes at the winter games in Nagano, Japan in 1998 rated strong team chemistry and chemistry between teams and coaches as critical determinants of performance (Gould, 1999). Teams with players who assumed strong leadership roles were also seen as more successful.

Cohesiveness Leads to Success and Vice Versa

There is general agreement that team cohesiveness and performance improvements are positively correlated. Disagreement exists as to whether cohesiveness causes performance improvements or successful performance results in cohesiveness. For example, among women's field hockey teams, midseason team records predicted postseason cohesiveness (Williams & Hacker, 1982). More successful teams at midseason were more likely to report interpersonal closeness and teamwork at postseason. Success and cohesiveness also predicted greater satisfaction with team participation. Among female athletes in a range of sports, the increase in team cohesiveness after successful performance was greater than the improvement in performance with increasing cohesiveness. Losing appeared to decrease the cohesiveness of teams in interactive sports to a greater degree than the cohesiveness of teams in coactive sports, at least for female athletes (Matheson & Mathes, 1997).

Cohesion and success (photo courtesy of Western Connecticut State University).

Cohesiveness and Success

Under head coach Bill Belichick, the New England Patriots won three Super Bowls in 4 years and an NFL record 21 straight games. The Patriot players demonstrated a unity of purpose that was recognized by opposing coaches such as Marvin Lewis of the Cincinnati Bengals.

"All of their players in every interview spoke about the concept of team," Lewis said. "They never spoke of having the best defensive line, or best quarterback. They spoke about their football team and how each member is important. In this day and age in professional athletics, they are the ultimate team. They believe in that, they have bought into that and it is working. What they have accomplished is tremendous and awesome . . . We are trying to get to where they are by doing it how they do it, and that is one game at a time. We are trying to stay on their heels and learn what they do and how they do it. They provide a great model for us" (Greenberg, 2005a, p. E9).

These results were contradicted in a carefully designed study with male and female collegiate field hockey players in England (Slater & Sewell, 1994). These contradictory results demonstrated that team cohesiveness midway through seasons predicted team performance after an additional four weeks. More cohesive teams at midseason were more successful, as determined by wins, ties, and losses, four weeks later. Team performance at the midway point did not predict cohesiveness after the four weeks.

Ultimately, the most comprehensive current research demonstrates that team cohesiveness promotes better performance and that successful performance enhances team cohesiveness (Carron et al., 2002b). Furthermore, teams that are cohesive in their pursuit of task and social goals are likely to be more successful.

Cohesiveness and Social Loafing

Team membership does not always result in improved performance. When group cohesion is low, team members sometimes **loaf** or goof off when they think other group members can make up for their reduction in effort. When cohesion is low, there is less concern for the success of the group (Everett, Smith, & Williams, 1992). In these groups that lack cohesion, there is a diffusion of responsibility, as individuals do not take personal responsibility and reason that jobs are the responsibility of other group members. Loafing is more likely to occur when individual contributions are not critical to the success of the group, when it appears that others are loafing, and when it is difficult to identify the contributions of individuals. Effort is increased in groups that lack cohesion when the performances of individual members are announced publicly (Paskevich et al., 2001).

Social loafing is less likely to occur in cohesive groups, and responsibility for failure is shared among the members of cohesive groups (Carron et al., 1998). Failure prompts **scapegoating** in groups that lack cohesion, as members blame teammates for failure. In scapegoating, team members attempt to enhance their image at the expense of teammates.

As has been emphasized at various points in this text, psychological variables such as team cohesiveness do not function in isolation from athletic skill, practice, and training. As will be described in the next sections, cohesiveness and team efficacy are positively correlated, and both are associated with better team performance.

Team Efficacy

As explained in Chapter 9, the belief that one has the capacity to organize and execute the actions necessary to realize goals in particular areas or domains of functioning is referred to as self-efficacy. Team members often hold efficacy beliefs not only about their potential for reaching athletic goals, but also about the efficacy of the team as a whole to act effectively and reach performance standards. Collective **team efficacy** is more closely tied to team performance than are the individual efficacy beliefs of team members, especially in interactive sports such as collegiate hockey. It is also a correlate of team cohesion in interactive sports such as basketball and handball (Heuze, Sarrazin, Masiero, Raimbault, & Thomas, 2006). Collective efficacy not only is the stronger predictor of hockey team performance, but is also more directly affected by the performance of hockey teams (Feltz & Lirgg, 2001). Team efficacy, but not individual efficacy, has been shown to increase and decrease, respectively, following wins and losses. With high collective team efficacy, team members exert more effort to reach goals, persevere when faced with difficulties and setbacks, and recover confidence more quickly after disappointing defeats.

Sources of Collective Efficacy

As was the case with individual self-efficacy, the most convincing source of collective or team efficacy is **enactive attainments** or actual team accomplishment. The efficacy of teams may increase across the course of athletic seasons, as coordination and teamwork increase. Team efficacy is also influenced by the play or enactive attainments of individual players. As with individual efficacy, observational learning, feedback, and physiological reactions also provide information about the efficacy of teams. Observational learning and feedback are provided as teams estimate their competence in comparison to other teams. Coaches influence teams, and effective coaches model confidence and provide persuasion to enhance team efficacy. Spectators provide feedback, and efficacy is affected by the reactions of the audience. Booing home crowds and hostile media can undermine team efficacy. Team members also monitor their physiological reactions in estimating efficacy (Bandura, 1997). For example, signs of physiological anxiety, physical dysfunction, fatigue, and emotional dysphoria erode efficacy.

Team cohesion also contributes to team efficacy or confidence that team goals will be accomplished, and with heightened team efficacy, team performance improves (Paskevich, Brawley, Dorsch, & Widmeyer, 1995). For example, intercollegiate and recreational collegiate volleyball teams with higher task cohesiveness, both GI-T and ATG-T, also demonstrated higher team efficacy (Paskevich, Brawley, Dorsch, & Widmeyer, 1999). The cohesive teams had confidence in their collective ability to overcome obstacles, sustain motivation and communicate effectively, and in their team's skills. Similar results were reported for elite Canadian male and female volleyball teams (Spink, 1990). However, in the Canadian study, the ATG-T and GI-S factors differentiated teams with high and low efficacy. Teams high in the ATG-T and GI-S factors also had higher efficacy. Teams with higher efficacy were more successful in a volleyball tournament. The experience of success enhances both team efficacy and cohesion.

Setting Team Goals

Simply put, a group goal is what sufficient numbers of a group such as a team attempt to accomplish. Cooperation and collaboration among teammates is necessary for the accomplishment of group goals. Goal setting for teams is complicated by the need to integrate team goals with the individual goals of team members.

Athletes generally endorse **team goals**, although team goals may not be specific and well defined. Team goals for practice are more likely to be process goals, and team goals for competition are likely to be process and outcome goals (Brawley, Carron, & Widmeyer, 1992). In Chapter 8, process goals were said to relate to objectives for specific skill enhancement and refinement, and outcome goals to results of competition that are defined in relation to competitors. An example of an outcome goal would be to win a particular game.

Group goals that are difficult and specific enhance performance (Widmeyer & Ducharme, 1997). In fact, group goals may increase performance more than individual goals because the criteria for group goals are more difficult (Burton, Naylor, & Holliday, 2001). Difficult goals motivate greater effort, and effort is also increased when team goals and individual responsibilities for reaching team goals are publicly disclosed. Social loafing is minimized when individual responsibilities for reaching team goals are defined. However, as was the case with individual goals, sportspersons must accept or buy into the team goals.

When athletes accept team goals, teams develop a shared focus and team cohesion improves. Indeed, athletes rated the acceptance of team goals as the most important source of task cohesion and the second most influential source of social cohesion. Team goals that lead to better team performance are also likely to promote cohesion. Team cohesion is enhanced when team members participate in the goal setting process. This process has been identified as a major component of team building or systematically enhancing team cohesion (Yukelson, 1997).

When team members participate in setting goals, they have opportunities to understand the responsibilities of individuals to the team and the degree of cooperation necessary to reach team goals. This collaboration is important if athletes are to prioritize team goals over individual goals.

Coaches and athletes have been encouraged to collaborate in setting long-term team goals or goals for entire athletic seasons. These goals should be specific and difficult, and team short-term goals should then determine the steps necessary to realize the long-term goals (Widmeyer & Ducharme, 1997). Continuing with this advice, short-term goals should involve outcome, performance, and process aspects. Outcome and process aspects were defined above, and athletic performance goals focus on results measured against individual or team baselines. An example of a performance goal for a basketball team would be to make 80 percent of free throws during practice and games by the end of a season. Finally, it is important for coaches to provide feedback about progress in meeting short- and long-term goals. This is easily accomplished by posting results and monitoring results in team meetings.

Summary and Conclusions

Team cohesion is associated with team success and successful teams are often more cohesive. Team cohesion does not last forever. It is a dynamic psychological quality that exists in relation to teammates and coaches. Its more indelible representation exists in the identities of athletes, as they take aspects of their identities from participation in teams.

Teams that stick together in pursuit of common goals experience a form of task or social cohesiveness. When individual members believe that teams provide opportunities for meeting task goals they experience individual attractions to the group – task (ATG-T), and when teams are understood to provide social opportunities, individuals acknowledge individual attractions to the group – social (ATG-S). Sportspersons also form opinions about the degree to which teammates are united in pursuit of task or social goals, and these opinions are represented on measures of group integration for task (GI-T) and social (GI-S) goals.

Opportunities for the development of cohesion occur when teammates spend time in the same sport venues and when they keep to similar schedules. Cohesion is enhanced when sportspersons take pride in team membership and are publicly recognized as a member of an elite corps. Regardless of sociological differences, athletes experience team cohesion when they recognize that team members share a unity of purpose. Coaches have a major role in determining team unity. People are more likely to loaf or avoid work on teams and in groups that lack cohesion.

Teams that are united in the pursuit of goals are more likely to be cohesive. Athletes are more likely to personally endorse goals when they take part in establishing goals and when they understand that teammates share the team goals.

Key Terms

Individual attractions to the group – task

Individual attractions to the group – social

Group integration – task goals

Group integration – social goals

Team cohesion: situational factors, personal characteristics, effective leadership, norms

Coactive and interactive sports

Social loafing

Scapegoating

Team efficacy

Enactive attainments

Team goals

Suggested Readings

Bray, C. D., & Whaley, D. E. (2001). Team cohesion, effort, and objective individual performance of high school basketball players. *The Sport Psychologist*, *15*, 260–275.

Burton, D., Naylor, S., & Holliday, B. (2001). Goal setting in sport: Investigating the goal effectiveness paradox. In R. N. Singer, H. A. Hausenblas, & C. M. Janelle (Eds.), *Handbook of sport psychology* (2nd ed., pp. 497–528). New York: Wiley.

Paskevich, D. M., Brawley, L. R., Dorsch, K. D., & Widmeyer, W. N. (1999). Relationship between collective efficacy and team cohesion: Conceptual and measurement issues. *Group Dynamics: Theory, Research, and Practice*, *3*, 210–222.

Widmeyer, W. N., & Ducharme, K. (1997). Team building through team goal setting. *Journal of Applied Sport Psychology*, *9*, 97–113.

References

Abernethy, B. (2001). Attention. In R. N. Singer, H. A. Hausenblas, & C. M. Janelle (Eds.), *Handbook of sport psychology* (2nd ed., pp. 53–85). New York: Wiley.

Abrahms, S. (2003). Cycle of life. *BJ's Journal, Early Fall*, 4–5.

Abramson, L. Y., Seligman, M. E. P., & Teasdale, J. D. (1978). Learned helplessness in humans: Critique and reformulation. *Journal of Abnormal Psychology, 87*, 49–74.

Acosta, R. V., & Carpenter, L. J. (1985). Status of women in athletics: Causes and changes. *Journal of Physical Education, Recreation & Dance, 56*, 35–37.

Acosta, R. V, & Carpenter, L. J. (1990). *Women in intercollegiate sport: A longitudinal study – thirteen year update, 1977–1990*. Unpublished manuscript, Brooklyn College, New York.

Adler, A. (1964). *Superiority and social interest: A collection of later writings* (H. L. Ansbacher & R. R. Ansbacher, Eds.). New York: Norton.

Agnew, G. A., & Carron, A. V. (1994). Crowd effects and the home advantage. *International Journal of Sport Psychology, 25*, 53–62.

Albinson, J. G., & Bull, S. J. (1988). *A mental game plan*. Eastbourne, UK: Spodyn.

Allen, J. B., & Howe, B. L. (1998). Player ability, coach feedback, and female adolescent athletes' perceived competence and satisfaction. *Journal of Sport & Exercise Psychology, 20*, 280–299.

Allison, M. T., & Meyer, C. (1988). Career problems and retirement among elite athletes: The female tennis professional. *Sociology of Sport Journal, 5*, 212–222.

Allsopp, J., Eysenck, H. J., & Eysenck, S. B. G. (1991). Machiavellianism as a component in psychoticism and extraversion. *Personality and Individual Differences, 12*, 29–41.

American College of Sports Medicine. (1982). Position stand: The use of alcohol in sports. *Medicine and Science in Sports and Exercise, 14*, ix–xi.

American Psychiatric Association. (2000). *Diagnostic and statistical manual of mental disorders* (4th ed., text revision). Washington, DC: American Psychiatric Association.

American Psychological Association. (2002). Ethical principles of psychologists and code of conduct. *American Psychologist, 57*, 1597–1611.

Ames, C., & Archer, J. (1987). Mothers' belief about the role of ability and effort in school learning. *Journal of Educational Psychology, 79*, 409–414.

Ames, C., & Archer, J. (1988). Achievement goals in the classroom: Students' learning strategies and motivation processes. *Journal of Educational Psychology, 80*, 260–267.

Amore, D. (2006, April 18). Rodriguez seeking perfection: Third baseman's obsessive drive causes concern for Torre. *Hartford Courant*, p. C2.

Amorose, A. J., & Horn, T. S. (2000). Intrinsic motivation: Relationships with collegiate athletes' gender, scholarship status, and perceptions of their coaches' behavior. *Journal of Sport and Exercise Psychology, 22,* 63–84.

Amorose, A. J., & Weiss, M. R. (1998). Coaching feedback as a source of information about perceptions of ability: A developmental examination. *Journal of Sport & Exercise Psychology, 20,* 395–420.

Andersen, M. B. (1993). Questionable sensitivity: A comment on Lee and Rotella. *The Sport Psychologist, 7,* 1–3.

Anderson, W. A., Albrecht, R. R., McKeag, D. B., Hough, D. O., & McGrew, C. A. (1991). A national survey of alcohol and drug use by college athletes. *The Physician and Sports-medicine, 19,* 91–104.

Andre, T., & Holland, A. (1995). Relationship of sport participation to sex role orientation and attitudes toward women among high school athletes. *Journal of Sport Behavior, 18,* 241–253.

Annesi, J. J. (1997). Three-dimensional state anxiety recall: Implications for individual zone of optimal functioning research and application. *The Sport Psychologist, 11,* 43–52.

Annesi, J. J. (1998). Applications of the Individual Zones of Optimal Functioning model for the multimodal treatment of precompetitive anxiety. *The Sport Psychologist, 12,* 300–316.

Anonymous. (1952). *Twelve steps and twelve traditions.* New York: Alcoholics Anonymous World Services.

Anshel, M. H. (1990). Perceptions of black intercollegiate football players: Implications for the sport psychology consultant. *The Sport Psychologist, 4,* 235–248.

Anshel, M. H. (1995). An examination of self-regulatory cognitive-behavioral strategies of Australian elite and non-elite competitive male swimmers. *Australian Psychologist, 30,* 78–83.

Anshel, M. H., & Delany, J. (2001). Sources of acute stress, cognitive appraisals, and coping strategies of male and female child athletes. *Journal of Sport Behavior, 24,* 329–354.

Anshel, M. H., & Kaissidis, A. N. (1997). Coping style and situational appraisals as predictors of coping strategies following stressful events in sport as a function of gender and skill level. *The British Journal of Psychology, 88,* 263–276.

Anshel, M. H., Kim, K.-W., Kim, B.-H., Chang, K.-J., & Eom, H.-J. (2001). A model for coping with stressful events in sport: Theory, application, and future directions. *International Journal of Sport Psychology, 32,* 43–75.

Anshel, M. H., & Mansouri, H. (2005). Influences of perfectionism on motor performance, affect, and causal attributions in response to critical information feedback. *Journal of Sport Behavior, 28,* 99–124.

Anshel, M. H., Porter, A., & Quek, J.-J. (1998). Coping with acute stress in sport as a function of gender: An exploratory study. *Journal of Sport Behavior, 21,* 363–376.

Anshel, M. H., & Sailes, G. (1990). Discrepant attitudes of intercollegiate team athletes as a function of race. *Journal of Sport Behavior, 13,* 68–77.

Arent, S. M., & Landers, D. M. (2003). Arousal, anxiety, and performance: A reexamination of the inverted-U hypothesis. *Research Quarterly for Exercise and Sport, 74,* 436–444.

Arkin, R. M., & Oleson, K. C. (1998). Self-handicapping. In J. M. Darley & J. Cooper (Eds.), *Attribution and social interaction* (pp. 313–347). Washington, DC: American Psychological Association.

Armstrong, L., & Jenkins, S. (2000). *It's not about the bike: My journey back to life.* New York: G. P. Putnam's Sons.

Armstrong, L., & Jenkins, S. (2003). *Every second counts.* New York: Broadway Books.

Ashe, A. (1993). *A hard road to glory: A history of the African American athlete.* New York: Amistad Press.

Ashton, C. H. (2001). Pharmacology and effects of cannabis: A brief review. *British Journal of Psychiatry, 178*, 101–106.

Associated Press. (2004, June 24). Lifetime ban possible: Montgomery, Collins targets of drug agency. *Hartford Courant*, pp. C1, C6.

Associated Press. (2005, January 16). Kwan wins ninth title: Ties Vinson's US record. *Hartford Courant*, p. E12.

Associated Press. (2005, March 23). Jury finds for Williams: Romanowski ordered to pay $340,000 in damages. *Hartford Courant*, p. C7.

Associated Press. (2005, May 18). Romanowski stayed step ahead. *Hartford Courant*, p. C2.

Associated Press. (2005, June 2). Racy 49ers video is a PR nightmare. *Hartford Courant*, p. C7.

Association for the Advancement of Applied Sport Psychology. (1994). *Ethical principles of the Association for the Advancement of Applied Sport Psychology.* [Brochure]. Boise, ID: AASP.

Atkins, R. (1990, June 24). Boris banks on bouncing back. *Observer*, pp. 3–5.

Atkinson, J. W. (1957). Motivational determinants of risk-taking behavior. *Psychological Review, 64*, 359–372.

Atkinson, J. W. (1964). *An introduction to motivation.* Princeton, NJ: Van Nostrand.

Atkinson, J. W. (1978). The mainsprings of achievement-oriented activity. In J. W. Atkinson & Joel O. Raynor (Eds.), *Personality, motivation, and achievement* (pp. 11–39). Washington, DC: Halsted Press.

Austin, J. T., & Vancouver, J. B. (1996). Goal constructs in psychology: Structure, process, and content. *Psychological Bulletin, 120*, 338–375.

Bagby, R. M., Costa, P. T. Jr., Widiger, T. A., Ryder, A. G., & Marshall, M. (2005). DSM-IV personality disorders and the five-factor model of personality: A multi-method examination of domain- and facet-level predictions. *European Journal of Psychology, 19*, 307–324.

Bahrke, M. S., Yesalis, C. E., & Brower, K. J. (1998). Anabolic–androgenic steroid abuse and performance-enhancing drugs among adolescents. *Child and Adolescent Psychiatric Clinics of North America, 7*, 821–838.

Bahrke, M. S., Yesalis, C. E., & Wright, J. E. (1996). Psychological and behavioral effects of endogenous testosterone and anabolic–androgenic steroids: An update. *Sports Medicine, 22*, 367–390.

Balaguer, I., Duda, J. L., Atienza, F. L., & Mayo, C. (2002). Situational and dispositional goals as predictors of perceptions of individual and team improvement, satisfaction, and coach ratings among elite female handball teams. *Psychology of Sport and Exercise, 3*, 293–308.

Balaguer, I., Duda, J. L., & Crespo, M. (1999). Motivational climate and goal orientations as predictors of perceptions of improvement, satisfaction and coach ratings among tennis players. *Scandinavian Journal of Medicine and Science in Sports, 9*, 1–8.

Ball, J. R., & Carron, A. V. (1976). The influence of team cohesion and participation motivation upon performance success in intercollegiate ice hockey. *Canadian Journal of Applied Sport Sciences, 1*, 271–275.

Bamberger, M. (2003). Annika Sorenstam: A woman among men. *Sports Illustrated, 98*, February 24, 62–67.

Bandura, A. (1986). *Social foundations of thought and action: A social cognitive theory.* Englewood Cliffs, NJ: Prentice-Hall.

Bandura, A. (1989a). Human agency in social cognitive theory. *American Psychologist, 44*, 1175–1184.

Bandura, A. (1989b). Self-regulation of motivation and action through internal standards and goal systems. In L. A. Pervin (Ed.), *Goal concepts on personality and social psychology* (pp. 19–85). Hillsdale, NJ: Lawrence Erlbaum Associates, Inc.

Bandura, A. (1991). Human agency: The rhetoric and the reality. *American Psychologist, 46,* 157–162.

Bandura, A. (1997). *Self-efficacy: The exercise of control.* New York: Freeman.

Bandura, A., & Cervone, D. (1983). Self-evaluative and self-efficacy mechanisms governing the motivational effects of goal systems. *Journal of Personality and Social Psychology, 45,* 1017–1028.

Bandura, A., & Cervone, D. (1986). Differential engagement of self-reactive influences in cognitive motivation. *Organizational Behavior and Human Decision Processes, 38,* 92–113.

Bandura, A., Jeffery, R. W., & Gajdos, E. (1975). Generalizing change through participant modeling with self-directed mastery. *Behaviour Research and Therapy, 13,* 141–152.

Bandura, A., & Simon, K. M. (1977). The role of proximal intentions in self-regulation of refractory behavior. *Cognitive Therapy and Research, 1,* 177–193.

Barber, H. (1998). Examining gender differences in sources and levels of perceived competence in interscholastic coaches. *The Sport Psychologist, 12,* 237–252.

Barnett, N. P., Smoll, F. L., & Smith, R. E. (1992). Effects of enhancing coach–athlete relationships on youth sport attrition. *The Sport Psychologist, 6,* 111–127.

Barron, K. E., & Harackiewicz, J. M. (2001). Achievement goals and optimal motivation: Testing multiple goal models. *Journal of Personality and Social Psychology, 80,* 706–722.

Bartlewski, P., Van Raalte, J. L., & Brewer, B. W. (1996). Effects of aerobic exercise on the social physique anxiety and body esteem of female college students. *Women in Sport and Physical Activity Journal, 5,* 49–62.

Bauer, P. J., Schwade, J. A., Wewerka, S. S., & Delaney, K. (1999). Planning ahead: Goal-directed problem solving by 2–7-year-olds. *Developmental Psychology, 35,* 1321–1337.

Baumeister, R. F. (1984). Choking under pressure: Self-consciousness and paradoxical effects of incentives on skillful performance. *Journal of Personality and Social Psychology, 46,* 610–620.

Baumeister, R. F. (1995). Disputing the effects of championship pressures and home audiences. *Journal of Personality and Social Psychology, 68,* 644–648.

Baumeister, R. F., Hamilton, J. C., & Tice, D. M. (1985). Public versus private expectancy of success: Confidence booster or performance pressure? *Journal of Personality and Social Psychology, 48,* 1447–1457.

Baumeister, R. F., Heatherton, T. F., & Tice, D. M. (1993). When ego threats lead to self-regulation failure: Negative consequences of high self-esteem. *Journal of Personality and Social Psychology, 64,* 141–156.

Baumeister, R. F., & Showers, C. J. (1986). A review of paradoxical performance effects: Choking under pressure in sports and mental tests. *European Journal of Social Psychology, 16,* 361–383.

Baumeister, R. F., & Steinhilber, A. (1984). Paradoxical effects of supportive audiences on performance under pressure: The home field disadvantage in sports championships. *Journal of Personality and Social Psychology, 47,* 85–93.

Baumgardner, A. H. (1991). Claiming depressive symptoms as a self-handicap: A protective self-presentation strategy. *Basic and Applied Social Psychology, 12,* 97–113.

Beauchamp, P. H., Halliwell, W. R., Fournier, J. F., & Koestner, R. (1996). Effects of cognitive-behavioral psychological skill training on motivation, preparation, and putting performance of novice golfers. *The Sport Psychologist, 10,* 157–170.

Beckham, D., & Watt, T. (2003). *Beckham: Both feet on the ground.* New York: Harper Collins.

Beilock, S. L., Afremow, J. A., Rabe, A. L., & Carr, T. H. (2001). "Don't miss!" The debilitating effects of suppressive imagery on golf putting performance. *Journal of Sport & Exercise Psychology*, 23, 200–221.

Beilock, S. L., & Carr, T. H. (2001). On the fragility of skilled performance: What governs choking under pressure? *Journal of Experimental Psychology: General*, 40, 701–725.

Beilock, S. L., Carr, T. H., MacMahon, C., & Starkes, J. L. (2002). When paying attention becomes counterproductive: Impact of divided versus skill-focused attention on novice and experienced performance of sensorimotor skills. *Journal of Experimental Psychology: Applied*, 8, 6–16.

Bem, S. L. (1974). The measurement of psychological androgyny. *Journal of Consulting and Clinical Psychology*, 42, 155–162.

Bem, S. L. (1978). Beyond androgyny: Some presumptuous prescriptions for a liberated sexual identity. In J. Sherman & F. Denmark (Eds.), *Psychology of women: Future directions for research* (pp. 1–23). New York: Psychological Dimensions.

Benoit, J., & Baker, S. (1987). *Running tide*. New York: Alfred A. Knopf.

Benson, H. (1983). The relaxation response: Its subjective and objective historical precedents and physiology. *Trends in Neurosciences*, 6, 281–284.

Benson, H., Greenwood, M. M., & Klemchuk, H. (1975). The relaxation response: Psychophysiologic aspects and clinical applications. *International Journal of Psychiatry in Medicine*, 6, 87–98.

Benson, H., Kotch, J. B., Crassweller, K. D., & Greenwood, M. M. (1977). Historical and clinical considerations of the relaxation response. *American Scientist*, 65, 441–445.

Bergandi, T. (1985). Psychological variables relating to the incidence of athletic injury. *International Journal of Sport Psychology*, 15, 141–149.

Berglas, S., & Jones, E. E. (1978). Drug choice as a self-handicapping strategy in response to noncontingent success. *Journal of Personality and Social Psychology*, 36, 405–417.

Berlet, B. (2001, June 18). Gag order: Misses force playoff. *Hartford Courant*, pp. C1, C6.

Berlet, B. (2005, June 2). Not all endorse Wie's career approach. *Hartford Courant*, p. C3.

Bianco, T. (2001). Social support and recovery from sport injury: Elite skiers share their experiences. *Research Quarterly for Exercise and Sport*, 72, 376–388.

Bianco, T., & Eklund, R. C. (2001). Conceptual considerations for social support research in sport and exercise settings: The case of sport injury. *Journal of Sport & Exercise Psychology*, 23, 85–107.

Biddle, S. (1989). Applied sport psychology: A view from Britain. *Applied Sport Psychology*, 1, 23–34.

Biddle, S. & Hanrahan, S. (1998). Attributions and attribution style. In J. Duda (Ed.), *Advances in Sport and Exercise Psychology Measurement* (pp. 3–20). Morgantown, WV: Fitness Information Technology.

Biddle, S. J. H., Hanrahan, S. J., & Sellars, C. N. (2001). Attributions: Past, present, and future. In N. Singer, H. A. Hausenblas, & C. M. Janelle (Eds.), *Handbook of sport psychology* (2nd ed., pp. 444–471). New York: Wiley.

Billing, J. (1980). An overview of task complexity. *Motor skills: Theory into practice*, 4, 18–23.

Black, S. J., & Weiss, M. R. (1992). The relationship among perceived coaching behaviors, perceptions of ability, and motivation in competitive age-group swimmers. *Journal of Sport & Exercise Psychology*, 14, 309–325.

Blanchard, C. Perreault, S., & Vallerand, R. J. (1998). Participation in team sport: A self-expansion perspective. *International Journal of Sport Psychology*, 29, 289–302.

Blatt, S. J. (1995). The destructiveness of perfectionism. *American Psychologist*, 50, 1003–1020.

Blatt, S. J., & Quinlan, P. (1967). Punctual and procrastinating students: A study of temporal parameters. *Journal of Consulting Psychology*, 31, 169–174.

Bloomberg News. (2005, February 1). Hamilton says do tread on me: Pistons guard promotes tire with his hair. *Hartford Courant*, p. C5.

Blount, R. (2004, March 26). Less than perfect; Keith Ballard becomes more effective when he learned not to dwell on his mistakes. *Star Tribune*, p. 10C.

Bluestein, G. (2004, September 20). Controlling their future: Athletes among those helping steer minority students toward automotive careers. *Hartford Courant*, p. C13.

Blunt, A. K., & Psychl, T. A. (2000). Task aversiveness and procrastination: A multidimensional approach to task aversiveness across stages of personal projects. *Personality and Individual Differences, 28*, 153–167.

Boggiano, A. K. (1998). Maladaptive achievement patterns: A test of a diathesis-stress analysis of helplessness. *Journal of Personality and Social Psychology, 74*, 1681–1695.

Boggiano, A. K., & Barrett, M. (1991). Strategies to motivate helpless and mastery-oriented children: The effects of gender based expectancies. *Sex Roles, 25*, 487–510.

Boggiano, A. K., Barrett, M., & Kellam, T. (1993). Competing theoretical analyses of helplessness: A social-developmental analysis. *Journal of Experimental Child Psychology, 55*, 194–207.

Boggiano, A. K., Shields, A., Barrett, M., Kellam, T., Thompson, E., Simons, J., & Katz, P. (1992). Helpless deficits in students: The role of motivational orientation. *Motivation and Emotion, 16*, 271–296.

Bois, J. E., Sarrazin, P. G., Brustad, R. J., Chanal, J. P., & Trouilloud, D. O. (2005). Parents' appraisals, reflected appraisals, and children's self-appraisals of sport competence: A yearlong study. *Journal of Applied Sport Psychology, 17*, 273–289.

Boixados, M., Cruz, J., Torregrosa, M., & Valiente, L. (2005). Relationships among motivational climate, satisfaction, perceived ability, and fair play attitudes in young soccer players. *Journal of Applied Sport Psychology, 16*, 301–317.

Boldizar, J. P. (1991). Assessing sex typing and androgyny in children: The Children's Sex Role Inventory. *Developmental Psychology, 27*, 505–515.

Bond, K. A., Biddle, S. J. H., & Ntoumanis, N. (2001). Self-efficacy and causal attribution in female golfers. *International Journal of Sport Psychology, 31*, 243–256.

Bonk, T. (2005, October 6). New pro Wie a $20 million teen. *Hartford Courant*, p. C5.

Borges, G., Walters, E. E., & Kessler, R. C. (2000). Associations of substance use, abuse, and dependence with subsequent suicidal behavior. *American Journal of Epidemiology, 151*, 781–789.

Borkovec, T. D., & Sides, J. K. (1979). Critical procedural variables related to the physiological effects of progressive relaxation: A review. *Behaviour Research and Therapy, 17*, 119–125.

Botterill, C. (1990). Sport psychology and professional hockey. *The Sport Psychologist, 4*, 358–368.

Boutcher, S. H., & Crews, D. J. (1987). The effect of a preshot attentional routine on a well-learned skill. *International Journal of Sports Psychology, 18*, 30–39.

Bower, B. L., & Martin, M. (1999). African American female basketball players: An examination of alcohol and drug behaviors. *College Health, 48*, 129–133.

Boyce, B. A., Wayda, V. K., Johnston, T., Bunker, L. K., & Eliot, J. (2001). The effects of three types of goal setting conditions on tennis performance: A field-based study. *Journal of Teaching in Physical Education, 20*, 188–200.

Boyce, W. T., & Sobolewski, S. (1989). Recurrent injuries in school children. *American Journal of the Disabled Child, 143*, 338–342.

Brackenridge, C. (2000). Sexual harassment and abuse. In B. L. Drinkwater (Ed.), *Women in sport* (pp. 342–350). Oxford: Blackwell Science.

Brawley, L. R., Carron, A. V., & Widmeyer, W. N. (1988). Exploring the relationship between cohesion and group resistance to disruption. *Journal of Sport & Exercise Psychology, 10*, 199–213.

Brawley, L. R., Carron, A. V., & Widmeyer, W. N. (1992). The nature of group goals in sport teams: A phenomenological analysis. *The Sport Psychologist, 6*, 323–333.

Bray, C. D., & Whaley, D. E. (2001). Team cohesion, effort, and objective individual performance of high school basketball players. *The Sport Psychologist, 15*, 260–275.

Brett, J. F., & VandeWalle, D. (1999). Goal orientation and goal content as predictors of performance in a training program. *Journal of Applied Psychology, 84*, 863–873.

Brewer, B. (1993). Self-identity and specific vulnerability to depressed mood. *Journal of Personality, 61*, 343–364.

Brewer, B. W. (2001). Psychology of sport rehabilitation. In R. N. Singer, H. A. Hausenblas, & C. M. Janelle (Eds.), *Handbook of sport psychology* (2nd ed., pp. 787–809). New York: Wiley.

Brewer, B. W., Cornelius, A. E., Van Raalte, J. L., Petitpas, A. J., Sklar, J. H., Pohlman, M. H., et al. (2000). Attributions for recovery and adherence to rehabilitation following anterior cruciate ligament reconstruction: A prospective analysis. *Psychology and Health, 15*, 283–291.

Brewer, B. W., Cornelius, A. E., Van Raalte, J. L., Petitpas, A. J., Sklar, J. H., Pohlman, M. H., Krushell, R. J., & Ditmar, T. D. (2003). Protection motivation theory and adherence to sport injury rehabilitation revisited. *The Sport Psychologist, 17*, 95–103

Brewer, B. W., Van Raalte, J. L., & Petitpas, A. J. (2000). Self-identity issues in sport career transitions. In D. Lavallee & P. Wylleman (Eds.), *Career transitions in sport: International perspectives* (pp. 29–43). Morgantown, WV: Fitness Information Technology.

Bricker, C. (2001, July 7). Rafter never backs down. *Hartford Courant*, pp. C1–C2.

Brook, J. S., Kessler, R. C., & Cohen, P. (1999). The onset of marijuana use from pre-adolescence and early adolescence to young adulthood. *Development and Psychopathology, 11*, 901–914.

Brooks, G., & Fahey, T. (1984). *Exercise physiology*. New York: Wiley.

Brown, E. J., Heimberg, R. G., Frost, R. O., Makris, G. S., Juster, H. R., & Leung, A. W. (1999). Relationship of perfectionism to affect, expectations, attributions and performance in the classroom. *Journal of Social and Clinical Psychology, 18*, 98–120.

Brown, J., & Delsohn, S. (1989). *Out of bounds*. New York: Zebra.

Brown, P., & Gaines, S. S. (1983). *The love you make: An insider's story of the Beatles*. New York: McGraw-Hill.

Brown, R. W., & Jewell, R. T. (1994). Is there consumer discrimination in college basketball? The premium fans pay for white players. *Social Science Quarterly, 75*, 401–413.

Brown, T. D. Jr., Van Raalte, J. L., Brewer, B. W., Winter, C. R., Cornelius, A. E., & Andersen, M. B. (2002). World Cup soccer home advantage. *Journal of Sport Behavior, 25*, 134–144.

Brustad, R. J. (1993). Who will go out and play? Parental and psychological influences on children's attraction to physical activity. *Pediatric Exercise Science, 5*, 210–223.

Buchanan, H. T., Blankenbaker, J., & Cotton, D. (1976). Academic and athletic ability as popularity factors in elementary school children. *Research Quarterly, 47*, 320–325.

Bull, S. J. (1991). Personal and situational influences on adherence to mental skills training. *Journal of Sport and Exercise Psychology, 13*, 121–132.

Bull, S. J., Shambrook, C. J., James, W., & Brooks, J. E. (2005). Towards an understanding of mental toughness in elite English cricketers. *Journal of Applied Sport Psychology, 17*, 209–227.

Burke, K. L. (1986). Comparison of psychological androgyny within a sample of female college athletes who participate in sports traditionally appropriate and traditionally inappropriate for competition by females. *Perceptual and Motor Skills, 63*, 779–782.

Burke, K. L. (1992). Concentration. *Sport Psychology Training Bulletin, 4*, 1–8.

Burns, D. (1993). *Ten days to self-esteem*. New York: William Morrow.

Burton, D. (2002). The Jekyll/Hyde nature of goals: Reconceptualizing goal setting in sport. In T. Horn (Ed.), *Advances in sport psychology* (pp. 267–297). Champaign, IL: Human Kinetics.

Burton, D., & Naylor, S. (1997). Is anxiety really facilitative? Reaction to the myth that cognitive anxiety always impairs sport performance. *Journal of Applied and Sport Psychology, 9*, 295–302.

Burton, D., Naylor, S., & Holliday, B. (2001). Goal setting in sport: Investigating the goal effectiveness paradox. In R. N. Singer, H. A. Hausenblas, & C. M. Janelle (Eds.), *Handbook of sport psychology* (2nd ed., pp. 497–528). New York: Wiley.

Burton, D., Weinberg, R., Yukelson, D., & Weigand, D. (1998). The goal effectiveness paradox in sport: Examining the goal practices of collegiate athletes. *The Sport Psychologist, 12*, 404–418.

Butcher, J., Lindner, K. J., & Johns, D. P. (2002). Withdrawal from competitive youth sport: A retrospective ten-year study. *Journal of Sport Behavior, 25*, 145–153.

Butler, J. L., & Baumeister, R. F. (1998). The trouble with friendly faces: Skilled performance with a supportive audience. *Journal of Personality and Social Psychology, 75*, 1213–1230.

Butryn, T. M. (2002). Critically examining white racial identity and privilege in sport psychology consulting. *The Sport Psychologist, 16*, 316–336.

Butt Why? Despite his actions, Zidane wins Golden Ball. (2006, July 11). *Hartford Courant*, p. C2.

Caesar, D. (2004, June 10). A (Jim) Gray spot for Bird. *Hartford Courant*, p. C7.

Callow, N., & Hardy, L. (2001). Types of imagery associated with sport confidence in netball players of varying skill levels. *Journal of Applied Sport Psychology, 13*, 1–17.

Callow, N., Hardy, L., & Hall, C. (2001). The effects of a motivational general-mastery imagery intervention on the sport confidence of high-level badminton players. *Research Quarterly in Exercise and Sport, 72*, 389–400.

Calmels, C., Berthoumieux, C., & d'Arripe-Longueville, F. (2004). Effects of an imagery training program on selective attention of national softball players. *The Sport Psychologist, 18*, 272–296.

Calmels, C., d'Arripe-Longueville, F., Fournier, J. F., & Soulard, A. (2003). Competitive strategies among elite female gymnasts: An exploration of the relative influences of psychological skills training and natural learning experiences. *International Journal of Sport & Exercise Psychology, 1*, 327–352.

Campo-Flores, A., & Kirsch, R. (2002). Sent to the penalty box. *Newsweek, 139*, January 21, 38.

Cantor, N., & Harlow, R. E. (1994). Personality, strategic behaviour and daily-life problem solving. *Current Directions in Psychological Science, 3*, 169–172.

Carlson, C. R., & Bernstein, D. A. (1995). Relaxation skills training: Abbreviated Progressive Relaxation. In W. O'Donohue & L. Krasner (Eds.), *Handbook of psychological skills training: Clinical applications and techniques*. Boston: Allyn & Bacon.

Carlson, R. C. (1988). The socialization of elite tennis players in Sweden: An analysis of the players' backgrounds and development. *Sociology of Sport Journal, 5*, 241–256.

Carlson, R. C. (1997). In search of the expert sport performer. *Science in the Olympic Sport, 1*, 1–13.

Carpenter, P. J., & Yates, B. (1997). Relationship between achievement goals and the perceived purposes of soccer for semiprofessional and amateur players. *Journal of Sport & Exercise Psychology, 19*, 302–311.

Carr, S., & Weigand, D. A. (2002). The influence of significant others on the goal orientations of youngsters in physical education. *Journal of Sport Behavior*, 25, 19–40.

Carron, A. V., Brawley, L. R., & Widmeyer, W. N. (1998). The measurement of cohesiveness in sport groups. In J. L. Duda (Ed.), *Advances in sport and exercise psychology* (pp. 213–226). Morgantown, WV: Fitness Information Technology.

Carron, A. V., Bray, S. R., & Eys, M. A. (2002a). Team cohesion and team success in sport. *Journal of Sport Sciences*, 20, 119–126.

Carron, A. V., & Chelladurai, P. (1981). The dynamics of group cohesion in sport. *Journal of Sport Psychology*, 3, 123–139.

Carron, A. V., Colman, M. M., Wheeler, J., & Stevens, D. (2002b). Cohesion and performance in sport: A meta analysis. *Journal of Sport and Exercise Psychology*, 24, 168–188.

Carron, A. V., & Dennis, P. W. (1998). The sport team as an effective group. In J. M. Williams (Ed.), *Applied sport psychology: Personal growth to peak performance* (3rd ed., pp. 127–141). Mountain View, CA: Mayfield.

Carron, A. V., & Dennis, P. W. (2001). The sport team as an effective group. In J. M. Williams (Ed.), *Applied sport psychology: Personal growth to peak performance* (4th ed., pp. 120–134). Mountain View, CA: Mayfield.

Carron, A. V., Prapavessis, H., & Grove, J. R. (1994). Group effects and self-handicapping. *Journal of Sport and Exercise Psychology*, 16, 246–257.

Carron, A. V., & Spink, K. S. (1993). Team building in an exercise setting. *The Sport Psychologist*, 7, 8–18.

Carron, A. V., & Spink, K. S. (1995). The group size–cohesion relationship in minimal groups. *Small Group Research*, 26, 86–105.

Carron, A. V., Widmeyer, W. N., & Brawley, L. R. (1985). The development of an instrument to assess cohesion in sport teams: The Group Environment Questionnaire. *Journal of Sport Psychology*, 7, 244–266.

Carver, C. S. (1996). Cognitive interference and the structure of behavior. In I. G. Sarason, G. R. Pierce, & B. R. Sarason (Eds.), *Cognitive interference theories, methods, & findings* (pp. 25–45). Mahwah, NJ: Lawrence Erlbaum Associates, Inc.

Carver, C. S., & Baird, E. (1998). The American dream revisited: Is it what you want or why you want it that matters? *Psychological Science*, 9, 289–292.

Carver, C. S., Lawrence, J. W., & Scheier, M. F. (1996). A control-process perspective on the origins of affect. In L. M. Martin & A. Tesser (Eds.), *Striving and feeling: Interactions among goals, affect, and self-regulation* (pp. 11–52). Mahwah, NJ: Lawrence Erlbaum Associates, Inc.

Carver, C. S., & Scheier, M. F. (1998a). A control-process perspective on anxiety. *Anxiety Research*, 1, 17–22.

Carver, C. S., & Scheier, M. F. (1998b). *On the self-regulation of behavior*. Cambridge, UK: Cambridge University Press.

Carver, C. S., & Scheier, M. F. (1992). Confidence, doubt and coping with anxiety. In D. G. Forgays, T. Sosnowski, & K Wresiewski (Eds.), *Anxiety: Recent developments in cognitive, psychophysiological and health research* (pp. 13–22). London: Hemisphere.

Castaneda, R., Sussman, N., Levy, R., O'Malley, M., & Westreich, L. (1998). A review of the effects of moderate alcohol intake on psychiatric and sleep disorders. *Recent Developments in Alcoholism*, 14, 197–251.

Castro, J. R., & Rice, K. G. (2003, August). *Attentional distraction and perfectionism: A test of competing models of moderation and mediation in the cognitive anxiety–performance relationship*. Poster presented at the Annual Convention of the American Psychological Association, Toronto, Canada.

Cavalli-Sforza, L. L., & Cavalli-Sforza, F. (1995). *The great human diasporas: The history of diversity and evolution*. Reading, MA: Perseus Books.

Centers for Disease Control and Prevention. (1998). *CDC surveillance summaries*. MMWR 49, SS-5. Atlanta, GA: CDCP.

Cerin, E. (2004). Predictors of competitive anxiety direction in male Tae Kwon Do practitioners: A multilevel mixed idiographic/nomothetic interactional approach. *Psychology of Sport and Exercise, 5*, 497–516.

Cervone, D. (2000). Thinking about self-efficacy. *Behavior Modification, 24*, 30–57.

Cervone, D., Kopp, D. A., Schaumann, L., & Scott, W. D. (1994). Mood, self-efficacy, and performance standards: Lower moods induce higher standards for performance. *Journal of Personality and Social Psychology, 67*, 499–512.

Cervone, D., & Wood, R. (1995). Goals, feedback, and the differential influence of self-regulatory processes on cognitively complex performance. *Cognitive Therapy and Research, 19*, 519–545.

Chait, L. D. (1990). Subjective and behavioral effects of marijuana the morning after smoking. *Psychopharmacology, 100*, 328–333.

Chase, M. A., & Dummer, G. M. (1992). The role of sports as a social status determinant for children. *Research Quarterly for Exercise and Sport, 63*, 418–424.

Chase, M. A., Lirgg, C. D., & Feltz, D. F. (1997). Do coaches' efficacy expectations for their teams predict team performance? *The Sport Psychologist, 11*, 8–23.

Chelladurai, P. (1980). Leadership in sports organizations. *Canadian Journal of Applied Sport Sciences, 5*, 226–231.

Chelladurai, P. (1984). Discrepancy between preferences and perceptions of leadership behavior and satisfaction of athletes in varying sports. *Journal of Sport Psychology, 6*, 27–41.

Chelladurai, P. (1990). Leadership in sports: A review. *International Journal of Sport Psychology, 21*, 328–354.

Chelladurai, P. (1993). Leadership. In R. N. Singer, M. Murphey, & L. K. Tennant (Eds.), *Handbook of research on sport psychology* (pp. 647–671). New York: Macmillan.

Chelladurai, P., & Arnott, M. (1985). Decision styles in coaching: Preferences of basketball players. *Research Quarterly for Exercise and Sport, 56*, 15–24.

Chelladurai, P., & Doherty, A. J. (1998). Styles of decision making in coaching. In J. M. Williams (Ed.), *Applied sport psychology: Personal growth to peak performance* (3rd ed., pp. 115–126). Mountain View, CA: Mayfield.

Chelladurai, P., Haggerty, T. R., & Baxter, P. R. (1989). Decision styles choices of university basketball coaches and players. *Journal of Sport and Exercise Psychology, 11*, 201–215.

Chelladurai, P., Imamura, H., Yamaguchi, Y., Oinuma, Y., & Miyauchi, T. (1988). Sport leadership in a cross-national setting: The case of Japanese and Canadian university athletes. *Journal of Sport & Exercise Psychology, 10*, 374–389.

Chelladurai, P., Malloy, D., Imamura, H., & Yamaguchi, Y. (1987). A cross-cultural study of preferred leadership in sports. *Canadian Journal of Sport Sciences, 12*, 106–110.

Chelladurai, P., & Quek, C. B. (1995). Decision style choices of high school coaches: The effects of situational and coach characteristics. *Journal of Sport Behavior, 18*, 91–108.

Chelladurai, P., & Reimer, H. A. (1998). Measurement of leadership in sport. In J. L. Duda (Ed.), Advances in sport and exercise psychology (pp. 227–253). Morgantown, WV: Fitness Information Technology.

Chelladurai, P., & Saleh, S. (1978). Preferred leadership in sports. *Canadian Journal of Applied Sport Sciences, 3*, 85–92.

Chelladurai, P., & Saleh, S. (1980). Dimensions of leader behavior in sports. *Journal of Sport Psychology, 2*, 34–45.

Chelladurai, P., & Turner, B. A. (2006). Styles of decision making in coaching. In J. M. Williams (Ed.), *Applied sport psychology: Personal growth to peak performance* (5th ed., pp. 140–154). New York: McGraw-Hill.

Chi, L., & Duda, J. L. (1995). Multi-sample confirmatory factor analysis of the task and ego orientation in sport questionnaire. *Research Quarterly for Exercise and Sport, 66,* 91–98.

Chu, D. (1982). *Dimensions of sport studies.* New York: Wiley.

Clark, R. D. (2002). Do professional golfers "choke"? *Perceptual and Motor Skills, 94,* 1124–1130.

Clearly, T., & Zimmerman, B. J. (2001). Self-regulation differences during athletic practice by experts, non-experts, and novices. *Journal of Applied Sport Psychology, 13,* 61–82.

Cloninger, C. R. (1987). Neurogenetic adaptive mechanisms in alcoholism. *Science, 236,* 410–416.

Coakley, J. (1992). Burnout among adolescent athletes: A personal failure or social problem? *Sociology of Sport Journal, 9,* 271–285.

Coakley, J. (2001). *Sport in society: Issues & controversies.* Boston: McGraw-Hill.

Coates, B. (1997, January 1). Workaholic Vermeil once considered "poster boy of coaching burnout". *St Louis Post-Dispatch,* p. C3.

Cochran, W., & Tesser, A. (1996). The "what the hell" effect: Some effects of goal proximity and goal framing on performance. In L. M. Martin & A. Tesser (Eds.), *Striving and feeling: Interactions among goals, affect, and self-regulation* (pp. 99–120). Mahwah, NJ: Lawrence Erlbaum Associates, Inc.

Coen, S. P., & Ogles, B. M. (1993). Psychological characteristics of the obligatory runner: A critical examination of the anorexia analogue hypothesis. *Journal of Sport and Exercise Psychology, 15,* 338–354.

Cogan, K. D., & Petrie, T. A. (1996). Diversity in sport. In J. L. Van Raalte & B. W. Brewer (Eds.), *Exploring exercise and sport psychology* (pp. 355–373). Washington, DC: American Psychological Association.

Cogan, K. D., & Petrie, T. A. (2002). Diversity in sport. In J. L. Van Raalte & B. W. Brewer (Eds.), *Exploring exercise and sport psychology* (2nd ed., pp. 417–436). Washington, DC: American Psychological Association.

Cohn, P. J. (1990a). An exploratory study on sources of stress and athlete burnout in youth golf. *The Sport Psychologist, 4,* 95–106.

Cohn, P. J. (1990b). Preperformance routines in sport: Theoretical support and practical applications. *The Sport Psychologist, 4,* 301–312.

Cohn, P. J. (1991). An exploratory study on peak performance in golf. *The Sport Psychologist, 5,* 1–14.

Compas, B. E., & Epping, J. E. (1993). Stress and coping in children and families. In C. F. Saylor (Ed.), *Children and disasters* (pp. 11–28). New York: Plenum Press.

Conroy, D. E. (2003). Representational models associated with fear of failure in adolescents and young adults. *Journal of Personality, 71,* 757–783.

Conroy, D. E. (2004). The unique psychological meanings of multidimensional fears of failing. *Journal of Sport & Exercise Psychology, 26,* 484–491.

Conroy, D. E., & Elliot, A. J. (2004). Fear of failure and achievement goals in sport: Addressing the issue of the chicken and the egg. *Anxiety, Stress, and Coping, 17,* 271–285.

Conroy, D. E., Elliot, A. J., & Hofer, S. M. (2003). Achievement goals questionnaire for sport: Evidence for factorial invariance, temporal stability, and external validity. *Journal of Sport & Exercise Psychology, 25,* 456–476.

Conroy, D. E., & Metzler, J. N. (2004). Patterns of self-talk associated with different forms of competitive anxiety. *Journal of Sport & Exercise Psychology, 26,* 69–89.

Conroy, D. E., Poczwardowski, A., & Henschen, K. P. (2001). Evaluative criteria and consequences associated with failure and success for elite athletes and performing artists. *Journal of Applied Sport Psychology, 13*, 300–322.

Constantian, C. A. (1981). *Attitudes, beliefs, and behavior in regard to spending time alone*. Unpublished doctoral dissertation. Harvard University, Cambridge, MA.

Cook, T. D., & Campbell, D. T. (1979). *Quasi-experimentation: Design & analysis issues for field settings*. Chicago: Rand McNally.

Cooper, M. L. (1994). Motivations for alcohol use among adolescents: Development and validation of a four-factor model. *Psychological Assessment, 6*, 117–128.

Cooper, M. L., Russell, M., Skinner, J. B., & Windle, M. (1992). Development and validation of a three-dimensional measure of drinking motives. *Psychological Assessment, 4*, 123–132.

Copeland, J., Peters, R., & Dillon, P. (2000). Anabolic–androgenic steroid use disorders among a sample of Australian competitive and recreational users. *Drug and Alcohol Dependence, 60*, 91–96.

Costa, P. T. Jr., & McCrae, R. R. (1992). *NEO PI-R professional manual*. Odessa, FL: Psychological Assessment Resources.

Costa, P. T. Jr., & McCrae, R. R. (1995). Primary traits of Eysenck's P-E-N system: three- and five-factor solutions. *Journal of Personality and Social Psychology, 69*, 308–317.

Costanzo, P. R., Woody, E., & Slater, P. (1992). On being psyched up but not psyched out: An optimal pressure model of achievement motivation. In A. K. Boggiano & T. S. Pittman (Eds.), *Achievement and motivation: A social developmental perspective*. New York: Cambridge University Press.

Cote, J. (1999). The influence of family in the development of talent. *The Sport Psychologist, 13*, 395–417.

Cote, J., & Salmela, J. H. (1996). The organizational tasks of high performance gymnastic coaches. *The Sport Psychologist, 10*, 247–260.

Cote, J., Salmela, J. H., & Russell, S. (1995a). The knowledge of high-performance gymnastic coaches: Competition and training considerations. *The Sport Psychologist, 9*, 76–95.

Cote, J., Salmela, J., Trudel, P., Baria, A., & Russell, S. (1995b). The coaching model: A grounded assessment of expert gymnastic coaches' knowledge. *Journal of Sport & Exercise Psychology, 17*, 1–17.

Courneya, K. S., & Carron, A. V. (1992). The home advantage in sport competitions: A literature review. *Journal of Sport & Exercise Psychology, 14*, 13–27.

Covassin, T., & Pero, S. (2004). The relationship between self-confidence, mood state, and anxiety among collegiate tennis players. *Journal of Sport Behavior, 27*, 230–241.

Covington, M. V. (1992). *Making the grade: A self-worth perspective on motivation and school reform*. New York: Cambridge University Press.

Cox, R. H. (2002). *Sport psychology: Concepts and applications* (5th ed.). New York: McGraw-Hill.

Cox, T. & Ferguson, E. (1991), Individual differences, stress, and coping. In C. L. Cooper & R. Payne (Eds.), *Personality and stress: Individual differences in the stress process* (pp. 7–30). Chichester, UK: Wiley.

Cox, T., & Kerr, J. H. (1990). Self-reported mood in competitive squash. *Personality and Individual Differences, 11*, 199–203.

Crant, J. M. (1996). Doing more harm than good: When is impression management likely to evoke a negative response? *Journal of Applied Social Psychology, 16*, 1454–1471.

Cresswell, S. L., & Eklund, R. C. (2005a). Changes in athlete burnout and motivation over a 12-week league tournament. *Medicine and Science in Sports and Exercise, 37*, 1957–1966.

Cresswell, S. L., & Eklund, R. C. (2005b). Motivation and burnout among top amateur rugby players. *Medicine and Science in Sports and Exercise, 37*, 469–477.

Cresswell, S. L., & Eklund, R. C. (2006a). Athlete burnout: Conceptual confusion, current research and future research directions. In S. Hanton & S. D. Mellalieu (Eds.), *Literature reviews in sport psychology* (pp. 91–126). New York: Nova Science Publishers.

Cresswell, S. L., & Eklund, R. C. (2006b). The convergent and discriminant validity of burnout measures in sport: A multi-trait/multi-method analysis. *Journal of Sport Sciences, 24*, 209–220.

Cresswell, S. L., & Eklund, R. C. (2006c). The nature of player burnout in rugby: Key characteristics and attributions. *Journal of Applied Sport Psychology, 18*, 219–239.

Cresswell, S., & Hodge, K. (2004). Coping skills: Role of trait sport confidence and trait anxiety. *Perceptual and Motor Skills, 98*, 433–438.

Crocker, P. R. E., & Graham, T. R. (1995). Coping by competitive athletes with performance stress: Gender differences and relationships with affect. *Sport Psychologist, 9*, 325–338.

Croft, R. J., Mackay, A. J., Mills, A. T. D., & Gruzelier, J. G. H. (2001). The relative contributions of ecstasy and cannabis to cognitive impairment. *Psychopharmacology, 153*, 373–379.

Csikszentmihalyi, M. (1990). *Flow: The psychology of optimal experience*. New York: Harper & Row.

Cumming, J., & Hall, C. (2002). Athletes' use of imagery in the off-season. *The Sport Psychologist, 16*, 160–172.

Cumming, J., Hall, C., Harwood, C., & Gammage, K. (2002). Motivational orientations and imagery use: A goal profiling analysis. *Journal of Sports Sciences, 20*, 127–136.

Cumming, J. L., & Ste-Marie, D. M. (2001). The cognitive and motivational effects of imagery training: A matter of perspective. *Sport Psychologist, 15*, 276–288.

Cupal, D. D. (1998). Psychological interventions in sport injury prevention and rehabilitation. *Journal of Applied Sport Psychology, 10*, 103–123.

Cury, F., Da Fonseca, D., Rufo, M., Peres, C., & Sarrazin, P. (2003). The trichotomous model and investment in learning to prepare a sport test: A mediational analysis. *British Journal of Educational Psychology, 73*, 529–543.

Cury, F., Elliot, A., Sarrazin, P., Da Fonseca, D., & Rufo, M. (2002). The trichotomous achievement goal model and intrinsic motivation: A sequential mediational analysis. *Journal of Experimental Social Psychology, 38*, 473–481.

Cyr, D. (2004). King of the court. *US Airways Attaché*, November, 32–36.

Daino, A. (1985). Personality traits of adolescent tennis players. *International Journal of Sport Psychology, 16*, 120–125.

Dale, G. A. (1997). Dealing with distractions. *Scholastic Coach & Athletic Director, 66*, 4–6.

Dale, G. A. (2000). Distractions and coping strategies of elite decathletes during their most memorable performances. *The Sport Psychologist, 14*, 17–41.

Dale, J., & Weinberg, R. S. (1989). The relationship between coaches' leadership style and burnout. *The Sport Psychologist, 3*, 1–13.

Daly, J. M., Brewer, B. W., Van-Raalte, J. L., Petitpas, A. J., & Sklar, J. H. (1995). Cognitive appraisals, emotional adjustment, and adherence to rehabilitation following knee surgery. *Journal of Sport Rehabilitation, 3*, 23–30.

D'Arripe-Longueville, F., Fournier, J. F., & Dubois, A. (1998). The perceived effectiveness of interactions between expert French judo coaches and elite female athletes. *The Sport Psychologist, 12*, 317–332.

Davidson, R., Goleman, D., & Schwartz, G. (1976). Attentional and affective concomitants of meditation: A cross-sectional study. *Journal of Abnormal Psychology, 85*, 235–238.

Davidson, R. J., & Schwartz, G. E. (1976). The psychobiology of relaxation and related states: A multi-process theory. In D. E. Mostofsky (Ed.), *Behavior control and modification of physiological activity* (pp. 399–442). Englewood Cliffs, NJ: Prentice-Hall.

Davis, C., Elliott, S., Dionne, M., & Mitchell, I. (1991). The relationship of personality factors and physical activity to body satisfaction in men. *Personality and Individual Differences, 12,* 689–694.

Davis, C., & Mogk, J. P. (1994). Some personality correlates of interest and excellence in sport. *International Journal of Sport Psychology, 25,* 131–143.

Davis, J. O. (1991). Sports injuries and stress management: An opportunity for research. *The Sport Psychologist, 5,* 175–182.

Davis, K. (2005, August 6). NCAA rejects "hostile" images. *Hartford Courant,* pp. A1 A4.

Davis, S. F., Huss, M. T., & Becker, A. H. (1995). Norman Triplett and the dawning of sport psychology. *The Sport Psychologist, 9,* 366–375.

Deci, E. L., & Ryan, R. M. (1985). *Intrinsic motivation and self-determination in human behavior.* New York: Plenum Press.

Deci, E. L., & Ryan, R. M. (1987). The support of autonomy and the control of behavior. *Journal of Personality and Social Psychology, 53,* 1024–1037.

Deford, F. (2003). Geno Auriemma + Dianna Taurasi = love, Italian style. *Sports Illustrated, 20,* 124–133.

DeFrancesco, C., & Burke, K. L. (1997). Performance enhancement strategies used in a professional tennis tournament. *International Journal of Sport Psychology, 28,* 185–195.

Denmark, F. L., & Fernandez, L. C. (1993). Historical development of the psychology of women. In F. L. Denmark & M. A. Paludi (Eds.), *Psychology of women: A handbook of issues and theories* (pp. 3–22). Westport, CT: Greenwood Press.

Deppe, R. K., & Harackiewicz, J. M. (1996). Self-handicapping and intrinsic motivation: Buffering intrinsic motivation from threat of failure. *Journal of Personality and Social Psychology, 70,* 868–875.

DeSimone, P. (1993). Linguistic assumptions in scientific language. *Contemporary Psychodynamics: Theory, Research & Application, 1,* 8–17.

Desjardins, G. Jr. (1996). The mission. In J. H. Salmela (Ed.), *Great job coach! Getting the edge from proven winners* (pp. 69–100). Ottawa, Canada: Potentium.

Developing your mental pacemaker. (1989). *Sport Psychology Training Bulletin,* September/October, 1–8.

Diehl, N., & Petrie, T. (1995). A longitudinal investigation of the effects of different exercise modalities on social physique anxiety. *Journal of Applied Sport Psychology, 7,* S55.

Diener, C. I., & Dweck, C. S. (1978). An analysis of learned helplessness: Continuous changes in performance, strategy, and achievement cognitions following failure. *Journal of Personality and Social Psychology, 36,* 451–462.

Dietrich, D. (1995). Gender differences in self-handicapping: Regardless of academic or social competence implications. *Social Behavior and Personality, 23,* 403–410.

Dillbeck, M. C., & Orme-Johnson, D. W. (1987). Physiological differences between Transcendental Meditation and rest. *American Psychologist, 42,* 879–881.

Dillman, L. (2004, August 22). Phelps: A gold watch. *Hartford Courant,* pp. E13–E14.

Dinges, M. M., & Oetting, E. R. (1993). Similarity in drug use patterns between adolescents and their friends. *Adolescence, 28,* 253–266.

Dirks, K. T. (2000). Trust in leadership and team performance: Evidence from NCAA basketball. *Journal of Applied Psychology, 85,* 1004–1012.

Doyle, P. (2005, January 5). Wade, Ryno get call. *Hartford Courant,* pp. C1, C5.

Draycott, S. G., & Kline, P. (1995). The big three or the big five – the EPQ-R vs the NEO-PI:

A research note, replication and elaboration. *Personality & Individual Differences, 18,* 801–804.

Drexler, L. P., Ahrens, A. H., & Haaga, D. A. F. (1995). The affective consequences of self-handicapping. *Journal of Social Behavior and Personality, 10,* 861–870.

Driskell, J. E., Copper, C., & Moran, A. (1994). Does mental practice enhance performance? *Journal of Applied Psychology, 79,* 481–492.

Druss, B. G., & Rosenheck, R. A. (1999). Patterns of health care costs associated with depression and substance abuse in a national sample. *Psychiatric Services, 50,* 214–218.

Duda, J. L. (1985). Goals and achievement orientations of Anglo and Mexican-American adolescents in sport and the classroom. *International Journal of Intercultural Relations, 9,* 131–155.

Duda, J. L. (1986). A cross-cultural analysis of achievement motivation in sport and the classroom. In L. VanderVelden & J. Humphrey (Eds.), *Current selected research in the psychology and sociology of sport* (pp. 115–132). New York: AMS Press.

Duda, J. L. (1988). The relationship between goal perspectives, persistence and behavioral intensity among male and female recreational sport participants. *Leisure Sciences, 10,* 95–106.

Duda, J. L. (1989a). Goal perspectives, participation, and persistence in sport. *International Journal of Sport Psychology, 20,* 42–56.

Duda, J. L. (1989b). The relationship between task and ego orientation and the perceived purpose of sport among male and female high school athletes. *Journal of Sport & Exercise Psychology, 11,* 318–335.

Duda, J. L. (1993). Goals: A social-cognitive approach to the study of achievement motivation in sport. In R. N. Singer, M. Murphey, & L. K. Tennant (Eds.), *Handbook of research on sport psychology* (pp. 421–436). New York: Macmillan.

Duda, J. L. (1997). Perpetuating myths: A response to Hardy's 1996 Coleman Griffith address. *Journal of Applied Sport Psychology, 9,* 303–309.

Duda, J. L. (2000). Psychological aspects of training. In B. L. Drinkwater (Ed.), *Women in sport* (pp. 108–119). Oxford: Blackwell Science.

Duda, J. L. (2001). Achievement goals research in sport: Pushing the boundaries and clarifying some misunderstandings. In G. C. Roberts (Ed.), *Advances in motivation in sport and exercise* (pp. 129–182). Champaign, IL: Human Kinetics.

Duda, J. L. (2005). Motivation in sport: The relevance of competence and achievement goals. In A. J. Elliot & C. S. Dweck (Eds.), *Handbook of competence and motivation* (pp. 318–335). New York: Guilford.

Duda, J. L., & Allison, M. T. (1982). The nature of sociocultural influences on achievement motivation: The case of the Navajo Indian. In J. W. Loy (Ed.), *Paradoxes of play* (pp. 188–197). West Point, NY: Leisure Press.

Duda, J., & Allison, M. (1990). Cross-cultural analysis in exercise and sport psychology: A void in the field. *Journal of Sport & Exercise Psychology, 12,* 114–131.

Duda, J. L., & Hall, H. (2001). Achievement goal theory in sport. Recent extensions and future directions. In R. N. Singer, H. A. Hausenblas, & C. M. Janelle (Eds.), *Handbook of sport psychology* (2nd ed., pp. 417–443). New York: Wiley.

Duda, J. L., & Kim, M. (1997). Parental and gym motivational climates and the development of eating disorders among young elite gymnasts. *Journal of Sport & Exercise Psychology, 19* (Suppl.), S48.

Duda, J. L., & Nicholls, J. G. (1992). Dimensions of achievement motivation in schoolwork and sport. *Journal of Educational Psychology 84,* 290–299.

Duda, J. L., Olson, L. K., & Templin, T. J. (1991). The relationship of task and ego orientation to sportsmanship attitudes and perceived legitimacy of injurious acts. *Research Quarterly for Exercise and Sport, 62,* 334–343.

Duda, J. L., & Roberts, G. C. (1980). Sex biases in general and causal attributions of outcome in co-ed sport competition. In C. H. Nadeau, W. R. Halliwell, K. M. Newell, & G. C. Roberts (Eds.), *Psychology of motor behavior and sport – 1979* (pp. 27–36). Champaign, IL: Human Kinetics.

Dugdale, J. R., & Eklund, R. C. (2002). Do *not* pay attention to the empires: Thought suppression and task-relevant focusing strategies. *Journal of Sport & Exercise Psychology, 24,* 306–319.

Dunn, J. G. H. (1999). A theoretical framework for structuring the content of competitive worry in ice hockey. *Journal of Sport & Exercise Psychology, 21,* 259–279.

Dunn, J. G. H., & Dunn, J. C. (1999). Goal orientations, perceptions, or aggression, and sportspersonship in elite male youth ice hockey players. *The Sport Psychologist, 13,* 183–200.

Dunn, J. G. H., Dunn, J. C., Gotwals, J. K., Vallance, J. K. H., Craft, J. M., & Syrotuik, D. G. (2006). Establishing construct validity evidence for the Sport Multidimensional Perfectionism Scale. *Psychology of Sport and Exercise, 7,* 57–79.

Dunn, J. G. H., Dunn, J.C., & Syrotuik, D. G. (2002). Relationship between multidimensional perfectionism and goal orientations in sport. *Journal of Sport & Exercise Psychology, 24,* 376–395.

Dunn, J. G. H., Gotwals, J. K., & Dunn, J. C. (2005). An examination of the domain specificity of perfectionism among intercollegiate student-athletes. *Personality and Individual Differences, 38,* 1439–1448.

Durand, M., Hall, C., & Haslam, I. R. (1997). The effects of combining mental and physical practice on motor skill acquisition: A review of the literature and some practical implications. *The Hong Kong Journal of Sports Medicine and Sports Science, 4,* 36–41.

Durtschi, S., & Weiss, M. (1986). Psychological characteristics of elite and nonelite marathon runners. In D. Landers (Ed.), *Sport and elite performers* (pp. 73–80). Champaign, IL: Human Kinetics.

Dweck, C. S. (1980). Learned helplessness in sport. In C. H. Nadeau, W. R. Halliwell, K. M. Newell, & G. C. Roberts (Eds.), *Psychology of motor behavior and sport – 1979* (pp. 1–11). Champaign, IL: Human Kinetics.

Dweck, C. S. (1986). Motivational processes affecting learning. *American Psychologist, 41,* 1040–1048.

Dweck, C. S. (1999). *Self-theories and goals: Their role in motivation, personality, and development.* Philadelphia: Taylor & Francis.

Dweck, C. S., & Bush, E. S. (1976). Sex differences in learned helplessness: I. Differential debilitation with peer and adult evaluators. *Developmental Psychology, 12,* 147–156.

Dweck, C., & Leggett, E. (1988). A social cognitive approach to motivation and personality. *Psychological Review, 95,* 256–273.

Eagan, M. & Gonzalez, R. (2005, May 19). Attack on coach resonates. *Hartford Courant,* pp. A1, A9.

Eccles, J., Adler, T., & Meece, J. L. (1984). Sex differences in achievement: A test of alternate theories. *Journal of Personality and Social Psychology, 46,* 26–43.

Eccles, J., & Harold, R. (1991). Gender differences in sport involvement: Applying the Eccles expectancy value model. *Journal of Applied Sport Psychology, 3,* 7–35.

Edwards, H. (1973). *Sociology of sport.* Homewood, IL: Dorsey Press.

Edwards, S. W., Gordin, R. D. Jr., & Henschen, K. P. (1984). Sex-role orientations of female NCAA championship gymnasts. *Perceptual and Motor Skills, 58,* 625–626.

Egan, S., & Stelmack, R. M. (2003). A personality profile of Mount Everest climbers. *Personality and Individual Differences, 34,* 1491–1494.

Egloff, B., & Gruhn, A. J. (1996). Personality and endurance sports. *Personality and Individual Differences, 21,* 223–229.

Eklund, R. C. (1994). A season long investigation of competitive cognition in collegiate wrestlers. *Research Quarterly for Exercise and Sport, 65,* 169–183.

Eklund, R. C. (1996). Preparing to compete: A season-long investigation with collegiate wrestlers. *The Sport Psychologist, 10,* 111–131.

Elliot, A. J. (1999). Approach and avoidance motivation and achievement goals. *Educational Psychologist, 34,* 169–189.

Elliot, A. J. (2005). A conceptual history of the achievement goal construct. In A. J. Elliot & C. S. Dweck (Eds.), *Handbook of competence and motivation* (pp. 52–72). New York: Guilford.

Elliot, A. J., & Church, M. A. (1997). A hierarchical model of approach achievement motivation. *Journal of Personality and Social Psychology, 72,* 218–232.

Elliot, A. J., & Harackiewicz, J. M. (1994). Goal setting, achievement orientation, and intrinsic motivation: A mediational analysis. *Journal of Personality and Social Psychology, 66,* 968–980.

Elliot, A. J., & Harackiewicz, J. M. (1996). Approach and avoidance achievement goals and intrinsic motivation: A mediational analysis. *Journal of Personality and Social Psychology, 70,* 461–475.

Elliot, A. J., & McGregor, H. A. (1999). Test anxiety and the hierarchical model of approach and avoidance achievement motivation. *Journal of Personality and Social Psychology, 76,* 628–644.

Elliot, A. J., & Sheldon, K. M. (1997). Avoidance achievement motivation: A personal goals analysis. *Journal of Personality and Social Psychology, 73,* 171–185.

Emmons, R. A., & Kaiser, H. A. (1996). A control-process perspective on the origins of affect. In L. M. Martin, & A. Tesser (Eds.), *Striving and feeling: Interactions among goals, affect, and self-regulation* (pp. 79–98). Mahwah, NJ: Lawrence Erlbaum Associates, Inc.

Escarti, A., & Guzman, J. F. (1999). Effects of feedback on self-efficacy, performance, and choice in an athletic task. *Journal of Applied Sport Psychology, 11,* 83–96.

Escarti, A., Roberts, G. C., Cervello, E. M., & Guzman, J. F. (1999). Adolescent goal orientations and the perception of criteria of success used by significant others. *International Journal of Sport Psychology, 30,* 309–324.

Eubank, M., Collins, D., Lovell, G., Dorling, D., & Talbot, S. (1997). Individual temporal differences in pre-competition anxiety and hormonal concentration. *Personality and Individual Differences, 23,* 1031–1039.

Evans, L., & Hardy, L. (1995). Sport injury and grief responses: A review. *Journal of Sport & Exercise Psychology, 17,* 227–245.

Evans, L., & Hardy, L. (2002a). Injury rehabilitation: A goal-setting intervention study. *Research Quarterly for Exercise and Sport, 73,* 310–319.

Evans, L., & Hardy, L. (2002b). Injury rehabilitation: A qualitative follow-up study. *Research Quarterly for Exercise and Sport, 73,* 320–329.

Evans, L., Hardy, L, & Fleming, S. (2000). Intervention strategies with injured athletes: An action research study. *The Sport Psychologist, 14,* 188–206.

Evans, L., Jones, L., & Mullen, R. (2004). An imagery intervention during the competitive season with an elite rugby union player. *The Sport Psychologist, 18,* 252–271.

Evans, M., Weinberg, R., & Jackson, A. (1992). Psychological factors related to drug use in college athletes. *The Sport Psychologist, 6,* 24–41.

Everett, J. L., Smith, R. E., & Williams, K. D. (1992). Effects of team cohesion and identifiability on social loafing in relay swimming performance. *International Journal of Sport Psychology, 23,* 311–324.

Everly, G. S., & Benson, H. (1989). Disorders of arousal and the relaxation response: Speculations on the nature and treatment of stress-related diseases. *International Journal of Psychosomatics, 36*, 15–21.

Ewing, M. E., Seefeldt, V. D., & Brown, T. P. (1996). *Role of organized sport in the education and health of American children and youth*. Background Report on the Role of Sports in Youth Development. New York: Carnegie Corporation of New York.

Eys, M. A., Burke, S. M., Carron, A. V., & Dennis, P. W. (2006). The sport team as an effective group. In J. M. Williams (Ed.), *Applied sport psychology: Personal growth to peak performance* (5th ed., pp. 157–173). New York: McGraw-Hill.

Eys, M. A., Hardy, J., Carron, A. V., & Beauchamp, M. R. (2003). The relationship between task cohesion and competitive state anxiety. *Journal of Sport and Exercise Psychology, 25*, 66–76.

Eysenck, H. J. (1952). *The scientific study of personality*. New York: Macmillan.

Eysenck, H. J. (1992). The definition and measurement of psychoticism. *Personality and Individual Differences, 13*, 757–785.

Eysenck, H. J. (1994). Personality: Biological foundations. In P. A. Vernon (Ed.), *The neuropsychology of individual differences* (pp. 151–207). London: Academic Press.

Eysenck, H. J., & Eysenck, M. W. (1985). *Personality and individual differences*. New York: Plenum.

Eysenck, H. J., & Eysenck, S. B. G. (1994). *Manual of the Eysenck Personality Questionnaire* (2nd ed.). London: Hodder & Stoughton.

Eysenck, H. J., Nias, D. K. B., & Cox, D. N. (1982). Sport and personality. *Advances in Behavior Research & Therapy, 4*, 1–56.

Eysenck, H. J., & Wilson, G. (1976). *Know your own personality*. New York: Barnes & Noble.

Eysenck, M. W., & Derakshan, N. (1997). Cognitive biases for future negative events as a function of trait anxiety and social desirability. *Personality and Individual Differences, 22*, 597–605.

Fanning, P. (1994). *Visualization for change* (2nd ed.). Oakland, CA: New Harbinger.

Farber, B. A. (1983). *Stress and burnout in the human service professions*. New York: Pergamon Press.

Farber, M. (2004). Code red. *Sports Illustrated, 100*, March 22, 56–59.

Farmer, H. S., & Vispoel, W. P. (1990). Attributions of female and male adolescents for real-life failure experiences. *Journal of Experimental Education, 58*, 127–140.

Fasting, K. (2000). Women's role in national and international sports governing bodies. In B. L. Drinkwater (Ed.), *Women in sport* (pp. 441–450). Oxford: Blackwell Science.

Farrell, A. (2002, Nov. 17). Golf: Sorenstam driven by perfection; the world's best golfer just gets better and better – and she keeps setting the goals higher. *Independent on Sunday*, p. 23.

Farthofer, A., & Brandstatter, H. (2001). Extraversion and optimal level of arousal at high-risk work. In A. Farthofer (Ed.), *Persons, situations, and emotions: An interactional approach* (pp. 133–146). New York: Oxford University Press.

Fatsis, S. (1998, March 6). At last! Here's a way to measure just how pathetic your team is. *Wall Street Journal*, p. B1.

Fawkner, H. J., McMurray, N. E., & Summers, J. J. (1999). Athletic injury and minor life events: A prospective study. *Journal of Science and Medicine in Sport, 2*, 117–124.

Feather, N. T. (1969). Attribution of responsibility and valence of success and failure in relation to initial confidence and task performance. *Journal of Personality and Social Psychology, 13*, 179–244.

Feher, P., & Meyers, M. C. (1998). Psychological profile of rock climbers: State and trait. *Journal of Sport Behavior, 21*, 167–183.

Feick, D. L., & Rhodewalt, F. (1997). The double-edged sword of self-handicapping: discounting, augmentation, and the protection and enhancement of self-esteem. *Motivation and Emotion, 21,* 147–163.

Feldhusen, J. F. (1995). Creativity: A knowledge base, metacognitive skills, and personality factors. *Journal of Creative Behavior, 29,* 255–268.

Feltz, D. L. (1982). Path analysis of the causal elements in Bandura's theory of self-efficacy and anxiety-based model of avoidance behavior. *Journal of Personality and Social Psychology, 42,* 764–781.

Feltz, D. L., Chase, M. A., Moritz, S. E., & Sullivan, P. J. (1999). Development of the multidimensional coaching effectiveness scale. *Journal of Educational Psychology, 91,* 765–776.

Feltz, D. L., & Landers, D. M. (1983). The effects of mental practice on motor skill learning and performance: A meta-analysis. *Journal of Sport Psychology 5,* 25–57.

Feltz, D. L., & Lirgg, C. D. (2001). Self-efficacy beliefs of athletes, teams, and coaches. In R. N. Singer, H. A. Hausenblas, & C. M. Janelle (Eds.), *Handbook of sport psychology* (2nd ed., pp. 340–361). New York: Wiley.

Feltz, D. L., & Mugno, D. A. (1983). A replication of the causal elements in Bandura's theory of self-efficacy and the influence of autonomic perception. *Journal of Sport Psychology, 5,* 263–277.

Ferrand, C., Tetard, S., & Fontayne, P. (2006). Self-handicapping in rock climbing: A qualitative approach. *Journal of Applied Sport Psychology, 18,* 271–280.

Ferrari, J. R. (1991). Self-handicapping by procrastinators: Protecting self-esteem, social-esteem, or both? *Journal of Research in Personality, 25,* 245–261.

Ferrari, J. R., Harriott, J. S., & Zimmerman, M. (1999). The social support networks of procrastinators: Friends or family in times of trouble? *Personality and Individual Differences, 26,* 321–331.

Ferrari, J. R., Johnson, J. L., & McCown, W. G. (1995). *Procrastination and task avoidance: Theory, research and treatment.* New York: Plenum.

Ferrari, J. R., & Tice, D. M. (2000). Procrastination as a self-handicap for men and women: A task-avoidance strategy in a laboratory setting. *Journal of Research in Personality, 34,* 73–83.

Filby, W. C. D., Maynard, I. W., & Graydon, J. K. (1999). The effect of multiple-goal strategies on performance outcomes in training and competition. *Journal of Applied Sport Psychology, 11,* 230–246.

Fincham, F. D., Hokoda, A., & Sanders, R. Jr. (1989). Learned helplessness, test anxiety, and academic achievement: A longitudinal analysis. *Child Development, 60,* 138–145.

Finn, R. (1994, September 26). The second time around for Jennifer Capriati. *New York Times,* pp. C1, C2.

Fisher, A., Mancini, V., Hirsch, R., Proulx, T., & Staurowsky, E. (1982). Coach–athlete interactions and team climate. *Journal of Sport Psychology, 4,* 388–404.

Fitzsimmons, P. A., Landers, D. M., Thomas, R. J., & Van der Mars, H. (1991). Does self-efficacy predict performance in experienced weightlifters? *Research Quarterly for Exercise and Sport, 62,* 424, 431.

Fleming, J., & Horner, M. S. (1992). The motive to avoid success. In C. P. Smith (Ed.), *Motivation and personality: Handbook of thematic content analysis* (pp. 278–310). New York: Cambridge University Press.

Flett, G. L., Blankstein, K. R., Hewitt, P. L., & Koledin, S. (1992). Components of perfectionism and procrastination in college students. *Social Behavior and Personality, 20,* 85–94.

Flett, G. L., Blankstein, K. R., & Martin, T. R. (1995). Procrastination, negative self-evaluation, and stress in depression and anxiety. In J. R. Ferrari, J. L. Johnson, &

W. G. McCown (Eds.), *Procrastination and task avoidance: Theory, research and treatment* (pp. 137–167). New York: Plenum.

Flett, G. L., & Hewitt, P. L. (1994). Perfectionism and components of state and trait anxiety. *Current Psychology, 13,* 326–349.

Flett, G. L., & Hewitt, P. L. (1995). Perfectionism, life events, and depressive symptoms: A test of a diathesis-stress mode. *Current Psychology, 14,* 112–138.

Flett, G. L., & Hewitt, P. L. (1998). Perfectionism in relation to attributions for success or failure. *Current Psychology, 17,* 249–263.

Flett, G., & Hewitt, P. (2005). The perils of perfectionism in sports and exercise. *Current Directions in Psychological Science. 14,* 14–18.

Flett, G. L., Hewitt, P. L., Blankstein, K. R., & Gray, L. (1998). Psychological distress and the frequency of perfectionistic thinking. *Journal of Personality and Social Psychology, 75,* 1363–1381.

Flett, G. L., Hewitt, P. L., & De Rosa, T. (1996). Dimensions of perfectionism, psychosocial adjustment, and social skills. *Personality and Individual Differences, 20,* 143–150.

Flett, G. L., Hewitt, P. L., & Martin, T. R. (1995). Dimensions of perfectionism and procrastination. In J. R. Ferrari, J. L. Johnson, & W. G. McCown (Eds.), *Procrastination and task avoidance: Theory, research and treatment* (pp. 113–136). New York: Plenum.

Flett, G. L., Sawatzky, D. L., & Hewitt, P. L. (1995). Dimensions of perfectionism and goal commitment: A further comparison of two perfectionism measures. *Journal of Psychopathology and Behavioral Assessment, 17,* 111–124.

Folkman, S., Chesney, M., McKusick, L., Ironson, G., Johnson, D. S., & Coates, T. J. (1991). Translating coping theory into an intervention. In J. Eckenrode (Ed.), *The social context of coping* (pp. 239–260). New York: Plenum.

Fortier, M. S., Vallerand, R. J., Briere, N. M., & Provencher, P. J. (1995). Competitive and recreational sport structures and gender: A test of their relationship with sport motivation. *International Journal of Sport Psychology, 26,* 24–39.

Foster, J. J., Weigand, D. A., & Baines, D. (2006). The effect of removing superstitious behavior and introducing a pre-performance routine on basketball free-throw performance. *Journal of Applied Sport Psychology, 18,* 167–172.

Fox, K., Goudas, M., Biddle, S., Duda, J., & Armstrong, N. (1994). Children's task and ego goal profiles in sport. *British Journal of Educational Psychology, 64,* 253–261.

Francis, L.J., Kelly, P., & Jones S.H. (1998). The personality profile of female students who play hockey. *Irish Journal of Psychology, 19,* 394–399.

Frankl, D., & Babbitt, D. G. III. (1998). Gender bias: A study of high school track & field athletes' perceptions of hypothetical male and female head coaches. *Journal of Sport Behavior, 21,* 396–407.

Franklin, K. (1989). Field of dreams: Little League's not so little anymore. *Sport,* September, 64–67.

Freixanet, M. G. (1991). Personality profile of subjects engaged in high physical risk sports. *Personality and Individual Differences, 12,* 1087–1093.

Freud, S. (1917). Mourning and melancholia. In J. Strachey (Ed. & Trans.), *The standard edition of the complete psychological works of Sigmund Freud* (Vol. 14, pp. 243–258). London: Hogarth Press.

Freud, S. (1920). *A general introduction to psychoanalysis.* New York: Washington Square Press.

Freud, S. (1923). The ego and the id. In J. Strachey (Ed. & Trans.), *The standard edition of the complete psychological works of Sigmund Freud* (Vol. 19, pp. 3–69). London: Hogarth Press.

Freud. S. (1927). The future of an illusion. In J. Strachey (Ed. & Trans.), *The standard edition of the complete psychological works of Sigmund Freud* (Vol. 21, pp. 5–56). London: Hogarth Press.

Freudenberger, H. J. (1974). Staff burnout. *Journal of Social Issues*, *30*, 159–165.

Freudenberger, H. J. (1975). The staff burnout syndrome in alternative institutions. *Psychotherapy: Theory, Research, & Practice*, *12*, 72–83.

Freudenberger, L. F., & Bergandi, T. A. (1994). Sport psychology research in American football: A review of the literature. *International Journal of Sport Psychology*, *25*, 425–434.

Friedman, E., & Berger, B. G. (1991). Influence of gender, masculinity, and feminity on the effectiveness of three stress reduction techniques: Jogging, relaxation response, and group interaction. *Journal of Applied Sport Psychology*, *3*, 61–86.

Frost, R. O., Heimberg, R. G., Holt, C. S., Mattia, J. I., & Neubauer, A. L. (1993). A comparison of two measures of perfectionism. *Personality and Individual Differences*, *14*, 119–126.

Frost, R. O., & Henderson, K. J. (1991). Perfectionism and reactions to athletic competition. *Journal of Sport and Exercise Psychology*, *13*, 323–335.

Frost, R. O., Lahart, C. M., & Rosenblate, R. (1991). The development of perfectionism: A study of daughters and their parents. *Cognitive Therapy and Research*, *15*, 469–489.

Frost, R. O., & Marten, P. A. (1990). Perfectionism and evaluative threat. *Cognitive Therapy and Research*, *14*, 559–572.

Frost, R. O., Marten, P., Lahart, C., & Rosenblate, R. (1990). The dimensions of perfectionism. *Cognitive Therapy and Research*, *14*, 449–468.

Frost, R. O., Turcotte, T. A., Heimberg, R. G., Mattia, J. I., Holt, C. S., & Hope, D. A. (1995). Reactions to mistakes among subjects high and low in perfectionistic concern over mistakes. *Cognitive Therapy and Research*, *19*, 195–205.

Furnham, A. (1990). Personality and demographic determinants of leisure and sports preference and performance. *International Journal of Sport Psychology*, *21*, 218–236.

Galassi, J. P., Frierson, H. T. Jr., & Sharer, R. (1981). Behavior of high, moderate, and low test-anxious students during an actual test situation. *Journal of Consulting and Clinical Psychology*, *49*, 51–62.

Galatzer-Levy, R., & Cohler, B. (1993). *The essential other*. New York: Basic Books.

Gallucci, N. T. (1997). On the identification of patterns of substance abuse with the MMPI-A. *Psychological Assessment*, *9*, 224–232.

Gammons, P. (1988, July 4). Inside baseball: Fatal distraction [Online]. *Sports Illustrated*. Available at www.elibrary.com

Gano-Overway, L. A., & Duda, J. L. (1999). Interrelationships between expressive individualism and other achievement goal orientations among African and European American athletes. *Journal of Black Psychology*, *25*, 544–563.

Garber, G., & Berlet, B. (1996, June 23). Major pressure: Norman regroups after collapse at Masters. *Hartford Courant*, pp. K1, K12.

Gardner, D. E. (1998). *The relationship between perceived coaching behaviors, team cohesion, and team motivational climates among Division I athletes*. Unpublished doctoral dissertation, Boston University, Boston, MA.

Garza, D. L., & Feltz, D. L. (1998). Effects of selected mental practice on performance, self-efficacy, and competition confidence of figure skaters. *The Sport Psychologist*, *12*, 1–15.

Gaudreau, P., & Blondin, J. P. (2002). Development of a questionnaire for the assessment of coping strategies employed by athletes in competitive sport settings. *Psychology of Sport and Exercise*, *3*, 1–34.

Gay, P. (1999). Sigmund Freud. *Time*, *153*, March, 2966–2969.

Gayton, W. F., Matthews, G. R., & Nickless, C. J. (1987). The home field disadvantage in sports championships: Does it exist in hockey? *Journal of Sport Psychology*, *9*, 183–185.

Gender-Equity Report, 2001–2002. (2002). Available at www.NCAA.org

George, T. R., & Feltz, D. L. (1995). Motivation in sport from a collective efficacy perspective. *International Journal of Sport Psychology, 26*, 98–116.

George, T. R., Feltz, D. L., & Chase, M. A. (1992). Effects of model similarity on self-efficacy and muscular endurance: A second look. *Journal of Sport and Exercise Psychology, 14*, 237–248.

Gernigon, C., Fleurance, P., & Reine, B. (2000). Effects of uncontrollability and failure on the development of learned helplessness in perceptual-motor tasks. *Research Quarterly for Exercise and Sport, 71*, 44–54.

Gernigon, C., Thill, E., & Fleurance, P. (1999). Learned helplessness: A survey of cognitive, motivational and perceptual-motor consequences in motor tasks. *Journal of Sports Sciences, 17*, 403–412.

Giacobbi, P. R. Jr., & Weinberg, R. S. (2000). An examination of coping in sport: Individual trait anxiety differences and situational consistency. *Sport Psychologist, 14*, 42–62.

Gilbourne, D., & Taylor, A. H. (1998). From theory to practice: The integration of goal perspective theory and life development approaches within an injury-specific goal-setting program. *Journal of Applied Sport Psychology, 10*, 124–139.

Gill, D. L. (1993). Competitiveness and competitive orientation in sport. In R. N. Singer, M. Murphey, & L. K. Tennant (Eds.), *Handbook of research on sport psychology* (pp. 314–327). New York: Macmillan.

Gill, D. L. (1995). Gender issues: A social-educational perspective. In S. M. Murphey (Ed.), *Sport psychology interventions* (pp. 205–234). Champaign, IL: Human Kinetics.

Gill, D. L. (1998a). Gender and competitive motivation: From recreation center to the Olympic arena. In D. Bernstein et al. (Eds.), *Nebraska symposium on motivation: Vol 45. Gender and motivation* (pp. 173–207). Lincoln: University of Nebraska Press.

Gill, D. L. (1998b). Gender and sport behavior. In T. S. Horn (Ed.), *Advances in sport psychology* (2nd ed.). Champaign, IL: Human Kinetics.

Gill, D. (2000). *Psychological dynamics of sport and exercise.* Champaign, IL: Human Kinetics.

Gill, D. L., & Deeter, T. E. (1988). Development of the Sports Orientation Questionnaire. *Research Quarterly for Exercise and Sport, 59*, 191–202.

Gill, D. L., Gross, J. B., & Huddleston, S. (1983). Participation motivation in youth sports. *International Journal of Sport Psychology, 14*, 1–14.

Gilovich, T., & Medvec, V. H. (1995). Some counterfactual determinants of satisfaction and regret. In N. J. Roese & J. M. Olson (Eds.), *What might have been: The social psychology of counterfactual thinking* (pp. 259–282). Mahwah, NJ: Lawrence Erlbaum Associates, Inc.

Glenn, S. D., & Horn, T. S. (1993). Psychological and personal predictors of leadership behavior in female soccer athletes. *Journal of Applied Sport Psychology, 5*, 17–34.

Gonzalez, R. (2005, May 27). Not injured, but insulted: Volleyball coach describes run-in with Picard. *Hartford Courant*, pp. C1, C8.

Gonzalez, R., & Courchesne, S. (2005, June 1). Batter up in court: Picard arraigned for assault. *Hartford Courant*, pp. C1, C6.

Goodgame, D. (2000). The game of risk: How the best golfer in the world got even better. *Time, 156*, August 14, 56–64, 65–66.

Goodger, K., Lavallee, D., Gorely, T., & Harwood, C. (2006). Burnout in sport: Understanding the process. In J. M. Williams (Ed.), *Applied sport psychology: Personal growth to peak performance* (5th ed., pp. 541–564). New York: McGraw-Hill.

Gordon, S. (1988). Decision styles and coaching effectiveness in university soccer. *Canadian Journal of Sport Sciences, 13*, 56–65.

Gotwals, J. K., Dunn, J. G. H., & Wayment, H. A. (2003). An examination of perfectionism and self-esteem in intercollegiate athletes. *Journal of Sport Behavior, 26*, 17–38.

Gould, D. (1999). Lessons from Nagano. *Olympic Coach, 9*, 2–5.

Gould, D. (2006). Goal setting for peak performance. In J. M. Williams (Ed.), *Applied sport psychology: Personal growth to peak performance* (5th ed., pp. 240–259), New York: McGraw-Hill.

Gould, D., & Damarjian, N. (1996). Imagery training for peak performance. In J. L. Van Raalte & B. W. Brewer (Eds.), *Exploring sport and exercise psychology* (pp. 25–50). Washington, DC: American Psychological Association.

Gould, D., Dieffenbach, K., & Moffett, A. (2002). Psychological characteristics and their development in Olympic champions. *Journal of Applied Sport Psychology, 14*, 172–204.

Gould, D., Eklund, R. C., & Jackson, S. A. (1992a). 1988 US Olympic wrestling excellence: I. Mental preparation, competitive cognition, and affect. *The Sport Psychologist, 6*, 358–382.

Gould, D., Eklund, R. C., & Jackson, S. A. (1992b). 1988 US Olympic wrestling excellence: II. Thoughts and affect occurring during competition. *The Sport Psychologist, 6*, 383–402.

Gould, D., Eklund, R. C., & Jackson, S. A. (1993a). Coping strategies used by US Olympic wrestlers. *Research Quarterly for Exercise and Sport, 64*, 83–93.

Gould, D., Eklund, R. C., Petlichkoff, L., Peterson, K., & Bump, L. (1991). Psychological predictors of state anxiety and performance in age-group wrestlers. *Pediatric Exercise Science, 3*, 198–206.

Gould, D., Feltz, D., & Weiss, M. R. (1985). Motives for participating in competitive youth swimming. *International Journal of Sport Psychology, 6*, 126–140.

Gould, D., Finch, L. M., & Jackson, S. A. (1993b). Coping strategies used by national champion figure skaters. *Research Quarterly for Exercise and Sport, 64*, 453–468.

Gould, D., Hodge, K., Peterson, K., & Giannini, J. (1989). An exploratory examination of strategies used by elite coaches to enhance self-efficacy in athletes. *Journal of Sport & Exercise Psychology, 11*, 128–140.

Gould, D., Horn, T., & Spreemann, J. (1983). Sources of stress in junior elite wrestlers. *Journal of Sport Psychology, 5*, 159–171.

Gould, D., & Petlichkoff, L. (1988). Participation motivation and attrition in young athletes. In F. Smoll, R. Magill, & M. Ash (Eds.), *Children in sport* (3rd ed., pp. 161–178). Champaign, IL: Human Kinetics.

Gould, D., Petlichkoff, L., Simons, J., & Vevera, M. (1987). Relationship between Competitive State Anxiety Inventory-2 subscale scores and pistol shooting performance. *Journal of Sport Psychology, 6*, 289–304.

Gould, D., & Pick, S. (1995). Sport psychology: The Griffith Era, 1920–1940. *The Sport Psychologist, 9*, 391–405.

Gould, D., Tuffey, S., Udry, E., & Loehr, J. (1996a). Burnout in competitive junior tennis players: II. Qualitative analysis. *The Sport Psychologist, 10*, 341–366.

Gould, D., Tuffey, S., Udry, E., & Loehr, J. (1997a). Burnout in competitive junior tennis players: III. Individual differences in the burnout experience. *The Sport Psychologist, 11*, 257–276.

Gould, D., & Udry, E. (1994). Psychological skills for enhancing performance: Arousal regulation strategies. *Medicine and Science in Sports and Exercise, 26*, 478–485.

Gould, D., Udry, E., Bridges, D., & Beck, L. (1997b). Stress sources encountered when rehabilitating from season-ending ski injuries. *The Sport Psychologist, 11*, 361–378.

Gould, D., Udry, E., Bridges, D., & Beck, L. (1997c). Coping with season-ending injuries. *The Sport Psychologist, 11*, 379–399.

Gould, D., Udry, E., Tuffey, S., & Loehr, J. (1996b). Burnout in competitive junior tennis players: I. A quantitative psychological assessment. *The Sport Psychologist, 10*, 322–340.

Gould, D., & Weiss, M. (1981). Effects of model similarity and model talk of self-efficacy and muscular endurance. *Journal of Sport Psychology, 3,* 17–29.

Graham, S., & Weiner, B. (1996). Theories and principles of motivation. In D. C. Berliner & R. C. Calfee (Eds.), *Handbook of educational psychology* (pp. 63–84). New York: Macmillan.

Graham, T. R., Kowalski, K. C., & Crocker, P. R. E. (2002). The contributions of goal characteristics and causal attributions to emotional experience in youth sport participants. *Psychology of Sport and Exercise, 3,* 273–291.

Granito, Jr., V. J. (2002). Psychological response to athletic injury: Gender differences. *Journal of Sport Behavior, 25,* 243–260.

Granito, V. J., & Rainey, D. W. (1988). Differences in cohesion between high school and college football teams and starters and nonstarters. *Perceptual and Motor Skills, 66,* 471–477.

Grant, B. F., DeBakey, S., & Zobeck, T. S. (1991). *Liver cirrhosis mortality in the United States, 1973–1988* (Surveillance Report No. 18). Rockville, MD: National Institute on Alcohol Abuse & Alcoholism.

Gray, G. (2004, June 23). Tyson looks in the mirror and sees a troubled man. *New York Times,* D1, D7.

Gray, J. (1992). *Men are from Mars, women are from Venus: A practical guide for improving communication and getting what you want in your relationships.* New York: Harper Collins.

Graydon, J., & Murphy, T. (1995). The effect of personality on social facilitation whilst performing a sports related task. *Personality and Individual Differences, 19,* 265–267.

Graziano, W. G., Feldesman, A. B., & Rahe, D. F. (1985). Extraversion, social cognition, and the salience of aversiveness in social encounters. *Journal of Personality and Social Psychology, 49,* 971–980.

Graziano, W. G., Hair, E. C., & Finch, J. F. (1997). Competitiveness mediates the link between personality and group performance. *Journal of Personality and Social Psychology, 73,* 1394–1408.

Green, S. L., & Weinberg, R. S. (2001). Relationships among athletic identity, coping skills, social support, and the psychological impact of injury in recreational participants. *Journal of Applied Sport Psychology, 13,* 40–59.

Greenberg, A. (2001a, June 18). Into the real world: Former Giant helps players make transition. *Hartford Courant,* p. C9.

Greenberg, A. (2001b, June 18). They have time for the pain: After the hitting stops, the hurting only starts. *Hartford Courant,* pp. C1, C8, C9.

Greenberg, A. (2005a, January 30). Super model: Patriots have set the example. *Hartford Courant,* pp. E1, E9.

Greenberg, A. (2005b, February 5). Reason to smile. Brady has world of interests, but football a clear priority. *Hartford Courant,* pp. C1, C7.

Greenlees, I., Jones, S., Holder, T., & Thelwell, R. (2006). The effects of self-handicapping on attributions and perceived judo competence. *Journal of Sports Sciences, 24,* 273–280.

Greenspan, M. J., & Feltz, D. L. (1989). Psychological interventions with athletes in competitive situations: A review. *The Sport Psychologist, 3,* 219–236.

Griffin, J., & Harris, M. B. (1996). Coaches' attitudes, knowledge, experiences, and recommendations regarding weight control. *The Sport Psychologist, 10,* 180–194.

Griffith, C. R. (1926). *Psychology of Coaching.* New York: Scribner.

Griffith, C. R. (1928). *Psychology of Athletics.* New York: Scribner.

Grove, J. R., & Heard, N. P. (1997). Optimism and sport confidence as correlates of slump-related coping among athletes. *The Sport Psychologist, 11,* 400–410.

Grove, J. R., Lavallee, D., Gordon, S., & Harvey, J. H. (1998). Account-making: A model of understanding and resolving distressful reactions to retirement from sport. *The Sport Psychologist, 12,* 52–67.

Gutgesell, M., & Canterbury, R. (1999). Alcohol usage in sport and exercise. *Addiction Biology, 4,* 373–383.

Haase, A. M., & Prapavessis, H. (2004). Assessing the factor structure and composition of the Positive and Negative Perfectionism Scale in sport. *Personality and Individual Differences, 36,* 1725–1740.

Haase, A. M., Prapavessis, H., & Owens, R. G. (2002). Perfectionism, social physique anxiety and disordered eating: A comparison of male and female elite athletes. *Psychology of Sport and Exercise, 3,* 209–222.

Hack, R. (2005). Golf's bizarre billionaire. *Golf, 47,* January, 84–92.

Hagan, A. L., & Hausenblas, H. A. (2003). The relationship between exercise dependence symptoms and perfectionism. *American Journal of Health Studies, 18,* 133–137.

Haggbloom, S. J., Warnick, R., Warnick, J. E., Jones, V. K., Yarbrough, G. L., Russell, T. M., et al. (2002). The 100 most eminent psychologists of the 20th century. *Review of General Psychology, 6,* 139–152.

Hale, B. D. (1993). Explanatory style as a predictor of academic and athletic achievement in college athletes. *Journal of Sport Behavior, 16,* 63–75.

Hale, B. D., & Whitehouse, A. (1998). The effects of imagery-manipulated appraisal on intensity and direction of competitive anxiety. *The Sport Psychologist, 12,* 40–51.

Hall, A. E., & Hardy, C. J. (1991). Ready, aim, fire . . . relaxation strategies for enhancing pistol marksmanship. *Perceptual and Motor Skills, 72,* 775–786.

Hall, C. R. (1985). Individual differences in the mental practice and imagery of motor skill performance. *Canadian Journal of Applied Sport Sciences, 10,* 17S–21S.

Hall, C. R. (2001). Imagery in sport and exercise. In R. N. Singer, H. A. Hausenblas, & C. M. Janelle (Eds.), *Handbook of sport psychology* (2nd ed., pp. 529–549). New York: Wiley.

Hall, C. R., Rodgers, W. M., & Barr, K. A. (1990). The use of imagery by athletes in selected sports. *The Sport Psychologist, 4,* 1–10.

Hall, H. K., Kerr, A. W., & Matthews, J. (1998). Precompetitive anxiety in sport: The contribution of achievement goals and perfectionism. *Journal of Sport and Exercise Psychology, 20,* 194–217.

Hall, J. K., & Kerr, A. W. (1997). Motivational antecedents of precompetitive anxiety in youth sport. *The Sport Psychologist, 11,* 24–42.

Hallagan, J. B., Hallagan, L. F., & Snyder, M. B. (1989). Anabolic-androgenic steroid use by athletes. *The New England Journal of Medicine, 321,* 1042–1045.

Halliwell, W. (1990). Providing sport psychology consulting services in professional hockey. *The Sport Psychologist, 4,* 369–377.

Halvari, H., & Kjormo, O. (1999). A structural model of achievement motives, performance approach and avoidance goals and performance among Norwegian Olympic athletes. *Perceptual and Motor Skills, 89,* 997–1022.

Hamachek, D. E. (1978). Psychodynamics of normal and neurotic perfectionism. *Psychology, 15,* 27–33.

Hamann, D. L. (1985). The other side of stage fright. *Music Educators Journal, 71,* 26–27.

Haney, C. J., & Long, B. C. (1995). Coping effectiveness: A path analysis of self-efficacy, control, coping, and performance in sport competitions. *Journal of Applied Social Psychology, 25,* 1726–1746.

Haney, M., Ward, A. S., Comer, S. D., Foltin, R. W., & Fischman, M. W. (1999). Abstinence symptoms following smoked marijuana in humans. *Psychopharmacology, 141,* 395–404.

Hanini, Y. L. (1980). A study of anxiety in sports. In W. F. Straub (Ed.), *Sport psychology: An analysis of athlete behavior* (pp. 236–249). Ithaca, NY: Mouvement.

Hanin, Y. L. (1986). State-trait research in sports in the USSR. In C. D. Spielberger & R. Diaz-Guerrero (Eds.), *Cross-cultural anxiety* (Vol. 3, pp. 45–64). Washington, DC: Hemisphere.

Hanin, Y. L. (2000a). *Emotions in sport*. Champaign, IL: Human Kinetics.

Hanin, Y. L. (2000b). Individual zones of optimal functioning (IZOF) model: Emotions–performance relationships in sport. In Y. L. Hanin (Ed.), *Emotions in sport* (pp. 65–89). Champaign, IL: Human Kinetics.

Hanin, Y. L. (2000c). Successful and poor performance and emotions. In Y. L. Hanin (Ed.), *Emotions in sport* (pp. 157–187). Champaign, IL: Human Kinetics.

Hanin, Y. L. (2004). Emotion in sports. In C. D. Spielberger (Ed.), *Encyclopedia of applied psychology* (Vol. 1, pp. 739–750). Oxford: Elsevier Academic Press.

Hanin, Y. L., & Stambulova, N. B. (2002). Metaphoric description of performance states: An application of the IZOF model. *The Sport Psychologist, 16*, 396–415.

Hanin, Y., & Syrja, P. (1995). Performance affect in junior ice hockey players: An application of the individual zones of optimal functioning model. *The Sport Psychologist, 9*, 169–187.

Hanin, Y., & Syrja, P. (1996). Predicted, actual, and recalled affect in Olympic-level soccer players: Idiographic assessments on individualized scales. *Journal of Sport & Exercise Psychology, 18*, 325–335.

Hanlon, T. (1994). *Sport parent*. Champaign, IL: Human Kinetics.

Hanton, S., & Connaughton, D. (2002). Perceived control of anxiety and its relationship to self-confidence and performance: A qualitative inquiry. *Research Quarterly for Exercise and Sport, 73*, 87–97.

Hanton, S., & Jones, G. (1999a). The acquisition and development of cognitive skills and strategies: I. Making the butterflies fly in formation. *The Sport Psychologist, 13*, 1–21.

Hanton, S., & Jones, G. (1999b). The effects of a multimodal intervention program on performers: II. Training the butterflies to fly in formation. *The Sport Psychologist, 13*, 22–41.

Hanton, S., Jones, G., & Mullen, R. (2000). Intensity and direction of competitive state anxiety as interpreted by rugby players and rifle shooters. *Perceptual and Motor Skills, 90*, 513–521.

Hanton, S., Mellalieu, S. D., & Hall, R. (2002). Re-examining the competitive anxiety trait-state relationship. *Personality and Individual Differences, 33*, 1125–1136.

Hanton, S., O'Brien, M., & Mellalieu, S. D. (2003). Individual differences, perceived control and competitive trait anxiety. *Journal of Sport Behavior, 26*, 39–55.

Hanton, S., Thomas, O., & Maynard, I. W. (2004). Competitive anxiety response in the week leading up to competition: The role of intensity, direction and frequency dimensions. *Psychology of Sport and Exercise, 5*, 169–181.

Harackiewicz, J. M., & Elliot, A. J. (1998). The joint effects of target and purpose goals on intrinsic motivation: A mediational analysis. *Personality and Social Psychology Bulletin, 24*, 675–689.

Hardy, J., Gammage, K., & Hall, C. (2001). A descriptive study of athlete self-talk. *The Sport Psychologist, 15*, 306–318.

Hardy, L. (1997). The Coleman Roberts Griffith Address: Three myths about applied consultancy work. *Journal of Applied Sport Psychology, 9*, 277–294.

Hardy, L., & Callow, N. (1999). Efficacy of external and internal visual imagery perspectives for the enhancement of performance on tasks in which form is important. *Journal of Sport & Exercise Psychology, 21*, 95–112.

Hardy, L., Jones, J. G., & Gould, D. (1996). *Understanding psychological preparation for sport: Theory and practice of elite performers*. Chichester, UK: Wiley.

Harger, G. J., & Raglin, J. S. (1994). Correspondence between actual and recalled precompetition anxiety in collegiate track and field athletes. *Journal of Sport and Exercise Psychology, 16*, 206–211.

Harris, D. V., & Harris, B. L. (1984). *The athlete's guide to sport psychology: Mental skills for physical people.* New York: Leisure Press.

Hart, C. L., van Gorp, W., Haney, M., Foltin, R. W., & Fischman, M. W. (2001). Effects of acute smoked marijuana on complex cognitive performance. *Neuropsychopharmacology, 25*, 757–765.

Hartford Courant. (1999, June 24). Baseball's best: Any Arguments?, p. C1.

Harwitt, S. (1992, January 22). Capriati is feeling the strain. *New York Times, 141*, pp. B7, B11.

Harwood, C. (2002). Assessing achievement goals in sport: Caveats for consultants and a case for contextualization. *Journal of Applied Sport Psychology, 14*, 106–119.

Harwood, C., Cumming, J., & Fletcher, D. (2004). Motivational profiles and psychological skills use within elite youth sport. *Journal of Applied Sport Psychology, 16*, 317–332.

Harwood, C. G., Cumming, J., & Hall, C. (2003). Imagery use in elite youth sport participants: Reinforcing the applied significance of achievement goal theory. *Research Quarterly for Exercise and Sport, 3*, 292–300.

Harwood, C., Hardy, L., & Swain, A. (2000). Achievement goals in sport: A critique of conceptual and measurement issues. *Journal of Sport & Exercise Psychology, 22*, 235–255.

Harwood, C., & Swain, A. (2002). The development and activation of achievement goals within tennis: II. A player, parent, and coach intervention. *The Sport Psychologist, 16*, 111–137.

Harwood, C. G., & Treasure, D. C. (2000). Point, counter-point goal profiling. *Association for the Advancement of Applied Sport Psychology Newsletter, 15*, 7–12.

Hasbrook, C. A., Hart, B. A., Mathes, S. A., & True, S. (1990). Sex bias and the validity of believed differences between male and female interscholastic athletic coaches. *Research Quarterly for Exercise and Sport, 61*, 259–267.

Hatfield, B. D., Landers, D. L., & Ray, W. J. (1984). Cognitive processes during self-paced motor performance: An electroencephalographic profile of skilled marksmen. *Journal of Sport Psychology, 6*, 42–59.

Hatzigeorgiadis, A., & Biddle, S. (1999). The effects of goal orientation and perceived competence on cognitive interference during tennis and snooker performance. *Journal of Sport Behavior, 22*, 479–501.

Hausenblas, H. A., & Carron, A. V. (1996). Group cohesion and self-handicapping in female and male athletes. *Journal of Sport and Exercise Psychology, 18*, 132–143.

Hausenblas, H. A., & Symons Downs, D. (2002). How much is too much? The development and validation of the Exercise Dependence Scale. *Psychology and Health, 17*, 387–404.

Hayashi, C. T. (1996). Achievement motivation among Anglo-American and Hawaiian male physical activities participants: Individual differences and social contextual factors. *Journal of Sport & Exercise Psychology, 18*, 194–215.

Heath, C., Larrick, R. P., & Wu, G. (1999). Goals as reference points. *Cognitive Psychology, 38*, 79–109.

Heath, T. (2004, July 17). Post-game planning. *Hartford Courant*, pp. E1, E8.

Heaton, A. W., & Sigall, H. (1991). Self-consciousness, self-presentation, and performance under pressure: Who chokes, and when? *Journal of Applied Social Psychology, 21*, 175–188.

Heide, F. J., & Borkovec, T. D. (1983). Relaxation-induced anxiety: Paradoxical anxiety enhancement due to relaxation training. *Journal of Consulting and Clinical Psychology, 51*, 171–182.

Heide, F. J., & Borkovec, T. D. (1984). Relaxation-induced anxiety: Mechanisms and theoretical implications. *Behavioral Research and Therapy*, *22*, 1–12.

Heider, F. (1958). *The psychology of interpersonal relations*. New York: Wiley.

Heil, J. (2000). The injured athlete. In Y. L. Hannin (Ed.), *Emotions in sport* (pp. 245–265). Champaign, IL: Human Kinetics.

Heishman, S. J., Arasteh, K., & Stitzer, M. L. (1997). Comparative effects of alcohol and marijuana on mood, memory, and performance. *Pharmacology, Biochemistry and Behavior*, *58*, 93–101.

Helmreich, R. L., & Spence, J. T. (1977). Sex roles and achievement. In R. W. Christiana & D. M. Landers (Eds.), *Psychology of motor behavior and sport – 1976* (Vol. 2, pp. 33–46). Champaign, IL: Human Kinetics.

Helms, J. E., Jernigan, M., & Maschler, J. (2005). The meaning of race in psychology and how to change it: A methodological perspective. *American Psychologist*, *60*, 16–26.

Helton, W. S., Dember, W. N., Warm, J. S., & Matthews, G. (1999). Optimism, pessimism, and false failure feedback: Effects on vigilance performance. *Current Psychology: Developmental, Learning, Personality, Social*, *18*, 311–325.

Hendrix, A. E., Acevedo, E. O., & Hebert, E. (2000). An examination of stress and burnout in certified athletic trainers at division 1-a universities. *Journal of Athletic Training*, *35*, 139–144.

Henschen, K. P. (1998). Athletic staleness and burnout: Diagnosis, prevention, and treatment. In J. M. Williams (Ed.), *Applied sport psychology: Personal growth to peak performance* (3rd ed., pp. 398–408). Mountain View, CA: Mayfield.

Hermann, E. (1921). The psychophysical significance of physical education. *American Physical Education Review*, *26*, 282–289.

Hersh, P. (2000, July 10). Just call him Slam-pras. *Hartford Courant*, pp. C1, C2.

Heuschkel, D. (2002, November 8). Pedro: No Cy, just why. *Hartford Courant*, pp. C1, C4.

Heuze, J.-P., Sarrazin, P., Masiero, M., Raimbault, N., & Thomas, J-P. (2006). The relationships of perceived motivational climate to cohesion and collective efficacy in elite female teams. *Journal of Applied Sport Psychology*, *18*, 201–218.

Hewitt, P. L., Flett, G. L., & Ediger, E. (1995). Perfectionism traits and perfectionistic self-presentation in eating disorder attitudes, characteristics, and symptoms. *International Journal of Eating Disorders*, *18*, 317–326.

Hewitt, P. J., Flett, G. L., & Ediger, E. (1996). Perfectionism and depression: Longitudinal assessment of a specific vulnerability hypothesis. *Journal of Abnormal Psychology*, *105*, 276–280.

Hewitt, P. L., Flett, G. L., Ediger, E., Norton, G. R., & Flynn, C. A. (1998). Perfectionism in chronic and state symptoms of depression. *Canadian Journal of Behavioral Science*, *30*, 234–242.

Heyman, G. D., Dweck, C. S., & Cain, K. M. (1992). Young children's vulnerability to self-blame and and state symptoms of depression. *Canadian Journal of Behavioural Science*, *30*, 234–242.

Heyman, J. (1993, March 23). Very superstitious. Boggs unashamed of his mind-boggling habits [Online]. *Newsday*. Available at www.elibrary.com

Heyman, S. R. (1982). Comparisons of successful and unsuccessful competitors: A reconsideration of methodological questions and data. *Journal of Sport Psychology*, *4*, 295–300.

Higgins, E. T. (1997). Beyond pleasure and pain. *American Psychologist*, *52*, 1280–1300.

Highlen, P. S., & Bennett, B. B. (1983). Elite divers and wrestlers: A comparison between open- and closed-skill athletes. *Journal of Sport Psychology*, *5*, 871–890.

Hildebrand, K. M., Johnson, D. J., & Bogle, K. (2001). Comparison of patterns of alcohol use between high school and college athletes and non-athletes. *College Student Journal, 35,* 358–365.

Hill, R. A., & Barton, R. A. (2005, May 19). Red enhances human performance in contests: Signals biologically attributed to red coloration in males may operate in the area of combat sports. *Nature, 435,* 293.

Hills, P., & Argyle, M. (1998). Positive moods derived from leisure and their relationship to happiness and personality. *Personality and Individual Differences, 25,* 523–535.

Hine, T. (2003a, January 18). Kwan shows others a fine old time. *Hartford Courant,* p. C1.

Hine, T. (2003b, January 19). National treasure: Kwan wins 7th title; Cohen 3rd behind Hughes. *Hartford Courant,* p. E2.

Hine, T. (2003c, March 30). As usual, count on Kwan. *Hartford Courant,* p. E3.

Hine, T. (2004a, January 10). A chance for pure excitement. *Hartford Courant,* p. C2.

Hine, T. (2004b, August 8). Swimming in hype. *Hartford Courant,* pp. E1, E10.

Hine, T. (2005, December 16). Great goalie still learning. *Hartford Courant,* pp. C1, C2.

Hirt, E. R., Deppe, R. K., & Gordon, L. J. (1991). Self-reported versus behavioral self-handicapping: Empirical evidence for a theoretical distinction. *Journal of Personality and Social Psychology, 61,* 981–991.

Hobden, K., & Pliner, P. (1995). Self-handicapping and dimensions of perfectionism: Self-presentation vs self-protection. *Journal of Research in Personality, 29,* 461–474.

Hodge, K., & Petlichkoff, L. (2000). Goal profiles in sport motivation: A cluster analysis. *Journal of Sport & Exercise Psychology, 22,* 256–272.

Hogan, R., & Kaiser, R. B. (2005). What we know about leadership. *Review of General Psychology, 9,* 169–180.

Hokoda, A., & Fincham, F. D. (1995). Orgins of children's helpless and mastery achievement patterns in the family. *Journal of Educational Psychology, 87,* 375–385.

Hollander, D. B., & Meyers, M. C. (1995). Psychological factors associated with over-training: Implications for youth sport coaches. *Journal of Sport Behavior, 18,* 3–20.

Hollembeak, J., & Amorose, A. J. (2005). Perceived coaching behaviors and college athletes' intrinsic motivation: A test of self-determination theory. *Journal of Applied Sport Psychology, 17,* 20–36.

Holmes, D. S. (1984). Meditation and somatic arousal reduction. A review of the experimental evidence. *American Psychologist, 39,* 1–10.

Holt, N. L., & Dunn, J. G. H. (2004). Toward a grounded theory of the psychosocial competencies and environmental conditions associated with soccer success. *Journal of Applied Sport Psychology, 16,* 199–219.

Holt, N. L., & Sparkes, A. C. (2001). An ethnographic study of cohesiveness in a college soccer team over a season. *The Sport Psychologist, 15,* 237–259.

Homme, L. E. (1970). *How to use contingency contracting in the classroom.* Champaign, IL: Research Press.

Horn, H. L., Duda, J. L., & Miller, A. (1993). Correlates of goal orientations among young athletes. *Pediatric Exercise Science, 5,* 168–176.

Horn, T. S. (1985). Coaches' feedback and changes in children's perception of their physical competence. *Journal of Educational Psychology, 77,* 174–186.

Horn, T. S. (1992). Leadership effectiveness in the sport domain. In T. S. Horn (Ed.), *Advances in sport psychology* (pp. 181–200). Champaign, IL: Human Kinetics.

Horn, T., & Carron, A. V. (1985). Compatibility in coach–athlete relationships. *Journal of Sport Psychology, 7,* 137–149.

Hornby, N. (1992). *Fever pitch.* New York: Penguin Books.

Horner, M. S. (1973). A psychological barrier to achievement in women: The motive to avoid success. In D. C. McClelland & R. S. Steele (Eds.), *Human motivation: A book of readings* (pp. 222–230). Morristown, NJ: General Learning Press.

Horner, M. S. (1978). The measurement and behavioral implications of fear of success in women. In J. W. Atkinson & J. O. Raynor (Eds.), *Personality, motivation, and achievement* (pp. 41–70). Washington, DC: Halsted Press.

Howard, J. (2002a, February 21). Michelle is experienced in knowing the pitfalls. *Newsday.* Available at www.Newsday.com

Howard, J. (2002b, February 22). Sarah tweaks, squeaks by foes. Hughes coach inject big finish into long routine. *Newsday.* Available at www.Newsday.com

Howard-Hamilton, M. (1993). African-American female athletes: Issues, implications, and imperatives for educators. *NASPA Journal, 30,* 153–195.

Hudson, J. (1978). Physical parameters used for female exclusion from law enforcement and athletics. In C. Oglesby (Ed.), *Women and sport: From myth to reality.* Philadelphia: Lea & Febiger.

Hughes, S. L., Case, H. S., Stuemple, K. J., & Evans, D. S. (2003). Personality profiles of Iditasport ultra-marathon participants. *Journal of Applied Sport Psychology, 15,* 256–261.

Humphreys, M. S, & Revelle, W. (1984). Personality, motivation, and performance: A theory of the relationship between individual differences and information processing. *Psychological Review, 91,* 153–184.

Hyde, J. S. (2005). The gender similarities hypothesis. *The American Psychologist, 60,* 581–592.

Infante, J. R., Peran, F., Martinez, M., Roldan, A., Poyatos, R., Ruiz, C., et al. (1998). ACTH and B-endorphin in transcendental meditation. *Physiology & Behavior, 64,* 311–315.

International Society of Sport Psychology. (1992). Physical activity and psychological benefits: A position statement. *The Sport Psychologist, 6,* 199–203.

Irving, P. G., & Goldstein, I. P. (1990). Effect of home-field advantage on peak performance of baseball pitchers. *Journal of Sport Behavior, 13,* 23–27.

Isberg, L. (2000). Anger, aggressive behavior, and athletic performance. In Y. L. Hanin (Ed.). *Emotions in sport.* Champaign, IL: Human Kinetics.

Italian admits to insult. (2006, July 12). *Hartford Courant,* p. C3.

Italian player ends mystery. (2006, September 6). *Hartford Courant,* p. C7.

Jack, S. J., & Ronan, K. R. (1998). Sensation seeking among high- and low-risk sports participants. *Personality and Individual Differences, 25,* 1063–1083.

Jackson, R. C., Ashford, K. J., & Norsworthy, G. (2006). Attentional focus, dispositional reinvestment, and skilled motor performance under pressure. *Journal of Sport & Exercise Psychology, 28,* 49–68.

Jackson, S. A. (1995). Factors influencing the occurrence of flow state in elite athletes. *Journal of Applied Sport Psychology, 7,* 138–166.

Jackson, S. A., & Csikszentmihalyi, M. (1999). *Flow in sports.* Champaign, IL: Human Kinetics.

Jackson, S. A., Kimiecik, J. C., Ford, S. K., & Marsh, H. W. (1998). Psychological correlates of flow in sport. *Journal of Sport & Exercise Psychology, 20,* 358–378.

Jackson, S. A., & Roberts, G. C. (1992). Positive performance states of athletes: Toward a conceptual understanding of peek performance. *The Sport Psychologist, 6,* 156–171.

Jacobi, M. (1877). *The question of rest for women during menstruation.* New York: G. P. Putnam & Sons.

Jacobs, G. D., Benson, H., & Friedman, R. (1996). Topographic EEG mapping of the relaxation response. *Biofeedback and Self-Regulation, 21,* 121–129.

Jacobs, J. (1999, September 11). It's now shaping up as the right move. *Hartford Courant*, pp. C1–C2.

Jacobs, J. (2005, February 20). She reshapes model standard. *Hartford Courant*, pp. E1, E14.

Jacobson, E. (1938). *Progressive relaxation*. Chicago: University of Chicago Press.

Jambor, E. A., & Zhang, J. J. (1997). Investigating leadership, gender and coaching level using the revised leadership scale for sport. *Journal of Sport Behavior, 20*, 313–322.

Janelle, C. M., Singer, R. N., & Williams, A. M. (1999). External distraction and attentional narrowing: Visual search evidence. *Journal of Sport & Exercise Psychology, 21*, 70–91.

Janssen, J., & Dale, G. (2002). *The seven secrets of successful coaches*. Cary, NC: Winning the Mental Game.

Jenkins, S. (1992). Teenage confidential. *Sports Illustrated, 76*, March 30, 26–29.

Jenkins, S., & Whiteside, K. (1994). Lost weekend. *Sports Illustrated, 80*, May 30, 14–18.

Jevning, R., Wallace, R. K., & Beidebach, M. (1992). The physiology of meditation: A review. A wakeful hypometabolic integrated response. *Neuroscience and Biobehavioral Reviews, 16*, 415–424.

Johnson, E. O., Roehrs, T., Roth, T., & Breslau, N. (1998). Epidemiology of alcohol and medication as aids to sleep in early adulthood. *Sleep, 21*, 178–186.

Johnson, J. J. M., Hrycaiko, D. W., Johnson, G. V., & Halas, J. M. (2004). Self-talk and female soccer performance. *The Sport Psychologist, 18*, 44–56.

Johnson, L., & Biddle, S. J. H. (1989). Persistence after failure: An exploratory look at "learned helplessness" in motor performance. *British Journal of Physical Education Research Supplement, 5*, 7–10.

Johnson, U., Ekengren, J., & Andersen, M. B. (2005). Injury prevention in Sweden: Helping soccer players at risk. *Journal of Sport & Exercise Psychology, 27*, 32–38.

Johnston, L. H., & Carroll, D. (1998). The context of emotional responses to athletic injury: A qualitative analysis. *Journal of Sport Rehabilitation, 7*, 206–220.

Johnston-O'Connor, E. J., & Kirschenbaum, D. S. (1986). Something succeeds like success: Positive self-monitoring for unskilled golfers. *Cognitive Therapy and Research, 10*, 123–136.

Jones, E. E., & Berglas, S. (1978). Control of attributions about the self through self-handicapping strategies: The appeal of alcohol and the role of underachievement. *Personality and Social Psychology Bulletin, 4*, 200–206.

Jones, E. E., & Davis, K. E. (1965). From acts to dispositions: The attribution process in person perception. In L. Berkowitz (Ed.), *Advances in experimental social psychology* (Vol. 2, pp. 219–266). London: Academic Press.

Jones, G. (1995). More than just a game: Research developments and issues in competitive anxiety in sport. *British Journal of Psychology, 86*, 449–478.

Jones, G., & Cale, A. (1989). Relationships between multidimensional competitive state anxiety and cognitive and motor subcomponents of performance. *Journal of Sports Sciences, 7*, 129–140.

Jones, G., & Hanton, S. (1996). Interpretation of competitive anxiety symptoms and goal attainment expectancies. *Journal of Sport and Exercise Psychology, 18*, 144–157.

Jones, G., & Hanton, S. (2001). Pre-competitive feeling states and directional anxiety interpretations. *Journal of Sports Sciences, 19*, 385–395.

Jones, G., Hanton, S., & Swain, A. B. J. (1994). Intensity and interpretation of anxiety symptoms in elite and non-elite sports performers. *Personality & Individual Differences, 17*, 657–663.

Jones, G., & Swain, A. (1995). Predispositions to experience debilitative and facilitative anxiety in elite and nonelite performers. *The Sport Psychologist, 9*, 201–211.

Jones, G., Swain, A., & Cale, A. (1991). Gender differences in precompetition temporal patterning and antecedents of anxiety and self-confidence. *Journal of Sport and Exercise Psychology, 13,* 1–15.

Jones, G., Swain, A. B. J., & Hardy, L. (1993). Intensity and direction dimensions of competitive state anxiety and relationships with performance. *Journal of Sport Sciences, 11,* 525–532.

Jones, K. A., Smith, N. C., & Holmes, P. S. (2004). Anxiety symptom interpretation and performance predictions in high-anxious, low-anxious and repressor sport performers. *Anxiety, Stress and Coping, 17,* 187–199.

Jordan, W. J. (1999). Black high school students' participation in school-sponsored sports activities: Effects of school engagement and achievement. *Journal of Negro Education, 68,* 54–71.

Jordet, G. (2005). Perceptual training in soccer: An imagery intervention study with elite players. *Journal of Applied Sport Psychology, 17,* 140–156.

Kagan, J. (1994). *Galen's prophecy: Temperament in human nature.* New York: Basic Books.

Kagan, J., Snidman, N., McManis, M., & Woodward, S. (2001). Temperamental contributions to the affect family of anxiety. *The Psychiatric Clinics of North America, 24,* 677–688.

Kahn, G. (2006, February 14). Climate of suspicion: High-tech forecasts are a turnoff in Turin. *Wall Street Journal,* p. A1.

Kahn, R. (1971). *The boys of summer.* New York: Harper & Row.

Kamen, L. P., & Seligman, M. E. P. (1986). *Explanatory style predicts college grade point average.* Unpublished manuscript, University of Pennsylvania, Philadelphia.

Kandel, D., Chen, K., Warner, L. A., Kessler, R. C., & Grant, B. (1997). Prevalence and demographic correlates of symptoms of last year dependence on alcohol, nicotine, marijuana, and cocaine in the US population. *Drug and Alcohol Dependence, 44,* 11–29.

Kane, M. J., & Engle, R. W. (2003). Working-memory capacity and the control of attention: The contributions of goal neglect, response competition, and task set to Stroop interference. *Journal of Experimental Psychology: General, 132,* 47–70.

Kane, T. D., Baltes, T. R., & Moss, M. C. (2001). Causes and consequences of free-set goals: An investigation of athletic self-regulation. *Journal of Sport & Exercise Psychology, 23,* 55–75.

Kane, T. D., Marks, M. A., Zaccaro, S. J., & Blair, V. (1996). Self-efficacy, personal goals, and wrestlers' self-regulation. *Journal of Sport and Exercise Psychology, 18,* 36–48.

Kanfer, R., & Ackerman, P. L. (1989). Motivation and cognitive abilities: An integrative/aptitude–treatment interaction approach to skill acquisition. *Journal of Applied Psychology, 74,* 657–690.

Kanfer, R., & Ackerman, P. L. (1996). A self-regulatory skills perspective to reducing cognitive interference. In I. G. Sarason, G. R. Pierce, & B. R. Sarason (Eds.), *Cognitive interference theories, methods, & findings* (pp. 153–171). Mahwah, NJ: Lawrence Erlbaum Associates, Inc.

Kareev, Y. (2000). Seven (indeed, plus or minus two) and the detection of correlations. *Psychological Review, 107,* 397–403.

Kasser, T., & Ryan, R. M. (1993). A dark side of the American dream: Correlates of financial success as a central life aspiration. *Journal of Personality and Social Psychology, 65,* 410–422.

Kasser, T., & Ryan, R. M. (1996). Further examining the American dream: Differential correlates of intrinsic and extrinsic goals. *Personality and Social Psychology Bulletin, 22,* 280–287.

Kavussanu, M., & Roberts, G. C. (1996). Motivation in physical activity contexts: The relationship of perceived motivational climate to intrinsic motivation and self-efficacy. *Journal of Sport and Exercise Psychology, 18*, 264–280.

Kelley, B. C., Eklund, R. C., & Ritter-Taylor, M. (1999). Stress and burnout among collegiate tennis coaches. *Journal of Sport & Exercise Psychology, 21*, 113–130.

Kelley, H. H. (1967). Attribution theory in social psychology. In D. Levine (Ed.), *Nebraska symposium on motivation* (Vol. 15, pp. 192–240). Lincoln: University of Nebraska Press.

Kelley, H. H. (1972). Causal schemata and the attribution process. In E. E. Jones, D. E. Kanouse, H. H. Kelley, R. E. Nisbett, S. Valins, & B. Weiner (Eds.), *Attribution: Perceiving the causes of behaviour* (pp. 1–26). Morristown, NJ: General Learning Press.

Kellmann, M., & Kallus, K. W. (2001). *Recovery–stress questionnaire for athletes: User manual.* Champaign, IL: Human Kinetics.

Kenow, L. J., & Williams, J. M. (1992). Relationship between anxiety, self-confidence, and evaluation of coaching behaviors. *The Sport Psychologist, 6*, 344–357.

Kerr, G., & Dacyshyn, A. (2001). The retirement experiences of elite, female gymnasts. *Journal of Applied Sport Psychology, 12*, 115–133.

Kerr, G., & Goss, J. (1996). The effects of a stress management program on injuries and stress levels. *Journal of Applied Sport Psychology, 8*, 109–117.

Kerr, J. H. (1997). *Motivation and emotion in sport: Reversal theory.* Hove, UK: Psychology Press.

Kerr, J. H., & Cox, T. (1991). Arousal and individual differences in sport. *Personality and Individual Differences, 12*, 1075–1085.

Kessler, R. C., Aguilar-Gaxiola, S., Berglund, P. A., Caraveo-Anduaga, J. J., DeWit, D. J., Greenfield, S. F., et al. (2001a). Patterns and predictors of treatment seeking after onset of a substance use disorder. *Archives of General Psychiatry, 58*, 1065–1071.

Kessler, R. C., Berglund, P. A., Bruce, M. L., Koch, J. R., Laska, E. M., Leaf, P. J., et al. (2001b). The prevalence and correlates of untreated serious mental illness. *Health Services Research, 36*, 987–1007.

Kessler, R. C., Berglund, P. A., Foster, C. L., Saunders, W. B., Stang, P. E., & Walters, E. E. (1997a). Social consequences of psychiatric disorders, II: Teenage parenthood. *American Journal of Psychiatry, 154*, 1405–1411.

Kessler, R. C., Crum, R. M., Warner, L. A., Nelson, C. B., Schulenberg, J., & Anthony, J. C. (1997b). Lifetime co-occurrence of DSM-III-R alcohol abuse and dependence with other psychiatric disorders in the National Comorbidity Survey. *Archives of General Psychiatry, 54*, 313–321.

Kessler, R. C., Foster, C. L., Saunders, W. B., & Stang, P. E. (1995). Social consequences of psychiatric disorders, I: Educational attainment. *American Journal of Psychiatry, 152*, 1026–1032.

Kessler, R. C., & Frank, R. G. (1997). The impact of psychiatric disorders on work loss days. *Psychological Medicine, 27*, 861–873.

Kessler, R. C., McGonagle, K. A., Zhao, S., Nelson, C. B., Hughes, M., Eshleman, S., et al. (1994). Lifetime and 12-month prevalence of DSM-III-R psychiatric disorders in the United States: Results from the national comorbidity survey. *Archives of General Psychiatry, 51*, 8–19.

Keteyian, A. (1999, October 31). The N.B.A.'s drug program is nothing more than a masquerade. *New York Times*, Section 8, p. 17.

Kilpatrick, M., Bartholomew, J., & Riemer, H. (2003). The measurement of goal orientations in exercise. *Journal of Sport Behavior, 26*, 121–136.

Kim, B. J., Williams, L., & Gill, D. L. (2003). A cross-cultural study of achievement orientation and intrinsic motivation in young USA and Korean athletes. *International Journal of Sport Psychology, 34*, 168–184.

King, P. (2000, February 9). Dick Vermeil: Back to the beginning [Online]. *Sports Illustrated.* Available at www.elibrary.com

Kingston, K. M., & Hardy, L. (1997). Effects of different types of goals on processes that support performance. *The Sport Psychologist, 11,* 277–293.

Kingston, K. M., Horrocks, C., & Hanton, S. (2006). Do multidimensional intrinsic and extrinsic motivational profiles discriminate between athlete scholarship status and gender? *European Journal of Sport Science, 6,* 53–63.

Kirkcaldy, B. D. (1980). An analysis of the relationship between psychophysiological variables connected to human performance and the personality variables extraversion and neuroticism. *International Journal of Sport Psychology, 11,* 276–289.

Kirkcaldy, B. D. (1984). Clinical psychology in sport. *International Journal of Sport Psychology, 15,* 127–136.

Kirsch, I., & Henry, D. (1979). Self-desensitization and public speaking in the reduction of public speaking anxiety. *Journal of Consulting and Clinical Psychology, 47,* 536–541.

Kirschenbaum, D. S. (1984). Self-regulation and sport psychology: Nurturing an emerging symbiosis. *Journal of Sport Psychology, 6,* 159–183.

Kirschenbaum, D. S., Ordman, A. M., Tomarken, A. J., & Holtzbauer, R. (1982). Effects of differential self-monitoring and level of mastery on sports performance. *Cognitive Therapy and Research, 6,* 335–342.

Kitsantas, A., & Zimmerman, B. J. (1998). Self-regulation of motoric learning: A strategic cycle view. *Journal of Applied Sport Psychology, 10,* 220–239.

Kitsantas, A., & Zimmerman, B. J. (2002). Comparing self-regulatory processes among novice, non-expert, and expert volleyball players: A microanalytic study. *Journal of Applied Sport Psychology, 14,* 91–105.

Kitsantas, A., Zimmerman, B. J., & Cleary, T. (2000). The role of observation and emulation in the development of athletic self-regulation. *Journal of Educational Psychology, 92,* 811–817.

Kleiber, D. A., & Brock, S. C. (1992). The effects of career-ending injuries on the subsequent well-being of elite college athletes. *Sociology of Sport Journal, 9,* 70–75.

Klein, H. J., Wesson, M. J., Hollenbeck, J. R., & Alge, B. J. (1999). Goal commitment and the goal-setting process: Conceptual clarification and empirical synthesis. *Journal of Applied Psychology, 84,* 885–896.

Klinger, E. (1996). The content of thoughts: Interference as the downside of adaptive normal mechanisms in thought flow. In I. G. Sarason, G. R. Pierce, & B. R. Sarason (Eds.), *Cognitive interference theories, methods, & findings* (pp. 3–23). Mahwah, NJ: Lawrence Erlbaum Associates, Inc.

Koca, C., Asci, F. H., & Kirazci, S. (2005). Gender role orientation of athletes and nonathletes in a patriarchal society: A study in Turkey. *Sex Roles, 52,* 217–225.

Kochman, T. (1981). *Black and white: Styles in conflict.* Chicago: University of Chicago Press.

Koivula, N. (1999). Sport participation: Differences in motivation and actual participation due to gender typing. *Journal of Sport Behavior, 22,* 360–371.

Koivula, N. (2001). Perceived characteristics of sports categorized as gender-neutral, feminine and masculine. *Journal of Sport Behavior, 24,* 377–393.

Koivula, N., Hassmen, P., & Fallby, J. (2002). Self-esteem and perfectionism in elite athletes: Effects on competitive anxiety and self-confidence. *Personality and Individual Differences, 32,* 865–875.

Kontos, A. P., & Breland-Noble, A. M. (2002). Racial/ethnic diversity in applied sport psychology: A multicultural introduction to working with athletes of color. *The Sport Psychologist, 16,* 296–315.

Kowal, J., & Fortier, M. S. (1999). Turning play into work: Effects of adult surveillance and extrinsic rewards on children's intrinsic motivation. *Journal of Personality and Social Psychology, 31,* 479–486.

Kowalski, K. C., & Crocker, P. R. E. (2001). Development and validation of the Coping Function Questionnaire for adolescents in sport. *Journal of Sport and Exercise Psychology, 23,* 136–155.

Kozar, B., Whitfield, K. E., Lord, R. H., & Mechikoff, R. A. (1993). Timeouts before free throws: Do the statistics support the strategy? *Perceptual and Motor Skills, 76,* 47–50.

Krane, V., & Baird, S M. (2005). Using ethnography in applied sport psychology. *Journal of Applied Sport Psychology, 17,* 87–107.

Krane, V., & Williams, J. M. (2006). Psychological characteristics of peak performance. In J. M. Williams (Ed.), *Applied sport psychology: Personal growth to peak performance* (5th ed., pp. 207–227), New York: McGraw-Hill.

Kraus, H., & Hirschland, P. (1954). Minimum muscular fitness tests in young children. *Research Quarterly, 25,* 178–188.

Krohne, H. W. (1993). Vigilance and cognitive avoidance as concepts in coping research. In H. W. Krohne (Ed.), *Attention and avoidance: Strategies in coping with aversiveness* (pp. 19–50). Seattle: Hogrefe & Huber.

Kubler-Ross, E. (1969). *On death and dying.* London: Tavistock.

Kuczka, K. K., & Treasure, D. C. (2005). Self-handicapping in competitive sport: Influence of the motivational climate, self-efficacy, and perceived importance. *Psychology of Sport and Exercise, 6,* 539–550.

Kuhn, C., Swartzwelder, S., & Wilson, W. (2000). *Pumped.* New York: Norton.

Kuhn, T. S. (1970). *The structure of scientific revolutions* (2nd ed.). Chicago: University of Chicago Press.

Kunz, J. L. (1997). Drink and be active? The associations between drinking and participation in sports. *Addiction Research, 5,* 439–450.

Kurosawa, K., & Harackiewicz, J. M. (1995). Test anxiety, self-awareness, and cognitive interference: A process analysis. *Journal of Personality, 63,* 931–951.

Kyllo, L. B., & Landers. D. M. (1995). Goal setting in sport and exercise: A research synthesis to resolve the controversy. *Journal of Sport & Exercise Psychology, 17,* 117–137.

Laios, A., Theodorakis, N., & Gargalianos, D. (2003). Leadership and power: Two important factors for effective coaching. *International Sports Journal,* Winter, 150–154.

Lamb, M. (1986). Self-concept and injury frequency among female college field hockey players. *Athletic Training, 21,* 220–224.

Landers, D. M. (1995). Sport psychology: The formative years, 1950–1980. *The Sport Psychologist, 9,* 406–417.

Landers, D. M., & Arent, S. M. (2006). Arousal–performance relationships. In J. M. Williams (Ed.), *Applied sport psychology: Personal growth to peak performance* (5th ed., pp. 260–284). New York: McGraw-Hill.

Landers, D. M. & Boutcher, S. H. (1993). Arousal–performance relationships. In J. M. Williams (Ed.), *Applied sport psychology: Personal growth to peak performance* (pp. 170–184). Palo Alto, CA: Mayfield.

Landers, L. M., & Petruzzello, S. J. (1994). Physical activity, fitness, and anxiety. In C. Bouchard, R. J. Shepard, & T. Stevens (Eds.), *Physical activity, fitness, and health* (pp. 868–882). Champaign, IL: Human Kinetics.

Landin, D., & Hebert, E. (1999). The influence of self-talk on the performance of skilled female tennis players. *Journal of Applied Sport Psychology, 111,* 263–282.

Lane, A. M., Jones, L., & Stevens, M. J. (2002). Coping with failure: The effects of self-esteem and coping on changes in self-efficacy. *Journal of Sport Behavior, 25,* 331–345.

Lanning, W., & Hisanaga, B. (1983). A study of the relation between the reduction of competition anxiety and an increase in athletic performance. *International Journal of Sport Psychology, 14,* 219–227.

Latham, G. P., & Seijts, G. H. (1999). The effects of proximal and distal goals on performance on a moderately complex task. *Journal of Organizational Behavior, 20,* 421–429.

Lay, C. H. (1986). At last, my research article on procrastination. *Journal of Research in Personality, 20,* 474–495.

Lay, C. H. (1995). Trait procrastination, agitation, dejection, and self-discrepancy. In J. R. Ferrari, J. L. Johnson, & W. G. McCown (Eds.), *Procrastination and task avoidance: Theory, research and treatment* (pp. 97–112). New York: Plenum.

Lay, C. H., Knish, S., & Zanatta, R. (1992). Self-handicappers and procrastinators: A comparison of their practice behavior prior to an evaluation. *Journal of Research in Personality, 26,* 242–257.

Lay, C., Kovacs, A., & Danto, D. (1998). The relation of trait procrastination to the big-five factor conscientiousness: An assessment with primary–junior school children based on self-report measures. *Personality and Individual Differences, 25,* 187–193.

Lazarus, R. S. (1991). *Emotion and adaptation.* New York: Oxford University Press.

Lazarus, R. S. (2000). Cognitive–motivational–relational theory of emotion. In Y. L. Hanin (Ed.), *Emotions in sport* (pp. 39–63). Champaign, IL: Human Kinetics.

Lazarus, R. S., & Folkman, S. (1984). *Stress, appraisal, and coping.* New York: Springer.

Leddy, M. H., Lambert, M. J., & Ogles, B. M. (1994). *Research Quarterly for Exercise and Sport, 65,* 347–354.

Lederman, D. (2005, October 21). Bradley's "Braves" stays on NCAA "hostile" list. Available at www.Insidehighered.com

Lee, C. C., & Rotella, R. J. (1991). Special concerns and considerations for sport psychology consulting with black student athletes. *The Sport Psychologist, 5,* 365–369.

Leerhsen, C. & Barrett, T. (1990). Teen queen of tennis. *Newsweek, 115,* May 14, 58–63.

Lefebvre, L. M., & Cunningham, J. D. (1977). The successful football team: Effects of coaching and team cohesiveness. *International Journal of Sport Psychology, 8,* 29–41.

Lehrer, P. M. (1982). How to relax and how not to relax: A re-evaluation of the work of Edmund Jacobson. *Behaviour Research and Therapy, 20,* 417–428.

Lehrer, P. M. (1987). A review of the approaches to the management of tension and stage fright in musical performance. *Journal of Research in Music Education, 35,* 143–152.

Lehrer, P., & Carr, R. (1997). Progressive relaxation. In W. T. Roth (Ed.), *Treating anxiety disorders* (pp. 83–116). San Francisco: Jossey-Bass.

Lehrer, P. M., Carr, R., Sargunaraj, D., Woolfolk, R. L. (1994). Stress management techniques: Are they all equivalent, or do they have specific effects? *Biofeedback and Self-Regulation, 19,* 353–401.

Lehrer, P. M., Woolfolk, R. L., Rooney, A. J., McCann, B., & Carrington, P. (1983). Progressive relaxation and meditation: A study of psychophysiological and therapeutic differences between two techniques. *Behaviour Research and Therapy, 21,* 651–662.

Leichliter, J., Meilman, P., Presley, C., & Cashin, J. (1998). Alcohol use and related consequences among college students with varying levels of involvement in college athletics. *Journal of College Health, 46,* 257–262.

Leith, K. P., & Baumeister, R. F. (1996). Why do bad moods increase self-defeating behavior? Emotion, risk taking and self-regulation. *Journal of Personality and Social Psychology, 71,* 1250–1267.

Lemyre, P.-N., Roberts, G. C., & Ommundsen, Y. (2002). Achievement goal orientations, perceived ability, and sportspersonship in youth soccer. *Journal of Applied Sport Psychology, 14,* 120–136.

Lemyre, P.-N, Treasure, D. C., & Roberts, G. C. (2006). Influence of variability in motivation and affect on elite athlete burnout susceptibility. *Journal of Sport & Exercise Psychology, 28,* 32–48.

Lennon, J., & McCartney, P. (1970). Let it be [Recorded by the Beatles]. On *Let it be* [Record]. London: Apple. (Recorded January 31, 1969, April 30, 1969 & January 4, 1970).

Leonard, W. M. (1989). The "home advantage": The case of the modern Olympiads. *Journal of Sport Behavior, 12,* 227–241.

Lerner, B. S., & Locke, E. A. (1995). The effects of goal setting, self-efficacy, competition, and personal traits on performance of an endurance task. *Journal of Sport & Exercise Psychology, 17,* 138–152.

LeUnes, A., & Burger, J. (2000). Profile of mood states research in sport and exercise psychology: Past, present, and future. *Journal of Applied Sport Psychology, 12,* 5–15.

Levitt, S., & Gutin, B. (1971). Multiple choice reaction time and movement time during physical exertion. *Research Quarterly, 42,* 405–410, 423–433.

Lewis, B. P., & Linder, D. E. (1997). Thinking about choking? Attentional processes and paradoxical performance. *Personality and Social Psychology Bulletin, 23,* 937–944.

Lidz, F. (1996). Different strokes. *Sports Illustrated, 85,* December 23, 122–123.

Lincoln, Y. S., & Guba, E. G. (1985). *Naturalistic inquiry.* Newbury Park, CA: Sage.

Linden, W. (1990). *Autogenic training: A clinical guide.* New York: Guilford.

Linden, W. (1994). Autogenic training: A narrative and quantitative review of clinical outcome. *Biofeedback and Self-Regulation, 19,* 227–264.

Linder, D. E., Brewer, B. W., Van Raalte, J. L., & De Lange, N. (1991). A negative halo for athletes who consult sport psychologists: Replication and extension. *Journal of Sport and Exercise Psychology, 13,* 133–148.

Lindman, H. R. (1974). *Analysis of variance in complex experimental designs.* San Francisco: W. H. Freeman.

Lindner, K. J., & Kerr, J. (2001). Predictability of sport participation motivation from meta-motivational dominances and orientations. *Personality and Individual Differences, 30,* 759–773.

Lindsley, D. H., Brass, D. J., & Thomas, J. B. (1995). Efficacy–performance spirals: A multilevel perspective. *Academy of Management Review, 20,* 645–678.

Lirgg, C. D. (1991). Gender differences in self-confidence in physical activity: A meta-analysis of recent studies. *Journal of Sport and Exercise Psychology, 8,* 294–310.

Lirgg, C. D., & Feltz, D. L. (1991). Teacher versus peer models revisited: Effects on motor performance and self-efficacy. *Research Quarterly for Exercise and Sport, 62,* 217–224.

Litsky, F. (2005, December 14). Steroids, expulsions & suspensions, track & field, drugs & sports. *New York Times,* p. D3.

Locke, E. A. (1996). Motivation through conscious goal setting. *Applied and Preventive Psychology, 5,* 117–124.

Locke, E. A., & Latham, G. P. (1994). Goal setting theory. In H. F. O'Neil Jr. & M. Drillings (Eds.), *Motivation: Theory and research* (pp. 13–29). Hillsdale, NJ: Lawrence Erlbaum Associates, Inc.

Locke, E. A., Latham, G. P., & Erez, M. (1988). The determinents of goal commitment. *Academy of Management Review, 13,* 22–39.

Logan, G. D. (1988). Towards an instance theory of automatization. *Psychological Review, 95,* 492–527.

Lohasz, P. G., & Leith, L. M. (1997). The effect of three mental preparation strategies on the performance of a complex response time task. *International Journal of Sport Psychology, 28,* 25–34.

Lopez-Frias, M., De La Fe Fernandez, M., Planells, E., Miranda, M. T., Mataix, J., & Llopis, J.

(2001). Alcohol consumption and academic performance in a population of Spanish high school students. *Journal of Studies on Alcohol, 62*, 741–744.

Luthe, W. (1970). *Autogenic therapy, Vol. IV: research and theory*. New York: Grune & Stratton.

Lynskey, M., & Hall, W. (2000). The effects of adolescent cannabis use on educational attainment: A review. *Addiction, 95*, 1621–1630.

MacAndrew, C. (1980). Male alcoholics, secondary psychopathy, and Eysenck's theory of personality. *Personality and Individual Differences, 1*, 151–160.

MacAndrew, C. (1981). What the MAC scale tells us about alcoholics: An interpretive review. *Journal of Studies on Alcohol, 42*, 604–625.

MacLean, C. R. K., Walton, K. G., Wenneberg, S. R., Levitsky, D. K., Mandarino, J. P., Waziri, R., et al. (1997). Effects of the Transcendental Meditation program on adaptive mechanisms: Changes in hormone levels and responses to stress after 4 months of practice. *Psychoneuroendocrinology, 22*, 277–295.

MacLeod, C. (1996). Anxiety and cognitive processes. In I. G. Sarason, G. R. Pierce, & B. R. Sarason (Eds.), *Cognitive interference theories, methods, & findings* (pp. 47–76). Mahwah, NJ: Lawrence Erlbaum Associates, Inc.

Madden, C. C., Kirkby, R. J., & McDonald, D. (1989). Coping styles of competitive middle distance runners. *International Journal of Sport Psychology, 20*, 287–296.

Magyar, T. M., & Duda, J. L. (2000). Confidence restoration following athletic injury. *The Sport Psychologist, 14*, 372–390.

Mahoney, M. J. (1989). Psychological predictors of elite and non-elite performance in Olympic weightlifting. *International Journal of Sport Psychology, 20*, 1–12.

Mahoney, M. J., & Avener, M. (1977). Psychology of the elite athlete: An exploratory study. *Cognitive Therapy and Research, 1*, 135–141.

Mahoney, M. J., Gabriel, T. J., & Perkins, T. S. (1987). Psychological skills and exceptional athletic performance. *The Sport Psychologist, 1*, 181–199.

Mahoney, P. J. (1997). Freud: Man at work. In C. W. Socarides and S. Kramer (Eds.), *Work and its inhibitions* (pp. 79–98). Psychoanalytic essays. Madison, CT: International Universities Press.

Majors, R. (1998). Cool pose: Black masculinity and sports. In G. Sailes (Ed.), *African Americans in sport* (pp. 15–22). New Brunswick, NJ: Transaction.

Malete, L., & Feltz, D. L. (2000). The effect of a coaching education program on coaching efficacy. *The Sport Psychologist, 14*, 410–417.

Mallett, C. J., & Hanrahan, S. J. (1997). Race modeling: An effective cognitive strategy for the 100m sprinter? *The Sport Psychologist, 11*, 72–85.

Mallett, C. J., & Hanrahan, S. J. (2004). Elite athletes: Why does the "fire" burn so brightly? *Psychology of Sport and Exercise, 5*, 183–200.

Malone, D. A., Dimeff, R. J., Lombardo, J. A., & Sample, R. H. B. (1995). Psychiatric effects and psychoactive substance use in anabolic-androgenic steroid users. *Clinical Journal of Sport Medicine, 5*, 25–31.

Mamassis, G., & Doganis, G. (2004). The effects of a mental training program on juniors pre-competitive anxiety, self-confidence, and tennis performance. *Journal of Applied Sport Psychology, 16*, 118–137.

Mandela, N. (1994). *Long walk to freedom: The autobiography of Nelson Mandela*. Boston: Little, Brown.

Maniar, S. D., Curry, L. A., Sommers-Flanagan, J., & Walsh, J. A. (2001). Student-athlete preferences in seeking help when confronted with sport performance problems. *The Sport Psychologist, 15*, 205–233.

Maraniss, D. (1999). *When pride still mattered: A life of Vince Lombardi*. New York: Simon & Schuster.

Marin, G. (1993). Influence of acculturation on familialism and self-identification among Hispanics. In M. E. Bernal & G. P. Knight (Eds.), *Ethnic identity: Formation and transmission among Hispanics and other minorities* (pp. 181–196). Albany: State University of New York Press.

Markus, H. R., & Kitayama, S. (1991). Culture and the self: Implications for cognition, emotion, and motivation. *Psychological Review, 98*, 224–253.

Martens, M. P., Mobley, M., & Zizzi, S. J. (2000). Multicultural training in applied sport psychology. *The Sport Psychologist, 14*, 81–97.

Martens, M. P., Watson, J. C. II, & Beck, N. C. (2006). Sport-type differences in alcohol use among intercollegiate athletes. *Journal of Applied Sport Psychology, 18*, 136–150.

Martens, R. (1977). *Sport Competition Anxiety Test*. Champaign, IL: Human Kinetics.

Martens, R. (1979). About smocks and jocks. *Journal of Sport Psychology, 1*, 94–99.

Martens, R. (1987). *Coaches' guide to sport psychology*. Champaign, IL: Human Kinetics.

Martens, R., Burton, D., Vealey, R., Bump, L., & Smith, D. (1990). The development of the Competitive State Anxiety Inventory–2. In R. Martens, R. S. Vealey, & D. Burton (Eds.), *Competitive anxiety in sport* (pp. 117–190). Champaign, IL: Human Kinetics.

Martin, A. J., Marsh, H. W., & Debus, R. L. (2001). Self-handicapping and defensive pessimism: Exploring a model of predictors and outcomes from a self-protection perspective. *Journal of Educational Psychology, 93*, 87–102.

Martin, B. A., & Martin, J. H. (1995). Comparing perceived sex role orientations of the ideal male and female athlete to the ideal male and female. *Journal of Sport Behavior, 18*, 286–301.

Martin, B. A., & Murberger, M. A. (1994). Effects of self-esteem and assigned goals on actual and perceived performance. *Journal of Social Behavior and Personality, 9*, 81–87.

Martin, J. J., Kelley, B., & Eklund, R. C. (1999). A model of stress and burnout in male high school athletic directors. *Journal of Sport and Exercise Psychology, 21*, 280–294.

Martin, K. A., & Brawley, L. R. (2002). Self-handicapping in physical achievement settings: The contributions of self-esteem and self-efficacy. *Self and Identity, 1*, 337–351.

Martin, K. A., & Hall, C. R. (1995). Using mental imagery to enhance intrinsic motivation. *Journal of Sport & Exercise Psychology, 17*, 54–69.

Martin, K. A., Moritz, S. E., & Hall, C. R. (1999). Imagery use in sport: A literature review and applied model. *The Sport Psychologist, 13*, 245–268.

Martin, S. B. (2005). High school and college athletes' attidudes toward sport psychology consulting. *Journal of Applied Sport Psychology, 17*, 127–139.

Martin, S. B., Akers, A., Jackson, A. W., Wrisberg, C. A., Nelson, L., Leslie, P. J., et al. (2001). Male and female athletes' and nonathletes' expectations about sport psychology consulting. *Journal of Applied Sport Psychology, 13*, 19–40.

Martin, S. B., Jackson, A. W., Richardson, P. A., & Weiller, K. H. (1999). Coaching preferences of adolescent youths and their parents. *Journal of Applied Sport Psychology, 11*, 247–262.

Martin, S. B., Wrisberg, C. A., Beitel, P. A., & Lounsbury, J. (1997). NCAA Division I athletes' attitudes toward seeking sport psychology consultation: The development of an objective instrument. *The Sport Psychologist, 11*, 201–218.

Martin-Krumm, C. P., Sarrazin, P. G., Peterson, C., & Famose, J.-P. (2003). Explanatory style and resilience after sports failure. *Personality and Individual Differences, 35*, 1685–1695.

Martinek, T. J. (1996). Fostering hope in youth: A model for explaining learned helplessness in physical activity. *Quest, 48*, 409–421.

Maslach, C., & Jackson, S. E. (1981). The measurement of experienced burnout. *Journal of Occupational Psychology, 2*, 99–113.

Maslach, C., & Jackson, S. E. (1986). *Maslach burnout inventory manual* (2nd ed.). Palo Alto, CA: Consulting Psychologists Press.

Maslach, C., & Schaufeli, W. B. (1993). Historical and conceptual development of burnout. In W. B. Schaufeli, C. Maslach, & T. Marek (Eds.), *Professional burnout: Recent developments in theory and research* (pp. 1–16). Philadelphia: Taylor & Francis.

Maslow, A. (1973). Deficiency motivation and growth motivation. In D. C. McClelland & R. S. Steele (Eds.), *Human motivation: A book of readings* (pp. 233–251). Morristown, NJ: General Learning Press.

Masson, J. F. (1985). *The complete letters of Sigmund Freud to Wilhelm Fliess*. Cambridge, MA: Harvard University Press. (Original work published 1897–1904).

Matheson, H., & Mathes, S. (1997). The effect of winning and losing on female interactive and coactive team cohesion. *Journal of Sport Behavior, 20*, 284–298.

May, J. R., & Brown, L. (1989). Delivery of psychological services to the US Alpine ski team prior to and during the Olympics in Calgary. *The Sport Psychologist, 3*, 320–329.

Maynard, I. W., Hemmings, B., & Warwick-Evans, L. (1995). The effects of a somatic intervention strategy on competitive state anxiety and performance in semiprofessional soccer players. *The Sport Psychologist, 9*, 51–64.

Maynard, I. W., Warwick-Evans, L., & Smith, M. J. (1995). The effects of a cognitive intervention strategy on competitive state anxiety and performance in semiprofessional soccer players. *Journal of Sport and Exercise Psychology, 17*, 428–446.

McAuley, E., Duncan, T. E., Wraith, S. C., & Lettunich, M. (1991). Self-efficacy, perceptions of success, and intrinsic motivation. *Journal of Applied Social Psychology, 21*, 139–155.

McCaffrey, N., & Orlick, T. (1989). Mental factors related to excellence among top professional golfers. *International Journal of Sport Psychology, 20*, 256–278.

McClelland, D. C. (1961). *The achieving society*. Princeton, NJ: Van Nostrand.

McClelland, D. C. (1985). How motives, skills, and values determine what people do. *American Psychologist, 40*, 812–825.

McCormick, R. E., & Tollison, R. D. (2001). Why do black basketball players work more for less money? *Journal of Economic Behavior & Organization, 44*, 201–219.

McCown, W., & Johnson, J. (1989), *Differential arousal gradients in chronic procrastination*. Paper presented at the American Psychological Society, Alexandria, Vancouver.

McCullagh, P. (1987). Model similarity effects on motor performance. *Journal of Sport Psychology, 4*, 249–260.

McCullagh, P., & Noble, J. M. (2002). Education for becoming a sport psychologist. In J. L. Van Raalte & B. W. Brewer (Eds.), *Exploring sport and exercise psychology* (2nd ed., pp. 439–458). Washington, DC: American Psychological Association.

McCullagh, P., & Weiss, M. R. (2001). Modeling: Considerations for motor skill performance and psychological responses. In R. N. Singer, H. A. Hausenblas, & C. M. Janelle (Eds.), *Handbook of sport psychology* (2nd ed., pp. 205–238). New York: Wiley.

McDermott, B. (1986). Stormin' Norman. *Sports Illustrated, 65*, August 25, 72–76, 78–76, 78–82, 84.

McDonald, S. A., & Hardy, C. J. (1990). Affective response patterns of the injured athlete: An exploratory analysis. *The Sport Psychologist, 4*, 261–274.

McElroy, M. A., & Willis, J. D. (1979). Women and the achievement conflict: A preliminary study. *Journal of Sport Psychology, 1*, 241–247.

McEnroe, J., & Kaplan, J. (2002). *You cannot be serious*. New York: G. P. Putnam's Sons.

McGinnis, J. M., & Foege, W. H. (1993). Actual causes of death in the United States. *Journal of the American Medical Association, 270*, 2207–2212.

McGlone, S. & Shrier, I. (2000), Does sex the night before competition decrease performance? *Clinical Journal of Sport Medicine, 10*, 233–234.

McGuire, E. J., Courneya, K. S., Widmeyer, W. N., & Carron, A. V. (1992). Aggression as a potential mediator of the home advantage in professional ice hockey. *Journal of Sport and Exercise Psychology, 14,* 148–158.

McIntosh, W. D. (1996). When does goal nonattainment lead to negative emotional reactions, and when doesn't it? The role of linking and rumination. In L. M. Martin & A. Tesser (Eds.), *Striving and feeling: Interactions among goals, affect, and self-regulation* (pp. 53–77). Mahwah, NJ: Lawrence Erlbaum Associates, Inc.

McKenzie, A. D., & Howe, B. L. (1997). The effect of imagery on self-efficacy for a motor skill. *International Journal of Sport Psychology, 28,* 196–210.

McKenzie, D. C. (1999). Markers of excessive exercise. *Canadian Journal of Applied Physiology, 24,* 66–73.

McNair, D. M., Lorr, M., & Droppleman, L. F. (1971). *Profile of mood states manual.* San Diego, CA: Educational and Industrial Testing Service.

McNally, J., & Orlick, T. (1975). Cooperative sport structures: A preliminary analysis. *Movement, 7,* 267–271.

Meaney, K. S., Dornier, L. A., & Owens, M. S. (2002). Sex-role stereotyping for selected sport and physical activities across age groups. *Perceptual and Motor Skills, 94,* 743–749.

Mednick, M. T., & Thomas, V. G. (1993). Women and the psychology of achievement: A view from the eighties. In F. L. Denmark & M. A. Paludi (Eds.), *Psychology of women: A handbook of issues and theories* (pp. 585–625). Westport, CT: Greenwood Press.

Medwechuk, N., & Crossman, J. (1994). Effects of gender bias on the evaluation of male and female swim coaches. *Perceptual and Motor Skills, 78,* 163–196.

Meeuwisse, W. H., & Fowler, P. J. (1988). Frequency and predictability of sports injuries in intercollegiate athletes. *Canadian Journal of Sport Sciences, 13,* 35–42.

Meilman, P. W., Leichliter, J. S., & Presley, C. A. (1999). Greeks and athletes: Who drinks more? *College Health, 47,* 187–190.

Mellalieu, S. D., Hanton, S., & Jones, G. (2003). Emotional labeling and competitive anxiety in preparation and competition. *The Sport Psychologist, 17,* 157–174.

Mellalieu, S. D., Hanton, S., & O'Brien, M. (2004). Intensity and direction of competitive anxiety as a function of sport type and experience. *Scandinavian Journal of Science and Medicine in Sport, 14,* 326–334.

Mend, H., & Federn, E. (1963). *Psychoanalysis and faith: The letters of Sigmund Freud and Oskar Pfister.* London: Hogarth Press.

Menzel, K. E., & Carrell, L. J. (1994). The relationship between preparation and performance in public speaking. *Communication Education, 43,* 17–26.

Merikangas, K. R., Mehta, R. L., Molnar, B. E., Walters, E. E., Swendsen, J. D., Aguilar-Gaziola, S., et al. (1998). Comorbidity of substance use disorders with mood and anxiety disorders: Results of the international consortium in psychiatric epidemiology. *Addictive Behaviors, 23,* 893–907.

Metheny, E. (1965). Symbolic forms of movement: The feminine image in sports. In E. Metheny (Ed.), *Connotations of movement in sport and dance* (pp. 43–56). Dubuque, IA: Brown.

Metzler, J. N., & Conroy, D. E. (2004). Structural validity of fear of success scale. *Measurement in Physical Education and Exercise Science, 8,* 89–108.

Meyers, A. W., Whelan, J. P., & Murphy, S. M. (1996). Cognitive behavioral strategies in athletic performance enhancement. In M. Hersen, R. M. Eisler, & P. M. Miller (Eds.), *Progress in behavioral modification* (Vol. 30, pp. 137–164). Pacific Grove, CA: Brooks/Cole.

Meyers, M. C., & LeUnes, A. (1996). Psychological skills assessment and athletic performance in collegiate rodeo athletes. *Journal of Sport Behavior, 19,* 132–147.

Meyers, M. C., & Sterling, J. C. (1990). Precompetitive mood state changes in collegiate rodeo athletes. *Journal of Sport Behavior, 13,* 114–122.

Mezzich, A., Tarter, R., Kirisci, L., Clark, D., Buckstein, O., & Martin, C. (1993). Subtypes of early age onset alcoholism. *Alcoholism: Clinical and Experimental Research, 17,* 767–770.

Midgley, C., Arunkumar, R., & Urdan, T. C. (1996). "If I don't do well tomorrow, there's a reason": Predictors of adolescents' use of academic self-handicapping strategies. *Journal of Educational Psychology, 88,* 423–434.

Midgley, C., & Urdan, T. (2001). Academic self-handicapping and achievement goals: A further examination. *Contemporary Educational Psychology, 26,* 61–75.

Mikulincer, M. (1986). Attributional processes in the learned helplessness paradigm: Behavioral effects of global attributions. *Journal of Personality and Social Psychology, 51,* 1248–1256.

Mikulincer, M. (1996). Mental rumination and learned helplessness: Cognitive shifts during helplessness training and their behavioral consequences. In I. G. Sarason, G. R. Pierce, & B. R. Sarason (Eds.), *Cognitive interference: Theories, methods, and findings* (pp. 191–209). Mahwah, NJ: Lawrence Erlbaum Associates, Inc.

Millard, L. (1996). Differences in coaching behaviors of male and female high school soccer coaches. *Journal of Sport Behavior, 19,* 19–31.

Miller, B. P., & Miller, A. J. (1985). Psychological correlates of success in elite sportswomen. *International Journal of Sport Psychology, 16,* 289–295.

Miller, G. A. (1956). The magic number seven plus or minus two: Some limits on our capacity for processing information. *Psychological Review, 63,* 81–97.

Ming, S., & Martin, G. L. (1996). Single-subject evaluation of a self-talk package for improving figure skating performance. *The Sport Psychologist, 10,* 227–238.

Mischel, W., & Shoda, Y. (1995). A cognitive–affective system theory of personality: Reconceptualizing situations, dispositions, dynamics, and invariance in personality structure. *Psychological Review, 102,* 246–268.

Miserandino, M. (1998). Attributional retraining as a method of improving athletic performance. *Journal of Sport Behavior, 21,* 286–297.

Mone, M. A., Baker, D. D., & Jeffries, F. (1995). Predictive validity and time dependency of self-efficacy, self-esteem, personal goals, and academic performance. *Educational and Psychological Measurement, 55,* 716–727.

Mor, S., Day, H. I., Flett, G. L., & Hewitt, P. L. (1995). Perfectionism, control, and components of performance anxiety in professional artists. *Cognitive Therapy and Research, 19,* 207–225.

Moran, A. (1995). How effective are psychological techniques used to enhance performance in tennis? The views of some international tennis coaches. In T. Reilly, M. Hughes, & A. Lees (Eds.), *Science and racket sports* (pp. 221–225). London: Spon.

Moran, A. (1996). *The psychology of concentration in sport performers.* Hove, UK: Psychology Press.

Moran, M. M., & Weiss, M. R. (2006). Peer leadership in sport: Links with friendship, peer acceptance, psychological characteristics, and athletic ability. *Journal of Applied Sport Psychology, 18,* 97–113.

Morgan, L. K., Griffin, J., & Heyward, V. H. (1996). Ethnicity, gender, and experience effects on attributional dimensions. *The Sport Psychologist, 10,* 4–16.

Morgan, M. (1985). Self-monitoring of attained subgoals in a private study. *Journal of Educational Psychology, 77,* 623–630.

Morgan, W. P. (1979). Prediction of performance in athletes. In P. Klavora & J. V. Daniel (Eds.), *Coach, athlete, and the sport psychologist* (pp. 173–186). Champaign, IL: Human Kinetics.

Morgan, W. P. (1980). Test of champions: The iceberg profile. *Psychology Today, 14*, 92–99, 101, 108.

Morgan, W. P., Brown, D. R., Raglin, J. S., O'Connor, P. J., & Ellickson, K. A. (1987). Psychological monitoring of overtraining and staleness. *British Journal of Sports Medicine, 21*, 107.

Morgan, W. P., & Johnson, R. W. (1978). Personality characteristics of successful and unsuccessful oarsmen. *International Journal of Sport Psychology, 9*, 119–133.

Morgan, W. P., & Pollock, M. L. (1977). Psychologic characterization of the elite distance runner. *Annals of the New York Academy of Sciences, 301*, 382–403.

Moritz, S. E., Martin, K. A., Hall, C. R., & Vadocz, E. (1996). What are confident athletes imaging? An examination of image content. *The Sport Psychologist, 10*, 171–197.

Morrell, E. M. (1986). Meditation and somatic arousal. *American Psychologist, 41*, 712–713.

Motl, R. W., Dishman, R. K., Saunders, R., Dowda, M., Felton, G., & Pate, R. R. (2001). Measuring enjoyment of physical activity in adolescent girls. *American Journal of Preventive Medicine, 21*, 110–117.

Mullen, B., & Cooper, C. (1994). The relation between group cohesiveness and performance: An integration. *Psychological Bulletin, 115*, 210–227.

Mumenthaler, M. S., & Taylor, J. L. (1999). Gender differences in moderate drinking effects. *Alcohol Health & Research World, 23*, 55–74.

Munroe, K., Giacobbi, P., Hall, C., & Weinberg, R. (2000). The 4 W's of imagery use: Where, when, why, and what. *Sport Psychologist, 14*, 119–137.

Murphy, A. (1998). Pro football: Taking his medicine. Broncos loopy linebacker Bill Romanowski pops a plethora of pills and powders to keep his minerals in balance. Too bad they don't do the same for his temper. *Sports Illustrated, 88*, May 25, 56–58, 61–63.

Murphy, J. B. (1993). *The moral economy of labor: Aristotelian themes in economic theory*. New Haven, CT: Yale University Press.

Murphy, L. R. (1983). A comparison of relaxation methods for reducing stress in nursing personnel. *Human Factors, 25*, 431–440.

Murphy, S. M. (1990). Models of imagery in sport psychology: A review. *Journal of Mental Imagery, 14*, 153–172.

Murphy, S. M. (1994). Imagery interventions in sport. *Medicine and Science in Sports and Exercise, 26*, 486–494.

Murphy, S. M., & Martin, K. A. (2002). The use of imagery in sport. In T. S. Horn (Ed.), *Advances in sport psychology*. Champaign, IL: Human Kinetics.

Murray, M. C., & Mann, B. L. (2006). Leadership effectiveness. In J. M. Williams (Ed.), *Applied sport psychology: Personal growth to peak performance* (5th ed., pp. 107–139). New York: McGraw-Hill.

Myers, D. G., & Diener, E. (1995). Who is happy? *Psychological Science, 6*, 10–19.

Nack, W. (2001). The wrecking yard. *Sports Illustrated, 94*, May 7, 60–66, 69–70, 72, 75.

Nagle, F. J., Morgan, W. P., Hellickson, R. O., Serfass, R. C., & Alexander, J. F. (1975). Spotting success traits in Olympic contenders. *The Physician and Sports Medicine, 3*, 31–34.

Nation, J. R., & LeUnes, A. (1983). A personality profile of the black athlete in college football. *Psychology, 20*, 1–3.

National Collegiate Athletic Association. (1992). *1991–1992 woman's volleyball injury surveillance system*. Overland Park, KS: NCAA.

National Collegiate Athletic Association. (1997). *The 1996–97 graduation report of student athletes*. Shawnee Mission, KS: NCAA.

National Safety Council. (1993). *Accident facts, 1993 edition*. Itasca, IL: NSC.

Nattiv, A., & Puffer, J. C. (1991). Lifestyles and health risks of collegiate athletes. *Journal of Family Practice, 33*, 585–590.

Naveh-Benjamin, M. (1991). A comparison of training programs intended for different types of test-anxious students: Further support for an information-processing mode. *Journal of Educational Psychology, 83*, 134–139.

Navratilova, M. (2006). *Shape your self: My 6-step diet and fitness plan to achieve the best shape of your life*. New York: Rodale.

NCAA Research Staff. (2001, June). *NCAA study of substance use habits of college student-athletes*. Indianapolis, IN: NCAA.

Nevill, A. M., & Holder, R. L. (1999). Home advantage in sport: An overview of studies on the advantage of playing at home. *Sports Medicine, 28*, 221–236.

Newcombe, P. A., & Boyle, G. J. (1995). High school students' sports personalities: Variations across participation level, gender, type of sport, and success. *International Journal of Sport Psychology, 26*, 277–294.

Newman, L. S., & Wadas, R. F. (1997). When the stakes are higher: Self-esteem instability and self-handicapping. *Journal of Social Behavior and Personality, 12*, 217–233.

Newton up to 388 lbs. – of pot. (2001, December 13). *Hartford Courant*, p. C2.

Nicholls, J. G. (1989). *The competitive ethos and democratic education*. Cambridge, MA: Harvard University Press.

Nicholls, J. G. (1992). The general and the specific in the development and expression of achievement motivation. In G. C. Roberts (Ed.), *Motivation in sport and exercise*. Champaign, IL: Human Kinetics.

Nicklaus, J. (1976). *Play better golf*. New York: King Features.

Nideffer, R. M. (1981a). *Predicting human behaviour: A theory and test of attentional and inter-personal style*. San Diego, CA: Enhanced Performance Associates.

Nideffer, R. M. (1981b). *The ethics and practice of applied sport psychology*. Ithaca, NY: Mouvement.

Nideffer, R. M. (1985). *Athletes' guide to mental training*. Champaign, IL: Human Kinetics.

Nideffer, R. M. (1993). Attention control training. In R. N. Singer, M. Murphy, & L. K. Tennant (Eds.), *Handbook of research on sport psychology* (pp. 542–556). New York: Macmillan.

Nideffer, R. M. & Sagal, M.-S. (2006). Concentration and attention control training. In J. M. Williams (Ed.), *Applied sport psychology: Personal growth to peak performance* (5th ed., pp. 382–403). New York: McGraw-Hill.

Nideffer, R. M., Sagal, M.-S., Lowry, M., & Bond, J. (2000). Identifying and developing world class performers. In *The practice of sport and exercise psychology: International perspectives*. Morgantown, WV: Fitness Information Technology.

Nixon, S. J. (1999). Neurocognitive performance in alcoholics: Is polysubstance abuse important? *Psychological Science, 10*, 181–185.

Noel, R. C. (1980). The effects of Visuo-motor Behavior Rehearsal on tennis performance. *Journal of Sport Psychology, 2*, 224–236.

Nolen-Hoeksema, S. (1990). *Sex differences in depression*. Stanford, CA: Stanford University Press.

Nolen-Hoeksema, S., Girgus, J. S., & Seligman, M. E. P. (1986). Learned helplessness in children: A longitudinal study of depression, achievement, and explanatory style. *Journal of Personality and Social Psychology, 51*, 435–442.

Nolen-Hoeksema, S., Girgus, J. S., & Seligman, M. E. P. (1992). Predictors and consequences of childhood depressive symptoms: A 5-year longitudinal study. *Journal of Abnormal Psychology, 101*, 405–422.

Nolen-Hoeksema, S., Parker, L. E., & Larson, J. (1994). Ruminative coping with depressed mood following loss. *Journal of Personality and Social Psychology, 67*, 92–104.

Norem, J. K., & Cantor, N. (1986a). Anticipatory and post hoc cushioning strategies: Optimism and defensive pessimism in "risky" situations. *Cognitive Therapy and Research, 10*, 347–362.

Norem, J. K., & Cantor, N. (1986b). Defensive pessimism: Harnessing anxiety as motivation. *Journal of Personality and Social Psychology, 51*, 1208–1217.

Norem, J. K., & Illingworth, K. S. S. (1993). Strategy-dependent effects of reflecting on self and tasks: Some implications of optimism and defensive pessimism. *Journal of Personality and Social Psychology, 65*, 822–835.

Norlander, T., & Archer, T. (2002). Predicting performance in ski and swim championships: Effectiveness of mood, perceived exertion, and dispositional optimism. *Perceptual and Motor Skills, 94*, 153–164.

Norton, G. R., & Johnson, W. E. (1983). A comparison of two relaxation procedures for reducing cognitive and somatic anxiety. *Journal of Behavior Therapy and Experimental Psychiatry, 14*, 209–214.

Norton, G. R., Rhodes, L., & Hauch, J. (1985). Characteristics of subjects experiencing relaxation and relaxation-induced anxiety. *Journal of Behavior Therapy and Experimental Psychiatry, 16*, 211–216.

Ntoumanis, N., & Jones, G. (1998). Interpretation of competitive trait anxiety symptoms as a function of locus of control beliefs. *International Journal of Sport Psychology, 29*, 99–114.

O'Connell, J. (1994, October 28). Bagwell can't ask for more: First from state to win award. *Hartford Courant*, p. C1.

Ogilvie, B. C., Haase, H., Jokl, E., Kranidiotis, D. T., Mahoney, M., & Nideffer, R. (1979). Critical issues in the application of clinical psychology in the sport setting. *International Journal of Sport Psychology, 10*, 178–183.

Ogilvie, B. C., & Tutko, T. A. (1966). *Problem athletes and how to handle them*. London: Palham Books.

Oglesby, C. A., & Hill, K. L. (1993). Gender and sport. In R. N. Singer, M. Murphey, & L. K. Tennant (Eds.), *Handbook of research on sport psychology* (pp. 718–728). New York: Macmillan.

Ommundsen, Y. (2001). Self-handicapping strategies in physical education classes: the influence of implicit theories of the nature of ability and achievement goal orientations. *Psychology of Sport and Exercise, 2*, 139–156.

Ommundsen, Y. (2004). Self-handicapping related to task and performance-approach and avoidance goals in physical education. *Journal of Applied Sport Psychology, 16*, 183–197.

Ommundsen, Y., & Roberts, G. C. (1999). Effect of motivational climate profiles on motivational indices in team sport. *Scandinavian Journal of Medicine and Science in Sports, 9*, 389–397.

Ommundsen, Y., Roberts, G. C., Lemyre, P. N., & Miller, B. W. (2005). Peer relationships in adolescent competitive soccer: Associations to perceived motivational climate, achievement goals and perfectionism. *Journal of Sports Sciences, 23*, 977–989.

Ommundsen, Y., Roberts, G. C., Lemyre, P. N., & Treasure, D. (2003). Perceived motivational climate in male youth soccer: relations to social–moral functioning, sportspersonship and team norm perceptions. *Psychology of Sport and Exercise, 4*, 397–413.

Onestak, D. M. (1991). The effects of progressive relaxation, mental practice, and hypnosis on athletic performance: A review. *Journal of Sport Behavior, 14*, 247–282.

Onestak, D. (1997). The effects of Visuo-Motor Behavior Rehearsal. *Journal of Sport Behavior, 20*, 185–198.

Orbach, I., Singer, R. N., & Murphey, M. (1997). Changing attributions with an attribution training technique related to basketball dribbling. *The Sport Psychologist, 11,* 294–304.

Orlick, T. D. (1986). *Psyching for sport.* Champaign, IL: Human Kinetics.

Orlick, T. (1992). *Freeing children from stress: Focusing and stress control activities for children.* Willits, CA: ITA Publications.

Orlick, T., & McCaffrey, N. (1991). Mental training with children for sport and life. *The Sport Psychologist, 5,* 322–334.

Orlick, T. D., & Mosher, R. (1978). Extrinsic awards and participant motivation in a sport related task. *International Journal of Sport Psychology, 9,* 27–39.

Orlick, T., & Partington, J. (1988). Mental links to excellence. *The Sport Psychologist, 2,* 105–130.

Orme-Johnson, D. W., Zimmerman, E., & Hawkins, M. (1997). Maharishi's vedic psychology. In H. R. R. Kao & D. Sinha (Eds.), *Asian perspectives on psychology* (pp. 282–308). New Delhi, India: Sage.

Oxendine, J. B. (1970). Emotional arousal and motor performance. *Quest, 13,* 23–32.

Oxendine, J. B. (1984). *Psychology of motor learning.* Englewood Cliffs, NJ: Prentice-Hall.

Pacht, A. R. (1984). Reflections on perfection. *American Psychologist, 39,* 386–390.

Page, S. J., Sime, W., & Nordell, K. (1999). The effects of imagery on female college swimmers' perceptions of anxiety. *The Sport Psychologist, 13,* 458–469.

Paivio, A. (1985). Cognitive and motivational functions of imagery in human performance. *Canadian Journal of Applied Sport Sciences, 10,* 22–28.

Pajares, F. (1996). Self-efficacy beliefs in academic settings. *Review of Educational Research, 66,* 543–578.

Papaioannou, A., March, H. W., & Theodorakis, Y. (2004). A multilevel approach to motivational climate in physical education and sport settings: An individual or group level construct. *Journal of Sport & Exercise Psychology, 26,* 90–118.

Pargman, D. (1998). *Understanding sport behavior.* Upper Saddle River, NJ: Prentice Hall.

Park, J.-K. (2000). Coping strategies used by Korean national athletes. *The Sport Psychologist, 14,* 63–80.

Parkhouse, B. L., & Williams, J. M. (1986). Differential effects of sex and status on evaluation of coaching ability. *Research Quarterly for Exercise and Sport, 57,* 53–59.

Parsons, C. A., & Soucie, D. (1988). Perceptions of the causes of procrastination by sport administrators. *Journal of Sport Management, 2,* 129–139.

Participation survey 1999–2000. (1999–2000). Indianapolis, IN: National Federation of State High School Associations.

Partington, J. T., & Shangi, G. M. (1992). Developing an understanding of team psychology. *International Journal of Sport Psychology, 23,* 28–47.

Paskevich, D. M., Brawley, L. R., Dorsch, K. D., & Widmeyer, W. N. (1995). Implications of individual and group level analyses applied to the study of collective efficacy and cohesion. *Journal of Applied Sport Psychology, 7,* S95.

Paskevich, D. M., Brawley, L. R., Dorsch, K. D., & Widmeyer, W. N. (1999). Relationship between collective efficacy and team cohesion: Conceptual and measurement issues. *Group Dynamics: Theory, Research, and Practice, 3,* 210–222.

Paskevich, D. M., Estabrooks, P. A., Brawley, L. R., & Carron, A. V. (2001). Group cohesion in sport and exercise. In R. N. Singer, H. A. Hausenblas, & C. M. Janelle (Eds.), *Handbook of sport psychology* (2nd ed., pp. 766–786). New York: Wiley.

Patrick, T. D., & Hrycaiko, D. W. (1998). Effects of a mental training package on an endurance performance. *The Sport Psychologist, 12,* 283–299.

Patterson, E. L., & Smith, R. E. (1998). Psychosocial factors as predictors of ballet injuries: Interactive effects of live stress and social support. *Journal of Sport Behavior, 21,* 101–113.

Patton, M. Q. (1990). *Qualitative evaluation and research methods*. Newbury Park, CA: Sage.

Pearson, R. E., & Petitpas, A. J. (1990). Transitions of athletes: Developmental and preventive perspectives. *Journal of Counseling & Development, 69*, 7–10.

Pelz, D. with Frank, J. A. (1999), *Dave Pelz's short game bible: Master the finesse swing and lower your score*. New York: Doubleday.

Penn State's Portland Fined in Bias Claim. (2006, April 19). *Hartford Courant*, p. C2.

Peretti-Watel, P., Beck, F., & Legleye, S. (2002). Beyond the U-curve: The relationship between sport and alcohol, cigarette and cannabis use in adolescents. *Addiction, 97*, 707–716.

Perkos, S., Theodorakis, Y., & Chroni, S. (2002). Enhancing performance and skill acquisition in novice basketball players with instructional self-talk. *Journal of Applied Sport Psychology, 14*, 14–26.

Perna, F. M., Ahlgren, R. L., & Zaichkowsky, L. (1999). The influence of career planning, race, and athletic injury on life satisfaction among recently retired collegiate male athletes. *The Sport Psychologist, 13*, 144–156.

Perna, F. M., Antoni, M. H., Baum, A., Gordon, P., & Schneiderman, N. (2003). Cognitive behavioral stress management effects on injury and illness among competitive athletes: A randomized clinical trial. *Annals of Behavioral Medicine, 25*, 66–73.

Perry, J. D., & Williams, J. M. (1998). Relationship of intensity and direction of competitive trait anxiety to skill level and gender in tennis. *The Sport Psychologist, 12*, 169–179.

Peters, H. J., & Williams, J. M. (2006). Moving cultural background to the foreground: An investigation of self-talk, performance, and persistence following feedback. *Journal of Applied Sport Psychology, 18*, 240–251.

Peters, M. F. (1981). Parenting in black families with young children: A historical perspective. In H. P. McAdoo (Ed.), *Black families* (pp. 211–244). Beverly Hills, CA: Sage.

Peterson, C., & Barrett, L. C. (1987). Explanatory style and academic performance among university freshmen. *Journal of Personality and Social Psychology, 53*, 603–607.

Peterson, C., & Bossio, L. M. (1989). Learned helplessness. In R. C. Curtis (Ed.), *Self-defeating behaviors: Experimental research, clinical impressions, and practical implications* (pp. 235–257). New York: Plenum.

Peterson, C., Maier, S. F., & Seligman, M. E. P. (1993). *Learned helplessness: A theory for the age of personal control*. New York: Oxford University Press.

Petherick, C. M., & Weigand, D. A. (2002). The relationship of dispositional goal orientations and perceived motivational climates on indices of motivation in male and female swimmers. *International Journal of Sport Psychology, 33*, 218–237.

Petitpas, A. J., Brewer, B. W., Rivera, P. M., & Van Raalte, J. L. (1994). Ethical beliefs and behaviors in applied sport psychology: The AAASP ethics survey. *Journal of Applied Sport Psychology, 6*, 135–151.

Petri, H. L., & Govern, J. (2004). *Motivation: Theory, research, and applications* (5th ed.). Belmont, CA: Wadsworth/Thomson Learning.

Petrie, T. A. (1992). Psychosocial antecedents of athletic injury: The effects of life stress and social support on female collegiate gymnasts. *Behavioral Medicine, 18*, 127–138.

Petrie, T. A. (1993). Coping skills, competitive trait anxiety, and playing status: Moderating effects on the life stress–injury relationship. *Journal of Sport & Exercise Psychology, 15*, 261–274.

Petrie, T. A. (1998). Anxiety management and the elite athlete: A case study. In K. F. Hayes (Ed.), *Integrating exercise, sports, movement, and mind: Therapeutic unity* (pp. 161–173). New York: Haworth Press.

Petrie, T. A., & Falkstein, D. L. (1998). Methodological, measurement, and statistical issues in research on sport injury prediction. *Journal of Applied Sport Psychology, 10,* 26–45.

Pfister, G. (2000). Women and the Olympic Games: 1900–97. In B. L. Drinkwater (Ed.), *Women in sport* (pp. 3–19). Oxford: Blackwell Science.

Phillips, J. M., & Gully, S. M. (1997). Role of goal orientation, ability, need for achievement, and locus of control in the self-efficacy and goal-setting process. *Journal of Applied Psychology, 82,* 792–802.

Pickworth, W. B., Rohrer, M. S., & Fant, R. V. (1997). Effects of abused drugs on psychomotor performance. *Experimental and Clinical Psychopharmacology, 5,* 235–241.

Piedmont, R. L. (1988). An interactional model of achievement motivation and fear of success. *Sex Roles, 10,* 89–100.

Piedmont, R. L., Hill, D. C., & Blanco, S. (1999). Predicting athletic performance using the five-factor model of personality. *Personality and Individual Differences, 27,* 769–777.

Pierce, B. E., & Burton, D. (1998). Scoring the perfect 10: Investigating the impact of goal-setting styles on a goal-setting program for female gymnasts. *The Sport Psychologist, 12,* 156–168.

Pierce, G. R., Henderson, C. A., Yost, J. H., & Loffredo, C. M. (1996). Cognitive interference and personality: Theoretical and methodological issues. In I. G. Sarason, G. R. Pierce, & B. R. Sarason (Eds.), *Cognitive interference theories, methods, & findings* (pp. 285–296). Mahwah, NJ: Lawrence Erlbaum Associates, Inc.

Pikoff, H. (1985). A critical review of autogenic training in America. *Clinical Psychology Review, 4,* 619–639.

Poczwardowski, A., & Conroy, D. E. (2002). Coping responses to failure and success among elite athletes and performing artists. *Journal of Applied Sport Psychology, 14,* 313–329.

Pollack, E. S., Franklin, G. M., Fulton-Kehoe, D., & Chowdhury, R. (1998). Risk of job-related injury among construction laborers with a diagnosis of substance abuse. *Journal of Environmental Medicine, 40,* 573–577.

Pope, H. G., & Katz, D. L. (1994). Psychiatric and medical effects of anabolic-androgenic steroid use. *Archives of General Psychiatry, 51,* 375–382.

Potter, S. (1947). *The theory and practice of gamesmanship.* Harmondsworth, UK: Penguin.

Poulton, R. G., Brooke, M., Moffitt, T. E., Stanton, W. R., & Silva, P. A. (1997). Prevalence and correlates of cannabis use and dependence in young New Zealanders. *New Zealand Medical Journal, 110,* 68–70.

Pragman, D. (1997). *Understanding sport behavior.* Upper Saddle River, NJ: Prentice Hall.

Prapavessis, H. (2000). The POMS and sports performance: A review. *Journal of Applied Sport Psychology, 12,* 34–48.

Prapavessis, H., & Carron, A. V. (1988). Learned helplessness in sport. *The Sport Psychologist, 2,* 189–201.

Prapavessis, H., & Carron, A. V. (1997). Sacrifice, cohesion, and conformity to norms in sport teams. *Group Dynamics: Theory, Research, and Practice, 1,* 231–240.

Prapavessis, H., & Gordon, S. (1991). Coach/player relationships in tennis. *Canadian Journal of Sport Science, 16,* 229–233.

Prapavessis, H., & Grove, J. R. (1991). Precompetitive emotions and shooting performance: The mental health and zone of optimal function models. *The Sport Psychologist, 5,* 223–234.

Prapavessis, H. & Grove, R. (1994). Personality variables as antecedents of precompetitive mood state temporal patterning. *International Journal of Sport Psychology, 22,* 347–365.

Prapavessis, H., & Grove, J. R. (1998). Self-handicapping and self-esteem. *Journal of Applied Sport Psychology, 10,* 175–184.

Prapavessis, H., Grove, J. R., & Eklund, R. C. (2004). Self-presentational issues in competition and sport. *Journal of Applied Sport Psychology, 16,* 19–40.

Prapavessis, H., Grove, J. R., Maddison, R., & Zillmann, N. (2003). Self-handicapping tendencies, coping, and anxiety responses among athletes. *Psychology of Sport and Exercise, 4,* 357–375.

Price, M. S., & Weiss, M. R. (2000). Relationships among coach burnout, coach behaviors, and athletes' psychological responses. *The Sport Psychologist, 14,* 391–409.

Price, S. L. (2001). Broken promise. *Sports Illustrated, 94,* May 28, 82–90.

Quinn, A. M., & Fallon, B. J. (1999). The changes in psychological characteristics and reactions of elite athletes from injury onset until full recovery. *Journal of Applied Sport Psychology, 11,* 210–229.

Raedeke, T. D. (1997). Is athlete burnout more than just stress? A sport commitment perspective. *Journal of Sport & Exercise Psychology, 19,* 396–417.

Raedeke, T. D. (2004). Coach commitment and burnout: A one-year follow-up. *Journal of Applied Sport Psychology, 16,* 333–349.

Raedeke, T. D., Granzyk, T. L., & Warren, A. (2000). Why coaches experience burnout: A commitment perspective. *Journal of Sport & Exercise Psychology, 22,* 85–105.

Raedeke, T. D., Lunney, K., & Venables, K. (2002). Understanding athlete burnout: Coach perspectives. *Journal of Sport Behavior, 25,* 181–206.

Raedeke, T. D., & Smith, A. L. (2001). Development and preliminary validation of an athlete burnout measure. *Journal of Sport & Exercise Psychology, 23,* 281–306.

Raffety, B. D., Smith, R. E., & Ptacek, J. T. (1997). Facilitating and debilitating trait anxiety, situational anxiety, and coping with an anticipated stressor: A process analysis. *Journal of Personality and Social Psychology, 72,* 892–906.

Raglin, J. S., & Turner, P. E. (1996). Variability in precompetition anxiety and performance in college track and field athletes. *Medicine & Science in Sports & Exercise, 28,* 378–385.

Raglin, J. S., & Wilson, G. S. (2000). Overtraining in athletes. In Y. L. Hanin (Ed.), *Emotions in sport* (pp. 191–207). Champaign, IL: Human Kinetics.

Raimy, V. C. (1950). *Training in clinical psychology.* New York: Prentice Hall.

Rain, J. S., Lane, I. M., & Steiner, D. D. (1991). A current look at the job satisfaction/life satisfaction relationship: Review and future considerations. *Human Relations, 44,* 287–307.

Ram, N., Starek, J., & Johnson, J. (2004). Race, ethnicity, and sexual orientation: Still a void in sport and exercise psychology? *Journal of Sport & Exercise Psychology, 26,* 250–268.

Rammsayer, T. H. (1998). Extraversion and dopamine: Individual differences in response to changes in dopaminergic activity as a possible biological basis of extraversion. *European Psychologist, 3,* 37–50.

Randle, S., & Weinberg, R. (1997). Multidimensional anxiety and performance: An exploratory examination of the zone of optimal functioning hypothesis. *The Sport Psychologist, 11,* 160–174.

Ranking the Dirtiest Teams (2006, July 8). *Hartford Courant,* p. C3.

Raskin, R., & Hall, C. S. (1981). The Narcissistic Personality Inventory: Alternate form reliability and further evidence of construct validity. *Journal of Personality Assessment, 45,* 159–162.

Raudsepp, L., & Liblik, R. (2002). Relationship of perceived and actual motor competence in children. *Perceptual and Motor Skills, 94,* 1059–1070.

Ravizza, K. (1988). Gaining entry with athletic personnel for season-long consulting. *The Sport Psychologist, 2,* 243–254.

Ravizza, K. (2006). Increasing awareness for sport performance. In J. M. Williams (Ed.),

Applied sport psychology: Personal growth to peak performance (5th ed., pp. 228–239). New York: McGraw-Hill.

Ray, O., & Ksir, C. (2002). *Drugs, society and human behavior* (9th ed.). Boston: McGraw-Hill.

Rees, T., & Hardy, L. (2000). An investigation of the social support experiences of high-level sports performers. *The Sport Psychologist, 14,* 327–347.

Rehm, L. P. (1982). Self-management in depression. In P. Karoly & F. H. Kanfer (Eds.), *Self-management and behavior change: From theory to practice* (pp. 522–567). New York: Pergamon.

Reilly, R. (1996). Master strokes. *Sports Illustrated, 84,* April 22, 24–29, 31.

Reilly, R. (2003). Hurts so good. *Sports Illustrated, 99,* August 4, 82.

Renger, R. (1993). A review of the Profile of Mood States (POMS) in the prediction of athletic success. *Journal of Applied Sport Psychology, 5,* 78–84.

Report finds economic cost of substance abuse exceeds $143 billion. (2002). *Alcoholism & Drug Abuse Weekly, 14,* January 28, 1, 4.

Report on the Committee on Training in Clinical Psychology of the American Psychological Association submitted at the Detroit meeting of the American Psychological Association, September 9–13, 1947. (1947). Recommended training program in clinical psychology. *American Psychologist, 2,* 539–558.

Requa, R. (1991, April). *The scope of the problem: The impact of sports-related injuries. Proceedings from the Conference on Sport Injuries in Youth: Surveillance Strategies.* Bethesda, MD: National Advisory Board for Arthritis and Musculoskeletal and Skin Diseases, National Institute of Arthritis and Musculoskeletal and Skin Diseases, and Centers for Disease Control.

Rettew, D., & Reivich, K. (1995). Sports and explanatory style. In G. M. Buchanan & M. E. P. Seligman (Eds.), *Explanatory style* (pp. 173–185). Hillsdale, NJ: Lawrence Erlbaum Associates, Inc.

Rheaume, J., Freeston, M. H., Ladouceur, R., Bouchard, C., Gallant, L., Talbot, F., & Vallieres, A. (2000). Functional and dysfunctional perfectionists: Are they different on compulsive-like behaviors? *Behaviour Research and Therapy, 38,* 119–128.

Rhoden, W. C. (1999, December 30). Just ranting and raving doesn't win. *New York Times,* p. D1.

Rhodewalt, F. (1994). Conceptions of ability, achievement goals, and individual differences in self-handicapping behavior: On the application of implicit theories. *Journal of Personality, 62,* 67–85.

Rhodewalt, F., Morf, C., Hazlett, S., & Fairfield, M. (1991). Self-handicapping: The role of discounting and augmentation in the preservation of self-esteem. *Journal of Personality and Social Psychology, 61,* 122–131.

Rhodewalt, F., Saltzman, A. T., & Wittmer, J. (1984). Self-handicapping among competitive athletes: The role of practice in self-esteem protection. *Basic and Applied Social Psychology, 5,* 197–209.

Rhodewalt, F., Sanbonmatsu, D. M., Tschanz, B., Feick, D. L., & Waller, A. (1995). Self-handicapping and interpersonal trade-offs: The effects of claimed self-handicaps on observers' performance evaluations and feedback. *Personality and Social Psychology Bulletin, 21,* 1042–1050.

Richardson, F. C., & Suinn, R. M. (1972). The Mathematics Anxiety Rating Scale: Psychometric data and interpersonal trade-offs: The effects of claimed self-handicaps on observers' performance evaluations and feedback. *Personality and Social Psychology Bulletin, 10,* 1042–1050.

Riggs, J. M. (1992). Self-handicapping and achievement. In A. K. Boggiano & T. S. Pittman

(Eds.), *Achievement and motivation: A social-developmental perspective* (pp. 244–267). New York: Cambridge University Press.

Riley, L. (2005, February 1). Working on a comeback: But Hunter may never play again. *Hartford Courant*, pp. C1, C3.

Riley, P. (1993). *The winner within: A life plan for team players*. New York: G.P. Putnam's Sons.

Robazza, C. (2006). Emotion in sport: An IZOF perspective. In S. Hanton & S. D. Mellalieu (Eds.), *Literature reviews in sport psychology* (pp. 127–158). New York: Nova Science Publishers.

Robazza, C., & Bortoli, L. (1998). Mental preparation strategies of Olympic archers during competition: An exploratory investigation. *High Ability Studies, 9*, 219–235.

Robazza, C., & Bortoli, L. (2003). Intensity, idiosyncratic content and functional impact of performance-related emotions in athletes. *Journal of Sport Sciences, 21*, 171–189.

Robazza, C., Pellizzari, M., & Hanin, Y. (2004). Emotion self-regulation and athletic performance: An application of the IZOF model. *Psychology of Sport and Exercise, 5*, 379–404.

Robbins, L. (2004, June 13). American marathoners cramming for Athens. *New York Times*, p. N6.

Roberts, G. C. (2001). Understanding the dynamics of motivation in physical activity: The influence of achievement goals on motivational processes. In G. C. Roberts (Ed.), *Advances in motivation in sport and exercise* (2nd ed., pp. 1–50). Champaign, IL: Human Kinetics.

Roberts, G. C., Spink, K. S., & Pemberton, C. L. (1999). *Learning experiences in sport psychology* (2nd ed.). Champaign, IL: Human Kinetics.

Roberts, G. C., & Treasure, D. C. (1999). Applied sport psychology. In A. M. Stec & D. A. Bernstein (Eds.), *Psychology: Fields of application* (pp. 116–126). Boston: Houghton Mifflin.

Roberts, G. C., Treasure, D. C., & Balague, G. (1998). Achievement goals in sport: The development and validation of the Perceptions of Success Questionnaire. *Journal of Sport Sciences, 16*, 337–347.

Roberts, S. (1997, October 26). N.B.A.'s uncontrolled substance. *New York Times*, Section 8, pp. 1, 7.

Robinson, D. W. (1990). An attributional analysis of student demoralization in physical education settings. *Quest, 42*, 27–39.

Robinson, D. W. (1993). Demoralization in recreation: A self-referent model and the role of the instructor. *Journal of Applied Recreation Research, 18*, 19–37.

Rodgers, J. (2000). Cognitive performance amongst recreational users of "ecstasy". *Psychopharmacology, 151*, 19–24.

Rodgers, W., Hall, C., & Buckolz, E. (1991). The effect of an imagery training program on imagery ability, imagery use, and figure skating performance. *Journal of Applied Sport Psychology, 3*, 109–125.

Rogers, C. (1954). *Becoming a person*. Oberlin, OH: Oberlin College.

Rogerson, L. J., & Hrycaiko, D. W. (2002). Enhancing competitive performance of ice hockey goaltenders using centering and self-talk. *Journal of Applied Sport Psychology, 14*, 14–26.

Roper, E. A. (2002). Women working in the applied domain: Examining the gender bias in applied sport psychology. *Journal of Applied Sport Psychology, 14*, 53–66.

Rose, J., & Jevne, R. F. J. (1993). Psychosocial processes associated with athletic injuries. *The Sport Psychologist, 7*, 309–328.

Ross, M. J., & Berger, R. S. (1996). Effects of stress inoculation training on athletes' postsurgical pain and rehabilitation after orthopedic injury. *Journal of Consulting and Clinical Psychology, 64,* 406–410.

Rotella, R. J., Gansneder, B., Ojala, D., & Billing, J. (1980). Cognitions and coping strategies of elite skiers: An exploratory study of young developing athletes. *Journal of Sport Psychology, 2,* 350–354.

Roth, S., & Cohen, L. J. (1986). Approach, avoidance, and coing with stress. *American Psychologist, 41,* 813–819.

Rowley, A. J., Landers, D. M., Kyllo, L. B., & Etnier, J. L. (1995). Does the iceberg profile discriminate between successful and less successful athletes? A meta-analysis. *Journal of Sport & Exercise Psychology, 17,* 185–199.

Rozell, E. J., Gundersen, D. E., & Terpstra, D. E. (1997). Gender differences in the factors affecting helplessness behavior and performance. *Journal of Social Behavior and Personality, 13,* 265–280.

Ruch, F. (1937). *Psychology and life.* New York: Scott, Foresman.

Ruiz, M. C., & Hanin, Y. L. (2004). Metaphoric description and individualized emotion profiling of performance related states in high-level karate athletes. *Journal of Applied Sport Psychology, 16,* 258–273.

Rushall, B., Hall, M., Roux, L., Sasseville, J., & Rushall, A. C. (1988). Effects of three types of thought content instructions on skiing performance. *The Sport Psychologist, 2,* 283–297.

Russell, P. (1976). *The TM technique.* London: Routledge & Kegan Paul.

Ryan, M. K., Williams, J. M., & Wimer, B. (1990). Athletic aggression: Perceived legitimacy and behavioral intentions in girls' high school basketball. *Journal of Sport & Exercise Psychology, 12,* 48–55.

Ryan, R. M., & Deci, E. L. (2000). Self-determination theory and the facilitation of intrinsic motivation, social development, and well-being. *American Psychologist, 55,* 68–78.

Ryba, T. V., Stambulova, N. B., & Wrisberg, C. A. (2005). The Russian origins of sport psychology: A translation of an early work of A. C. Puni. *Journal of Applied Sport Psychology, 17,* 157–169.

Ryska, T. A. (2001). The impact of acculturation on sport motivation among Mexican-American adolescent athletes. *The Psychological Record, 51,* 533–547.

Ryska, T. A., & Yin, Z. (1998). Effects of trait and situational self-handicapping on competitive anxiety among athletes. *Current Psychology, 17,* 48–56.

Ryska, T. A., & Yin, Z. (1999). The role of dispositional goal orientation and team climate on situational self-handicapping among young athletes. *Journal of Sport Behavior, 22,* 410–425.

Ryska, T. A., Yin, Z., Cooley, D., & Ginn, R. (1999). Developing team cohesion: A comparison of cognitive-behavioral strategies of US and Australian sport coaches. *Journal of Psychology, 133,* 523–539.

Sage, G. H., & Loudermilk, S. (1979). The female athlete and role conflict. *Research Quarterly, 50,* 88–96.

Sailes, G. A. (1993). An investigation of campus stereotypes: The myth of black athletic superiority and the dumb jock stereotype. *Sociology of Sport Journal, 10,* 88–97.

Salazar, W., Landers, D. M., Petruzello, S. J., Han, M., Crews, D. J., & Kubitz, K. A. (1990). Hemispheric asymmetry, cardiac response, and performance in elite archers. *Research Quarterly for Exercise and Sport, 61,* 351–359.

Salminen, S. (1990). Sex role and participation in traditionally inappropriate sports. *Perceptual & Motor Skills, 71,* 1216–1218.

Salmon, J., Hall, C., & Haslam, I. (1994). The use of imagery by soccer players. *Journal of Applied Sport Psychology, 6,* 116–133.

Sanders, G. S., Baron, R. S., & Moore, D. L. (1978). Distraction and social comparison as mediators of social facilitation effects. *Journal of Experimental Social Psychology, 14,* 291–303.

Sanna, L. J. (1998). Defensive pessimism and optimism: The bitter-sweet influence of mood on performance and prefactual and counterfactual thinking. *Cognition and Emotion, 12,* 635–665.

Sarason, I. G. (1972). Test anxiety and the model who fails. *Journal of Personality and Social Psychology, 22,* 410–413.

Sarason, I. G. (1973). Test anxiety and cognitive modeling. *Journal of Personality and Social Psychology, 28,* 58–61.

Sarason, I. G. (1981). Test anxiety, stress, and social support. *Journal of Personality, 49,* 101–114.

Sarason, I. G., Pierce, G. R., & Sarason, B. R. (1996). Domains of cognitive interference. In I. G. Sarason, G. R. Pierce, & B. R. Sarason (Eds.), *Cognitive interference theories, methods, & findings* (pp. 139–152). Mahwah, NJ: Lawrence Erlbaum Associates, Inc.

Sarason, I. G., Potter, E. H., & Sarason, B. R. (1986). Recording and recall of personal events: Effects on cognitions and behavior. *Journal of Personality and Social Psychology, 51,* 347–356.

Sarason, I. G., & Sarason, B. R. (1986). Experimentally provided social support. *Journal of Personality and Social Psychology, 50,* 1222–1225.

Sarason, I. G., Sarason, B. R., & Pierce, G. R. (1995). Cognitive interference: At the intelligence–personality crossroads. In D. H. Saklofske & M. Zeidner (Eds.), *International handbook of personality and intelligence* (pp. 285–296). New York: Plenum Press.

Sarrazin, P., Biddle, S., Famose, J. P., Cury, F., Fox, K., & Durand, M. (1996). Goal orientations and conceptions of the nature of sport ability in children: A social cognitive approach. *British Journal of Social Psychology, 35,* 399–414.

Savis, J. C. (1994). Sleep and athletic performance: Overview and implications for sport psychology. *The Sport Psychologist, 8,* 111–125.

Scanlan, T. K., & Lewthwaite, R. (1984). Social psychological aspects of competition for male youth sport participants: I Predictors of competitive stress. *Journal of Sport Psychology, 6,* 208–226.

Scanlan, T. K., Lewthwaite, R., & Jackson, B. L. (1984). Social psychological aspects of competition for male youth sport participants: II Predictors of performance outcomes. *Journal of Sport Psychology, 6,* 422–429.

Scheiber, D. (1990). Tennis' new legend in the making. *Saturday Evening Post, 262,* Issue 5, 68–71.

Scherzer, C. B., Brewer, B. W., Cornelius, A. E., Van Raalte, J. L., Petitpas, A. J., Sklar, J. H., et al. (2001). Psychological skills and adherence to rehabilitation after reconstruction of the anterior cruciate ligament. *Journal of Sport Rehabilitation, 10,* 165–172.

Schlenker, B. R., Phillips, S. T., Boniecki, K. A., & Schlenker, D. R. (1995). Championship pressures: Choking or triumphing in one's own territory. *Journal of Personality and Social Psychology, 68,* 632–643.

Schmid, A., & Peper, E. (1993). Training strategies for concentration. In J. M. Williams (Ed.), *Applied sport psychology: Personal growth to peak performance* (2nd ed., pp. 262–273). Mountain View, CA: Mayfield.

Schmidt, G. W., & Stein, G. L. (1991). Sport commitment: A model integrating enjoyment, dropout, and burnout. *Journal of Sport & Exercise Psychology, 8,* 254–265.

Schneider, R. H., Alexander, C. N., & Wallace, R. K. (1992). In search of an optimal behavioral treatment for hypertension: A review and focus on Transcendental Meditation. In E. H. Johnson, W. D. Gentry, & S. Julius (Eds.), *Personality, elevated blood pressure, & essential hypertension* (pp. 291–316). Washington, DC: Hemis-phere.

Schouwenburg, H. C. (1995). Academic procrastination: Theoretical notions, measurement, and research. In J. R. Ferrari, J. L. Johnson, & W. G. McCown (Eds.), *Procrastination and task avoidance: Theory, research and treatment* (pp. 71–96). New York: Plenum.

Schuckit, M. A. (1994). Low level of response to alcohol as a predictor of future alcoholism. *American Journal of Psychiatry, 151,* 184–189.

Schultz, R. W., Eom, H. J., Smoll, F. L., & Smith, R. E. (1994). Examination of the factorial validity of the Group Environment Questionnaire. *Research Quarterly for Exercise and Sport, 65,* 226–236.

Schulz, J. (1932). *Das Autogene Training (Konzentrative Selbstentspannung).* Leipzig, Germany: Thieme.

Schunk, D. H. (1989). Self-efficacy and achievement behaviors. *Educational Psychology Review, 1,* 173–208.

Schunk, D. H. (1995). Self-efficacy, motivation, and performance. *Journal of Applied Sport Psychology, 7,* 112–137.

Schurr, K. T., Ashley, M. A., & Joy, K. L. (1977). A multivariate analysis of male athlete personality characteristics: Sport type and success. *Multivariate Experimental Clinical Research, 3,* 53–68.

Schwartz, G. E., Davidson, R. J., & Goleman, D. J. (1978). Patterning of cognitive and somatic processes in the self-regulation of anxiety: Effects of meditation versus exercise. *Psychosomatic Medicine, 40,* 321–328.

Schwarzenegger, A., & Hall, D. K. (1977). *Arnold: The education of a bodybuilder.* New York: Simon & Schuster.

Schwarzer, R. (1996). Thought control of action: Interfering self-doubts. In I. G. Sarason, G. R. Pierce, & B. R. Sarason (Eds.), *Cognitive interference theories, methods, & findings* (pp. 99–115). Mahwah, NJ: Lawrence Erlbaum Associates, Inc.

Schwenk, C. R. (1998). Marijuana and job performance: Comparing the major streams of research. *Journal of Drug Issues, 28,* 941–970.

Scripture, E. W. (1900). Cross-education. *Popular Science, 56,* 589–596.

Seabourne, T. G., Weinberg, R. S., Jackson, A., & Suinn, R. M. (1985). Effect of individual-ized, nonindividualized and package intervention strategies on karate performance. *Journal of Sport Psychology, 7,* 40–50.

Sędek, G., & Kofta, M. (1990). When cognitive exertion does not yield cognitive gain: Toward an informational explanation of learned helplessness. *Journal of Personality and Social Psychology, 58,* 729–743.

Segal, B. (1986). Confirmatory analyses of reasons for experiencing psychoactive drugs during adolescence. *International Journal of the Addictions, 20,* 1649–1662.

Seligman, M. (1975). *Helplessness: On depression, development, and death.* San Francisco: Freeman.

Seligman, M. E. P. (1990). *Learned optimism.* New York: Pocket Books.

Seligman, M. E. P., Abramson, L. Y., Semmel, A., & von Baeyer, C. (1979). Depressive attributional style. *Journal of Abnormal Psychology, 88,* 242–247.

Seligman, M. E. P., Nolen-Hoeksema, S., Thornton, N., & Thornton, K. M. (1990). Explana-tory style as a mechanism of disappointing athletic performance. *Psychological Science, 1,* 143–146.

Shain, J. (2001, July 23). Du-validation: Leaves field behind for 1st major title. *Hartford Courant,* pp. C1, C7.

Shambrook, C. J., & Bull, S. J. (1999). Adherence to psychological preparation in sport. In S. J. Bull (Ed.), *Adherence issues in sport and exercise* (pp. 169–196). Chichester, UK: Wiley.

Shaq, Lakers Play It Cool Open West Finals with Road Victory (2004, May 22). *Hartford Courant*, p. C2.

Shaw, L., & Sichel, H. (1971). *Accident proneness*. London: Penguin.

Shea, J. (2002). Buzz on: Caffeine spreads from coffee to soft drinks, candy, even soap. *Hartford Courant*, p. D1.

Sheldon, J. P., & Eccles, J. S. (2005). Physical and psychological predictors of perceived ability in adult male and female tennis players. *Journal of Applied Sport Psychology, 17,* 48–63.

Sheldon, K. M., & Elliot, A. J. (1999). Goal striving, need satisfaction, and longitudinal well-being: The self-concordance model. *Journal of Personality and Social Psychology, 76,* 482–497.

Sheldon, W. H. (1940). *The varieties of human physique*. New York: Harper.

Sheldon, W. H. (1942). *The varieties of human temperament*. New York: Harper.

Sherman, C. A., Fuller, R., & Speed, H. D. (2000). Gender comparisons of preferred coaching behaviors in Australian sports. *Journal of Sport Behavior, 23,* 389–406.

Sherman, E. (2001, July 23). Those extra drivers: Extra club costs Woosnam. *Hartford Courant*, p. C7.

Shields, C. A., Paskevich, D. M., & Brawley, L. R. (2003). Self-handicapping in structured and unstructured exercise: Toward a measurable construct. *Journal of Sport & Exercise Psychology, 25,* 267–283.

Short, M. W. (2002). The effect of imagery function and imagery direction on self-efficacy and performance on a golf-putting task. *The Sport Psychologist, 16,* 47–67.

Short, S. E., Bruggeman, J. M., Engel, S. G., Marback, T. L., Wang, L. J., Willandsen, A., & Short, M. W. (2002). The effect of imagery function and imagery direction on self-efficacy and performance on a golf-putting task. *The Sport Psychologist, 16,* 48–67.

Short, S. E., Monsma, E. A., & Short, M. W. (2004). Is what you see really what you get? Athletes' perceptions of imagery's functions. *The Sport Psychologist, 10,* 341–349.

Showers, C. (1992). The motivational and emotional consequences of considering positive or negative possibilities for an upcoming event. *Journal of Personality and Social Psychology 63,* 474–484.

Siedentop, D. (2002). Junior sport and the evolution of sport cultures. *Journal of Teaching in Physical Education, 21,* 392–401.

Silva, J. M. III. (1982). An evaluation of fear of success in female and male athletes and nonathletes. *Journal of Sport Psychology, 4,* 92–96.

Silva, J. M. III. (1989). The evolution of the Association for the Advancement of Applied Sport Psychology and the *Journal of Applied Sport Psychology. Journal of Applied Sport Psychology, 1,* 1–3.

Silva, J. M. III. (1990). An analysis of the training stress syndrome in competitive athletics. *Applied Sport Psychology, 2,* 5–20.

Silva, J. M. III, & Andrew, J. A. (1987). An analysis of game location and basketball performance in the Atlantic Coast Conference. *International Journal of Sport Psychology, 18,* 188–204.

Silva, J. M. III, & Conroy, D. E. (1995). Understand aggressive behavior and its effects upon athletic performance. In K. P. Henschen & W. F. Straub (Eds.), *Sport psychology: An analysis of athlete behavior* (3rd ed., pp. 149–159). Longmeadow, MA: Mouvement.

Silva, J. M. III, Conroy, D. E., & Zizzi, S. J. (1999). Critical issues confronting the advancement of applied sport psychology. *Journal of Applied Sport Psychology, 11,* 298–320.

Singer, R. N. (1989). Applied sport psychology in the United States. *Applied Sport Psychology, 1,* 61–80.

Singer, R. N. (2002). Preperformance state, routines, and automaticity: What does it take to realize expertise in self-paced events? *Journal of Sport & Exercise Psychology, 24,* 359–375.

Sinnot, K., & Biddle, S. (1998). Changes in attributions, expectations of success and intrinsic motivation after attributional retraining in children's sport. *International Journal of Adolescence and Youth, 7,* 137–144.

Siri, S., & Martin, G. L. (1996). Single-subject evaluation of a self-talk package for improving figure skating performance. *The Sport Psychologist, 10,* 227–238.

Sisley, B. L., Weiss, M. R., Barber, H., & Ebbeck, V. (1990). Developing competence and confidence in novice women coaches – A study of attitudes, motives, and perceptions of ability. *Journal of Physical Education, Recreation & Dance, 61,* 60–64.

Slade, L. A., & Rush, M. C. (1991). Achievement motivation and the dynamics of task difficult choices. *Journal of Personality and Social Psychology, 60,* 165–172.

Slanger, E., & Rudestam, K. E. (1997). Motivation and disinhibition in high risk sports: Sensation seeking and self-efficacy. *Journal of Research in Personality, 31,* 355–373.

Slater, M. R., & Sewell, D. F. (1994). An examination of the cohesion–performance relationship in university hockey teams. *Journal of Sports Sciences, 12,* 423–431.

Slobounov, S., Yukelson, D., & O'Brien, R. (1997). Self-efficacy and movement variability of Olympic-level springboard divers. *Journal of Applied Sport Psychology, 9,* 171–190.

Smedley, A., & Smedley, B. D. (2005). Race as biology is fiction, racism as a social problem is real: Anthropological and historical perspectives on the social construction of race. *American Psychologist, 60,* 16–26.

Smith, H. W. (1994). *The 10 natural laws of successful time and life management: Proven strategies for increased productivity and inner peace.* New York: Warner.

Smith, J. C. (1990). *Cognitive-behavioral relaxation training: A new system of strategies for treatment and assessment.* New York: Springer.

Smith, J. C., Amutio, A., Anderson, J. P., & Aria, L. A. (1996). Relaxation: Mapping an uncharted world. *Biofeedback and Self-Regulation, 21,* 63–90.

Smith, M., & Lee, C. (1992). Goal setting and performance in a novel coordination task: Mediating mechanisms. *Journal of Sport & Exercise Psychology, 14,* 169–176.

Smith, R. E. (1986). Toward a cognitive-affective model of athletic burnout. *Journal of Sport Psychology, 8,* 36–50.

Smith, R. E. (1996). Performance anxiety, cognitive interference, and concentration enhancement strategies in sports. In I. G. Sarason, G. R. Pierce, & B. R. Sarason (Eds.), *Cognitive interference theories, methods, & findings* (pp. 261–283). Mahwah, NJ: Lawrence Erlbaum Associates, Inc.

Smith, R. E. (1999). Generalization effects in coping skills training. *Journal of Sport and Exercise Psychology, 21,* 189–204.

Smith, R. E. (2006a). Positive reinforcement, performance feedback, and performance enhancement. In J. M. Williams (Ed.), *Applied sport psychology: Personal growth to peak performance* (5th ed., pp. 40–56). New York: McGraw-Hill.

Smith, R. E. (2006b). Understanding sport behavior: A cognitive-affective processing systems approach. *Journal of Applied Sport Psychology, 18,* 1–27.

Smith, R. E., & Christensen, D. S. (1995). Psychological skills as predictors of performance and survival in professional baseball. *Journal of Sport & Exercise Psychology, 17,* 399–415.

Smith, R. E., Ptacek, J. T., & Smoll, E. L. (1992). Sensation seeking, stress, and adolescent injuries: A test of stress-buffering, risk-taking, and coping skills hypotheses. *Journal of Personality and Social Psychology, 62,* 1016–1024.

Smith, R. E., Schutz, R. W., Smoll, F. L., & Ptacek, J. T. (1995a). Development and validation of a multidimensional measure of sport-specific psychological skills: The Athletic Coping Skills Inventory–28. *Journal of Sport & Exercise Psychology, 17,* 379–398.

Smith, R. E., & Smoll F. L. (1990). Self-esteem and children's reactions to youth sport coaching behaviors: A field study of self-enhancement processes. *Developmental Psychology, 26,* 987–993.

Smith, R. E., & Smoll, F. L. (1997). Coach-mediated team building in youth sports. *Journal of Applied Sport Psychology, 9,* 114–132.

Smith, R. E., & Smoll, F. L. (2002a). *Way to go, coach! A scientifically-proven approach to coaching effectiveness.* Portola Valley, CA: Warde.

Smith, R. E., & Smoll, F. L. (2002b). Youth sports as a behavior setting for psychosocial interventions. In J. L. Van Raalte & B. W. Brewer (Eds.), *Exploring sport and exercise psychology* (2nd ed., pp. 341–372). Washington, DC: American Psychological Association.

Smith, R. E., Smoll, F. L., & Barnett, N. P. (1995b). Reduction of children's sport performance anxiety through social support and stress-reduction training for coaches. *Journal of Applied Developmental Psychology, 16,* 125–142.

Smith, R. E., Smoll, R. L., & Curtis, B. (1979). Coach effectiveness training: A cognitive-behavioral approach to enhancing relationship skills in youth sport coaches. *Journal of Sport Psychology, 1,* 59–75.

Smith, R. E., Smoll, F. L., & Passer, M. W. (2002). Sport performance anxiety in young athletes. In F. L. Smoll & R. E. Smith (Eds.), *Children and youth in sport: A biosocial perspective* (2nd ed.). Dubuque, IA: Kendall/Hunt.

Smith, R. E., Smoll, E. L., & Ptacek, J. T. (1990a). Conjunctive moderator variables in vulnerability and resiliency research: Life stress, social support, coping skills, and adolescent sport injuries. *Journal of Personality and Social Psychology, 58,* 360–370.

Smith, R. E., Smoll, F. L., & Schutz, R. W. (1990b). Measurement and correlates of sport-specific cognitive and somatic trait anxiety: The Sport Anxiety Scale. *Anxiety Research, 2,* 263–280.

Smith, R. E., Smoll, F., & Smith, N. J. (1989). *Parents' complete guide to youth sports.* Costa Mesa, CA: HDL.

Smith, R. E., Zane, N. W. S., Smoll, F. L., & Coppel, D. B. (1983). Behavioral assessment in youth sports: Coaching behaviors and children's attitudes. *Medicine and Science in Sports and Exercise, 15,* 208–214.

Smith, S. L., Fry, M. D., Ethington, C. A., & Li, Y. (2005). The effects of female athletes' perceptions of their coaches' behaviors on their perceptions of the motivational climate. *Journal of Applied Sport Psychology, 17,* 170–177.

Smith, T. W. (1998, October 14). Report says Tyson has mental woes, but is fit. *New York Times,* pp. D1, D2.

Smith, T. W., Snyder, C. R., & Handelsman, M. M. (1982). On the self-serving function of an academic wooden leg: Test anxiety as a self-handicapping strategy. *Journal of Personality and Social Psychology, 42,* 314–321.

Smoll, F. L. (1998). Improving the quality of coach–parent relationships in youth sports. In J. M. Williams (Ed.), *Applied sport psychology: Personal growth to peak performance* (3rd ed., pp. 63–73). Mountain View, CA: Mayfield.

Smoll, F. L., & Cumming, S. (2006). Enhancing coach–parent relationships in youth sports: Increasing harmony and minimizing hassle. In J. M. Williams (Ed.), *Applied sport psychology: Personal growth to peak performance* (5th ed., pp. 192–204). New York: McGraw-Hill.

Smoll, F. L., & Smith, R. E. (1988). Reducing stress in youth sport: Theory and application.

In F. L. Smoll, R. A. Magill, & M. J. Ash (Eds.), *Children in sport* (3rd. ed., pp. 229–249). Champaign, IL: Human Kinetics.

Smoll, F. L., & Smith, R. E. (1989). Leadership behaviors in sport: A theoretical model and research paradigm. *Journal of Applied Social Psychology, 19,* 1522–1551.

Smoll, F. L., & Smith, R. E. (2006). Development and implementation of coach-training programs. In J. M. Williams (Ed.), *Applied sport psychology: Personal growth to peak performance* (5th ed., pp. 458–480). New York: McGraw-Hill.

Solomon, G. B., Wiegardt, P. A., Wayda, V. K., Yusuf, F. R., Kosmitzki, C., Williams, J., et al. (1996). Expectancies and ethnicity: The self-fulfilling prophecy in college basketball. *Journal of Sport & Exercise Psychology, 18,* 83–88.

Solowij, N., Stephens, R. S., Roffman, R. A., Babor, T., Kadden, R., Miller, M., et al. (2002). Cognitive functioning of long-term heavy cannabis users seeking treatment. *Journal of the American Medical Association, 287,* 1123–1131.

Sordoni, C., Hall, C., & Forwell, L. (2000). The use of imagery by athletes during injury rehabilitation. *Journal of Sport Rehabilitation, 9,* 329–338.

Spalding, L. R., & Hardin, C. D. (1999). Unconscious unease and self-handicapping: Behavioral consequences of individual differences in implicit and explicit self-esteem. *Psychological Science, 10,* 535–539.

Spencer, J. (2006, February 8). For some athletes, the road to victory starts with restraint. *Wall Street Journal,* p. A1.

Spencer, S. J., Steele, C. M., & Quinn, D. M. (1999). Stereotype threat and women's math performance. *Journal of Experimental Social Psychology, 35,* 4–28.

Spielberger, C. D., Gorsuch, R. L., & Lushene, R. E. (1970). *Manual for the State-Trait Anxiety Inventory (STAI).* Palo Alto, CA: Consulting Psychologists Press.

Spielberger, C. D., & Vagg, P. R. (1995). Test anxiety: A transactional process model. In C. D. Spielberger & P. R. Vagg (Eds.), *Test anxiety: Theory, assessment, and treatment* (pp. 3–13). Washington, DC: Taylor & Francis.

Spink, K. S. (1990). Group cohesion and collective efficacy of volleyball teams. *Journal of Sport & Exercise Psychology, 12,* 301–311.

Spink, K. S. (1995). Cohesion and intention to participate of female sport team athletes. *Journal of Sport & Exercise Psychology, 17,* 416–427.

Stainback, R. D. (1997). *Alcohol and sport.* Champaign, IL: Human Kinetics.

Stambulova, N. B., Wrisberg, C. A., & Ryba, T. V. (2006). A tale of two traditions in applied sport psychology: The heyday of Soviet sport and wake-up calls for North America. *Journal of Applied Sport Psychology, 18,* 173–184.

Starr, M. (2002a). Kwan Song. *Newsweek, 139,* February 18, 50–55.

Starr, M. (2002b). Sarah-dipity! *Newsweek, 139,* March 4, 34–37.

Starr, M., & Reiss, S. (1994, September 30). Fault, Miss Capriati. *Newsweek, 123,* 70–72.

Stavrou, N. A., & Zervas, Y. (2004). The confirmatory factor analysis of the slow state scale in sports. *International Journal of Sport and Exercise Psychology, 2,* 161–181.

Steel, P., Brothen, T., & Wambach, C. (2001). Procrastination and personality, performance, and mood. *Personality and Individual Differences, 30,* 95–106.

Steele, C. M. (1997). A threat in the air: How stereotypes shape intellectual ability and performance. *American Psychologist, 52,* 613–629.

Steele, C. M., & Aronson, J. (1995). Stereotype threat and the intellectual test performance of African Americans. *Journal of Personality and Social Psychology, 69,* 797–811.

Steenland, K., & Deddens, J. A. (1997). Effect of travel and rest on performance of professional basketball players. *Sleep, 20,* 366–369.

Steinberg, G. M., Singer, R. N., & Murphey, M. (2000). The benefits to sport achievement when a multiple goal orientation is emphasized. *Journal of Sport Behavior*, 23, 407–423.

Stone, J., Lynch, C. I., Sjomeling, M., & Darley, J. M. (1999). Stereotype threat effects on Black and White athletic performance. *Journal of Personality and Social Psychology*, 77, 1213–1227.

Stone, J., Perry, Z. W., & Darley, J. M. (1997). "White men can't jump": Evidence for the perceptual confirmation of racial stereotypes following a basketball game. *Basic and Applied Social Psychology*, 19, 291–306.

Strean, W. B. (1995). Youth sport contexts: Coaches' perceptions and implications for intervention. *Journal of Applied Sport Psychology*, 7, 23–37.

Stroebel, C. F. (1982). *QR: The quieting reflex*. New York: Berkley Books.

Students' Vote on the Graduate Training Accreditation Issue. (1997, September 25). The Annual Conference of the Association for the Advancement of Applied Sport Psychology, San Diego, CA.

Substance Abuse and Mental Health Services Administration. (2006). *Results from the 2005 national household survey on drug abuse: National findings* (Office of Applied Studies, USDUH Series H-30, DHHS Publication SMA 06-4194). Rockville, MD.

Sue, D. W., & Sue, D. (1999). *Counseling the culturally different: Theory and practice* (3rd ed.). New York: Wiley.

Suinn, R. M. (1980). *Psychology in sport: Methods and applications*. Minneapolis, MN: Burgess.

Suinn, R. M. (1985). The 1984 Olympics and sport psychology. *Journal of Sport Psychology*, 7, 321–329.

Suinn, R. M. (1986). *Seven steps to peak performance: The mental training manual for athletes*. Toronto, Canada: H. Huber.

Suinn, R. M. (1987). Behavioral approaches to stress management in sport. In J. R. May & M. J. Asken (Eds.), *Sport psychology* (pp. 59–75). New York: PMA.

Swift, E. M. (1989). Facing the music: Wade Boggs stayed cool despite his ex-lover's steamy revelations. *Sports Illustrated*, March 6, pp. 38–40, 45.

Tallis, F., & Eysenck, M. W. (1994). Worry: Mechanisms and modulating influences. *Behavioural and Cognitive Psychotherapy*, 22, 37–56.

Tang, T. L., & Reynolds, D. B. (1993). Effects of self-esteem and perceived goal difficulty on goal setting, certainty, task performance, and attributions. *Human Resource Development Quarterly*, 4, 153–170.

Taylor, D. R., Poulton, R., Moffitt, T. E., Ramankutty, P., & Sears, M. R. (2000). The respiratory effects of cannabis dependence in young adults. *Addiction*, 95, 1669–1677.

Taylor, J. (1996). Intensity regulation and athletic performance. In J. L. Van Raalte & B. W. Brewer (Eds.), *Exploring sport and exercise psychology* (pp. 75–106). Washington, DC: American Psychological Association.

Taylor, J., & Ogilvie, B. C. (2001). Career termination among athletes. In R. N. Singer, H. A. Hausenblas, & C. M. Janelle (Eds.), *Handbook of sport psychology* (2nd ed., pp. 787–809). New York: Wiley.

Taylor, J., Ogilvie, B. C., & Lavallee, D. (2006). Career transition among athletes: Is there life after sports? In J. M. Williams (Ed.), *Applied sport psychology: Personal growth to peak performance* (5th ed., pp. 595–615). New York: McGraw-Hill.

Taylor, J., & Wilson, G. S. (2002). Intensity regulation and sport performance. In J. L. Van Raalte & B. W. Brewer (Eds.), *Exploring sport and exercise psychology* (2nd ed., pp. 99–130). Washington, DC: American Psychological Association.

Taylor, S. E., Pham, L. B., Rivkin, I. D., & Armor, D. A. (1998). Harnessing the imagination: Mental simulation, self-regulation, and coping. *American Psychologist*, 53, 429–439.

Tellegen, A. (1981). Practicing the two disciplines for relaxation and enlightenment:

Comment on "Role of the feedback signal in electromyograph biofeedback: The relevance of attention" by Qualls and Sheehan. *Journal of Experimental Psychology: General, 110,* 217–226.

Tenenbaum, G., Stewart, E., Singer, R. N., & Duda, J. (1996). Aggression and violence in sport: An ISSP position stand. *International Journal of Sport Psychology, 27,* 229–236.

Terry, P. C. (1993). Mood state profiles as indicators of performance among Olympic and World Championship athletes. In S. Serpa, J. Alves, V. Ferreira, & A. Paulo-Brito (Eds.), *Proceedings of the VIIIth ISSP World Congress of Sport Psychology* (pp. 963–967). Lisbon, Portugal: International Society of Sport Psychology.

Terry, P. (1995). The efficacy of mood state profiling with elite performers: A review and synthesis. *The Sport Psychologist, 9,* 309–324.

Terry-Short, L. A., Owens, R. G., Slade, P. D., & Dewey, M. E. (1995). Positive and negative perfectionism. *Personality and Individual Differences, 18,* 663–668.

Tests show impairment at low BACs (2000). *Alcoholism and Drug Abuse Weekly, 33,* August 21, 8.

The new kid in town (1989). *Time,* January 2, 105.

The Queen (2002). *Sports Illustrated,* December/January, 63.

Thelwell, R. C., & Greenlees, I. A. (2003). Developing competitive endurance performance using mental skills training. *The Sport Psychologist, 17,* 318–337.

Thelwell, R. C., Greenlees, I. A., & Weston, N. J. V. (2006). Using psychological skills training to develop soccer performance. *Journal of Applied Sport Psychology, 18,* 254–270.

Thelwell, R. C., & Maynard, I. W. (1998). Anxiety–performance relationships in cricketers: Testing the zone of optimal functioning hypothesis. *Perceptual and Motor Skills, 87,* 675–698.

Thelwell, R. C., & Maynard, I. W. (2002). A triangulation of findings of three studies investigating repeatable good performance in professional cricketers. *International Journal of Sport Psychology, 33,* 247–268.

Theodorakis, Y. (1995). Effects of self-efficacy, satisfaction, and personal goals on swimming performance. *The Sport Psychologist, 9,* 245–253.

Theodorakis, Y. (1996). The influence of goals, commitment, self-efficacy and self-satisfaction on motor performance. *Journal of Applied Sport Psychology, 8,* 171–182.

Theodorakis, Y., Weinberg, R., Natsis, P., Douma, I., & Kazakas, P. (2000). The effects of motivational versus instructional self-talk on improving motor performance. *The Sport Psychologist, 14,* 253–272.

Theodosiou, A., & Papaioannou, A. (2006). Motivational climate, achievement goals and metacognitive activity in physical education and exercise involvement in out-of-school settings. *Psychology of Sport and Exercise, 7,* 361–379.

Thomas, G. (1996). Learned helplessness and basketball playoff performance. *Journal of Sport Behavior, 19,* 347–353.

Thomas, P. R., & Fogarty, G. J. (1997). Psychological skills training in golf: The role of individual differences in cognitive preferences. *The Sport Psychologist, 11,* 86–106.

Thomas, P. R., & Over, R. (1994). Psychological and psychomotor skills associated with performance in golf. *The Sport Psychologist, 8,* 73–86.

Thompson, T. (2004). Re-examining the effects of noncontingent success on self-handicapping behaviour. *British Journal of Educational Psychology, 74,* 239–260.

Thompson, T., Davidson, J. A., & Barber, J. G. (1995). Self-worth protection in achievement motivation: Performance effects and attributional behavior. *Journal of Educational Psychology, 87,* 598–610.

Thompson, T., & Richardson, A. (2001). Self-handicapping status, claimed self-handicaps and reduced practice effort following success and failure feedback. *British Journal of Educational Psychology, 71*, 151–170.

Throll, D. A. (1981). Transcendental Meditation and progress relaxation: Their psychological effects. *Journal of Clinical Psychology, 37*, 776–781.

Throll, D. A. (1982). Transcendental Meditation and progressive relaxation: Their physiological effects. *Journal of Clinical Psychology, 38*, 522–530.

Thurber, J. (1939). The secret life of Walter Mitty. In *My world – And welcome to it*. New York: Harcourt, Brace, & World.

Tice, D. M. (1991). Esteem protection or enhancement? Self-handicapping motives and attributions differ by trait self-esteem. *Journal of Personality and Social Psychology, 60*, 711–725.

Tice, D. M., & Baumeister, R. F. (1990). Self-esteem, self-handicapping, and self-presentation: The strategy of inadequate practice. *Journal of Personality, 58*, 443–464.

Tice, D. M., & Baumeister, R. F. (1997). Longitudinal study of procrastination, performance, stress, and health: The costs and benefits of dawdling. *Psychological Science, 8*, 454–458.

Top 10 Chokes in Majors (2002, December). *Golf Magazine, 44*, 117.

Top of the world: Italy wins shootout with France for fourth Cup title. (2006, July 9). www.SI.com

Torre, J., & Dreher, H. (1999). *Joe Torre's ground rules for winners*. New York: Hyperion.

Tracey, J. (2003). The emotional response to the injury and rehabilitation process. *Journal of Applied Sport Psychology, 15*, 279–293.

Travis, R. (1994). The junction point model: A field model of waking, sleeping, and dreaming, relating dream witnessing, the waking/sleeping transition, and transcendental meditation in terms of a common psychophysiologic state. *Dreaming, 4*, 91–104.

Treasure, D. C., Duda, J. L., Hall, H. K., Roberts, G. C., Ames, C., & Maehr, M. L. (2001). Clarifying misconceptions and misrepresentations in achievement goal research in sport: A response to Harwood, Hardy, and Swain. *Journal of Sport & Exercise Psychology, 23*, 317–329.

Treasure, D. C., Monson, J., & Lox, C. L. (1996). Relationship between self-efficacy, wrestling performance, and affect prior to competition. *The Sport Psychologist, 10*, 73–83.

Treasure, D. C., & Roberts, G. C. (1998). Relationship between female adolescents' achievement goal orientations, perceptions of the motivational climate, belief about success and sources of satisfaction in basketball. *International Journal of Sport Psychology, 29*, 211–230.

Triplett, N. L. (1898). Dynamogenic factors in pacemaking and competition. *The American Journal of Psychology, 9*, 507–533.

Udry, E. (1996). Social support: Exploring its role in the context of athletic injuries. *Journal of Sport Rehabilitation, 5*, 151–163.

Udry, E. (1997). Coping and social support among injured athletes following surgery. *Journal of Sport & Exercise Psychology, 19*, 71–90.

Udry, E. (1999). The paradox of injuries: Unexpected positive consequences. In D. Pargman (Ed.), *Psychological bases of sport injuries* (pp. 79–88). Morgantown, WV: Fitness Information Technology.

Udry, E., Gould, D., Bridges, D., & Beck, L. (1997a). Down but not out: Athlete responses to season-ending injuries. *Journal of Sport & Exercise Psychology, 19*, 229–248.

Udry, E., Gould, D., Bridges, D., & Tuffey, S. (1997b). People helping people? Examining the social ties of athletes coping with burnout and injury stress. *Journal of Sport & Exercise Psychology, 19*, 368–395.

Ungerleider, S. (2001). *Faust's gold: Inside the East German doping machine*. New York: Thomas Dunne.

Upthegrove, T. R., Roscigno, V. J., & Charles, C. Z. (1999). Big money collegiate sports: Racial concentration, contradictory pressures, and academic performance. *Social Science Quarterly, 80*, 718–737.

Urdan, T., Midgley, C., & Anderman, E. (1998). The role of classroom goal structure in students' use of self-handicapping strategies. *American Educational Research Journal, 35*, 101–122.

US Department of Education. (1972). *Nondiscrimination on the basis of sex in education programs or activities receiving federal financial assistance*. Available at www.ed.gov/legislation/FedRegister

US Department of Education. (2002). *Postsecondary institutions in the United States: Fall 2000 and degrees and other awards conferred: 1999–2000*. Washington, DC: National Center for Education Statistics.

US Olympic Committee. (1983). US Olympic Committee establishes guidelines for sport psychology services. *Journal of Sport Psychology, 5*, 4–7.

Utman, C. H. (1997). Performance effects of motivational state: A meta-analysis. *Personality and Social Psychology Review, 2*, 170–182.

Vallee, C. N., & Bloom, G. A. (2005). Building a successful university program: Key and common elements of expert coaches. *Journal of Applied Sport Psychology, 17*, 179–196.

Vallerand, R. J. (2001). A hierarchical model of intrinsic and extrinsic motivation in sport and exercise. In G. C. Roberts (Ed.), *Advances in motivation in sport and exercise* (2nd ed., pp. 263–319). Champaign, IL: Human Kinetics.

Vallerand, R. J., Deci, E. L., & Ryan, R. M. (1987). Intrinsic motivation in sport. *Exercise and Sport Sciences Reviews, 15*, 389–425.

Vallerand, R. J., & Losier, G. F. (1994). Self-determined motivation and sportsmanship orientations: An assessment of their temporal relationship. *Journal of Sport & Exercise Psychology, 16*, 229–245.

Vallerand, R. J., & Losier, G. F. (1999). An integrative analysis of intrinsic and extrinsic motivation in sport. *Journal of Applied Sport Psychology, 11*, 142–169.

Vallerand, R. J., & Rousseau, F. L. (2001). Intrinsic and extrinsic motivation in sport and exercise: A review using the hierarchial model of intrinsic and extrinsic motivation. In R. N. Singer, H. A. Hausenblas, & C. M. Janelle (Eds.), *Handbook of sport psychology* (2nd ed., pp. 389–416). New York: Wiley.

Van Eerde, W. (2000). Procrastination: Self-regulation in initiating aversive goals. *Applied Psychology: An International Review, 49*, 372–389.

Van Raalte, J. L., Brewer, B. W., Linder, D. E., & DeLange, N. (1990). Perceptions of sport-oriented professionals: A multidimensional scaling analysis. *The Sport Psychologist, 4*, 228–234.

Van Raalte, J. L., Brewer, D. D., Brewer, B. W., & Linder, D. E. (1992). NCAA division II college football players' perceptions of an athlete who consults a sport psychologist. *Journal of Sport & Exercise Psychology, 14*, 273–282.

Van Raalte, J. L., Brewer, D. D., Matheson, H., & Brewer, B. W. (1996). British athletes' perceptions of sport and mental health practitioners. *Journal of Applied Sport Psychology, 8*, 102–108.

Van Raalte, J. L., Brewer, B. W., Rivera, P. M., & Petitpas, A. J. (1994). The relationship between self-talk and performance of competitive junior tennis players. *NASPSPA Conference Abstracts, 16 Supplement*, S118 (abstract).

Van Raalte, J. L., Cornelius, A. E., Hatten, S. J., & Brewer, B. W. (2000). The antecedents and consequences of self-talk in competitive tennis. *Journal of Sport and Exercise Psychology,* *22*, 345–356.

Van Vianen, A. E. M., & De Dreu, C. K. W. (2001). Personality in teams: Its relationship to social cohesion, task cohesion, and term performance. *European Journal of Work and Organizational Psychology, 10*, 97–120.

VanYperen, N. W. (1995). Interpersonal stress, performance level, and parental support: A longitudinal study among highly skilled young soccer players. *The Sport Psychologist, 9*, 225–241.

Vealey, R. S. (2001). Understanding and enhancing self-confidence in athletes. In R. N. Singer, H. A. Hausenblas, & C. M. Janelle (Eds.), *Handbook of sport psychology* (2nd ed., pp. 550–565). New York: Wiley.

Vealey, R. S., Armstrong, L., Comar, W., & Greenleaf, C. A. (1998). Influence of perceived coaching behaviors on burnout and competitive anxiety in female college athletes. *Journal of Applied Sport Psychology, 10*, 297–318.

Vealey, R. S., & Greenleaf, C. A. (2006). Seeing is believing: Understanding and using imagery in sport. In J. M. Williams (Ed.), *Applied sport psychology: Personal growth to peak performance* (5th ed., pp. 306–343). New York: McGraw-Hill.

Vealey, R. S., Hayashi, S. W., Garner-Holman, G., & Giacobbi, P. (1998). Sources of sport-confidence: Conceptualization and instrument development. *Journal of Sport & Exercise Psychology, 20*, 54–80.

Vealey, R. S., Udry, E. M., Zimmerman, V., & Soliday, J. (1992). Intrapersonal and situational predictors of coaching burnout. *Journal of Sport & Exercise Psychology, 14*, 40–58.

Vealey, R. S., & Walter, S. M. (1993). Imagery training for performance enhancement and personal development. In J. M. Williams (Ed.), *Applied sport psychology: Personal growth to peak performance* (2nd ed., pp. 200–224). Mountain View, CA: Mayfield.

Veroff, J. (1992). Power motivation. In C. P. Smith (Ed.), *Motivation and personality: Handbook of thematic content analysis* (pp. 278–310). New York: Cambridge University Press.

Vickers, J. N. (1996). Visual control when aiming at a far target. *Journal of Experimental Psychology: Human Perception and Performance, 22*, 342–354.

Voy, R. (1991). *Drugs, sport, and politics*. Champaign, IL: Human Kinetics.

Wahl, G., Wertheim, L. J., & Dohrmann, G. (2001). Special Report: Passion Play. *Sports Illustrated, 95*, September 10, 58–70.

Wallace, H. M., & Baumeister, R. F. (2002). The performance of narcissists rises and falls with perceived opportunity for glory. *Journal of Personality and Social Psychology, 82*, 819–834.

Wallace, H. M., Baumeister, R. F., & Vohs, K. D. (2005). Audience support and choking under pressure: A home disadvantage? *Journal of Sports Sciences, 23*, 429–438.

Wallace, R. K., & Benson, H. (1972). The physiology of meditation. *Scientific American, 226*, 84–90.

Walling, M. D., Duda, J. L., & Chi, L. (1993). The Perceived Motivational Climate in Sport Questionnaire: Construct and predictive validity. *Journal of Sport and Exercise Psychology, 15*, 172–183.

Walling, M., & Martinek, T. (1995). Learned helplessness: A case study of a middle school student. *Journal of Teaching in Physical Education, 14*, 454–456.

Wang, J., Marchant, D., & Morris, T. (2004). Coping style and susceptibility to choking. *Journal of Sport Behavior, 27*, 75–92.

Ward, P., & Williams, A. M. (2003). Perceptual and cognitive skill development in soccer: The multidimensional nature of expert performance. *Journal of Sport & Exercise Psychology, 25*, 93–111.

Watkins, C. E. Jr., Terrell, F., Miller, F. S., & Terrell, S. L. (1989). Cultural mistrust and its effects on expectational variables in Black client–White counselor relationships. *Journal of Counseling Psychology, 36*, 447–450.

Watson, A. E., & Pulford, B. D. (2004). Personality differences in high risk sports amateurs and instructors. *Perceptual and Motor Skills, 99*, 83–94.

Watson, D. C. (2001). Procrastination and the five-factor model: A facet level analysis. *Personality and Individual Differences, 30*, 149–158.

Watson, G. G. (1986). Approach–avoidance behaviour in team sports: An application to leading Australian national hockey players. *International Journal of Sport Psychology, 17*, 136–155.

Weber, M. (1930). *The Protestant work ethic and the spirit of capitalism* (T. Parsons, Trans.). New York: Scribner. (Original work published 1904).

Wechsler, H., Davenport, A. E., Dowdall, G. W., Grossman, S. J., & Zanakos, S. I. (1997). Binge drinking, tobacco, and illicit drug use and involvement in college athletics: A survey of students at 140 American colleges. *College Health, 45*, 195–200.

Wegner, D. M. (1994). Ironic processes of mental control. *Psychological Review, 101*, 34–52.

Wegner, D. M. (1997a). When the antidote is the poison: Ironic mental control processes. *Psychological Science, 8*, 148–150.

Wegner, D. M. (1997b). Why the mind wanders. In J. D. Cohen & J. W. Schooler (Eds.), *Scientific approaches to consciousness* (pp. 295–315). Hillsdale, NJ: Lawrence Erlbaum Associates, Inc.

Wegner, D. M., Broome, A., & Blumberg, S. J. (1997). Ironic effects of trying to relax under stress. *Behavioral Research and Therapy, 35*, 11–21.

Weinberg, R. S. (1977). Anxiety and motor behavior: A new direction. In R. W. Christina & D. M. Landers (Eds.), *Psychology of motor behavior and sport – 1976* (Vol. 2, pp. 132–139). Champaign, IL: Human Kinetics.

Weinberg, R. S. (1996). Goal setting in sport and exercise: Research to practice. In J. L. Van Raalte & B. W. Brewer (Eds.), *Exploring sport and exercise psychology* (pp. 3–24). Washington, DC: American Psychological Association.

Weinberg, R., Bruya, L., & Jackson, A. (1985). The effects of goal proximity and goal specificity on endurance performance. *Journal of Sport & Exercise Psychology, 7*, 296–305.

Weinberg, R., Bruya, L., Jackson, A., & Garland, H. (1987). Goal difficulty and endurance performance: A challenge to the goal attainability assumption. *Journal of Sport Psychology, 10*, 82–92.

Weinberg, R. S., Burke, K. L., & Jackson, A. W. (1997). Coaches' and players' perceptions of goal setting in junior tennis: An exploratory investigation. *The Sport Psychologist, 11*, 426–439.

Weinberg, R. S., Burton, D., Yukelson, D., & Weigand, D. (1993). Goal setting in competitive sport: An exploratory investigation of practices of collegiate athletes. *The Sport Psychologist, 7*, 275–289.

Weinberg, R. S., Burton, D., Yukelson, D., & Weigand, D. (2000a). Perceived goal setting practices of Olympic athletes: An exploratory investigation. *The Sport Psychologist, 14*, 279–295.

Weinberg, R., Butt, J., & Knight, B. (2001). High school coaches' perceptions of the process of goal setting. *The Sport Psychologist, 15*, 20–47.

Weinberg, R. S., & Gould, D. (2007). *Foundations of sport and exercise psychology* (4th ed.). Champaign, IL: Human Kinetics Press.

Weinberg, R., Grove, R., & Jackson, A. (1992). Strategies for building self-efficacy in tennis players: A comparative analysis of Australian and American coaches. *The Sport Psychologist, 6*, 3–13.

Weinberg, R., & Jackson, A. (1990). Building self-efficacy in tennis players: A coach's perspective. *Applied Sport Psychology*, 2, 164–174.

Weinberg, R. S., Seabourne, T. G., & Jackson, A. (1981). Effects of visuomotor behavior rehearsal, relaxation, and imagery on karate performance. *Journal of Sport Psychology*, 3, 228–238.

Weinberg, R., Tenenbaum, G., McKenzie, A., Jackson, S., Anshel, M., Grove, R., et al. (2000b). Motivation for youth participation in sport and physical activity: Relationships to culture, self-reported activity levels, and gender. *International Journal of Sport Psychology*, 31, 321–346.

Weinstein, M., & Smith, J. C. (1992). Isometric squeeze relaxation (Progressive Relaxation) vs meditation: Absorption and focusing as predictors of state effects. *Perceptual and Motor Skills*, 75, 1263–1271.

Weisenberg, M., Gerby, Y., & Mikulincer, M. (1993). Aerobic exercise and chocolate as means for reducing learned helplessness. *Cognitive Therapy and Research*, 17, 579–592.

Weiss, H. M., Suckow, K., & Rakestraw, T. L. (1999). Influence of modeling on self-set goals: Direct and mediated effects. *Human Performance*, 12, 89–114.

Weiss, M. R. (1991). Psychological skill development in children and adolescents. *The Sport Psychologist*, 5, 335–354.

Weiss, M. R., Amorose, A. J., & Allen, J. B. (2000). The young elite athlete: The good, the bad, and the ugly. In B. L. Drinkwater (Ed.), *Women in sport* (pp. 409–429). Oxford: Blackwell Science.

Weiss, M. R., & Barber, H. (1995). Socialization influences of collegiate female athletes: A tale of two decades. *Sex Roles*, 33, 129–140.

Weiss, M. R., Barber, H., Ebbeck, V., & Sisley, B. L. (1991). Developing competence and confidence in novice female coaches: II. Perceptions of ability and affective experiences following a season-long coaching internship. *Journal of Sport & Exercise Psychology*, 13, 336–363.

Weiss, M. R., & Chaumeton, N. (2002). Motivational orientations in sport. In T. S. Horn (Ed.), *Advances in sport psychology* (2nd ed., pp. 61–99). Champaign, IL: Human Kinetics.

Weiss, M. R., Ebbeck, V., & Horn, T. S. (1997). Children's self-perceptions and sources of physical competence information: A cluster analysis. *Journal of Sport and Exercise Psychology*, 19, 52–70.

Weiss, M., & Friedrichs, W. (1986). The influence of leader behaviors, coach attributes, and institutional variables on performance and satisfaction of collegiate basketball teams. *Journal of Sport Psychology*, 8, 332–346.

Weiss, M. R., & Gill, D. L. (2005). What goes around comes around: Re-emerging themes in sport and exercise psychology. *Research Quarterly for Exercise and Sport*, 76, S71–S87.

Weiss, M. R., McCullagh, P., Smith, A. L., & Berlant, A. R. (1998). Observational learning and the fearful child: Influence of peer models on swimming skill performance and psychological responses. *Research Quarterly for Exercise and Sport*, 69, 380–394.

Weiss, M. R., Smith, A. L., & Theeboom, M. (1996). "That's what friends are for": Children's and teenagers' perceptions of peer relationships in the sport domain. *Journal of Sport & Exercise Psychology*, 18, 347–379.

Weiss, M. R., & Stevens, C. (1993). Motivation and attrition of female coaches: An application of social exchange theory. *The Sport Psychologist*, 7, 244–261.

Weitlauf, J. C., Cervone, D., Smith, R. E., & Wright, P. M. (2001). Assessing generalization in perceived self-efficacy: Multidomain and global assessments of the effects of self-defense training for women. *Personality and Social Psychology Bulletin*, 27, 1683–1691.

Weitlauf, J. C., Smith, R. E., & Cervone, D. (2000). Generalization effects of coping skills training: Influence of self-defense training on women's efficacy beliefs, assertiveness, and aggression. *Journal of Applied Psychology, 85,* 625–633.

Wertheim, L. J. (2001a). Jenny come lately. *Sports Illustrated, 94,* February 5, 54–57.

Wertheim, L. J. (2001b). How Jenny got her groove back: Hard work and harder workouts have helped Jennifer Capriati become a force in tennis once again. *Sports Illustrated for Women, 3,* May 1, 73–76.

Westermeyer, J., Eames, S. L., & Nugent, S. (1998). Comorbid dysthymic and substance disorder: Treatment history and cost. *American Journal of Psychiatry, 155,* 1556–1560.

Westre, K., & Weiss, M. (1991). The relationship between perceived coaching behaviors and group cohesion in high school football teams. *The Sport Psychologist, 5,* 41–54.

Wethe, D. (2004, March 11). Suddenly on sidelines. *Hartford Courant,* pp. E1, E6.

Whelan, J. P., Epkins, C. C., & Meyers, A. W. (1990). Arousal interventions for athletic performance: Influence of mental preparation and competitive experience. *Anxiety Research, 2,* 293–307.

Whelan, J. P., Meyers, A. W., & Elkins, T. D. (2002). Ethics in sport and exercise psychology. In J. L. Van Raalte & B. W. Brewer (Eds.), *Exploring sport and exercise psychology* (2nd ed., pp. 503–524). Washington, DC: American Psychological Association.

White, A., & Hardy, L. (1995). Use of different imagery perspectives on the learning and performance of different motor skills. *British Journal of Psychology, 86,* 169–180.

White, A., & Hardy, L. (1998). An in-depth analysis of the uses of imagery by high level slalom canoeists and artistic gymnasts. *Sport Psychologist, 12,* 387–403.

White, S. A. (1993a). The effects of gender and age on causal attribution in softball players. *International Journal of Sport Psychology, 24,* 49–58.

White, S. A. (1993b). The relationship between psychological skills, experience, and practice commitment among collegiate male and female skiers. *The Sport Psychologist, 7,* 49–57.

White, S. A. (1995). The perceived purposes of sport among male and female intercollegiate and recreational sport participants. *International Journal of Sport Psychology, 26,* 490–502.

White, S. A., & Duda, J. L. (1994). The relationship of gender, level of sport involvement, and participation motivation to task and ego orientation. *International Journal of Sport Psychology, 25,* 4–18.

White, S. A., Duda, J. L., & Keller, M. R. (1998). The relationship between goal orientation and perceived purposes of sport among youth sport participants. *Journal of Sport Behavior, 21,* 474–483.

White, S. A., & Zellner, S. R. (1996). The relationship between goal orientation, beliefs about the causes of sport success, and trait anxiety among high school, intercollegiate, and recreational sport participants. *The Sport Psychologist, 10,* 58–72.

WHO (2007). *International Classification of Diseases and Related Health Problems* (10th Revision). Geneva, Switzerland: World Health Organization.

Wickersham, S. (2004). Pat hand: After taking back control of his life, Tom Brady is once again playing like a champ. *ESPN Magazine, 7,* Issue 2, January 19, 40–43.

Widmeyer, W. N., & Birch, J. S. (1979). The relationship between aggression and performance outcome in ice hockey. *Canadian Journal of Applied Sport Science, 4,* 91–94.

Widmeyer, W. N., Brawley, L. R., & Carron, A. V. (1990). The effects of group size in sport. *Journal of Sport & Exercise Psychology, 12,* 177–190.

Widmeyer, W. N., Brawley, L. R., & Carron, A. V. (2002). Group dynamics in sport. In T. S. Horn (Ed.), *Advances in sport psychology* (2nd ed., pp. 163–180). Champaign, IL: Human Kinetics.

Widmeyer, W. N., & Ducharme, K. (1997). Team building through team goal setting. *Journal of Applied Sport Psychology, 9,* 97–113.

Widmeyer, W. N., & Williams, J. M. (1991). Predicting cohesion in a coaching sport. *Small Group Research, 22,* 548–570.

Wiese-Bjornstal, D. M., Smith, A. S., Shaffer, S. M., & Morrey, M. A. (1998). An integrated model of response to sport injury: Psychological and sociological dynamics. *Journal of Applied Sport Psychology, 10,* 46–69.

Wiggins, D. K. (1984). The history of sport psychology in North America. In J. M. Silva & R. S. Weinberg (Eds.), *Psychological foundations of sport* (pp. 9–22). Champaign, IL: Human Kinetics.

Wiggins, D. K. (1997). "Great speed but little stamina": The historical debate over Black athletic superiority. In S. W. Pope (Ed.), *The new American sport history: Recent approaches and perspectives* (pp. 312–338). Urbana: University of Illinois Press.

Wiggins, M. S. (1998). Anxiety intensity and direction: Preperformance temporal patterns and expectations in athletes. *Journal of Applied Sport Psychology, 10,* 201–211.

Williams, A. M., & Elliott, D. (1999). Anxiety, expertise, and visual search strategy in karate. *Journal of Sport & Exercise Psychology, 21,* 362–375.

Williams, A. M., Janelle, C. M., & Davids, K. (2004). Constraints on the search for visual information in sport. *International Journal of Sport and Exercise Psychology, 2,* 301–318.

Williams, A. M., Singer, R. N., & Frehlich, S. G. (2002). Quiet eye duration, expertise, and task complexity in near and far aiming tasks. *Journal of Motor Behavior, 34,* 197–207.

Williams, A. M., Vickers, J., & Rodrigues, S. (2002a). The effects of anxiety on visual search, movement kinematics, and performance in table tennis: A test of Eysenck and Calvo's Processing Efficiency Theory. *Journal of Sport & Exercise Psychology, 24,* 438–455.

Williams, A. M., Ward, P., Knowles, J. M., & Smeeton, N. J. (2002b). Anticipation skill in a real-world task: Measurement, training, and transfer in tennis. *Journal of Experimental Psychology: Applied, 8,* 259–270.

Williams, A. M., Ward, P., Smeeton, N. J., & Allen, D. (2004). Developing anticipation skills in tennis using on-court instruction: Perception versus perception and action. *Journal of Applied Sport Psychology, 16,* 350–360.

Williams, J. E. (1996). The relation between efficacy for self-regulated learning and domain-specific academic performance, controlling for test anxiety. *Journal of Research and Development in Education, 29,* 77–80.

Williams, J. M. (2001). Psychology of injury risk and prevention. In R. N. Singer, H. A. Hausenblas, & C. M. Janelle (Eds.), *Handbook of sport psychology* (2nd ed., pp. 766–786). New York: Wiley.

Williams, J. M., & Hacker, C. M. (1982). Causal relationships among cohesion, satisfaction, and performance in women's intercollegiate field hockey teams. *Journal of Sport Psychology, 4,* 324–337.

Williams, J. M., & Harris, D. V. (2006). Relaxation and energizing techniques for regulation of arousal. In J. M. Williams (Ed.), *Applied sport psychology: Personal growth to peak performance* (5th ed., pp. 285–305). New York: McGraw-Hill.

Williams, J. M., Hogan, T. D., & Andersen, M. B. (1993). Positive states of mind and athletic injury risk. *Psychosomatic Medicine 55,* 468–472.

Williams, J. M., & Leffingwell, T. R. (1996). Cognitive strategies in sport and exercise psychology. In J. L. Van Raalte & B. W. Brewer (Eds), *Exploring sport and exercise psychology* (pp. 25–50). Washington, DC: American Psychological Association.

Williams, J. M., & Parkhouse, B. L. (1988). Social learning theory as a foundation for examining sex bias in evaluation of coaches. *Journal of Sport & Exercise Psychology, 10,* 322–333.

Williams, J. M., & Scherzer, C. B. (2003). Tracking the training and careers of graduates of advanced degree programs in sport psychology, 1994 to 1999. *Journal of Applied Sport Psychology, 15,* 335–353.

Williams, J. M., & Scherzer, C. B. (2006). Injury risk and rehabilitation: Psychological considerations. In J. M. Williams (Ed.), *Applied sport psychology: Personal growth to peak performance* (5th ed., pp. 456–479). New York: McGraw-Hill.

Williams, J. M., & Straub, W. F. (2006). Sport psychology: Past, present, future. In J. M. Williams (Ed.), *Applied sport psychology: Personal growth to peak performance* (5th ed., pp. 1–13). New York: McGraw-Hill.

Williams, J. M., Tonymon, P., & Andersen, M. B. (1991). The effects of stressors and coping resources on anxiety and peripheral narrowing. *Journal of Applied Sport Psychology, 3,* 126–141.

Williams, K. J., Donovan, J. J., & Dodge, T. L. (2000). Self-regulation of performance: Goal establishment and goal revision processes in athletes. *Human Performance, 13,* 159–180.

Williams, L. (1994). Goal orientations and athletes' preferences for competence information sources. *Journal of Sport & Exercise Psychology, 16,* 416–430.

Williams, R., & Youssef, Z. (1975). Division of labor in college football along racial lines. *International Journal of Sport Psychology, 3,* 3–11.

Williams, T., & Underwood, J. (1970). *The science of hitting.* New York: Simon & Schuster.

Wilson, V. E., Peper, E., & Schmid, A. (2006). Strategies for training concentration. In J. M. Williams (Ed.), *Applied sport psychology: Personal growth to peak performance* (5th ed., pp. 404–422). New York: McGraw-Hill.

Winter, D. G. (1992). Power motivation revisited. In C. P. Smith (Ed.), *Motivation and personality: Handbook of thematic content analysis* (pp. 301–310). New York: Cambridge University Press.

Wise, M. (2000, February 2). N.B.A. finds minimal use of marijuana in first tests. *New York Times,* p. D1.

Wolf, E. S. (1997). A self psychological perspective of work and its inhibitions. In C. W. Socarides and S. Kramer (Eds.), *Work and its inhibitions: Psychoanalytic essays* (pp. 99–114). Madison, CT: International Universities Press.

Wolfe, R. N., & Kasmer, J. A. (1988). Type versus trait: Extraversion, impulsivity, sociability, and preferences for cooperative and competitive activities. *Journal of Personality and Social Psychology, 54,* 864–871.

Wolfenden, L. E., & Holt, N. L. (2005). Talent development in elite junior tennis: Perceptions of players, parents, and coaches. *Journal of Applied Sport Psychology, 17,* 1–19.

Wood, R., & Bandura, A. (1989). Impact of conceptions of ability on self-regulatory mechanisms and complex decision-making. *Journal of Personality and Social Psychology, 56,* 407–415.

Woodman, T., Albinson, J. G., & Hardy, L. (1997). An investigation of the zones of optimal functioning hypothesis within a multidimensional framework. *Journal of Sport and Exercise Psychology, 19,* 131–141.

Woodman, T., & Hardy, L. (2001). Stress and anxiety. In R. N. Singer, H. A. Hausenblas, & C. M. Janelle (Eds.), *Handbook of sport psychology* (2nd ed., pp. 290–318). New York: Wiley.

Woods, T. (2001). *How I play golf.* New York: Warner Books.

Worthington, E. L., Tipton, R. M., Cromley, J. S., Richards, T., & Janke, R. H. (1984). Speech and coping skills training and paradox as a treatment for college students anxious about public speaking. *Perceptual and Motor Skills, 59,* 394.

Wright, E. F., Jackson, W., Christie, S. D., McGuire, G. R., & Wright, R. D. (1991). The home-course disadvantage in golf championships: Further evidence for the undermining effect of supportive audiences on performance under pressure. *Journal of Sport Behavior, 14,* 51–60.

Wright, E. F., & Voyer, D. (1995). Supporting audiences and performance under pressure: The home-ice disadvantage in hockey championships. *Journal of Sport Behavior, 18,* 21–28.

Wurtele, S. K. (1986). Self-efficacy and athletic performance: A review. *Journal of Social and Clinical Psychology, 4,* 290–301.

Yaeger, D. (2000). Rx for trouble: Did Romo's fondness for pharmaceuticals go too far? *Sports Illustrated, 93,* August 21, 27–28.

Yantz, T. (2002, October 25). Coach's four-letter word: Stop. *Hartford Courant,* p. C6.

Yasunaga, M., & Inomata, K. (2004). Factors associated with helplessness among Japanese collegiate swimmers. *Perceptual and Motor Skills, 99,* 581–590.

Yee, P. L., & Vaughan, J. (1996). Integrating cognitive, personality, and social approaches to cognitive interference and distractibility. In I. G. Sarason, G. R. Pierce, & B. R. Sarason (Eds.), *Cognitive interference theories, methods, & findings* (pp. 77–97). Mahwah, NJ: Lawrence Erlbaum Associates, Inc.

Yerkes, R. M., & Dodson, J. D. (1908). The relation of strength of stimulus to rapidity of habit formation. *Journal of Comparative Neurology of Psychology, 18,* 459–482.

Yocom, G., Woods, T., Williams, T., Cooke, A., Venturi, K., Bush, G., et al. (2000). 50 greatest golfers of all time and what they taught us. *Golf Digest, 51,* July, 87–174.

Yoo, J. (2000). Factorial validity of the coping scale for Korean athletes. *International Journal of Sport Psychology, 31,* 391–404.

Yoo, J. (2001). Coping profile of Korean competitive athletes. *International Journal of Sport Psychology, 32,* 290–303.

Yoo, J., & Park, S. J. (1998a). Development of a sport coping scale. *Korean Journal of Physical Education, 37,* 151–168.

Yoo, J., & Park, S. J. (1998b). A test of the causal–structural model on coping effectiveness in sport. *Korean Journal of Physical Education, 37,* 141–152.

York, J. L., Hirsch, J. A., Pendergast, D. R., & Glavy, J. S. (1999). Muscle performance in detoxified alcoholics. *Journal of Studies on Alcohol, 60,* 413–421.

Yukelson, D. (1997). Principles of effective team building interventions in sport: A direct services approach at Penn State University. *Journal of Applied Sport Psychology, 9,* 73–96.

Yukelson, D. (2006). Communicating effectively. In J. M. Williams (Ed.), *Applied sport psychology: Personal growth to peak performance* (5th ed., pp. 174–191). New York: McGraw-Hill.

Zacharatos, A., Barling, J., & Kelloway, E. K. (2000). Development and effects of trans-formational leadership in adolescents. *Leadership Quarterly, 11,* 211–226.

Zador, P. L. (1991). Alcohol-related relative risk of fatal driver injuries in relation to driver age and sex. *Journal of Studies on Alcohol, 52,* 302–310.

Zaichkowsky, L. D., & Baltzell, A. (2001). Arousal and performance. In R. N. Singer, H. A. Hausenblas, & C. M. Janelle (Eds.), *Handbook of sport psychology* (2nd ed., pp. 319–339). New York: Wiley.

Zajonc, R. B. (1965). Social facilitation. *Science, 149,* 269–274.

Zanich, M. L., & Grover, D. E. (1989). Introductory psychology from the standpoint of the consumer. *Teaching of Psychology, 16,* 72–74.

Zeidner, M. (1994). Personal and contextual determinants of coping and anxiety in an evaluative situation: A prospective study. *Personality and Individual Differences, 16,* 899–918.

Zidane: "I don't regret anything that happened." (2006, July 13). *Hartford Courant,* p. C5.

Ziegler, S. G. (1987). Effects of stimulus cueing on the acquisition of ground strokes by beginning tennis players. *Journal of Applied Behavior Analysis, 20,* 405–411.

Zimmerman, B. J. (2000). Attaining self-regulation: A social cognitive perspective. In M. Boekaerts, P. Pintich, & M. Seidner (Eds.), *Self-regulation: Theory, research and application* (pp. 13–39). Orlando, FL: Academic Press.

Zinsser, N., Bunker, L., & Williams, J. M. (1998). Cognitive techniques for building confidence and enhancing performance. In J. M. Williams (Ed.), *Applied sport psychology: Personal growth to peak performance* (3rd ed., pp. 270–295). Mountain View, CA: Mayfield.

Zinsser, N., Bunker, L., & Williams, J. M. (2006). Cognitive techniques for building confidence and enhancing performance. In J. M. Williams (Ed.), *Applied sport psychology: Personal growth to peak performance* (5th ed., pp. 349–381). New York: McGraw-Hill.

Zizzi, S., Zaichkowsky, L., & Perna, F. M. (2002). Certification in sport and exercise psychology. In J. L. Van Raalte & B. W. Brewer (Eds.), *Exploring exercise and sport psychology* (2nd ed., pp. 417–436). Washington, DC: American Psychological Association.

Zohar, D. (1998). An additive model of test anxiety: Role of exam-specific expectations. *Journal of Educational Psychology, 90,* 330–340.

Zuckerman, M. (1994). *Behavioral expressions and biosocial bases of sensation seeking.* Cambridge, UK: Cambridge University Press.

Zuckerman, M., Kieffer, S. C., & Knee, C. R. (1998). Consequences of self-handicapping: Effects on coping, academic performance, and adjustment. *Journal of Personality and Social Psychology, 74,* 1619–1628.

Zuckerman, M., & Wheeler, L. (1975). To dispel fantasies about the fantasy-based measure of fear of success. *Psychological Bulletin, 82,* 932–946.

Zuroff, D. C., & Schwarz, J. C. (1978). Effects of Transcendental Meditation and muscle relaxation on trait anxiety, maladjustment, locus of control, and drug use. *Journal of Consulting and Clinical Psychology, 46,* 264–271.

Appendix

Test Anxiety

Like choking, **test anxiety** is paradoxical because it impairs performance when people are highly motivated to perform optimally. The literature about test anxiety is largely consistent with that of choking and in addition there is information about how to ameliorate test anxiety that may have applications in sport settings.

Returning to the model of stress discussed at the beginning of Chapter 10 (Lazarus & Folkman, 1984), test anxiety occurs in the inter-action of the test and the test taker. The test represents the stressor, and tests are interpreted as *threatening* if they are important and test takers do not believe that they can make the grade or perform adequately (Spielberger & Vagg, 1995). The degree of threat posed by a test is deter-mined by the nature of the test questions, students' ability in the subject area of the test, the level of the students' preparation for the test, and their trait anxiety. Students who have not prepared adequately and who lack sophisticated test-taking skills may become increasingly anxious during the course of an examination. This occurs when students cannot answer individual questions and prematurely conclude that they will fail. This definition of threat is similar to the definition of pressure that was dis-cussed in the section on choking in Chapter 10.

Tests that are interpreted to be more threatening cause more state anxiety with physiological anxiety and cognitive interference. The cogni-tive interference includes self-centered and self-critical thoughts, worry about falling behind others, recall of previous test situations that resulted in disaster, anticipated poor grades, and concern about how instructors will view one's performance. Cognitive interference has been more detrimental to test performance than physiological anxiety. As is often the case with cognitive anxiety, the cognitive interference that occurs in test situations has been described as peremptory and automatic. It occurs without conscious volition and preempts concentration on the test itself.

Cognitive interference in the form of self-deprecatory thoughts and test-related worries interferes with concentration, retrieval of information from memory, and decision-making, and is especially disruptive on mathematics tasks (Sarason, Sarason, & Pierce, 1995). Approximately one third of students who sought therapy for test anxiety were most anxious about mathematics tests (Richardson & Suinn, 1972).

Self-Focused Attention and Test Anxiety

The combination of **self-focused attention** and high levels of test anxiety produces performance deficits, off-task thinking, and a wish to quit (Carver & Scheier, 1992; Kurosawa and Harackiewicz, 1995). This combination is associated with a lack of persistence in solving difficult problems. The single most common thought among anxious students who focus on themselves during examinations was the wish to be somewhere else (Galassi, Frierson, & Sharer, 1981). The experience of test anxiety is unpleasant, and some people avoid situations in which they are evaluated so as to avoid the experience of this anxiety. This avoidance spares people the discomfort of anxiety at the cost of missing opportunities for accomplishments and for the mastery of test anxiety by performing successfully in these evaluations (Sarason et al., 1995).

Social Comparisons and Performance Anxiety

Children as young as 10 to 13 years of age have identified **social comparisons** as the primary source of information about their competence in sports and academics. This process of comparing oneself to others, and finding oneself less capable, is an important source of the anxiety that children in this age range have about evaluations (Weiss, Ebbeck, & Horn, 1997). When forces from the outside issue goals and challenges, people are more likely to have concerns about whether they will be successful. Of course students are routinely faced with the imposition of challenges from the outside in the form of tests and examinations.

Trait Test Anxiety

Some people experience test anxiety during almost all of their examinations and therefore show a trait of test anxiety. This trait test anxiety is similar to the **fear of failure** motive that was described in Chapter 2. Trait test anxiety may lead to the adoption of **performance-avoidance goals** with which performers focus on avoiding failure and the demonstration of incompetence (Elliot & McGregor, 1999). With fear of failure and performance-avoidance goals, people may withdraw from situations involving threat and pressure and conclude that they "don't test well" or are "choke artists." With performance-avoidance goals, standards for successful performance are considered beyond one's reach. Recall that efficacy or confidence that one is capable of realizing performance standards contains cognitive interference, decreases the experience of stress, and limits choking under pressure.

Test Anxiety and Defensive Pessimism

Optimists have been shown to have higher expectations and better performances than pessimists and people who do not identify any expectations for their performances. Optimists are not particularly fearful of failure. If optimists fail, they protect their self-esteem by attributing the causes of failure to external, temporary factors that are outside their control rather than to their talent (Norem & Cantor, 1986a, 1986b). However, some people marshal their resources to prepare for evaluations by considering the consequences of a poor performance. This occurs when people set their expectations at a lower level than would be expected on the basis of their prior performance. With the prospect of performing at a level beneath their usual standards, they experience facilitative anxiety that motivates appropriate preparation for the evaluation. They prepare for examinations to avoid the pain of failure. This pessimism does not lead to lower performance on cognitive tasks, and shields performers from some of the sting of failure. Failure that is anticipated is less aversive than unanticipated failure, and unexpected success is more satisfying than expected success (Feather, 1969).

Although this strategy has been referred to as **defensive pessimism**, it is not the same as the personality trait of pessimism, which inhibits effort and performance. Defensive pessimism is not a global trait, but consists of pessimism in specific domains such as academic and social functioning. These pessimists acknowledge that their performances generally exceed their gloomy predictions. They therefore appear to be somewhat aware that their expectations for poor performances are cognitive tricks to motivate them to work hard to avoid failure. Defensive pessimists are deliberate in approaching problems and think through possible solutions and outcomes to problems as well as worst-case scenarios. Optimists tend to consider fewer outcomes and to look on the bright side (Norem & Illingworth, 1993).

Defensive Pessimism and Reactions of Others

Performance suffers if defensive pessimists experience positive moods and if optimists realize negative moods prior to evaluations. The performance of defensive pessimists also suffers if others make efforts to convince them that their performance will be good (Sanna, 1998). The negative focus of defensive pessimists apparently mobilizes them or "psyches them up" to meet a stressor.

How Adaptive is Defensive Pessimism?

The effects of defensive pessimism on sport performance have not been determined. However, as emphasized in this appendix, efficacy that one will meet and surpass standards necessary for success limits choking under pressure. As noted in Chapter 9, the time for doubt about one's readiness to perform successfully is distal to performances, when there is ample time to train and hone skills. Self-doubts during preparatory stages may function similarly to defensive pessimism and motivate more thorough preparation for competition.

However, in the long run defensive pessimism may be a less effective strategy than optimism for students. Over time, defensive pessimists experience more burnout, loss of intrinsic motivation in academics, and ultimately, diminished achievement (Cantor & Harlow, 1994).

Help for Test Anxiety

A simple and straightforward way of limiting test anxiety is to give instructions to concentrate and avoid distractions (Norem & Cantor, 1986b). Apparently people with both high and low test anxiety follow these instructions, as college students reported less cognitive interference when coached in this manner. The benefits of the instructions to concentrate and avoid distractions may reflect the students' lack of skill in identifying cognitive interference and redirecting attention when interference is detected. Instructions to increase attention to cognitive tasks and decrease negative emotions such as worry or upset following errors have been show to increase the speed of performance and decrease the number of errors on a variety of cognitive tests (Kanfer & Ackerman, 1996). These instructions were most influential with those that were least skilled and most likely to make errors.

Social support appears to be an important source of protection from cognitive interference and test anxiety (Yee & Vaughan, 1996). College students who experienced little social support in their personal lives profited from interventions in which authoritative adults demonstrated an interest in their wellbeing and offered assistance on tests. Apparently there is a threshold of social support below which test anxiety and cognitive interference disrupt test performance and above which additional support is less influential. For example, the performance of students who reported higher levels of social support in their personal lives did not show additional improvement as a result of expressions of interest and assistance by authoritative adults (Sarason & Sarason, 1986) or apparent college students (Sarason, 1981).

Unfortunately, people with low social support are often inhibited and less able to ask for the support of others. Those with low social support rate themselves as less interesting and less worthy of helpful interventions from others, and they are more likely to have social anxiety and lower self-esteem.

Students with high levels of test anxiety also profit from *watching* authoritative adults solve problems and *enunciate principles* for solving problems. Whether this intervention provided information about how to solve test problems or again provided social support was not clear, but it did promote attention to the test items and contained cognitive interference (Sarason, 1973). Conversely, the performance of students with high test anxiety deteriorates when they observe other students fail on the same test (Sarason, 1972).

As discussed in Chapter 3, it is unrealistic to expect excellent performance without thorough preparation. Test anxiety is also more likely when students have an inadequate knowledge of the subject matter. Interventions to decrease cognitive interference will be ineffective in improving the performance of people who are not adequately prepared for evaluations (Naveh-Benjamin, 1991).

Self-Efficacy Contains Cognitive Interference and Anxiety

At this point in this book, the construct of self-efficacy is quite familiar. At this point in the Appendix, it should be clear that self-efficacy contains cognitive interference and performance anxiety. A leitmotiv in the choking and test anxiety literature has been that anxiety and performance deficits result from a lack of efficacy or belief that one can meet and exceed the standards necessary for successful performances (Jones, 1995; Williams, 1996; Zohar, 1998). A lack of efficacy contributes to attention to the costs of defeat, the formidableness of competitors, and the difficulty of tasks. Attention may also be given to signs of physiological anxiety. The inability to control physiological anxiety may further erode self-efficacy, and performance deteriorates as this spiral continues. Cognitive interference is more likely to occur if a person believes that all of their self-esteem will be lost if they fail an examination or have a poor performance. Less threat will be experienced if success or failure is understood to extend simply to the task at hand and not to the validation of the entire self or person.

People who believe they can handle threats demonstrate fewer cognitive and physiological signs of anxiety. At both the cognitive and the physiological level, they act as if they have nothing to be afraid of. They also take action to alleviate the stress related to their performance. For example, by carefully preparing for evaluations, following preperformance routines, developing game plans, engaging in visualization and self-talk, becoming practiced in reducing physiological arousal, predicting contents of evaluations and strategies of opponents, and having a Plan B, performers enhance their personal control and limit their anxiety.

Preparation and belief in one's capacity to execute components of a performance make worry unnecessary. It is unrealistic and probably unproductive to expect to experience little cognitive and physiological anxiety and cognitive interference during examinations and performances when one has not prepared sufficiently to realize success. Focusing on aspects in a performance over which one has control supports efficacy beliefs. Focusing on aspects that are not under the performer's control, such as the strength of an opponent, diminishes efficacy.

Although self-efficacy is a stable characteristic, **focusing on the positive** prior to evaluations and competitions enhances it. For example, students "primed" to recall accomplishments experienced less cognitive interference when working on insolvable mazes (Sarason, Potter, & Sarason, 1986). US Coast Guard Academy cadets who kept diaries of stressful experiences during an intense six-week summer training period found their training to be more difficult and stressful than a comparable group of cadets that kept a diary of the "good things" that happened to them during the same period. The cadets with the positive focus reported less stress and fewer feelings of defeat. It appears that negative or positive experiences are not recalled in isolation. Their retrieval initiates the recall of thoughts that are related in both content and mood. Focusing on inadequacies prior to evaluations can therefore erode confidence and efficacy. As explained above and in Chapter 9, the time to recognize weaknesses is prior to evaluations while there is still time to ameliorate them. Self-talk and mental imagery prior to performances should focus on mastery so that feelings of efficacy can dominate thoughts and moods.

Key Terms

Test anxiety

Self-focused attention

Social comparisons and
performance anxiety

Fear of failure

Performance-avoidance goals

Defensive pessimism

Social support

Focusing on the positive

Author Index

Subject Index

Figures and tables denoted in **bold**. Page entries for headings with subheadings refer to general aspects of that topic.